Lecture Notes in Computer Science   16476

The series Lecture Notes in Computer Science (LNCS), including its subseries Lecture Notes in Artificial Intelligence (LNAI) and Lecture Notes in Bioinformatics (LNBI), has established itself as a medium for the publication of new developments in computer science and information technology research, teaching, and education.

LNCS enjoys close cooperation with the computer science R & D community, the series counts many renowned academics among its volume editors and paper authors, and collaborates with prestigious societies. Its mission is to serve this international community by providing an invaluable service, mainly focused on the publication of conference and workshop proceedings and postproceedings. LNCS commenced publication in 1973.

Kaoru Sumi · Raian Ali · Roberto Legaspi

Editors

Persuasive Technology

21st International Conference, PERSUASIVE 2026
Hakodate, Japan, March 10–13, 2026
Proceedings

 Springer

Editors
Kaoru Sumi
Future University Hakodate
Hokkaido, Japan

Raian Ali
Hamad Bin Khalifa University
Doha, Qatar

Roberto Legaspi
KDDI Research
Saitama, Japan

ISSN 0302-9743   ISSN 1611-3349 (electronic)
Lecture Notes in Computer Science
ISBN 978-3-032-19686-6   ISBN 978-3-032-19687-3 (eBook)
https://doi.org/10.1007/978-3-032-19687-3

This Springer imprint is published by the registered company Springer Nature Switzerland AG
The registered company address is: Gewerbestrasse 11, 6330 Cham, Switzerland

If disposing of this product, please recycle the paper.

Preface

In a world in which technology has become increasingly embedded in people's everyday lives, influencing human behavior and attitudes has emerged as a key factor in addressing many societal and personal challenges. Persuasive Technology is a vibrant interdisciplinary research field that focuses on the design, development, and evaluation of interactive systems aimed at influencing people's attitudes and behaviors through persuasion, rather than coercion or deception. By supporting individuals in setting and achieving their own goals, persuasive technologies have contributed to improving well-being and quality of life across domains such as health, education, sustainability, and social interaction.

The International Conference on Persuasive Technology (PERSUASIVE) is the leading international forum for researchers and practitioners to present and discuss theoretical, methodological, and technical advances in this field. Over the years, the conference series has been hosted in many locations around the world, fostering a diverse and active research community.

The 21st International Conference on Persuasive Technology (PERSUASIVE 2026) was held in Hakodate, Japan, from March 10 to 13, 2026. This edition marked the first time that the PERSUASIVE conference was hosted in Japan. A distinctive feature of PERSUASIVE 2026 was its co-location with ABC 2026, a new collaborative initiative that brought together complementary research communities. In addition, the Academy of Behavior Transformation by AIoT (BTI), a Japanese academic society focusing on behavior change, contributed to the conference by organizing a dedicated workshop.

On March 10, 2026, the conference hosted a rich program of workshops and a tutorial, including:

Workshops

- *Personalizing Persuasive Technologies Workshop 2026 (PPT 2026)*
- *The 1st International Workshop on Trust and Blame in Social Agents (TBSA 2026)*
- *The 2nd International Workshop on Upholding Ethical Designs (I-WOULD 2026)*
- *The 3rd BTI International Workshop (BTIW3)*

Tutorial

- *Self-Regulated Learning Tool for Academic Success*

In addition, a special workshop on Behavior Change Support Systems (BCSS) was held, continuing the long-standing tradition of BCSS events within the PERSUASIVE community.

The main conference took place from March 11 to 13, 2026, and featured a single-track program comprising oral presentations of accepted papers, poster and demo sessions, and opportunities for discussion and networking. The conference also included keynote addresses by Catherine Pelachaud and Hiroshi Ishiguro, whose pioneering work has had a profound impact on research in human–agent interaction, social agents, and human-centered intelligent systems.

This volume contains the accepted Full and Short Papers of the main conference. A total of 104 submissions, a record number for the conference, were received and evaluated through a double-blind peer-review process conducted using EasyChair. A total of 88 program committee members and reviewers contributed to the review process, with each paper receiving at least three detailed and constructive reviews, thereby ensuring high-quality feedback for the authors. Following careful review assessment, 25 Full Papers and 8 Short Papers were accepted, resulting in a full-paper acceptance rate of 24.0%.

We would like to express our sincere gratitude to all authors who submitted their work to PERSUASIVE 2026. We also warmly thank the members of the program committee and the reviewers for their time, expertise, and dedication, which were essential to maintaining the high scientific quality of the conference. Finally, we thank all organizers, workshop and tutorial chairs, as well as the supporting institutions whose efforts made PERSUASIVE 2026 possible.

<table>
<tr><td>Hakodate, Japan</td><td>Kaoru Sumi</td></tr>
<tr><td>March 2026</td><td>Raian Ali</td></tr>
<tr><td></td><td>Roberto Legaspi</td></tr>
</table>

Organization

General Chair

Kaoru Sumi   Future University Hakodate, Japan

Program Chairs

Raian Ali   Hamad Bin Khalifa University, Qatar
Roberto Legaspi   KDDI Research, Japan

Late Breaking Results (LBR) Chairs

Rhodora Abadia   Adelaide University, Australia
Ala Yankouskaya   Bournemouth University, UK

Doctoral Consortium Chairs

Yutaka Arakawa   Kyushu University, Japan
Harri Oinas-Kukkonen   University of Oulu, Finland
Khin Than Win   University of Wollongong, Australia

Demo, Poster and Artefacts Track Chairs

Antonio Garcia-Cabot   University of Alcalá, Spain
Yugo Nakamura   Kyushu University, Japan

Workshops and Tutorial Chairs

Kiemute Oyibo   York University, Canada
Thomas James Tiam-Lee   De La Salle University, Philippines

Proceedings Chairs

Elena Vlahu-Gjorgievska   University of Wollongong, Australia
Tadashi Okoshi   Keio University, Japan
Ahmed Salem   Future University Hakodate, Japan

Publicity Chairs

Ifeoma Adaji   University of British Columbia, Canada
Yasuyuki Sumi   Future University Hakodate, Japan

Program Committee

Rhodora Abadia   Adelaide University, Australia
Stanley Abhadiomhen   York University, Canada
Ifeoma Adaji   University of British Columbia, Canada
Dena Al-Thani   Hamad Bin Khalifa University, Qatar
Aftab Alam   Hamad Bin Khalifa University, Qatar
Mona Alhasani   Dalhousie University, Canada
Raian Ali   Hamad Bin Khalifa University, Qatar
Alaa Ali S. Almohanna   Northern Border University, Saudi Arabia
Nawaf Almutairi   University of Hail, Saudi Arabia
Sameha Ahmed Ali Alshakhsi   Hamad Bin Khalifa University, Qatar
Alaa Alslaity   Dalhousie University, Canada
Saleh Altuwayrib   University of Hail, Saudi Arabia
Yutaka Arakawa   Kyushu University, Japan
Emily Arden-Close   Bournemouth University, UK
Judith Azcarraga   De La Salle University, Philippines
Rafael Cabredo   De La Salle University, Philippines
Barbara Caci   University of Palermo, Italy
Luca Chittaro   University of Udine, Italy
Nelly Condori Fernández   Universidad Santiago de Compostela, Spain
Peter De Vries   University of Twente, Netherlands
Shital Desai   York University, Canada
Alia El Bolock   American University in Cairo, Egypt
Sandra Famador   University of the Philippines, Philippines
Alexander Felfernig   TU Graz, Austria
Mark Freeman   University of Sydney, Australia
Ken-ichi Fukui   Kansai University, Japan
Nanami Furue   Hitotsubashi University, Japan

Antonio Garcia-Cabot	University of Alcalá, Spain
Jaap Ham	Eindhoven University of Technology, Netherlands
Hooman Hoghooghi Esfahani	University of Isfahan, Iran
Tahera Hossain	Nagoya University, Japan
Hung-Hsuan Huang	Fukuchiyama Public University, Japan
Tetsunari Inamura	Tamagawa University, Japan
Paul Inventado	California State University Fullerton, USA
Sriram Iyengar	University of Arizona, USA
Elaheh Jafari	University of Saskatchewan, Canada
Heejin Jeong	Arizona State University, USA
Nitchan Jianwattanapaisarn	ATR Interaction Science Laboratories, Japan
Nirattaya Khamsemanan	Thammasat University, Thailand
Divesh Lala	Kyoto University, Japan
Roberto Legaspi	KDDI Research, Japan
Magnus Liebherr	University of Duisburg-Essen, Germany
Kohei Matsumura	Ritsumeikan University, Japan
Shahla Meedya	Western Sydney University, Australia
Mark Mensah	University of Ghana, Ghana
Alexander Meschtscherjakov	University of Salzburg, Austria
Cees Midden	Eindhoven University of Technology, Netherlands
George Mikros	National and Kapodistrian University of Athens, Greece
Niko Männikkö	Oulu University of Applied Sciences, Finland
Yugo Nakamura	Kyushu University, Japan
Cholwich Nattee	Thammasat University, Thailand
Fakhroddin Noorbehbahani	University of Isfahan, Iran
Kohei Ogawa	Nagoya University, Japan
Harri Oinas-Kukkonen	University of Oulu, Finland
Tadashi Okoshi	Keio University, Japan
Ethel Ong	De La Salle University, Philippines
Fidelia Orji	Dalhousie University, Canada
Rita Orji	Dalhousie University, Canada
Oladapo Oyebode	Dalhousie University, Canada
Kiemute Oyibo	York University, Canada
Zelinna Pablo	Torrens University, Australia
Constantina Panourgia	Bournemouth University, UK
George Angelos Papadopoulos	University of Cyprus, Cyprus
John Rooksby	Northumbria University, UK
Ahmed Salem	Future University Hakodate, Japan
Briane Paul Samson	De La Salle University, Philippines
Akihiro Sasaki	KDDI Research, Japan
Marta Serafini	University of Udine, Italy

Zubair Shah	Hamad Bin Khalifa University, Qatar
Nili Steinfeld	Ariel University, Israel
Agnis Stibe	RMIT University, Vietnam
Merlin Teodosia Suarez	De La Salle Lipa, Philippines
Kaoru Sumi	Future University Hakodate, Japan
Yasuyuki Sumi	Future University Hakodate, Japan
Asuka Terai	Future University Hakodate, Japan
Katja Tiefengrabner	Salzburg Research Forschungs mbH, Austria
Akira Utsumi	ATR Intelligent Interaction Research Laboratories, Japan
Evangelia Vanezi	University of Cyprus, Cyprus
Elena Vlahu-Gjorgievska	University of Wollongong, Australia
Isaac Wiafe	University of Ghana, Ghana
Khin Than Win	University of Wollongong, Australia
Burkhard Wuensche	University of Auckland, New Zealand
Wenzhen Xu	Hitotsubashi University, Japan
Ala Yankouskaya	Bournemouth University, UK
Affan Yasin	Xi'an Jiaotong-Liverpool University, China
Keiichi Yasumoto	Nara Institute of Science and Technology, Japan
Tomoko Yonezawa	Kansai University, Japan
Donghuo Zeng	KDDI Research, Japan
Junpei Zhong	UOW College Hong Kong, China

Additional Reviewers

Thomas Photiadis	Pongpisit Thanasutives
Nat Pavasant	Alexandros Yeratziotis
Rabby Lavilles	Savvas Savvides
Christos Mettouris	

Contents

HyperCare: An AI-Driven, Personalized, and Adaptive Persuasive Technology for Continuous Hypertension Prevention and Management

Josteve Adekanbi[1]([⊠]) [iD], Japheth Kimeu[1] [iD], Gladwin Irudayaraj[1] [iD],
Olumide Thomas Adeleke[2] [iD], Ibukun Okunade[2] [iD], Rita Orji[1] [iD],
and Oladapo Oyebode[1] [iD]

[1] Faculty of Computer Science, Dalhousie University, Halifax, Nova Scotia, Canada
`josteve.adekanbi@dal.ca`
[2] College of Health Sciences, Bowen University, Iwo, Osun State, Nigeria

Abstract. Hypertension is a major global health problem linked to heart disease, stroke, and premature death, affecting more than one billion adults worldwide. Its complex interplay of physiological and behavioural determinants, combined with infrequent clinical visits and reliance on self-reported readings, makes its control challenging and contributes to its growing prevalence. Digital health technologies, including wearable devices, mobile health (mHealth) apps, and artificial intelligence (AI), have emerged to enable continuous health monitoring and adaptive feedback. However, most existing apps track only isolated determinants (e.g., sleep or physical activity) and lack explainability, thereby limiting accurate risk assessment and clinical trust. To address these gaps, we present HyperCare – a novel, AI-driven, personalized, and adaptive persuasive technology that integrates multimodal sensing of health determinants, persuasive strategies (PS), and explainability to prevent and manage hypertension. The technology continuously collects multimodal data, including blood alcohol content, blood glucose, body weight, sleep patterns, and activity level (step count). These data are then automatically analyzed using a retrieval-augmented generation (RAG)-based and explainable large language model (LLM) to recommend evidence-based interventions in real time while operationalizing 11 PS. Next, we conduct an expert evaluation with clinicians using 20 well-established heuristics across three hypertension-risk scenarios. The clinicians rate HyperCare with mean scores of 100% for clinical relevance, 98.9% for transparency and explainability, 100% for persuasion, 100% for ethics, and 100% for usability. Strong inter-rater agreement is observed (Krippendorff's $\alpha = 0.92$, 95% CI [0.75, 1]; Cohen's $\kappa = 0.90$, $p < .001$), confirming the system's overall effectiveness. These findings demonstrate the potential of integrating multimodal sensing, PS, and explainable AI into a technology (HyperCare) for continuous and personalized hypertension prevention and management.

Keywords: Hypertension · Artificial Intelligence (AI) · Persuasive Technology · Multimodal Sensing · Mobile Health (mHealth) · Explainable AI (XAI) · Retrieval-Augmented Generation (RAG)

K. Sumi et al. (Eds.): PERSUASIVE 2026, LNCS 16476, pp. 1–16, 2026.
https://doi.org/10.1007/978-3-032-19687-3_1

1 Introduction

Hypertension, or high blood pressure, is a leading global health problem associated with heart disease, stroke, and premature death [1]. The World Health Organization (WHO) estimates that approximately 1.4 billion adults aged 30–79 years worldwide have hypertension, and about 600 million (44%) of them are unaware of their condition [2]. Hypertension develops from a combination of physiological and behavioural determinants (or risk factors) such as excessive alcohol intake, poor sleep quality, and high blood glucose, making its prevention and control a complex challenge [3]. Despite advances in clinical care, its prevalence continues to rise, driven by infrequent clinical visits and self-reported readings, which limit data accuracy, authenticity, and timeliness, thereby reducing the reliability of personalized feedback, real-time clinical assessment, and intervention delivery [4].

Over the past decade, digital health technologies, including wearable devices, mobile health (mHealth) apps, and artificial intelligence, have advanced hypertension management by enabling continuous monitoring and adaptive feedback [5]. Yet most existing systems track isolated determinants, depend on manual data entry, and lack explainability, limiting their accuracy, adherence, and clinical trust [6, 7]. Moreover, recent work with large language models (LLMs) and retrieval-augmented generation (RAG) shows potential for evidence-grounded personalization but remains underexplored in hypertension care [8].

Therefore, this study aims to address these gaps by examining two key research questions: **RQ1:** *How can an explainable, AI-driven persuasive technology integrate multimodal data and retrieval-augmented reasoning to deliver personalized, evidence-based interventions for hypertension prevention and management?* **RQ2:** *How clinically relevant, transparent, persuasive, ethical, and usable are the AI-generated interventions in promoting effective hypertension prevention and management?*

To address these questions, we developed and evaluated *HyperCare*, an AI-driven, mobile-based, personalized, and adaptive persuasive technology for hypertension prevention and management that employs 11 persuasive strategies, such as self-monitoring, suggestion, and goal setting, from the Persuasive Systems Design (PSD) framework [9] to drive motivation and engagement. HyperCare enables continuous, passive multimodal sensing of key clinically recognized hypertension determinants [10], including blood alcohol content, blood glucose, body weight, sleep duration, and step count. It integrates data from connected wearables and home-monitoring devices (e.g., breathalyzers, glucose monitors, smartwatches, and sleep trackers) to collect data automatically without user input. In addition to sensor data, the app collects basic demographic information (e.g., age, gender, and family history of hypertension) during account setup, as these factors also influence hypertension risk [11]. The system analyzes these data in real time using a RAG-based LLM that grounds its reasoning in established clinical evidence, including peer-reviewed articles from PubMed, as well as the WHO and the American Heart Association (AHA) guidelines. It then generates personalized and clinically grounded interventions (insights, goals, and suggestions) accompanied by explanations. HyperCare also provides a built-in conversational coach that supports multimodal interaction, helping users interpret their data and recommendations through context-aware, evidence-grounded guidance.

To assess HyperCare's interventions, we conducted an expert evaluation with two clinicians (each with extensive experience managing hypertensive patients) across three hypertension-risk scenarios (low, moderate, and high) using 20 well-recognized heuristics in the field of Human-Computer Interaction (HCI), adapted from the clinical healthcare domain [12, 13]. The clinicians rated HyperCare with mean scores of 100% for clinical relevance, 98.9% for transparency and explainability, 100% for persuasiveness, 100% for ethics, and 100% for usability, validating its overall effectiveness across all scenarios. The inter-rater reliability was computed using Krippendorff's alpha (α) [14], with a value of 0.92, 95% CI [0.75,1], as well as Cohen's kappa (κ) [15] with a value of 0.90 ($p < .001$), indicating strong agreement between the clinicians.

We contribute to the fields of HCI, persuasive technology, and digital health in three ways. First, we design and develop *HyperCare*, a personalized, AI-driven, persuasive mHealth system that integrates physiological, behavioural, and demographic data through continuous, passive multimodal sensing and retrieval-augmented reasoning to support hypertension prevention and management. Second, we conduct a clinician-based heuristic evaluation using 20 adapted heuristics across three hypertension-risk scenarios, demonstrating strong inter-rater agreement and consistently high ratings for clinical relevance, transparency, persuasion, ethics, and usability. Finally, we provide practical recommendations for designing trustworthy, explainable, and persuasive health technologies that combine large language models with real-time, passive, multimodal sensing to enhance user engagement and clinical reliability.

2 Background and Related Work

2.1 Hypertension Determinants

Hypertension arises from a complex interplay of physiological, behavioural, and demographic determinants [3]. Among the behavioural and physiological determinants, five have been consistently identified in the literature as strongly predictive of hypertension onset and progression: First, excessive alcohol consumption raises blood pressure through sympathetic activation and vascular resistance [16]. Second, blood glucose dysregulation, often linked to insulin resistance, contributes to endothelial dysfunction and arterial stiffness, both of which accelerate hypertensive pathology [17]. Third, excess body weight increases cardiac output and vascular resistance, with epidemiological studies showing that each 10 kg increase in weight corresponds to an approximately 3–4 mmHg increase in systolic pressure [18]. Fourth, sleep duration and quality are also critical; both short sleep (less than 6 h per night) and fragmented sleep are associated with a higher risk of developing hypertension due to hormonal and autonomic imbalance [19]. Fifth, physical inactivity, typically reflected in reduced daily step count or low cardiorespiratory fitness, has been shown to increase hypertension risk by up to 30% compared with active individuals [20].

In addition to these modifiable determinants, non-modifiable factors such as age, gender, and family history significantly affect baseline risk and can mediate the impact of behavioural factors [2]. For instance, men tend to develop hypertension earlier than women [21], and individuals with hypertensive parents face more than double the lifetime risk compared with those without such a history [22].

As these determinants interact dynamically and interdependently, addressing hypertension requires approaches that continuously monitor them rather than focusing on a single risk factor. Recognizing these relationships provides the foundation for designing intelligent, data-driven systems that deliver effective interventions.

2.2 Digital Interventions for Hypertension Prevention and Management

Digital interventions have transformed how hypertension is prevented and managed by extending care beyond traditional clinical settings. Over the past decade, three major technologies have shaped this progress – mobile health applications, wearable devices, and artificial intelligence. Mobile health (mHealth) apps allow users to record blood pressure, track habits, and receive behaviour-based feedback [23]. Research shows that app-supported self-monitoring leads to measurable improvements; for instance, a meta-analysis of more than 7,000 adults found that app-based interventions reduced systolic blood pressure by approximately 1.6 mmHg [24]. Building on these apps, wearable devices such as smartwatches, smart scales, and sleep trackers have introduced passive data collection, enabling continuous tracking of heart rate, activity, and sleep without manual entry. Studies integrating wearables with home blood pressure monitors report greater reductions in blood pressure and stronger engagement over time [25]. Artificial intelligence has further advanced these systems by analyzing large, continuous data streams to predict risk, detect abnormal patterns, and adapt recommendations using techniques such as machine learning and deep learning [26]. More recently, large language LLMs have been explored to enhance personalization and communication, allowing systems to generate natural, conversational health guidance [27]. However, because LLMs can sometimes produce inaccurate or unsupported statements, the RAG technique has emerged as a way to ground model outputs in verified medical literature and reduce hallucination, thereby improving reliability and clinical trust [28].

Despite these advances, existing systems still face three main limitations. First, many require manual data entry for meals, exercise, or readings, which increases effort and reduces adherence. Second, most focus on a single determinant rather than considering how multiple factors interact to influence blood pressure. Third, few systems explain how their AI-generated recommendations are produced, which limits clinician confidence and user understanding. Addressing these challenges requires integrated, evidence-based systems capable of passively collecting data from multiple sources, interpreting it holistically, and communicating insights through clear, explainable feedback.

3 Method

3.1 System Design and Architecture

As shown in Fig. 1, HyperCare operates as a continuous feedback loop connecting data collection, reasoning, intervention delivery, explainability, and refinement (RQ1). The multimodal data are collected passively from connected devices and stored in a central database. This data is then analyzed to generate and deliver personalized interventions, including *insights* (clinically relevant interpretations of the user's current data), recommended goals, and suggestions. After delivery, the user may provide feedback on the intervention's usefulness or relevance, which is used to refine subsequent generations. The system then continues to monitor incoming sensor data to assess progress of the goals and whether the suggestions are being followed, and to automatically generate new interventions whenever changes in the user's data warrant revised guidance. HyperCare also features a conversational coach that ingests the user's data and generated interventions to guide users on hypertension prevention and management.

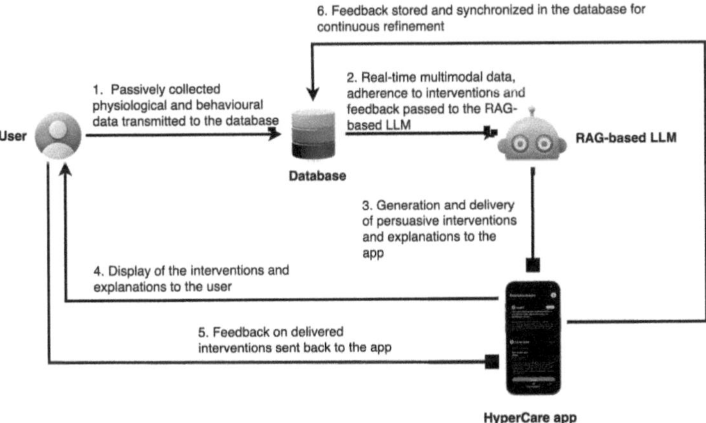

Fig. 1. Architecture of HyperCare, showing a continuous feedback loop for hypertension prevention and management.

3.2 Passive Multimodal Sensing

HyperCare integrates five authenticated sensing devices (Fig. 2) to enable continuous, passive, and multimodal sensing of key hypertension determinants via secure Open Authentication (OAuth) Application Programming Interfaces (APIs) or native Software Development Kit (SDK), ensuring real-time data retrieval without manual entry.

Specifically, blood alcohol concentration (BAC), reported in % BAC, is obtained from the BACtrack C6 Breathalyzer (Fig. 2a) via its SDK [29]. Blood-glucose levels are captured every five minutes from the Dexcom G6 Continuous Glucose Monitor (Fig. 2b) through OAuth-based access to the Dexcom API [30], providing continuous readings in mg/dL. Body weight is recorded in kilograms (kg) from the Withings Body Smart scale (Fig. 2c) via the Withings OAuth API [31]. Sleep duration (in seconds) is retrieved nightly from the Withings Sleep (Fig. 2d) using the same API, while step count is continuously streamed from the Google Pixel Watch 3 (Fig. 2e) through the Google Fit Android API [32].

These data are then stored on a Firebase Firestore [33] database alongside the user's age, gender, and family history of hypertension for secure, real-time data storage and synchronization.

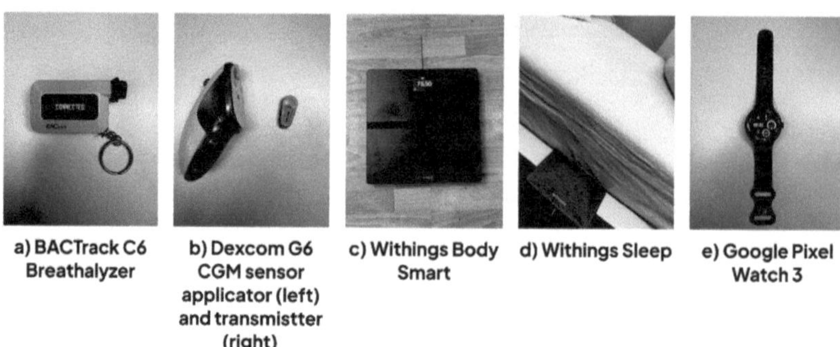

Fig. 2. The five passive multimodal sensing devices integrated into HyperCare.

3.3 Explainable AI-Driven Interventions Generation

When new data arrives from any sensing device, a locally hosted backend service initializes a pipeline which processes the recent values for blood alcohol content, blood glucose, body weight, sleep duration, step count, age, gender, and family history, then generates persuasive and personalized interventions including one insight, up to three recommended goals, and up to three recommended suggestions, each accompanied by explanations grounded in peer-reviewed clinical research and established medical guidelines.

The pipeline uses a RAG-based LLM built on GPT-OSS 120B (using the default hyperparameters, i.e., temperature = 1) [34] running through the Groq API for low-latency execution [35]. Before each generation, the system retrieves context from an open-source vector database (Chroma [36]) that includes six PubMed articles focused on the key determinants monitored in HyperCare, as well as the WHO hypertension guidelines [2]. We selected these articles by running determinant-specific PubMed queries such as:

("hypertension" OR "blood pressure") AND ("sleep duration") AND human AND English AND ("cohort" OR "trial" OR "meta-analysis")

Analogous queries were used for alcohol consumption, blood glucose, body weight, and physical activity, with each search returning several hundred to several thousand results. Following methods consistent with structured evidence retrieval frameworks and systematic reviews used in biomedical informatics and clinical decision-support research [37], we applied multi-step filtering. First, we ranked records by relevance score using PubMed's default algorithm, then limited the results to the top 50 per determinant. From these, we manually screened titles and abstracts to identify those reporting associations between the determinant and blood pressure or hypertension.

For alcohol consumption, we included a recent systematic review and meta-analysis that supports a causal association between alcohol intake and incident hypertension, especially above roughly 12 g per day [38]. For sleep, we included a meta-analysis showing that short sleep duration is associated with a higher risk of incident hypertension [39]. For physical activity, we included evidence that walking and higher levels of physical activity lower blood pressure and reduce the risk of hypertension [40]. For body weight, we included meta-analytic and cohort evidence that higher body mass index (BMI) and weight gain increase hypertension risk and that weight loss reduces blood pressure [41]. For blood glucose, we included a recent review and cohort evidence showing that elevated fasting blood glucose, even within the normal range, is independently associated with higher prevalence and incidence of hypertension [42]. We also included guidelines from the American College of Cardiology (ACC) and the AHA to anchor the thresholds and lifestyle targets used in the recommended goals [43].

The pipeline formats the latest user data, retrieves the top passages from the vector database, and sends a structured prompt (Fig. 3) to the model. The model then returns a JavaScript Object Notation (JSON) object with the insight, recommended goal, suggestions, and corresponding explanations. These interventions are then stored in the database for retrieval by the mobile app.

The coach also runs on the same backend service, using the same data and the same vector database, but responds to user queries in real time. It applies the identical retrieval step and returns answers with explanations that reference the retrieved passages. This keeps on-demand coaching consistent with the batch interventions produced by the pipeline.

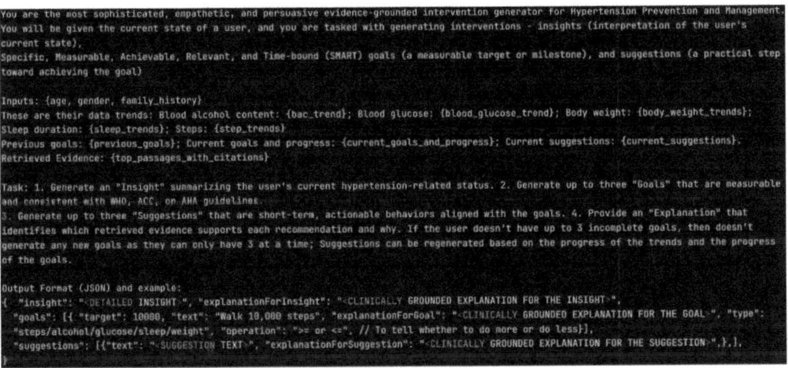

Fig. 3. Prompt used to guide the retrieval-augmented generation model for interventions generation in HyperCare.

3.4 Interventions Delivery

We developed HyperCare by integrating insights from recent studies showing that digital health interventions incorporating persuasive and behaviour-change strategies, such as personalization and goal setting, can enhance adherence and support hypertension prevention and management [44, 45]. Guided by this evidence and the Persuasive Systems Design (PSD) framework [9], we implemented 11 persuasive strategies (Table 1) as app features across five primary user interfaces: Trends, Track Alcohol, Recommendations, Coach, and Profile (Fig. 4).

The **Trends** interface (Fig. 4a) aggregates longitudinal readings for blood alcohol content, blood glucose, body weight, step count, and sleep duration. Users can view daily, weekly, monthly, or yearly patterns, with automatic updates as new data arrives. The **Track Alcohol** interface (Fig. 4b) integrates with the BACtrack C6 breathalyzer to record and analyze the blood alcohol content; each measurement is timestamped, stored, and triggers the interventions generation pipeline in real time.

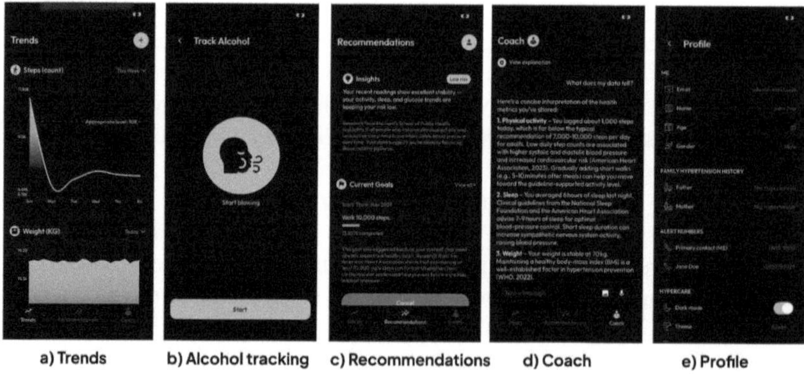

a) Trends   b) Alcohol tracking   c) Recommendations   d) Coach   e) Profile

Fig. 4. Dark-mode user interfaces of HyperCare showing: (a) Trends, (b) Track Alcohol, (c) Recommendations, (d) Coach, and (e) Profile.

The **Recommendations** interface (Fig. 4c) displays the generated insights, goals, and suggestions, each accompanied by explanations referencing the user's data and clinical evidence. Goals, which can be accepted, rejected, or cancelled, define measurable outcomes (e.g., step targets, alcohol-free days), while suggestions provide short-term actions. To maintain focus, the system supports up to three active goals and suggestions, automatically tracking progress as new data is retrieved and storing completed or canceled ones in history. In case of high-risk trends (e.g., poor sleep or abnormal blood glucose levels), the system issues alerts to the user and their emergency contacts. The **Coach** interface (Fig. 4d) enables a conversational multimodal (text, images, or audio) interaction, explains user data, clarifies recommendations, and provides evidence-based explanations with a consistent persona. The **Profile** interface (Fig. 4e) displays demographic details, family history, and emergency contacts, with customization options for dark mode and color themes.

Table 1. Implementation of features based on the PSD framework [9]

Persuasive Strategy	Description	Implementation in HyperCare
Self-Monitoring	Enables users to observe their own behaviour and outcomes.	Displays daily, weekly, and monthly trends for all tracked determinants.
Reduction	Lowers effort by simplifying data collection and actions.	Connects devices for automatic data capture, removing manual entry.

(continued)

Table 1. (continued)

Persuasive Strategy	Description	Implementation in HyperCare
Suggestion	Offers actionable guidance at appropriate moments.	Issues real-time, context-based suggestions when new data is received.
Goal Setting	Helps users commit to specific, measurable targets.	Generates goals derived from individual data patterns.
Verifiability	Allows users to confirm the source and basis of feedback.	Each recommendation cites related data and supporting evidence.
Reminders	Prompts users to maintain engagement and follow targets.	Sends notifications for tracking progress and goal completion.
Customization	Allows users to adjust the interface to personal preferences.	Provides options for enabling different modes and changing color themes,
Social Role	Maintains a supportive, consistent system persona.	The coach explains recommendations and interprets user trends with a consistent persona.
Social Support	Facilitates help or alerts in high-risk situations.	Sends automatic alerts to emergency contacts when risks arise.
Tunneling	Guides users step by step toward healthier behaviour.	Links explanations and follow-ups to build gradual behaviour change.
Personalization	Adjusts system content and feedback based on user data and state.	Continuously adapts to users' data trends and progress.

4 Evaluation

To answer RQ2, we conducted a heuristic evaluation with two practicing clinicians (each with over 10 years of experience managing hypertensive patients) on the clinical appropriateness, explainability, persuasive design quality, and usability of the technology across three hypertension-risk scenarios: *low*, *moderate*, and *high*. The clinicians independently reviewed the HyperCare using 20 well-recognized heuristics from the HCI field, adapted from the healthcare domain [12, 13, 46–48]. As shown in Table 2, the 20 heuristics are organized into five groups, each comprising four heuristics: Clinical Validity and Safety, Transparency and Explainability, Persuasive Design and Behavioural Support, Ethical and Privacy Considerations, and Usability and Presentation – included because expert evaluations can identify most usability issues early in digital-health systems [47], and clinicians have been shown to detect domain-specific usability problems during heuristic evaluations of digital health technologies [48].

Table 2. The five heuristic groups and the corresponding heuristics used to evaluate HyperCare, adapted from the healthcare domain [12, 13, 46–48]

Heuristic group	Heuristics
Clinical Validity and Safety	— Recommendations align with established hypertension guidelines. — No recommendation could cause direct or indirect clinical harm. — Risk thresholds and suggested actions are clinically appropriate. — Alerts convey urgency accurately without alarmism.
Transparency and Explainability	— Each recommendation includes a clear and traceable rationale. — Reasoning is expressed in accessible language. — Data sources and recency are identifiable. — The system communicates uncertainty or confidence when relevant.
Persuasive Design and Behavioural Support	— Goals are specific, measurable, achievable, relevant, and time bound. — Feedback reinforces progress constructively. — Personalization enhances relevance without intrusiveness. — The AI coach maintains a professional and supportive tone.
Ethical and Privacy Considerations	— Sensitive data are handled appropriately. — Recommendations respect cultural and gender diversity. — AI reasoning and data use are transparent. — No recommendation compromises confidentiality or ethical standards.
Usability and Presentation	— Text and layout are concise and easy to interpret. — Terminology conforms to clinical standards. — Interaction and feedback options are visible and intuitive. — The interface remains legible in both light and dark modes.

4.1 Procedure

We provided an instruction document to each clinician that detailed the HyperCare system, the evaluation's purpose, the definition of the heuristics, and the steps for conducting the review. Along with the instruction document, a structured evaluation workbook containing five sheets was provided. The first sheet outlined the overall evaluation procedure, definitions of the heuristic groups, and examples of how to interpret and rate each item. The next three sheets represented the hypertension-risk scenarios which included user data (blood alcohol content, blood glucose level, body weight, step count, and sleep duration) and a brief patient profile specifying age, gender, and a family history of hypertension, as well as the generated interventions, consisting of one insight, three goals, and three suggestions, each accompanied by an explanation. The clinicians' qualitative overall feedback on the evaluation was entered in the provided sheet.

Across the scenarios, each heuristic was rated on a four-point ordinal scale (0 = Not applicable; 1 = Excellent/No issue; 2 = Minor issue; 3 = Major issue; 4 = Critical issue), adapted from previous heuristic evaluation studies in digital health technologies and clinical decision-support systems [12, 49], where such scaling has been shown to provide a reliable and interpretable measure of usability and clinical validity.

4.2 Results

Table 3 summarizes the mean ratings for each heuristic group across all hypertension-risk scenarios. The system achieved uniformly high scores, with mean ratings of 100% for Clinical Validity and Safety, Persuasive Design, Ethical and Privacy, and Usability, and 98.9% for Transparency and Explainability. The inter-rater reliability across the scenarios was computed using Krippendorff's α (ordinal) [14] and Cohen's κ [15] to determine the overall agreement, with values $\alpha = 0.917$ (95% CI [0.75, 1.00]) and $\kappa = 0.901$ ($p < .001$), indicating excellent inter-rater reliability as coefficients above 0.80 are generally interpreted as strong or almost perfect agreement [14].

Beyond the quantitative ratings, qualitative feedback from the clinicians emphasized the system's practical and clinical value. One clinician stated that the app *"will promote healthy lifestyle choices, lower blood pressure, and mitigate the burden of non-communicable diseases. Ultimately, it will reduce cardiovascular morbidity and mortality and help to attain the third Sustainable Development Goal (SDG)."* [C1]. The other described HyperCare as *"innovative and patient-friendly; it will vitally improve patient care."* [C2].

Table 3. Mean heuristic ratings (%) across heuristic groups.

Heuristic group	Clinician 1 (%)	Clinician 2 (%)	Mean (%)
Clinical Validity and Safety	100	100	100
Transparency and Explainability	100	98	99
Persuasive Design and Behavioural Support	100	100	100
Ethical and Privacy Considerations	100	100	100
Usability and Presentation	100	100	100

5 Discussion

This study explored how an explainable, AI-driven persuasive technology can integrate multimodal data and retrieval-augmented reasoning to deliver personalized, evidence-based interventions for hypertension prevention and management (RQ1), and how these interventions are clinically relevant, transparent, persuasive, ethical, and usable (RQ2). The evaluation showed that HyperCare successfully combined continuous multimodal data with explainable AI reasoning to generate adaptive, evidence-based interventions. Clinicians rated these interventions highly across all heuristic groups, indicating strong clinical relevance, transparency, persuasion, ethics, and usability. These findings align with prior work showing that persuasive design features drive motivation and engagement in digital health interventions [44, 45]. They also extend this evidence by demonstrating that integrating these strategies into an explainable, AI-driven system enhances transparency.

These findings have strong implications for clinicians, individuals, and researchers in digital health. For clinicians, beyond reducing workload, HyperCare extends visibility between visits by providing continuous, data-driven insight into behavioural and physiological trends. Passive data reveal how users respond to goals and manage risks in daily life, enabling better-informed clinical decisions and more personalized advice. For individuals, this work shows that hypertension can be prevented and managed continuously without manual tracking. By combining multiple passive data streams, HyperCare delivers feedback unattainable through self-report, shifting health management toward real-time, automatic, and data-informed support. For researchers, the results confirm that passive multimodal sensing provides a robust foundation for personalized and adaptive care. Chronic diseases like hypertension stem from interacting determinants, and integrating multimodal sensing with explainable, persuasive interventions directly addresses this complexity, demonstrating that AI can unify data interpretation and behaviour support within a validated framework.

Next, we reflect on our findings to offer three design recommendations for the future development of persuasive digital health technologies.

5.1 Design Recommendations

Integrate continuous, passive, multimodal sensing with adaptive, persuasive strategies to sustain engagement. The evaluation showed that HyperCare's passive multimodal sensing of alcohol intake, glucose, sleep, weight, and activity reduced perceived user burden (from the clinicians) while maintaining relevance through adaptive feedback. Prior studies have also demonstrated that passive data collection improves adherence, and persuasive mechanisms such as goal setting, reminders, and self-monitoring enhance motivation and behavioural consistency [50]. Future systems should therefore combine passive multimodal sensing with adaptive feedback that interprets real-time data and responds dynamically. For example, a system could detect poor sleep patterns and send a personalized reminder to rest earlier, followed by a progress message when improvement is observed.

Prioritize transparency and explainability in AI-powered technologies. Clinicians consistently rated transparency and traceability as key strengths of HyperCare, noting that clear explanations increased their confidence in the system's reasoning. Prior research in clinical decision-support systems also shows that explainable models enhance trust, accountability, and safe use by allowing users to verify how data influence recommendations [51]. Systems should therefore pair each recommendation with an interpretable explanation directly linked to input data and supporting evidence. For example, when suggesting adjustments to alcohol intake or sleep duration, the system should display the specific readings that triggered the advice and reference the hypertension guideline that supports it.

Extend persuasive strategies through contextual and adaptive personalization. Beyond prior research showing that persuasive and behaviour-change strategies such as reminders, goal setting, and self-monitoring enhance adherence and engagement [44], our findings further demonstrate that these strategies are most effective when dynamically adapted to each user's context. The implication is that persuasion should not be static but evolve with the user's changing state, preferences, and progress. Therefore, future persuasive health systems should implement adaptive feedback loops that learn from user responses to deliver timely, context-sensitive interventions. For example, if a user repeatedly misses activity goals, the system might simplify the target, offer encouragement, and reschedule reminders to align with their daily rhythm.

6   Limitations and Future Work

Although this study does not include a user study, prior work in digital health has established that expert evaluation is an essential step before testing such systems with end users [12]. This study, therefore, focused on clinician-based evaluation to first verify the system's clinical soundness, transparency, and usability. While the number of experts is limited, their specific clinical insights established a necessary foundation for this initial verification. Future work will extend this by conducting a longitudinal user study to examine how individuals with different hypertension-risk levels engage with HyperCare in real-world contexts, assess adherence and trust over time, and evaluate long-term behavioural outcomes. Following the user study, the final stage of this research will involve real-world deployment and continuous refinement of HyperCare in collaboration with healthcare providers to validate integration within clinical workflows, assess population-level scalability, and measure sustained impact on hypertension prevention and management.

7   Conclusion

This study introduced *HyperCare*, an explainable, AI-driven, persuasive technology for hypertension prevention and management that integrates passive multimodal sensing, retrieval-augmented reasoning, and personalized intervention delivery. Through clinician-based evaluation, HyperCare demonstrated high clinical relevance, transparency, persuasion, ethical compliance, and usability, confirming its potential as a clinically sound and trustworthy system. The findings show that combining passive sensing with explainable AI can support continuous hypertension care by providing real-time, evidence-grounded, and personalized recommendations without increasing clinician workload or user burden. Future work will extend this evaluation through a longitudinal user study to examine real-world engagement, adherence, and behavioural outcomes, followed by deployment in clinical settings to validate integration, scalability, and sustained impact on hypertension prevention and management.

Acknowledgments. We acknowledge the support of the Natural Sciences and Engineering Research Council of Canada (NSERC) through the Discovery Grant.

References

1. Kibone, W., et al.: High blood pressure prevalence, awareness, treatment, and blood pressure control among Ugandans with rheumatic and musculoskeletal disorders. PLoS One. **18**, e0289546 (2023)
2. Hypertension: https://www.who.int/news-room/fact-sheets/detail/hypertension, last accessed 2025/11/05.
3. Zhou, B., et al.: Worldwide trends in hypertension prevalence and progress in treatment and control from 1990 to 2019: a pooled analysis of 1201 population-representative studies with 104 million participants. Lancet. **398**, 957 (2021)
4. Prince, S.A., et al.: A comparison of direct versus self-report measures for assessing physical activity in adults: a systematic review. Int. J. Behav. Nutr. Phys. Act. **5**, 1–24 (2008)
5. Leitner, J., et al.: The effect of an AI-based, autonomous, digital health intervention using precise lifestyle guidance on blood pressure in adults with hypertension: single-arm nonrandomized trial. JMIR Cardio. **8**, e51916 (2024)
6. Abdelaal, Y., et al.: Exploring the applications of Explainability in wearable data analytics: systematic literature review. J. Med. Internet Res. **26**, e53863 (2024)
7. Cho, J.S., Park, J.H.: Application of artificial intelligence in hypertension. Clin. Hypertens. **30**(1), 1–9 (2024)
8. Aguzzi, G., et al.: Applying retrieval-augmented generation on open LLMs for a medical Chatbot supporting hypertensive patients. In: Proceedings of the 3rd AIxIA Workshop on Artificial Intelligence for Healthcare (HC@AIxIA 2024), pp. 1–12 (2024)
9. Oinas-Kukkonen, H., et al.: Persuasive systems design: key issues, process model, and system features. Commun. Assoc. Inf. Syst. **24**, 28 (2009)
10. Know Your Risk Factors for High Blood Pressure | American Heart Association: https://www.heart.org/en/health-topics/high-blood-pressure/know-your-risk-factors-for-high-blood-pressure, Accessed 10 Nov 2025.
11. Ranasinghe, P., et al.: The influence of family history of hypertension on disease prevalence and associated metabolic risk factors among Sri Lankan adults. BMC Public Health. **15**(1), 1–9 (2015)
12. Cho, H., et al.: Assessing the usability of a clinical decision support system: heuristic evaluation. JMIR Hum. Factors. **9**, e31758 (2022)
13. Galavi, Z., et al.: Heuristics used for evaluating the usability of mobile health applications: a systematic literature review. Digit Health. **10**, 20552076241253540 (2024)
14. Krippendorff, K.: Content Analysis: an Introduction to its Methodology, 4th edn. Sage Publications (2019)
15. McHugh, M.L.: Interrater reliability: the kappa statistic. Biochem Med (Zagreb). **22**, 276 (2012)
16. Di Federico, S., et al.: Alcohol intake and blood pressure levels: a dose-response meta-analysis of nonexperimental cohort studies. Hypertension. **80**, 1961–1969 (2023)
17. Sakr, H.F., et al.: Insulin resistance and hypertension: mechanisms involved and modifying factors for effective glucose control. Biomedicine. **11**, 2271 (2023)
18. Sabaka, P., et al.: The effects of body weight loss and gain on arterial hypertension control: an observational prospective study. Eur. J. Med. Res. **22**, 43 (2017)
19. Calhoun, D.A., Harding, S.M.: Sleep and hypertension. Chest. **138**, 434 (2010)

20. Hayes, P., et al.: Physical activity and hypertension. Rev. Cardiovasc. Med. **23**, 302 (2022)
21. Gillis, E.E., Sullivan, J.C.: Sex differences in hypertension: recent advances. Hypertension. **68**, 1322–1327 (2016)
22. Wang, N.Y., Young, J.H., Meoni, L.A., Ford, D.E., Erlinger, T.P., Klag, M.J.: Blood pressure change and risk of hypertension associated with parental hypertension: the Johns Hopkins precursors study. Arch. Intern. Med. **168**, 643–648 (2008)
23. Abe, M., et al.: Smartphone application-based intervention to lower blood pressure: a systematic review and meta-analysis. Hypertens. Res. **48**, 492–505 (2025)
24. Kassavou, A., et al.: The association between smartphone app-based self-monitoring of hypertension-related behaviors and reductions in high blood pressure: systematic review and meta-analysis. JMIR Mhealth Uhealth. **10**, e34767 (2022)
25. Sinou, N., et al.: The role of wearable devices in blood pressure monitoring and hypertension management: a systematic review. Cureus. **16**, e75050 (2024)
26. Skalidis, I., et al.: Artificial intelligence and advanced digital health for hypertension: evolving tools for precision cardiovascular care. Medicina. **61**, 1597 (2025)
27. Layton, A.T.: AI, machine learning, and ChatGPT in hypertension. Hypertension. **81**, 709–716 (2024)
28. Ke, Y.H., et al.: Retrieval augmented generation for 10 large language models and its generalizability in assessing medical fitness. npj Digital Med. **8**, 1–11 (2025)
29. BACtrack SDK: https://sdk.bactrack.com/, Accessed 10 Nov 2025.
30. Dexcom API | Home: https://developer.dexcom.com/home, Accessed 10 Nov 2025.
31. Public API | Withings: https://developer.withings.com/developer-guide/v3/withings-soluti ons/app-to-app-solution/, Accessed 10 Nov 2025.
32. Read the Daily Step Total | Google Fit | Google for Developers: https://developers.google. com/fit/scenarios/read-daily-step-total, Accessed 10 Nov 2025
33. Firestore | Firebase: https://firebase.google.com/docs/firestore, Accessed 10 Nov 2025
34. Agarwal, S., et al.: gpt-oss-120b & gpt-oss-20b Model Card. arXiv preprint arXiv:2508.10925 (2025).
35. Groq is fast, low cost inference: https://groq.com/, Accessed 10 Nov 2025
36. Chroma: https://www.trychroma.com/, Accessed 12 Nov 2025
37. Chapter 4: Searching for and selecting studies | Cochrane: https://www.cochrane.org/authors/ handbooks-and-manuals/handbook/current/chapter-04, Accessed 11 Nov 2025
38. Cecchini, M., et al.: Alcohol intake and risk of hypertension: a systematic review and dose-response meta-analysis of nonexperimental cohort studies. Hypertension. **81**, 1701–1715 (2024)
39. Hosseini, K., et al.: Association between sleep duration and hypertension incidence: systematic review and meta-analysis of cohort studies. PLoS One. **19**, e0307120 (2024)
40. Lee, L.L., et al.: Walking for hypertension. Cochrane Database Syst. Rev. (2) (2021)
41. Yuan, L., et al.: Dose-response relationship between body mass index and hypertension: a cross-sectional study from eastern China. Prev. Med. Rep. **46**, 102852 (2024)
42. Yan, Q., et al.: Association of blood glucose level and hypertension in elderly Chinese subjects: a community-based study. BMC Endocr. Disord. **16**, 40 (2016)
43. Whelton, P.K., et al.: 2017 ACC / AHA / AAPA / ABC / ACPM / AGS / APhA / ASH / ASPC / NMA / PCNA Guideline for the Prevention, Detection, Evaluation, and Management of High Blood Pressure in Adults: A Report of the American College of Cardiology/American Heart Association Task Force on Clinical Practice Guidelines….Hypertension. 71, E13–E115 (2018).
44. Gosetto, L., et al.: Personalizing mobile applications for health based on user profiles: a preference matrix from a scoping review. PLOS Digit. Health. **4**(8), e0000978 (2025)

45. Zhou, Y., et al.: Behavior change techniques used in self-management interventions based on mHealth apps for adults with hypertension: systematic review and meta-analysis of randomized controlled trials. J. Med. Internet Res. **26**, e54978 (2024)
46. Zhang, J., et al.: Using usability heuristics to evaluate patient safety of medical devices. J. Biomed. Inform. **36**, 23–30 (2003)
47. de, R.,.T.J., et al.: Usability assessment of a digital tool to enhance person–clinician communication in the memory clinic: an expert evaluation. Digit Health. **11** (2025)
48. Scandurra, I., et al.: Heuristic evaluation performed by usability-educated clinicians: education and attitudes. Stud. Health Technol. Inform. **130**, 205–216 (2007)
49. Jones, E.K., et al.: Combined expert and user-driven usability assessment of trauma decision support systems improves user-centered design. Surgery. **172**, 1537–1548 (2022)
50. Nebeker, C., et al.: Applying a digital health checklist and readability tools to improve informed consent for digital Health Research. Front Digit Health. **3**, 690901 (2021)
51. Anjara, S.G., et al.: Examining explainable clinical decision support systems with think aloud protocols. PLoS One. **18**, e0291443 (2023)

Dual Dimensions of Media Diversity: Cross-Platform News Use and Partisan Exposure

Soo Young Bae[1]([⊠]) [ID] and Meeyoung Cha[2] [ID]

[1] University of Massachusetts, Amherst, MA 01003, USA
sooyoungbae@umass.edu
[2] Max Planck Institute for Security and Privacy, 44799 Bochum, Germany

Abstract. The rise of personalized and algorithmically curated media environments has transformed how influence operates in the digital public sphere. As users increasingly rely on platform-specific news feeds and partisan outlets, concerns have grown that selective exposure may limit citizens' ability to engage with diverse viewpoints and resist misinformation. This study conceptualizes diverse media use as a key dimension of digital media exposure that shapes how individuals encounter information across contrasting communicative environments. Drawing on a national online survey of South Korean adults (N = 1,000), this study differentiates media platform diversity and media partisan diversity and examines how each is associated with political knowledge and conspiracy beliefs about the #MeToo movement. The analyses reveal a dual pattern. High levels of platform-diverse news use, while seemingly satisfying users' information needs across different platforms, were unrelated to political knowledge yet positively associated with belief in #MeToo conspiracies, suggesting that cross-platform repetition may amplify misinformation rather than broaden understanding. These findings indicate that users exposed to news across multiple platforms may develop a perceived sense of being well informed, even in the absence of substantive knowledge gains. In contrast, higher levels of partisan diversity in digital media use were positively related to political knowledge and negatively associated with conspiracy beliefs, pointing to the potential of ideologically diverse exposure to support more balanced information processing. Overall, the study extends ongoing discussions of media diversity by demonstrating that greater exposure across platforms does not necessarily correspond to more informed or reflective beliefs. By highlighting how different forms of diversity shape belief formation, the study offers new insights into the subtle, system-level mechanisms through which digital information environments exert persuasive influence.

Keywords: Information Systems · Platform Diversity · Partisan Diversity · Algorithmic Persuasion · Misinformation

1 Introduction

In an era dominated by algorithmic curation and personalized recommendation systems, citizens' encounters with information are increasingly fragmented and selective. Social media feeds, search algorithms, and mobile news apps filter content in ways that reinforce existing interests, potentially narrowing the range of perspectives to which users

K. Sumi et al. (Eds.): PERSUASIVE 2026, LNCS 16476, pp. 17–24, 2026.
https://doi.org/10.1007/978-3-032-19687-3_2

are exposed. This transformation in news delivery has revived long-standing questions about how diversity in media exposure shapes political learning and persuasion. Traditional theories of democratic communication emphasize the normative value of diverse information environments, arguing that exposure to a broad range of viewpoints enables citizens to make informed judgments and resist misinformation. Yet, the meaning of "diversity" has become more complex in algorithmic contexts. Whereas earlier studies treated diversity largely as variation in ideological content, today's media users navigate multiple platforms, each with its own architecture, affordances, and algorithmic logic, that influence what information is encountered and how it is interpreted.

This study examines the persuasive implications of these new forms of diversity. Specifically, it differentiates between platform diversity (exposure to news across multiple types of media platforms), and partisan diversity (exposure to ideologically varied outlets). By comparing these two dimensions, this research seeks to illuminate how distinct pathways of media diversity may differentially shape citizens' political knowledge and susceptibility to misinformation.

2 Literature Review

The selective exposure tradition argues that individuals gravitate toward congenial information that confirms prior beliefs [1]. However, algorithmic personalization complicates this process. Personalized news feeds are not simply reflections of user preferences, but products of algorithmic inferences designed to maximize engagement [2]. Empirical work suggests that personalization can reinforce existing biases by filtering out counter-attitudinal information, creating "filter bubbles" or "echo chambers" [3]. Yet, others contend that algorithmic systems may occasionally increase incidental exposure to diverse content [4]. These mixed findings underscore the need to specify what kind of diversity matters.

Media diversity is multidimensional. Platform diversity refers to the range of distinct channels, television, newspapers, social media, portals, messengers, through which individuals obtain news. This diversity reflects technological multiplicity rather than ideological variation. Prior research shows that cross-platform use can expand perceived exposure [5] and provide a sense of being well-informed, even when substantive knowledge remains limited [6]. The repetitive circulation of similar stories across platforms can foster redundant learning, reinforcing beliefs through repetition rather than comprehension.

Partisan diversity, in contrast, captures exposure to ideologically diverse sources. Cross-cutting exposure, which refers to encounters with viewpoints from opposing sides, has been linked to increased political knowledge and tolerance [7, 8]. Ideological heterogeneity encourages deliberative reflection and reduces susceptibility to misinformation [9]. In polarized environments, however, ideologically one-sided media diets may intensify affective polarization.

From a persuasion perspective, the sense of being informed can itself be influential. Exposure across multiple platforms may produce perceived knowledge gain, enhancing confidence without necessarily improving factual understanding, a form of illusory fluency [10]. Such perceived expertise can make individuals more resistant to corrective information and more receptive to conspiratorial frames that "fit" pre-existing schemas. Conversely, ideologically diverse exposure introduces cognitive dissonance that can foster critical evaluation, counter-arguing, and deeper learning. Taken together, these insights suggest that media diversity exerts dual persuasive effects, one rooted in technological diversity (platform-based) and another in ideological diversity (partisan). Building on this framework, the present study asks the following research question:

RQ: How do the two forms of media diversity – platform and partisan – differentially relate to citizens' political understanding and susceptibility to conspiracy beliefs?

3 Methods

3.1 Data

The study draws on survey data from South Korea collected in November 2020, administered online by the national polling firm *Embrain*. Stratified quota sampling matched official census distributions for age, gender, and region. A total of 1,000 adults (ages 19–69; M = 40.95, SD = 13.69; 51.2% male) completed the questionnaire. Key demographic characteristics of the sample closely resemble population figures reported by Statistics Korea for age (sample mean = 40.95; population mean = 42.4), gender (sample = 51.2% male; population = 50.1% male), and monthly household income (sample median = KRW 2,000,000–3,000,000; population median ≈ KRW 2,970,000). The sample includes a higher proportion of respondents with higher education (84.9%) compared to the general South Korean population, where approximately 50% hold a college diploma. While we acknowledge this overrepresentation, it is reflective of the digitally literate segment that predominantly engages with digital media in South Korea.

Our study was conducted in the context of the #MeToo movement in South Korea, which provided a useful opportunity to examine the theorized relationships. The series of accusations in the #MeToo movement gave rise to political rumors and conspiracy theories that revolved around the perpetrators, the victims, and the movement itself. In addition, South Korea presents an ideal context for examining the use of various media platforms, with a high usage rate of social and mobile platforms and news portals [11].

3.2 Independent Variables

Platform Diversity Index
To measure the diversity of media platforms used for news, participants indicated how frequently they used each of 11 distinct sources, spanning traditional, digital, and interpersonal channels. These included newspapers, TV news, radio, social media platforms (e.g., Facebook, X/Twitter, Instagram, TikTok), Internet forums, online video platforms (e.g., YouTube), personalized news feeds (e.g., Google News, Apple News), podcasts, web portals (e.g., NAVER), mobile messengers (e.g., WhatsApp, KakaoTalk, Telegram), and offline conversations with acquaintances. Responses were measured on a 5-point scale (1 = never, 5 = several times a day).

These items were used to calculate each user's platform diversity using the Shannon diversity index, also known as "Shannon entropy" [12]. Originally proposed by Claude

Shannon in 1948 as a measure of informational uncertainty, the index captures the degree to which observations are spread across different categories. In systems with low entropy, where most activity is concentrated in only a few categories, outcomes are relatively predictable; in high-entropy systems, where activity is distributed more evenly, outcomes become more uncertain. Because it reflects both variety and distribution, the Shannon index has become one of the most widely used measures of diversity in fields such as ecology and biological monitoring. In the context of media use, it emphasizes the *richness* of an individual's news environment. This represents the number of different platforms they rely on, rather than simple frequency or uniformity of use. The Shannon entropy index was calculated as:

$$H = -\sum_i P_i \ln P_i \tag{1}$$

P_i represents the proportion of an individual's total news use that comes from platform i, calculated by dividing the amount of use for each platform by the individual's overall media use. For example, consider a respondent who uses social media, YouTube, and portal services several times a day (coded as 5), and watches TV news three times a week (coded as 3). Responses of "never" were coded as 0. In this case, the respondent's total media use equals 18, yielding proportional values such as P(social media) = 5/18, P(YouTube) = 5/18, P(portal) = 5/18, and P(TV news) = 3/18. The Shannon index is then computed by multiplying each proportion by its natural logarithm, summing these products, and multiplying the result by -1. Higher values of the Platform Diversity Index indicate greater diversity in the media platforms an individual uses for news (0 = no diversity; 2.4 = maximum diversity). In this study, respondents' Platform Diversty Index scores ranged up to 2.4 (M = 1.81, SD = 0.42).

Partisan Diversity Index

Partisan diversity was measured using participants' reported use of 26 news outlets that were classified into three ideological categories: right-leaning (n = 5), left-leaning (n = 5), and central/neutral (n = 16), based on prior research [13], see Table 1]. Respondents indicated which of these outlets they used regularly. To capture the breadth and the range of ideological perspectives represented in a participant's media diet, we created a two-component index.

First, we calculated a baseline outlet-use score:

$$U = (Number\ of\ outlets\ used\ by\ individual)/26 \tag{2}$$

Second, we identified how many of the three ideological categories were represented in the individual's selected outlets:

$$D = Number\ of\ ideological\ categories\ used\ (1, 2, or\ 3) \tag{3}$$

The final Partisan Diversity Index is the product of these two components:

$$Partisan\ Diversity = U \times D = \frac{Number\ of\ Outlets\ Used}{26} \times D \tag{4}$$

This operationalization ensures that a participant receives a higher score only when they both (1) use a greater number of outlets overall and (2) draw on outlets from a wider range of ideological categories (ranging from right-leaning to left-leaning). Thus, the index captures not just quantity of outlet use but the *ideological heterogeneity* of individuals' media exposure.

Table 1. Media Outlets by Ideological Leaning

Score	Example	Number of Outlets
Right leaning	Chosunilbo, JoongAng Ilbo, Dong-A Ilbo, TV chosun, Channel A	5 items
Left leaning	Hankyoreh, Kyunghyang Shinmun, Ohmynews, Newstapa, JTBC	5 items
Central/Neutral	Munhwa Ilbo, Kookmin Ilbo, PRESSIAN, Money Today, Insight, E-daily, Dailian, NoCutNews, Dispatch, MBC, SBS, KBS, YTN, MBN, Local broadcasting, and all others	26 items

3.3 Dependent Variables

Political Knowledge. Eight factual items assessed the respondent's knowledge of South Korea's politics and issues (e.g., name of prime minister, minimum wage, recent legislation outcomes related to #MeToo). Correct answers were coded 1, summed to yield a score ranging from 0 to 8 ($M - 4.37$, $SD = 1.66$).

#MeToo Conspiracy Beliefs. Belief in the #MeToo conspiracy was measured using a 5-point Likert scale (1 = completely disagree, 5 = completely agree). Respondents indicated their agreement with four statements depicting the #MeToo movement as politically motivated: (1) the #MeToo movement is a conspiracy to attack liberal politicians; (2) the #MeToo movement is a conspiracy to attack conservative politicians; (3) the movement is a campaign deliberately devised by specific groups for strategic gain; and (4) the movement is being used as a political maneuver to undermine a particular politician or party. Responses were averaged to create a single index of conspiracy belief (Cronbach's $\alpha = .90$, $M = 2.51$, $SD = 0.91$).

3.4 Control Variables

Several demographic and political factors were included as controls: age, gender, income, education, and political interest. Political interest ($M = 3.30$, $SD = 1.01$) was measured with the item, "How interested are you in politics?" (1 = not at all interested, 5 = very interested).

3.5 Analysis

Ordinary least squares (OLS) regressions tested main and interaction effects using the StatsModels library in Python.

4 Results

The central aim of this study was to assess how different forms of media diversity – platform-based and partisan – shape individuals' political understanding and susceptibility to conspiracy beliefs. To address this, our analyses first examined the baseline associations between the full set of control variables and each key outcome. As shown in Table 2, the block of control variables demonstrates significant relationships with the outcome variables political knowledge and conspiracy beliefs. Overall, education was a positive predictor of political knowledge (β = .28, p < .001) and negative predictor of beliefs in #MeToo conspiracies (β = −.19, p < .001). Similarly, respondents with higher levels of political interest scored higher in political knowledge (β = .34, p < .001) while showing lower levels of #MeToo conspiracy beliefs (β = −.14, p < .001).

Further analyses reveal the contrasting outcomes of platform-diverse news use and partisan diversity in predicting the two outcome variables. First, platform diversity did now show a significant relationship with political knowledge. However, platform diversity was positively related to belief in the #MeToo conspiracy (β = .15, p < .001). This finding suggests that citizens who consumed news across many different types of platforms were not necessarily more politically knowledgeable, yet they were more likely to endorse conspiratorial interpretations of the #MeToo movement, even after controls. In contrast, partisan diversity was positively associated with political knowledge (β = .35, p < .001) and negatively associated with #MeToo conspiracy belief (β = −.10, p < .10). This suggests that users with ideologically varied media diets were more informed and less prone to conspiratorial reasoning.

Table 2. Regression Outputs

Predictors	Political Knowledge (β, t)	#MeToo Conspiracy Belief (β, t)
Age	.03***, 3.50	−.01*, −2.10
Gender (male = 1)	.60***, 6.20	.49***, 5.80
Education	.28***, 7.10	−.19***, −4.50
Income	.07*, 2.20	n.s.
Political Interest	.34***, 8.90	−.14***, −3.80
Platform Diversity Index	n.s.	.15***, 4.10
Partisan Diversity Index	.35***, 9.00	−.10#, −1.80
Total R^2 (%)	20.6%	11.8%

Note: Entries are standardized regression coefficients. # p < .10; * p < .05; ** p < .01; *** p < .001.

5 Discussion

This study expands our understanding of media diversity by offering a more nuanced and empirically grounded account of how users' media diets and habits shape political learning and misperceptions. A key contribution lies in distinguishing platform diversity from partisan diversity, two forms of media diversity that are often conflated in existing scholarship. By conceptualizing these as distinct technological and ideological dimensions of media exposure, this study provides a more precise approach to capturing the complexity of individuals' media repertoires.

In addition, this study adopts the "Shannon entropy index" to operationalize platform diversity. This methodological extension allows us to move beyond simple counts of news sources to assess the distribution and balance of exposure across platforms and ideological outlets, offering a more robust and theoretically informed measure of diversity.

The findings of this study reveal that these two forms of diversity yield fundamentally different outcomes. Partisan diversity is shown to foster the acquisition of political knowledge, while platform diversity contributes no significant gains. Consistent with prior theorization of cross-cutting exposure, our results also show that encountering ideologically heterogeneous sources can facilitate cognitive elaboration that may ultimately reduce belief in conspiracy theories. In contrast, platform diversity exhibits a positive association with conspiracy beliefs surrounding #MeToo. Taken together, these results highlight a nuanced but crucial paradox: technological diversity without ideological diversity may reinforce misperceptions rather than mitigate them, enabling users to confirm existing beliefs across multiple platforms. Although individuals traverse many platforms, they may encounter redundant content driven by similar algorithmic logics. Such repetition may reinforce familiarity and confidence without improving factual understanding, leaving users more susceptible to conspiratorial narratives that gain credibility through repeated cross-platform exposure.

Nevertheless, this study has several limitations to be addressed. Because the data are cross-sectional, causal interpretations should be made with caution. It remains unclear whether diverse platform use leads to conspiratorial belief or whether individuals prone to such beliefs seek out multiple sources for confirmation. Future research should employ longitudinal or experimental designs to clarify these relationships. Additionally, qualitative approaches could offer deeper insight into how individuals subjectively interpret "diversity" in their daily media routines, whether they equate platform switching with informational variety or recognize ideological sameness across channels. Finally, expanding the scope of inquiry beyond the #MeToo movement to other issues of social controversy will help assess the generalizability of the dual-diversity framework proposed here.

Overall, by disentangling technological from ideological diversity and applying a distribution-sensitive entropy measure, this study provides a more nuanced theoretical and empirical foundation for understanding how diverse media environments shape political knowledge, perceived knowledge, and conspiracy beliefs in the algorithmic public sphere.

References

1. Stroud, N.J.: Niche News: the Politics of News Choice. Oxford University Press, Oxford (2011)
2. Pariser, E.: The Filter Bubble: What the Internet Is Hiding from you. Penguin, New York (2011)

3. Bakshy, E., Messing, S., Adamic, L.A.: Exposure to ideologically diverse news and opinion on Facebook. Science. **348**(6239), 1130–1132 (2015)
4. Fletcher, R., Nielsen, R.K.: Are people incidentally exposed to news on social media? New Media Soc. **20**(7), 2450–2468 (2017)
5. Kim, Y., Chen, H.-T., Gil de Zúñiga, H.: Stumbling upon news on the internet. Comput. Hum. Behav. **29**(6), 2607–2614 (2013)
6. Park, J., Mostafa, N.A., Han, H.-J.: StoryWeb: a storytelling-based knowledge-sharing application among multiple stakeholders. Creat. Innov. Manag. **29**(2), 224–236 (2020)
7. Mutz, D.C.: Cross-cutting social networks: testing democratic theory in practice. Am. Polit. Sci. Rev. **96**(1), 111–126 (2002)
8. Wojcieszak, M., Price, V.: Bridging the divide or intensifying the conflict? J. Commun. **60**(4), 656–675 (2010)
9. Garrett, R.K., Nisbet, E.C., Lynch, E.K.: Undermining the corrective effects of media exposure: the role of confirmation bias. J. Commun. **63**(4), 617–637 (2013)
10. Oppenheimer, D.M.: The secret life of fluency. Trends Cogn. Sci. **12**(6), 237–241 (2008)
11. Reuters Institute: Digital news report 2023. Reuters Institute for the Study of Journalism, Oxford (2023)
12. Shannon, C.E.: A mathematical theory of communication. Bell Syst. Tech. J. **27**(3), 379–423 (1948)
13. Park, S.: Political news use on internet: use patterns and users' characteristics. Korean J. Journalism Commun. Stud. **48**(3), 436–465 (2004)

From Bytes to Blocks: Motivating Students to Learn Microprogramming with Minecraft

Roan Cedric Campo, Enzo Arkin Panugayan$^{(\boxtimes)}$, Clive Jarel Ang, and Roger Luis Uy

College of Computer Studies, De La Salle University, Manila, Philippines
{roan_campo,enzo_arkin_panugayan,clive_jarel_c_ang,roger.uy}@dlsu.edu.ph

Abstract. Computer Architecture is a core subject in Computer Science that involves understanding the structure, function, and design of computer systems. However, the traditional method of educating students with Computer Architecture can be difficult for students to understand without visual simulation. Minecraft is a sandbox game with electrical components called Redstone, which allows players to replicate circuits like Logic Gates, Combinational Logic, Flip Flops, Memory Units, and even a fully functional Computer. Redstone circuits in Minecraft have been proven to be Turing Complete, allowing the creation of computational systems similar to real digital systems. This study explores the use of Minecraft as a supplementary educational platform for learning Computer Architecture through gamified and visual simulations, and examines how it can affect the motivation and understanding of students. We designed a 16-bit Von Neumann architecture where the Control Unit, responsible for coordinating CPU operations, is left as a blank template for students to encode proper microcode signals for the correct cycle to emulate instruction execution. The project was implemented as a major course output for an undergraduate computer architecture course at a Philippine university where instruction is conducted primarily in English, as is standard in Philippine higher education for computer science programs. Student understanding on Microprogramming was assessed using a pre-test administered after traditional lectures and a post-test following the completion of the Minecraft-based project.

Keywords: Computer Architecture · Gamified Learning · Minecraft Redstone · Central Processing Unit · Microprogramming

1 Introduction

The study of computer architecture requires students to work across multiple levels of abstraction simultaneously. The execution of a single instruction has multiple aspects, including transistor physics, gate logic, datapath organization, and ISA semantics. Sweller's cognitive load theory [21] suggests that this density of

K. Sumi et al. (Eds.): PERSUASIVE 2026, LNCS 16476, pp. 25–40, 2026.
https://doi.org/10.1007/978-3-032-19687-3_3

information can exceed working memory capacity. The problem is compounded by what might be called the "invisibility" of hardware: unlike software, where print statements can be used to reveal a program's state, important processes in computer architecture, such as clock propagation, occur without observable side effects. Students cannot see data moving through a datapath until results appear in registers. However, Nikolic et al. [12] found that visualization was the most requested feature in architecture education tools.

1.1   Minecraft and the Validation Problem

Minecraft's Redstone system has been proven to be Turing-complete and has been used to build processors by community members [20]. However, the system's behavior differs from physical hardware in ways that matter pedagogically. For example, signals propagate instantly through Redstone dust within a game tick, while components like torches introduce delays. This inverts real electronics, where wire delay is often the dominant factor.

In addition, there is limited empirical support for Minecraft in education. Prayaga et al. [18] explored using Minecraft to teach digital logic to secondary students through hands-on activities. Alawajee and Delafield-Butt [2] conducted a systematic review of 42 studies and found that only 19% included control groups, highlighting methodological limitations in the field. LeRoy [8] compared Minecraft and PowerPoint lessons on logic gates with varying levels of multimedia support, finding mixed results where Minecraft groups performed significantly better on construction-based retention tasks while PowerPoint groups reported higher cognitive processing demands.

What exists is a validation gap. Official curricula like Minecraft: Education Edition may undergo testing, but they coexist with numerous community tutorials that claim educational value without pedagogical design or assessment. The popularity of the platform has outpaced the research needed to establish its effectiveness. Microsoft's ownership of Minecraft adds another layer of complexity to independent validation. Though there were still instances of testing the capabilities of Minecraft for education, where motivation shows positive results especially with children as Minecraft is widely popular amongst them [23].

Other game-based environments offer different approaches. Factorio uses logic combinators and conveyor systems that align with dataflow architectures [4]. The game Turing Complete provides structured puzzles that progress from NAND gates to complete CPUs [11]. Moreover, Zachtronics programming games (e.g. ExaPunks) present constrained, assembly-like programming that emphasizes optimization. Each platform embodies different pedagogical assumptions about how students should engage with computational concepts.

1.2   Microprogramming Simulators

Microprogramming persists in education despite its decline in commercial processors. Parker and Becker [16] argue that it makes control unit operation visible in ways that hardwired control does not. The writing of microcode requires specifying every register transfer and control signal for each instruction cycle. This builds a detailed model of processor operation. Educational architectures like MARIE [13], MIPS [17], and DLX [5] balance complexity with accessibility at different levels of abstraction.

Existing tools fall into three categories, each with limitations. Educational processors like SEP (Simple Enough Processor) [7] provide structured environments for understanding CPU operation but may limit exploration of alternative designs. Interactive simulators such as those described by Wolffe et al. [24] provide microcode editors but often lack adequate debugging support, making error correction difficult for students. Constructive environments like Logisim let students build processors from the gates up, but this buries control unit concepts under the mechanics of low-level wiring, contradicting constructionist principles that emphasize learning through active construction [15].

These tools force a choice between abstraction and construction. Students would have to observe without building or build while managing details unrelated to control logic.

1.3 Research Gaps and Synthesis

In general, two problems emerge from this analysis. Game-based platforms engage students but face questions of hardware fidelity and the lack of research validation. Microprogramming simulators offer either too much abstraction or too little, failing to support learning at the appropriate level. The gap between these approaches suggests the need for tools that enable the construction of control units without requiring gate-level implementation or accepting passive observation. Such tools would need to balance student agency with conceptual focus, motivation, and technical friction, although how to achieve this balance and whether this 'productive' failure can be quantitatively captured beyond surface level sentiment remains to be an open question.

2 Methodology

2.1 Computer Architecture in Minecraft

The implementation of computer architecture within Minecraft relies on different redstone components to emulate logic gates, which constitutes as the fundamental building blocks of digital systems. Minecraft provides four primary redstone components: Redstone Wire, Redstone Torch, Redstone Repeater, and Redstone Comparator. Through a systematic combination of these elements, it is possible to create the complete set of logical operations (AND, OR, XOR, NOT). By default, redstone wires operate on a signal range of 0–15, where 0 represents a logical low state and values 1–15 represent logical high states. The Redstone Torch functions inherently as a NOT gate, producing output when unpowered and deactivating when powered. The Redstone Repeater acts as a buffer gate, propagating signals to connected redstone wires to construct OR gates. Implementing an AND gate follows from the composition of NOT gates according to De Morgan's laws. The Redstone Comparator performs comparison and subtraction operations on signals; when configured through specific means, it can be used to replicate an XOR gate. Through these approaches, the research team were able to successfully implement the complete set of fundamental logical operations within the Minecraft environment.

The initial phase of implementation drew upon established community resources, including a YouTube tutorial series on Minecraft Redstone by mattbatwings [10], which provided foundational examples of the different implementations of logic gates. Subsequent development phases proceeded independently through iterative design and testing by the research team.

2.2 Architecture Overview

The hierarchical composition of logic gates enables the construction of higher-level components, including the Arithmetic Logic Unit (ALU), Main Memory (MM), Control Unit (CU), and register file. These components constitute the minimal architecture required for a functional Von Neumann Central Processing Unit (CPU) capable of executing programs stored in main memory (Fig. 1).

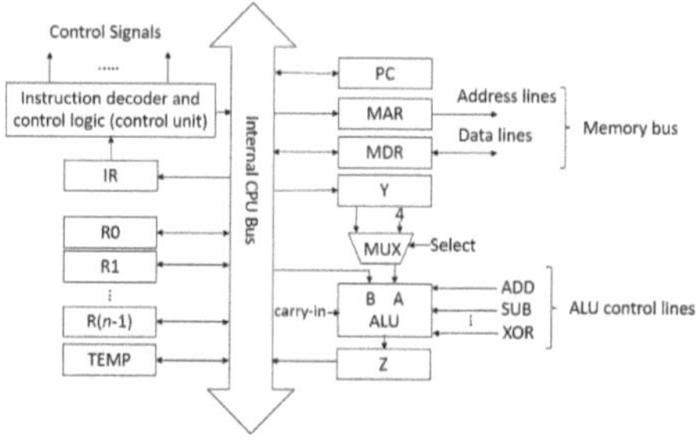

Fig. 1. Example of a single-bus CPU architecture

The **Arithmetic Logic Unit (ALU)** performs all arithmetic and logical operations of the CPU. It supports eight operations: (ADD, SUB, MUL, DIV, AND, OR, XOR, NOT). The ALU updates conditional flags automatically to support branching instructions such as JZ and JNZ. The **Main Memory (MM)** provides 16-bit storage per address and supports READ and WRITE operations via the Memory Address Register (MAR) and Memory Data Register (MDR). The **Control Unit (CU)** coordinates instruction execution by generating precisely timed microcode signals for the ALU, memory, and register file. The system supports 16 operation codes, encoded in a fixed instruction format consisting of an operation field, operand identifiers, and a buffer for immediate values (OPERATION OPERAND BUFFER OPERAND).

Design Constraints and Pedagogical Considerations. Given that the primary goal is to motivate student engagement with microprogramming concepts through visual representation, the computer was designed in a way that prioritizes accessibility over complexity. The implementation constrains the system to a 16-bit architecture with 16 operation codes, a limitation made because of the performance of Minecraft's rendering engines on lower-end machines. Larger implementations encounter runtime errors when components exceed the simulation distance boundary, causing those components to not be rendered and, therefore, to break mid-execution. The instruction format also simplifies the interpretation of OP codes and emphasizes microprogramming behavior (Fig. 2).

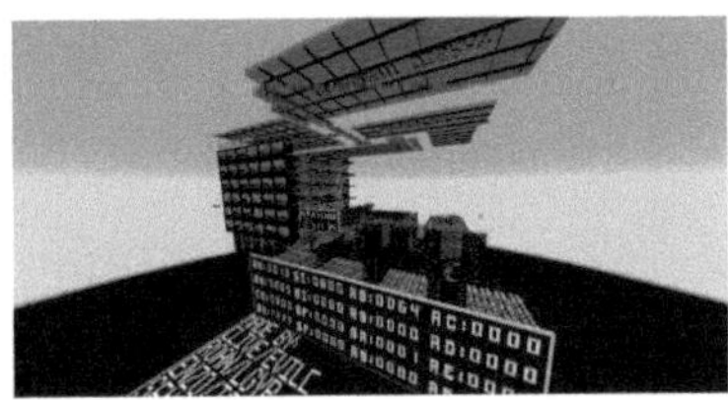

Fig. 2. Implementation of 16-Bit Control Bus

2.3   Research Design

The study used an iterative design methodology, beginning with a pilot implementation conducted with an initial cohort of students in the preceding academic term. This preliminary case study served as a beta test, with the pilot cohort achieving a mean project grade of 82%, a passing but modest result that suggested room for improvement. The students also provided valuable feedback, outlining several concerns and suggestions for improvements which were incorporated into the next iteration of ArchCraft. This paper focuses on the second iteration of ArchCraft. This is also where improvements were incorporated to the current iteration. Whereas the initial iteration emphasized the hardware connections between the Control Unit and system components, the second and current iteration prioritized microprogramming concepts and microcode mapping strategies.

Students were first taught microprogramming through the traditional lecture-based approach, followed by a formative assessment to evaluate their conceptual understanding. This assessment incorporated theoretical machine code problems designed to distinguish true comprehension from rote memorization. Subsequently, students became involved with ArchCraft as their summative project, tasked with encoding the appropriate control signals for their assigned assembly instructions and executing complete programs loaded into main memory according to the provided specifications. The assignment included architectural constraints and theoretical assembly code with specified behavioral requirements, which enabled the researchers to assess the students' ability to apply the concepts they learned in microprogramming to special applications.

2.4   Reflection Analysis

Data Collection and Preprocessing. Reflections were collected from 69 students across four sections of a university computer science course following a Minecraft-based microprogramming activity. As is common in Philippine higher education, students wrote their reflections in a mixture of English and Filipino, a code-switching style locally known as "Taglish." To ensure a granular analysis of the system's persuasive impact, paragraphs were segmented into individual sentences, resulting in a dataset of 1563 units. The text was then cleaned using regex and NLTK to remove noise while preserving the bilingual content for contextual validity.

Thematic Modeling. We employed **BERTopic** with the *paraphrase-multilingual-MiniLM-L12-v2* transformer to capture bilingual semantic nuances. Dimensionality was reduced via UMAP to five components, followed by HDB-SCAN for initial clustering. We applied **Agglomerative Clustering** optimized by Silhouette Score to refine these into "Broad Themes" representing distinct areas of student engagement.

Theoretical Mapping. Following [22], we modeled the environment as a Persuasive System where design features act as antecedents to psychological outcomes [14].

- **PSD Support Areas**: We quantified four categories from the Persuasive Systems Design (PSD) framework: Primary Task (PTS), Dialogue (DS), System Credibility (SC), and Social Support (SS) [22].
- **Motivational States**: We measured the three pillars of Self-Determination Theory (SDT)—Autonomy (AT), Competence (CM), and Relatedness (RD) [19]. We additionally operationalized **Resilience (PF)** through the lens of Productive Failure [6], quantifying persistence despite technical friction [9].

Multi-Dimensional Semantic Analysis. To help assign a score to PSD, SDT, and PF, we devised a two lens approach to have multiple ways to understand:

- **Lens 1 (Lexical Salience)**: Here, direct thematic alignment is measured between student reflections and theoretical framework. We calculated cosine similarity (CS) to measure literal alignment with anchors that we made. Each metric's defining anchor was handcrafted by us such that it saturates its definition. This serves mostly as to validate the second lens.

– **Lens 2 (Logical Entailment)**: To capture "higher-order" meaning, we employed Natural Language Inference (NLI) using `BART-large-mnli`. NLI classifies the relationship between a "premise" (student reflection) and a "hypothesis" (e.g., "This student shows competence") [1]. This zero-shot approach provides an entailment probability (EP) that bypasses literal terminology to discover latent behaviors, such as resilience, that are statistically invisible to lexical tools.

By triangulating these lenses, we can evaluate the effectiveness of the persuasive support areas and motivational states present in the environment. This methodology allows us to separate between literal surface-level thematic overlap and the deep internalization. Statistical validation, using Kruskal-Wallis test, Dunn's test, and a Correlation tests, can be used identify statistically significant differences in metrics of semantics.

Thematic and Sentiment Analysis. Student sentiment of the reflections was captured using *twitter-XLM-roBERTa-base*; it is chosen for its robustness in multilingual, informal text - notably a mixture of Filipino and English commonly known as Taglish [3]. This ML-based approach provided probability scores ranging from positive (+1) to negative (-1) indicating the emotional significance of a student. Then, we explored how sentiment is distributed across themes and is correlated to the motivation of students.

Interaction Matrix Analysis. To investigate the structural relationship between system features and psychological outcomes, we implemented an Interaction Matrix using Spearman's Rank Correlation (ρ). Building on the structural modeling established by [14], our approach replaces linear Pearson correlations with NLI-derived Entailment Probabilities (EP) to better capture non-linear relationships within the technical sandbox environment. This method triangulates design-level interventions (PSD) with experiential outcomes (SDT and PF) across all engagement themes. High correlation coefficients in the resulting matrix quantify the efficacy of specific persuasive support areas in stimulating fundamental psychological needs, providing a granular map of how system design influences motivational states.

3   Results

3.1   Performance Assessment

The grading scheme emphasized students' ability to implement theoretical instructions and algorithms rather than reproduce lecture-demonstrated microcode. Students were required to encode assembly instructions to a custom instruction. Optimization constraints were enforced through cycle-count limits and penalties for inefficiencies. Project tasks included instructions such as SQUARE DST, SRC, which squares a source register and stores the result in a destination register under a two-cycle execution constraint, as well as LOAD-THREE, which assessed understanding of register positioning and ALU operand routing. Performance data were collected from 14 groups of five students each. The cohort achieved a mean project grade of 97.70% (out of 100), a substantial improvement over the pilot cohort's 82% and indicates a generally better grasp at the concepts learned throughout the course. Error analysis indicated that mistakes resulted primarily from carelessness rather than conceptual misunderstanding, as all groups successfully implemented the required theoretical instructions and integrated them into functional algorithms.

3.2   Thematic Labelling and Feature Classification

BERTopic identified 18 optimal clusters based on Silhouette Score maximization. These themes, summarized in Table 1, represent the primary dimensions of student engagement, ranging from technical implementation to emotional balancing.

Table 1. Theme Category from Student Reflections

ID	Labeled Theme	Top Keywords
0	Conceptual Understanding	computer architecture, architecture, concepts
1	Learner Interest	would, subjects, learning
2	Performance Constraints	tick, testing, time
3	Game-Based Motivation	gamebased, academic, love
4	Technical Engagement	unit, control, memory
5	Learning via Minecraft	microprogramming, microprogramming minecraft, minecraft
6	Transcription Noise	micr, comput er, er
7	Instructional Materials	videos, video, module videos
8	Hands-On CPU Operations	cpu, see cpu, minecraft
9	Problem Solving	solution, challenges, however
10	Platform Limitations	limitations, minecraft, run minecraft
11	Digital Logic / Redstone	redstone, circuits, redstone circuits
12	Project Value	opinion, think idea, project lot
13	Future Recommendation	batches, future batches, future
14	Balancing Emotions	project, academics, fun
15	Deepening Concepts	microprogramming, learning microprogramming, text
16	Creative Architecture	architecture, computer architecture, computer
17	Real-World Design	realworld, systems, computer systems

3.3   Mean Entailment Score Distribution

Distribution of Persuasive Support Area Scores. Overall, System Credibility (SC) maintained the highest Mean EP across all major themes, **reflecting a strong student perception** on the platform's technical authority and the accuracy of the Redstone-based feedback loop throughout the project. Notably, High alignment of SC and Primary Task Support (PTS) and themes like Project Value (T12) and Hands-On CPU Operations (T8) **indicates that perceived reliability was closely tied** to the constructionist nature of the assignment (Fig. 3).

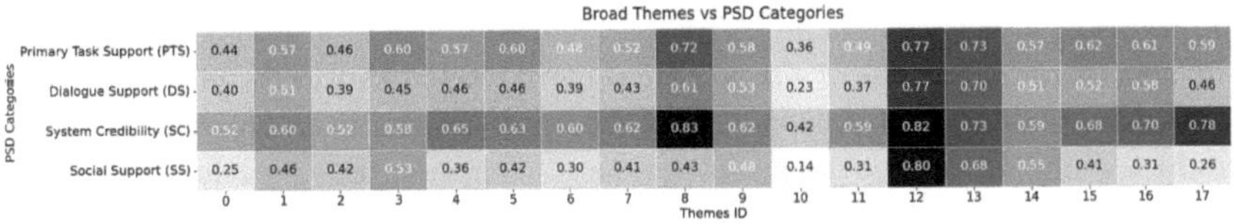

Broad Themes vs PSD Categories

PSD Categories	0	1	2	3	4	5	6	7	8	9	10	11	12	13	14	15	16	17
Primary Task Support (PTS)	0.44	0.57	0.46	0.60	0.57	0.60	0.48	0.52	0.72	0.58	0.36	0.49	0.77	0.73	0.57	0.62	0.61	0.59
Dialogue Support (DS)	0.40	0.51	0.39	0.45	0.46	0.46	0.39	0.43	0.61	0.53	0.23	0.37	0.77	0.70	0.51	0.52	0.58	0.46
System Credibility (SC)	0.52	0.60	0.52	0.58	0.65	0.63	0.60	0.62	0.83	0.62	0.42	0.59	0.82	0.73	0.59	0.68	0.70	0.78
Social Support (SS)	0.25	0.46	0.42	0.53	0.36	0.42	0.30	0.41	0.43	0.48	0.14	0.31	0.80	0.68	0.55	0.41	0.31	0.26

Themes ID

Fig. 3. EP Distribution of PSD Support Categories/Areas across Broad Themes

Mean EP scores identify Hands-On CPU Operations (T8) as the psychological "peak," where direct datapath interaction co-occurred with maximized CM (0.95) and RD (0.97). A distinct PF signature emerged in Problem Solving (T9), where Resilience (0.75) significantly outweighed AT (0.66), statistically capturing a "productive struggle" of high persistence despite reduced environmental control.

Conversely, Platform Limitations (T10) functioned as a persuasive deterrent; low AT (0.42) and Resilience (0.38) mark the threshold where technical friction **appears to hinder** engagement (Fig. 4).

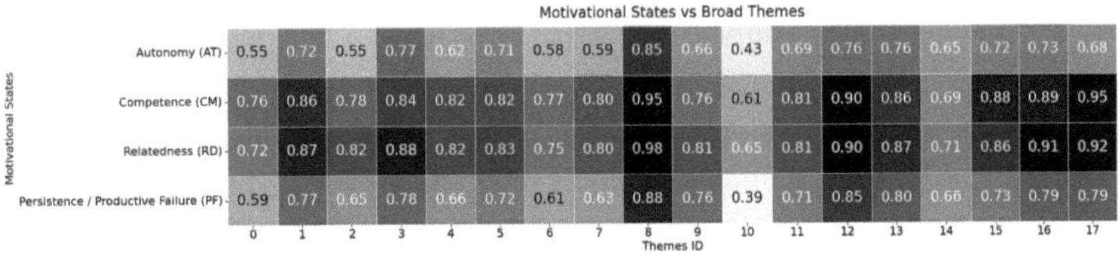

Motivational States vs Broad Themes

Motivational States	0	1	2	3	4	5	6	7	8	9	10	11	12	13	14	15	16	17
Autonomy (AT)	0.55	0.72	0.55	0.77	0.62	0.71	0.58	0.59	0.85	0.66	0.43	0.69	0.76	0.76	0.65	0.72	0.73	0.68
Competence (CM)	0.76	0.86	0.78	0.84	0.82	0.82	0.77	0.80	0.95	0.76	0.61	0.81	0.90	0.86	0.69	0.88	0.89	0.95
Relatedness (RD)	0.72	0.87	0.82	0.88	0.82	0.83	0.75	0.80	0.98	0.81	0.65	0.81	0.90	0.87	0.71	0.86	0.91	0.92
Persistence / Productive Failure (PF)	0.59	0.77	0.65	0.78	0.66	0.72	0.61	0.63	0.88	0.76	0.39	0.71	0.85	0.80	0.66	0.73	0.79	0.79

Themes ID

Fig. 4. EP Distribution of Motivation State across Broad Themes

3.4   Model Validation

Persuasive Support Area Validation. Spearman correlation between Lens 1 (CS) and Lens 2 (NLI) scores showed significant alignment ($p < .001$), peaking in Dialogue Support (DS) and System Credibility (SC) ($r \approx 0.37$). The lower correlation in Social Support (SS) ($r \approx 0.22$) suggests a "lexical bottleneck," where students use diverse language that NLI captures more effectively than keyword-based CS. Kruskal-Wallis tests for both NLI ($H = 248.40, p < .001$) and CS ($H = 593.82, p < .001$) confirm that ArchCraft support areas distinct support areas across thematic modules. Post-hoc Dunn's tests revealed significant differences ($p < .001$) except for CS scores between SC and DS ($p = .2758$). This convergence indicates that students perceive system feedback and technical authority as a unified experience, which NLI disambiguates through logical entailment.

Motivational State and Resilience Validation. Significant correlations were found between CS and NLI for Autonomy ($\rho \approx .163$), Competence ($\rho \approx .35$), and Relatedness ($\rho \approx .217$) ($p < .001$). However, Resilience failed to show significant correlation ($p \approx .188$), as students expressed agency via domain-specific Redstone terminology (e.g., "logic gating") rather than formal academic language—a latent behavior identified exclusively by Lens 2. Kruskal-Wallis tests (NLI: $H = 189.46$; CS: $H = 450.75$; $p < .001$) confirm the curriculum triggers varied motivational states. While Dunn's tests generally showed significant differences, NLI scores for CM and Autonomy were logically similar ($p \approx .164$), reflecting the shared, community-driven nature of task execution within the ArchCraft sandbox.

3.5   Thematic and Sentiment Results

Sentiment Distribution and Impact. Sentiment across the 18 themes leaned positive, peaking in *Hands-On CPU Operations* (Theme 8) and *Real-World Design* (Theme 17). Conversely, *Performance Constraints* (Theme 2) and *Platform Limitations* (Theme 10) elicited the lowest sentiment, reflecting the technical friction of the Redstone environment. Spearman correlation confirmed that positive sentiment is significantly associated with all PSD and SDT constructs ($p < .001$), with the strongest associations found in Primary Task Support ($\rho \approx .43$) and Dialogue Support ($\rho \approx .41$) (Fig. 5).

SDT Sensitivity on Themes. Kruskal-Wallis tests revealed that the system's impact on motivation is highly context-dependent across themes ($p < .001$), with Resilience emerging as the most sensitive construct ($H = 71.89$). This sensitivity is most evident in the inverse relationship between sentiment and resilience found in 'friction' themes; for example, in Performance Constraints (Theme 2) and Problem Solving (Theme 9), students maintained high resilience scores ($M = 0.65$ and $M = 0.76$ respectively) despite negative sentiment valences ($M = -0.32$ and $M = -0.21$). This divergence validates the PF framework, where technical hurdles catalyzed deeper engagement rather than withdrawal. However, the Spearman correlation ($\rho = 0.3709, p < .001$) across all friction themes also identifies a 'breaking point' in Platform Limitations (Theme 10), where a sharp decline in sentiment ($M = -0.58$) eventually coincided with a

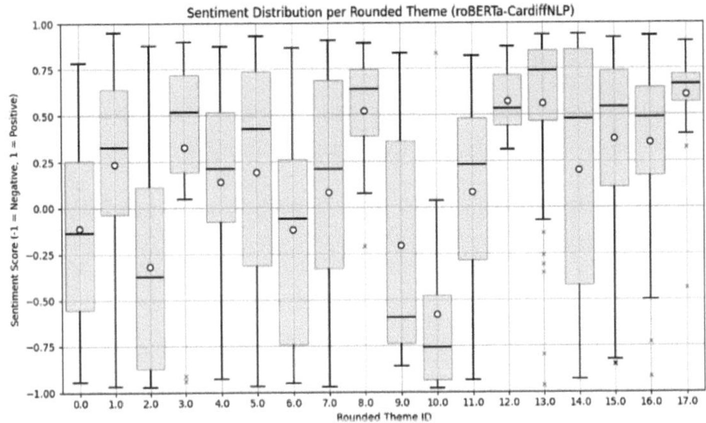

Fig. 5. Sentiment Distribution across themes

drop in resilience ($M = 0.39$), marking the threshold where technical friction ceases to be productive.

Qualitative Thematic Interpretation. Sentiments were diverse, with mixed positive and negative reflections. Students found that Minecraft has limitations that can affect the performance of the build. Redstone has its limitations on tick delays and signal sending, relying on repeaters to send signal, adding more tick delay. The Minecraft computer was also a large scaled build so this posed problems in execution runtime.

> "Speaking on the performance, I really did not like how slow it was to debug and test the programs and the control unit connections as it took us almost an hour to let the program run." – Student 36

Despite the limitations, students found the Minecraft Project interesting and helpful in learning Microprogramming. Being able to visualize how each bit flows through each part of the CPU allowed them to visualize data flow concepts and optimizations. It also felt more engaging for them since they get to interact with actual components but in a safe and fun manner without needing to deal with actual electrical components. Some students found the project intimidating at first but ended up having fun doing the project in the long run.

> "Minecraft, to me, as an interactive game, encourages a more fun, and hands-on approach to computer architecture that is impossible to achieve in a traditional classroom environment. " – Student 26

It can also be seen that the understanding side of the project has the highest mean value, showing that the project was effective in helping students visualize and understand not just theoretical CPU concepts, but also Real-World Computer Systems as actual full simulations show the restrictions that theoretical learning does not have.

"More importantly, this project made me genuinely appreciate what professors always say: "computers only understand 0s and 1s." I'd heard that phrase countless times before, but I never really understood what it meant until now." – Student 15

3.6   Interaction Matrix Analysis

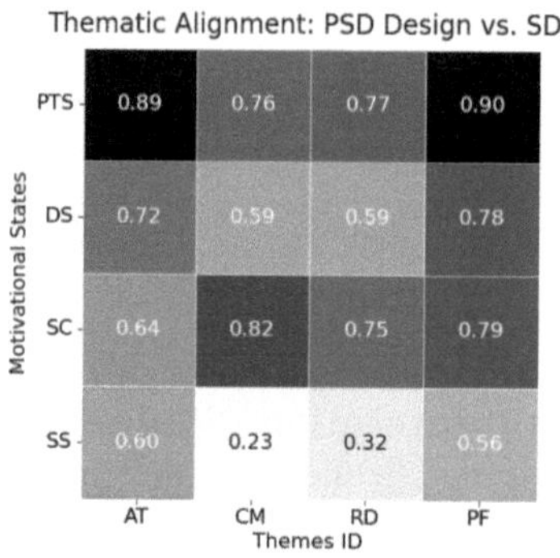

Fig. 6. Interaction Matrix

A Spearmann correlation test confirmed that specfic PSD support areas correlate more with specific SDT outcomes across all 18 themes. Notably, PTS showed a strong association with Autonomy and Resilience (both $\rho \approx 0.89$), **suggesting that the provided tools facilitated** student agency. It suggests that what tools the Archcraft learning environment provides is associated positively with how students feel more agency and stay more resilient when they fail. Furthermore, the high correlation between SC and CM (0.82) **indicates that technical accuracy is a primary antecedent** to a student's sense of mastery within the simulation (Fig. 6).

Limitations. This study uses a one-group post-test-only design, which limits causal claims because there is no control group using a traditional architecture simulator, making it impossible to determine whether the observed motivational gains were caused by ArchCraft itself or by novelty effects from using Minecraft.

The lexical salience analysis depends on semantic anchors defined by the authors, which introduces researcher bias despite being grounded in established SDT and PSD definitions. Future studies should use peer-validated or standardized anchors to ensure a higher inter-rater reliability.

The reliance on Natural Language Inference to infer latent motivational behaviors further constrains interpretation, as entailment scores reflect the logical patterns in a student rather than direct evidence of their internal psychological states, meaning high scores do not guarantee that students actually experienced the corresponding motivation.

In addition, the findings are context-specific, as the participants were drawn from a single university within a particular educational and cultural setting. Factors such as local attitudes toward game-based learning may have influenced student engagement and their responses, limiting the extent to which the results can be generalized to other institutions or learning environments.

4   Conclusion

This study examined whether Minecraft could support microprogramming instruction through *ArchCraft*, a 16-bit CPU implementation that uses redstone components. The approach attempted to solve a problem in existing educational tools: simulators that abstract away control details fail to build the mental models that microprogramming instruction requires. ArchCraft provided students with direct manipulation of microcode signals without the need to wire individual logic gates.

Post-hoc analysis using Natural Language Inference (NLI) revealed that the environment functioned as a sophisticated persuasive system, mapping technical features to psychological needs. By triangulating Persuasive Systems Design (PSD) support areas with Self-Determination Theory (SDT) and Productive Failure (PF) constructs, we identified that System Credibility (SC) and Primary Task Support (PTS) served as primary drivers for students' autonomy and competence in this system. Most notably, the high mean project grade (97.70%) suggests that the technical "friction" inherent in the platform did not impede learning. Instead, as framed by the Productive Failure (PF) framework [6], the unconstrained design environment of ArchCraft necessitated exploratory design, requiring students to build and test their own control-signal mappings and develop resilience ($H = 71.89, p < .001$) to overcome platform-specific hurdles. Persistence was not a static trait, but a dynamic response to the varying technical complexities of the ArchCraft modules. These indicated that students found value in visualizing datapath operations and understanding control signal coordination during instruction execution.

However, the analysis also showed that Minecraft's technical properties imposed constraints that directly affected the learning process. Redstone signal propagation and rendering delays disrupted debugging during microprogram implementation. This indicates a trade-off between a circuit's visibility and system performance rather than a minor usability issue. Because all entities, including Redstone components, operate on Minecraft ticks, execution time increases with the size of a circuit: small circuits require only a few ticks based on the number of sequential logic gates, while large-scale structures such as a full CPU incur larger delays. In this case study, the implemented Minecraft computer required 396 ticks per instruction cycle to ensure correct execution, with each instruction spanning eight cycles, resulting in 3,168 ticks per line of assembly code, excluding additional delays from memory operations. Although the tick rate can be increased, the effective execution speed remains dependent on the student's hardware capabilities.

Based on these constraints and the student sentiment analysis, the findings point to clear directions for future refinement of the approach, including practices that should be adopted, practices that should be avoided, and targeted improvements to better balance pedagogical visibility with technical performance.

- **Recommended practices**
  - Provide a visual simulation of microprogramming and visible logic.
  - Use Minecraft as a 3D gamified visualization to leverage the sandbox environment and support learner autonomy, reflected in the strong correlation between PTS and Autonomy ($\rho \approx 0.89$).
- **Practices to avoid**
  - Requiring students to implement complex circuitry (e.g., a full CPU) in pure vanilla Minecraft.
- **Directions for further improvement**
  - Develop or adopt stable Minecraft mods that support modular, small-scale representations of combinational circuits and signals.
  - Optimize circuit design to reduce tick requirements, improving system performance and System Credibility (SC), which strongly correlates with student Competence ($\rho \approx 0.82$).

The results contribute to the literature where game-based platforms have been adopted faster than they have been validated. The validation gap noted in the introduction remains. Although this study provides evidence that Minecraft can support certain aspects of microprogramming instruction, particularly those related to visualization and construction, it also demonstrates that platform constraints impose real limits on what can be accomplished. Whether these limits are acceptable depends on instructional priorities. If the goal is to understand how control signals coordinate datapath operations, the platform provides a workable environment. If students need to develop and test complex programs through rapid iteration, the performance characteristics become prohibitive.

The question of how to balance abstraction and construction in computer architecture education persists. ArchCraft addresses part of this problem by enabling control unit manipulation without gate-level detail, but it introduces new constraints through platform limitations. Future research should compare Minecraft-based instruction against traditional simulators using controlled experimental designs to determine under what conditions construction-based approaches provide instructional benefits beyond engagement effects. Until such comparisons exist, claims about the educational value of game-based platforms remain incompletely supported.

Acknowledgments. We would like to thank Sean Benedict Bernardo and Mariella Jeanne Dellosa for assisting us through the project.

References

1. Afşin, Y., Temizel, T.T.: Harnessing large language models for automatic evaluation of mobile health applications based on persuasive system design principles. In: Persuasive Technology. PERSUASIVE 2024. Lecture Notes in Computer Science. vol. 14646, pp. 3–17. Springer, Cham (2024). https://doi.org/10.1007/978-3-031-58226-4_1
2. Alawajee, O., Delafield-Butt, J.: Minecraft in education benefits learning and social engagement. Int. J. Game-Based Learn. **11**(4), 19–56 (2021). https://doi.org/10.4018/IJGBL.2021100102
3. Barbieri, F., Camacho-Collados, J., Neves, L., Espinosa-Anke, L.: Tweeteval: unified benchmark and comparative evaluation for tweet classification. Snap Inc./Cardiff University (2020)
4. Boardman, B.S., Killingsworth, C.C.: Simulation of production and inventory control using the computer game factorio. In: Proceedings of the 2021 ASEE Gulf-Southwest Annual Conference. Baylor University, Waco, TX, USA (March 24–26 2021)
5. Hennessy, J.L., Patterson, D.A.: Computer Architecture: A Quantitative Approach. Morgan Kaufmann (1990)
6. Kapur, M.: Productive failure. Cogn. Instr. **26**(3), 379–424 (2008). https://doi.org/10.1080/07370000802212669
7. Kara, A., Mostefai, M.: Simple enough processor: from scratch elaborated simulated educational CPU. IEEE Transactions on Education (2023), in preparation
8. LeRoy, W., Kathleen, A.: A mixed methods approach to understanding the effect of applying multimedia principles to a Minecraft STEM lesson. Doctoral dissertation, University of California, Santa Barbara (2022)
9. Liu, Y., Huang, X.: Effects of basic psychological needs on resilience: a human agency model. Front. Psychol. **12**, 700035 (2021). https://doi.org/10.3389/fpsyg.2021.700035
10. mattbattwings: Logical redstone reloaded. YouTube playlist (2023). https://youtube.com/playlist?list=PL5LiOvrbVo8keeEWRZVaHfprU4zQTCsV4
11. McKanna, E., Hassan, F.: Enhancing student understanding of digital logic and computer architecture through turing complete game challenges. In: Proceedings of the 2024 ASEE North Central Section Conference. Kalamazoo, Michigan (March 2024). https://peer.asee.org/45615
12. Nikolic, B., Radivojevic, Z., Djordjevic, J., Milutinovic, V.: A survey and evaluation of simulators suitable for teaching courses in computer architecture and organization. IEEE Trans. Educ. **52**(4), 449–458 (2009). https://doi.org/10.1109/TE.2008.930097
13. Null, L., Lobur, J.: The Essentials of Computer Organization and Architecture. Jones & Bartlett Learning, 4th edn. (2014)
14. Orji, F.A., Gutierrez, F.J., Vassileva, J.: Exploring the influence of persuasive strategies on student motivation: self-determination theory perspective. In: Baghaei, N., et al. (eds.) PERSUASIVE 2024. Lecture Notes in Computer Science, vol. 14636, pp. 222–236. Springer Nature Switzerland AG (2024)
15. Papert, S., Harel, I.: Situating constructionism. In: Constructionism. Ablex Publishing (1991)
16. Parker, J.R., Becker, K.: A microprogramming simulator for instructional use. Tech. rep., Department of Computer Science, University of Calgary, 2500 University Drive N.W., Calgary, Alberta, Canada T2N-IN4 (1992)

17. Patterson, D.A., Hennessy, J.L.: Computer Organization and Design: The Hardware/Software Interface. Morgan Kaufmann, 5th edn. (2017). https://www.elsevier.com/books/computer-organization-and-design-risc-v-edition/patterson/978-0-12-812275-4
18. Prayaga, L., Davis, J., Whiteside, A., Riffle, A.: An exploration in the use of minecraft to teach digital logic to secondary school students. Int. J. Inform. Technol., Eng. Sci. **2**(1), 33–40 (2016), iSSN: 2249-0515
19. Ryan, R.M., Deci, E.L.: Self-determination theory and the facilitation of intrinsic motivation, social development, and well-being. Am. Psychol. **55**(1), 68–78 (2000). https://doi.org/10.1037110003-066X.55.1.68
20. sammyuri: Chungus 2 - a very powerful 1hz minecraft cpu (2021). https://www.youtube.com/watch?v=FDiapbD0Xfg, youTube video
21. Sweller, J., Ayres, P., Kalyuga, S.: Cognitive Load Theory. Springer (2011). https://doi.org/10.1007/978-1-4419-8126-4
22. Tikka, P., Tiitinen, S., Ilomäki, S., Ruusuvuori, J., Oinas-Kukkonen, H.: Persuasive systems design and self determination theory: Mapping system features to intervention framework to foster motivation. In: BCSS 2025: The 13th International Workshop on Behavior Change Support Systems. Limassol, Cyprus (May 2025)
23. Voštinár, P., Dobrota, R.: Minecraft as a tool for teaching online programming. In: Matej Bel University, Department of Computer Science. Banská Bystrica, Slovakia (2021)
24. Wolffe, G., Yurcik, W., Osborne, M., Holliday, M.: Teaching computer organization/architecture with limited resources using simulators. In: Proceedings of the 33rd SIGCSE Technical Symposium on Computer Science Education, pp. 176–180 (2002), https://doi.org/10.1145/563517.563408

Wellnify.Ai: Insights from the Longitudinal Use of an mHealth App for Health and Wellness

Gerry Chan[1]([✉]) [iD], Brendon Ferguson[2] [iD], Sam Ross[2] [iD], and Rita Orji[1] [iD]

[1] Faculty of Computer Science, Dalhousie University, Halifax, NS, Canada
gerry.chan@dal.ca
[2] Wellnify.ai, Halifax, NS, Canada

Abstract. This paper is an evaluation of Wellnify.ai, a customizable, mobile-friendly wellness app that leverages gamification and behavior change techniques to encourage healthier, more active communities. Wellnify.ai contains a suite of wellness tools, to include a library of workouts, online challenges, and educational content. The app allows organizations to upload and gamify their own content. Moreover, this app allows participants to engage in wellness challenges and competitive and cooperative tasks that reward movement and health behaviors using augmented reality and other physical experiences. After a three-month deployment across multiple organizations, anonymized real-life usage data and logs of participant activity were analyzed to assess engagement, participation in challenges, and interactions with wellness content. Results show that through gamification and community support, the app can support prolonged engagement with wellness challenges. The results demonstrate the effectiveness of Wellnify.ai to sustain participatory wellness over time and present a favorable view of the app's future development and larger implementation opportunities.

Keywords: Augmented reality (AR) · Gamification · mobile health (mHealth) · health and wellness · persuasive technology · physical activity · user engagement

1 Introduction

Participation in regular physical activity (PA) is important for maintaining overall health and wellbeing [1]. Technology has potential promote PA and encourage healthy behaviors over time. For example, mobile applications and other digital technologies can track users' PA capabilities, as well as their daily mobility patterns, and even provide feedback on their PA progress. These applications remind the user to keep active, provide advice tailored to their needs, and support continued motivation through various forms of reward or challenge. Research suggests that digital interventions, particularly those incorporating gamification and social features, can increase user motivation and adherence to PA over time [2, 3]. Researchers and designers are exploring how to incorporate design features that promote motivation and user engagement in PA [4–6].

Mobile Health (mHealth) applications or apps are gaining much popularity because of their multiple functionalities and broad potential benefits. Research has shown these

K. Sumi et al. (Eds.): PERSUASIVE 2026, LNCS 16476, pp. 41–50, 2026.
https://doi.org/10.1007/978-3-032-19687-3_4

applications to be effective for diverse purposes, including supporting exercise adherence, especially in the short-term [7], and promoting well-being and decreasing workplace stress [8]. In particular, mHealth gamified applications are more effective compared to non-gamified ones [9], and that incorporating social features, such as leaderboards and cooperative challenges can increase the level of enjoyment [10]. However, few studies have examined the long-term effectiveness of mobile health applications, as well as what design features are optimal to encourage sustained use. This in-the-wild study assessed user engagement and participation in wellness challenges using Wellnify.ai,[1] a customizable, mobile-friendly wellness mHealth app that applies gamification and behavior change strategies to support healthier, active communities. We analyzed anonymized behavioral usage data collected in real-life settings for three-month deployment across different organizations to explore engagement patterns. Our results show that gamification, particularly Augmented Reality (AR) and the types of activities, can enable sustained participation in wellness over time and provide valuable implications for how to design digital applications to encourage long-term behavior change.

2 Related Work

mHealth apps, such as fitness apps, have been shown to promote PA and reduce sedentary behavior. Previous studies suggest that these apps positively impact users' PA levels and overall health outcomes [11–13], and can improve user experience and promote long-term use when gamified features are included [14]. For example, Caro et al. [6] investigated how a social mobile gamified health app, StepQuest, can sustain PA over time. Two user studies were conducted over six-months and found that pre-existing social relationships (e.g., friendships) positively impacted engagement and PA levels. However, PA declined after week four, suggesting that social relationships and various game elements are not sufficient to motivate continued PA behavior change.

In a different study, Odenigbo et al. [15] examined AR Dancee, a mobile AR-driven intervention to increase PA and improve mood. A 15-day study with 104 participants showed increased PA across genders, stronger among younger adults, and improved mood with reduced anxiety, highlighting AR's potential for stress management and well-being. More recently, Srivastava et al. [13] explored AR and persuasive game design in PetBuddy, promoting PA via virtual pet interactions. Sixty-five young adults played for 10 days, reporting increased PA, achievement meeting PA levels recommended by the World Health Organization (WHO) guidelines and adoption of healthier behaviors. Features such as competition, rewards, self-monitoring, and customization motivated sustained engagement, suggesting the importance of enjoyment and interactive elements in mobile health games.

To summarize, mHealth applications have the potential to support PA. Gamification and social interactions are effective at increasing engagement, but diminishes after the initial novelty. AR adds further benefits by enhancing enjoyment, providing immediate feedback, and improving mental health. Strategically combining gamification, AR, and persuasive design can promote sustained PA and positive health outcomes.

---

[1] https://wellnify.ai/

3   Wellnify.ai

(a) Home screen   (b) Badges   (c) Leaderboard   (d) Profile

(e) Augmented reality interactions

Fig. 1. Example features of the Wellnify.ai mHealth application.

Wellnify.ai is an mHealth application (Fig. 1) that supports physical health and overall wellbeing through social and fun movement, and healthy habit changes. The app makes changing to healthy habits more engaging by employing behavior-change strategies, gamification and social connectivity. With a web-based admin panel and white label option, the app makes it easy for organizations to work with their employees, students and community members to engage with the app. Organizations can set up with custom participant challenges and engagement levels for their groups, ensuring each organization can use the app regardless of the number of participants. Wellnify.ai creates a unique experience that enables users to monitor their activity levels, engage in challenges and competitions, and consume personalized wellness content.

Users can earn rewards such as badges (Fig. 1b) and levels for completing steps, exercises, or wellness tasks. Users can also participate or collaborate as part of a team and have access to a review of content across a range of movement and education (workouts, video and educational, mindfulness) supported by AR-based exercise monitoring that provides interactive movement feedback (Fig. 1e). Administrators (anyone responsible for the management of users on the app) interact with a dashboard in a web browser-based format to manage content on the app, plan activities, and track the number of participants. The application is designed based on the idea that tracking and encouraging wellness helps support longer-term commitment and engagement, when tracking is fun and social [16]. It applies principles of persuasive design to enhance motivation and adherence to healthy behaviours. Wellnify.ai incorporates features for primary task support, dialogue, system credibility, and social support according to the Persuasive Systems Design (PSD) model developed by Oinas-Kukkonen and Harjumaa [17], which creates continual user engagement and support for changing behaviour. Table 1 shows how each of the features is mapped to persuasive strategies described in the PSD model.

Table 1. Wellnify.ai features mapped to persuasive strategies in the PSD model [17].

Features	Persuasive Strategy	Description
Activity tracking, goal setting, progress indicators	Self-monitoring, goal setting, reduction	Enables users to monitor physical activity and visualize progress, simplifying behavior change into manageable steps.
Push notifications, reminders, feedback messages	Reminders, praise, reinforcement	Timely prompts and feedback keep users engaged and encourages continued participation.
Team challenges, leaderboards (Fig. 1c), community feeds	Social comparison, social facilitation, competition, cooperation	Encourages motivation through social interaction, peer recognition, and shared goals.
Badges (Fig. b), XP points, levels, and rewards	Rewards, conditioning	Reinforces desired behaviors by providing positive feedback and tangible incentives.
Professional wellness content, educational videos, AR exercise tracking (Fig. e)	Expertise, surface credibility	Reliable and well-designed content enhances user trust in the system's legitimacy and guidance.
Tailored content and adaptive experience (Fig. 1d)	Personalization, tailoring	Delivers relevant activities and wellness content aligned with users' preferences and goals, enhancing perceived relevance and autonomy.

4   Method

We analyzed data from 356 users aged 18–65 across Canada who used the Wellnify.ai application between June 2025 and August 2025. The dataset included user-generated records related to PA, including timed exercise reports, step count results, and overall activity summaries. These data were automatically recorded by the app through users' interactions with activity tracking and AR-based exercise monitoring features. For example, when referring to "timed exercise reports," this indicates sessions in which users completed specific workouts that recorded duration, repetitions, and completion time. Similarly, "step results" refer to data captured through users' daily walking or movement tracking integrated with the app.

Before analysis, the dataset was cleaned to ensure quality and reliability. The data records containing missing, duplicated and inconsistent values were identified and removed. Outliers (e.g., unrealistic step count or incomplete exercise duration) were checked for and removed, when surpassing pre-specified thresholds (e.g., as defined by greater than three standard deviations from the mean value). Additionally, the data were checked for internal consistency contradiction among categories of activity to ensure that duration, frequency and completion, for example, made logical sense. Only validated and complete user entries were retained for further analysis. To ensure accuracy and representativeness, only complete user records were included in the analysis; entries containing missing or incomplete data were excluded. Descriptive statistics were first computed to summarize user engagement levels across activity types. Frequency distributions were then applied to visualize trends in users' exercise duration, step counts, and overall activity levels, allowing identification of common participation patterns and engagement intensity among users.

5   Results

This section presents the results ($N = 356$) based on data collected during the first three months of usage of the Wellnify.ai application. The analysis begins with an overview of user activity patterns, starting with cumulative step counts, which provide a broad measure of overall PA. This is followed by an analysis of exercise engagement, including total time spent on different activities and trends across the three months. Finally, we examine the use of AR features in exercises to understand how AR-based activities influence engagement and preferences compared with traditional, non-AR exercises.

5.1   Step Count Analysis

This section presents an analysis of cumulative step counts over the first three months of using the Wellnify.ai application. Because established step-count classifications are based on daily step counts, custom categories were defined for the 3-month totals to better reflect meaningful differences in activity levels. Step counts were grouped into three categories: Low (0–300,000 steps), Medium (300,001–700,000 steps), and High (700,001–1,000,000 steps). These categories allow for a clear interpretation of overall activity and identification of patterns within the dataset. Figure 2 shows that the majority of participants fell within the High category, indicating that most users achieved substantial cumulative step counts over the three-month period.

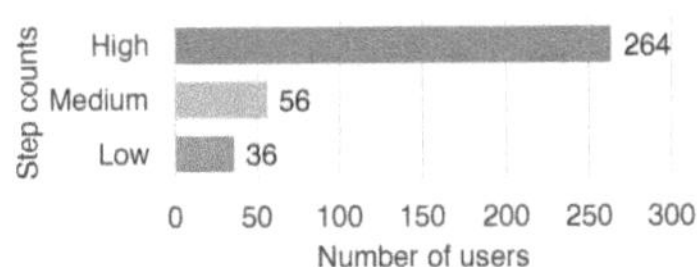

Fig. 2. Cumulative step counts over the first three months.

5.2 Activity Analysis

An analysis of the total minutes spent on different exercises shows which ones were the most participated (Fig. 3). Cycling had the most total time with more than 23,600 min, suggesting that it is popular for endurance and cardiovascular fitness. Meditating had the second most time with about 3,700 min, suggesting mental wellness and relaxation are also significant focus. Mountain Biking is the third most time-intensive task with a total of 3,645 min. This fitness option combines adventure with the demands of a physical workout. Walking is next with about 2,500 min, indicating how regular exercise of low intensity can add up. Weightlifting with a total of 1,330 min, while functional strength training was 985 min and offers a versatile approach to fitness. Swimming had 960 min and can provide total body, low intensity, fitness. Finally, in eighth place is Pilates with 600 min, which promotes core strength, flexibility, and balance. This analysis shows not only the total time spent on activities, but also the variety of ways that users prioritize endurance, strength, and wellness in a routine.

Next, an analysis of the top eight (8) exercises by month shows interesting patterns in how physical activity is distributed over time (Fig. 4). Cycling appeared most consistently in total minutes in June, July, and August, which likely reflects both its popularity and long activity time. Meditating shows up heavily in June, suggesting a month focused on wellness. Activities such as Mountain Biking and Walking were less pronounced and showed moderate variation with peaks in June for Mountain Biking and minimal variation in Walking as an activity three months. Gardening and Weightlifting are present into June and July, indicating trends of seasonal activity. Likewise, Functional Strength Training and Swimming occurred primarily in June. Overall, during the summer, the monthly groupings show that outdoor and exploratory activities stand out across the summer months while indoor or organized activities such as Strength Training, to some degree, have stable much lower total activity times.

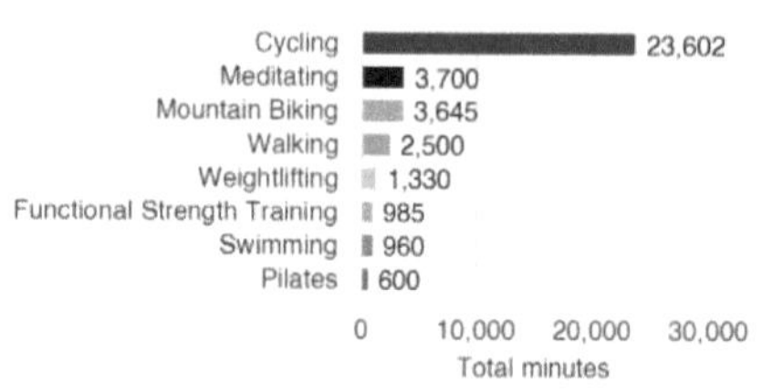

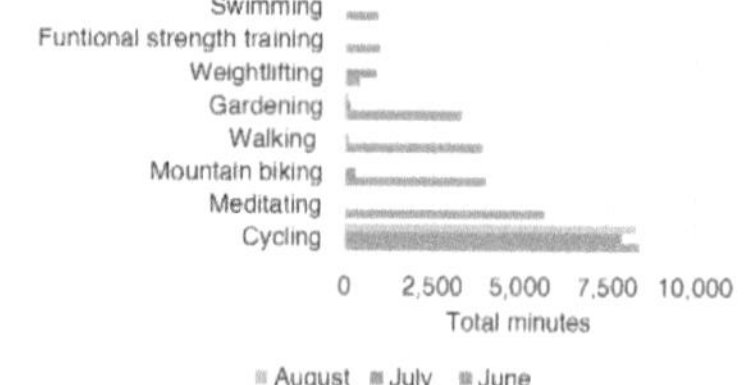

Fig. 3. Analysis of the total minutes spent on different exercises.

Fig. 4. Top eight (8) exercises by month.

5.3 AR Feature Analysis

Results (Table 2) showed that users generally prefer non-AR for core strength and cardio exercises (e.g., Squats, Push Ups, High Knees), while AR is favored for unique, guided, or playful activities (e.g., like dance, meditation, or skill-based moves). Moreover, there is a distinction in user preferences between AR and non-AR activities across different months and types of exercises. AR is favored for unique, guided, or playful activities, such as "Fun & Short Hip Hop Dance" and "Learn the Crow Pose". These activities that incorporate AR show heightened levels of engagement during the months of June and August, providing evidence that AR is highly favored for new or social interactions. Traditional exercises experienced heavy engagement during the months of June and July. For example, during these months, exercises that included squats, push-ups, mountain climbers, high knees, shoulder taps, dead bug, and butt kicks were mostly carried out without AR. This suggests that users prefer non-AR formats for their core strength and cardio, as well as standard workouts.

As for the months, it remains consistent that June shows strong engagement with AR specialty activities, yet users are consistent with non-AR activity in standard core/strength exercises. The month of July appears to consist mainly of non-AR exercises in both specialty and standard activities. In the month of August, AR is used slightly more in meditation and some skill-based movement patterns, however, non-AR engagement remains high for most core, strength and, cardio exercises. Overall, patterns suggest that AR creates an engaging context for social, fun, guided, and/or skill-based activities while non-AR remains most popular format for regular, high activity levels experienced during exercise.

Table 2. Activity and the number of repeats for non-AR vs. AR, by month.

Activity	Non-AR	AR	Month(s)
Fun & Short Hip Hop Dance	1,047	0	June
Learn the Crow Pose	1,011	0	June
Butt Kicks	0	506	June, July and August
High Knees	112	309	June, July and August
Squats	422	0	June, July and August
Mountain Climbers	41	265	June, July and August
Shoulder Taps	92	409	June, and July
Dead Bug / Dead Bug Isometric Hold	0	137	June, July and August

6   Discussion

We sought to understand user engagement, PA, and user preferences for AR features of the Wellnify.ai app over the first three months of use. Our analysis focused on the distribution of activity across different types of exercise and the use of AR-based and traditional exercise. Data from step counts, exercise sessions, and AR usage reveal overall trends in standard exercise and guided or playful activity, identifying what features increased engagement and continued usage of the app. The results contribute to our understanding of how mHealth apps can promote PA and wellness through features that promote interactivity and social engagement.

6.1 Design Recommendations

Based on our observations, we propose three recommendations for designing and researching mHealth apps, particularly those that are gamified and encourage PA.

Design Recommendation 1: Use AR for Guided, Playful, and Skill-Based Activities. Research suggests that the gradual release of game features can increase the level of motivation and sustained engagement in PA [9, 18]. In the current study, our findings show that AR tasks (i.e., dance, meditation, or skill-based movement) demonstrated greater engagement than standard workouts, whereas core strength and cardiovascular exercises were typically performed without the use of AR. Thus, designers should focus on using AR for guided, playful, or skill-based activities where feedback, novelty, and social interactions can enhance value. For example, the AR system could include challenges for learning new movements or group-based guided exercises to increase the level of engagement and enjoyment.

Design Recommendation 2: Introduce Gamified Rewards for Low- and High-Intensity Activities. Previous research shows that gamification (e.g., badges, level-ups, and collectables) can enhance engagement and adherence to PA [19, 20]. Our data suggests that it is important to include rewards in both endurance-based and lower-intensity wellness activities, meaning that rewards should not be exclusive to high-intensity exercise. Designers should have gamified rewards for both types of exercise. Therefore, the system should also award points for completing meditation sessions, walking, or strength exercise, encouraging people to stay engaged and complete multiple physical and wellness activities.

Design Recommendation 3: Use Seasonal Engagement Strategies to Sustain Activity Levels. Beyond studies showing that a user's engagement in PA is dependent upon weather conditions [21], our results revealed activity levels were at their highest during June and July, but dropped dramatically by August, suggesting generalized withdrawal from PA. Designers should plan for these seasonal declines and develop seasonal engagement strategies. For example, the system could implement short-term challenges (one day to one week), indoor summer exercise, or timely motivational notifications during activity-specific drop-off months to assist users in staying engaged consistently throughout the year.

6.2 Limitations and Directions for Future Work

Although we found some interesting results, there are a few limitations to this study. First, in this analysis, we only considered the first three months of app usage, meaning long-term engagement or behavior change may not be captured. Second, the dataset consisted of self-selected users (i.e., users chose to take part), which could have contributed to selection bias and limited generalizability of the findings. Third, we did not examine user demographics or contextual factors (e.g., location, environmental conditions,) that may influence activity patterns. Therefore, in future research, we must investigate longer-term usage, including examining more diverse user populations and contextual and personal factors influencing engagement with AR and gamified features. Additionally, collecting qualitative feedback would provide richer insights into user preferences and help optimize the app for sustained behavior change.

7 Conclusion

In closing, this study shows how users interacted with the Wellnify.ai app during their first three months. By analyzing activity patterns, we found that AR and non-AR features contribute to participation in different ways: AR activities encouraged deeper, sustained involvement, while non-AR activities offered accessible engagement. These insights highlight the value of combining interactive elements with flexible activity options to promote long-term behavior change. We offer three key takeaways. First, users were active, indicating potential engagement in PA, particularly in cumulative step counts. Second, activity profiles fluctuated across exercise type and seasonality, reflecting users' benefit from flexible activities tailored to individual and contextual preferences. Third, AR was most effective for guided, playful, and skill-based activities, as users preferred traditional exercises without AR, suggesting AR should enhance rather than replace workouts. Collectively, these findings highlight the advantage of gamified, flexible activity planning with targeted AR features to increase engagement, encourage healthier behaviors, and demonstrate that mHealth applications like Wellnify.ai can support ongoing engagement in real-world settings.

Acknowledgements. This research was undertaken, in part, thanks to funding from the Canada Research Chairs Program. We acknowledge the support of the Natural Sciences and Engineering Research Council of Canada (NSERC) through the Discovery Grant and the Mitacs Elevate Program. The research is conducted as part of the Dalhousie University Persuasive Computing Lab.

References

1. Alpert, P.T.: Exercise works. Home Health Care Manag. Pract. **21**, 371–374 (2009). https://doi.org/10.1177/1084822309334032
2. Zhao, Z., Arya, A., Orji, R., Chan, G.: Effects of a personalized fitness recommender system using gamification and continuous player modeling: system design and long-term validation study. JMIR Serious Games. **8** (2020). https://doi.org/10.2196/19968
3. Chan, G., Arya, A., Orji, R., Zhao, Z., Whitehead, A.: Increasing motivation in social exercise games: personalising gamification elements to player type. Behav. Inf. Technol., 1–31 (2023). https://doi.org/10.1080/0144929X.2023.2255293
4. Rhodes, R.E., Beauchamp, M.R., Blanchard, C.M., Bredin, S.S.D., Warburton, D.E.R., Maddison, R.: Predictors of stationary cycling exergame use among inactive children in the family home. Psychol. Sport Exerc. **41**, 181–190 (2019). https://doi.org/10.1016/j.psychsport.2018.03.009
5. Morrison, A., Bakayov, V.: Stickers for steps: a study of an activity tracking system with face-to-face social engagement. Proc. ACM Human-Computer Interact. **1**, 1–10 (2017). https://doi.org/10.1145/3134717

6. Caro, K., Feng, Y., Day, T., Freed, E., Fox, B., Zhu, J.: Understanding the effect of existing positive relationships on a social motion-based game for health. In: Proceedings of the 12th EAI International Conference on Pervasive Computing Technologies for Healthcare, pp. 77–87 (2018). https://doi.org/10.1145/3240925.3240942

7. Borst, F., Reuss-Borst, M., Boschmann, J., Schwarz, P.: Can mobile-health applications contribute to long-term increase in physical activity after medical rehabilitation?-a pilot-study. PLOS Digit. Heal. **2**, e0000359 (2023). https://doi.org/10.1371/journal.pdig.0000359

8. Herold, M., Simbula, S., Gallucci, M.: Can smartphone applications and wearable technologies improve workplace Well-being and help manage stress? A systematic review. Curr. Psychol., 28650–28673 (2024). https://doi.org/10.1007/s12144-024-06534-z

9. Maher, C.A., et al.: Gamification in a physical activity app: what gamification features are being used, by whom, and does it make a difference? Games Health J. **11**, 193–199 (2022). https://doi.org/10.1089/g4h.2021.0207

10. Chan, G., Arya, A., Orji, R., Zhao, Z., Stojmenovic, M., Whitehead, A.: Player matching for social Exergame retention. In: Extended Abstracts of the 2020 Annual Symposium on Computer-Human Interaction in Play, pp. 198–203. ACM, New York, NY, USA (2020). https://doi.org/10.1145/3383668.3419879

11. Schoeppe, S., et al.: Apps to improve diet, physical activity and sedentary behaviour in children and adolescents: a review of quality, features and behaviour change techniques. Int. J. Behav. Nutr. Phys. Act. **14**, 83 (2017). https://doi.org/10.1186/s12966-017-0538-3

12. F., H., Wright, A., Shill, J., Stephens, H., Uccellini, M.: Using health and Well-being apps for behavior change: a systematic search and rating of apps. JMIR Mhealth Uhealth. **7**(7), e11926. https//mhealth.jmir.org/2019/7/e11926 (2019). https://doi.org/10.2196/11926

13. Srivastava, P., Chan, G., Oyebode, O., Orji, R.: PetBuddy: an examination of augmented reality Mobile health game for promoting physical activity. Lect. Notes Comput. Sci. 15711 LNCS, 264–280 (2025). https://doi.org/10.1007/978-3-031-94959-3_19

14. Gong, Y., Yi, J.: Gamified features as a mediator of fitness app engagement: a cross-sectional study. Int. J. Bus. Emerg. Mark. **17**, 1–29 (2025). https://doi.org/10.1504/IJBEM.2025.100 74543

15. Odenigbo, I.P., Alslaity, A., Chan, G., Orji, R.: AR Dancee: an augmented reality-based Mobile persuasive intervention for promoting physical activity through dancing. Int. J. Hum. Comput. Interact., 6765–6785 (2024). https://doi.org/10.1080/10447318.2024.2384136

16. Spotswood, F., Shankar, A., Piwek, L.: Changing emotional engagement with running through communal self-tracking: the implications of 'teleoaffective shaping' for public health. Sociol. Heal. Illn. **42**, 772–788 (2020). https://doi.org/10.1111/1467-9566.13057

17. Harjumaa, M., Oinas-Kukkonen, H.: Persuasive systems design: key issues, process model, and system features. Commun. Assoc. Inf. Syst. **24** (2009). https://doi.org/10.17705/1CAIS. 02428

18. Zhao, Z., Arya, A., Whitehead, A., Chan, G., Etemad, S.A.: Keeping users engaged through feature updates: a long-term study of using wearable-based Exergames. In: Proceedings of the 2017 CHI Conference Human Factors in Computer Systems - CHI '17, pp. 1053–1064 (2017). https://doi.org/10.1145/3025453.3025982

19. Nicolaidou, I., Aristeidis, L., Lambrinos, L.: A gamified app for supporting undergraduate students' mental health: a feasibility and usability study. Digit. Heal. **8**, 20552076221109059 (2022). https://doi.org/10.1177/20552076221109059

20. Laine, T.H., Duong, N., Lindvall, H., Oyelere, S.S., Rutberg, S., Lindqvist, A.K.: A reusable multiplayer game for promoting active school transport: development study. JMIR Serious Games. **10**, e31638 (2022). https://doi.org/10.2196/31638

21. Wagner, A.L., Keusch, F., Yan, T., Clarke, P.J.: The impact of weather on summer and winter exercise behaviors. J. Sport Heal. Sci. **8**, 39–45 (2019). https://doi.org/10.1016/j.jshs.2016. 07.007

A Value Sensitive Design Approach to Enhancing Eye Donation Informed Consent

Waraporn Chumkasian[1,2]($\boxtimes$) [ID], Elena Vlahu-Gjorgievska[1] [ID],
Constantinos Petsoglou[2] [ID], and Khin Than Win[1] [ID]

[1] University of Wollongong, Wollongong, Australia
`wc817@uowmail.edu.au`, `{elenavg,win}@uow.edu.au`
[2] Sydney Eye Hospital, Sydney, Australia

Abstract. The persistent scarcity of eye donations remains a significant concern. Various measures have been implemented to increase eye donation rates and mitigate supply shortages. Central to these efforts is the enhancement of awareness and knowledge, which are essential in overcoming barriers to donation. Persuasive Technology Design was employed to ensure the artefact was developed to increase individual awareness and knowledge of donation voluntarily. Nevertheless, the ethical advancement of eye donation procedures requires that informed consent be obtained from donors. The core values related to eye donation were identified by stakeholders with expertise in the field who participate actively in the design and development of the application. These values have guided the development of the app's content and features, utilizing the Persuasive System Design and Value Sensitive Design frameworks as the theoretical foundation. The study aims to identify and clarify the primary values associated with eye donation artefacts, potentially informing the development of similar artefacts for other organ donations. Further research is needed to assess the significance of these values in enhancing awareness and understanding of donation, thereby facilitating an increase in eye donation rates.

Keywords: Eye donation · Ethical values · Mobile health · Value sensitive design

1 Introduction

Corneal opacity remains a significant global health concern, affecting approximately 1.9 million individuals and accounting for 5% of blindness cases worldwide [1]. In Australia, eye donation operates under an opt-in system, which places emphasis on voluntary participation. While promoting eye donation is essential to address the shortage of corneal tissue, consent processes must uphold ethical standards. Specifically, individuals should receive clear, accessible, and comprehensive information, enabling informed decision-making without coercion or deceptive design practices.

Ensuring transparency and avoiding manipulative elements such as dark patterns are critical to maintaining trust and respecting autonomy in digital consent mechanisms.

K. Sumi et al. (Eds.): PERSUASIVE 2026, LNCS 16476, pp. 51–65, 2026.
https://doi.org/10.1007/978-3-032-19687-3_5

Furthermore, ethical perspectives have been of concern and ethical controversies and tensions that occurred with the use of technology in healthcare lead users not to adopt the systems [2]. Thus, there is a moral obligation to ensure that information provided in health information systems, such as mHealth applications, is accurate, beneficial and does not impose harm on the individuals.

The value and ethical aspects of designing information systems for healthcare are very important. Berdichevsky and Neuenschwander (1999) presented the ethics of persuasive technology, indicating that designers should follow the privacy, disclosure and the golden principles [3]. As ethical concerns play an important role in the design of persuasive technology, there is an indispensable need to consider users' values [4, 5].

2 Background

The Australian government has supported eye donation through the DonateLife program since 2009 [6]. DonateLife helps develop programs and campaigns to raise awareness of eye donation, as mandated by the Australian Organ and Tissue Donation and Transplantation Authority Act 2008 [7]. As the need for eye donation continues to grow each year (increasing by 6% in 2024), there is an effort to raise awareness of eye donation among both the government and the public using health technology [6, 8, 9]. However, the health information technology developers must adhere to ethical principles when developing artefacts to increase eye donation rates. Ethical values in eye donation involve balancing the benefits against potential harm, while respecting bodily integrity (including beauty). The social and symbolic significance of body parts (such as identity) [10, 11], as well as the principles of informed consent, autonomy, voluntariness in donation, shared benefit to all, and altruism [12].

Balancing benefits against potential harms (beneficence). Almost all eye donation occurs after the donor's death. This noble act is unlikely to harm the donor, but the donor needs to ensure that the purpose of the donation is purely altruistic, not driven by fame, competition, fashion, or peer/social pressure [13, 14]. The donation needs to be based on the benefits for the recipients, improving their quality of life and enabling them to live independently [15]. Another aspect is the eye tissue donation, such as limbal stem cells, that can be obtained from a living donor and transplanted into an eye with limbal stem cell deficiency [14]. In this case, the donor may face risks, so this donation depends on the donor's autonomous judgement, as well as the surgeon's, to ensure that the benefit to the recipient outweighs the harm to the donor [14].

Informed consent forms the foundation of law regarding the removal of organs and tissues, as well as their intended purpose [20, 21]. It is essential and can be either subjective or objective, reflecting the donor's will, and it enhances the donor's autonomy in deciding on eye donation [22]. There are four key elements: 1) the donor must have the capacity to decide freely, 2) receive sufficient information, 3) possess the capacity to understand, and 4) be able to make an informed decision [20–23]. Informed consent helps ensure that the donor's decision was made voluntarily and without coercion, thereby preventing harm [18, 21, 24]. Overinforming can compromise patient safety (delaying the treatment) or reduce the benefit of violating nonmaleficence and beneficence, while underinforming can leave the donor inadequately informed [16].

There are two types of consent for organ donation: presumed consent and explicit consent. Presumed consent (opt-out) is a system that allows eyes to be removed from the deceased's body for transplantation or research unless the deceased has stated their objection to the relevant authority [17, 18]. The right of all potential donors to object is upheld as an ethical fundamental of eye donation [19, 20]. Presumed consent has been shown to increase eye donations in many countries [18, 21, 22]. The explicit consent (opt-in) requires the donor or next of kin (in some countries) to permit the removal of their eye during life or after death [17]. With this type, donors are encouraged to opt in or inform their family, next of kin, friends, and significant others of their decision to donate their eyes [17].

Autonomy is the ability of a person to make their own choices and decisions [20, 23]. Autonomy is crucial because it involves considering individual and family perspectives to enable voluntary decision-making regarding donation [24]. Manipulation undermines autonomy by taking control of an individual. The three main influences on individuals are coercion, manipulation, and persuasion [25]. Although the literature argues that both consent types (opt-in or opt-out) give individuals the freedom of choice [10], the ethical dilemma surrounding autonomy arises from the presumed consent [10]. Some argue that dead bodies have no rights, allowing society to remove their eyes; this raises questions about autonomy in this context [21].

Voluntariness in donation refers to the condition in which an individual makes a donation decision freely, without manipulation or coercion by others [25, 26]. The decision-making process for eye donation should occur in circumstances designed to minimize the risk of coercion or undue influence, which can result in physical, psychological, or economic harm [27]. Pressure from family, emotion, or other influences can affect the donor's voluntary choice [28]. In healthcare, most manipulation occurs through informational manipulation, in which information is deliberately managed or withheld to mislead individuals into acting in accordance with the agency's preferences [22].

Shared benefits for all. Since organ donation is for everyone in society, some might say that using organs in a particular way is a poor choice [17]. For example, in some countries, such as Israel, there is a law that allows donors to donate organs to specific recipients, including family members or friends, and this can be applied to particular religious or ethnic groups [13].

Altruism is a behaviour that involves helping others selflessly without expecting anything in return [30], and it is the primary reason for donation [32]. It serves as a social motivator for doing good and is essential for eye donation [18, 30].

Informed consent in the Australian context. Australia uses an opt-in (explicit) consent, requiring donors' consent and additional approval from their next of kin [28, 29]. Therefore, donors must ensure their desire to donate eyes is known to their loved ones through family discussions, registering with the national organ donation registry or carrying an organ donor card [8]. Australians also have a soft opt-out system, meaning that if the deceased has not expressed a wish regarding eye donation, they can be considered as eye donors [29]. In these cases, the next of kin or family are approached to obtain their consent [29].

3 The Value-Sensitive Design (VSD)

The aim of this study is to identify values related to the informed consent for eye donation. The value identification was done by using Value Sensitive Design (VSD), a theoretical framework for designing technology that systematically incorporates human values throughout the entire design process [30, 31].

The VSD employs a three-part approach, comprising conceptual, empirical, and technical components [35]. The informed consent for eye donation was first conceptualised based on the literature [24, 32]. The second step involved identifying the stakeholders, as presented in Table 1. Furthermore, the values that support informed consent for eye donation were identified through empirical investigations of discussions from 44 meetings with health professionals, human-computer interaction experts and health informatics specialists, including eye specialists from the eye bank and the national organ and tissue authority. The study validated the values presented in the application by collecting feedback from consumers. A total of 166 participants participated in the survey. The study was approved by the South Eastern Sydney Local Health District ethics committee.

Table 1. Illustrates the stakeholders involved in the study.

Groups	Type of stakeholders	Stakeholders
App users	Direct stakeholders	Patients, carers and eye clinic visitors.
Health professionals	Direct stakeholders	Cornea specialist, ophthalmic nurse, physician, nurse, and student nurse.
IT professionals	Direct stakeholders	Human-computer interaction experts, health informatics specialist, and app developer.
Healthcare organisations	Indirect stakeholders	NSW Health, NSW Eye and Tissue Bank, NSW Organ and Tissue Service, Save Sight Institute, and Sydney Eye Hospital.
Educational organisations	Direct stakeholders	University of Sydney, and University of Wollongong.

Nineteen values related to the development of the eye donation content app were consistently identified throughout the meetings.

Accessibility was identified as a value that enables eye donation to be open to everyone regardless of age [38], so anyone can donate without bias or restrictions based on race, socioeconomic status, gender, or other social factors [38]. The stakeholder advised that since the eye donation system is intended for users aged 16 years and over, the appearance must be suitable for all age groups ("should be available to all members in the public aged 16 years and older, including the ones with vision impairment...", "Make the app that design for vast age range... not too fancy...", "The information can be in text, video, or image format...", "Help users learn better..."). Therefore, the content needs to be designed to be accessible for a broad age range of readers, using plain language suitable for the general public of all religious beliefs and cultural backgrounds, ensuring no offence is caused.

Eye donation enables treatment for corneal blindness, which can be caused by infections from bacteria, viruses, fungi, or protozoa, as well as by trauma, contact lens use, or steroid use [38–40]. Therefore, **Beneficence and non-maleficence** define the benefits of eye donation and the outcomes of transplantation, illustrating how it can transform an individual's life from dependence to independence ("increase awareness for eye donation and donation knowledge…").

As most people lack personal experience with eye donation, one way to raise awareness and increase eye donation rates is to expose potential donors to people who directly benefit from donation, as stakeholders indicated, "Testimonial videos featuring recipients and their families can be very effective in inspiring others to donate their eyes…". Providing the videos of recipients and their families could emotionally convince users to understand how the donated organ could drastically improve the quality of the recipient's life and their loved ones', as if they were the ones needing the organ, presenting the value of **Relatedness.**

Stakeholders also highlighted the **Trust,** recommending the disclosure of the sponsor and source of information, "Use the official logo of the Hospital, Australia Organ and Tissue Donation Service, UOW and University of Sydney…". Stakeholders also indicated the need of using credible and verified resources "Use the verified multimedia, including the image…". Thus, to promote users' trust in the designed technology, an authoritative resource with involvement of expert stakeholders in content development are essential.

Usability refers to the extent of use or suitability, which is vital for creating a user-centred artefact and for assessing whether it performs tasks efficiently and as designed [38]. For this study, stakeholders suggested the solution not to be intrusive to users ("Do not include the feature of notification as it is annoying the users…"), easy navigation, user guidance towards providing consent to donate and visually appealing design ("Display web link for registration at many places in the app, to assist and remind them to do so when they are ready…", "Use colour for each content category so the users can follow it easily…", "The video must be able to rotate so users can watch both vertical and horizontal…").

Health literacy is the ability of individuals to obtain, read, understand, or use health-related information, navigate the healthcare system, or make informed medical decisions [36]. Recent research found that only 40% of donors read the consent form thoroughly, paying attention to technical terms and complex language, and that the consent form often failed to meet readability standards [34]. The stakeholders suggested that the information content should include eye donation education in different formats, such as text, images, and videos, to improve users' health literacy ("Provide more information about the donation so consumers will have more knowledge and understand…", "have information at the 7th-grade level", "include different formats, text, image, video"). Thus, the health education content should be evaluated for readability using the Flesch-Kincaid Reading Ease [36]. These tests that are commonly used to measure how easily the reader can understand the material, and are often utilised by researchers, policymakers, and marketers.

The stakeholders emphasised on the domain Expertise, "the educator from NSW Eye and Tissue Bank and Australian Organ and Tissue Donation Service can provide proper content…". Informing the individual about the expert organisations that endorsed the artefact through written documentation and visual representations, can enhance the individual's confidence in utilising the application.

Stakeholders stressed the importance of **Inclusivity,** "Let users know that all religions support eye donation…". One obstacle to eye donation is religious misconceptions suggesting conflicts with certain beliefs [19]. Therefore, stakeholders proposed a dedicated page offering information, highlighting that the five major religions endorse eye donation and have relevant perspectives. Past research indicates that limited knowledge about donation can serve as a barrier [36].

Respect is vital to ensure that all parties involved in eye donation are treated with dignity and autonomy [33]. The individual's decision to donate or not should be respected, and the entire process must be transparent, adhering to policies, regulations, and stakeholder requirements [33]. The stakeholders noted, "Since in Australia we use the opt-in consent system, the family must be aware of the deceased's wish to donate their eyes…", "Do not use images that might offend some religious beliefs, such as pictures of the Bible or temples…". Thus, the content utilises language that positively encourages individuals to donate and refrains from blaming or disrespecting those who choose not to register for donation. Additionally, avoiding rushing or persistently nudging with numerous notifications.

Stakeholders advised that the solution should supports this value of **Transparency** by displaying and listing the information it collects from users and indicating this on the disclaimer page, "Include the data we collect in the information and privacy". The purpose of the artefact needs to be clearly stated including details about the staff involved in developing the content.

Autonomy is fundamental to eye donation [23], and stakeholders stated that the solution should support this value, "provide the user with the option to provide consent".

The stakeholders also suggested placing a link to the source of eye donation knowledge content allowing users to verify the accuracy of the content and access additional information, which support the **Credibility** of the solution, ("Add the content reference link at the bottom of the page so they can read more if they want…").

Altruism-promoting. Altruism is the core ethical principle and value underpinning eye donation [13, 26]. It is regarded as the highest form of generosity towards strangers, serving as the motivation behind donation [38]. The previous study showed that the awareness of eye donation could increase the willingness to donate/altruism [34] the stakeholders recommend as to "Include information about corneal transplants in the content to ensure users…".

Interactive. Stakeholders expressed concerns that the solution should better engage users, "Include interaction, use the eligible eye donation questions to increase the engagement and provide knowledge as well…". Eye donation experts in the field developed the 7-question eligibility criteria for eye donation aiming to educate users about the requirements to become an eye donor, thus could improve users engagement and their health literacy.

Compliance. One piece of advice from the stakeholder was to develop the information content in accordance with the Australian National Eye Donation Guidelines ("Content must adhere to the National Organ and Tissue Donation guidelines…").

Availability. Stakeholders agreed that the developed artefact (mobile application) should be freely available to all members of the public and potential eye donors on both iOS and Android platforms, thereby reaching a broader audience, ("the app free of charge and available for iOS and Android platforms…", "The app should be promoted on the NSW website and on social media so users can benefit from it…").

Informative. The eye donation information can help raise awareness, leading to an increase in eye donors [30]. Furthermore, precise donation information is substantially associated with eye donation registration [35]. The stakeholder proposed that offering detailed and evidence-based donation information would aid in increasing eye donation rates ("Provide all very important eye donation knowledge they should know, so they can decide to donate..").

Connectivity. The stakeholders commented that the solution should enable users to share it with friends and loved ones so they can use it ("Should be compatible with social media, so they can get more support or share their wish to become an eye donor on social media…").

The final, third step focused on Technical Investigations, designing the artefact - mHealth app for eye donation - based on the design requirements raising from identified values and corresponding norms (Table 2). According to the values and context, persuasive strategies were identified. For example, Primary Task Support category such as reduction and tunnelling are applied for "eligibility for donation". Dialogue support category, Similarity is applied by providing recipient and family testimonies. Credibility support category is applied by providing trusted source of stakeholders (Expertise), reliable sources of information (Trustworthiness), registration access for eye donation, national organ donation registry (Verifiability). Additionally, the Social support category is included through the possibility of sharing donation wishes to next of kin through SMS from the template and accessing the DonateLife Facebook page, promoting social connection and cooperation.

4   The Values Implicated in the Contents of the App

4.1   Fundamental Knowledge for Eye Donation

To uphold the principles of usability, the content has been meticulously crafted to be visually engaging, with explicit navigation instructions provided within the application (Fig. 1). This section presents colour-coded content categorised to assist individuals in selecting their preferred starting point, offering clear and visually appealing information within the same category. The content has been carefully designed to be self-contained and complete. It does not require chronological exploration, thereby also enhancing health literacy. This content emphasises the essential aspects of eye donation that influence an individual's decision to contribute, fostering awareness and expanding knowledge regarding donation.

Table 2. The implication of the values in the application's design.

Value	Norms	Design requirements
Accessibility	To provide the instructions to use the app and for assisting users with vision impairment	Present the icon of speaker. Include text reading feature. Enable flexibility of font size.
Beneficence and non-maleficence	To improve health literacy. To provide insight into how organ donation is a valuable gift. To provide the donation criteria.	Include eye donation education content using different formats, such as video, image, and text regarding. Include video content regarding the corneal recipients and family. Include the means to assess the donor eligibility of the user.
Relatedness	To provide the means for individuals to sympathise with patients with corneal blindness.	Utilise the video content of the recipient and family donor testimonies.
Trust	To demonstrate the use of reliable content and trusted sources in app development.	Display the organisation's logos and branding that endorsed the app's design and development.
Usability	To provide eye donation content in categories.	Use colour coded content.
	To enhance engagement.	Visually appealing.
Health literacy	To assist users in better understanding eye donation information.	Utilised information should be tailored for reading ability suitable for the target users, incorporating multimedia, reading texts, and images to facilitate a better understanding of eye donation information.
Expertise	To provide the list of organisations endorsing the app design and development.	Display the list of organisations endorsing the application on the main screen of the app, as well as in the terms and conditions outlining the copyrights associated with the application.
Inclusivity	To present the concentrated information in a single location.	Nominate specific screens for each category of information.
Respect	To show respect to all users' donation decisions.	Do not include notifications or reminders intended to continually prompt users to register for donations.

(continued)

Table 2. (*continued*)

Value	Norms	Design requirements
Transparency	To provide the user with the list of data collection information.	Display on the main screen the details of information collection, such as the date and time of downloading, as well as deletion.
Autonomy	To provide an opportunity for the user to decide whether they want to proceed with using this app. Provide a way to confirm the eye donor's wish.	Provide option for the user to accept the user agreement. Include a feature (e.g. sending sms) to provide opportunity of informing others about the wish to become an eye donor.
Credibility	To provide evidence of trusted sources for users to comprehend.	Display the web links and references at the bottom of each screen for the source of the content.
Altruism promotion	To increase altruism of users.	Provide video content of the recipient and family's testimonies.
Interactive	To present the information actively in a manner that allows users to respond.	Use an educational tool and eligibility questionnaire for eye donation (yes-or-no questions).
Increase engagement	To provide users with various learning options.	Utilise an active set of eligibility questions for eye donation which can serve as an alternative approach to educate users about eye donation, supplementing traditional methods such as text, videos, and images.
Compliance	To provide evidence of reliable sources for app development.	Adhere to the Australian Eye Donation Guidelines and ensure compliance with app store regulations during the development of the application's features.
Availability	To facilitate access for all potential eye donors.	Disseminate the application across both iOS and Android platforms at no cost.

(*continued*)

Table 2. (*continued*)

Value	Norms	Design requirements
Informative	To provide the concise information regarding eye donation.	Provide comprehensive and accurate information in the respective categories from the outset, including eye donation, processes, and transplantation.
Connectivity	To promote information and communication among users/organisation staff.	Allow navigation from app to websites and social media of the NSW eye and tissue donation service.
		Allow user to review the app on the app's website and leave comments.
	To facilitate easy app sharing.	Provide option for the app to be shared.

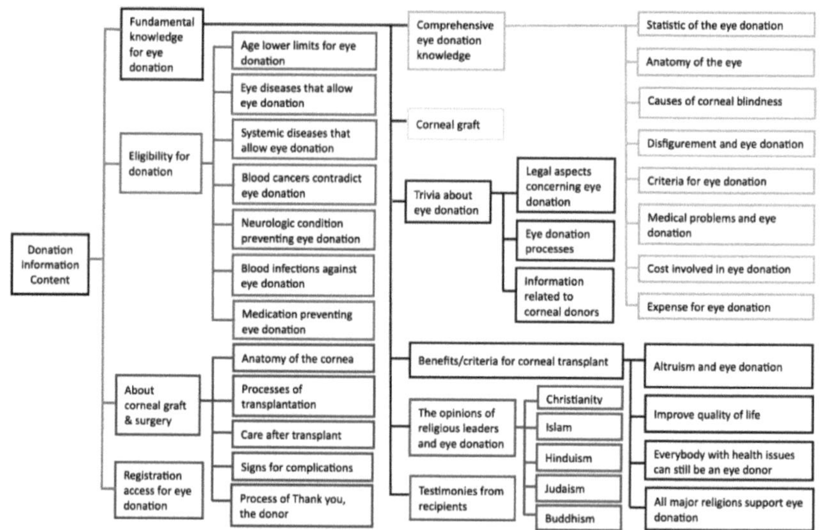

Fig. 1. The information architecture of the eye donation app

A lack of awareness and knowledge regarding the act of donation constitutes a significant barrier to eye donation. Consequently, this subsection presents statistical data on eye donation to enhance awareness, a factor previously demonstrated to influence the willingness to donate eyes [36] significantly. This content provides comprehensive information about eye donation, which is essential for assisting individuals in making informed decisions about donation. It emphasises the importance of being well-informed and underscores the value of informative content. The information is evidence-based and aligns with national eye donation guidelines, thereby promoting trust in the eye donation app.

The second subsection provides a detailed elaboration on the anatomy of the eye, the causes of corneal blindness, and the appropriate treatment methods. The age criteria for donation, as per Australian guidelines, specify that the minimum age for eye donation is two years, with no upper age limit. However, individuals under the age of 18 must obtain additional consent from a parent or guardian before donation [37]. Consequently, the content must be designed to be accessible to a broad age group of readers, employing plain language suitable for the general public across various religious beliefs and cultural backgrounds. Additionally, the content includes images and text that enhance learning for some individuals, ensuring that no offence is caused and underscoring the importance of accessibility. Given that the target audience spans a wide age range, the material was carefully developed and validated using the Flesch-Kincaid readability scale [38, 39], achieving a score of 77. This indicates that the material is appropriate for students in Year 8 or higher, or individuals aged 13 years and above, to read and comprehend effectively, thereby reflecting an emphasis on health literacy.

Limited knowledge regarding all aspects of eye donation can serve as a considerable obstacle to the act. This third subsection outlines the criteria for eye donation, noting that the most common health issues do not preclude individuals from undergoing eye donation [40]. It further details the processes involved and elucidates the procedures for registration. Donors shall be treated with dignity, and confidentiality shall be maintained for both the donor and the recipient. Additionally, the donation will not result in disfigurement and will not interfere with funeral arrangements. Furthermore, this section advocates for individuals to participate in the commendable act of becoming eye donors, thereby exemplifying the principle of altruism.

The subsequent subsection highlights the importance of addressing prevalent misconceptions concerning eligibility for eye donation, particularly in relation to age and health conditions, most of which do not prevent donation. Furthermore, the majority of religious doctrines endorse eye donation. This initiative has the potential to benefit numerous individuals affected by corneal blindness, potentially transforming their lives from dependence to independence, thereby upholding the principles of beneficence and non-maleficence.

The section on religions and eye donation explores the perspectives of religious leaders to motivate individuals to follow their guidance and act in accordance with their faith [41, 42]. This highlights the significance of the relatedness values. Additionally, the information provided was thorough and relevant to eye donation, reinforcing the importance of informative content.

The final subsection in this category encompasses the testimonies from the recipient and their family. This segment presents video evidence illustrating their gratitude and the significant changes in their lives after receiving the donation. This subsection highlights the importance of both relatedness and beneficence values.

4.2 Information Regarding Eligibility for Eye Donation

Questionnaires regarding the eligibility of eye donation were presented. This section is provided as an informative as well as promoting interactivity. The users can answer 7 questions and receive relevant information enhancing user engagement and increased health literacy.

4.3 Information about the Content of Corneal Grafts and Surgery

This part covers the details of what should happen to the corneal donation recipient after the transplant and how to care for it. Clear and concise information from the national guidelines and corneal specialists, with references to ensure content accuracy, supports the value of compliance and credibility. It features an image of the eye on the first day after surgery, along with a video explaining the surgical process in simple language, accompanied by subtitles to support health literacy. The content can be accessed with just one click, enhancing usability and accessibility, which will be especially helpful for senior individuals with vision impairments.

5 Empirical Investigation with Consumers

In order to evaluate the importance of the identified values and information architecture of the app in relation to the eye donation knowledge, a cross-sectional study was conducted at a tertiary hospital's eye clinics outpatient department. The survey was completed by 166 patients aged 16 years and over who attended the clinic with their carers, recruited through convenience sampling.

The consumers were asked to reflect on eye donation app. Based on the results (Table 3 and 4), the consumers identified the values included in the application and no significant differences were found among the different user groups.

Table 3. Logistic regression for high eye donation knowledge and demographic variables

Variables	Group	Odd Ratio (95% CI)	P value
Gender	Male and female	.750 (0.37–1.48)	0.40
Age	Age16–45	1	0.35
	Age 46–65	.563 (0.24–1.33)	0.19
	Age 65 up	.885 (0.35–2.27)	0.80
Ethnicity	Caucasian	1	0.41
	Asian	.640 (0.20–2.02)	0.45
	Other	.460 (0.13–1.58)	0.22
Religion	Christian	1	0.90
	Non-Christian religion	.765 (0.18–3.26)	0.72
	Non religion	.867 (0.41–1.83)	0.71

Table 4. Verified scores of the eye donation content

Eye Donation Values identified	Percentage	Eye Donation Values identified	Percentage	Eye Donation Values identified	Percentage
Respect	97%	Beneficence	88%	Availability	78.9%
Connectivity	94%	Altruism promotion	86.7%	Inclusivity	54.2%
Transparency	91%	Usability	84.29%		
Informative	89.2%	Health literacy	80.7%		

6 Discussion and Conclusion

Ethical values are crucial in developing eye donation content because they promote informed consent, respect donors and recipients, uphold public trust, and help prevent misinformation. Such content also considers cultural sensitivities and ensures fair treatment of all individuals, fostering a positive view of eye donation. This encourages more participation and ensures that the eye donation process is conducted with respect to individuals' dignity and adheres to ethical standards [43].

Previous studies [44, 45] on app design provided how value considerations are incorporated through translating stakeholder values into persuasive systems design and the development of the system. While stakeholders identified 19 key values related to eye donation, consumers ranked 10 values highly. Nevertheless, some values, such as transparency, can encompass credibility and trust. Thus, entangling values in system design could be a daunting task. Smit and Nacar [46] indicated that translating values into health applications has not been easy and highlighted the need for clarity.

This study presented how values should be considered in the development of an eye donation consent promotion app and validated the application's values with consumers to determine whether the identified values are aligned. While the knowledge of eye donation, usability, and other app values can be studied, the effectiveness of the app on actual eye donation registration rates can be studied only longitudinally from the Government registry. Nevertheless, this study demonstrated how value considerations could be embedded in promoting eye donation registration and informed consent, and that this approach could be applicable to other organ donation studies.

References

1. Tidke, S.C., Tidake, P.: A review of corneal blindness: causes and management. Cureus. **14** (2022)
2. Phillips, W.: Ethical controversies about proper health informatics practices. Mo. Med. **112**, 53–57 (2015)
3. Berdichevsky, D., Neuenschwander, E.: Toward an ethics of persuasive technology. Commun. ACM. **42**, 51–58 (1999)

4. Jacobs, N.: Two ethical concerns about the use of persuasive technology for vulnerable people. Bioethics. **34**, 519–526 (2020)
5. Kuonanoja, L., Meedya, S., Win, K.T., Oinas-Kukkonen, H.: Ethical Evaluation of a Value Sensitive Persuasive System: Case Milky Way. Proceedings of Pacific Asia Conference of Information Systems (PACIS). Association for Information Systems, (2018)
6. Australian Government Organ and Tissue Authority: Registering is easy and only takes one minute become an organ and tissue donor.
7. Australian Government Organ and Tissue Authority: Who we are.
8. Chumkasian, W., et al.: Design and development of mHealth app: eye donor Aust. In: International Conference on Persuasive Technology, pp. 75–88. Springer (2024)
9. Australian Organ and Tissue Donation and Transplantation Authority: Australian Donation and Transplantation Activity Report 2024. (2025)
10. Schicktanz, S., Wiesemann, C., Wöhlke, S., Carmi, A.: Teaching Ethics in Organ Transplantation and Tissue Donation-Cases and Movies. Universitätsverlag Göttingen (2010)
11. Lawlor, M., Kerridge, I.: Understanding selective refusal of eye donation: identity, beauty, and interpersonal relationships. J. Bioethical Inquiry. **11**, 57–64 (2014)
12. Centre for Eye Research Australia: Aussie lead the way in protecting the rights of the eye donors. (2018)
13. Rabinowich, A., Jotkowitz, A.: Altruism and religion: a new paradigm for organ donation. J. Relig. Health. **57**, 360–365 (2018)
14. Ayorinde, J.O., Saeb-Parsy, K., Hossain, A.: Opportunities and challenges in using social media in organ donation. JAMA Surg. **155**, 797–798 (2020)
15. Drzyzga, K., Krupka-Matuszczyk, I., Drzyzga, Ł., Mrukwa-Kominek, E., Kucia, K.: Quality of life and mental state after sight restoration by corneal transplantation. Psychosomatics. **57**, 414–422 (2016)
16. Veatch, R.M.: Implied, presumed and waived consent: the relative moral wrongs of under-and over-informing. Am. J. Bioeth. **7**, 39–41 (2007)
17. Dalal, A.R.: Philosophy of organ donation: review of ethical facets. World J. Transplant. **5**, 44 (2015)
18. Price, D.: Human Tissue in Transplantation and Research: a Model Legal and Ethical Donation Framework, vol. 10. Cambridge University Press (2009)
19. Hickson, M.: Research Handbook for Health Care Professionals. John Wiley & Sons (2013)
20. Zina, O.: The essential guide to doing your research project. Sage (2021)
21. Saab, S., Saggi, S.S., Akbar, M., Choi, G.: Presumed consent: a potential tool for countries experiencing an organ donation crisis. Dig. Dis. Sci. **64**, 1346–1355 (2019)
22. Prous, M., Ponto, M.: Barriers to ocular tissue donation in acute clinical settings. Progress in Health Sciences. **5**, 134–141 (2015)
23. Vandemeulebroucke, T., Denier, Y., Mertens, E., Gastmans, C.: Which framework to use? A systematic review of ethical frameworks for the screening or evaluation of health technology innovations. Sci. Eng. Ethics. **28**, 26 (2022)
24. Hyde, M.K., Masser, B.M., Edwards, A.R., Ferguson, E.: Australian perspectives on opt-in and opt-out consent systems for deceased organ donation. Prog. Transplant. **31**, 357–367 (2021)
25. Pace, N., Hendry, R.: Consent: ethical considerations. Anaesth. Intensive Care Med. **7**, 107–109 (2006)
26. Dopelt, K., Siton, L., Harrison, T., Davidovitch, N.: Revisiting the relationship between altruism and organ donation: insights from Israel. Int. J. Environ. Res. Public Health. **19**, 7404 (2022)
27. Resnik, D.B.: The Ethics of Research with Human Subjects: Protecting People, Advancing Science, Promoting Trust. Springer (2018)

28. Pham, T.: Ethical and legal considerations in healthcare AI: innovation and policy for safe and fair use. R. Soc. Open Sci. **12**, 241873 (2025)
29. Jenkin, R.A., Garrett, S.A., Keay, K.A.: Altruism in death: attitudes to body and organ donation in Australian students. Anat. Sci. Educ. **16**, 27–46 (2023)
30. Wilbanks, J.: Ethical issues in consumer informatics and online content. In: Consumer Informatics and Digital Health: Solutions for Health and Health Care, pp. 327–336. Springer (2019)
31. Yetim, F.: Bringing discourse ethics to value sensitive design: pathways toward a deliberative future. AIS Trans. Hum.-Comput. Interact. **3**, 133–155 (2011)
32. Nicholls, R.: Reform in Australia: a focus on informed consent. Glob. Priv. Law Rev. **3** (2022)
33. Aslam, S., Adler, E., Mekeel, K., Little, S.J.: Clinical effectiveness of COVID-19 vaccination in solid organ transplant recipients. Transpl. Infect. Dis. **23**, e13705 (2021)
34. AlHejaili, W., Almalik, F., Albrahim, L., Alkhaldi, F., AlHejaili, A., Al Sayyari, A.: Scores of awareness and altruism in organ transplantation among Saudi health colleges students-impact of gender, year of study, and field of specialization. Saudi J. Kidney Dis. Transpl. **29**, 1028–1034 (2018)
35. Ryckman, R.M., van den Borne, B., Thornton, B., Gold, J.A.: Value priorities and organ donation in young adults. J. Appl. Soc. Psychol. **35**, 2421–2435 (2005)
36. Ackuaku-Dogbe, E., Abaidoo, B.: Eye donation: awareness and willingness among patients attending a tertiary eye center in Ghana. West Afr. J. Med. **33**, 258–263 (2014)
37. Australian Government Organ and Tissue Authority: Who can donate? ,
38. Neuhoff, E., Feeser, K.M., Sutherland, K., Hovatter, T.: Flesch-Kincaid reading grade level re-examined: creating a uniform method for calculating readability on a certification exam. Online J. Workforce Educ. Dev. **9**, 2 (2016)
39. Walsh, T., Volsko, T.: Readability assessment of internet-based consumer health information. Respir. Care. **53**, 1310–1315 (2008)
40. Inc, A.T.C.-o.A.: National guidelines for organ and tissue donation. Australasian Transplant Co-Ordinators Association (2008)
41. Williams, A.M., Muir, K.W.: Awareness and attitudes toward corneal donation: challenges and opportunities. Clin. Ophthalmol., 1049–1059 (2018)
42. Chumkasian, W., et al.: Prevalence and predictors of knowledge and attitudes toward eye donation among the general population: a systematic review. Cornea. **42**, 520–528 (2023)
43. Layman, E.: Health informatics: ethical issues. Health Care Manag. **22**, 2–15 (2003)
44. Altuwayrib, S., Win, K.T., Freeman, M.: Medication adherence support applications for chronic arthritis patients: healthcare providers. In: Perspective in Saudi Arabia. Medinfo 2023. IOS Press, Sydney (2023)
45. Almutairi, N., Vlahu-Gjorgievska, E., Win, K.T.: mHealth asthma management app's content creation, stakeholders' values and design features. Int. J. of Hum.–Comput. Interact. **41**, 3352–3368 (2025)
46. Smits, M., Nacar, M., Ludden, D.S., G., van Goor, H.: Stepwise design and evaluation of a values-oriented ambient intelligence healthcare monitoring platform. Value Health. **25**, 914–923 (2022)

Parent-Child Dialogue Support Through Semi-autonomous Para-operated Robot in Home Learning

Eiki Go[1]([✉]) [iD], Tomonori Kubota[1] [iD], Masaya Iwasaki[2] [iD], Satoshi Sato[1] [iD], and Kohei Ogawa[1] [iD]

[1] Graduate School of Engineering, Nagoya University, Nagoya, Japan
go.eiki.j1@s.mail.nagoya-u.ac.jp
[2] Graduate School of Engineering Science, The University of Osaka, Suita, Japan

Abstract. The efficacy of educational robots in children's school education and home learning has been established. There has been a growing demand for robots that effectively support parent-child learning at home, but the design of robots that can assist without disrupting their dialogue has remained unclear. This study proposes a novel form of robot for supporting home learning while promoting parent-child dialogue: a semi-autonomous para-operated robot, which is partially controlled by the parent from the side. We hypothesized that this approach, unlike autonomous robots which may reduce parental burden but lead to parental disengagement, would increase parental involvement through active operation. To validate this hypothesis, we conducted an experiment with parent-child pairs comparing three conditions: (1) no robot, (2) autonomous robot, and (3) the proposed semi-autonomous robot. The results revealed that the proposed robot significantly increased parental utterances without increasing parental burden compared to the other conditions, supporting our hypothesis. This study contributes by demonstrating the effectiveness of semi-autonomous para-operated robots in facilitating parent-child home learning.

Keywords: Semi-autonomous robot · Para-operated robot · Home learning · Parent-child dialogue · Human-robot interaction

1 Introduction

As research and real-world applications of social robots capable of interacting with humans expand, the effectiveness of educational robots used for children's school education and home learning has been demonstrated. A previous study has shown that children who study with robots can improve their concentration in repetitive learning tasks, such as memorizing vocabulary [15]. Other research has revealed that children can develop friendly relationships with robots placed

E. Go and T. Kubota—Co-first authors.

Fig. 1. Parent-child learning scene during the experiment using the proposed semi-autonomous para-operated robot. The robot speaks and proceeds with the learning task based on the parent's operation.

in schools and interact with them as if they were friends [14]. There are various ways to use robots in education, including tutor-type robots that directly instruct children [13], learning partners that engage in interactive learning [12], and models where children take on the role of teaching the robot [11,23]. All of these approaches have been shown to improve learning outcomes.

On the other hand, concerns have been raised about introducing robots in children's education. Dependence on robots may negatively impact human relationships [24], and it is argued that the introduction of robots into education may diminish parental and teacher engagement, thereby weakening their relationships with children [1,8]. Some concerns suggest that the use of robots to replace human interaction in education may impair children's communication skills [19].

Parents play an important role in their children's knowledge acquisition and social skills, and past studies have confirmed that parents' active involvement in education has a positive effect on their children's academic performance [3,4,7,20]. In particular, it has been shown that learning through interaction between parents and children contributes to the improvement of children's motivation to learn and their level of understanding, and the facilitation of dialogue between parents and children during learning is an important issue [5,6,18]. Educational support robots must be designed to facilitate human communication, while enhancing learning effectiveness, rather than interfering with it.

Previous research on educational support robots has predominantly focused on studies of one-on-one interactions between children and robots [2,10]. However, in recent years, there has been increasing attention to studies examining the triadic relationship among parents, children, and robots [1,8]. Above previous research studies have shown that robots are expected not only to support children's learning, but also to contribute to strengthening parent-child relationships. However, little is known about how to design robots that effectively support parentâĂŞchild learning at home, highlighting a gap in current research.

We propose that a semi-autonomous para-operated robot is promising as a form of robot that can support home learning while facilitating dialogue between parents and children (Fig. 1). In this model, the parent, child, and robot engage in a collaborative learning task while the parent secretly partially operates the robot. Semi-autonomous robots are shown to be able to perform tasks while reducing operator workload by integrating human operation with the robot's autonomous functions [22]. Para-operated robots, which allow operators to participate in triadic interactions through nearby control, have been suggested to possess the potential to serve as catalysts for enhanced human relationships [16,17]. This paper focuses on the possibility that the act of parents operating robots could serve as a factor in promoting parent-child interaction.

On the other hand, from the perspective of reducing parental workload, an autonomous robot that requires no operation may be more effective. While an autonomous robot can lessen parental workload compared to a para-operated form, it risks transforming the parent into a passive observer as the learning task occurs solely between the child and the robot. Conversely, the proposed semi-autonomous para-operated robot enables parents to be more actively engaged in the learning task through partial operation without significantly increasing their workload, thereby fostering dialogue between parent and child. We hypothesize that semi-autonomous operation encourages parents to engage more actively in the task, thereby facilitating significantly more utterances than autonomous robots

By demonstrating the effectiveness of the semi-autonomous para-operated robot, this study addresses an important research gap in designing practical robots to support parent-child home learning. Specifically, we revealed that employing a semi-autonomous para-operated robot, partially controlled by the parent, promotes parent-child dialogue without increasing parental burden, in contrast to autonomous robots that prioritize parental convenience. This paper covers related research (Sect. 2), experimental methods (Sect. 3), results (Sect. 4), and discussion (Sect. 5).

2   Related Work

2.1   Parent-Child Home Learning Support Robots

Parent-child home learning support robots, the focus of this paper, have recently begun to gain attention. Ho et al. explored the roles and design that parents prefer for the robot in parent-child education while reading picture books [8]. The results show that many parents are positive about delegating monotonous tasks such as picture book reading to a robot, indicating a demand for a robot that can support parent-child home learning. In addition, as discussed in Sect. 1, it is also clear that such robots need to be designed to facilitate dialogue between parents and children [1,8].

On the other hand, in home learning, parents prefer to maintain control over the robot [1,10]. For example, field experiments in which robots autonomously generate educational content and conduct home learning have highlighted the need for a mechanism that allows parents to review and approve the robot's utterances [9]. Such a design is essential to prevent autonomous robot utterances from contradicting parental intentions in children's learning.

However, previous research has not yet revealed a design for robots that can support home parent-child learning by facilitating parent-child dialogue, while allowing parents to control the robot. In the context of this research, this paper proposes a semi-autonomous para-operated robot as a robot facilitating dialogue between parents and children. Although this form, in which parents operate the robot, may also satisfy the requirement that parents can control the robot, this paper focuses solely on the effect of promoting parent-child dialogue.

2.2 Para-operated Robot

Research on para-operated robots is still limited, but its effectiveness is being demonstrated. Para-operated robots are a type of robot in which the operator, the robot, and the interlocutor exist in the same space, allowing the operator to engage in conversation while controlling the robot [17]. By controlling the robot's utterances during a triadic conversation, operators are expected to guide the dialogue according to their intentions and facilitate human-human interaction through the robot. Past studies have shown that when shop staff operate a robot during customer services, it reduces their workload and fosters customer rapport [16]. Shimaya et al. further demonstrated their effectiveness in promoting self-disclosure and reducing psychological burden in counseling [21].

However, previous robots of this type were fully operator-controlled and lacked autonomy, resulting in a significant workload on the operator. To address this issue, this paper presents a system in which the robot autonomously generates appropriate utterances based on the situation, allowing the operator to engage in dialogue with minimal operation. Although this paper focuses on research on home learning support robots between parents and children, it is novel in that it incorporates semi-autonomous control into para-operated robot research. Furthermore, there have been no prior examples of applying para-operated robots to parent-child home education. This study also demonstrates the effectiveness of proximity operation in the context of home education.

3   Method

3.1   Experimental Design

To test the hypothesis, a laboratory experiment was conducted in which parents and children performed a learning task using the robot. This experiment was designed with the assumption that parents assist their children with learning tasks at home.

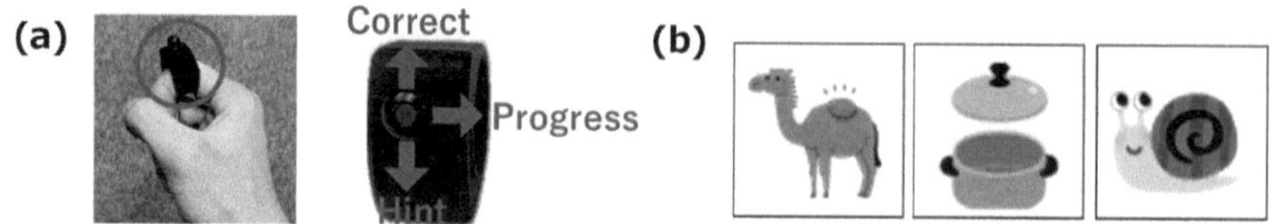

Fig. 2. (a) The ring-shaped controller used by parents to operate the robot, and (b) a sample of the cards used in the card memorization game.

For the experimental learning task, we adopted a card memorization game commonly used in Japanese home learning. In this task, the child memorizes the order of 25 cards by listening to a story crafted based on the card order, which is told by the parent to help the child recall the order. After the cards are shuffled, the child attempts to arrange them in the original order. As an example of the story, if the cards were arranged as shown in Fig. 2(b), the parent might say, "A camel was taking a walk when it found a pot. Inside the pot, there was a snail."

To examine the effects of a semi-autonomous para-operated robot in this task, we compared three conditions using a within-participant design:

- **No-robot condition (NR):** The parent and child performed the learning task without the robot.
- **Semi-autonomous robot condition (SAR):** The parent, child, and a semi-autonomous para-operated robot, operated by the parent, performed the learning task.
- **Autonomous robot condition (AR):** The parent, child, and autonomous robot performed the learning task.

3.2   Learning Task Flow

The learning task described above followed a specific flow (Fig. 3), which consisted of three main parts: ice-breaking with the robot, memorizing the card order, and arranging the cards. The robot was operated using a ring-shaped controller that allows input operations via Bluetooth connectivity. This controller is equipped with a lever, which enables the operator to send their intentions to the robot by tilting it to issue the three types of commands detailed below (Fig. 2(a)).

- **Progress command (right):** Triggers the robot's utterance to advance the learning task during icebreaking and memorizing the card order part (detailed in the following section).
- **Correct command (up):** Triggers the robot to praise the child when they place a card correctly.
- **Hint command (down):** Triggers the robot to provide a hint when the child is struggling.

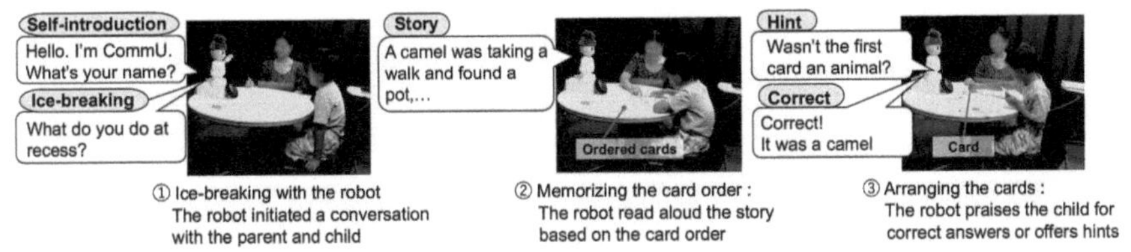

① Ice-breaking with the robot
The robot initiated a conversation
with the parent and child

② Memorizing the card order :
The robot read aloud the story
based on the card order

③ Arranging the cards :
The robot praises the child for
correct answers or offers hints

Fig. 3. Task flow, experimental scenes (AR and SAR conditions), and examples of the robot's utterances. In NR condition, the task was carried out solely by the parent and child.

In SAR condition, the parent used this device and operated the robot without the child noticing. In AR condition, the experimenter operated the robot remotely from another room, using a Wizard of Oz method to simulate an autonomous condition.

Ice-Breaking with the Robot: When the task began, each input of the *progress command* by the parent triggered a single robot utterance for the ice-breaking interaction, facilitating a conversation between the parent and child about topics such as their favorite activities and birthday gifts. Once the robot had completed 8 utterances, the robot asked, "Shall we begin the card memorization game?" and waited for the child's response before proceeding to the next step. In the NR condition, the ice-breaking phase was omitted.

Memorizing the Card Order: Next, the child memorized the order of the cards by looking at the cards and listening to the story. Continuing to use the *progress command*, the robot first instructed the parent, "Point to the cards as the story progresses." Each subsequent input of the *progress command* then triggered the robot to read aloud one segment of the story. Additionally, the robot was designed to accommodate requests from the child, such as repeating a part of the story. Once the story reading was completed, the next *progress command* triggered the robot to ask, "Did you remember the story?" and instructed the parent to shuffle the cards. In NR condition, the parent read the story aloud instead of the robot.

Arranging the Cards: Finally, the child arranges the cards in their original sequence, following the memorized story. Upon the child's correct placement of a card, the input of the *correct command* produced a confirmation sound, and the robot praised the child, weaving in elements of the story, for example, "Correct! First, the camel was taking a walk, right?" The robot prompted the parent to praise the child after every fourth *correct command* input. Additionally, if the child struggled with the card order, the *hint command* could be input, and the robot would provide an appropriate hint. Even if the *hint command* was input multiple times for the same card, the robot generated a different hint each time. It was considered that these robot behaviors would save parents the effort of thinking of hints and further promote conversations, such as praising the child.

In NR condition, the parent provided hints and confirmed whether the cards were correctly arranged instead of the robot.

3.3 System

In the system, the robot's speech content is generated autonomously by GPT-4o to ensure situational appropriateness, while the parent's intervention is limited to triggering the timing and flow of interaction using a discreet ring-shaped controller.

Apparatus. We developed an educational support robot that parents can easily operate to support dialogue and learning with their children. We used CommU, a communication robot manufactured by Vstone Co., Ltd. This robot is a humanoid communication robot approximately 30 cm in height, equipped with nine degrees of freedom in its head, neck, and arms, allowing it to interact with users through gestures and facial expressions. The robot's utterance was synthesized using the NSSS speech engine on macOS. While speaking, the robot performed behaviors such as bowing, waving, and nodding to facilitate more interactive communication. The ring-shaped controller used to operate the robot was the ArcX Smart Ring, a wearable device manufactured by ArcX Technology Ltd.

Robot Utterance Generation. We adopted OpenAI's GPT-4o API to generate the robot's utterances and used prompt engineering techniques to control their content. In the ice-breaking and memorizing the card order parts, the system prompt describes detailed conversation strategies, including instructions to engage in a small talk consisting of 8 robot utterances on topics such as favorite activities and birthday gifts, and to ask the child to begin the card memorization game after the small talk. Furthermore, the story crafted based on the card order is described in the prompt in small segments, and each time the parent inputs the *progress command*, the system output the next passage of the story. The system was designed to process the most recent speech recognition log and the parent's *progress command*, enabling it to judge the context and respond to mid-task requests from the child, such as, "Read that part again."

During the arranging part, for the robot to provide appropriate hints, the system needed to recognize which card the child was currently struggling with. To achieve this, an experimenter monitored the card arranging process via a camera from another room and manually input the number of the card the child was currently struggling with into the system in real time. Depending on the parent's input of the *hint command* or the *correct command*, the system generated an appropriate hint or praise based on the number of the card that the child had correctly placed or was struggling with.

3.4   Procedure

The experiment involved parent-child instruction, task performance, and questionnaire evaluation, repeated across three counterbalanced conditions to mitigate order effects. Additionally, three distinct card orders were prepared and counterbalanced to minimize potential sequence bias during task performance.

Initially, both the parent and child received a general briefing on the learning task. This briefing emphasized that they were encouraged to engage in conversation throughout the task and provided an overview of the questionnaire. Subsequently, the child was relocated to a separate room, and the parent received condition-specific instructions. In SAR condition, the parent was trained on the robot's operation and given practice, with specific guidance to ensure that the child remained unaware of the operation. Conversely, in AR condition, it was explained that the robot would act autonomously. In NR condition, the parent was instructed on how to proceed with the task without the robot's involvement. Following the completion of each condition's task, participants completed the questionnaire, as detailed in the following section.

3.5   Measurement

To investigate whether the semi-autonomous para-operated robot successfully facilitated the parent's utterances, we analyzed the number of times the parent spoke to the child using recorded video of the experiment. First, three annotators classified all of the parent's utterances into five categories: *Monologue*, *Hint*, *Praise*, *Chatting*, and *Phatic Expressions* (e.g., back-channeling or repetition to facilitate smooth conversation [25]). To ensure reliability, only utterances agreed upon by at least two of the three annotators were adopted as data. For the AR and SAR conditions, utterances during the Ice-breaking part were excluded from the utterance count, as this part did not exist in the NR condition. Additionally, utterances identified as the parent's monologues and utterances related to hints about the card order, which depended on the child's memorization, were also excluded. Finally, the sum of the three categories (*Praise*, *Chatting*, and *Phatic Expressions*) was defined as the parent's utterance count, and this study first conducted a comparison of this total utterance count across conditions. If significant differences were found, supplementary analyses were also conducted for each category to investigate what specific types of utterances differed.

In addition to the analysis of parental utterances described above, questionnaires were administered to both the children and the parents. Regarding the parents, if operating the semi-autonomous para-operated robot proposed in this study imposes an excessive burden, its practical applicability may be compromised. Therefore, to assess parental workload across all conditions and the operational burden in the SAR condition, parents completed the following questionnaire (9-point Likert scale; 1: not at all - 9: very much). Specifically, parents were asked about their workload (Q1) after each of the three conditions, and about the difficulty of operating the robot (Q2) specifically after the SAR condition:

- **Q1:** Did you feel that this task had a high workload?
- **Q2:** Did you find it difficult to operate the robot?

On the other hand, to evaluate their task experience, children were asked about *task enjoyment* and *liking of the robot* on a 9-point Likert scale after completing the task in each condition.

3.6   Statistical Analysis

For the utterance count, a Friedman test was performed to determine whether there were significant differences among the conditions. If the Friedman test indicated significant differences, two-tailed Wilcoxon signed-rank tests were conducted as post hoc analyses to identify which conditions differed. Since multiple comparisons were performed, Bonferroni correction was applied by multiplying the p-values by three. In addition to the total utterance analysis described above, multiple statistical analyses were conducted to examine differences between conditions for each utterance category. Because these analyses were considered additional and exploratory, correction for multiplicity was not deemed strictly necessary.

To analyze the questionnaire results, two-tailed Mann-Whitney U tests were conducted to determine whether the ratings for workload (Q1) in all conditions and operation difficulty (Q2) in the SAR condition were significantly lower than the chance level (5: Neutral). Additionally, for Q1, a Friedman test was performed to verify differences in parental workload between the three conditions. The statistical analyses were conducted using Python, utilizing the NumPy, pandas, SciPy.stats, and Statsmodels libraries, with a significance level of 5%.

3.7   Participants

Twelve parent-child pairs, consisting of fourth-grade children (6 boys, 6 girls; age $M = 9.5, SD = 0.52$) and their parents (12 mothers, age $M = 44.42, SD = 3.85$), participated in the experiment. The experiment was approved by an ethics review board, and written informed consent was obtained from both the children and their parents prior to the study.

Twelve parent-child pairs, consisting of fourth-grade children (6 boys, 6 girls; age $M = 9.5, SD = 0.52$) and their parents (12 mothers, age $M = 44.42, SD = 3.85$), participated in the experiment. They were recruited through a local crowd-sourcing platform.** The experiment was approved by the ethics review board **of Nagoya University. Before the experiment, the parents were fully informed about the study's purpose and the recording of video and audio data. Written informed consent was obtained from all parents prior to participation. To ensure privacy, all collected data were anonymized and stored on a password-protected secure drive.

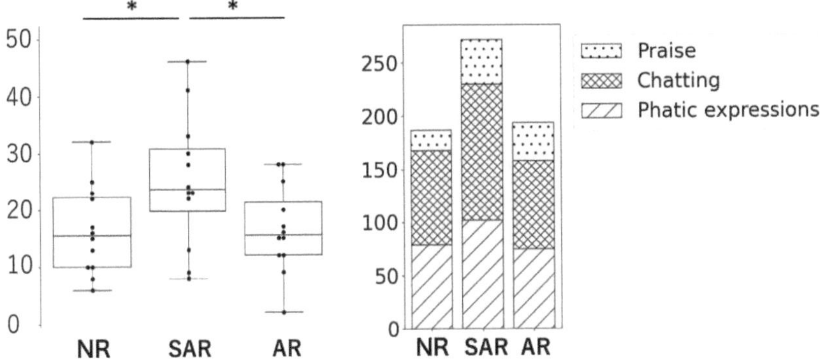

Fig. 4. Results of the total number of parental utterances (left) and the breakdown of utterances by category (right) (*: $p < .05$).

4   Results

The results for the number of parental utterances toward their children are shown in Fig. 4 (left) (NR: $Mdn = 15.5, IQR = [10.0, 21.5]$; SAR: $Mdn = 23.5, IQR = [19.75, 30.75]$; AR: $Mdn = 15.5, IQR = [12.0, 21.25]$). A Friedman test revealed a significant difference in utterance count among the conditions ($\chi^2(2) = 6.93, p = .0312$). Post hoc two-tailed Wilcoxon signed-rank tests with Bonferroni correction revealed that utterance counts were significantly higher in SAR condition compared to both AR condition ($W = 4.0$, adjusted $p = .0293$) and NR condition ($W = 5.5$, adjusted $p = .0430$). No significant difference was observed between AR and NR conditions ($W = 32.5$, adjusted $p = 1.0$). Thus, the results indicate that the number of parental utterances toward their children was significantly higher in SAR than in the other conditions. Here, the median interaction duration was 348.5s (IQR: 308.5–446.5) for NR, 364.5s (IQR: 343.5–453.0) for SAR, and 354.0s (IQR: 327.0–408.5) for AR. We consider that no substantial differences of interaction duration were observed between conditions, suggesting that session length did not influence the frequency of utterances.

Figure 4(right) shows the breakdown of the parent's utterances. A Friedman test was conducted for each of the three categories of the parent's utterances (*Praise*, *Chatting*, and *Phatic expressions*). The results revealed a significant difference among conditions for *Chatting* ($\chi^2(2) = 7.24, p = .0267$), whereas *Praise* showed a marginal trend ($\chi^2(2) = 4.85, p = .0885$), and no significant difference was observed for *Phatic expressions* ($\chi^2(2) = 1.23, p = .5414$). Next, though these analyses were exploratory (Sect. 3.6), post hoc two-tailed Wilcoxon signed-rank tests with Bonferroni correction were additionally conducted for *Chatting*. As a result, for *Chatting*, the utterance count was shown to be significantly higher in the SAR condition compared to the AR condition ($W = 9.0$, adjusted $p = .0483$).

Figure 5(a) presents the results for the parental workload for each condition. First, a Mann-Whitney U test was conducted to compare these values against the

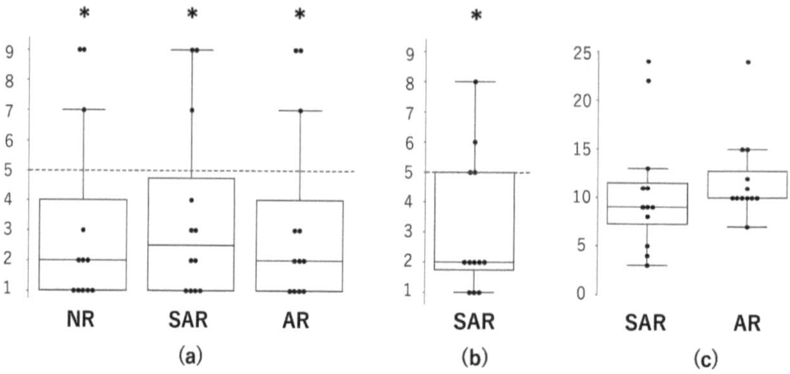

Fig. 5. Results of (a) parental workload across all conditions (asterisks indicate a significant difference from the chance level 5), (b) parental operation difficulty in the SAR condition, and (c) the number of robot's utterances in the SAR and AR conditions ($*: p < .05$).

chance level (5: neutral). The results showed that the scores for all conditions—No Robot (NR, $p = .0275$), Semi-Autonomous Robot (SAR, $p = .0280$), and Autonomous Robot (AR, $p = .0279$)—were significantly lower than the chance level. Furthermore, a Friedman test confirmed no significant difference in parental workload across the three conditions ($\chi^2(2) = 1.68, p = .4308$). These findings indicate that parents did not perceive an excessive workload during the learning activity regardless of the robot's presence or level of autonomy, and there was no significant difference in workload across conditions.

Next, Fig. 5(b) presents the results for the operation difficulty in the SAR condition. Similarly, a comparison with the chance level was conducted, and the results showed that the scores were significantly lower than the chance level ($p = .021$). These findings indicate that parents did not find the operation of the proposed robot particularly difficult, suggesting that its operability was within an acceptable range and did not pose a problem for task execution.

In addition to the above evaluation, this study also examined the number of the robot's utterances. This analysis was necessary to accurately assess the effect on parental utterance promotion, as a large difference in the robot's utterance count between the SAR and AR conditions might bias the results. The results for the robot's utterance count are shown in Fig. 5(c) (SAR: $Mdn = 9.0, IQR = [7.25, 11.5]$; AR: $Mdn = 10.0, IQR = [10.0, 12.75]$). A two-tailed Wilcoxon signed-rank test revealed no significant difference in the number of utterances between the two conditions ($W = 29.0, p = .47$). Consequently, it is unlikely that differences in the robot's utterance frequency influenced the observed effect on parental utterance promotion.

Finally, the questionnaire results regarding the children's task experience were analyzed. The results showed a tendency toward a ceiling effect for items such as "Did you find this activity very enjoyable?" and "Did you like the robot?", with evaluations skewed toward the highest score. Specifically, for the "enjoyable" question, over 91% (33 out of 36 responses) across all three conditions were the highest rating of "9". For the "Did you like the robot?" question, ratings of "8" or higher accounted for approximately 67% (16 out of 24 responses) across the two conditions with the robot.

5   Discussion

This study tested the hypothesis that, compared to scenarios without a robot or with an autonomous robot, a semi-autonomous para-operated robot facilitates increased parental utterances to their children. Analysis of parental utterance frequency revealed that parents in the semi-autonomous robot condition spoke significantly more to their child than those in the no-robot and autonomous robot conditions, supporting this study's hypothesis that a semi-autonomous para-operated robot, which is partly operated by the parent, was found to be the most effective in facilitating parental utterances. Furthermore, the evaluation of perceived operation difficulty and workload revealed that this partial operation did not impose an excessive burden on the parents. In addition, the questionnaire for children suggested that the robot used in this study was positively accepted by them, and post-experiment interviews confirmed that no child noticed their parent operating the robot in the semi-autonomous robot condition.

These results demonstrate that introducing a semi-autonomous para-operated robot in parent-child home learning can significantly promote parental utterances through the parent's engagement in robot operation. This finding indicates the effectiveness of the semi-autonomous para-operated robot in promoting parent-child dialogue in home learning, and presents one effective design for the research gap identified in the introduction: a home learning support robot that promotes dialogue without diminishing parental engagement. While robot research often focuses on achieving autonomy to assist humans, the results of this study suggest that deliberate human operation can, in some cases, be more beneficial, highlighting an intriguing aspect of human-robot interaction.

A potential explanation for the increase in parental utterances with the semi-autonomous robot is that robot operation facilitated task engagement, resulting in increased parental responsibility. Compared to using an autonomous robot, operating a semi-autonomous robot may require more active participation in the task. To prevent operational errors or delays in the robot's speech timing, parents may have had more responsibility, leading to increased involvement in the task. However, this aspect was not explicitly examined in the current experiment, and why robot operation facilitates parental utterances remains a question for future research.

As shown in Fig. 4(right), in the breakdown of the parent's utterances, parental *Chatting* significantly increased, particularly in the SAR condition. This might be explained by the mechanism that allowed parents in the SAR condition to control the timing of utterances. Whereas the robot in the AR (fully autonomous) condition might proceed with the task without considering the parent-child conversation and interrupt them, the robot in the SAR condition spoke only upon the parent's command input.

We consider that this parent-led design avoided the problem specific to triadic interactions where the robot intervenes when humans want to talk. With the proposed method, the operator can advance the task at their own timing. This prevents scenarios where the robot autonomously proceeds to the next step, thereby interrupting the parent-child dialogue just as the parent intended to speak, and creates space for natural conversation to emerge between tasks. For example, during one task in the SAR condition, after the robot read a line of the story, a parent was observed pointing to a card and saying to their child, "This bike looks like your dad's," which sparked a brief chat.

While conventional research in educational robotics emphasizes the importance of involving parents rather than focusing solely on the child-robot dyad, approaches that prioritize parent-led interaction remain under-explored. Our proposed semi-autonomous para-operated approach addresses this gap by granting parents a leading role in the interaction. By controlling the timing of the robot's dialogue, parents can provide precise and adaptive support at the exact moment their child encounters a challenge. Consequently, the robot does not replace the parental role; instead, it functions as an inter-personal infrastructure that keeps the parent at the heart of the learning process, thereby fostering deeper and more meaningful parent-child engagement.

Although this was not the primary focus of this study, the experiment suggested that the use of a robot may provide parents with new insights about their children. For instance, the robot's inquiries about school experiences or birthday wishes enabled parents to gain insights they might not have otherwise obtained or found challenging to elicit directly. Future research should further investigate this aspect of usefulness as a potential benefit of robots in parent-child learning.

The findings of this study are limited by the small and homogeneous sample, particularly the exclusive participation of mothers. While we believe the demonstrated effectiveness of the semi-autonomous robot in mother-child interactions warrants reporting, to improve generalizability, future research should involve larger, more diverse samples, including fathers, to explore potential differences in father-child interactions within home learning contexts. Additionally, parental operation of the robot was concealed from the child, which would raise ethical consideration regarding transparency and trust. Future studies should investigate the psychological impact of revealing the parent's role to the child.

Although this study primarily focused on parental evaluations, children's acceptance of the robot was also a critical factor. In fact, a questionnaire was administered to assess children's acceptance, but many children gave the highest possible ratings for all questions, resulting in a ceiling effect, raising concerns about the reliability of the responses. We consider that the children seemed receptive to the robot during the experiment, but future research should incorporate methodologies to assess children's perspectives. Furthermore, we also aim to improve our system to increase its autonomy, eliminating the need for the Wizard of Oz method and enabling broader field studies in the future.

Acknowledgements. This work was supported by Toyota Motor Corporation (fundamental study), JST Moonshot R&D Grant Number JPMJMS2011 (system development), and JSPS KAKENHI Grant Number JP25K21248 (analysis and presentation).

Disclosure of Interests. This study was partially funded by Toyota Motor Corporation.

References

1. Cagiltay, B., Ho, H.R., Michaelis, J.E., Mutlu, B.: Investigating family perceptions and design preferences for an in-home robot. In: Proceedings IDC, pp. 229–242 (2020)
2. Chen, H., Ostrowski, A.K., Jang, S.J., Breazeal, C., Park, H.W.: Designing long-term parent-child-robot triadic interaction at home through lived technology experiences and interviews. In: Proceedings of the RO-MAN, pp. 401–408 (2022)
3. Duncan, G.J., et al.: School readiness and later achievement. Dev. Psychol. **43**(6), 1428 (2007)
4. Fehrmann, P.G., Keith, T.Z., Reimers, T.M.: Home influence on school learning: direct and indirect effects of parental involvement on high school grades. J. Educ. Res. **80**(6), 330–337 (1987)
5. Greenberg, M.T., et al.: Enhancing school-based prevention and youth development through coordinated social, emotional, and academic learning. Am. Psychol. **58**(6–7), 466 (2003)
6. Harris, A., Goodall, J.: Do parents know they matter? engaging all parents in learning. Educ. Res. **50**(3), 277–289 (2008)
7. Hill, N.E., et al.: Parent academic involvement as related to school behavior, achievement, and aspirations: Demographic variations across adolescence. Child Dev. **75**(5), 1491–1509 (2004)
8. Ho, H.R., Hubbard, E.M., Mutlu, B.: "It's not a replacement:" enabling parent-robot collaboration to support in-home learning experiences of young children. In: Proceedings of the CHI, pp. 1–18 (2024)
9. Ho, H.R., Kargeti, N., Liu, Z., Mutlu, B.: Set-paired: Designing for parental involvement in learning with an ai-assisted educational robot. arXiv preprint arXiv:2502.17623 (2025)
10. Ho, H.R., White, N.T., Hubbard, E.M., Mutlu, B.: Designing parent-child-robot interactions to facilitate in-home parental math talk with young children. In: Proceedings of IDC, pp. 355–366 (2023)
11. Hood, D., Lemaignan, S., Dillenbourg, P.: When children teach a robot to write: an autonomous teachable humanoid which uses simulated handwriting. In: Proceedings of the HRI, pp. 83–90 (2015)
12. Kanda, T., Shimada, M., Koizumi, S.: Children learning with a social robot. In: Proceedings of the HRI, pp. 351–358 (2012)
13. Kennedy, J., Baxter, P., Senft, E., Belpaeme, T.: Social robot tutoring for child second language learning. In: Proceedings of the HRI, pp. 231–238 (2016)
14. Komatsubara, T., Shiomi, M., Kanda, T., Ishiguro, H., Hagita, N.: Can a social robot help children's understanding of science in classrooms? In: Proceedings of the HAI, pp. 83–90 (2014)
15. Konijn, E.A., Smakman, M., Berghe, R.: Use of robots in education. Int. Encycl. Media Psychol. 1–8 (2020)

16. Kubota, T., Isowa, T., Ogawa, K., Ishiguro, H.: Development and verification of an onsite-operated android robot working cooperatively with humans in a real store (in Japanese). Trans. Hum. Interface Soc. **22**(3), 275–290 (2020)
17. Kubota, T., Ogawa, K.: Effects of the behavior of a para-operated robot on the impression of the operator: a preliminary online study considering the robot-operator distance. In: Proceedings of the HAI, pp. 356–358 (2023)
18. Ma, X., Shen, J., Krenn, H.Y., Hu, S., Yuan, J.: A meta-analysis of the relationship between learning outcomes and parental involvement during early childhood education and early elementary education. Educ. Psychol. Rev. **28**, 771–801 (2016)
19. Park, S.J., Han, J.H., Kang, B.H., Shin, K.C.: Teaching assistant robot, robosem, in English class and practical issues for its diffusion. In: Proceedings of the ARSO, pp. 8–11 (2011)
20. Peck, C.A., Carlson, P., Helmstetter, E.: Parent and teacher perceptions of outcomes for typically developing children enrolled in integrated early childhood programs: A statewide survey. J. Early Interv. **16**(1), 53–63 (1992)
21. Shimaya, J., Yoshikawa, Y., Kumazaki, H., Matsumoto, Y., Miyao, M., Ishiguro, H.: Communication support via a tele-operated robot for easier talking: case/laboratory study of individuals with/without autism spectrum disorder. Int. J. Soc. Robot. **11**, 171–184 (2019)
22. Shiomi, M., Sakamoto, D., Kanda, T., Ishi, C.T., Ishiguro, H., Hagita, N.: A semi-autonomous communication robot: a field trial at a train station. In: Proceedings of the HRI. pp. 303–310 (2008)
23. Tanaka, F., Kimura, T.: The use of robots in early education: a scenario based on ethical consideration. In: Proceedings of the RO-MAN, pp. 558–560 (2009)
24. Turkle, S.: Why these friendly robots can't be good friends to our kids. Wash. Post **7** (2017)
25. Žegarac, V., Clark, B.: Phatic interpretations and phatic communication. J. Linguist. **35**(2), 321–346 (1999)

KosmoWalker: Designing a Social Step-Based Mobile Game for Motivating Physical Activity

Mausd Imran[1]([✉]) [iD], Gerry Chan[1] [iD], Oladapo Oyebode[1] [iD], Rebecca Moyer[2] [iD], and Rita Orji[1] [iD]

[1] Faculty of Computer Science, Dalhousie University, Halifax, NS, Canada
`masud.imran@dal.ca`
[2] Faculty of Health, School of Physiotherapy, Dalhousie University, Halifax, NS, Canada

Abstract. Physical activity apps have been receiving much research attention because of their potential to promote healthier lifestyles. However, despite established benefits from being physically active and the potential for new activity apps, global activity levels are still low. Many gamified systems have been created to increase enjoyment during exercise, yet most focus on single-player interactions and do not enhance long-term engagement. In this paper, we present our initial design and findings of *KosmoWalker*, a social space-themed, step-based mobile game that turns walking into cooperative missions by converting real-world step counts into virtual points that move teams through space via goal setting and team challenges. Results showed that the prototype is engaging and persuasive, particularly the experience of participating in competitive challenges and shared goals, and that the user interface is usable and easy to navigate. Overall, these findings illustrate the promise of social and collaborative exergame design and inform the development of a functional version for broader evaluation.

Keywords: Gamification · mobile health (mHealth) · persuasive technology · physical activity · social exergames

1 Introduction

Online exercise programs can improve physical activity (PA), physical function, and mental health in healthy adults, suggesting digital interventions may help combat physical inactivity while supporting overall well-being [1]. However, global PA levels remain insufficient, especially among individuals who are sedentary at work [2, 3]. While gamified applications and exergames are enjoyable alternatives to traditional exercise [4–6], most existing systems focus on single-player interactions and do not adequately support long-term engagement or motivation [7]. In this paper, we present the design, development, and preliminary evaluation of "KosmoWalker", a social, step-based exergame that transforms walking into virtual rewards and cooperative missions. *KosmoWalker* is grounded in principles of gamification, persuasive technology, and social facilitation, using real-world step counts to advance players through a space-themed narrative while encouraging team-based goal setting and collaboration. Prior research suggests that collaborative gameplay can increase motivation, enjoyment, and adherence to PA [6, 8,

K. Sumi et al. (Eds.): PERSUASIVE 2026, LNCS 16476, pp. 81–92, 2026.
https://doi.org/10.1007/978-3-032-19687-3_7

9], yet there is little evidence on the design and impact of early-stage prototypes that embed these features. The goal of this research is to examine *KosmoWalker's* potential to promote sustained PA engagement through socially interactive gameplay. We conducted a mixed-methods study with participants interacting with a low-fidelity prototype to answer the research question: *"To what extent can a collaborative, step-based exergame motivate users to engage in regular physical activity and experience positive social interactions?"*.

This work builds on previous research on designing social exergames [10–13], as well as mHealth apps that support PA and motivate sustained participation [14–16]. Early results suggest that the *KosmoWalker* prototype is motivating and perceived as usable and intuitive. Participants particularly valued team-based challenges and shared goals, which elicited a sense of relatedness. These results provide valuable insights for designing functional versions of socially interactive exergames and testing them with broader audiences. We contribute to the field of Human-Computer Interaction (HCI) and persuasive technology in three ways. First, we introduce a collaborative exergame prototype designed to motivate PA through meaningful social interactions. Second, we provide preliminary evidence on how social gameplay features influence engagement and motivation in a PA context. Third, we offer design principles for developing interactive, socially engaging exergames that support sustained health behavior change.

2 Related Work

2.1 Exergames, Persuasive Design Principles and Theories in Digital Health

Exergames, videogames that provide encouragement to exercise [17], have been shown to promote PA and reduce loneliness [18] but often struggle to sustain long-term engagement [7, 8]. Recent research on social exergames show that adding social interaction increases intrinsic motivation and enjoyment compared to single-player versions and are likely to have greater appeal to young adults who are not typically interested in traditional exergames [13]. Similarly, digital health apps have been shown to promote PA and reduce sedentary behavior [19, 20]. Previous studies suggest that these apps positively impact users' PA levels and overall health outcomes [21, 22]. Both exergames and digital health apps face the challenge of maintaining user motivation over time. Effective digital health programs often apply theories of persuasive design to elicit certain behaviours from users. One established model is Fogg's Behaviour Model (FBM), which states that behaviour only occurs when Motivation, Ability, and a Prompt (trigger) exist at the same time [23]. Self-Determination Theory (SDT) is a useful framework to understand how to support intrinsic motivation through satisfying the following three basic psychological needs: (1) autonomy, (2) competence, and (3) relatedness. Evidence suggests that interventions that support user autonomy, reinforce user's sense of competence and develop social connectedness lead to greater engagement and internal motivation, particularly for health behaviour change [24]. A review of SDT-based PA interventions showed that programs supporting autonomy, providing positive feedback to enhance competence, and encouraging social relationships increased motivation and intentions to remain physically active [25]. Thus, designing digital health apps with these motivational and social components can promote sustained engagement, intrinsic motivation, and long-term adherence to PA behaviors.

2.2 Gamification Strategies and their Effectiveness

Gamification, the use of game elements in non-game contexts [26], has shown to be an effective approach to increase user engagement in health behavior interventions [27, 28]. Some common examples of gamification strategies are point systems, leaderboards, badges, and rewards for goal attainment. Recent studies show that gamification elements can promote behavior change [29, 30]. For example, a meta-analysis examined the effect of gamification within health apps found that the addition of gamification encouraged individuals engaging with the app to walk a little more each day and had a small, but significant, impact on weight-related outcomes for individuals who used the gamified app compared to those who used the same app but did not have any gamified elements [31]. Another systematic review found that gamified interventions were related to levels of moderate-to-vigorous PA (MVPA) that increased and body mass index (BMI) that decreased for children and adolescents [32]. These findings demonstrate the potential of gamification elements to not only engage users but support meaningful change in health behavior with a thoughtful application in interventions. However, very little research has explored how gamification interacts with users' psychological needs and motivational processes over the long term, suggesting an important area for future study [33, 34].

3 KosmoWalker Game Prototype Design

KosmoWalker is a social mobile step-based exergame that turns walking through space exploration. Guided by the Persuasive System Design model developed by Oinas-Kukkonen and Harjumaa [35], the game incorporates strategies such as self-monitoring, simulation, rewards, and social influence to motivate sustained PA. *KosmoWalker's* design is structured across five (5) key layers that integrate persuasive strategies as game features to support behavior change. We iteratively developed the prototype, starting with a low-fidelity version (Fig. 1) to test core mechanics and interactions, then progressing to a high-fidelity version (Fig. 2) to refine visual design and navigation.

(1) **Core Gameplay Loop**: *KosmoWalker's* transforms real-world walking into in-game progress, where steps evolve barren planets into habitable worlds. This creates an immediate feedback loop (walk → progress → transformation; Figs. 1and 2a) facilitating **self-monitoring** [35] to reinforce competence and engagement. Additionally, social mechanics like leaderboards (Figs. 1 and 2b) and a "planet peek" feature promote **social comparison** [35] and shared motivation. The core loop thus blends goal setting, feedback, and social engagement to gamify everyday PA.

(2) **Theming and Visual Progression**: Capitalizing on the popularity of space themes in PA interventions [9, 36, 37], the app features dynamic visual progression where planets evolve from barren to lush as users accumulate steps. This transformation offers real-time feedback, while narrative rewards such as unlocking story snippets

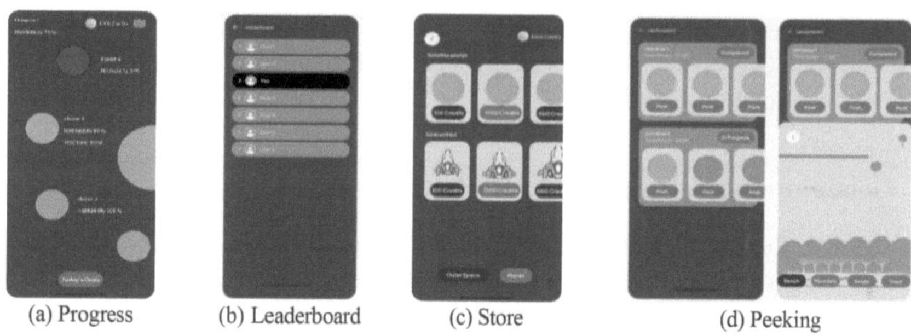

(a) Progress   (b) Leaderboard   (c) Store   (d) Peeking

Fig. 1. Lo-fidelity prototype of *KosmoWalker* app features and user interface.

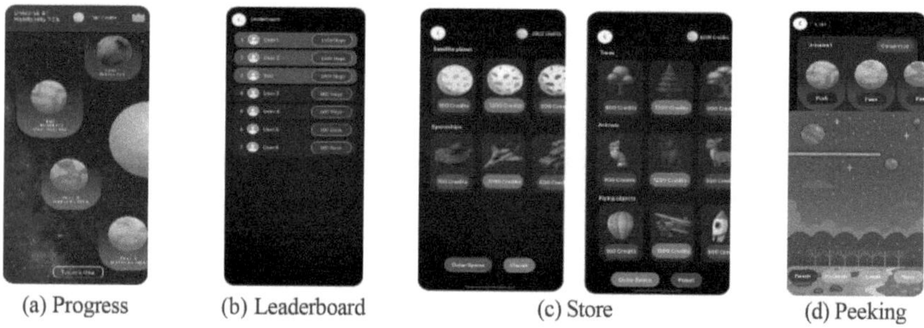

(a) Progress   (b) Leaderboard   (c) Store   (d) Peeking

Fig. 2. Hi-fidelity prototype of *KosmoWalker* app features and user interface.

deepen engagement. These visual and narrative cues utilize persuasive strategies of simulation and reward, reinforcing **self-monitoring** and motivating long-term interest.

(3) Customization Layer: Users earn credits (1 step = 1 credit) to purchase decorative items in the KosmoStore (Figs. 1 and 2c), allowing for the personalization of habitable planets. This system merges extrinsic rewards with intrinsic creative satisfaction, promoting autonomy and owner-ship. By tying exercise to tangible in-game value, the customization layer transforms PA into a personally meaningful and continuously engaging experience.

(4) Social Layer: The social layer supports a sense of social relatedness through leaderboards and a "ghost view" feature (Figs. 1 and 2d), which allows users to observe peers' planets. These elements facilitate social comparison and **social facilitation** [35], where seeing others' achievements motivates performance. By leveraging strategies of **social influence** and **competition**, *KosmoWalker* transforms solitary walking into a community-driven journey characterized by accountability and playful rivalry.

(5) Reminders and Notifications: An adaptive notification system (Fig. 3) sustains engagement by delivering timely, thematic nudges based on activity patterns. From a persuasive design perspective, it aligns with Fogg's Behavior Model [23], where timely prompts bridge the gap between intention and action. By offering **praise** and **tailoring** messages to context reminding during inactivity and reinforcing after success, the feature sustains motivation and reduces attrition. Serving as gentle behavioral triggers, these **reminders** help embed walking and app interaction into users' routines, ensuring continued participation and long-term habit formation.

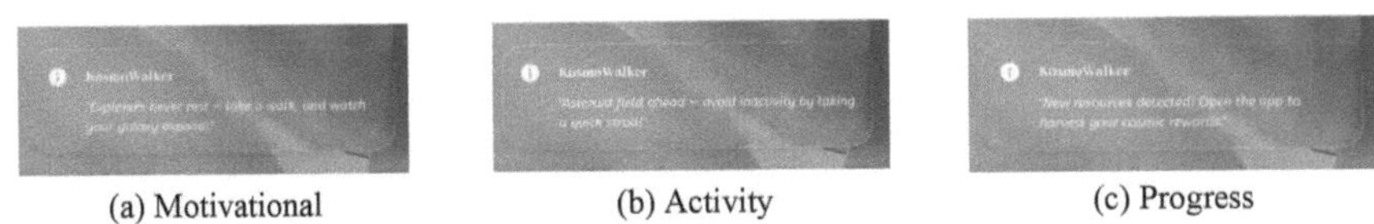

(a) Motivational   (b) Activity   (c) Progress

Fig. 3. Reminders and notifications.

4   User Study Design

To evaluate the usability and user perception of the prototype, a mixed-methods study approach was used. The evaluation was divided into three parts: (1) a usability test, (2) a semi-structured interview, and (3) a post-study questionnaire.

4.1   Participants

Participants were recruited by email. Six (6) participants (4 males, 2 females), ranging in age between 18 to 35 years, agreed and completed the user study. This number is informed by previous research suggesting that approximately 3 to 5 users is adequate to uncover the majority of usability issues during formative evaluations [38]. Two participants hold Bachelor's degrees and four hold Master's degrees in Computer Science specializing in Human-Computer Interaction and related fields. All participants had prior experience with digital games and interactive applications, making them well-suited to evaluate the usability and overall user experience of the game prototype.

4.2   Recruitment and Procedures

After receiving approval from our university ethics review board, the recruitment for participants commenced. To participate in the study, participants had to be over 18 years and understand English. Participants who met the inclusion criteria proceeded with the following three-part procedure:

Part 1 Usability Test: After reading the consent form and accepting it, participants completed 8 tasks (Table 1) using the prototype. Upon completion of each task, participants were asked to rate the level of difficulty for completing each task on a 5-point Likert scale (1 = very hard, to 5 = very easy) using the Single-Ease Question [39] and provide a rationale for that rating. Participants were also invited to think aloud [40] while performing that tasks. The think-aloud technique is commonly employed in HCI research and usability studies to gain insight into users' decision-making processes and the motivations behind their actions.

Part 2 Semi-Structured Interview: Participants evaluated the game concept and interface in two sections. First, they assessed the effectiveness of sample lock-screen notifications (Fig. 3) for promoting engagement and PA. Second, they discussed overall impressions, usability challenges, and suggestions for improvement to complement the think-aloud findings.

Part 3 Post-Study Questionnaire: Participants evaluated their perception of the game prototype using the system usability scale (SUS) [41], and the perceived persuasiveness scale [42]. Participants indicated their level of agreement using a 5-point Likert scale (1 = strongly disagree to 5 = strongly agree).

5   Results

5.1   Usability Test Results

The results of the usability test are summarized in Table 1. The SEQ scores showed that the average easiness ratings for all tasks were above 4.00, indicating a generally positive user experience. From the think-aloud comments, users expressed that most features were intuitive and straightforward, with one participant saying, *"Navigating to view my planet was very easy and clear"* [P1]. However, some users noted minor difficulties during the "Enter planet" task, with one mentioning, *"I wasn't immediately sure how to enter the planet, it took a moment to find the button"* [P3]. Overall, these findings suggest that the app prototype demonstrates strong usability across core functions, though a few areas could benefit from enhanced guidance or clearer navigation cues to further improve user experience.

Table 1. Summary of usability test results ($N = 6$).

Tasks	*M*	*SD*	Key comments and issues from think-aloud data
Enter planet	4.17	1.33	*"I was able to do it easily"* [P1]. *"I wouldn't expect every planet to share the same life or civilization"* [P5].
Find planet origin	4.08	1.20	*"The planets reminded me of childhood documentaries on Discovery Channel, the stories felt similar to those I used to watch"* [P5]. *"Yeah, this one's really good and interesting it motivates me to do my steps and unlock the redacted story"* [P6].
View leaderboard	4.17	0.98	*"I guess it was nice, being able to compete with both friends and strangers would be nice"* [P4]. *"For me it was very intuitive"* [P5].
Peek at others' planets	4.17	1.17	*"It was really nice to see what other people are doing in their universe, it makes you feel more competitive to do your steps"* [P4].

(continued)

Table 1. (*continued*)

Tasks	*M*	*SD*	Key comments and issues from think-aloud data
Customize planet	4.17	1.17	*"Maybe little games, small puzzle games or something to earn credits rather than just walking"* [P3].

5.2 Semi-Structured Interview Results

Section 1 Feedback on Notification Types: Participant reception regarding daily motivation was mixed. While some were indifferent, others valued reminders if they were personalized and timed to avoid busy periods, with tailored messages linking personal progress to specific goals viewed as the most engaging approach. Regarding health and activity prompts, participants supported specific reminders to break sedentary periods, noting they effectively reduced inactivity, particularly when delivered midday to afternoon. Finally, notifications regarding milestones, leaderboards, and unlocked resources were found to be highly motivating and generated curiosity, and while some users felt certain alerts lacked context, the majority found these updates effective for sustaining motivation and participation.

Section 2 General Impressions: Interview recordings were transcribed, and thematic analysis, as outlined by Braun and Clarke [43], was used to identify patterns and themes in the data. The transcripts were reviewed to detect recurring patterns, which were then categorized into meaningful themes. Each theme was labeled and organized to reflect the key findings of the analysis. Our analysis revealed three themes, which are discussed in the following sections. Excerpts from the interviews are presented with minor spelling and grammatical corrections for clarity.

Theme 1: Gamification elements such as leaderboards and planet unlocking increases motivation and engagement. The app's gamified features, particularly the leaderboard and the unlocking and organization of planets, were significant motivators for participants. Several users expressed that these elements encouraged them to walk more and engage with the app. For example, one participant said, "leaderboard always encourages" [P03], and another shared, *"my walking is creating a planet, it felt amazing"* [P1]. Participants also compared the leaderboard to familiar apps with streaks, noting that competition helped maintain their motivation, as one remarked, *"adding some streak – if continue, some of my friends don't want to break it"* [P2]. These insights highlight that gamification strategies effectively enhance user engagement by providing a sense of accomplishment and friendly competition.

Theme 2: Visual design and meaningful content improvements could enhance user experience and motivation. Several participants suggested that improving the app's visual appeal and integrating more meaningful, educational content could strengthen motivation and overall experience. One participant recommended *"more engaging content – the app could have motivation and educational value to it"* [P4]. Others suggested adding real images and scientific information to deepen the learning aspect, such as *"If it can teach something meaningful like scientific aspects, it would be better*" [P6]. Participants also talked about the need for clearer tutorials and tips to ease onboarding, with one saying, "*some tips and guidelines before starting the game would be better*" [P1]. These responses suggest that better aesthetics and content relevance could increase the app's motivational impact and user satisfaction.

Theme 3: Physical activity and walking are central motivators and experiences within the app. Participants frequently mentioned how the app's design encouraged them to increase their PA, particularly walking. Many expressed that the concept of building and unlocking planets through their steps provided meaningful motivation to be active. For example, one participant stated, "*after walking the planet would be completed and inside the planet was meaningful*" [P5], while another shared, "*my walking is creating a planet, it felt amazing*" [P1]. The app's emphasis on step-based progress made users more aware of their activity levels and helped them set tangible goals related to physical movement. Another participant noted, "*health thing – motivated do something good for the planet, steps motivation wise it's very nice!*" [P2]. These comments illustrate that linking PA with engaging visual and narrative elements helped reinforce motivation for exercise.

5.3   Questionnaire Results

The SUS scores and item means were reported to provide a high-level view of the app's usability. The SUS revealed an average score of 83.52 ($SD = 3.55$), indicating that the overall usability of the app is "excellent" [44]. One-sample t-tests were conducted to compare perceived persuasiveness scores to the mid-point of 3. Results showed that the features were perceived as persuasive ($t(5) = 11.62, p = .001$). Furthermore, 100% stacked bar charts were generated to visualize each item in the perceived persuasiveness scale. Fig. 4 shows that the scores leaned strongly toward the positive end of the scale, with most participants selecting agree/strongly agree for items evaluating the persuasiveness of the app's features and their ability to motivate user engagement.

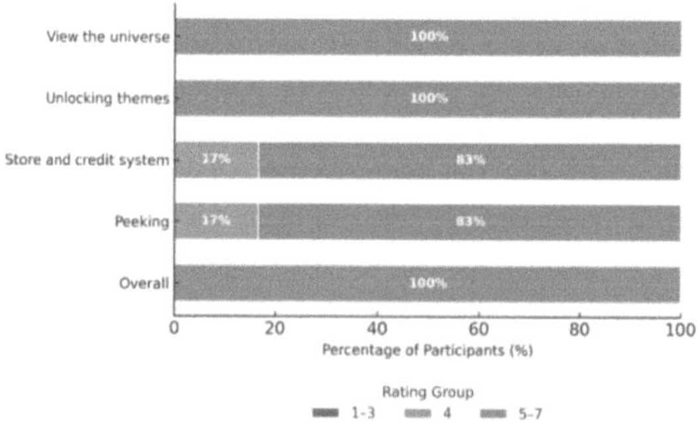

Fig. 4. 100% stacked bar chats of perceived persuasiveness scores for each feature.

6 Discussion

The current research investigated the usability and perceived persuasiveness of *KosmoWalker*, with specific interest in evaluating how the features might drive user engagement and align with health-related behaviors and motivations. Results suggest that the overall app interface supports good usability and the features were perceived as persuasive. Participants found the features of the app to be motiving, which is an encouraging sign that this app may support some positive enhancement of users' activity habits. However, facets related to dynamic complexity received lower ratings, suggesting that certain interactions were not entirely predictable, and users were sometimes uncertain about the next steps. This observation was corroborated by think-aloud comments, which indicated that participants had some confusion with the crown icon for representing the leaderboard, and that the guidance provided regarding some features could be improved. For example, some participants experienced temporarily confusion associated with a lack of instructional support for navigation. To improve usability, labels, tooltips, or short tutorial could be implemented to better assist the user in navigating the app. Participants also suggested adding an educational component (e.g., learning about evolution) and time-based challenges which could further enhance the level of engagement and provide the user with a sense of achievement.

While the findings are positive, one important limitation was the prototype was not a fully developed app. Exploring the app with intended participants in a real-world context will be important for full validation of app effectiveness and persuasive capability. Future work involves refining the app interface based on findings and also additional usability testing, and a long-term, in-the-wild study with intended participants to again explore both quantitative measures (e.g., total unfinished, step counts) but also qualitative feedback (e.g., enjoyment, engagement, motivation) to determine how the app might support continuing PA.

7 Conclusion

This study examined the usability, ease of use, and perceived persuasive features of *KosmoWalker* as a tool for promoting PA. The results provide important insights into the development of a fully functional app. The findings suggest that the design is easy to use and has content that is motivational, appealing to potential users in a way that elicits engagement. Overall, participants had positive attitudes toward the content and user interface, providing further evidence for the use of the app to promote PA and to support everyday behavior change and repeat use. Although participants point to a few areas that may require some redesign including the explicit provision of instructions on use, and avoiding dynamic complexity of use, the findings are useful for future iterative development of the app. Future studies will involve the continued development of the app, evaluation in more open and natural contexts, as well as a long-term study of the app potential to sustain PA engagement.

Acknowledgements. This research was undertaken, in part, thanks to funding from the Canada Research Chairs Program. We acknowledge the support of the Natural Sciences and Engineering

Research Council of Canada (NSERC) through the Discovery Grant. The research is conducted as part of the Dalhousie University Persuasive Computing Lab.

References

1. Bhundoo, A.K., Pillay, J.D., Wilke, J.: The effectiveness of online exercise on physical activity, motor function, and mental health: systematic review and meta-analysis. J. Med. Internet Res. **27**, e64856 (2025). https://doi.org/10.2196/64856
2. Clemes, S.A., Oêconnell, S.E., Edwardson, C.L.: Office workersê objectively measured sedentary behavior and physical activity during and outside working hours. J. Occup. Environ. Med. **56**, 298–303 (2014). https://doi.org/10.1097/JOM.0000000000000101
3. Lin, C.Y., et al.: Workplace neighbourhood built environment and workers' physically-active and sedentary behaviour: a systematic review of observational studies. Int. J. Behav. Nutr. Phys. Act. **17**, 148 (2020). https://doi.org/10.1186/s12966-020-01055-x
4. Moholdt, T., Weie, S., Chorianopoulos, K., Wang, A.I., Hagen, K.: Exergaming can be an innovative way of enjoyable high-intensity interval training. BMJ Open Sport Exerc. Med. **3** (2017). https://doi.org/10.1136/bmjsem-2017-000258
5. Lin, Y., Wang, J., Luo, Z., Li, S., Zhang, Y., Wünsche, B.C.: Dragon hunter: loss aversion for increasing physical activity in AR Exergames. In: ACM International Conference Proceeding Series, pp. 212–221 (2023). https://doi.org/10.1145/3579375.3579403
6. Chan, G., Whitehead, A., Parush, A.: Dynamic player pairing: quantifying the effects of competitive versus cooperative attitudes. In: Korn, O., Lee, N. (eds.) Game Dynamics: Best Practices in Procedural and Dynamic Game Content Generation, pp. 71–93. Springer International Publishing, Cham (2017). https://doi.org/10.1007/978-3-319-53088-8_5
7. Chan, G., Arya, A., Orji, R., Zhao, Z.: Motivational strategies and approaches for single and multi-player exergames: a social perspective. PeerJ Comput. Sci. **5**, e230 (2019). https://doi.org/10.7717/peerj-cs.230
8. Caro, K., Feng, Y., Day, T., Freed, E., Fox, B., Zhu, J.: Understanding the effect of existing positive relationships on a social motion-based game for health. In: Proceedings of the 12th EAI International Conference on Pervasive Computing Technologies for Healthcare, pp. 77–87 (2018). https://doi.org/10.1145/3240925.3240942
9. Saksono, H., et al.: Spaceship launch: designing a collaborative exergame for families. In: Proceedings of the 18th ACM Conference on Computer Supported Cooperative Work \& Social Computing, pp. 1776–1787 (2015). https://doi.org/10.1145/2675133.2675159
10. Ren, X., Hollander, L., Van Der Marel, R., Molenaar, L., Lu, Y.: Step-by-step: exploring a social exergame to encourage physical activity and social dynamics among office workers. In: Extended Abstracts of the 2019 CHI Conference on Human Factors in Computing Systems (2019). https://doi.org/10.1145/3290607.3312788
11. Kaos, M.D., Rhodes, R.E., Hämäläinen, P., Graham, T.C.N.: Social play in an Exergame: how the need to belong predicts adherence. In: BT Proceedings of the 2019 CHI Conference on Human Factors in Computing Systems, CHI 2019, Glasgow, Scotland, UK (2019). https://doi.org/10.1145/3290605.3300660
12. Chan, G., et al.: Social Exergames in health and wellness: a systematic review of trends, effectiveness, challenges, and directions for future research. Int. J. Hum. Comput. Interact. **41**, 5894–5925 (2024). https://doi.org/10.1080/10447318.2024.2371686
13. Yansun, E., Kim, D., Wünsche, B.C.: CoXercise - perceptions of a social exercise game and its effect on intrinsic motivation. In: ACSW '22: Proceedings of the 2022 Australasian Computer Science Week, pp. 176–185 (2022). https://doi.org/10.1145/3511616.3513113

14. Oyebode, O., Ganesh, A., Orji, R.: TreeCare: development and evaluation of a persuasive Mobile game for promoting physical activity. In: 2021 IEEE Conference on Games (CoG) (2021). https://doi.org/10.1109/CoG52621.2021.9619035

15. Tong, H.L., et al.: Efficacy of a mobile social networking intervention in promoting physical activity: quasi-experimental study. JMIR Mhealth Uhealth. **7**, e12181 (2019). https://doi.org/10.2196/12181

16. Faizah, A., Hardian, A.F.A., Nandini, R.D., Handayani, P.W., Harahap, N.C.: The influence of incentive-based Mobile fitness apps on users' continuance intention with gender moderation effects: quantitative and qualitative study. JMIR Hum. Factors. **11**, e50957 (2024). https://doi.org/10.2196/50957

17. Whitehead, A., Johnston, H., Nixon, N., Welch, J.: Exergame effectiveness: what the numbers can tell us. In: Proceedings of the 5th ACM SIGGRAPH Symposium on Video Games - Sandbox '10, pp. 55–62. ACM Press, New York, USA (2010). https://doi.org/10.1145/1836135.1836144

18. Brox, E., Luque, L.F., Evertsen, G.J., Hernandez, J.E.G.: Exergames for elderly: social exergames to persuade seniors to increase physical activity. In: 2011 5th International Conference on Pervasive Computing Technologies for Healthcare (PervasiveHealth) and Workshops, pp. 546–549 (2011). https://doi.org/10.4108/icst.pervasivehealth.2011.246049

19. Srivastava, P., Chan, G., Oyebode, O., Orji, R.: PetBuddy: an examination of augmented reality Mobile health game for promoting physical activity. In: International Conference on Persuasive Technology, vol. 15711. LNCS, pp. 264–280 (2025). https://doi.org/10.1007/978-3-031-94959-3_19

20. Odenigbo, I.P., Alslaity, A., Chan, G., Orji, R.: AR Dancee: an augmented reality-based Mobile persuasive intervention for promoting physical activity through dancing. Int. J. Hum. Comput. Interact. **41** (2024). https://doi.org/10.1080/10447318.2024.2384136

21. Schoeppe, S., et al.: Apps to improve diet, physical activity and sedentary behaviour in children and adolescents: a review of quality, features and behaviour change techniques. Int. J. Behav. Nutr. Phys. Act. **14**, 83 (2017). https://doi.org/10.1186/s12966-017-0538-3

22. F., H., Wright, A., Shill, J., Stephens, H., Uccellini, M.: Using health and Well-being apps for behavior change: a systematic search and rating of apps. JMIR Mhealth Uhealth. **7**(7), e11926. https//mhealth.jmir.org/2019/7/e11926 (2019). https://doi.org/10.2196/11926

23. Fogg, B.: A behavior model for persuasive design. In: ACM International Conference Proceeding Series, p. 350 (2009). https://doi.org/10.1145/1541948.1541999

24. Gillison, F.B., Rouse, P., Standage, M., Sebire, S.J., Ryan, R.M.: A meta-analysis of techniques to promote motivation for health behaviour change from a self-determination theory perspective. Health Psychol. Rev. **13**, 110–130 (2019). https://doi.org/10.1080/17437199.2018.1534071

25. Sheeran, P., et al.: Self-determination theory interventions for health behavior change: meta-analysis and meta-analytic structural equation modeling of randomized controlled trials. J. Consult. Clin. Psychol. **88**, 726–737 (2020). https://doi.org/10.1037/ccp0000501

26. Deterding, S., Dixon, D., Khaled, R., Nacke, L.: From game design elements to gamefulness: defining gamification. In: Proceedings of the 15th International Academic MindTrek Conference: Envisioning Future Media Environments, MindTrek 2011 (2011). https://doi.org/10.1145/2181037.2181040

27. Mulchandani, D., Alslaity, A., Orji, R.: Exploring the effectiveness of persuasive games for disease prevention and awareness and the impact of tailoring to the stages of change. Hum. Comput. Interact. **38**, 459–494 (2022). https://doi.org/10.1080/07370024.2022.2057858

28. Xu, L., et al.: Smartphone-based gamification intervention to increase physical activity participation among patients with coronary heart disease: a randomized controlled trial. J. Telemed. Telecare. **30**, 1425–1436 (2023). https://doi.org/10.1177/1357633X221150943

29. H., M.A.: Maintenance of behaviour change following a community-wide gamification based physical activity intervention. Prev. Med. Rep. **13**, 37–40 (2019)
30. Alslaity, A., Chan, G., Orji, R.: A panoramic view of personalization based on individual differences in persuasive and behavior change interventions. Front. Artif. Intell. **6**, 1125191 (2023). https://doi.org/10.3389/frai.2023.1125191
31. Nishi, M., Nagamitsu, R., Matoba, S.: Association between daily step counts and healthy life years: a national cross-sectional study in Japan. BMJ Heal. Care Inf. **31**, e101051 (2024). https://doi.org/10.1136/bmjhci-2024-101051
32. Wang, M., Xu, J., Zhou, X., Li, X., Zheng, Y.: Effectiveness of gamification interventions to improve physical activity and sedentary behavior in children and adolescents: systematic review and meta-analysis. JMIR Serious Games. **13**, e68151 (2025). https://doi.org/10.2196/68151
33. Mazeas, A., Duclos, M., Pereira, B., Chalabaev, A.: Evaluating the effectiveness of gamification on physical activity: systematic review and meta-analysis of randomized controlled trials. J. Med. Internet Res. **24**, e26779 (2022). https://doi.org/10.2196/26779
34. Sal-de-Rellán, A., Hernández-Suárez, Á., Hernaiz-Sánchez, A.: gamification and motivation in adolescents. Systematic review from physical education. Front. Psychol. **16**, 1575104 (2025). https://doi.org/10.3389/fpsyg.2025.1575104
35. Oinas-Kukkonen, H., Harjumaa, M.: Persuasive systems design: key issues, process model, and system features. Commun. Assoc. Inf. Syst. **24**, 485–500 (2009). https://doi.org/10.17705/1cais.02428
36. Finkelstein, S.L., Nickel, A., Barnes, T., Suma, E.A.: Astrojumper: designing a virtual reality exergame to motivate children with autism to exercise. In: 2010 IEEE Virtual Reality Conference (VR), pp. 267–268 (2010). https://doi.org/10.1109/VR.2010.5444770
37. Feltz, D.L., et al.: Simulated partners and collaborative exercise (SPACE) to boost motivation for astronauts: study protocol. BMC Psychol. **4**, 54 (2016). https://doi.org/10.1186/s40359-016-0165-9
38. Nielsen, J.: Usability inspection methods. In: Conference Human Factors Computer Systems Proceedings 1994, pp. 413–414 (1994). https://doi.org/10.1145/259963.260531
39. Wetzlinger, W., Auinger, A., Dörflinger, M.: Comparing effectiveness, efficiency, ease of use, usability and user experience when using tablets and laptops. In: International Conference of Design, User Experience, and Usability, vol. 8517. LNCS, pp. 402–412 (2014). https://doi.org/10.1007/978-3-319-07668-3_39
40. Solomon, P.: The think aloud method: A practical guide to modelling cognitive processes. (1995). doi:https://doi.org/10.1016/0306-4573(95)90031-4.
41. Brooke, J.: SUS - a quick and dirty usability scale, 4–7 (1996). https://doi.org/10.1002/hbm.20701
42. Drozd, F., Lehto, T., Oinas-Kukkonen, H.: Exploring perceived persuasiveness of a behavior change support system: a structural model. In: Proceedings of the 7th International Conference on Persuasive Technology: Design for Health and Safety, vol. 7284. LNCS, pp. 157–168 (2012). https://doi.org/10.1007/978-3-642-31037-9_14
43. Braun, V., Clarke, V.: Using thematic analysis in psychology. Qual. Res. Psychol. **3**, 77–101 (2006). https://doi.org/10.1191/1478088706qp063oa
44. Bangor, A., Kortum, P., Miller, J.: Determining what individual SUS scores mean. J. Usability Stud. **4**, 114–123 (2009). https://doi.org/10.5555/2835587.2835589

Towards Personalized Conversations: How Rhetorical Framing Shapes User Trust and Acceptance in Healthcare Chatbots

Rutuja Joshi[1]([✉]) [ID], Klaus Bengler[1] [ID], and Julia Augustyniak[2]

[1] Technical University of Munich, Garching, Germany
{rutuja.joshi,bengler}@tum.de
[2] University of Trento, Trento, Italy
julia.augustyniak@studenti.unitn.it

Abstract. Conversational agents (CAs) are emerging as potential solutions in healthcare for triage, symptom checking, and patient guidance. However, despite technological advances, the acceptance of such systems continues to remain low. Along with functional aspects, the interaction layer plays an important role in enhancing user trust and acceptance. Building on this, the study investigates whether rhetorical persuasive communication styles can improve users' perceived trust and acceptance of healthcare CAs. Based on Aristotelian rhetoric, three conversational styles were designed—*Ethos* (credibility), *Pathos* (emotional appeal), and *Logos* (rationality) and implemented in a Wizard-of-Oz within-subject experiment (N = 36) along with a neutral Baseline style across four non-critical medical scenarios. Results show that communication style significantly influenced system acceptance but not trust, suggesting that trust in healthcare chatbots is probably based on reliability and competence than conversational style. *Ethos* and *Pathos* were perceived as most useful; *Logos* was ranked highest while *Baseline* was least preferred. Further analyses revealed that user traits did not moderate the effects on trust and system acceptance.

Keywords: Conversational Agents · Chatbots · Human-AI Interaction · Healthcare · Dialogue Design · Conversation Design · Persuasive Technology · Rhetorical Strategies · Adaptive Interaction · Personalization

1 Introduction

Chatbots or conversational agents (CAs) have emerged as promising tools in healthcare supporting tasks like symptom checking, triage and patient education [25,38]. Despite their potential to enhance efficiency and accessibility, healthcare chatbots struggle with low user trust and acceptance - a paradox at the core of their adoption challenge [43]. Apart from the technical challenges regarding accuracy, reliability and data security, studies have also reported challenges in adoption due to lack of transparency, empathy and mismatch between user expectations and CA's responses [12,43]. These challenges highlight that beyond functional performance, the interaction layer also plays a crucial role in shaping the users' experience [5].

User-adaptive interaction or providing personalized experience have shown potential in improving user engagement and acceptance in various domains including healthcare [2,33]. However, operationalizing these adaptive strategies still remains a challenge. Persuasive conversation design with emotional support and transparent reasoning shows potential in increasing adoption of healthcare chatbots [44]. Applying persuasive rhetorical principles—such as credibility *(Ethos)*, emotional connection *(Pathos)*, and logical reasoning *(Logos)*—could be thus one approach to improve trust and acceptance of healthcare chatbots [16]. These rhetorical dimensions can then act as mechanisms to personalize user interactions. However, prior to implementing these aspects in context of adaptive interactions, it is important to understand how users perceive these individual dialogue strategies. While rhetorical strategies have been studied in healthcare communication and persuasive contexts [8,34,42], they have rarely been empirically tested as standalone interaction mechanisms in healthcare chatbots.

This study examines how different rhetorical communication styles influence users' perceived trust and acceptance of a symptom-checking CA. Participants interacted with a Wizard-of-Oz (WoOz) chatbot simulating four styles: *Baseline*, *Ethos*, *Pathos*, and *Logos* in a within-subject WoOz experimental design. The study provides empirical evidence on effects of communication style by addressing the following research question: *How do rhetorical communication styles in healthcare CAs influence users' perceived trust, system acceptance, and communication preferences?*

2 Related Work

2.1 Trust and Acceptance in Healthcare CAs

In medical scenarios trust between doctors and patient is imperative [30], particularly given the inherent vulnerability and information asymmetry [31]. When CAs enter this space, the nature of trust changes—while humanâĂŞhuman trust often stems from affective factors such as empathy and interpersonal rapport, trust in CAs is primarily cognitive, grounded in perceptions of reliability, competence, and transparency [20,35]. Acceptance, on the other hand, can be defined based on user's willingness to use the system, and is typically explained by models such as the Technology Acceptance Model (TAM) [7] or the Unified Theory of Acceptance and Use of Technology (UTAUT2) [40]. Recent research has shown that apart from the known factors from UTAUT2, additional factors like trust in provider and system, perceived compatibility, privacy risk expectancy, experience in e-diagnosis, and access to health systems also influence acceptance of CAs in medical diagnosis [19].

2.2   Personalization in Chatbot Communication

Personalization has been identified as one of the approaches to increase user trust and acceptance regarding CAs [21]. In healthcare chatbots, personalization has shown to increase therapeutic bonding and willingness to use [41], user satisfaction, user engagement and dialogue quality [17]. According to [22], personalization in combination with credibility through source expertise positively affected user's perceived benefits and self-efficacy regarding healthcare chatbots. Furthermore, [11] identified that contextual factors like type of disease along with personality traits proved to be effective parameters for personalizing interactions. In adaptivity, user traits are used to lay ground rules and states are used to trigger short term adaptations [6]. In this study, we explore the user needs regarding personalization by utilizing individual rhetorical strategies and examine if user traits moderate the effects these styles.

2.3   Rhetorics in Human-Computer Interaction (HCI)

Rhetorical strategies have been historically used in politics - speeches and monologues, persuasive discourse and marketing. However, the Aristotelian rhetorical dimensions of *Ethos*, *Pathos* and *Logos* also offer a framework for adaptivity and persuasion in human technology interaction. In healthcare, [34] investigated the impact of pathos, ethos and logos-based communication on AI adoption and found that pathos and logos-based communication help in addressing patient's trust issues in AI-based technology. Furthermore, [32] introduces the concept of machine ethos and highlights that the "derived ethos" can be shaped by direct interactions with the system. [37] also proposes a theoretical framework for AI-chatbots based on intelligent quotient (rational component), emotional quotient (emotional component) and trustworthy quotient (credibility component). Previous research identifies transparency and explanations, empathy and anthropomorphism, and expertise and professionalism positively influence user engagement and satisfaction [34, 43]. These individual factors highlight the attributes of ethos, pathos, and logos. Based on this, [16] proposed a framework to integrate the rhetorical dimensions as an adaptivity mechanism in healthcare CAs. However, rhetorical strategies in healthcare CAs need to be implemented carefully and in accordance with defined ethical guidelines to avoid misleading the user [32, 34].

3   Conversation Design Using Rhetorical Strategies

The medical dialogues for the study were developed in a two-stage process. Semi-structured interviews with medical professionals (n = 5) ensured medical accuracy and comparability of selected symptoms and diseases, all of which represented low-severity conditions not requiring medical visits. Four medical scenarios were defined to minimize interaction fatigue: common cold, mild tension headache, mouth ulcer, and swollen bug bite. Dialogues were then written in four communication styles—*Baseline, Ethos, Pathos*, and *Logos*. A focus group with linguistics experts (n = 6) reviewed and refined the dialogues to ensure sufficient and consistent representation of the styles in the conversations. Thematic analysis of transcripts and expert feedback guided final revisions in the 16 dialogues (4 Styles x 4 Scenarios). Prior to the main study, 2 pilot tests were conducted to verify intended manipulations and minor changes were made in the dialog transcripts and study procedure.

Table 1. Examples of introductory chatbot messages across Styles

Style	Chatbot Message
Baseline	"Hello! I'm a healthcare diagnostic chatbot... I will ask you a few questions to understand your condition and propose the most likely diagnosis."
Ethos	"...I was **created by the Technical University of Munich** with **medical experts** from Poland and Germany, using data from recent diagnostic manuals... "
Pathos	"Hello **[User Name]! Thank you for reaching out**... Let's go through some questions together so we can **help you** get back in shape."
Logos	"...I will ask you a few questions to understand your condition and propose the most likely diagnosis **based on my data**. What are your symptoms?"

Drawing inspiration from Aristotelian rhetoric, this study transfers these persuasive appeals in designing medical dialogues. The *Ethos* conversation focused on highlighting credentials, using a professional tone, and giving proactive recommendations - building the CA's character as a speaker. Similarly, the *Pathos* driven dialog emphasized affective engagement of the CA through empathy, use of supportive language and offering reassurance. The *Logos* style incorporated rational persuasion by providing data-driven insights, explanations or justifications, and transparency about underlying processes. In addition, a *Baseline* strategy was developed that avoided specific rhetorical elements, serving as a neutral control. Table 1 gives examples of introductory statements in each style.

4   Methodology

4.1   Study Design and Procedure

A mixed-method approach including a WoOz study was used to evaluate user trust and acceptance for different chatbot communication styles. In this setup, a human "wizard" posed as the CA, facilitating consistent interaction experiences across participants. The study was conducted online via Google Meets using a prototypical web application messenger interface allowing subjects to participate from their preferred location and setup.

Each participant experienced all four styles across different scenarios, counterbalanced through Latin-square randomization to mitigate order effects. In a pre-study survey after receiving information about the study and consenting to participation, demographics and personality traits, including Affinity for Technology Interaction (ATI) [10], Rational-Experiential Inventory (REI-10) [26,28]; Need for Affect (NFA) [1], Trusting Stance (TS) and Faith in General Technology (FIGT) [24] were gathered. During the study, participants (n = 36) experienced four chatbot interactions corresponding to the four communication styles through the web-based prototype. After each interaction, trust was measured using Trust in Automation (TiA) scale [18] (14 items, subscales: Reliability, Understanding, Trust in Automation, Familiarity) on a 5-point Likert scale and system acceptance using the Van der Laan Acceptance Scale [39] (8 items, subscales: Satisfaction, Usefulness) on a semantic differential between -2 to +2. In addition, users also rated perception of the style on a 10 item, 5-point Likert scale after every interaction, that was used to evaluate whether the rhetorical dialog styles were perceived as intended. At the end of the session, participants ranked the four styles based on preference. The participants were informed about the WoOz nature of the study after completing all four interactions. The study was approved by the Ethics Committee of the Technical University of Munich (Ref No.: 2024-471-S-CB).

4.2 Data Analysis

The collected data was reviewed for completeness and 36 valid datasets were considered for further analyses. The descriptive analyses including means (M) and standard deviation (SD) are reported in the subsequent sections. To evaluate overall effects of style, repeated measures MANOVAs using Pillai's trace (V) were planned for the dependent variables trust and acceptance [27]. Subscales showing significant style effects were further examined using linear mixed-effect models (LMM) implemented with the *afex* package [36]. The analyses considered the counterbalanced two factorial design, with *Style* (4 levels) as a repeated measures factor, *Scenarios* (4 levels) as a fixed blocking variable, and *Participant-ID* as a random-effect using the Kenward-Roger approximation for small-sample inference [13].

Models were estimated using restricted maximum likelihood (REML), and Type III sums of squares were used for hypothesis testing [36]. Post-hoc pairwise comparisons were conducted using the *emmeans* package in R with Tukey adjustment [9, p. 431] for multiple comparisons. Random slopes were avoided due to the limited sample size. The trait scores were z-standardized before entry into the models. Model robustness was verified using the *performance* package [23], and if necessary modified models were refitted and compared with the original LMM. The moderating effects of user traits were explored using separate models, developed for technology-trust traits, cognitive style and affective orientation. The interaction effects between style and user trait tested the moderation effects of traits on trust and acceptance.

The differences in perception of style and the ranking data were analysed using the non-parametric Friedman test. All model assumptions were verified before each test, and non-parametric alternatives were used when necessary. Analyses were performed in RStudio.

4.3   Sample

The sample size (N = 36) was determined a priori using G*Power to detect medium effect sizes with a statistical power of 0.95 in a within-subject design. Participants were recruited through convenience sampling at the university and online. The study's prerequisites included understanding and communicating in English language, minimum age of 18 years, and access to a laptop or computer and internet. A total of 36 participants (20 Female, 14 Male, 2 Non-binary; $M = 29.6 \pm 11.2$ years) took part in the study. The sample was predominantly highly educated with 58.3% having a Bachelor's degree, 36.1% having a Master's degree and 5.6% having a high school education. Most participants showed high proficiency in English language with $n = 7$ native language speakers and $n = 18$ participants having C1 or C2 level proficiency, $n = 11$ subjects were at B1 or B2 level English proficiency. The subjects also showed previous exposure to chatbots with $n = 32$ participants having used a chatbot before.

The results of technological affinity measured using ATI on a 6-point Likert scale indicated that the sample had a moderate to high affinity towards technology ($M = 3.67 \pm 0.69$). The *Need for Cognition* (NFC) and *Faith in Intuition* (FI), both measured using the REI-10 on a 5-point Likert scale, were moderate ($M_{NFC} = 3.52 \pm 0.85$; $M_{FI} = 3.59 \pm 0.73$), suggesting that participants tend to engage in both rational and intuitive modes of information processing. The NFA rated on a scale from -2 to +2, showed slightly positive tendencies ($M_{NFA} = 0.83 \pm 0.35$), indicating a slight inclination toward affective experiences. TS and FIGT, derived from McKnight's model of trust in technology [24] and scored on a 5-point Likert scale, resulted in a moderate range ($M_{TS} = 3.25 \pm 0.84$; $M_{FIGT} = 3.46 \pm 0.52$). These ratings depicted a generally neutral but open orientation toward technological systems. Overall, the trait profile suggests a young, digitally proficient sample with generally positive orientations toward technology and moderate cognitive engagement tendencies. The relatively low variability across traits indicates a fairly homogeneous participant group.

5   Results

5.1   Trust

Descriptive results (Fig. 1) show that trust ratings across most subscales were on the higher end of the 5-point Likert scale, other than *Familiarity*. All subscales showed acceptable to excellent internal consistency (Cronbach's $\alpha = .67 - .95$), comparable to the original TiA validation [18]. The subscale *Understanding* received highest mean scores in the following order for the styles: *Ethos* ($M_{Und} = 4.11 \pm 0.75$), *Pathos* ($M_{Und} = 4.06 \pm 0.69$), *Logos* ($M_{Und} = 4.03 \pm 0.82$) and

Baseline ($M_{Und} = 3.99 \pm 0.79$), followed by *Reliability* and *Trust in Automation*. *Familiarity* was rated lower than the other subscales with *Ethos* ($M_F = 2.96 \pm 1.19$) and *Pathos* ($M_F = 2.96 \pm 1.23$) scoring slightly more than *Logos* ($M_F = 2.92 \pm 1.18$) and *Baseline* ($M_F = 2.90 \pm 1.21$). The styles *Ethos* and *Pathos* showed slightly higher ratings than others across all subscales.

A repeated measures MANOVA ($V = 0.12$, $F(12, 312) = 1.05$, $p = .41$) revealed no significant multivariate effect of communication style, indicating that stylistic differences did not substantially influence users' perceived trust.

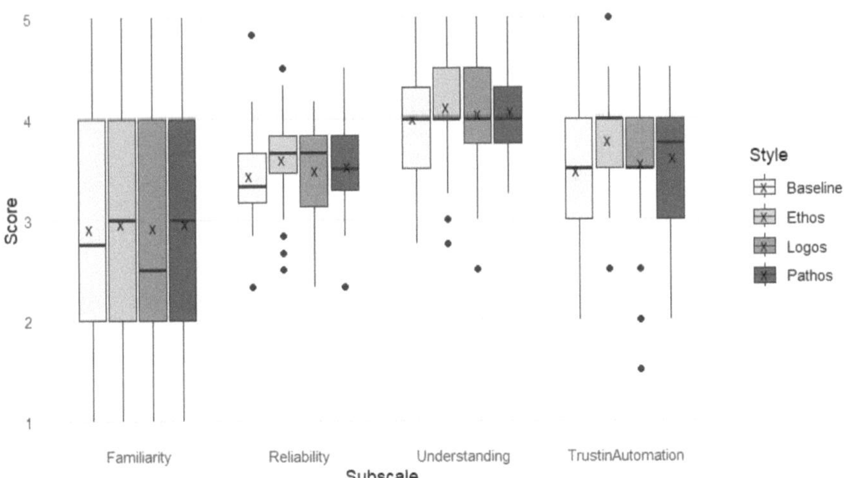

Fig. 1. Trust based on Trust in Automation Scale [18].

5.2 Acceptance

As for acceptance rated on a semantic differential ranging from -2 to +2, the descriptive results indicate a positive trend in general with all means for both subscales lying above zero (see Fig. 2). Both subscales showed good internal consistency (Cronbach's α_S & $\alpha_{Use} = .85$). *Pathos* style showed highest scores on the *Satisfaction* subscale ($M_S = 1.25 \pm 0.69$), followed by *Ethos* ($M_S = 1.08 \pm 0.68$). The styles *Baseline* ($M_S = 0.94 \pm 0.72$) and *Logos* ($M_S = 0.93 \pm 0.82$) received lower scores. On the *Usefulness* subscale, *Ethos*, ($M_{Use} = 1.42 \pm 0.56$) was rated better than *Pathos* ($M_{Use} = 1.41 \pm 0.54$), *Logos* ($M_{Use} = 1.38 \pm 0.60$) and *Baseline* ($M_{Use} = 1.17 \pm 0.69$).

A repeated measures MANOVA ($V = 0.19$, $F(6, 210) = 3.79$, $p = .001$) indicated that the styles seem to have a significant differential effect on the acceptance subscales when tested at a 5% level of significance. The post-hoc univariate ANOVA analysis with Greenhouse-Geisser correction showed significant effects of style for both *Satisfaction* ($F(2.47, 86.44) = 3.26$, $p = .034$, partial $\eta^2 = 0.09$)

and *Usefulness* (F(2.77, 96.80) = 4.67, p =.005, partial η^2 = 0.12). The pairwise Tukey comparisons further specify that *Ethos* (p =.008) and *Pathos* (p =.025) were rated significantly more useful than the *Baseline*. No significant group differences were found in *Satisfaction*.

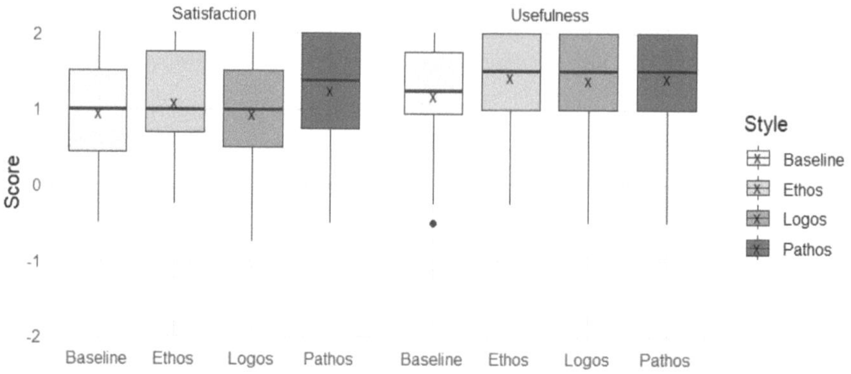

Fig. 2. Acceptance based on Van der Laan [39].

In addition, to verify robustness and explore potential moderation effects of user traits and scenario on *Usefulness*, linear mixed-effects models were tested using the Kenward-Roger approximation for small-sample inference. Starting from a full model including *Scenario* and theoretically relevant individual trait moderators (*NFC*; *NFA*; *ATI,TS,FIGT*), stepwise model comparisons *(KRmodcomp)* confirmed that only the main effect of *Style* contributed significantly ((F(3, 105) = 4.67, p = .004)), using the Kenward-Roger adjusted degrees of freedom, no significant moderation effects of the theoretically relevant chosen user traits were found. The model explained substantial participant-level variance ($R^2_{conditional}$ = .72) but only limited fixed-effect variance ($R^2_{marginal}$ = .03).

Model diagnostics confirmed approximate normality and homoscedasticity of residuals. Autocorrelation tests showed minor within-subject correlation (ϕ = −0.06). To examine model robustness, the model was refitted excluding five outliers (Cook's distance > 0.5). The reduced model exhibited similar fixed-effect estimates and identical significance patterns (p < .05 for *Style*), indicating that the results were not driven by these outliers. The model fit slightly improved ($R^2_{conditional}$ = .81, $R^2_{marginal}$ = .01), confirming the stability of the findings.

5.3   Rankings

Participants ranked the four communication styles from 1 (most preferred) to 4 (least preferred). As seen in Fig. 3, *Logos* was most preferred (M_R = 2.14±1.07) followed by *Pathos* (M_R = 2.19±1.01) and *Ethos* (M_R = 2.28±1.11), whereas *Baseline* was least preferred (M_R = 3.39±0.8). A Friedman test ($\chi^2(3)$ = 22.97, p < .001) indicated significant differences across styles. Post-hoc Wilcoxon signed rank tests revealed that *Ethos* ($p = .003$) , *Pathos* ($p < .001$) and *Logos* ($p < .001$) were all preferred over the *Baseline*. The within-subject agreement, Kendall's $W = 0.21$, suggested some shared preferences across participants but also considerable individual variation in preferred styles.

A further exploratory Spearman correlation analysis examined possible relationships between ranks, trust, acceptance, and user traits. The results revealed significant weak to moderate negative correlations for *Reliability* ($\rho = -0.22$, $p = .008$), *Trust in Automation* ($\rho = -0.18$, $p = .02$), *Satisfaction* ($\rho = -0.25$, $p = .003$) and *Usefulness* ($\rho = -0.25$, $p = .003$). On the other hand, no significant correlations emerged between each participant's traits and their ranks for each style.

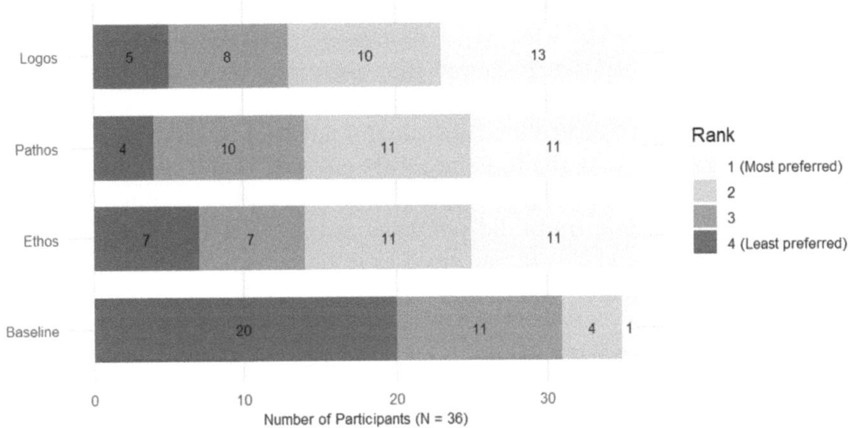

Fig. 3. Ranking of Styles according to Preference.

5.4   Perception

The items for perception of style were rated on a 5-point likert scale. For data analysis, these items were categorized into four dimensions: Pathos-based (Empathy, Supportiveness, and Reassurance), Ethos-based (Professionalism, Credentials, and Proactivity), Logos-based (Data-driven, Transparency, and Explanations), and Neutrality. To verify whether the intended styles were perceived as designed, a Friedman comparison was conducted across these dimensions. Significant effects of style were found for *Pathos* ($\chi^2(3) = 39.627$, $p < .001$), *Ethos* ($\chi^2(3) = 36$, $p < .001$), *Logos* ($\chi^2(3) = 18.33$, $p < .001$) and *Neutrality* ($\chi^2(3) = 12.26$, $p = .006$). Post-hoc Wilcoxon comparisons with Holm correction showed that the *Pathos* style was rated significantly higher on Pathos-related items ($p < .001$, $r = .75 - .80$, large effect) and *Ethos* style was rated significantly higher on Ethos-related items ($p < .01$, $r = .58 - .86$, large effect). In case of Logos-related perception items, both *Ethos* and *Logos* styles received significantly higher ratings than *Baseline* ($p < .05$, $r = .38 - .69$, medium to large effect) indicating conceptual overlaps between both communication strategies. Baseline was perceived as most neutral among all four styles; however, the differences were not statistically significant. Overall, the results confirm that style manipulations were successful except for intersections between *Logos* and *Ethos* styles.

6   Discussion

The presented study investigated influences of three different communication styles on user's perceived trust and acceptance through a WoOz setting. The rhetorical styles invoked slightly higher trust and acceptance than the baseline. The findings indicate that participants' perceived acceptance of a chatbot varied with communication style, while trust remained relatively stable across conditions. The inferential statistics showed that rhetorical styles *Ethos* and *Pathos* were rated significantly better on the *Usefulness* subscale of acceptance while the post-hoc tests for *Satisfaction* subscale did not lead to significant group differences. Contrary to that the ranking results showed that *Logos* was preferred over all other styles and the rhetorical styles were ranked significantly better than *Baseline*. The user traits did not have any moderating effects on acceptance and almost all styles were perceived as intended apart from some overlaps between *Logos* and *Ethos*.

6.1   Trust vs Acceptance

Trust and acceptance ratings followed different trajectories - trust remained stable while system acceptance changed with conversation style. This is in accordance with previous research, where trust is primarily grounded in perceptions of system accuracy, competence, and domain reliability [20]. In this study, users experienced only a short scripted interaction in each style and these brief singular interactions also mean that results likely captured initial impressions rather than stable trust calibrations [4] which may explain the limited stylistic influence on trust. Similarly, the WoOz nature may have affected trust scores and further reduced sensitivity to stylistic differences. Moreover, the non-critical scenarios allowed diagnoses to be easily inferred, even with limited medical knowledge potentially leading to ceiling effects in trust ratings. Furthermore, the TiA questionnaire measures trust as a general construct and may not fully capture affective variations that could be influenced by communication style.

In contrast to trust, communication style significantly affected perceived usefulness of the chatbot with *Ethos* being perceived as most useful, closely followed by *Pathos*. These findings align with persuasion theory, which emphasizes that credibility and emotional engagement enhance perceived value [14, 15]. These differences in results between trust and acceptance further strengthen the theory that in healthcare systems, trust is epistemic whereas acceptance is relational

[31]. From a design perspective, this suggests that technical transparency promotes trust, while adaptive or personalized communication enhance acceptance and engagement.

6.2 User Traits, User States and Adaptivity

The analysis of moderating effects of user traits on perceived usefulness as a subscale of system acceptance did not result in significant outputs, contrary to expectations that individual differences such as need for cognition, need for affect, affinity towards technology interaction, trusting stance etc., would moderate acceptance outcomes. This was also seen in the ranking data where no significant correlations between user traits and preferences were found.

While this may partly reflect the limited and relatively homogeneous sample, it also suggests that stable personality traits might not be the most effective basis for tailoring chatbot communication. Instead, adapting style dynamically using situational cues in the user's message may provide a more robust approach towards personalization in case of short interactions. This aligns with recent research in adaptive interaction that emphasizes state-based adaptation for short term interactions over static trait-based profiling for improving engagement and user experience [6]. The trait-based data can still be used to determine ground rules for adaptations [6].

6.3 Conceptual Overlap Between Rhetorical Aspects

Beyond trust and acceptance, the perception checks largely confirmed that style manipulations were understood as indicated. *Pathos* and *Ethos* were perceived consistently with their rhetorical framing, while *Logos* intersected with *Ethos* attributes. This suggests that some characteristics are not exclusive to the assigned rhetorical dimension. This overlap is not unexpected: credibility (ethos) and evidence-based reasoning (logos) are both critical in medical communication [29, 42]. This highlights the methodological challenge of considering individual rhetorical constructs in applied dialogue design. Nevertheless, the manipulation results confirm that participants broadly recognized the intended stylistic differences, validating the experimental framework. Further research must refine the dialogue strategies to accommodate these conceptual overlaps between the rhetorical dimensions.

6.4   Limitations and Ethical Considerations

The WoOz setup allowed for a controlled experience across all participants. However, that also meant that human errors could not be eliminated - varying response timings, sending the wrong message or a message that does not accurately address user's intention might have influenced the overall ratings, especially for the *Reliability/Competence* subscale of Trust in Automation. Apart from that, the limited homogeneous sample size ($N = 36$) met the minimum requirement for a within-subject design, but may have limited statistical power to detect smaller effects. In addition, as revealed by the perception of style, *Logos* was often not distinctively perceived, this was also seen in the participant comments where they failed to distinguish between *Logos* and *Baseline*, suggesting a need for stronger rhetorical differentiation in future designs.

The use of persuasive personalization in healthcare chatbots has its advantages but also raises important ethical considerations. The adaptive styles *Ethos* and *Pathos* enhanced acceptance of the CA, but if not implemented carefully these cues risk inappropriate trust [3], especially in safety critical systems. Thus, transparency about system capabilities, limitations and intent is imperative. Furthermore, individual trait-based adaptation may lead to stereotyping risks and induce bias in conversation. The dialog design must balance persuasive engagement with user autonomy and transparency.

7   Conclusion

This study examined the effect of rhetorical communication styles on trust and acceptance of medical diagnosis chatbots. The Aristotelian rhetorical dimensions were used to investigate user preferences and moderation effects of user traits. Results revealed that while the rhetorical conversational style impacts system acceptance, especially perceived usefulness, it does not significantly improve trust. *Ethos* and *Pathos* were perceived to be the most useful persuasive styles, highlighting the importance of credibility and empathy in medical dialogue systems. In contrast to the acceptance results, *Logos* was ranked the best, emphasizing that rational and reasoning aspects are most valued in healthcare conversations. The perception check indicated some conceptual overlap between rhetorical dimensions *Ethos* and *Logos*, suggesting that these constructs need to be considered in combination rather than individually. Furthermore, moderation analyses for user traits did not yield significant effects, reinforcing that the chatbot should adapt its communication style based on contextual cues within the interaction rather than using stable personality traits, especially in short-term interactions. From a design perspective, this implies that trust and acceptance need different interaction approaches in healthcare conversational design. Trust needs functional reliability and transparency, whereas acceptance can be improved by personalizing interactions. Future work should thus explore dynamic, context-aware interaction elements relevant for adaptation and their effects on trust and acceptance in singular and long-term interactions.

Acknowledgments. This research was conducted at the Chair of Ergonomics, Technical University of Munich. We are deeply grateful to Yu-Jou Lee for developing the prototype. Special thanks to Verena Pongratz and Amrita Bhattacherjee for their valuable input, particularly in data analysis, which significantly aided the development of this work.

Disclosure of Interests. The authors have no competing interests to declare that are relevant to the content of this article. AI Tools were used for proof-reading and paraphrasing.

References

1. Appel, M., Gnambs, T., Maio, G.R.: A short measure of the need for affect. J. Pers. Assess. **94**(4), 418–426 (2012)
2. Barange, M., Rasendrasoa, S., Bouabdelli, M., Saunier, J., Pauchet, A.: Impact of adaptive multimodal empathic behavior on the user interaction. In: Martinho, C., Dias, J., Campos, J., Heylen, D. (eds.) Proceedings of the 22nd ACM International Conference on Intelligent Virtual Agents. pp. 1–8. ACM, New York, NY, USA (2022). https://doi.org/10.1145/3514197.3549675
3. Bickmore, T.W., Ólafsson, S., O'Leary, T.K.: Mitigating patient and consumer safety risks when using conversational assistants for medical information: exploratory mixed methods experiment. J. Med. Internet Res. **23**(11), e30704 (2021). https://doi.org/10.2196/30704
4. Bickmore, T.W., Picard, R.W.: Establishing and maintaining long-term human-computer relationships. ACM Trans. Comput.-Human Interact. **12**(2), 293–327 (2005). https://doi.org/10.1145/1067860.1067867
5. Biro, J., Linder, C., Neyens, D.: The effects of a health care chatbot's complexity and persona on user trust, perceived usability, and effectiveness: mixed methods study. JMIR Hum. Factors **10**, e41017 (2023). https://doi.org/10.2196/41017
6. Braun, M., Alt, F.: Affective assistants. In: Brewster, S., Fitzpatrick, G., Cox, A., Kostakos, V. (eds.) Extended Abstracts of the 2019 CHI Conference on Human Factors in Computing Systems, pp. 1–6. ACM, New York, NY, USA (2019) https://doi.org/10.1145/3290607.3313051
7. Davis, F.D.: Perceived usefulness, perceived ease of use, and user acceptance of information technology. MIS Q. **13**(3), 319 (1989). https://doi.org/10.2307/249008
8. Dubov, A.: Ethical persuasion: the rhetoric of communication in critical care. J. Eval. Clin. Pract. **21**(3), 496–502 (2015). https://doi.org/10.1111/jep.12356
9. Field, A., Field, Z., Miles, J.: Discovering Statistics Using R. Sage (2012). https://www.torrossa.com/en/resources/an/4913501
10. Franke, T., Attig, C., Wessel, D.: A personal resource for technology interaction: development and validation of the affinity for technology interaction (ATI) scale. Int. J. Human-Comput. Interact. **35**(6), 456–467 (2019). https://doi.org/10.1080/10447318.2018.1456150
11. Furini, M., Mariani, M., Montagna, S., Ferretti, S.: Conversational skills of LLM-based healthcare chatbot for personalized communications. In: Proceedings of the 2024 International Conference on Information Technology for Social Good, pp. 429–432. ACM, New York, NY, USA (2024).https://doi.org/10.1145/3677525.3678693

12. Ghosh, D., Faik, I.: Practical empathy: the duality of social and transactional roles of conversational agents in giving health advice. In: ICIS 2020 Proceedings., vol. 5. https://aisel.aisnet.org/icis2020/ishealth/ishealth/5
13. Halekoh, U., Højsgaard, S.: A Kenward-Roger approximation and parametric bootstrap methods for tests in linear mixed models – The R Package pbkrtest. J. Stat. Softw. **59**(9) (2014). https://doi.org/10.18637/jss.v059.i09
14. Han, J., Balabanis, G.: Meta-analysis of social media influencer impact: key antecedents and theoretical foundations. Psychol. Market. **41**(2), 394–426 (2024). https://doi.org/10.1002/mar.21927
15. Higgins, E.T.: Value from hedonic experience and engagement. Psychol. Rev. **113**(3), 439–460 (2006). https://doi.org/10.1037/0033-295X.113.3.439
16. Joshi, R., Bengler, K.: Crafting human-AI interaction: a rhetorical approach to adaptive interaction in conversational agents. In: Ahmad, M.I., Lohan, K., Foster, M.E., Holthaus, P., Nagai, Y. (eds.) Proceedings of the 12th International Conference on Human-Agent Interaction, pp. 314–322. ACM, New York, NY, USA (11242024). https://doi.org/10.1145/3687272.3688297
17. Kocaballi, A.B., et al.: The personalization of conversational agents in health care: systematic review. J. Med. Internet Res. **21**(11), e15360 (2019). https://doi.org/10.2196/15360
18. Körber, M.: Theoretical considerations and development of a questionnaire to measure trust in automation. In: Bagnara, S., Tartaglia, R., Albolino, S., Alexander, T., Fujita, Y. (eds.) IEA 2018. AISC, vol. 823, pp. 13–30. Springer, Cham (2019). https://doi.org/10.1007/978-3-319-96074-6_2
19. Laumer, S., Maier, C., Gubler, F.: Chatbot Acceptance in Healthcare: Explaining User Adoption of Conversational Agents for Disease Diagnosis. Research Papers (2019). https://aisel.aisnet.org/ecis2019_rp/88
20. Lee, J.D., See, K.A.: Trust in automation: designing for appropriate reliance. Hum. Factors **46**(1), 50–80 (2004). https://doi.org/10.1518/hfes.46.1.50_30392
21. Liu, K., Da,: Tao: The roles of trust, personalization, loss of privacy, and anthropomorphism in public acceptance of smart healthcare services. Comput. Hum. Behav. **127**, 107026 (2022). https://doi.org/10.1016/j.chb.2021.107026
22. Liu, Y.L., Yan, W., Hu, B., Li, Z., Lai, Y.L.: Effects of personalization and source expertise on users' health beliefs and usage intention toward health chatbots: Evidence from an online experiment. Digital health **8**, 20552076221129718 (2022). https://doi.org/10.1177/20552076221129718
23. Lüdecke, D., Ben-Shachar, M., Patil, I., Waggoner, P., Makowski, D.: performance: an R Package for Assessment, Comparison and Testing of Statistical Models. J. Open Source Softw. **6**(60), 3139 (2021). https://doi.org/10.21105/joss.03139
24. Mcknight, D.H., Carter, M., Thatcher, J.B., Clay, P.F.: Trust in a specific technology. ACM Trans. Manag. Inf. Syst. **2**(2), 1–25 (2011). https://doi.org/10.1145/1985347.1985353
25. Milne-Ives, M., et al.: The effectiveness of conversational agents in health care: systematic review. J. Med. Internet Res. **22**(10) (2020). https://doi.org/10.2196/16934
26. Norris, P., Pacini, R., Epstein, S.: The Rational-Experiential Inventory, short form
27. Olson, Chester L.: Comparative robustness of six tests in multivariate analysis of variance. J. Am. Stat. Assoc. **69**(348), 894–908 (1974). https://doi.org/10.1080/01621459.1974.10480224
28. Pacini, R., Epstein, S.: The relation of rational and experiential information processing styles to personality, basic beliefs, and the ratio-bias phenomenon. J. Pers. Soc. Psychol. **76**(6), 972–987 (1999). https://doi.org/10.1037//0022-3514.76.6.972

29. Page, M., Crampton, P., Viney, R., Rich, A., Griffin, A.: Teaching medical professionalism: a qualitative exploration of persuasive communication as an educational strategy. BMC Med. Educ. **20**(1), 74 (2020). https://doi.org/10.1186/s12909-020-1993-0

30. Pearson, S.D., Raeke, L.H.: Patients' trust in physicians: many theories, few measures, and little data. J. Gen. Intern. Med. **15**(7), 509–513 (2000). https://doi.org/10.1046/j.1525-1497.2000.11002.x

31. Rowe, R., Calnan, M.: Trust relations in health care–the new agenda. Eur. J. Pub. Health **16**(1), 4–6 (2006). https://doi.org/10.1093/eurpub/ckl004

32. Sætra, H.S.: A machine's ethos? An inquiry into artificial ethos and trust. Comput. Hum. Behav. **153**, 108108 (2024). https://doi.org/10.1016/j.chb.2023.108108

33. SCHUBART, J.R., STUCKEY, H.L., GANESHAMOORTHY, A., SCIAMANNA, C.N.: Chronic health conditions and internet behavioral interventions: a review of factors to enhance user engagement. CIN: Computers, Informatics, Nursing **29**(2 Suppl), TC9–20 (2011). https://doi.org/10.1097/NCN.0b013e3182155274

34. Schubart, J.R., Stuckey, H.L., Ganeshamoorthy, A., Sciamanna, C.N.: Chronic health conditions and internet behavioral interventions: a review of factors to enhance user engagement. CIN: Comput., Inform., Nurs. **29**(2 Suppl), TC9–20 (2011). https://doi.org/10.1097/NCN.0b013e3182155274

35. Seitz, L., Bekmeier-Feuerhahn, S., Gohil, K.: Can we trust a chatbot like a physician? A qualitative study on understanding the emergence of trust toward diagnostic chatbots. Int. J. Human-Comput. Stud. **165**, 102848 (2022). https://doi.org/10.1016/j.ijhcs.2022.102848

36. Singmann, H., Kellen, D.: An introduction to mixed models for experimental psychology. New Methods in Cognitive Psychology, Routledge, New York, US (2019). https://discovery.ucl.ac.uk/id/eprint/10107874/

37. Sucameli, I.: Improving the level of trust in human-machine conversation. Adv. Robot. **35**(9), 553–560 (2021). https://doi.org/10.1080/01691864.2021.1884132

38. Tudor Car, L., et al.: Conversational agents in health care: scoping review and conceptual analysis. J. Med. Internet Res. **22**(8), e17158 (2020). https://doi.org/10.2196/17158

39. van der Laan, J.D., Heino, A., de Waard, D.: A simple procedure for the assessment of acceptance of advanced transport telematics. Transport. Res. Part C. Emerg. Technol. **5**(1), 1–10 (1997). https://doi.org/10.1016/S0968-090X(96)00025-3

40. Venkatesh, V., Thong, J.Y., Xu, X.: Consumer Acceptance and Use of Information Technology: Extending the Unified Theory of Acceptance and Use of Technology (2012)

41. Vossen, W., Szymanski, M., Verbert, K.: The effect of personalizing a psychotherapy conversational agent on therapeutic bond and usage intentions. In: Proceedings of the 29th International Conference on Intelligent User Interfaces, pp. 761–771 (2024). https://doi.org/10.1145/3640543.3645195

42. Walker, M.J., Rogers, W.A.: Reasonableness, credibility, and clinical disagreement. AMA J. Ethics **19**(2), 176–182 (2017). https://doi.org/10.1001/journalofethics.2017.19.2.stas1-1702

43. Wutz, M., Hermes, M., Winter, V., Köberlein-Neu, J.: Factors influencing the acceptability, acceptance, and adoption of conversational agents in health care: integrative review. J. Med. Internet Res. **25**, e46548 (2023). https://doi.org/10.2196/46548
44. You, Y., Tsai, C.H., Li, Y., Ma, F., Heron, C., Gui, X.: Beyond self-diagnosis: how a chatbot-based symptom checker should respond. ACM Trans. Comput.-Human Interact. **30**(4), 1–44 (2023) https://doi.org/10.1145/3589959

Understanding User Perspectives on Persuasive Systems Design Principles in mHealth Applications Using Deep Learning Techniques

Sudarshan Khadka and Elena Vlahu-Gjorgievska^(✉)

University of Wollongong, Wollongong, Australia
{skhadka,elenavg}@uow.edu.au

Abstract. With the increasing use of mHealth applications for well-being, support, and monitoring, the Persuasive Systems Design (PSD) model has also become more prevalent in digital health interventions. However, understanding how users perceive and respond to these persuasive strategies remains limited. Harnessing machine learning models, this study proposes a novel methodological approach to examine the user sentiments and their link with the PSD features as expressed in the app reviews. Sentiment analysis was performed on reviews extracted from 10 applications in the Google Play Store, followed by automatic classification of reviews into PSD categories using a transformer. The results revealed a polarised perception across categories, with primary task support predominantly receiving positive sentiment, while system credibility support attracting more negative sentiment. These findings suggest that the implementation of the primary task support features aligns well with users' needs, and their positive perception can further enhance user engagement. However, the developers need to reconsider the way the credibility support features are embedded since it may be counterintuitive and reduce users' trust.

Keywords: Persuasive Systems Design (PSD) · mHealth Applications · Sentiment Analysis · Transformer-based classification

1 Introduction

Today, the population is facing an increasingly fast-paced lifestyle, where the pursuit of healthier eating habits and fitness integrated in sustainable weight management strategies has become of great importance. In this context, mobile health (mHealth) applications have emerged as a widely adopted solution, offering effective reach and potential impact [1]. However, despite the popularity of the mHealth weight management applications, the long-term user engagement with those remains a challenge [2].

The effectiveness of these applications is often closely associated with the successful implementation of Persuasive System Design (PSD) principles. The

K. Sumi et al. (Eds.): PERSUASIVE 2026, LNCS 16476, pp. 109–120, 2026.
https://doi.org/10.1007/978-3-032-19687-3_9

findings indicate that the use of applications with persuasive features results in better weight management outcomes [3–5]. A recent evaluation shows that among 120 diabetes management applications, applications used only a median of 3 out of 28 PSD principles [6]. While most of the applications utilised primary task support features and dialogue support features, social support features were not implemented adequately [6]. This inconsistent implementation suggests that although developers seem to be aware of the importance of persuasive features, they lack an understanding of how these features are perceived by users and the complexity in implementing the underrepresented features. However, while persuasive features can improve user engagement and outcomes, simply adding more does not always lead to better usability or satisfaction. In some cases, users may even react negatively to certain features, especially if they feel intrusive or overwhelming [7]. Therefore, understanding user perspectives on persuasive features is crucial for creating mHealth applications that resonate with end users.

Most studies [7–9] in this area rely on expert evaluation of persuasive features and manual mapping. While these approaches provide valuable insights, they are time-consuming and cannot be scaled to a large volume ofÂăuser feedback, such as users' reviews. To overcome this gap, this study proposes a novel approach to explore the user sentiments and their link with the persuasive features as expressed in the app reviews. The proposed approach combines natural language processing methods with the established PSD model to evaluate how real users feel and respond to persuasive features in mHealth weight management applications, answering the research question: "How do end users perceive the use of persuasive features in mHealth applications for weight management?"

2   Methodology

The research was carried out in four stages: collecting user reviews, sentiment analysis, identifying persuasive design features with machine learning, and Bigram analysis.

2.1   Data Collection and Preprocessing

To select the eligible application, the search terms "weight management apps", "food and fitness apps", and "weight loss apps" were used in the Google Play Store. The search identified more than 30 applications, which were further narrowed based on their rating (more than 3 stars) and the inclusion of features that support both diets and physical activities, resulting in 13 applications selected for the study.

Users' reviews were collected using automated web scraping techniques implemented via the Google Play Scraper library, following best practices for ethical gathering of publicly available information. Additionally, language filtering was performed to keep only English-language reviews.

For dataset preparation and model training, a subset of 3,000 reviews was manually annotated using the Persuasive System Design (PSD) framework.

These reviews were drawn from three applications randomly selected from the full set. The purpose of this annotated subset was to provide a seed dataset enabling supervised learning for scalable PSD classification. The remaining 82,143 reviews, of the remaining ten applications, were used for model testing and analysis. The length of the reviews varied from 3 to 847 words (M = 23.4 words; SD = 31.2) with applications providing 3 to 20,000 reviews to the pool of reviews to be analyzed.

2.2 Sentiment Analysis

After preprocessing and data cleaning, sentiment analysis was performed on user reviews to determine the overall positive or negative sentiment using a pretrained BERT-based model. The chosen model was applied to predict the sentiment polarity within the clean review texts. Hence, each review was tagged with a positive sentiment classification (usually praise or satisfaction) or a negative sentiment classification (criticism or dissatisfaction).

2.3 PSD Classification

Data Preparation. In order to train a classifier to recognise the PSD categories in text, a labelled dataset through manual annotation was created. A random sample of the collected reviews from three selected applications was used for coding to maintain a mix of different applications and sentiment directions, obtaining variability in the content. The annotation was based on the PSD model and formal definitions by [10]. The annotation process was done independently by the two authors, with any discrepancies resolved through discussion. The reviewed text was tagged with one or more PSD tags (multi-label), depending on the context of the review.

Model Training. The annotated review dataset was used to train a multi-label text classification model to automatically categorise user reviews into PSD categories. The pre-trained `bert-base-uncased` model provided by the Hugging Face Transformers library [11], which implements the Bidirectional Encoder Representations from Transformers (BERT) architecture [12] was employed. This particular implementation was selected for its reproducibility, extensive empirical validation, and widespread adoption in natural language processing research.

The main advantages of BERT include ability to model bidirectional contextual dependencies and capture implicit semantic cues in short, informal, and often ambiguous user-generated text (such as reviews). In contrast to lexicon-based and bag-of-words approaches, which rely on surface-level keyword matching, transformer-based models can infer meaning from context, enabling the identification of persuasive features that are expressed indirectly. Prior work has demonstrated that fine-tuned BERT models consistently outperform traditional machine learning methods on sentiment analysis and text classification tasks involving noisy, domain-specific user reviews [13,14].

A custom classification layer was added on top of the model, consisting of five sigmoid-activated output neurons, one for each PSD category: Primary Task Support, Dialogue Support, System Credibility Support and Social Support, and one for General Review.

In order to confidently evaluate model performance, 5-fold stratified cross-validation with proportional representation in each fold was employed. The model was trained on 80% of the data and validated on the remaining 20% within each fold. Performance was monitored with macro-averaged precision, recall, and F1-score, calculated after choosing an optimal decision threshold. To avoid reliance on a random choice of decision threshold (e.g., 0.5), threshold tuning between 0.3 and 0.7 was carried out for each fold, selecting the value that attained the highest macro F1-score on the validation set. In each iteration, the model was reinitialised and fine-tuned independently to account for any learning variations through different training subsets. The performance of the model across five folds was uniform with minimal fluctuation on metrics of evaluation (a sign of stable generalisation), as shown in Table 1. This iterative process of training and testing led to a highly optimised BERT-based classifier capable of predicting persuasive design principles in applications' reviews.

Table 1. Fold-wise Evaluation Metrics for PSD Classification Model

Fold	Precision	Recall	F1-Score	Best Threshold
1	0.9431	0.9380	0.9405	0.70
2	0.9426	0.9386	0.9399	0.70
3	0.9064	0.9423	0.9237	0.50
4	0.9426	0.9324	0.9371	0.60
5	0.9512	0.9356	0.9375	0.60

2.4   Bigram Analysis

In addition to the multi-label classification into persuasive principles and sentiment polarity, bigram analysis was carried out for identifying commonly expressed concerns and themes in user reviews. This linguistic approach was employed for identifying which word pairs (bigrams) most commonly co-occur and are used to convey satisfaction or dissatisfaction. Bigram analysis was utilised as a complementary method to support quantitative findings of sentiment classification and PSD prediction.

3   Results

The results of the sentiment analysis, followed by the automated PSD prediction, resulted in an association between the sentiments and the underlying PSD category for each application. The results were generated on the individual app level and overall (Tables 2, 3 and 4).

Only 29% of reviews were classified as PSD-related (Table 2). Namely, the reviews were assigned to PSD categories only when the predicted confidence for at least one persuasive principle exceeded the predefined threshold of 0.6. Reviews that did not meet this criteria were categorised as General Reviews, representing feedback unrelated to persuasive features, such as pricing, usability issues, or general satisfaction. This threshold-based approach prioritised precision and reduced false positive PSD assignments in the presence of class imbalance.

Table 2. Overall Summary of Sentiment and Review Type

Metric	Value	Percentage
Total Reviews	82,143	100%
Positive Reviews	54,880	66.81%
Negative Reviews	27,262	33.19%
PSD-related Reviews	23,829	29.01%
General Reviews	58,314	70.99%
Positive PSD Reviews	13,866	58.19%
Negative PSD Reviews	9,962	41.18%

Table 3. Overall Per-Category PSD Sentiment Summary

Category	Total Reviews	Positive (%)	Negative (%)
Primary Task Support	11535	90.08	9.91
Dialogue Support	9198	77.15	22.85
Social Support	1966	84.03	15.97
System Credibility Support	10396	23.57	76.43

3.1   Sentiment Distribution Across Applications

The analysis of 82143 aggregate reviews for 10 health and fitness applications presented highly heterogeneous user satisfaction, as shown in Table 4. The aggregate positive review rates ranged from 37.62% (OMO) to 87.57% (8Fitness), and were indicative of varying user experiences for different applications and functionalities. 8Fitness emerged as the most well-received app with 87.57% positive reviews, followed by Cronometer (77.11%) and Healthi (73.2%). In contrast,

Table 4. Overall and PSD-related Reviews Sentiment by App

App	Total Reviews	Positive (%)	Negative (%)	PSD-Related	PSD- Related (%)	PSD Positive (%)	PSD Negative (%)
8Fitness	23478	87.57	12.43	2951	12.57	84.95	15.05
Cronometer	4936	77.11	22.89	2157	43.70	76.96	23.04
Foodvisor	2436	57.55	42.45	911	37.40	59.93	40.07
Healthi	4284	73.20	26.80	1059	24.72	62.32	37.68
MyFitnessPal	9845	39.78	60.22	3606	36.63	36.83	63.17
Noom	16481	63.79	36.21	6484	39.34	59.02	40.98
OMO	2919	37.62	62.38	868	29.74	34.33	65.67
Simple	6962	61.81	38.19	2659	38.19	64.57	35.43
WeightWatchers	7935	62.51	37.49	2279	28.72	48.92	51.08
YAZIO	2867	41.37	58.63	855	29.82	24.44	75.56

OMO had the lowest user satisfaction with only 37.62% positive reviews, followed by MyFitnessPal (39.78%) and YAZIO (41.37%).

The prevalence of PSD-related reviews varied significantly across applications, ranging from 12.57% (8Fitness) to 43.7% (Cronometer). 8Fitness excelled in PSD-related reviews with 84.95% positive sentiment that closely matched its overall positive review rate (87.57%). Similarly, Cronometer, Healthi and Simple also had considerably high positive sentiment in PSD-related reviews. This alignment suggests smooth fusion of features that address nutrition concerns and fitness exercises with user expectations. Conversely, YAZIO, OMO and MyFitnessPal exhibited poor PSD-related sentiment, with more than 60% of the PSD-related reviews skewing towards negative sentiment.

The sentiment distribution across PSD categories is presented in Table 5. In general, the applications had high positive sentiment for Primary Task Support, with 8Fitness and Cronometer scoring over 90% positive sentiment, indicating a good mapping of core functionality to user intent.

Notably, the applications received widespread criticism for System Credibility Support features, with negative sentiment consistently exceeding 65%. Even widely adopted applications, like Noom and WeightWatcherswith (with 10M+ user downloads and substantial user feedback), suffered from credibility-related pushback, despite their high brand recognition and user engagement. Dialogue Support and Social Support features were overall well-received, particularly for applications like Simple, Healthi, and Noom.

3.2 Linguistic Patterns in PSD-Related Reviews

To examine user language patterns, bigram frequency analysis was conducted for each PSD category. This analysis identified recurring themes and lexical patterns characterising user feedback across PSD categories.

Primary Task Support reviews, characterised by overwhelmingly positive sentiment, demonstrated consistent emphasis on monitoring and personalisation capabilities (Fig. 1). The most frequent bigrams included "track foods", "track calories" and "easy track". These patterns reflect users' focus on behavioural tracking, goal monitoring, and interface usability, consistent with the category's high positive sentiment.

Table 5. App level Sentiment distribution across PSD categories

PSD Category	Positive (%)	Negative (%)	Positive Count	Negative Count	App
Primary Task Support	94.18	5.82	2811	173	8Fitness
Dialogue Support	90.93	9.07	1874	187	
System Credibility Support	37.37	62.63	179	300	
Social Support	93.02	6.98	293	22	
Primary Task Support	93.78	6.22	1041	69	Cronometer
Dialogue Support	74.51	25.49	152	52	
System Credibility Support	60.04	39.96	652	434	
Social Support	88.57	11.42	31	4	
Primary Task Support	78.59	21.41	279	76	Foodvisor
Dialogue Support	71.48	28.52	208	83	
System Credibility Support	32.36	67.64	122	255	
Social Support	70.00	30.00	28	12	
Primary Task Support	87.36	12.64	394	57	Healthi
Dialogue Support	52.32	47.68	79	72	
System Credibility Support	33.86	66.14	171	334	
Social Support	84.42	15.58	103	19	
Primary Task Support	78.14	21.86	1696	475	MyFitnessPal
Dialogue Support	57.59	42.41	258	190	
System Credibility Support	16.50	83.50	382	1933	
Social Support	72.52	27.48	95	36	
Primary Task Support	76.65	23.35	2154	681	Noom
Dialogue Support	79.14	20.86	2679	706	
System Credibility Support	17.73	82.27	449	2083	
Social Support	82.90	17.10	805	166	
Primary Task Support	61.29	38.71	114	72	OMO
Dialogue Support	50.41	49.59	183	180	
System Credibility Support	10.56	89.44	49	415	
Social Support	60.00	40.00	12	8	
Primary Task Support	81.43	18.57	1315	299	Simple
Dialogue Support	79.67	20.33	1313	335	
System Credibility Support	19.64	80.36	174	712	
Social Support	93.98	6.02	156	10	
Primary Task Support	73.78	26.22	681	242	Weight Watchers
Dialogue Support	62.76	37.24	300	178	
System Credibility Support	16.84	83.16	196	968	
Social Support	69.65	30.35	101	44	
Primary Task Support	54.11	45.89	112	95	YAZIO
Dialogue Support	29.59	70.41	50	119	
System Credibility Support	12.93	87.07	76	512	
Social Support	52.38	47.62	11	10	

Dialogue Support reviews exhibited balanced language patterns reflecting both positive and negative experiences with system interactions (Fig. 2). Common bigrams included "daily reminder", "keeps motivated", "timely notification". These patterns suggest varied user experiences with system-generated prompts and feedback mechanisms.

Social Support reviews revealed a strong emphasis on community interaction and peer engagement (Fig. 3). Dominant bigrams included "share progress", and "good community". The prevalence of these community-focused terms underscores the importance of peer-based features for user satisfaction within this category.

System Credibility Support reviews displayed distinctly different linguistic patterns, reflecting the category's predominantly negative sentiment (Fig. 4). Frequent bigrams included "false information" (n =225), "behind paywall", and "free version". These patterns indicate user concerns about trustworthiness, feature accessibility, and monetisation transparency. The co-occurrence of "false information" with broader accuracy concerns and "behind paywall" with accessibility complaints highlights specific credibility issues affecting user trust.

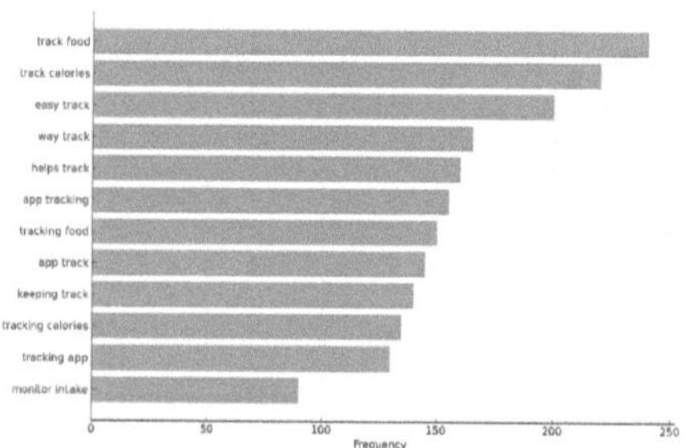

Fig. 1.   Primary   Task   Support Bigrams.

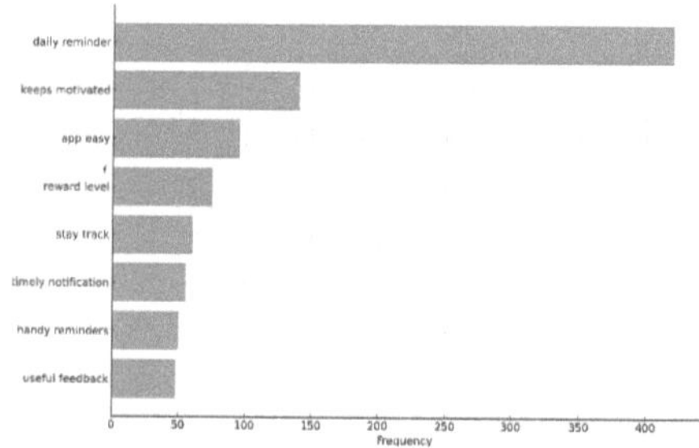

Fig. 2. Dialogue Support Bigrams.

4   Discussion

This study successfully leveraged user reviews to understand the impact of PSD principles in mHealth applications, utilising the potential of transformer models. The results suggest that using PSD principles in mHealth applications for weight management is perceived positively by the users. The overall sentiment towards the persuasive features was positive, similarly to the findings of previous studies [15,16]. This indicates that persuasive features play an important role in shaping the user's perspective towards applications.

The key findings are related to the prevalence of the Primary Task Support category in the user reviews and significantly higher positive sentiments towards it. This implies that users highly value applications' core functionalities

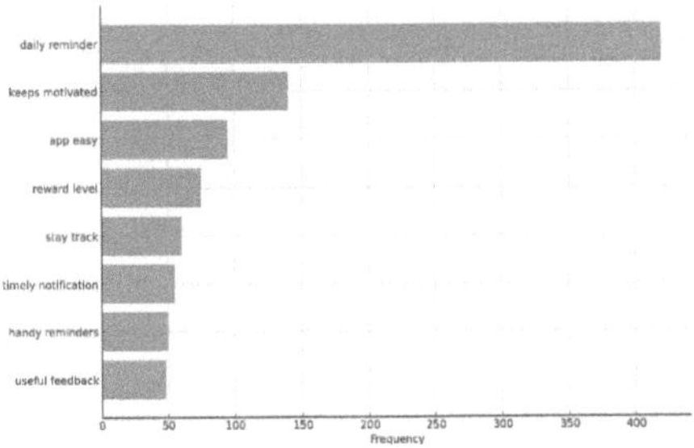

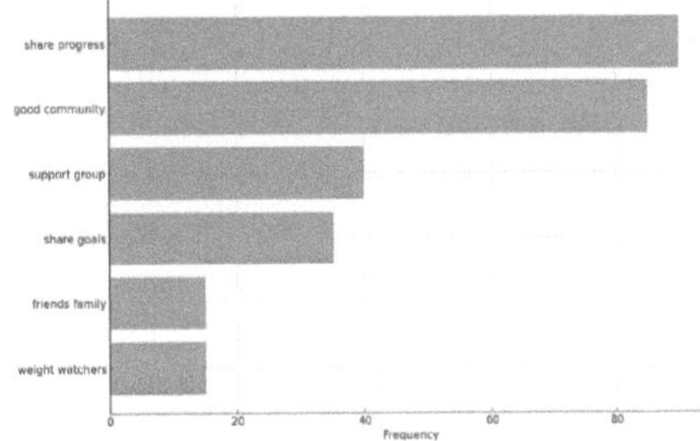

Fig. 3. Social Support Bigrams.

Fig. 4. System Credibility Support Bigrams.

and features that allow them to achieve their goals (as managing their weight). The positive reviews suggest that when an app effectively assists users in their primary objectives – i.e., by breaking down complex behaviours into simple step-by-step instructions, monitoring their progress, or providing personalised content – users respond with satisfaction and appreciation. This is reflected in user comments, with common bigrams of Primary Task Support related reviews including "easy track", "monitor intake", and "keeping track". These results indicate that users value the tracking and self-monitoring features, which make their health-related goals more achievable. This also aligns with the research by Bansal et al. [17], that the self-monitoring and personalisation features can lead to user satisfaction.

The Primary Task Support predominance in reviews supports the observation that mHealth app developers should prioritise robust primary task features – ensuring the core capabilities of the app are clear, effective, and closely linked to the user's goals. These conclusions correspond to previous research [18] which found that self-monitoring and goal setting were the principles most frequently used.

Social Support features, which capitalise on social influence and peer engagement, were also positively perceived in consumer reviews. The majority of users highlighted features like community forums, group challenges, sharing progress with friends or family, leaderboards, or support from other users. The general attitude towards these mentions was positive, indicating that users enjoy the social elements of mHealth applications. Bigrams such as "share progress", "support group", or "good community" were indicative and frequent, highlighting that a sense of being able to compare and relate to others can be an engaging factor for the users. This is evidence that social forces can play a key role in driving individuals, so users are more likely to be responsible and motivated due to social reasons [19]. For example, knowing one's friends/family can see how one does, or participating in a group step-counting challenge, can give a sense of responsibility or competition that will cause them to continue using it.

A notable finding from the results of sentiment distribution in the social support category is the contradiction with previous research. Previous research

[7] stated that the use of more social support features might lead to a decrease in user experience, whereas our results showed that the social support features are well perceived by the users, and more than 90% of reviews that mentioned social support features exhibited positive sentiment. In some applications, such as Simple and Noom, social support had the highest positive sentiments among the PSD categories. These stand-out positive sentiment, and good overall positive sentiments, further suggests that incorporating Social Support features in mHealth applications can attract a positive attitude in users. On the other hand, the considerably lower number of user reviews in the social support category can be an indication that the social support features have been underestimated and underrepresented in the analyzed applications, despite their ability to receive positive feedback from users, as stated in [5].

The dialogue support features were also highly popular in the user reviews, affirming the findings of previous research [6]. These interactive and feedback-triggered functionalities in the applications, such as reminders, prompts, motivational messages, rewards, and other forms of system-triggered dialogues, can increase users' engagement. The results of bigram analysis revealed that terms like "daily reminder" and "useful feedback" are frequent in the reviews, asserting that timely reminders and inspiring feedback are memorable in the user experience. Their popularity and positivity in sentiment analysis show that while users enjoyed these prompts, those also motivated users to adhere to their healthy habits.

Unlike the other PSD categories, System Credibility Support had significantly higher negative sentiment in user reviews - approximately 60% of references under this category were negative. System Credibility Support involves qualities that make the system more credible, trustworthy, and transparent, such as displaying third-party indications of approval, providing evidence behind assertions, protecting privacy, and making sure the content and appearance of the app convey credibility. Bigram analysis in this category highlighted terms "false information", "behind paywall". These findings complement the Nutrokpor et al.[7] outcomes, which stated that using more system credibility features does not always guarantee increased trust. Similarly, as indicated by bigrams "behind paywall", another concern impacting the credibility of the applications is the trend to attract users by setting all the features as free (at the initial installation of the app), and down the line of the user's journey to manage weight, those features are put behind the paywall, forcing users to subscribe to the pro version to retain the progress statistics. The users frequently complained that they were tricked into subscribing to the app, instead of being informed transparently. A similar finding confirmed that being transparent can increase user perception of fairness with respect to persuasive systems, lessen the feeling of being "tricked" by the system and give the user a sense of control [20].

4.1   Limitations and Future Work

This research has a few limitations which should be considered while interpreting its findings. The dataset used for the PSD prediction model was manually annotated by the researchers, introducing subjectivity bias. The future work could be focused on engineering the training data to enhance the model's performance. The identification of the common topics or terms was done using bigram analysis. However, bigrams can bring the most frequent terms, which might not be related to the topics being discussed [21]. Another limitation of this research is the context of the PSD sentiments since the analysed reviews were for the weight-management applications. Therefore, future research is needed to broaden the scope. In some cases, the negative sentiment towards a persuasive feature can be due to its implementation and functionality issues rather than the persuasive principles used [9]. Future research can consider this by separating the functionality-related sentiments and PSD principle-related sentiments.

5 Conclusion

This research utilised sentiment analysis and deep learning-based classification to examine users' attitudes towards persuasive system design (PSD) principles in mHealth applications. The research identified significant differences in users' sentiments across PSD categories. Features categorised under Primary Task Support - e.g., monitoring, goal-setting, and personalisation - were extremely popular across the board, with more than 90% positive reviews. Similarly, Social Support and Dialogue Support features also had very positive reviews. Conversely, System Credibility Support features elicited negative sentiments, with users mentioning false advertisements, deceptive paywalls, and misleading information.

The integration of PSD classification with the use of a transformer-based review analysis led to a scalable and fine-grained approach for the analysis of users' feedback. The findings from this research have a variety of implications for the design of mHealth applications, such as prioritising core primary task features, utilising more social support features, and carefully designing the system credibility features. Persuasive features can make a significant contribution to user satisfaction - if appropriately utilised. Facilitating users' primary objectives, fostering good social interactions, and building credibility are all essential in the design of impactful and credible mHealth applications.

References

1. Okolo, C.A., Babawarun, O., Arowoogun, J.O., Adeniyi, A.O., Chidi, R.: The role of mobile health applications in improving patient engagement and health outcomes: a critical review. Int. J. Sci. Res. Arch. (2024)
2. Mustafa, A.S., Ali, N., Dhillon, J.S., Alkawsi, G., Baashar, Y.: User engagement and abandonment of mhealth: a cross-sectional survey. Healthcare **10**(2), 221 (2022)
3. Sittig, S., McGowan, A., Iyengar, S.: Extensive review of persuasive system design categories and principles: behavioral obesity interventions. J. Med. Syst. **44**, 128 (2020)

4. Alnaabi, Y.A.H.Y.A., Ibrahim, N.A.Z.R.I.T.A., Dhillon, J.S.: A systematic literature review of persuasive design features utilized by mobile-based obesity interventions. J. Theor. Appl. Inform. Technol. **99**(2), 530–539 (2021)
5. Asbjørnsen, R.A., et al.:. Persuasive system design principles and behavior change techniques to stimulate motivation and adherence in electronic health interventions to support weight loss maintenance: Scoping review. J. Med. Internet Res. **21**(6), e14265, (2019)
6. Geirhos, A., Stephan, M., Wehrle, M., et al.: Standardized evaluation of the quality and persuasiveness of mobile health applications for diabetes management. Sci. Rep. **12**, 3639 (2022)
7. Nutrokpor, C., Ekpezu, A.O., Wiafe, A., Wiafe, I.: Exploring the impact of persuasive system features on user sentiments in health and fitness apps. In: Proceedings of the 9th International Workshop on Behavior Change Support Systems (BCSS 2021), Aachen, Germany, 2021. RWTH Aachen University (2021)
8. Meyer, J., Okuboyejo, S.: User reviews of depression app features: Sentiment analysis. JMIR Form. Res. **5**(12), e17062 (2021)
9. Camacho-Rivera, M., Vo, H., Huang, X., Lau, J., Lawal, A., Kawaguchi, A.: Evaluating asthma mobile apps to improve asthma self-management: User ratings and sentiment analysis of publicly available apps. JMIR Mhealth Uhealth **8**(10), e15076 (2020)
10. Oinas-Kukkonen, H., Harjumaa, M.: Persuasive systems design: Key issues, process model, and system features. Commun. Assoc. Inform. Syst. **24** (2009)
11. Wolf, T., et al.: Transformers: state-of-the-art natural language processing. In: Liu, Q., Schlangen, D., eds. In: Proceedings of the 2020 Conference on Empirical Methods in Natural Language Processing: System Demonstrations, pp. 38–45, Online, October 2020. Association for Computational Linguistics
12. Devlin, J., Chang, M.-W., Lee, K., Toutanova, K.: Pre-training of deep bidirectional transformers for language understanding, Bert (2019)
13. Zhang, L., Wang, S., Liu, B.: Deep learning for sentiment analysis: a survey. WIREs Data Min. Knowl. Discovery **8**(4), e1253 (2018)
14. Sun, C., Qiu, X., Xu, Y., Huang, X.: How to fine-tune bert for text classification? (2020)
15. Win, K.T., Mullan, J., Howard, S., Oinas-Kukkonen, H.: Persuasive systems design features in promoting medication management for consumers. In: Hawaii International Conference on System Sciences. IEEE Computer Society (2017)
16. Almutairi, N., Vlahu-Gjorgievska, E., Win, K.: Persuasive features for patient engagement through mhealth applications in managing chronic conditions: a systematic literature review and meta-analysis. Inform. Health Soc. Care **48**(3), 267–291 (2023)
17. Bansal, S., Monika: Advances in emotion text analysis: a systematic review of machine learning and deep learning techniques. SSRN Electron. J. (May 2024)
18. Orji, R., Moffatt, K.: Persuasive technology for health and wellness: state-of-the-art and emerging trends. Health Inform. J. **24**(1), 66–91 (2016)
19. Milne-Ives, M., de Cock, C., Kostkova, P.: Potential associations between behavior change techniques and engagement with mobile health apps: Systematic review. Front. Psychol. **14**, 1227443 (2023)
20. Cemiloglu, D., Arden-Close, E., Hodge, S.E., Ali, R.: Explainable persuasion for interactive design: the case of online gambling. J. Syst. Softw. **195**, 111517 (2023)
21. Hachaj, T., Ogiela, M.R.: What can be learned from bigrams analysis of messages in social network? In: 2018 11th International Congress on Image and Signal Processing, BioMedical Engineering and Informatics (CISP-BMEI), pp. 1–4 (2018)

Story2Change: Towards an AI-Driven Persuasive Technology for Depression Management through Narrative Storytelling

Japheth Mumo Kimeu[1]([✉]) [iD], Gladwin Irudayaraj[1] [iD], Josteve Adekanbi[1] [iD],
Gloria Obuobi-Donkor[2] [iD], Medard Adu[2] [iD], Ejemai Eboreime[2] [iD], Grace Ataguba[1] [iD],
Rita Orji[1] [iD], and Oladapo Oyebode[1] [iD]

[1] Faculty of Computer Science, Dalhousie University, Halifax, Nova Scotia, Canada
japheth.kimeu@dal.ca
[2] Department of Psychiatry, Dalhousie University, Halifax, Nova Scotia, Canada

Abstract. Storytelling can reduce resistance to health messages by increasing identification, but the narrative elements, persuasive strategies, and emotional features that make recovery stories effective are poorly understood, thereby limiting real-time story generation for behaviour change. To address this gap, we developed and evaluated an artificial intelligence (AI) agent for generating persuasive recovery stories in real-time. From 156,871 Reddit posts in a depression community, we identified 988 inspiring recovery stories and used an explainable large language model to extract their narrative elements, persuasive strategies, and emotional trajectories. We encoded these elements in a retrieval-augmented generation (RAG) agent and evaluated 100 generated stories with mental health experts. Ratings showed near-perfect agreement (Cohen's $\kappa = 0.993, p < .001$) and supported the stories' clinical relevance and potential to motivate positive change. The next step is to integrate our AI agent into persuasive technology (PT) to enable real-time generation of tailored and clinically grounded recovery narratives that motivate behaviour change at scale, with potential applicability beyond depression.

Keywords: Narrative Persuasion · Depression Management · Storytelling · Artificial Intelligence (AI) · Large Language Model (LLM) · AI Agent · Mental Health

1 Introduction

Depression is one of the most prevalent mental health conditions worldwide, which has remained under-recognized and under-supported for decades [1, 2]. It affects how people feel, think, and act, often leading to persistent sadness, loss of interest, self-harm, suicidal thoughts, and reduced ability to function in daily life [3]. According to the World Health Organization, 332 million people worldwide experience depression each year, yet the majority struggle to have access to timely emotional support and care – with no fewer than 10% receiving treatment in low-income countries [4]. Storytelling as a narrative-based intervention can provide mental health support, as people tend to share

K. Sumi et al. (Eds.): PERSUASIVE 2026, LNCS 16476, pp. 121–132, 2026.
https://doi.org/10.1007/978-3-032-19687-3_10

their experiences, find hope, and inspire others [5]. An emotional connection is often created when people share their personal stories on how they overcame depression, which professional advice may sometimes not provide [6]. Through these stories, readers feel understood, supported, and motivated to take small steps towards recovery. With social media platforms, people are now able to discuss mental health issues and share their recovery stories to a wider population.

Over the years, researchers have used social media data from Reddit, X (formerly Twitter), and Facebook, among other platforms, to examine the influence of online discussion on mental health outcomes. For example, online communities on Reddit, such as *r/depression*, provide an open platform where people narratively share their experiences with depression, including coping/recovery mechanisms and outcomes, and receive feedback from peers [7]. However, most research analyzes social media posts or narratives without assessing whether they have the potential to inspire or motivate desirable behaviour change in others, which goes beyond mere sentiment analysis [8]. In recent years, artificial intelligence (AI) techniques such as machine learning and deep learning have been explored to deliver interventions to support depression [9]. Yet, existing systems deliver these interventions without offering clinically grounded explanations, thereby limiting trust and reducing adoption [10]. Another important gap is the lack of persuasive systems that can automatically generate inspiring and persuasive stories geared to support individuals suffering from depression [8]. Without such systems, the potential of using technology to create supportive and inspiring recovery stories at scale remains unexplored. To address these gaps, we ask the following research questions:

RQ1: *What narrative elements, emotional trajectories, and persuasive strategies make a recovery story inspiring and persuasive in addressing depression?*

RQ2: *How can such inspiring and persuasive recovery stories be computationally generated at scale using technology?*

RQ3: *How clinically relevant and persuasive are these generated stories in motivating positive behavioural change among individuals experiencing depression?*

To address these research questions, we selected Reddit data over other social media platforms because it hosts active mental health communities where users frequently share detailed narratives. In contrast, platforms like Twitter impose character limits that restrict content depth. Reddit's relative anonymity also supports user privacy, making it a suitable choice for this study. In total, we collected 156,871 posts and 430,112 comments from the depression community (*r/depression*) on Reddit, which we analyzed and identified 988 inspiring recovery narratives or stories motivating at least one commenter to act positively towards behaviour change, as supporting even just one person suffering from depression is important. We then extracted and analyzed the narrative elements, persuasive strategies, and emotional trajectories present in these recovery stories. For example, our analysis revealed that stories that combined multiple persuasive strategies had a higher chance of increasing motivational impact, especially those that offered emotional support with actionable advice. Based on these findings, we developed an AI agent leveraging a retrieval-augmented generation (RAG)-based large language model (LLM) to generate inspiring stories that offer hope and recovery for readers experiencing depressive episodes. To assess the clinical and persuasive effectiveness, we generated

100 inspiring stories and conducted a heuristic evaluation on these stories with two mental health experts (clinicians) using 8 well-established heuristics in the healthcare domain and the field of human computer interaction (HCI) [11]. Our results showed high rating, with mean score of 92% for clinical effectiveness and 89% for persuasive effectiveness. The inter-rater reliability was computed using Cohen's Kappa [12] ($\kappa = 0.993$, $p < .001$), indicating high agreement in clinicians.

This study offers four key contributions to the field of HCI, persuasive technology, and digital health. First, we offer an extensive analysis of Reddit posts to identify narrative elements, persuasive strategies, and emotional flows that contribute to an inspiring and behaviour-change story. Second, we established a computational approach for generating persuasive recovery stories that inspire or motivate behaviour change in individuals experiencing depression using advanced AI. Third, we provide empirical insights from expert evaluation of AI-generated inspiring and persuasive recovery stories to demonstrate their clinical and persuasive effectiveness, as well as their potential to drive behavior change (depression management). Finally, we offer practical recommendations for designing and developing persuasive technologies that leverage our findings to generate inspiring, persuasive stories in real-time to support depression management.

2 Background and Related Work

2.1 Storytelling in Digital Technologies to Support Depression Management

This section covers existing studies that applied storytelling in depression management. While these studies have shown the potential of storytelling, there is limited evidence on the impact of persuasive storytelling. More so, most of the approaches employed in existing studies are criticized as they lack theoretical grounding and clinical validity [13, 14]. For example, Kumar et al. [15] analyzed 100 Twitter stories to detect depression patterns. However, they offered no evidence on how these stories could persuade or drive behavioral change among readers. Similarly, Shen et al. [8] demonstrated how Twitter users' posting behaviors were linked with depression more than the content within the posts. However, their study exclusively focused on depression detection. Overall, these studies have shown a limited connection between the persuasiveness of stories on social media platforms and depression management, highlighting the essential need for a study that employs theory-grounded approaches to establish a connection between the persuasiveness of stories on social media platforms and depression management.

2.2 Theoretical Foundations

Narrative Transportation Theory. To explore what makes a story persuasive, we first examined theories that describe how readers become emotionally immersed in narratives – a process referred to as narrative transportation [16]. The narrative transportation theory developed by Melanie Green and Timothy Brock [17], provides the foundation for understanding persuasive effects on stories, highlighting that transportation occurs when readers are fully immersed in a narrative, creating vivid mental simulations and experiencing behavioural changes. This theory is facilitated by three elements: (1) identification, (2) empathy, and (3) vivid imagery with character. Transported individuals tend to adopt the beliefs, attitudes, and behaviors from the narrative.

Aristotle's Poetic Theory. Next, we examined how Aristotle's poetics theory grounds narrative storytelling through structural coherence [18]. The theory remains foundational, identifying the five key core narrative elements in stories: *plot, setting, conflict, theme,* and *characters* [19]. The plot informs the sequence of events that organizes a story's action. A story may begin with a struggle, followed by coping mechanisms, and finally end with a resolution [20]. The setting encompasses the where, when, and circumstances in which the story unfolds and characters act [21]. The conflict element represents the struggle that creates narrative tension, acting as the structural hinge linking narrative form, persuasive intent, and the emotional transformation [22]. Theme informs the character captured from a story. It reflects personal growth, transformation, hope, and resilience [23]. The characters are people whose actions and decisions the story unfolds.

Persuasive Systems Design (PSD) Model. The PSD model is a framework designed to aid in the design of computerized systems that influence user attitudes or behaviors to achieve their goal without coercion [24]. It comprises 28 persuasive strategies classified into four categories, namely: primary task, dialogue support, system credibility support, and social support as shown in Table 1.

Table 1. Categories of persuasive strategies [24]

Persuasive strategies categories	Example of strategies
Primary task support	Reduction, tailoring, tunneling, personalization
Dialogue support	Praise, rewards, reminders, suggestion, similarity
System credibility support	Trustworthiness, expertise, credibility
Social support strategies	Social learning, social comparison, normative influence

Ekman's Emotional Theory. While persuasive strategies inform how stories motivate behaviour change, understanding the emotional trajectories fosters empathy and engagement. Ekman's Theory provides this affective lens. Developed by Paul Ekman, this theory identifies six basic emotions, which are anger, disgust, fear, happiness, sadness, and surprise [25]. We examined the emotional trajectory to assess whether stories that began with sadness and ended with happiness or relief contributed to hope and empathy, raising persuasion.

3   Methodology

As shown in Fig. 1, we followed a workflow with two stages. To address RQ1, we first analyzed the posts and comments retrieved from Reddit subcommunity on depression (r/depression). Then, to address RQs 2 and 3, we generated 100 inspiring stories to support depression based on our findings and conducted a heuristic evaluation (using eight well-established heuristics from the healthcare domain and the field of HCI) of these stories with two clinicians (psychiatrists) with over three years of work experience in mental health. Each clinician was involved in the heuristics design; after approving it, they validated the generated stories, provided their ratings independently, and finally, their inter-rater agreement level was determined. For all analysis and extraction across this study, we utilized the open source GPT-OSS-120B LLM [26] via the Groq Application Programming Interface (API) [27], and we refer to it as *"the LLM"*.

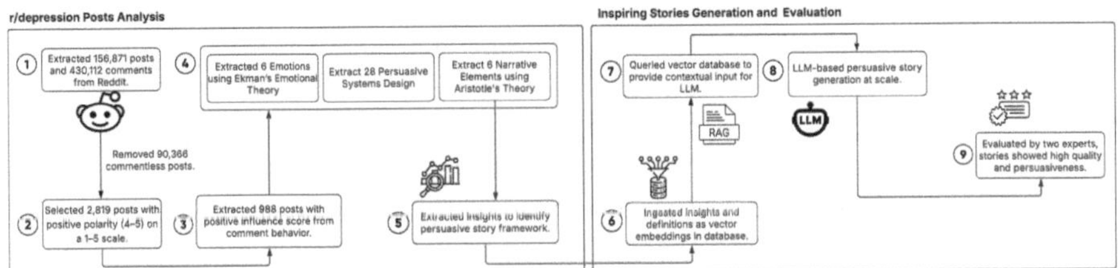

Fig. 1. Methodological stages.

3.1 R/Depression Posts Analysis

We extracted 156,871 posts and 430,112 comments spanning from September 2024 to September 2025, from the subcommunity using the arctic shift photon reddit downloader [28], which provided a streamlined access to depression post metadata. We then identified and retained 66,505 posts with atleast one comment, excluding the rest without comments (n = 90,366 posts). Next, we prompted the LLM to analyze the sentiments of each retained posts on a scale of 1 to 5, where 1 was extremely negative and 5 was extremely positive, conveying hope, relief, motivation, or inspiration to overcome depression. The LLM then generated a sentiment score and a reason for the score, which we reviewed to verify justification for the score. We identified 2,819 positive posts (with scores 4 or 5), 55,322 negative posts (with scores 1 or 2) and 3,863 neutral posts (with score of 3). Next, we analyzed the comments of the 2,819 posts by prompting the LLM to assess whether at least one comment found each post to be influential in a positive way towards behavioral change or self-efficacy in overcoming depression (we chose at least one comment as supporting even a single person suffering from depression is important). The output of the LLM included a score, either 0 or 1, with 0 implying that no comment found the post to be influential, and 1 meaning that at least one comment found the post to be influential, as well as a reason for the score which we reviewed to verify the justification for the score. This analysis revealed 988 posts with influential narrative or stories (with a score of 1), and 1,831 non-influential posts (with a score of 0). Finally, we leveraged the LLM to extract the narrative elements (plots, setting, conflict, theme, and characters), flow of the persuasive strategies (the order in which each strategy was introduced in the post), and emotional trajectories (anger, disgust, fear, happiness, sadness, and surprise) of the 988 influential posts. The output of the LLM included the narrative elements, persuasive strategies, and the emotional trajectories found in the posts, as well as the reasons for each extracted information, which we reviewed to verify the justification for the extracted information. We then conducted an inductive thematic analysis on the 988 posts to find and analyze recurring categories and patterns.

3.2 Inspiring Stories Generation and Evaluation

Based on our findings, we prepared a structured document that lists the top 30 recurring patterns (or categories) across the narrative elements (e.g., recovery stories for plot, present day for setting, self-worth crisis for conflict, community support for theme, and self-narrator for character), the top 30 trajectories of persuasive strategies (e.g., *social support → suggestions → recognition*), and the top 30 emotional trajectories (e.g., *sadness → fear → happiness*). Next, we indexed this document using an open-source vector database (Chroma [29]) for retrieval-augmented generation, and then generated 100 inspiring stories by prompting a RAG-based AI agent (leveraging the LLM) to automatically craft the stories based on the information extracted from the vector database. Finally, we conducted a heuristic evaluation with two clinicians (each with over 5 years of experience in the mental health domain) to assess the clinical and persuasive effectiveness of the 100 inspiring stories generated. The clinicians evaluated the stories using 8 well-established heuristics in the healthcare domain and the field of HCI [11]. As shown in Table 2, the 8 heuristics are organized into two categories: the first 4 heuristics assess clinical effectiveness of the stories, while the remaining 4 heuristics assess persuasiveness of the stories.

We provided an instruction document to each clinician that detailed the study, evaluation purpose, heuristics definition, and the steps for conducting the review. We also provided evaluation workbook containing three sheets. The first sheet outlined the overall evaluation procedure. The second sheet included the 100 generated inspiring stories in one column, eight different columns representing the rating for each heuristic, and one column for comments on each story. The last sheet was provided to enter overall feedback on the evaluation of the stories. The heuristics were rated on a 5-point ordinal scale (1 = lowest quality/not acceptable, 2 = weak/important problems present, 3 = acceptable but needs improvement, 4 = good/minor issues only, and 5 = excellent/meets the goal clearly) adapted from previous heuristic evaluation studies in HCI [30–34].

4   Results

4.1 Extraction of Narrative Elements

Across the 988 influential posts, we identified 285 recurring patterns (or categories) for Plot, 122 for Setting, 256 for Conflict, 306 for Theme, and 91 for Characters. The top 7 categories under the Plot narrative element were *recovery stories* (n = 238), *encouraging messages* (n = 227), *suicidal ideation* (n = 173), *therapy journeys* (n = 165), *self-compassion* (n = 134), *support requests* (n = 125), and *social isolation* (n = 86). The dominance of encouraging messages, recovery stories, and therapy journeys in the plot suggests a preference among readers for structured, hopeful narratives. The top 7 categories under Setting were *present-day* (n = 662), *home setting* (n = 433), *internal reflection* (n = 265), *online forum* (n = 248), *social media* (n = 172), *support group* (n =

Table 2. The heuristics used in the evaluation and the corresponding descriptions.

Heuristic	Description
Clinical Accuracy and Safety	The story should not: (i) include unsafe or misleading claims, (ii) discourage therapy or medication, (iii) give harmful advice.
Therapeutic Alignment	The story reflects known helpful methods such as cognitive reframing, behavioural activation, problem solving, or self-efficacy building.
Emotional Safety and Sensitivity	The story acknowledges distress without causing harm. It uses respectful, non-judgmental language.
Recovery Orientation and Help-Seeking	The story shows that improvement is possible and points toward safe help when needed. It avoids false promises.
Credibility and Trustworthiness	The story feels genuine and believable. It avoids exaggerated claims.
Emotional Engagement and Identification	The story holds attention and helps the reader identify with the narrator.
Self-Efficacy and Social Support Cues	The story increases the reader's sense that small steps are possible and shows support from others when relevant.
Actionability and Behavioural Trigger	The story suggests a safe, specific next step that a reader could try.

75), and *workplace setting* (n = 54). The top 7 categories under Conflict were *self-worth crisis* (n = 226), *existential crisis* (n = 167), *suicidal ideation* (n = 165), *anxiety* (n = 122), *hope vs despair* (n = 105), *self-efficacy* (n = 102), and *loneliness* (n = 95). These categories highlight the emotional hurdles that precede resolution, providing insights into the structure of pervasive recovery narratives. The top 7 Theme categories were *community support* (n = 249), *hope* (n = 216), *resilience* (n = 158), *self-efficacy* (n = 158), *self-care* (n = 142), *motivation* (n = 123), and *self-advocacy* (n = 96). The top 7 categories under Characters were: *self-narrator* (n = 809), *inner self* (n = 293), *patient* (n = 206), *support group* (n = 201), *personified depression* (n = 169), *young adults* (n = 145), and *trauma survivor* (n = 118). The high frequency of the self-narrator suggested that first-person storytelling is more likely to enhance relatability and persuasive impact. Taken together, these narrative elements form a persuasive and coherent arc that enhances emotional transportation.

4.2 Extraction of Persuasive Strategies

Among the 28 persuasive strategies from the PSD framework [24], eight (8) persuasive strategies were found within the posts or stories: *social support* (n = 915), *suggestions* (n = 659), *goal setting* (n = 406), *recognition* (n = 321), *praise* (n = 312), *and reminders* (n = 156). Social support offers emotional or practical assistance to someone in need, suggestions provided ideas or recommendations to help someone; Goal setting helps individuals establish objectives to work towards; Praise expresses approval or admiration for someone's actions or qualities; Reminders prompt individuals to remember important tasks or information; and Recognition acknowledges individuals' efforts or achievements in depression management. The top trajectories of persuasive strategies were *social support → suggestions* (n = 110), *suggestions → social support* (n = 42), *social support → recognition* (n = 32), *social support → suggestions → recognition* (n = 23), and *social support → goal setting* (n = 21). This indicates that stories combining multiple strategies (while offering emotional support alongside actionable advice) are more likely to enhance motivational and behaviour change impact.

4.3 Extraction of Emotional Trajectories

Across the 988 influential posts, our findings revealed 1675 occurrences of *sadness*, 1440 of *happiness*, 908 of *fear*, 367 of *surprise*, 341 of *anger*, and 242 of *disgust*. The top emotional trajectories were *sadness → happiness* (n = 67), *sadness → fear → happiness* (n = 37), *sadness → happiness → sadness → happiness* (n = 22), and *happiness → sadness → happiness* (n = 21).

4.4 Stories Generation and Evaluation

As shown in Table 3, the clinicians rated the 100 stories generated by our RAG-based agent highly across the eight heuristics.

Table 3. Mean ratings (%) across heuristics.

Heuristic Category	Clinician 1 (%)	Clinician 2 (%)	Mean (%)
Clinical Accuracy & Safety	99.4	80.0	89.7
Therapeutic Alignment	99.6	80.0	89.8
Emotional Safety & Sensitivity	99.8	100.0	99.9
Help & Recovery Orientation	92.4	80.0	86.2
Credibility & Trustworthiness	100.0	80.0	90.0
Emotional Engagement & Identification	99.8	80.0	89.9
Social & Self-Efficacy Influence	97.0	80.0	88.5
Behavioural Trigger / Call to Action	95.4	80.0	87.7

As shown in Table 4, we performed an inductive thematic analysis on the qualitative feedback (comments on each story) from the clinicians based on the procedure from Braun and Clarke [35].

Table 4. Thematic analysis of the clinical and persuasive effectiveness top themes.

Theme	Description	Clinicians' Quotes (CQ)
Emotional and therapeutic support	Potential to provide therapeutic support.	*"A compassionate, realistic recovery narrative that models emotional support."* [C1]
Behavioural adaptations	Potential to drive behavioural change.	*"Strong emphasis on gentle social support and small behavioural steps."* [C2]
Social support	Potential to drive social bonding with communities,	*"A safe and recovery-oriented narrative that models gradual community support."* [C1]

5 Discussion

This study examined what makes recovery stories inspiring and behaviour-changing in depression, how such stories can be computationally generated, and how clinicians evaluate them. By analyzing 988 influential narratives, we found that stories that use a clear first-person arc, emphasize self-worth struggles, therapy engagement, and community support, and combine persuasive strategies such as social support and actionable suggestions are more likely to motivate positive responses. These patterns align with evidence that narrative transportation, identification, and supportive framing enhance receptivity to mental-health interventions. Based on these findings, a RAG-based agent generated 100 stories that clinicians rated highly for clinical appropriateness and persuasive value, indicating that data-driven narrative structures can produce content that is emotionally supportive, safe, and clinically relevant. For clinicians, these results suggest that AI-generated recovery narratives could serve as a low-intensity complement to treatment by reinforcing therapeutic themes between sessions. For people experiencing depression, they highlight the motivational impact of relatable stories that acknowledge distress yet model small, credible steps toward improvement. For researchers, this work demonstrates how large-scale peer narratives can be transformed into operational design for generating supportive, explainable, and persuasive content.

5.1 Design Recommendations

Recommendation 1: Use first-person recovery arcs that acknowledge struggle and model small steps forward. The most influential stories used first-person voice and moved from distress toward realistic improvement, consistent with evidence that identification and recovery-oriented framing enhance openness to change [36]. This structure validates users' emotions while modelling achievable progress. Systems should therefore generate stories that begin with honest difficulty and end with hopeful action.

Recommendation 2: Combine persuasive strategies rather than using them in isolation. The strongest stories blended social support with suggestions, recognition, and goal setting, reflecting findings that layered strategies increase persuasive impact. In mental-health contexts, this combination makes guidance feel both empathetic and actionable [37]. Systems should structure persuasive elements as short sequences (support followed by practical advice) to mirror effective peer interactions.

Recommendation 3: Use emotional trajectories that start in negative affect and resolve toward relief. Effective stories frequently followed trajectories such as *sadness → happiness*, a pattern supported by research showing that emotional resolution strengthens engagement and empathy [38]. Acknowledging distress before shifting to stability avoids forced positivity while maintaining therapeutic safety. Systems should therefore model gentle upward emotional transitions aligning with real recovery experiences.

5.2 Limitations and Future Work

One limitation of this study is the absence of a user study involving people experiencing depression. However, clinical guidelines emphasize expert review as an essential first step for establishing therapeutic safety before exposing vulnerable users to novel interventions, making our clinician evaluation an appropriate and necessary foundation for this work [39]. As part of future work, we will develop an AI-driven persuasive technology that integrates our RAG-based AI agent to generate inspiring stories in real time. This technology will then be deployed and evaluated in real-world settings. Furthermore, given that persuasive AI for depression is a sensitive application domain, future work will address ethical concerns through explainability, diverse data sources, and clinical oversight.

6 Conclusion

This study showed how large-scale peer recovery narratives can inform the development of an AI-driven persuasive technology for depression management. By analyzing influential stories from r/depression, we identified the narrative structures, persuasive strategy combinations, and emotional trajectories that underpin impactful recovery communication. These insights enabled a RAG-based agent to generate clinically appropriate and persuasive stories, which clinicians rated highly for therapeutic safety and behavioural relevance. Overall, the findings demonstrate that AI-generated narratives can complement mental-health support by offering relatable, recovery-oriented stories grounded in real experiences and scalable for personalized use.

Acknowledgement. We acknowledge the support of the Natural Sciences and Engineering Research Council of Canada (NSERC) through the Discovery Grant.

References

1. Stratton, E., et al.: Deciding to disclose a mental health condition in male dominated workplaces; a focus-group study. Front. Psych. **9**, 422834 (2018)

2. Rojas-Andrade, R., et al.: Teachers as school mental health professionals and their daily practices. Sch. Ment. Heal. **16**(2), 566–576 (2024)
3. Depression., https://www.who.int/health-topics/depression/#tab=tab_1.
4. Mental health., https://www.who.int/health-topics/mental-health#tab=tab_1.
5. Naslund, J.A., et al.: The future of mental health care: peer-to-peer support and social media. Epidemiol. Psychiatr. Sci. **25**, 113–122 (2016)
6. Alexander, K.J., et al.: Young children's emotional attachments to stories. Soc. Dev. **10**, 374–398 (2001)
7. Barnetz, Z., et al.: From "patient" to "activist": treatment experiences, changing perceptions, and resistance of mental health survivors. J. Progress. Hum. Serv. **33**, 8–39 (2022)
8. Liu, D., et al.: Detecting and measuring depression on social media using a machine learning approach: systematic review. JMIR Mental Health. **9**, e27244 (2022)
9. Li, H., et al.: Systematic review and meta-analysis of AI-based conversational agents for promoting mental health and Well-being. npj Digital Med. **6**(1), 236 (2023)
10. Alam, L., Mueller, S.: Examining the effect of explanation on satisfaction and trust in AI diagnostic systems. BMC Med. Inform. Decis. Mak. **21**(1), 178 (2021)
11. Khowaja, K., Al-Thani, D.: New checklist for the heuristic evaluation of mHealth apps (HE4EH): development and usability study. JMIR Mhealth Uhealth. **8**, e20353 (2020)
12. McHugh, M.L.: Interrater reliability: the kappa statistic. Biochem Med (Zagreb). **22**, 276–282 (2012)
13. Kendellt, R.E.: Clinical validity*. Psychol. Med. **19**, 45–55 (1989)
14. Chiovitti, R.F., et al.: Rigour and grounded theory research. J. Adv. Nurs. **44**, 427–435 (2003)
15. Kumar, A., et al.: Anxious depression prediction in real-time social data. In: International Conference on Advances in Engineering Science Management & Technology (ICAESMT) - 2019, pp. 1–7. Uttaranchal University, Dehradun, India., Available at SSRN (2019)
16. Van Laer, T., et al.: The extended transportation-imagery model: a meta-analysis of the antecedents and consequences of consumers' narrative transportation. J. Consum. Res. **40**, 797–817 (2014)
17. Green, M.C., Brock, T.C.: The role of transportation in the persuasiveness of public narratives. J. Pers. Soc. Psychol. **79**, 701–721 (2000)
18. Aristotle's Poetics - Stephen Halliwell - Google Books: University of Chicago Press. 1–67 (1998).
19. Ferdinal et al.: Introduction to literary studies, Padang, 1–162 (2020).
20. Downing, S.J.: Learning the plot. Manag. Learn. **28**, 27–44 (1997)
21. An Integral Setting Tells More than When and Where on JSTOR: https://www.jstor.org/stable/20200766.
22. Kösen, M.G.: Emotions and Narratives: a Brief Literature Discussion, pp. 1–43. DAAD-TÜBİTAK Project, İstanbul Bilgi University, European Institute (2024)
23. Rennick-Egglestone, S., et al.: The impact of mental health recovery narratives on recipients experiencing mental health problems: qualitative analysis and change model. PLoS One. **14**, e0226201 (2019)
24. Oinas-Kukkonen, H., et al.: Persuasive systems design: key issues, process model, and system features. Commun. Assoc. Inf. Syst., 1–16 (2009)
25. Shiota, M.N.: Theory of Basic Emotions. The SAGE Encyclopedia of Theory in Psychology. 249–250 (2016).
26. Kumar, D., et al.: GPT-OSS-20B: A Comprehensive Deployment-Centric Analysis of OpenAI's Open-Weight Mixture of Experts Model. arXiv:2508.16700. (2025)
27. Groq is fast: low-cost inference., https://groq.com/.
28. Arctic Shift.: https://arctic-shift.photon-reddit.com/.
29. Chroma.: https://www.trychroma.com/.

30. Langevin, R., et al.: Heuristic evaluation of conversational agents. In: Proceedings of the 2021 CHI Conference on Human Factors in Computing Systems, pp. 1–15, ACM, Yokohama, Japan (2021)
31. Leamy, M., Bird, V., Le Boutillier, C., Williams, J., Slade, M.: Conceptual framework for personal recovery in mental health: systematic review and narrative synthesis. Br. J. Psychiatry. **199**(6), 445-452 (2011). https://doi.org/10.1192/bjp.bp.110.083733. PMID: 22130746
32. Corrigan, P. W., Giffort, D., Rashid, F., Leary, M., Okeke, I.: Recovery as a psychological construct. Community Ment. Health. J. **35**(3), 231-239 (1999). https://doi.org/10.1023/a:101 8741302682. PMID: 10401893
33. Baumel, A, Faber, K,. Mathur, N., Kane, J. M.: Muench F enlight: a comprehensive quality and therapeutic potential evaluation tool for mobile and web-based eHealth interventions, J. Med. Internet Res. **19**(3), e82 (2017). https://doi.org/10.2196/jmir.7270. PMID: 28325712, PMCID: 5380814
34. Baumel, A., Muench, F.: Heuristic evaluation of Ehealth interventions: establishing standards that relate to the therapeutic process perspective. JMIR Ment. Health, **3**(1), e5 (2016). https://doi.org/10.2196/mental.4563. PMID: 26764209, PMCID: 4730107
35. Willig, C., Stainton Rogers, W.: The SAGE Handbook of Qualitative Research in Psychology, 2nd edn. SAGE Publications Ltd, London (2017)
36. Ng, F., et al.: The mechanisms and processes of connection: developing a causal chain model capturing impacts of receiving recorded mental health recovery narratives. BMC Psychiatry. **19**, 413 (2019)
37. Mutter, A., et al.: Persuasive design principle of social support in digital interventions targeting mental health symptoms: a systematic review and meta-analysis. BMJ Open. **14**, e086728 (2024)
38. Nabi, R.L., et al.: The role of a narrative's emotional flow in promoting persuasive outcomes. Media Psychol. **18**, 137–162 (2015)
39. Cho, H., et al.: Assessing the usability of a clinical decision support system: heuristic evaluation. JMIR Hum. Factors. **9**, e31758 (2022)

Developing a Persuasive Nutrition App Based on the Australian Dietary Guidelines

Joohyun Lee(✉) ⓘ, Elizabeth Neale ⓘ, and Khin Than Win ⓘ

University of Wollongong, Wollongong, NSW, Australia
`jr1970@uowmail.edu.au`

Abstract. This study presents the design and development of a credible, evidence-based nutrition tracking system grounded in the Design Science Research (DSR) and Persuasive Systems Design (PSD) frameworks. Drawing on insights from large-scale user reviews and established nutrition science, the research integrates Australia's official dietary standards, the Australian Dietary Guidelines (ADG), Nutrient Reference Values (NRV), and the national food composition database to enhance feedback interpretability, behavioural guidance, and potential clinical credibility. The system architecture combines voice-enabled meal logging, semantic food matching, and ADG/NRV-aligned analytics to provide persuasive, guideline-driven feedback while minimising logging effort. The study contributes a replicable methodological approach for translating evidence-based nutrition frameworks and persuasive systems design into practical, user-centred mHealth applications.

Keywords: Human–Computer Interaction · Dietary Monitoring System · mHealth · Persuasive Technology · Design Science Research

1 Introduction

With the technology advancements and the global adoption of mobile technologies, diet-tracking applications have become widely used tools to support healthier eating habits. However, most dietary apps still face high user attrition, limited interpretability of feedback, and poor alignment with dietary standards [1–4]. Existing applications typically emphasize calorie counting and macronutrient tracking while neglecting usability, evidence-based design, and verified nutritional data [3].

Recent research in mobile health (mHealth) has demonstrated that applying Design Science Research (DSR) and Persuasive Systems Design (PSD) frameworks can provide a structured, theory-driven pathway for developing persuasive, evidence-based interventions. Studies such as Guracho et al. (2025) on mobile mental health interventions and Chumkasian et al. (2024) on the Eye Donor Aust application have shown that DSR enables the systematic translation of theoretical principles into effective, credible mHealth artifacts [5–7]. Their work demonstrates how persuasive design mechanisms such as primary task support, dialogue support, and credibility support, can meaningfully

K. Sumi et al. (Eds.): PERSUASIVE 2026, LNCS 16476, pp. 133–147, 2026.
https://doi.org/10.1007/978-3-032-19687-3_11

improve engagement and trust across different health domains [8]. Building on these theoretical advances, this study grounds its design in Australia's evidence-based nutrition guidelines, the Australian Dietary Guidelines (ADG) and Nutrient Reference Values (NRV) and a food composition database the Australian Food and Nutrient Database (AUSNUT) [9–11].

The ADG provides population-level recommendations regarding consumption of foods, food groups, and dietary patterns to promote health and reduce risk of chronic disease, which are expressed as food-group serves in the food selection guide the Australian Guide to Healthy Eating [12]. In comparison, the NRVs define daily nutrient intakes required for health maintenance and disease prevention. AUSNUT serves as the data backbone linking foods consumed to their nutrient profiles, enabling translation between food serves and nutrient adequacy [9, 10]. The series of databases are government-maintained food composition databases that provide a comprehensive breakdown of both macro and micronutrients for Australian foods. Developed and updated by Food Standards Australia New Zealand (FSANZ), databases are based on nationally representative dietary survey data. It allows evidence-based analysis of nutrients to move beyond simple calorie tracking toward a clinically relevant understanding of nutrient balance and adequacy. At the time of app development, the most recent AUSNUT database was AUSNUT 2011–13 [11].

Prior evidence-based nutrition-app and commercial platforms have typically focused only on ADG-based serves, overlooking nutrient-level insight and thereby limiting clinical interpretability [2, 13]. By combining comparison to ADGs and NRVs (informed by AUSNUT 2011–13) within a persuasive, evidence-driven framework, this study advances a more credible and interpretable model of dietary feedback, one that bridges behavioural guidance with scientific accuracy and addresses the theoretical and practical gaps identified in previous systems [9, 10].

Thus, this paper provides a framework for utilising DSR in the conceptual design of developing mHealth applications.

2 Research Framework – Design Science Research

Accordingly, this research addresses the overarching goal of designing and developing a credible nutrition system informed by real-world user insights and grounded in evidence-based dietary frameworks. To address these gaps and limitations, this study integrates the PSD model as a theoretical lens for enhancing motivation, credibility, and user adherence in behaviour change systems. Complementing this, Design Science Research (DSR) is adopted as the methodological framework to ensure a rigorous and iterative development process encompassing the relevance, rigor, and design cycles [7, 14]. DSR provides a structured approach for developing and evaluating innovative artifacts that address real-world problems while contributing to theoretical knowledge [7, 14]. This research has been approved by the university with approval 2025/291.

In the context of this research, the artifact, a voice-enabled, evidence-based diet-tracking app, serves as a design instantiation that links user needs, persuasive system theory, and nutrition informatics.

According to Hevner's model, DSR operates through three interrelated cycles: relevance, rigor, and design cycles. The relevance cycle connects the research to the problem environment, ensuring that the developed artifact addresses genuine user and stakeholder needs [7, 14]. In this study, the relevance cycle was informed by the analysis of commercial diet-tracking app user reviews [2]. which identified key design challenges such as high logging effort, lack of credible feedback, and poor adherence Fig. 1.

DSR Cycle (Hevner)

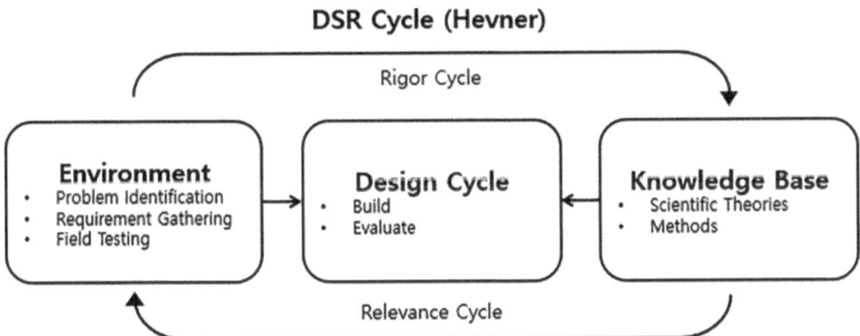

Fig. 1. Design Science Research Cycle by Hevner.

The rigor cycle links the study to the existing body of scientific knowledge by, drawing from established theories, models, and technical methods. Here, the Persuasive Systems Design (PSD) model forms the primary theoretical foundation for embedding persuasive features that enhance motivation, credibility, and engagement. In addition, nutrition science resources such as the ADG and NRV provide evidence-based standards for generating clinically interpretable dietary feedback [8–10]. The rigor cycle also encompasses the technical foundations used to implement the artifact, including speech recognition, natural language processing (NLP), and embedding-based food retrieval [2, 6, 7].

The design cycle represents the iterative process of building and evaluating the artifact. The app design requirements are identified through ongoing consultations with stakeholders including, medical scientists, dietitian, health informatician, and consumers group. Within this study, the design cycle involved integrating stakeholders and theoretical requirements into a working prototype that combines voice-enabled meal logging, AUSNUT 2011–13-based food data retrieval, and ADG/NRV-aligned feedback. Evaluation at this stage was ex-ante and analytical, focusing on theoretical alignment expert and clinical heuristic reviews, and technical verification of speech/NLP and nutrition-mapping pipelines.

3 Relevance Cycle: Problem Context and Requirements Derivation

The relevance cycle establishes the connection between the problem environment and the research activities, ensuring that the developed artifact directly addresses real-world needs and stakeholder expectations [14]. In this study, the environment is defined by the rapidly expanding ecosystem of commercial diet-tracking applications and their role in promoting healthier eating behaviours through mobile technology [3, 15]. Despite their popularity, most existing tools suffer from high user attrition, limited data credibility, and weak integration with evidence-based dietary frameworks such as the ADG and NRV [9, 10]. Consequently, users frequently encounter usability challenges, inconsistent data, and unclear feedback, which collectively undermine trust and the behavioural intent of these systems [16–18].

3.1 Problem Identification

Prior research on diet-tracking apps consistently reports three persistent problem dimensions. Review-based analyses indicate that high logging effort, fragmented workflows, and search friction are major barriers to sustained use [3], a pattern mirrored in engineering studies that translate user comments into evolving requirements [1]. Commercial apps frequently surface inconsistent or unverifiable entries, limiting confidence and interpretability against national standards [2]. Furthermore, features tend to emphasise calorie counting with limited persuasive or adaptive support, contributing to attrition over time [2, 16, 17]. Collectively, findings across recent nutrition-app studies converge on usability, credibility, and motivation as the key design challenges to be addressed through a PSD model framework [2]. These gaps motivate a design response that couple's friction-reducing capture, evidence-aligned feedback, and persuasive mechanisms [2, 8]

3.2 Empirical Investigation and Stakeholder Perspectives

Building upon the gaps identified in prior literature [1, 3] and the need for a more evidence-driven approach to nutrition app design, as part of this current research, an empirical analysis was conducted on approximately 99,000 user reviews from two leading commercial diet-tracking applications, MyFitnessPal and Lose It! [2]. The purpose of this investigation was to transform large-scale user feedback into actionable design knowledge that could address the usability, credibility, and motivational issues consistently reported across previous studies. Through topic modelling and sentiment analysis, the review data revealed distinct clusters of user experiences that informed the formulation of design requirements in the next stage of development. Topic modelling was conducted using K-Means clustering, while sentiment polarity was computed using roBERTa-based model. Reviews were pre-processed through tokenisation, lemmatisation, and stop-word removal. This ensured reproducibility and methodological transparency."

The first major finding related to usability burden, as clusters such as *"logging effort,"* *"search frustration,"* and *"time-consuming process"* were strongly associated with negative sentiment. Users consistently described manual logging as tedious and cognitively demanding, suggesting that simplified or automated input mechanisms are essential for maintaining long-term engagement [2]. This challenge was particularly evident among casual users and individuals with limited digital or health literacy, reinforcing the need for features that reduce cognitive load and streamline task flow [2].

The second theme concerned credibility and accuracy. Many reviews expressed frustration with missing Australian food items, unverified nutrient data, and inconsistencies across databases [2]. These findings underscored the necessity of integrating authoritative data sources such as AUSNUT 2011–2013 [11] and aligning feedback mechanisms with evidence-based frameworks including the ADG [9] and the NRV [10]. By grounding feedback in these standards, nutritional outputs could become not only more accurate but also clinically interpretable and trustworthy [18].

A third pattern reflected a motivational deficit in existing applications. Most commercial systems focused narrowly on calorie counting, offering limited adaptive or persuasive support to sustain user engagement. In contrast, positive sentiment clustered around features such as progress visualisation, reminders, and encouraging feedback, highlighting the behavioural importance of personalisation and persuasive reinforcement [16, 17]. Users appeared to respond more favourably to systems that acknowledged progress and provided motivational cues tailored to their goals.

These empirical findings validated and extended the trends identified in prior research, while revealing nuanced expectations from three stakeholder groups. End users emphasised the importance of ease of logging and data credibility, health professionals required clinically interpretable and standardised nutritional outputs, and researchers prioritised transparency and evidence-based data pipelines for reproducibility and scientific reliability [1]. By capturing the intersection of these perspectives, the analysis provided a grounded understanding of both user experience and professional needs within the diet-tracking context.

3.3 Deriving the Design Requirements Catalogue (DRC)

From the empirical investigation that was structured through the PSD model [8],a Design Requirements Catalogue was formulated to capture user-centred and evidence-based requirements for artifact development. Each requirement reflects a critical user need validated through the review analysis and is mapped to corresponding PSD categories and design principles that will inform later implementation.

These requirements translate real-world user experiences into structured design knowledge, establishing a direct link between empirical evidence, persuasive design theory, and nutritional science [14]. By aligning validated user needs with PSD principles and ADG/NRV frameworks, the DRC ensures that the resulting artifact is contextually relevant, clinically credible, and behaviourally persuasive, fulfilling the central objective of the DSR relevance cycle [7–10].

4 Rigor Cycle: Theoretical and Knowledge Foundations

The rigor cycle connects the design process to established scientific knowledge, ensuring that the developed artifact is both theoretically grounded and methodologically sound [7, 14]. In this study, the rigor cycle integrates conceptual models from persuasive technology, evidence-based dietary frameworks, and advanced natural language processing (NLP) to inform artifact construction and design decisions [2, 19]. Together, these foundations ensure that the system design reflects both behavioural and technical validity.

Table 1. Design Requirements derived from Empirical Evidence to be Mapped to PSD Strategies

Code	Requirement Description	Empirical Evidence [2]	Design Features
R1	Enable low-effort and intuitive meal logging through voice input and semantic search to reduce cognitive load.	Negative sentiment clusters on logging effort, search frustration, and time-consuming process.	Simplified input and automation to reduce effort.
R2	Integrate verified AUSNUT data and generate feedback aligned with ADG/NRV standards.	Complaints about inaccurate or outdated nutrient information and missing local foods.	Use of verified data and evidence-based standards.
R3	Provide adaptive, positive feedback linked to dietary progress and nutrient balance.	Limited persuasive/adaptive features; positive reviews favoured progress tracking and social support.	Adaptive, motivational, and personalised feedback.
R4	Ensure transparency of data provenance and user control over entries (edit/undo).	Frustration with database errors and lack of editability.	Transparent data and reversible user actions.
R5	Protect privacy and data security to maintain trust and clinical applicability.	Concerns about data sharing and commercial bias in reviews.	Clear privacy, consent, and data security practices.

4.1 Theoretical Foundations: Persuasive Systems Design Model

The PSD model provides the central theoretical framework for embedding persuasive elements into the artifact. The model outlines four primary categories, Primary Task, Dialogue, Credibility, and Social Support — that define the design strategies to influence user motivation and adherence. Within this study, the PSD model serves two key purposes:

To guide the translation of user needs and sentiment-based insights into persuasive design requirements [16, 17].

To structure the logic of the user interface and feedback mechanisms.

Specifically, Primary Task Support informed the integration of friction-reducing features such as voice-based meal logging and semantic food search, addressing the usability burden identified in the relevance cycle [2]. Dialogue Support guided the inclusion of adaptive, encouraging feedback, while System Credibility Support underpinned the incorporation of verified nutrient data and transparent data provenance [18]. Together, these align with persuasive strategies of reduction, suggestion, trustworthiness, and personalization, all contributing to enhanced motivation, engagement, and trust [8, 16].

4.2 Evidence-Based Foundations: Nutrition Informatics

Beyond behavioural persuasion, the rigor cycle draws upon nutrition informatics and dietary science to ensure that the app's outputs are clinically interpretable. The system's nutrient feedback framework is grounded in two authoritative Australian standards:

1. The ADG, provide recommendations for food and food group consumption [9] expressed as food group serves in the food selection guide the Australian Guide to Healthy Eating [12].
2. The NRV, which define population-level nutrient intake recommendations [10]

By aligning user feedback with these standards, the app provides interpretable, evidence-based feedback rather than abstract calorie counts. This alignment directly responds to the credibility and interpretability issues highlighted in user reviews [2, 18]. Furthermore, the use of the AUSNUT 2011–2013 food composition database ensures data accuracy, local relevance, and transparency [11], key components of System Credibility Support in the PSD model [8].

4.3 Technical Foundations: Speech and NLP Pipeline

The rigor cycle also includes the technical rigor required to operationalise persuasive and nutritional theories. The artifact integrates Automatic Speech Recognition (ASR) and NLP to reduce the cognitive load of manual entry [19]. The ASR component leverages a speech-to-text pipeline using Google Speech Recognition, while the NLP module employs a Named Entity Recognition (NER) model for food item extraction and embedding-based retrieval for semantically matching food entities with AUSNUT 2011–13 records [20, 21].

To operationalise the persuasive and nutritional theories within the rigor cycle, the artifact implements an ASR to NLP pipeline tailored to food logging. Automatic Speech Recognition is handled by a speech-to-text service - Google Speech Recognition to obtain a verbatim transcript of the user's utterance. On this transcript, a custom food domain NER model spaCy v3 identifies four target entity types [22]:

- FOOD_ITEM: e.g., "grilled chicken", "Greek yogurt", "flat white"
- F_QUANTITY: "one", "two", "half", numeric tokens ("1.5")
- SERVING: container or unit terms ("cup", "slice", "tablespoon", "packet")
- MEAL_TYPE: "breakfast", "lunch", "dinner", "snack"

The NER output feeds a hybrid retrieval layer that combines semantic matching via Sentence-Transformers and cosine similarity to rank candidate AUSNUT 2011–13 records and fuzzy string matching using RapidFuzz to stabilise matches when user phrasing is informal or noisy. The retrieval stage returns the most probable AUSNUT 2011–13Food Survey ID and Measure ID, which are then used to compute macro and micro-nutrient totals from the official composition fields. This end-to-end design reduces cognitive load of voice input, preserves interpretability for explicit entities and measures, and anchors outputs in AUSNUT's verified nutrient tables, enabling clinically relevant feedback rather than calorie-only summaries.

This integration enables intuitive, hands-free logging and ensures that user-generated inputs are accurately mapped to verified food records, supporting both usability and credibility [18]. Each pipeline component was validated through technical verification tests, ensuring acceptable precision, recall, and mapping accuracy [23]. These processes represent the rigor of the technical design, connecting computational methods to nutrition informatics principles [7, 23].

Collectively, these theoretical, evidential, and technical foundations represent the knowledge base from which the artifact's design principles and utility hypotheses were derived [7, 8]. Table 1 maps each design principle to its corresponding PSD construct, empirical evidence, and nutritional standard, forming a traceable framework that links behavioural theory, empirical need, and technical implementation.

By situating the design within this established body of knowledge, the rigor cycle ensures that the artifact is not merely a prototype, but a scientifically grounded, theory-informed persuasive system [7]. This foundation enables systematic evaluation in subsequent DSR stages and supports the contribution of this work to both Persuasive Technology theory and evidence-based nutrition informatics.

5 Design Cycle: Artifact Development and Analytical Evaluation

The design cycle operationalises the knowledge gathered from the relevance and rigor cycles through the iterative construction and evaluation of the artifact [7, 14]. In this study, the design cycle focuses on translating theoretical foundations of the PSD model, evidence-based nutrition frameworks, and NLP-driven automation into a functional, theory-aligned prototype [8, 11]. This stage encompasses two major activities: artifact design and instantiation, and ex-ante analytical evaluation [23].

5.1 Artifact Design and Instantiation

Before empirical user testing, a structured ex-ante analytical evaluation was conducted to assess the artifact's compliance with the PSD model and theoretical coherence with behaviour change and nutrition informatics standards [8, 11].

The PSD Compliance Matrix assessed how well each design element operationalised persuasive design principles. Each implemented feature was evaluated across the four PSD domains: Primary Task, Dialogue, Social, and Credibility Support and subsequent mHealth adaptation studies [16, 17] Table 2.

Transparency, reversibility, privacy, and security are not explicitly defined strategies in the original Persuasive Systems Design (PSD) model (Oinas-Kukkonen & Harjumaa, 2009). In this study, these constructs are treated as complementary credibility-supporting mechanisms that operationalise core PSD principles such as trustworthiness, authority, and verifiability, consistent with prior mHealth adaptations of PSD. The matrix demonstrated that, all critical persuasive dimensions were successfully embedded, with strength in task reduction, adaptive dialogue, and credibility assurance [8, 16]. These alignments verified theoretical fidelity between empirical insights and design realisation [7]

Table 2. PSD Compliance Matrix

Code	Design Feature Direction	Compliance Evidence / Theoretical Link	PSD Category	Design Principle
R1	Simplified input and automation to reduce effort.	Voice and semantic logging reduce cognitive load and support self-tracking.	Primary Task	Reduction, Self-monitoring
R2	Use of verified data and evidence-based standards.	AUSNUT and ADG/NRV integration enhance feedback credibility.	System Credibility	Authority, Trustworthiness
R3	Adaptive, motivational, and personalised feedback.	Context-aware prompts sustain engagement and motivation.	Dialogue	Suggestion, Praise, Personalisation
R4	Transparent data and reversible user actions.	Visible data provenance and edit options build user trust.	System Credibility	Transparency*, Reversibility*
R5	Clear privacy, consent, and data security practices.	Secure storage and consent controls ensure ethical compliance.	System Credibility	Privacy*, Security*

5.2   Analytical Evaluation Criteria

The analytical evaluation followed Sonnenberg & vom Brocke's (2012) evaluation logic, focusing on:

Theoretical Alignment: The extent to which design elements reflect PSD and public health frameworks.

Design Integrity: Consistency between R1–R5 and implemented functionalities

Construct Validity: Whether implemented features accurately instantiate the intended persuasive mechanisms.

Feasibility and Usability Heuristics: Expert walkthroughs to ensure the artifact remains usable and intuitive prior to empirical testing.

Preliminary results confirmed strong alignment between theoretical intentions and functional realization, providing confidence that subsequent ex-post evaluations such as Cognitive Walkthroughs will validate behavioural effectiveness and user experience robustness [24, 25].

This Design Cycle completes the DSR framework by translating the relevance cycle's empirical user needs into functional modules, and the rigor cycle's theoretical models and evidence bases such as PSD, ADG, and NRV, into technical and behavioural logic [7].

5.3 Artifact Architecture and Functional Components

The developed artifact is a voice enabled persuasive nutrition tracking application designed to address the three empirically derived problem domains: usability burden, data credibility, and motivational deficit. Guided by Hevner's DSR principles, the artifact's design ensures iterative synthesis between theoretical constructs and practical implementation, thereby maintaining traceability across the relevance, rigor, design cycle.

The core architectural components:

Meal Logging Module: Integrates voice recognition and semantic search to reduce cognitive effort (R1).

Nutrition Intelligence Engine: Links the AUSNUT 2011–13 food database to the ADG and NRV for context-aware nutrient feedback (R2).

Feedback and Motivation System: Provides adaptive, personalised feedback loops informed by progress tracking and nutrient balance (R3).

Transparency and Control Functions: Allow users to edit, undo, and review entries (R4).

Privacy and Security Layer: Implements robust data encryption, local storage options, and clear privacy disclosures (R5).

The architecture ensures modular traceability between requirements, PSD constructs, and implemented features, represented through a Traceability Matrix (Table 1). This matrix allows clear mapping between user needs, persuasive principles, and system components, reinforcing theoretical transparency and design accountability.

5.4 Conflicts and Difficulties in the Development Process

The derived design requirements (R1–R5) provided a clear conceptual framework that guided the overall system architecture and module design.

The primary development challenge emerged in the implementation of the voice-enabled meal logging module (R1), which integrates ASR, NLP, and database retrieval into a single interaction flow.

This module, highlighted in Fig. 2 as the Voice Log and ASR/NER pipeline, introduced complexity due to the need to coordinate multiple AI components, including open-source language models and a custom-trained food-domain NER model.

As illustrated in Fig. 2, most system components, such as the nutrition analysis engine (R2), feedback and visualisation modules (R3), and privacy and control functions (R4–R5) which were implemented without major technical conflict, as they relied on well-established data pipelines and interface patterns. A key difficulty arose from the variability and ambiguity of spoken food descriptions, which often include informal food names, brand references, quantities, and serving expressions. Accurately identifying food items,

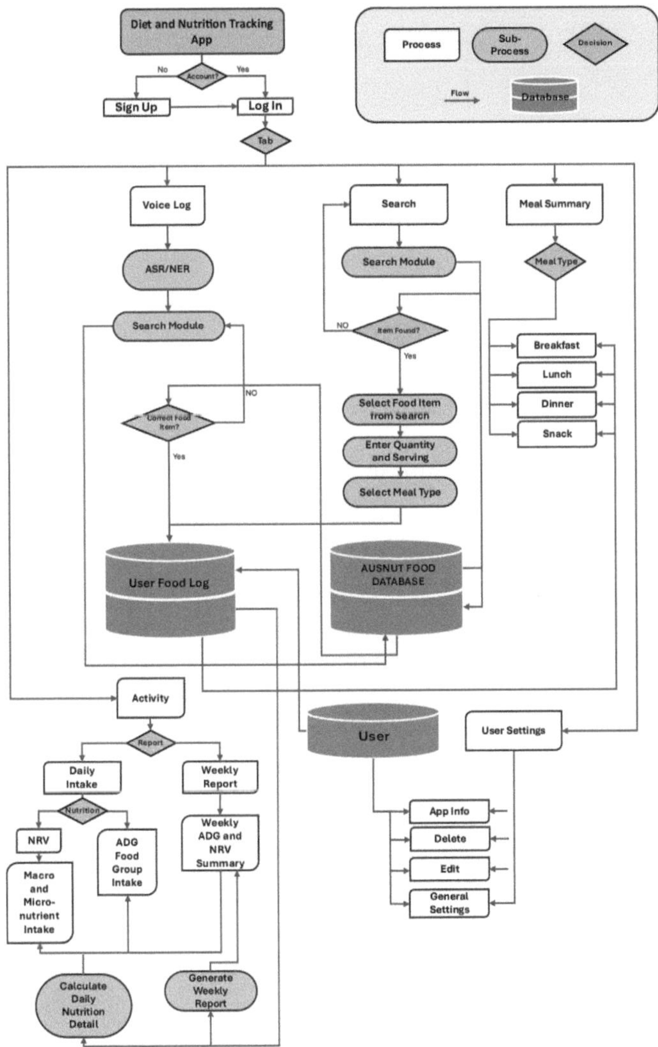

Fig. 2. System-augmented data flow diagram

quantities, and serving units while maintaining low user effort created tension between usability objectives (task reduction) and data accuracy requirements. To resolve this conflict, a hybrid embedding-based retrieval approach was adopted, transforming extracted entities into vector representations and matching them against AUSNUT records using semantic similarity rather than exact string matching Fig. 3.

Fig. 3. Screenshot of Application Design

6   Design Evaluation and Theoretical Implications

This stage of the Design Science Research process evaluates the artifact's theoretical coherence, persuasive functionality, and design integrity, connecting the analytical results to their broader theoretical implications for persuasive technology and nutrition informatics [7, 8, 23]. Evaluation in this phase remains ex-ante and analytical, focusing on conceptual alignment, construct validity, and design fidelity rather than empirical outcomes [26]. The goal is to confirm that the system, as built, effectively embodies persuasive principles, evidence-based nutritional logic, and user-centred design requirements [11]

6.1 Evaluation Outcomes: Theoretical Coherence and Design Integrity

The evaluation outcomes reported in this section reflect an ex-ante analytical assessment of the finalised application, rather than empirical user testing or completed cognitive walkthroughs. The PSD Compliance Matrix and Traceability Matrix were used as theoretical inspection instruments to examine the coherence between empirically derived user needs, Persuasive Systems Design constructs, and implemented system features [8, 23]. This analytical alignment demonstrates that design decisions were systematically grounded in established persuasive principles prior to empirical evaluation.

Primary Task Support was analytically assessed through inspection of the voice-based logging and semantic food search modules, which instantiate the PSD principle of Reduction and directly address the empirically identified usability burden [2].

Dialogue Support was examined through the structure of adaptive feedback and progress visualisation mechanisms, which align with Suggestion, Praise, and Personalisation principles intended to enhance motivation and engagement [16, 17].

System Credibility Support was evaluated through design-level inspection of the nutrition analysis pipeline, including the integration of AUSNUT 2011–13 data and comparison against ADG and NRV standards. These design elements operationalise Authority and Trustworthiness principles, while privacy-preserving data handling and user control mechanisms conceptually support credibility expectations relevant to mHealth systems [18].

Social Support elements, although planned for future iterations, were conceptually integrated into the design framework, aligning with Social Facilitation and Recognition mechanisms commonly applied in persuasive health interventions.

Overall, this analytical evaluation confirms construct fidelity at the design level, indicating that each implemented component is theoretically consistent with its intended persuasive function. These findings provide a justified foundation for subsequent ex-post empirical evaluations, including expert-led cognitive walkthroughs and user-centred usability testing, which will be required to assess behavioural effectiveness and experiential robustness [23].

7 Conclusion

This study demonstrates how applying DSR methodology and PSD principles can guide the creation of a credible and interpretable nutrition tracking system that bridges behavioural theory, clinical evidence, and technological innovation [8, 14, 16]. By integrating verified nutritional data from AUSNUT 2011–13 with Australia's evidence-based dietary frameworks of the ADG and NRV, the artifact delivers feedback that is both scientifically accurate and behaviourally actionable. This dual-layered design transforms raw nutrient information into persuasive, guideline-aligned insights that can improve user trust and motivation, addressing the long-standing gap between consumer diet apps and clinically credible dietary tools [3, 15].

Beyond the artifact, the study provides a methodological blueprint for applying DSR to mHealth system design, showing how empirical user insights and theoretical models can be systematically translated into verifiable, persuasive features [2, 14]. Together, this work advances the understanding of how persuasive design mechanisms and nutrition informatics can be integrated to produce health technologies that are usable, credible, and evidence-driven, providing a replicable model for future research and clinical applications [8, 11]

References

1. Carreño, L.V.G., Winbladh, K.: Analysis of user comments: an approach for software requirements evolution. In: Proceedings of the 2013 International Conference on Software Engineering, pp. 582–591. IEEE Press, San Francisco, CA, USA (2013)
2. Lee, J., Guan, V., Win, K.T.: Analysing user feedback on commercial diet tracking app. In: Win, K.T., Ali, R., Karapanos, E., Papadopoulos, G.A., Oyibo, K., Vlahu-Gjorgievska, E. (eds.) Persuasive Technology, pp. 18–31. Springer Nature Switzerland, Cham (2025)
3. Zečević, M., Mijatović, D., Kos Koklič, M., Žabkar, V., Gidaković, P.: User perspectives of diet-tracking apps: reviews content analysis and topic modeling. J. Med. Internet Res. **23**(4), e25160 (2021). https://doi.org/10.2196/25160
4. Hyzy, M., Bond, R., Mulvenna, M., Bai, L., Dix, A., Leigh, S., et al.: System usability scale benchmarking for digital health apps: meta-analysis. JMIR Mhealth Uhealth. **10**(8), e37290 (2022). https://doi.org/10.2196/37290
5. Chumkasian, W., Win, K.T., Vlahu-Gjorgievska, E., Freeman, M., Fernandez, R., Green, H., et al.: Design and development of mHealth app: eye donor Aust. Persuasive technology. In: 19th International Conference, PERSUASIVE 2024, Wollongong, NSW, Australia, April 10–12, 2024, Proceedings, pp. 75–88. Springer, Wollongong, NSW, Australia (2024)
6. Guracho, Y.D., Thomas, S.J., Ammutairi, N., Win, K.T.: Design and development of a mobile mental health application for individuals with depression and anxiety: design science research methods. Behav. Inform. Technol., 1–16 (2024). https://doi.org/10.1080/0144929X.2025.248 1639
7. vom Brocke, J., Hevner, A., Maedche, A.: Introduction to design science research. In: vom Brocke, J., Hevner, A., Maedche, A. (eds.) Design Science Research Cases, pp. 1–13. Springer International Publishing, Cham (2020)
8. Oinas-Kukkonen, H., Harjumaa, M.: Persuasive systems design: key issues, process model, and system features. Commun. Assoc. Inf. Syst., 24 (2009). https://doi.org/10.17705/1CAIS. 02428
9. National Health and Medical Research Council (NHMRC): Australian Dietary Guidelines. In: Care AGDoHaA, editor. Canberra: National Health and Medical Research Council; (2013)
10. National Health and Medical Research Council and New Zealand Ministry of Health: Nutrient Reference Values for Australia and New Zealand Including Recommended Dietary Intakes. Updated 2017 ed. Canberra: National Health and Medical Research Council (2006)
11. Food Standards Australia New Zealand: AUSNUT 2011–2013 – Australian Food Composition Database. In: (FSANZ) FSANZ, editor. (2019)
12. National Health and Medical Research Council (NHMRC): Australian Guide to Healthy Eating. National Health and Medical Research Council, Canberra; (2013)
13. Guan, V., Zhou, C., Wan, H., Zhou, R., Zhang, D., Zhang, S., et al.: A novel Mobile app for personalized dietary advice leveraging persuasive technology, computer vision, and cloud computing: development and usability study. JMIR Form Res. **7**, e46839 (2023). https://doi. org/10.2196/46839
14. Hevner, A.: A three cycle view of design science research. Scand. J. Inf. Syst. **19** (2007)
15. Scarry, A., Rice, J., O'Connor, E.M., Tierney, A.C.: Usage of Mobile applications or Mobile health technology to improve diet quality in adults. Nutrients. **14**(12) (2022). https://doi.org/ 10.3390/nu14122437

16. Dennison, L., Morrison, L., Conway, G., Yardley, L.: Opportunities and challenges for smartphone applications in supporting health behavior change: qualitative study. J. Med. Internet Res. **15**(4), e86 (2013). https://doi.org/10.2196/jmir.2583

17. Kwon, J.-Y., Lee, J.-S., Park, T.-S.: Analysis of strategies to increase user retention of fitness Mobile apps during and after the COVID-19 pandemic. Int. J. Environ. Res. Public Health. **19**, 10814 (2022). https://doi.org/10.3390/ijerph191710814

18. Lin, A.W., Morgan, N., Ward, D., Tangney, C., Alshurafa, N., Van Horn, L., et al.: Comparative validity of mostly unprocessed and minimally processed food items differs among popular commercial nutrition apps compared with a research food database. J. Acad. Nutr. Diet. **122**(4), 825–32.e1 (2022). https://doi.org/10.1016/j.jand.2021.10.015

19. Medhat, W., Hassan, A., Korashy, H.: Sentiment analysis algorithms and applications: a survey. Ain Shams Eng. J. **5**(4), 1093–1113 (2014). https://doi.org/10.1016/j.asej.2014.04.011

20. He, Q., Veldkamp, B.P., Glas, C.A., de Vries, T.: Automated assessment of patients' self-narratives for posttraumatic stress disorder screening using natural language processing and text mining. Assessment. **24**(2), 157–172 (2017). https://doi.org/10.1177/1073191115602551

21. Liu Y, Ott M, Goyal N, Du J, Joshi M, Chen D, et al.: RoBERTa: A Robustly Optimized BERT Pretraining Approach. (2019)

22. Shelar, H., Kaur, G., Heda, N., Agrawal, P.: Named entity recognition approaches and their comparison for custom NER model. Sci. Technol. Libr. **39**(3), 324–337 (2020). https://doi.org/10.1080/0194262X.2020.1759479

23. Sonnenberg C, vom Brocke J. Evaluations in the science of the artificial – reconsidering the build-evaluate pattern in design science research. In: Peffers K, Rothenberger M, Kuechler B, editors. Design Science Research in Information Systems Advances in Theory and Practice. Berlin, Heidelberg: Springer Berlin Heidelberg; p. 381–397.(2012)

24. Bagheri, F., Abbasi, F., Sadeghi, M., Khajouei, R.: Evaluating the usability of a cancer registry system using cognitive walkthrough, and assessing user agreement with its problems. BMC Med. Inform. Decis. Mak. **23**(1), 23 (2023). https://doi.org/10.1186/s12911-023-02120-8

25. Farzandipour, M., Nabovati, E., Tadayon, H., Sadeqi, J.M.: Usability evaluation of a nursing information system by applying cognitive walkthrough method. Int. J. Med. Inform. **152**, 104459 (2021). https://doi.org/10.1016/j.ijmedinf.2021.104459

26. Bligård, L.-O., Osvalder, A.-L.: Enhanced cognitive walkthrough: development of the cognitive walkthrough method to better predict, identify, and present usability problems. Adv. Hum. Comput. Interact. **2013**(1), 931698 (2013). https://doi.org/10.1155/2013/931698

CalcQuest: A Gamified Abacus Learning Support System for Enhancing Operational Proficiency

Yuki Matsuda[1,2]($\boxtimes$) [ORCID] and Taizo Kozaki[2]

[1] Okayama University, Okayama 700-0082, Japan
`yukimat@okayama-u.ac.jp`
[2] Nara Institute of Science and Technology, Nara 630-0192, Japan
`kozaki.taizo.kv7@is.naist.jp`

Abstract. Abacus learning improves calculation speed, memory retention, and concentration. However, learners often encounter difficulties with specific operations, leading to reduced learning efficiency and repetitive practice of similar operations, which can cause mental fatigue and a decline in motivation. To address these challenges, this study proposes CalcQuest, a gamified learning support system designed to help learners overcome operational weaknesses through structured and engaging practice. CalcQuest incorporates an abacus board recognition system using a document camera with AR markers, a mechanism for detecting operational weaknesses and generating personalized problems, and a gamified user interface to integrate these components. Through a two-week exploratory study with six novice learners, we compared CalcQuest with a baseline system in terms of calculation accuracy, calculation speed, and observed behavioral trends. The results suggest the potential of integrating personalized feedback and gamification to support abacus learning.

Keywords: Abacus · Education · Learning Support · Gamification

1 Introduction

The abacus (*Soroban*) is a traditional calculating tool to represent numbers and perform arithmetic operations by sliding beads along rods (Fig. 1). Beyond its primary function as a calculator, the abacus is widely recognized for its educational benefits, including calculation speed, memory retention, and concentration [1,2,8,10,15,18–20]. In recent years, the widespread adoption of calculators and computers has reduced the practical need for the abacus. Nevertheless, abacus learning remains popular, not only in Japan but also in many countries worldwide.

One of the key challenges in abacus learning is addressing "operational weaknesses," defined as recurrent procedural errors such as the omission of complementary addition or incorrect carry operations. Learners often encounter difficulties with specific operations, leading to repeated errors that hinder progress and

K. Sumi et al. (Eds.): PERSUASIVE 2026, LNCS 16476, pp. 148–162, 2026.
https://doi.org/10.1007/978-3-032-19687-3_12

reduce learning efficiency. Furthermore, repetitive practice of similar operations can result in mental fatigue, which may negatively affect learner motivation. Most existing abacus learning support systems do not explicitly focus on the identification of such operational weaknesses and instead rely on learners or instructors to manually diagnose these difficulties [3].

To address these challenges, we propose a novel abacus learning support system called "CalcQuest" as shown in Fig. 2. This system introduces an approach to identifying learners' operational weaknesses by leveraging our prior work, an abacus input value estimation method that utilizes a document camera as a sensor [12]. Based on the identified weaknesses, the system automatically generates personalized calculation problems designed to help learners naturally overcome their difficulties and improve proficiency. These problems are seamlessly integrated into a gamified interface, encouraging learners to engage with the exercises in a fun and motivating way, thereby fostering sustained learning and mastery.

This paper presents the design, implementation, and evaluation of CalcQuest. Through a two-week exploratory study with six novice university students, we examined the use of CalcQuest in comparison with a baseline system and observed trends related to operational weaknesses, calculation speed, accuracy, and learner behavior. The results suggest that integrating personalized problem generation with gamification may support learners in addressing operational weaknesses while sustaining engagement during abacus practice. By focusing on both operational challenges and mental fatigue, CalcQuest demonstrates the potential of gamified learning support for abacus education.

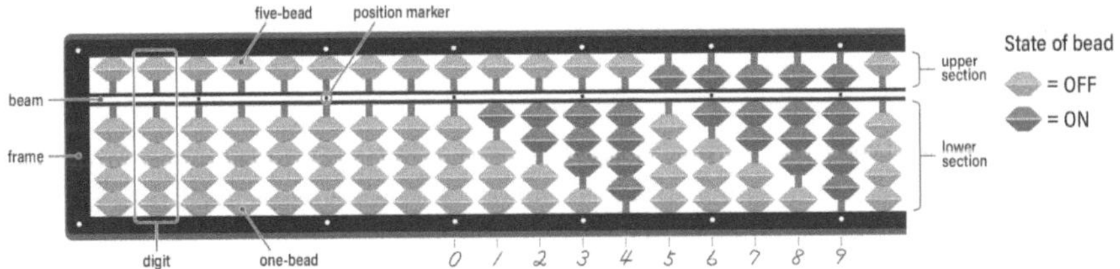

Fig. 1. Components and number representation of the abacus.

Fig. 2. Overview of CalcQuest, a gamified abacus learning support system.

2   Basic Knowledge of Abacus

An abacus is an assistive tool for various calculations such as the four arithmetic operations by expressing numbers with the positions of five beads which can be moved vertically. This section provides summary of the preliminary knowledge of the abacus.

2.1   Numerical Representation Using Abacus

First, the components of the abacus are shown in Fig. 1 (left). A *digit* corresponds to one digit in base 10, and the placement of five beads can represent numbers from "0 ∼ 9." Each *digit* is divided into an upper and lower section by a *beam*, and the single bead in the upper section (`five-bead`) represents the base-10 number "5," while the four beads in the lower section (`one-beads`) represent base-10 numbers "1" each. A specific example of numerical representation is shown in Fig. 1 (right). There is a space half the height of the beads in both the upper and lower sections, and the state of each bead is represented by moving the beads up and down. In the upper section, the bead in the raised position represents OFF (0), while the lowered position represents ON (5); conversely, in the lower section, the raised position represents ON (1), and the lowered position represents OFF (0). The sum of the beads in the same digit (the total of the numerical values represented by the beads in the ON state) represents the value of that digit. The *position marker* in Fig. 1 is indicated on the beam every three digits and is used as a marker to determine the ones place. The digits to the right of the determined position marker are used to represent decimals.

2.2   Calculation Methods with the Abacus

Calculations using the abacus are characterized by the extensive use of complementary combinations of 5 and 10. Specifically, there are three types of manipulations. In the following, we explain the procedure for each manipulation with addition as an example, but subtraction can also be represented in a similar manner by performing the inverse manipulation of it.

First, the **Calculations involving either one-beads or five-bead** is the simplest manipulation, which can be completed by moving either `one-beads` or `five-bead`. The following are examples of addition. First, for the calculation of $1 + 2$, starting from the state with only one `one-bead` raised (1), a manipulation to raise two more `one-beads` (+2) can be performed, resulting in the state representing 3. For the calculation of $3 + 5$, with three `one-beads` raised (3), the manipulation of lowering the `five-bead` (+5) can be performed, resulting in the state representing 8.

Second, the **Calculations involving one-beads and five-bead** requires simultaneous movement of `one-beads` and `five-bead`. Specifically, it corresponds to the manipulation where the state changes from 0 ∼ 4 to 5 ∼ 9 (or the reverse). The following are examples of addition. The calculation of $1 + 6$ can be obtained by combining manipulation (1), adding 6 (i.e., 5 and 1) to the state with one bead raised (1), resulting in the calculated result of 7. On the other hand, the calculation of $2 + 4$ requires adding 4 to the state with two beads raised (2), but since there are only four one-beads per digit, this calculation cannot be represented by the combination of only one-beads. Therefore, the concept of the complement of 5 is introduced. Since 4 can be expressed as $5 - 1$, performing the manipulations of "subtracting 1 (lowering one one-bead)" and "adding 5 (lowering the five-bead)" simultaneously from the current input value of 2 results in the calculated result of $2 + 4$, which is 6.

Third, the **Calculations involving two digits (carrying and borrowing)** requires the movement of beads over two digits. Specifically, it corresponds to the manipulation where the state changes from $0 \sim 9$, which can be represented in one digit, to a number of 10 or greater (or the reverse), i.e., carrying or borrowing. The following are examples of addition. In the calculation of $3 + 8$, 8 will be added to the state with three beads raised (3), however since it cannot be represented within a single digit, the concept of the complement of 10 is introduced. Since 8 can be expressed as $10 - 2$, performing the manipulations of "subtracting 2" and "adding 10" simultaneously from the current input value of 3 results in the calculated result of $3 + 8$, which is 11. In addition, there are cases where the complement of 5 must also be considered. For example, in the calculation of $6 + 8$, although 8 requires considering the complement of 10 as mentioned above, and subtracting 2 from the one's place, subtracting 2 from 6 requires considering the complement of 5 $(5 - 3)$. Thus, to obtain the calculated result of $6 + 8$, which is 14, it is necessary to perform the three manipulations of "adding 3", "subtracting 5", and "adding 10" simultaneously.

3   Related Work

There are several existing works for supporting abacus learning. Arakawa *et al.* [3] proposed a Learning Management System (LMS) for abacus education, managing learning software such as flash mental arithmetic, reading aloud arithmetic, and quick-view arithmetic on the LMS, and combining it with individual grades and learning progress to enable learning anywhere with a PC equipped with the software. Kitagawa *et al.*[1] proposed an abacus learning support system consisting of a board estimation system using a camera and a projection mapping system that overlays images on the beads to convey manipulation methods. The system estimates input values on the abacus using an RGB camera placed at the backside of a transparent table. Based on estimated results, the projector provides various instructions about abacus manipulations on the table or on the beads of the abacus. There are also approaches to support abacus learning by reproducing the abacus on the screens of smartphones and tablet devices. Saito *et al.* [13] proposed an electronic abacus feature as a plugin for a learning support system designed for smartphones. By reproducing the abacus on the screen, basic abacus manipulations can be performed, and the process

---

[1] This paper is published only in Japanese: http://www.interaction-ipsj.org/proceedings/2022/data/pdf/6D04.pdf.

of calculation using the electronic abacus can also be displayed as a formula. Baharudin *et al.* [5] proposed an interactive abacus learning application, which was implemented as PC software, for beginners. Digika offers a service called *Soro Touch* [14], which provides mental arithmetic learning instruction based on the abacus UI and manipulation methods. The system reproduces an abacus-like interface on tablet devices and adopts a calculation method that operates buttons corresponding to beads with both hands. Tokuda *et al.* [16] proposed a method for estimating abacus learners' performance using matrix factorization on student-generated learning data with the Sorotouch app.

Our previous work proposed the method to recognize input values on the abacus in real-time using a document camera as a sensor [12], and also developed an abacus learning support system using a commercially available abacus and a table-top interface to provide coaching content based on abacus input value estimation [11]. The system presents calculation problems on a table-top interface and shows instructions near the corresponding digits where calculation mistakes occur. In addition to addressing cognitive difficulties, sustaining learner motivation is a critical challenge in abacus learning due to the repetitive nature of procedural practice.

To improve the skills of abacus learners, it is essential to identify weaknesses or errors in their calculation processes and provide tailored guidance accordingly. However, these processes have traditionally relied on direct instruction from lecturers, presenting a challenge in realizing ICT-based learning support systems. Existing abacus learning support systems have focused primarily on fundamental instruction for abacus operations and calculation processes. Few systems have incorporated functionalities to identify and address learners' individual weaknesses. Additionally, while gamification has been explored as a means to enhance learning motivation, its application to abacus-specific learning remains limited. This study aims to provide tailored learning support to overcome these difficulties by detecting operational weaknesses of each learner using the abacus operation sensing based on our previous work [12]. Moreover, the integration of gamification elements seeks to enhance learner engagement and motivation, addressing the psychological challenges of repetitive practice.

In recent years, gamification and game-based learning have been widely explored as effective approaches for enhancing learner motivation and engagement in educational contexts. Prior studies have shown that embedding learning tasks directly into core gameplay mechanics, rather than presenting them as auxiliary quizzes, leads to higher engagement and improved learning outcomes. Habgood and Ainsworth demonstrated that intrinsically integrated educational games, in which solving academic problems directly advances in-game progress (e.g., defeating enemies), significantly outperform extrinsically integrated designs in both learning gains and time-on-task [6]. RPG-inspired learning environments have also been shown to be effective in mathematics education. Turn-based battle metaphors, where learners solve problems to attack opponents or avoid damage, provide immediate and meaningful feedback that sustains engagement and supports persistence. Such designs have been reported to be particularly effective for novice learners and those with lower initial performance, as they frame repeated practice as goal-oriented and enjoyable activities rather than monotonous drills [4,7]. Furthermore, recent research highlights the importance of learner autonomy in gamified systems. Allowing learners to voluntarily select more challenging tasks, especially when accompanied by higher in-game rewards, has been shown to increase intrinsic motivation. Studies on self-selected difficulty indicate that learners are more willing to engage with challenging problems when they perceive the challenge as a choice rather than an obligation [9,17]. These findings suggest that gamification designs that positively reinforce voluntary engagement with difficult tasks can effectively promote learning behaviors, particularly in domains that require repeated procedural practice such as arithmetic learning.

4   CalcQuest

CalcQuest is a novel abacus learning support system designed to address operational weaknesses and improve learning efficiency by reducing learners' mental fatigue and promoting sustained motivation through gamified elements that make the learning process enjoyable and engaging, as shown in Fig. 3 and Fig. 4. It features two core functionalities: identifying operational weaknesses from calculation logs to enhance proficiency, and providing gamified learning materials to mitigate mental fatigue and foster sustained engagement. The following sections delve into the details of each functionality.

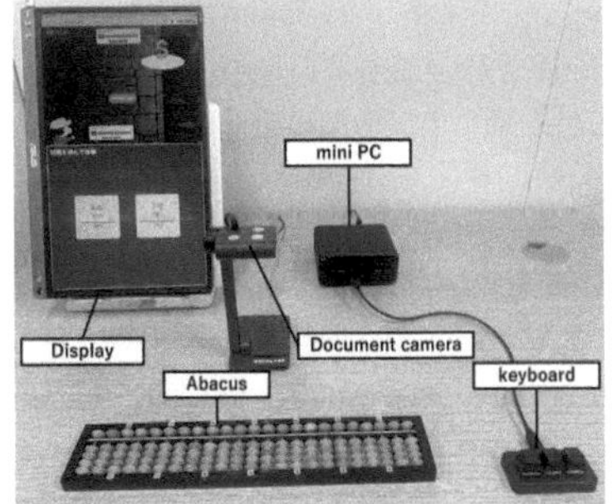

Fig. 3. CalcQuest System Setup.

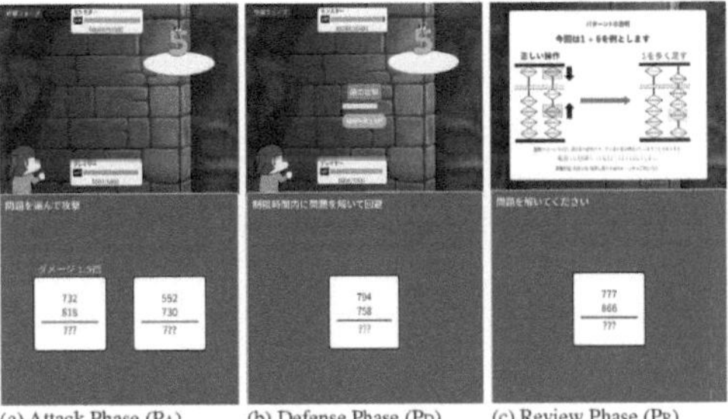

(a) Attack Phase (P_A)   (b) Defense Phase (P_D)   (c) Review Phase (P_R)

Fig. 4. CalcQuest Interfaces.

4.1   Functionality for Enhancing Operational Proficiency

Definition of Operational Weaknesses Operational weaknesses of abacus refer to specific errors that learners repeatedly encounter during calculations.

Based on an analysis of common errors faced by learners, we originally categorize these weaknesses into the following six patterns.

First, **Pattern 1 (*omission of addition*)** refers to cases where required addition operations are not performed, e.g., skipping "add 3" operation in the calculation of $6 + 8$. **Pattern 2 (*omission of subtraction*)** refers to cases where required subtraction steps are not performed, which is the inverse of Pattern 1. Next, **Pattern 3 (*errors in addition amount*)** refers to cases where an incorrect value is added. For example, in the calculation of $1 + 6$, adding 1 more than necessary represents this pattern. **Pattern 4 (*errors in subtraction amount*)** refers to cases where an incorrect value is subtracted, which is the inverse of Pattern 3. Then, **Pattern 5 (*confusion of five- and one-beads*)** occur when different types of beads are operated. For example, in the calculation of $3 + 5$, mistakenly adding 10 instead of 5 categorizes this pattern. Finally, **Pattern 6 (*reversal of addition and subtraction*)** refers to cases where addition is mistakenly performed instead of subtraction, or vice versa. For example, in the calculation of $8 + 3$, incorrectly subtracting 7 by misinterpreting the complement of 10 and subtracting 3 instead represents this pattern.

Method for Identifying Operational Weaknesses. The operational weaknesses are identified based on the tendency of the repeative errors. It suggests that the learner may misunderstand or may have forgotten the specific abacus operation procedures. CalcQuest adopts a method to identify the operational weakness pattern based on calculating the digit-wise differences between the learner's answer and the correct answer of the given calculation problems when the learner's answer is wrong. Specifically, the difference values for each digit between leaner's answer and correct answer are calculated to estimate the possible reasons of error. Accumulating these estimations, the frequent patterns of operational weaknesses can be identified from the six predefined patterns mentioned above. For example, consider the calculation "$6 + 8$," where the recognized result is 11. In this case, the correct answer is 14, resulting in a difference value of -3. This difference value of -3 indicates that the operation to "add 3" was omitted. This can be identified as Pattern 1 of the operational weaknesses (omission of addition).

Method for Detecting Operational Weaknesses in Multi-Digit Calculations. In multi-digit calculations, operations such as carrying and borrowing can influence other digits. As a specific example, consider the calculation "$12 + 48$," where the result is recognized as 70. The method for detecting operational weaknesses in this case is as follows: First, in multi-digit calculations, errors are estimated sequentially from the highest digit. In this case, the recognized result for the tens digit is 7, while the correct value is 6, resulting in a difference value of 1. Based on this difference, the system verifies whether the carrying operation affecting the calculation "$1 + 4$" was performed correctly. The program refers to the calculation result of the lower digit, "$2 + 8$," to determine whether the carrying operation was appropriately executed. The difference value of 1 suggests two possible errors: (1) the omission of the operation to "subtract 1" during the calculation "$1 + 4$," or (2) the correct execution of "$1 + 4$," but an error in the calculation "$2 + 8$," where the operation to lift one bead ($+10$) in the leftmost column was mistakenly performed as lifting two beads ($+20$). By analyzing these difference values, the system can detect Pattern 2 (omission of subtraction) and Pattern 3 (errors in addition amount) as operational weaknesses. This method is not limited to two-digit calculations and can also be applied to three-digit or higher calculations. Even as the number of digits increases, the system can break down the calculation into individual digits and verify the results to detect operational weaknesses using the same procedure. Detected operational weaknesses are recorded in the database according to their corresponding patterns. Even when multiple operational weaknesses are identified simultaneously, each is independently detected and recorded appropriately. Additionally, if an error does not match any of the predefined six patterns, it is categorized and recorded as "Other."

Problem Generation Method for Enhancing Operational Proficiency. Based on the detection results of operational weakness patterns, problems containing the identified weaknesses are generated. Specifically, as a particular pattern is repeatedly detected, the detection count for that pattern increases. When the detection count exceeds five, the system flags it as an operational weakness. Once flagged, problems containing the corresponding operational weakness are prioritized for presentation. When a learner answers a problem containing the flagged operational weakness correctly, the accumulated detection count for that pattern decreases by one. This process continues, and when the detection count falls to three or below, the weakness is considered resolved, and the flag is removed. Once the flag is removed, problems containing that operational weakness are no longer presented. However, if the same pattern is detected again and its detection count exceeds five, the operational weakness is flagged once more, and problems containing it are prioritized following the same procedure. If no operational weakness patterns are detected, random problems are generated instead.

4.2 Functionality of Gamified Learning Materials

The gamified learning materials in CalcQuest were designed based on prior findings in educational gamification and game-based learning research. In particular, the system adopts an RPG-style turn-based battle metaphor, in which solving calculation problems directly affects the state of the game, such as attacking an enemy or avoiding damage. This design aims to intrinsically integrate learning activities into gameplay so that calculation itself becomes a meaningful in-game action rather than an auxiliary task [6]. The overall system flow is shown in Fig. 5. The gameplay is structured into four sequential phases: Attack, Defense, Judgment, and Review.

First is the **Attack Phase** (P_A) as shown in Fig. 4 (a). At the top of the screen, the enemy's illustration and hit points (HP_E) are displayed, while the

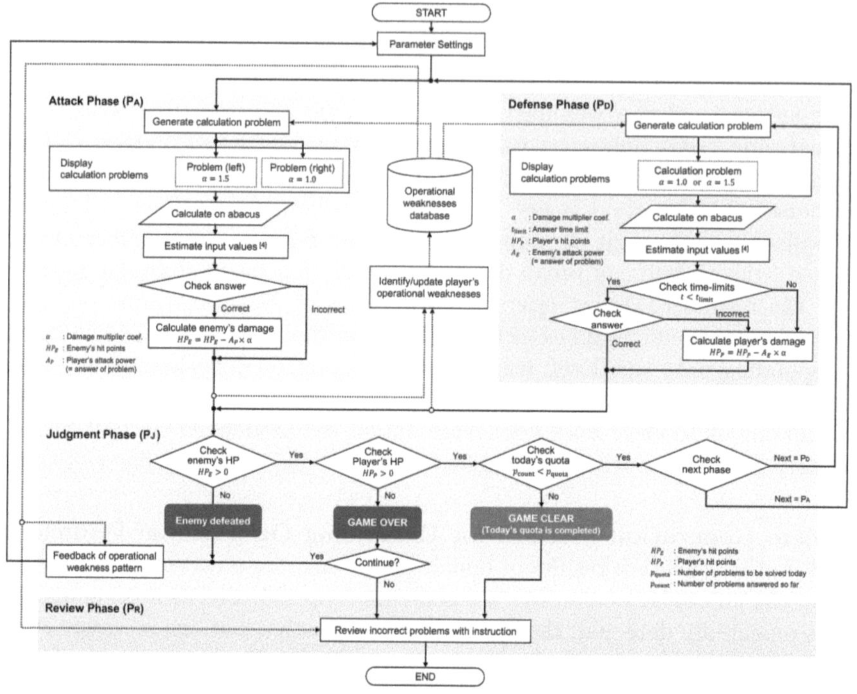

Fig. 5. System flow of the gamified abacus learning support system.

player's illustration and hit points (HP_P) are shown in the center. Two calculation problems of varying difficulty are presented at the bottom of the screen during this phase. The problem on the left includes the player's operational weaknesses, while the problem on the right is a randomly generated problem. The player selects and solves one of the two problems. To encourage engagement with operational weaknesses, the damage dealt to the enemy is adjusted based on the selected problem. When the learner correctly solves a problem containing operational weaknesses, a higher damage multiplier ($\alpha = 1.5$) is applied, resulting in greater damage. In contrast, solving a randomly generated problem applies a standard multiplier ($\alpha = 1.0$). This design allows learners to voluntarily choose whether to engage with more challenging, weakness-related problems, rather than forcing repeated exposure to them. Such self-selected challenge-taking behavior has been shown to play a crucial role in sustaining intrinsic motivation in gamified learning environments, particularly when higher rewards are associated with more challenging tasks [9,17]. The system automatically infers which problem was selected by comparing the calculation result with the correct answers of both problems. If the player's answer is correct, damage is dealt to the enemy according to $A_P \times \alpha$, where the answer of the solved problem is used as the player's attack power A_P. If the answer is incorrect, no damage is dealt to the enemy.

Next is the **Defense Phase** (P_D) as shown in Fig. 4 (b). At the top of the screen, the enemy's illustration and hit points (HP_E) are displayed, with the player's illustration and hit points (HP_P) in the center. A single calculation problem is shown at the bottom of the screen. A bar between the enemy and the player represents the time-limit (t_{limit}). During the Defense Phase, the player is presented with a problem that includes their operational weaknesses. If no weaknesses have been detected, a random problem is presented instead. If the player answers the problem correctly within the time limit, the enemy's attack is avoided. However, if the time limit expires or the answer is incorrect, the player takes damage ($A_E \times \alpha$, the answer of solved problem will be enemy's attack power A_E).

Judgment Phase. (P_J) checks status of the game. In this phase. the remaining health points of the player (HP_P) and the enemy (HP_E) are evaluated, and the next phase is determined. If the player's health points reach zero ($HP_P \leq 0$), the game enters a *Game Over* state, and the player is prompted to decide whether to continue the game. If the player chooses to continue, a new game begins with updated parameters. If the player chooses not to continue, the game is finished. If the number of answered problems (p_{count}) reaches today's quota (p_{quota}), the game enters a *Game Clear* state, and finishes. A single round consists of the Attack Phase (P_A), followed by the Judgment Phase (P_J), the Defense Phase (P_D), and another Judgment Phase (P_J), and it will repeat multiple rounds until the end of the game.

After finishing the game, **Review Phase** (P_R) as shown in Fig. 4 (c) provides the problems they answered incorrectly during the game, and the player revisits and solves them. Each review problem will be provided with explanations of the correspond operational weakness pattern at the top of the screen.

5   Evaluation and Discussion

5.1   Experiment and Evaluation Method

In this experiment, we evaluated the proposed system, CalcQuest, to enhance abacus proficiency. The purpose of the experiment was to verify the effectiveness of features such as operational weakness detection, problem generation, and UI feedback incorporating gamification elements in overcoming operational weaknesses and improving abacus proficiency. This study was conducted with the approval of the "Research Ethics Committee for Studies Involving Human Subjects" at Nara Institute of Science and Technology (approval No.: 2022-I-63-1).

The experiment was conducted over 14 days, with the proposed system installed to university campus at Nara Institute of Science and Technology. The participants were six graduate students (gender: male 5, female 1; age: 22–25) who had no prior experience in learning abacus. Before the experiment, the purpose of the study, instructions for using the system, and the basics of abacus operation were explained to them. Then, a pre-test was conducted, and the participants were divided into the following two groups (CalcQuest: n=3, Baseline: n=3) based on their scores to ensure balance between the groups. The difficulty level of calculation problems is set as three-digit two-term problems based on their scores for evaluating the improvement of participants' calculation abilities. All participants solve 50 calculation problems using the abacus every day ($p_{\mathrm{quota}} = 50$). After the experiment, short semi-structured interviews (5âĂŞ10 min) were conducted. Responses were recorded and qualitatively analyzed.

CalcQuest Group is the experimental group, they use the proposed system with all functionalities as described in Sect. 4. The time-limit for each problem (t_{limit}) was set to 10 s, regardless of the participants' skill levels. Each time they reach *Game Over*, *Game Clear*, and *Enemy defeated*, participants can review the summary of learning (the number of correct answers, incorrect answers, and elapsed time), and explanations of the operational weakness patterns corresponding to the incorrect answers. At the review phase, participants can view and solve problems that were not correctly answered by revisiting the explanations of the operational weakness patterns shown at the top of the screen. (Figure 4 (c)).

Baseline Group is control group, they use the basic system same as the CalcQuest group, but proposed functionalities (operational weakness detection, and gamified learning materials) are not included. After finishing today's quota (p_{quota}), the system automatically check the answers, and shows the summary of today's study (the number of correct answers, incorrect answers, and elapsed time). At the review phase (P_{R}), participants can solve problems which were not correctly answered, but no explanation about operational weakness pattern will be provided. This baseline configuration was designed as a minimal comparison condition and does not isolate individual system components.

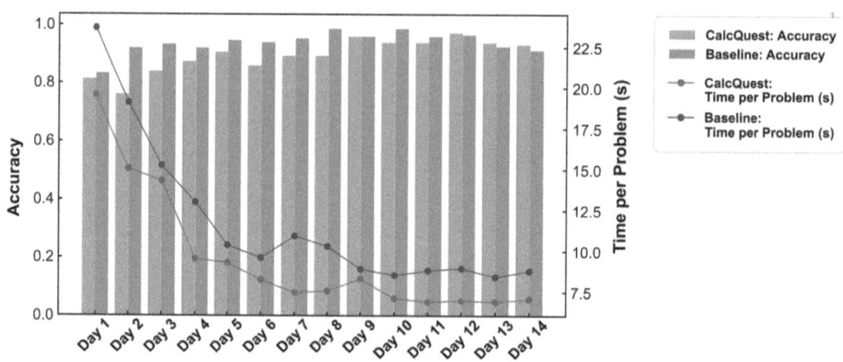

Fig. 6. Daily trends in accuracy rates and calculation time per problem for CalcQuest and Baseline groups.

5.2   Calculation Accuracy and Calculation Speed

From the results shown in Fig. 6, the CalcQuest group exhibited lower accuracy rates in the first half of the experiment but tended to surpass the Baseline group in the latter half. Possible reasons for the lower accuracy rates in the early phase for the CalcQuest group include pressure caused by the time limit as a game element, which may have led to increased errors due to rushing, and frequent exposure to problems containing operational weaknesses, which could have suppressed accuracy rates at the initial stage. On the other hand, the improved accuracy rates observed in the latter half may be related to continued engagement with weakness-focused practice and the motivational features of the game scenario. These observations suggest trends toward improvements in learning performance, reflected in increases in both accuracy rates and calculation speed. In contrast, the Baseline group recorded the highest accuracy rates around the midpoint of the experiment but showed a decline in the latter half. According to interviews, some participants (P5, P6) mentioned *"losing interest in the latter half"* and *"feeling like it was just repetitive work,"* suggesting that the monotonous learning environment may have led to reduced engagement. Additionally, comments such as *"I couldn't maintain focus"* and *"My calculation errors increased"* were reported, which may have been associated with the observed decline in accuracy rates in the later stages. In the CalcQuest group, participants provided feedback such as *"The game scenario and the operational weakness-overcoming feature were motivating"* (P2, P3). Furthermore, one participant suggested that *"if there was a mechanism to increase the speed during the attack phase, it would further boost motivation"* (P2), indicating potential areas for future improvement in supporting learner engagement. These qualitative observations suggest that the game elements in CalcQuest may have contributed to sustaining engagement during the learning process.

Additionally, in terms of calculation speed per problem, the CalcQuest group consistently solved problems faster than the Baseline group, with the observed difference reaching approximately two seconds by the 14th day. This trend may be related to the requirement for quick responses under the time limit imposed in CalcQuest. In contrast, the Baseline group, which did not include a time limit, was able to solve problems more slowly and accurately. As a result, although the Baseline group gradually increased their calculation speed, they did not exceed the performance observed in the CalcQuest group.

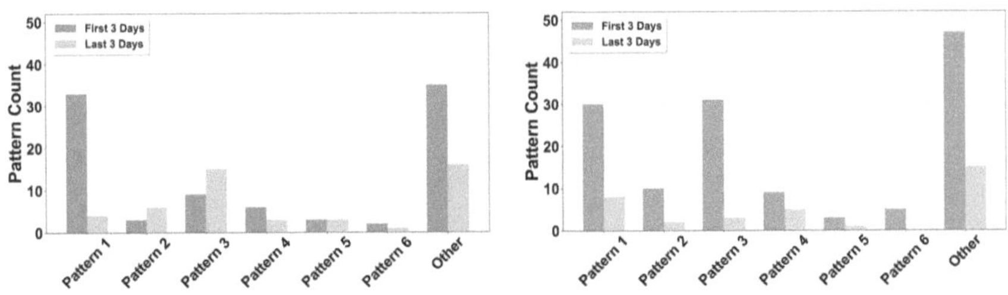

Fig. 7. Operational weakness patterns of each group detected at the first and last three days of the experiment.

5.3   Changes in Patterns of Operational Weaknesses

Figure 7 shows the total number of detected operational weaknesses in each group during the first and last three days of the experiment. In the CalcQuest group, a decreasing trend in detected operational weaknesses was observed, with particularly notable reductions in Patterns 1 and 3. This result suggests that the feedback functionality in CalcQuest may have helped reduce the frequency of repeated errors. Specifically, the feedback provided during the review phase may have supported learners in reflecting on their mistakes and adjusting their calculation processes. Due to the experimental scenario, participants in the CalcQuest group were exposed to a larger number of problems containing operational weaknesses compared to those in the Baseline group. While such exposure would typically be expected to increase the number of detected weaknesses, a decrease was observed over time. This observation suggests that the weakness-focused practice and feedback mechanisms in CalcQuest may have contributed to reducing repeated operational errors. In contrast, the Baseline group exhibited an increasing trend in the detection of Pattern 3 during the latter half of the experiment. This trend suggests that operational weaknesses may not have been sufficiently addressed in the absence of explicit feedback targeting specific error patterns. Although the Baseline group also included a review phase, the lack of targeted feedback on operational weaknesses may have increased the tendency for learners to repeat similar errors. These observations highlight the potential importance of feedback that not only allows learners to retry problems but also supports understanding of the underlying causes of errors.

Furthermore, both groups showed a high frequency of operations classified as "Other," indicating the need to reevaluate the current definitions of operational weaknesses and consider the inclusion of additional patterns in future work. In the CalcQuest group, the selection rate for problems containing operational weaknesses was 100%. This observation suggests that the damage multiplier mechanism may have encouraged learners to select weakness-related problems, thereby promoting engagement with challenging operations.

5.4   Limitations

This study has several limitations that should be considered when interpreting the results. First, the sample size was small, consisting of six novice participants, which limits the generalizability of the findings. The study was designed as an exploratory investigation, and the observed results should be interpreted as indicative trends rather than conclusive evidence. Second, the experimental period was limited to two weeks. While short-term changes in calculation performance and learner behavior were observed, the current study does not assess long-term retention, transfer of skills, or sustained motivation. Longer-term studies are required to evaluate the enduring effects of the proposed system. Third, the current experimental design does not isolate the individual contributions of personalized problem generation, gamification elements, and practice frequency. As a result, it is not possible to attribute observed effects to specific components of the system. Future work will employ more controlled experimental designs to examine the role of each factor in greater detail. Finally, participants were novice university students, which may introduce sampling bias and limit applicability to other learner populations, such as children or experienced abacus users. Future studies with more diverse participants are necessary to further validate the effectiveness of the proposed approach.

6   Conclusion

This study proposed CalcQuest, a gamified abacus learning support system designed to help learners improve their skills while reducing mental fatigue. The system identifies operational weaknesses and generates personalized problems to address them, supporting learners in overcoming challenges. By incorporating gamification, it aims to support learner engagement and promote continuous skill development in an engaging learning environment. The effectiveness of CalcQuest was explored through a two-week experiment involving novice learners. The results showed trends of improvement in both calculation accuracy and speed, suggesting that personalized problem generation and gamification elements may have contributed to enhanced learning outcomes. Future research will explore large-scale evaluations, long-term impacts, and refinements to weakness detection and problem generation to further investigate the effectiveness of the proposed approach.

Acknowledgments. This study was supported in part by the 2021 KDDI Foundation Research Grant Program.

Disclosure of Interests. The authors have no competing interests to declare that are relevant to the content of this article.

References

1. Amaiwa, S.: The effects of abacus learning on solving arithmetic problems: a comparative study of elementary / junior high school students at upper level and inexperienced students. J. Faculty Educ., Shinshu Univ. **96**, 145–156 (1999)
2. Amaiwa, S., Hatano, G.: Effects of abacus learning on 3rd-graders' performance in paper-and-pencil tests of calculation. Jpn. Psychol. Res. **31**, 161–168 (1989)
3. Arakawa, K., Kawasaki, K., Sawada, K., Futatsuishi, Y., Kakehi, M., Watanabe, I.: Web learning support system development in abacus education. J. Faculty Sci. Technol., Seikei Univ. **48**, 75–79 (2011)
4. Babazadeh, M., Maffioli, M., Falcade, R.: Transforming math anxiety into engagement: the impact of rpg-based gamification on middle school students. In: Proceedings of the 19th European Conference on Games-Based Learning (ECGBL 2025), pp. 54–63 (2025). https://doi.org/10.34190/ecgbl.19.1.4084
5. Baharudin, S., Rias, R.M., Ahmad, M.F.: Designing an interactive abacus learning application for beginners: A prototype. In: 2010 International Conference on User Science and Engineering (i-USEr), pp. 89–92 (2010).https://doi.org/10.1109/IUSER.2010.5716729

6. Habgood, M.P.J., Ainsworth, S.E.: Motivating children to learn effectively: exploring the value of intrinsic integration in educational games. J. Learn. Sci. **20**(2), 169–206 (2011). https://doi.org/10.1080/10508406.2010.508029

7. Hieftje, K., Pendergrass, T., Kyriakides, T.C., Gilliam, W.S., Fiellin, L.E.: An evaluation of an educational video game on mathematics achievement in first grade students. Technologies **5**(2), 1–8 (2017). https://doi.org/10.3390/technologies5020030

8. Hu, Y., et al.: Enhanced white matter tracts integrity in children with abacus training. Hum. Brain Mapp. **32**(1), 10–21 (2011). https://doi.org/10.1002/hbm.20996

9. Lomas, J.D., Koedinger, K.R., Patel, N., Shodhan, S., Poonwala, N., Forlizzi, J.L.: Is difficulty overrated?: the effects of choice, novelty and suspense on intrinsic motivation in educational games. In: Proceedings of the 2017 CHI Conference on Human Factors in Computing Systems (CHI '17). pp. 1028–1039 (2017). https://doi.org/10.1145/3025453.3025638

10. Lu, Y., Li, M., Cui, Z., Wang, L., Hu, Y., Zhou, X.: Transfer effects of abacus training on cognition. Curr. Psychol. **42**, 6271–6286 (2023) https://doi.org/10.1007/s12144-021-01968-1

11. Matsuda, Y.: A table-top interface for real-time coaching in abacus learning. In: The 10th International Conference on Smart Computing (SmartComp '24), pp. 243–245 (2024). https://doi.org/10.1109/SMARTCOMP61445.2024.00056

12. Matsuda, Y.: Abacus manipulation understanding by behavior sensing utilizing document camera as a sensor. Int. J. Activity Behav. Comput. **2024**(1), 1–16 (2024). https://doi.org/10.60401/ijabc.2

13. Saito, K., Sasaki, H., Mizuno, K.: Development of learning support tools using the mobile phone. In: Proceedings of Forum on Information Technology. FIT'09, vol. 8, pp. 653–654 (2009)

14. Sorotouch Co., Ltd.: Sorotouch. https://www.sorotouch.jp/ (2016). Accessed 01 Aug 2026

15. Stigler, J.W.: "mental abacus": The effect of abacus training on Chinese children's mental calculation. Cogn. Psychol. **16**(2), 145–176 (1984). https://doi.org/10.1016/0010-0285(84)90006-9

16. Tokuda, K., Kaschub, D., Ota, T., Hashimoto, Y., Fujiwara, N., Sudo, A.: Prediction of student performance in abacus-based calculation using matrix factorization. In: Adjunct Publication of the 28th ACM Conference on User Modeling, Adaptation and Personalization, pp. 114–118. UMAP '20 Adjunct (2020). https://doi.org/10.1145/3386392.3399309

17. Tyni, J., Bednarik, R., Kahila, J., Tedre, M.: A bird matching game: Difficulty, rewards and intrinsic motivation. Int. J. Serious Games **11**(4), 57–77 (2024). https://doi.org/10.17083/ijsg.v11i4.602

18. Wang, C.: A review of the effects of abacus training on cognitive functions and neural systems in humans. Front. Neurosci. **14**(913), 1–12 (2020). https://doi.org/10.3389/fnins.2020.00913

19. Wang, C., et al.: Training on abacus-based mental calculation enhances visuospatial working memory in children. J. Neurosci. **39**(33), 6439–6448 (2019). https://doi.org/10.1523/JNEUROSCI.3195-18.2019

20. Xie, Y., et al.: Long-term abacus training gains in children are predicted by medial temporal lobe anatomy and circuitry. Dev. Sci. **27**(4), e13489 (2024). https://doi.org/10.1111/desc.13489

Persuasive Art Experience in the Metaverse: Case of the Finnish Metagallery

Juho Mattila[1]([🖂])[iD], Iikka Paajala[1][iD], Sameera Bandaranayake[1][iD], and Pasi Karppinen[2][iD]

[1] Oulu Advanced Research on Service and Information Systems (OASIS), Faculty of Information Technology and Electrical Engineering, University of Oulu, Oulu, Finland
`juho.e.mattila@oulu.fi`
[2] imec-SMIT, Vrije Universiteit Brussel, Brussels, Belgium

Abstract. The metaverse opens new possibilities for digital art and cultural participation, yet the persuasive dynamics of virtual art encounters remain little understood. This study applies the Persuasive Systems Design (PSD) model to analyze audience engagement in the Finnish Metagallery, a virtual exhibition hosted by the Finnish National Gallery in Decentraland. Thirteen interviews were thematically analyzed to examine how PSD features—usefulness and ease of use, liking, tailoring, authority, and social facilitation—shape the art experience. Participants found the gallery accessible and visually appealing, but its value often centered on convenience rather than deep immersion or social presence, and institutional authority raised expectations that were not always met. The findings show how aesthetic experience can act as a persuasive mechanism in metaverse exhibitions, and suggest that persuasive impact in virtual art spaces depends less on technical novelty than on the alignment of aesthetic, experiential, and social design qualities that sustain meaningful engagement.

Keywords: Metaverse · Persuasive Systems Design model · Liking feature · Virtual art experience

1 Introduction

The concept of the metaverse is still emerging, as both researchers and industry actors continue to shape its meaning [22]. It is commonly described as a network of immersive digital realms not constrained by physical space, distance, or materiality. These environments include three-dimensional games, extended reality (XR) spaces, and social platforms [12,19,21]. They offer opportunities for entertainment, education, and social connection, while enabling simulations of historical, fantastical, or real-world locations [14]. Virtual museums and art exhibitions have become an important development within this landscape, demonstrating how digital platforms can connect audiences with artworks and cultural heritage in new ways [11].

K. Sumi et al. (Eds.): PERSUASIVE 2026, LNCS 16476, pp. 163–177, 2026.
https://doi.org/10.1007/978-3-032-19687-3_13

An art experience is more than viewing an artwork—it involves emotional response, interpretation, and meaning-making shaped by the creator, the viewer, and the surrounding cultural context [7]. Prior research suggests that virtual reality (VR) can evoke art experiences comparable to physical galleries [15], yet virtual exhibitions still struggle to replicate the social dimension and embodied qualities of museum visits. Interaction with other visitors or virtual humans remains limited, but the metaverse offers potential to overcome these constraints by enabling shared presence and social engagement [9]. As XR exhibitions evolve, the challenge is to understand how immersive technologies can enrich engagement and support the interpretive, emotional, and social aspects of artistic experience [6].

Although immersive art and VR exhibitions have been studied within HCI, cultural heritage, and digital media research, their potential as persuasive systems remains underexplored. The Persuasive Systems Design (PSD) model provides a structured framework for analyzing how interactive systems influence users [16], yet no prior study has applied PSD to virtual art environments where persuasion occurs subtly through atmosphere, clarity, beauty, and the perceived authenticity of the experience. This gap is particularly relevant in metaverse exhibitions, where spatial immersion and aesthetic impact can shape users' attitudes, emotions, and openness to new cultural formats. Here, persuasion is approached in terms of experiential and affective engagement rather than direct behavior change. To address this gap, our guiding research question is: *How does the Finnish Metagallery succeed in creating an art experience for gallery visitors?*

Based on interviews with 13 participants this study extends the PSD model to metaverse-based cultural experiences by showing how principles of *usefulness and ease of use, liking, tailoring, authority, and social facilitation* manifest in a virtual gallery. It offers design implications for creating credible, emotionally rich, and socially meaningful virtual art environments.

2   Background

Although there are still several definitions for the metaverse, it generally represents a transformative shift in online experiences [14,21]. It can be described as a network of immersive digital realms where users interact, trade goods, and explore shared virtual worlds [22]. These environments can be tailored to users' interests, ranging from historical reconstructions to fantasy settings or futuristic simulations. The metaverse also enables social interaction and collaboration, thus creating shared narratives and experiences [9]. Users can design personalized environments that integrate real-time data and interactive content, and these virtual spaces often foster new forms of digital economies based on blockchain technologies [23].

Some metaverse platforms are specifically dedicated to cultural exhibitions, while others, such as Decentraland, host a variety of user-generated experiences [5,10]. This versatility makes them promising venues for digital art and museum experimentation. The Finnish Metagallery was built within Decentraland as a pilot project exploring how a metaverse-based gallery could support public access to art and participatory cultural experiences [8, 18].

Virtual art exhibitions, as a novel medium, redefine the relationship between art institutions and their audiences. They encourage participation, interaction, and agency in ways not possible within traditional gallery settings [19]. Virtual artworks are not bound by materiality but exist through interactions between visual form, digital space, and the viewer's interpretation [6]. Such exhibitions expand audiences beyond geographical limits, attracting younger and more global visitors who may not typically attend physical museums [9].

Technologies such as virtual, augmented, and mixed reality enhance the aesthetic experience by providing immersive and emotionally engaging ways to interact with artworks. Viewers can explore additional information, contextual narratives, or multisensory features such as sound design and motion [2]. Furthermore, blockchain technologies can ensure digital ownership and authenticity of art through Non-Fungible Tokens (NFTs), offering artists new ways to monetize and distribute their work [13].

The PSD model [16] offers a theoretical framework for understanding how interactive technologies can influence users' attitudes and behaviors through design features. It identifies seven underlying postulates and 28 design principles that guide the development of persuasive systems. The postulates emphasize, for example, that information technology is never neutral, persuasion is often incremental, and persuasive systems should aim to be both *useful* and *easy to use*. The persuasive system features are divided into four categories. *Primary task support* focuses on helping users achieve their main goals efficiently; *System credibility support* builds trust and legitimacy through expertise and transparency; and *Social support* leverages social influence and collaboration to enhance engagement. *Dialogue support* concerns the interactive feedback and communicative elements, and maintains an ongoing persuasive dialogue with the user. The feature of *liking* plays a particularly central role in this study, since it captures the aesthetic dimension of interaction: "A system that is visually attractive for its users is likely to be more persuasive" [16]. A well-designed virtual gallery that is visually harmonious, responsive, and immersive can subtly guide users toward deeper engagement.

Research in human–computer interaction supports the link between aesthetics and perceived system effectiveness. Tractinsky [20] demonstrated the "what is beautiful is usable" effect, where visual appeal enhances perceived usability. Cyr, Head, and Ivanov [4] found that design aesthetics strengthen trust and loyalty, while Silvennoinen and Jokinen [17] showed that aesthetic pleasure elicits positive affect that promotes sustained interaction. These studies suggest that visual aesthetics act as persuasive cues by shaping both emotional response and cognitive evaluation.

3   Methodology

This research adopts a qualitative case study approach to explore user experiences of the Finnish Metagallery hosted in the Decentraland metaverse. The Finnish National Gallery (FNG) was the first museum in Finland to establish an exhibition space in a metaverse platform in October 2022 [8]. The Decentraland community donated the virtual land parcel on which the Metagallery was built, underscoring the collaborative and experimental nature of the initiative [18].

Decentraland enables users to create, explore, and monetize digital content in a decentralized, community-governed environment [5,10]. Built on the Ethereum and Polygon blockchains, it allows users to own virtual land parcels (LAND) represented as Non-Fungible Tokens (NFTs) and to take part in governance through a Decentralized Autonomous Organization (DAO) [23]. At the time of data collection, Decentraland was primarily accessed through desktop applications using keyboard and mouse, without full VR functionality.

The Finnish Metagallery digitally reconstructs the Finnish Pavilion from the 1900 Paris World Fair, originally designed by Armas Lindgren, Herman Gesellius, and Eliel Saarinen. The interior of the Metagallery environment is illustrated in Fig. 1a. The exhibition includes canonical works by artists such as Akseli Gallen-Kallela, Venny Soldan-Brofeldt, and Albert Edelfelt. Thematically, the gallery presented five curatorial narratives: *Peace, Queer, Animals, Works by 20th-century female artists*, and *Works by 20th-century male artists*. Each artwork offers contextual information about the artist and painting. The 3D model and technical implementation were developed by the design studio Adventure Club [1], and the project received support from the Museum District community and the Decentraland DAO.

The exhibition included a social participation feature: visitors who signed the in-world guestbook (Fig. 1b) received an NFT wearable for their Decentraland avatar, which they could use to vote on forthcoming exhibition themes via the platform's blockchain-based system.

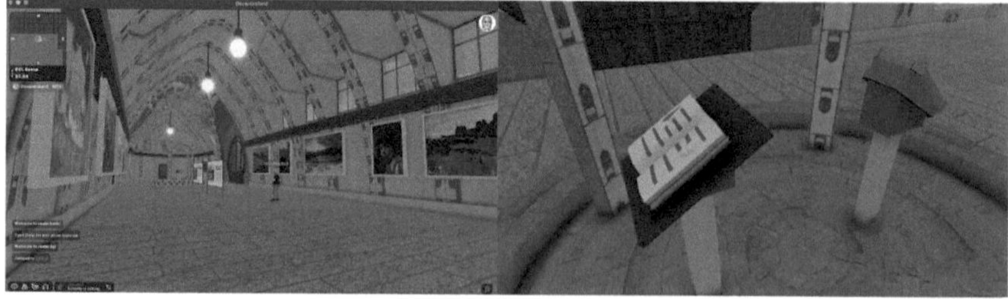

Fig. 1. Examples from the study: (a) virtual Metagallery space showing reconstructed pavilion and (b) the guestbook that enabled blockchain interactions.

A total of 13 participants were interviewed using a semi-structured protocol. The participants had either professional or personal familiarity with art, metaverse technologies, or both. Recruitment targeted individuals who had visited the Finnish Metagallery, ensuring first-hand experience of the virtual exhibition. Table 1 summarizes demographic and background information.

Table 1. Participant information

No.	Gender	Age	Occupation/Interest
1	F	44	Librarian – Art
2	M	23	Entrepreneur – Both
3	M	34	Software Developer – Metaverse
4	M	65	CEO/Teacher – Both
5	F	21	Student – Metaverse
6	F	48	Teacher – Art
7	M	48	Entrepreneur – Metaverse
8	F	40	System Expert – Metaverse
9	F	39	Project Manager – Art
10	F	52	Expert – Art
11	F	26	Product Designer – Art
12	F	49	Graphics Designer – Art
13	M	55	Head of Digital Management – Art

The semi-structured interview guide included 57 questions, and for this study, analysis focused on themes that examined participants' perceptions of the art experience, comparison with physical exhibitions, usability, and suggestions for improvement. Questions were for example: *"Can you describe your art experience? How would you compare it to a physical museum visit?"* and *"How could the art experience in virtual worlds be improved?"* Interviews lasted between 30 and 60 min and were conducted online mostly in Finnish. All sessions were recorded and transcribed. Data were analyzed using reflexive thematic analysis following Braun and Clarke [3]. The process involved iterative reading, coding, and theme development to identify patterns across participants' accounts. Codes were then clustered into higher-level themes that reflected participants' experiences of art and interaction with and within the metaverse. The PSD model [16] was applied after initial inductive coding as an interpretive lens to structure and theorize experiential findings, rather than to predetermine categories during data collection.

To interpret the findings through the PSD model [16], thematic categories were mapped onto relevant postulates and design principles. Although several persuasive elements were identified across the data, this study focuses on the most prominent postulate and feature within each PSD category. Participants' reflections on the usability and functionality of the metaverse environment were linked to the PSD postulate of *usefulness and ease of use*. Descriptions of the virtual art experience—particularly in terms of clarity, immersion, and aesthetic pleasure—were associated with the *liking* feature under *Dialogue support*. Their views on museums, art, and physical exhibitions content corresponded to the principle of *tailoring* within *Primary task support*. Statements concerning authenticity and institutional trust related to *System credibility support*, while comments about shared spaces, voting features, or social presence were mapped to *Social support*. This analytical mapping structured the interpretation of participants' experiences in relation to persuasive and aesthetic system features of the Metagallery. Analytical validity was supported through researcher cross-checking and triangulation with interview field notes. Coding and theme development were discussed iteratively among the authors, and discrepancies were resolved through collaborative refinement. The analysis combined inductive theme generation with deductive interpretation guided by the PSD framework. All procedures followed institutional ethical guidelines: participants gave informed consent, could withdraw at any time, and all personal identifiers were removed with transcripts stored on secure drives accessible only to the research team.

4   Results

The thematic analysis produced five main dimensions corresponding to postulate "Persuasive systems should aim at being both useful and easy to use" and system feature categories: Dialogue Support; Primary Task Support; Credibility Support; Social Support. These dimensions summarize how participants experienced the Finnish Metagallery and how persuasive system features were reflected in participant experiences.

Postulate Usefulness and Ease of Use. According to the PSD postulate [16], the system must be useful to users while remaining easy to use. Convenience and accessibility emerged as important positive factors amongst participants. Several appreciated the ability to explore national art collections remotely as participant 4 remarked, *"Online is super practical, you can do it right from your living room."* Most participants described their initial interaction with the Metagallery as smooth. Even those with limited experience in virtual worlds found the basic controls manageable. One respondent summarized this by noting that *"It was easy; there was nothing counterintuitive about that experience"* (P2). For participant 7 the technical implementation even hijacked the aesthetic experience, *"I notice that I don't examine art, I examine pixels and polygons."*

However, some participants also mentioned usability problems, such as difficulties in enlarging artwork for a detailed view. *"The artworks, it was difficult to target to open them large, so that you would have gotten a direct view. As I struggled, I ended up viewing them less"* (P1). Several also noted that the system required a powerful computer: *"The biggest stumbling block was the machine running a little poorly"* (P9). Participant 6 suggested a lighter version for mobile devices and improved safety measures: *"So far, it's heavy for an ordinary computer. They should do a lighter version, mobile, tablets. Main threat technically.*

Security, safety for children and women especially, safety for everybody. Two main things that should be solved in the first place. Accessibility and safety."

Several participants described account and wallet setup as a hurdle: *"The login itself is not so clear if you haven't done it before. The wallet was confusing at first..."* (P5). One visitor switched paths: *"I downloaded the client, but couldn't get the wallet to work. So I went with the browser"* (P2). Wallet requirements blocked participation in voting: "need a crypto wallet, so couldn't" (P1). Others preferred web-first alternatives: *"Voting could have be done on the website?"* (P4). Beyond wallets, wayfinding added friction: *"difficult to find (the gallery)"* and the *"link to the correct spawn location"* (P2).

Field-of-view and zoom limitations hindered close reading: *"I couldn't see the whole dome, only pieces every corner; the console structure in the middle made it impossible to see the dome as a whole, so I had to move to different angles"* (P6). Proximity also caused label occlusion: *"If you are too close to the ceiling fresco in the middle, it may cover the texts of the nearest paintings; it depends on where you stand, not what you look at"* (P5). Participants asked for basic readability improvements such as "larger text" (P4).

Dialogue Support - Liking. Within the PSD framework, the principle of *Liking* under *Dialogue support* emphasizes that visually and emotionally appealing systems are more persuasive [16]. In the Metagallery, participants' perceived art experience revealed both appreciation and disappointment. Those who had a positive experience appreciated the digital transformation of the artworks and the convenience it offered. Participants 4 and 5 regarded the whole experience positively: *"Nice to have information on everything. The same experience as if you were there in person""* (P5); *"When you think about the concept, the art experience has deepened and gives broader thinking about what this can be and what this can become. The art experience is expectantly positive"* (P4). Participant 6 found the immersive aspect of the Metagallery appealing: *"I really like the concept of using the gallery for presenting the art... It was more immersive than just browsing through images on my computer. So, it was interesting, it was a good idea to showcase the pieces in the gallery."* Participant 2 also appreciated the clarity and presentation of the artworks, *"It was a pleasant experience to see the paintings. They looked surprisingly good. As I recall when I was there, I was surprised. They were clear, well-lit, and easily approachable."*

Additionally, participants articulated concrete levers that could further enhance aesthetic impact, including *"ability to zoom into frescoes and paintings and larger, clearer labels"* (P4) and *"soundscapes that set the mood"* (P10).

However, several respondents expected a more affectively powerful experience than what the digital gallery could provide. One participant reflected, *"At first, it wasn't impressive, due to being used to getting high-resolution images... but then I started to see what this can become"* (P4). Negative feedback often concerned insufficient image resolution or a lack of emotional presence compared to real museums. Some participants commented that museums are more than paintings and that the surroundings are an important part when exploring exhibitions: *"As a heavy consumer of art, I don't see the trace of humanity in the metaverse in the same way as in a real museum"* (P10). Participant 1 said that *"art experience isn't comparable with real experience at a physical gallery, as it was a flat experience"*, and participant 13 stated bluntly: *"Can't say I had an art experience."*

Several interviewees expressed a desire for a more immersive experience and suggested that digital art designed specifically for the metaverse would be more impactful, *"There should be visually more wow effect, to get a proper experience from it"* (P12). Since technology can enable novel ways to exhibit art, some respondents wished there would have been more added value to be present in the metaverse. Participant 8 suggested that visitors could enter the painting's world, and respondent 2 also pointed out the unique possibilities of digital exhibits: *"I would have hoped that the exhibition would have had something only virtually, and surprising and innovative, which would have startled from the perspective of art ... But it was traditional. There could have been something in it, which would have been possible to implement only with technology."*

Primary Task Support – Tailoring. Most interviewed participants had found the Metagallery through the FNG's website or social media, which established trust but also shaped the perceived audience. As one participant noted, *"I saw the advertisement on Facebook and went to explore it. Museums and galleries are close to my heart and virtual worlds are interesting"* (P12). The exhibition thus reached users who were already culturally oriented.

The Metagallery was frequently described as a culturally valuable project, important for Finland and for the future of digital art, yet participants often perceived it as something meaningful for others rather than for themselves. Participant 10 observed that the Metagallery would suit *"those who can't get to the National Gallery in person, for tourists to some extent. I can't imagine that the youth would be excited about this."* Participant 9 argued on the contrary that the younger generation would gradually form the natural audience for such environments: *"This world is built for them. Younger people will grow into these worlds and become the audience."* Several others envisioned that the virtual format is an easy way for foreigners or people living far away to experience Finnish art.

Tailoring needs were explicit and often framed as parallel visit modes. Participants highlighted the importance of music and sound to set different atmospheres—historical or relaxing—*"To get into the mood, the sound world is very important—different versions for historical or relaxing atmospheres"* (P10). Building on this, participants described *"old Paris or relaxation music"* options and *"different levels for present day versus history"* to match varying intentions (P10).

Enthusiast-oriented layers were also requested, including *"alternative versions of the works, short videos showing how pieces were made and what materials were used, and expert commentary explaining why the works are interesting"* (P11). Together, these suggestions point to a tailoring strategy that offers lightweight mode switches for casual visits while providing deeper process and context layers for motivated audiences.

Credibility support – Authority. The Authority feature within the PSD framework refers to the system's credibility derived from institutional reputation, expertise, or endorsement [16]. In the context of the Finnish Metagallery, credibility was strongly linked to the presence of the FNG as the organizing institution. For many participants, the FNG brand signified cultural legitimacy, professionalism, and safety, which encouraged them to explore an otherwise unfamiliar metaverse environment.

The association with a national cultural institution reassured users that the project was authentic and non-commercial. Several respondents expressed that they might not have entered Decentraland or created a crypto wallet without the institutional guarantee. Participant 6 described this trust explicitly: *"I thought that the National Gallery could be a safe frame for my first metaverse experience."* High level of expectation was particularly evident among participants with strong art-historical or museological expertise. One art historian noted that certain details were missing from the reconstruction: *"I knew there was furniture inside and other objects inside the pavilion, and actually, the pavilion that is in the metaverse is mainly the structure, the pure structure"* (P6). Participants anticipated a certain level of artistic and technical excellence—expectations that were not always met. One respondent noted, *"I expected more when the National Museum, a big organization, is behind it"* (P12).

Social Support – Social Facilitation. Within the PSD model, *Social Facilitation* refers to situations in which the mere presence of other users performing the same task enhances motivation or engagement [16]. In the Finnish Metagallery, social interaction features such as chat or voice were available but seldom used. Most participants reported visiting the gallery alone and described minimal engagement with others, reflecting the individualized nature of the experience. As one participant noted humorously, *"Didn't even notice the chat—we are introverts"* (P9).

Despite the low level of direct interaction, several respondents spontaneously commented on the perception of others' presence in the space. For instance, participant 11 recalled: *"There was also another avatar; it felt like there was another person looking at the art too. That added to the communal experience."* Similarly, participant 9 appreciated the subtle awareness of company: *"It's nice to know that you are somewhere where there are others. Makes it a nicer experience; it's a good thing to see others."* These remarks indicate that even without explicit communication, co-presence contributed to a faint sense of shared experience—an embryonic form of social facilitation.

Conversely, the absence of social cues could also diminish the perceived realism and emotional resonance of the virtual museum. One participant described this explicitly: *"It's a strange experience to go to a museum and you are all alone"* (P8). Others suggested that seeing avatars or familiar users could make the experience more engaging and authentic. As participant 11 concluded, *"Seeing other people makes the experience more communal."*

Participants proposed low-pressure ways to make others perceptible without forced conversation, such as thematic role-play through *"evening costumes, parasols, or walking sticks aligned with the 1900 setting"* (P9), alongside calls for *"more user participation and interactive functionality"* (P7).

Several participants engaged with community voting features: *"I voted for a piece of art that fit in the theme"* (P12), and others endorsed the idea for future exhibitions—*"Metagallery had the opportunity to vote on future exhibitions. Yes, absolutely, opinion matters"* (P13)—framing it as *"meaningful empowerment of users"* (P14).

5   Discussion and Conclusion

This study explored how the Finnish Metagallery in Decentraland succeeded in creating meaningful art experiences in a metaverse context. By applying the PSD model [16] as an analytical lens, the research illuminates how usefulness and ease of use, liking, tailoring, authority, and social facilitation were reflected in participants' accounts of engagement and perception in a virtual art exhibition. In doing so, the case adds nuance to optimistic claims that metaverse-based galleries could replicate or extend museum experiences [10,20] by showing how persuasive potential depends on the alignment of aesthetic, technical, and institutional factors.

Usefulness and Ease of Use. Convenience and accessibility were key drivers of positive engagement. The possibility to explore a national collection "from the living room" exemplifies how virtual exhibitions can lower spatial and temporal barriers, echoing prior work on the metaverse as an infrastructure for remote cultural participation [10,20,22,23]. From a PSD perspective, this aligns with the postulate that persuasive systems must be both useful and easy to use [16]. However, our findings also highlight that usability in metaverse environments is fragile. Performance issues, limited zoom, small labels, and hardware requirements broke the "flow" of experience for several participants. This resonates with the observation that current metaverse platforms often remain technically demanding and unevenly accessible [11,21].

Liking as Aesthetic Persuasion. Participants' accounts strongly confirm the central role of the PSD principle of liking [16]. When the Metagallery was perceived as visually coherent, users described the experience as immersive, "surprisingly good," and clearly better than "just browsing images on a computer." This aligns with the "what is beautiful is usable" effect [20] and HCI research showing that aesthetic pleasure fosters positive affect, perceived usability, and longer-term engagement [4,18]. At the same time, the results expose limits of aesthetic persuasion in metaverse art. Several participants, especially experienced museum-goers, found the exhibition "flat" and not comparable to a physical art experience. Their expectations had been shaped both by high-resolution digital imagery in other contexts and by the cultural weight of the FNG. This tension mirrors broader debates on whether virtual art can reproduce the embodied, social, and atmospheric qualities of museum visits [6,6,12,20]. Our findings suggest that liking in this context is not only a property of the interface but an interplay between artwork, spatial reconstruction and sensory design (e.g., soundscapes [2]). Interestingly, several participants explicitly asked for "more wow effect" and forms of interaction "only possible virtually," such as entering the world of the paintings or adding fantastical, historically inspired elements. This supports the view that metaverse art should not merely remediate physical exhibitions but explore genuinely new aesthetic affordances [12,14]. From a PSD standpoint, liking in virtual art may be strongest when aesthetic design highlights the medium's distinct possibilities rather than offering a conservative digital replica of a physical gallery.

Tailoring and Audience Expectations. The findings on tailoring show that the Metagallery primarily reached already culturally oriented audiences, especially people who follow the FNG. This is consistent with earlier work showing that early adopters of metaverse cultural experiences often already possess high cultural or technological capital [10,19]. Participants' reflections on potential audiences point toward tailoring strategies that differentiate between quick, lightweight visits and deeper, context-rich explorations. Their suggestions – multiple sound "modes" (historical vs.\ relaxing), options for more detailed process information, and expert commentary – map onto the tailoring feature as well [16]. Rather than a single, one-size-fits-all gallery, designers could provide layered experiences: highlight tours and translations for remote or casual visitors, and more demanding interpretive content and making-of materials for enthusiasts. This resonates with proposals in museum technology research to design virtual exhibitions as configurable experiences with varying levels of narrative and interaction [2,19].

Authority as Double-Edged Sword. The presence of the FNG as the organizing institution clearly enhanced credibility and trust. Participants described the gallery as a "safe frame" for their first metaverse experience, consistent with the PSD category of System credibility support [16] and prior work on how institutional authority underpins trust in digital cultural services [10,12]. For some, this credibility lowered psychological barriers to engaging with blockchain-based environments and wallets [23], which might otherwise be perceived as risky or overly technical. Yet institutional authority also raised expectations of curatorial and technical excellence. When image resolution, reconstruction detail, or interaction design fell short, disappointment was amplified by the strong brand behind the project. Authority thus acted as a double-edged cue: it increased initial motivation but also sharpened perceived shortcomings.

Social and Participatory Persuasion. The category of Social support in the PSD model [16] was only partially realized in the Metagallery. On the one hand, participants described a weak but meaningful form of social facilitation: simply seeing another avatar occasionally made the experience feel less lonely and more "communal." This is in line with the idea that even minimal awareness of others can enhance motivation in shared digital spaces [10]. On the other hand, most visits remained solitary, and features such as chat were often unnoticed or unused, which contrasts with visions of the metaverse as inherently social and co-present [10,20]. This may reflect not only design limitations but also the early-stage nature of metaverse museum use, where visitors, especially art enthusiasts, have not yet developed shared conventions for social interaction in such environments. The blockchain-based voting feature illustrates a different form of social persuasion: participatory decision-making about future exhibitions and NFTs as recognition of contribution [14,22]. Several participants experienced voting as a meaningful way to influence the gallery, suggesting that soft forms of co-curation can foster a sense of ownership even in low-interaction environments, in line with cultural heritage research on participatory and co-creative practices [10,18]. For future designs, it may be more important to offer multiple social support mechanisms – from unobtrusive co-presence to more interactive tools – than to rely on any single channel, especially given that the metaverse was a new medium for many participants and some features were only lightly used.

Table 2. PSD postulates and design implications

PSD postulate and features	Design implication
Usefulness & Ease of Use	Keep frictionless entry; add direct full-view for artworks; ensure adaptive performance so heaviness doesn't undermine usefulness.
Dialogue Support—Liking	Invest in higher-resolution assets, guided viewpoints and lighting, plus opt-in metaverse-only moments to avoid a flat feel.
Primary Task Support—Tailoring	Tailor to distinct audiences: highlight tours and translations; adjustable soundscapes and pacing; depth-on-demand context for enthusiasts; uniquely virtual features to engage younger users.
System Credibility—Authority	Surface curator/FNG provenance; maintain craftsmanship and accuracy; set expectations clearly to reinforce institutional credibility.
Social Support—Social Facilitation	Provide ambient co-presence (visible occupancy, gentle proximity cues, scheduled tours) and low-friction participation (in-gallery/web voting with clear outcomes).

Integrating PSD Features in Metaverse Art Design. Taken together, the Finnish Metagallery case suggests that the persuasive potential of art in the metaverse does not stem from technological novelty alone but from the orchestration of PSD features: usefulness and ease of use, liking, tailoring, credibility, and social support [16]. Table 2 synthesizes how these features manifested in the Finnish Metagallery and translates them into actionable design implications. For example, suggestions for better zoom, larger labels, and lighter technical requirements highlight how usefulness and ease of use are preconditions for aesthetic persuasion; proposals for multiple sound and content "modes" illustrate tailoring; and calls for more visible others and participatory mechanisms signal the need to strengthen social support.

In relation to prior work on virtual art and museums, the case both confirms and complicates earlier findings. Like Lin et al. [15], we observe that virtual environments can support meaningful art experiences, but our results stress that such experiences are unevenly distributed and easily undermined by technical and design shortcomings. Echoing Sylaiou et al. [19] and Giannini and Bowen [10], the study suggests that metaverse exhibitions indeed expand access and experimentation, yet the promise of "museum beyond museums" remains contingent on resolving issues of accessibility, atmosphere, and sociality.

Contributions and Future Research. This study extends persuasive technology research by applying the PSD framework to digital culture and art, illustrating how aesthetic experience can be conceptualized as a persuasive mechanism in metaverse exhibitions. Although the Metagallery did not explicitly aim to change user behavior, it embodied an implicit persuasive intent common to cultural institutions: encouraging repeated visits, sustained interest, and continued engagement with art in new formats. In this sense, persuasion operates as an infrastructural assumption rather than an overt design strategy. Rather than explicit nudging, persuasion here emerges through visual and experiential qualities that invite voluntary, reflective engagement with artworks and their context.

For designers and institutions, a key implication is to treat visual quality, accessibility, institutional credibility, and participatory features as interdependent goals, and to leverage metaverse-specific affordances such as tailored visit modes and richer sensory environments. At the same time, this study does not directly measure attitude or behavior change but focuses on participants' self-reported experiences and perceived persuasive potential; the findings should therefore be interpreted as insights into experiential persuasion rather than confirmed behavioral outcomes.

Future work should compare platforms and experimentally vary aesthetic and interactive features to examine their effects on attention, emotion, and cultural learning over time. Exploration of metaverse-specific incentives, such as NFT-based rewards that function as motivational cues within virtual cultural spaces, also warrants further investigation. There is particular value in exploratory and longitudinal studies that combine interviews with behavioral observation across different technical pilots, enabling more systematic investigation of how virtual environments can be designed to support meaningful engagement and potential behavior change over time. Overall, the Finnish Metagallery case suggests that metaverse-based exhibitions can offer a convincing and emotionally resonant experience when aesthetics, usability, tailoring, credibility, and social support are carefully aligned.

Acknowledgement. We gratefully acknowledge the Finnish National Gallery for enabling the study of the Metagallery and inspiring its exploration of virtual art spaces. We also thank Sitra, the Finnish Innovation Fund, for their valuable support. Our sincere appreciation goes to all participants whose insights were essential to understanding virtual art experiences.

References

1. Adventure club: meta-gallery project (2022). https://competitionentries.adventureclub.io/2022/meta-gallery/. Accessed 31 Oct 2025
2. Baratè, A., Ludovico, L.A., Presti, G.: Sound design for paintings in virtual art exhibitions. J. New Music Res. (2023)
3. Braun, V., Clarke, V.: Using thematic analysis in psychology. Qual. Res. Psychol. **3**(2), 77–101 (2006)
4. Cyr, D., Head, M., Ivanov, A.: Design aesthetics leading to web trust, satisfaction, and loyalty in online business. Int. J. Hum Comput Stud. **67**(10), 850–869 (2009)
5. Decentraland: Official website. https://decentraland.org/. Accessed 31 Oct 2025
6. Deleuze, G., Wolfe, C.T.: The actual and the virtual. Architecture New York, ANY (1997)
7. Dewey, J.: Having an Experience. Minton, Balch and Company (1934)
8. Finnish Metagallery: Official website. https://web.archive.org/web/20230330195603/https://finnishmetagallery.fi/. Accessed 31 Oct 2025
9. Giannini, T., Bowen, J.P.: Museums and the metaverse: new signs of computational art and life. Digital Creativity (2023)
10. Guidi, B., Michienzi, A.: Social games and blockchain: exploring the metaverse of decentraland. In: IEEE 42nd International Conference on Distributed Computing Systems Workshops (ICDCSW), pp. 190–195 (2022)
11. Hurst, W., et al.: Digital art and the metaverse: benefits and challenges. Future Internet **15**(6), 188 (2023)
12. Kalpokas, I., Kalpokienė, J.: Regulating the Metaverse: A Critical Assessment. Routledge (2023)
13. Kępińska, A., Wiśniewski, R.: Metaverse and its creative potential for visual arts. Acta Universitatis Lodziensis. Folia Sociologica **85**, 57–75 (2023)
14. Lee, L., et al.: All one needs to know about metaverse: a complete survey on technological singularity, virtual ecosystem, and research agenda. Found. Trends Hum. Comput. Interact. **18**(2–3), 100–337 (2024)
15. Lin, C.L., Chen, S.J., Lin, R.: Efficacy of virtual reality in painting art exhibitions appreciation. Appl. Sci. **10**(9), 3012 (2020)
16. Oinas-Kukkonen, H., Harjumaa, M.: Persuasive systems design: key issues, process model, and system features. Commun. Assoc. Inf. Syst. **24**, 485–500 (2009)
17. Silvennoinen, J.M., Jokinen, J.P.P.: Aesthetics and affect in human–computer interaction. Comput. Hum. Behav. **59**, 197–207 (2016)
18. Sitra: Sitra and the finnish national gallery pilot an interactive virtual art exhibition to explore the metaverse. https://www.sitra.fi/en/news/sitra-and-the-finnish-national-gallery-pilot-an-interactive-virtual-artexhibition-to-explore-the-metaverse/ (2022). Accessed 31 Oct 2025
19. Sylaiou, S., et al.: From physical to virtual art exhibitions and beyond: survey and some issues for consideration for the metaverse. J. Cult. Herit. **66**, 86–98 (2024)
20. Tractinsky, N.: Toward the study of aesthetics in information technology. In: Proceedings of the International Conference on Information Systems (ICIS) (2004)
21. Venugopal, J.P., Subramanian, A.A.V., Peatchimuthu, J.: The realm of metaverse: a survey. Comput. Animation Virtual Worlds **34**(5), e2150 (2023)

22. Wang, H., et al.: A survey on the metaverse: the state-of-the-art, technologies, applications, and challenges. IEEE Internet Things J. **10**(16), 14671–14688 (2023)
23. Wang, S., Ding, W., Li, J., Yuan, Y., Ouyang, L., Wang, F.Y.: Decentralized autonomous organizations: concept, model, and applications. IEEE Trans. Comput. Soc. Syst. **6**(5), 870–878 (2019)

Estimating the Perceived Burden
of Disaster Preparedness Using Location
Data: An Exploratory Study

Mizuki Miura[1(✉)], Zhixiong Chen[1], Akihiro Kobayashi[2], Masato Taya[1],
and Daisuke Kamisaka[1]

[1] KDDI Research, Inc., Saitama 356-8502, Japan
`{mi-miura,zh-chen,ma-taya,da-kamisaka}@kddi.com`
[2] KDDI Corporation, Tokyo 108-0074, Japan
`ao-kobayashi@kddi.com`

Abstract. As natural disasters intensify, translating awareness into concrete preparedness remains difficult. We propose a framework to estimate individuals' perceived burdens for disaster preparedness by integrating location data with psychological indicators. A BERT-based location encoder models GPS trajectories as token sequences to learn contextual mobility embeddings, which are combined with daily mobility, demographics, personality, and preparedness stage. Using five months of GPS data from 61,846 users for pre-training and survey data from 500 participants for classification, the framework estimates perceived burdens across eight behaviors. Three main insights emerged. First, mobility-informed modeling effectively estimated preparedness-related attitudes at the individual level, with higher accuracy for routine behaviors such as checking home safety or stocking supplies than for socially coordinated actions like community drills. Second, incorporating temporal and personal contextual embeddings—particularly home and workplace locations—yielded the best performance, suggesting that personal spatial context captures lifestyle patterns relevant to perceived burden. Third, adding psychological and attitudinal features, including GRIT, Big Five traits, and preparedness stage, improved classification accuracy beyond mobility features alone. Overall, these findings indicate that combining mobility and psychological factors supports more precise, personalized modeling of preparedness tendencies, providing a foundation for adaptive persuasive systems that encourage proactive, user-centered disaster preparedness.

Keywords: Disaster preparedness · BERT · Smartphone location data

1 Introduction

As natural disasters intensify, fostering individual preparedness—such as securing emergency supplies or confirming evacuation routes—has become increasingly important. Despite innovations including chatbot-based evacuation prompts [1], weather-linked risk information [2], and VR/AR disaster training [3,4], many people remain unprepared. This persistent gap between awareness and action, known as the risk perception paradox [5], continues to challenge disaster research [6,7]. Although cognitive biases such as risk underestimation [8] and present bias [9] have been identified, effective ways to translate awareness into concrete preparedness behavior remain limited. For adaptive persuasive systems, inferring users' psychological traits from everyday behavior is therefore crucial, as traditional surveys mainly capture intentions and rely on self-reports that often diverge from real actions [10–12].

This study focuses on human mobility—time-series data of movements and stays obtained from GPS and related sensors—as a behavioral lens into psychology. Prior work has shown that smartphone-based mobility data can reveal stable personality traits [13,14], but it remains unclear whether such data can estimate disaster preparedness tendencies, particularly attitudes and willingness to take protective action. Building on this, we hypothesize that mobility patterns encode attitudinal preparedness. Recent advances in Natural Language Processing (NLP) and Large Language Models (LLMs) [15] enable sequence-based modeling that represents spatiotemporal trajectories as tokens embedding both context and intent.

We propose a perceived-burden estimation framework using a Bidirectional Encoder Representations from Transformers (BERT)-based Location Encoder [16], combined with psychological indicators such as personality traits (Big Five) [17,18] and persistence and consistency (GRIT) [19,20]. The model was pre-trained on unlabeled GPS data from 61,846 users and trained using questionnaire data from 500 participants. Extending prior mobility-based personality studies [13,14], this work estimates disaster preparedness tendencies by focusing on individuals' perceived burdens in preparedness actions, suggesting the potential of mobility-informed language modeling for future context-aware persuasive approaches.

2   Related Work

2.1   Disaster Preparedness and Behavioral Discrepancies

The persistent gap between disaster awareness and protective behavior—known as the risk perception paradox [5]—has long challenged disaster research [6]. Studies on action prioritization [7], risk underestimation [8], and present bias [9] have clarified cognitive mechanisms but have not sufficiently explained how awareness translates into sustained preparedness action.

In persuasive technology, personalization is a well-established strategy for behavior change [21,22]. However, in disaster preparedness, practical applications remain limited, as many systems rely on static profiles or self-reported data that overlook changing contexts and motivations. Traditional surveys assess perception and self-efficacy [12] but often diverge from real behavior and lack temporal granularity [10,11], limiting insight into everyday preparedness practices.

2.2   NLP and LLMs-Based Behavioral Modeling

This study conceptualizes mobility as everyday human movement represented as sequential GPS records, such as trips between home, work, and activity locations. While earlier mobility studies relied on supervised learning or clustering [23–25], more recent work applies Natural Language Processing (NLP) and Large Language Models (LLMs) by treating location sequences as tokens. Models such as BERT [16] and Generative Pre-trained Transformer (GPT) [15] enable sequence-based modeling that captures contextual semantics of spatiotemporal trajectories.

Prior research has shown that mobility data can serve as proxies for psychological traits. For example, de Montjoye et al. clustered users by Big Five personality dimensions using mobility logs [13], and Stachl et al. predicted personality traits from large-scale smartphone sensor data [14], indicating that traits are reflected in mobility regularities. Ziepert et al. [26] further linked GPS-derived features to psychological constructs, and together with recent LLM-based personality inference from user interactions [27,28], these studies provide growing evidence that behavioral traces can be used to estimate psychological and attitudinal states.

2.3   Research Gap and Motivation

Prior work in persuasive technology, personality modeling, and mobility analysis emphasizes integrating psychological and behavioral perspectives to understand human action. Although mobility data offer ecologically valid behavioral information, they have rarely been used to estimate psychological or attitudinal states related to disaster preparedness. Practical frameworks linking real-world mobility with psychological estimation in this domain remain limited.

To address this gap, we introduce a perceived-burden estimation framework using a BERT-based location encoder. By focusing on everyday mobility and psychological states, this study explores a foundational approach for understanding the gap between cognition and action, contributing to persuasive technology in disaster preparedness.

3   Proposed Approach

3.1   Overview of the Framework

This study estimates individuals' perceived burden in disaster preparedness by modeling mobility behavior with a BERT-based location encoder and integrating psychological and behavioral features. The framework consists of three components: a location encoder trained on large-scale GPS data, feature construction combining mobility and survey variables, and a classifier predicting perceived burdens (Fig. 1).

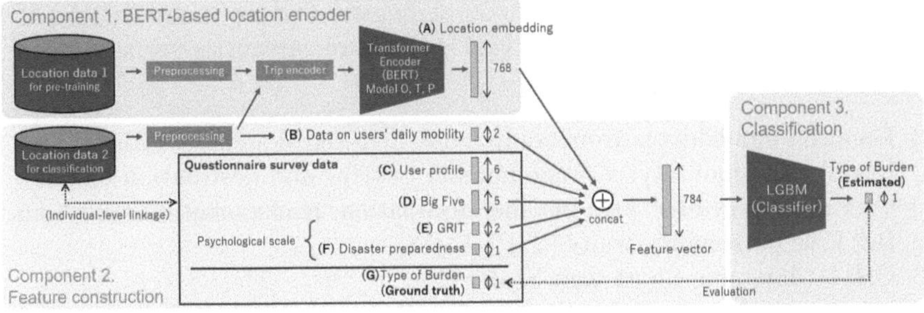

Fig. 1. Analytical framework of the perceived burden estimation system.

The approach follows hierarchical learning: generalized mobility representations are learned from large unlabeled GPS data, refined using a smaller labeled dataset with psychological information, and finally classified using a Light Gradient Boosting Machine (LGBM) [29]. This design links everyday mobility patterns with psychological predispositions, providing a basis for context-aware persuasive modeling.

Component 1: BERT-Based Location Encoder. The BERT-based location encoder transforms raw GPS trajectories into embeddings that capture the spatio-temporal patterns of individual mobility. Each trip is treated as a sequence of grid cell IDs—unique identifiers assigned to evenly divided areas on a geographic grid, analogous to words in a sentence—and trained with the Masked Language Modeling (MLM) [30] to learn contextual dependencies between locations without explicit labels. Three tokenization settings are applied: Model O (location grid IDs only), Model T (including temporal context: day/night and weekday/holiday), and Model P (including personal context: estimated home and workplace). These contextual variations serve as sub-word augmentations, allowing the model to learn how spatial and personal contexts shape movement semantics. The encoder outputs 768-dimensional embeddings for each trip and functions as a fixed feature extractor for classification.

Component 2: Feature Construction. Embeddings from the BERT-based location encoder (feature A) are combined with behavioral and psychological variables (features B-F) to create a comprehensive feature vector for classifying perceived burden (variable G) (see Fig. 1). Feature categories are as follows:

(A) Location embeddings from component 1, using Model O, T and P.
(B) Users' daily mobility: average number of trips and destination distance.
(C) User profile: gender, age, income, occupation, transportation, and housing.
(D) Big Five personality traits (TIPI-J) [18].
(E) GRIT (Japanese Short Grit Scale) [20].
(F) Disaster preparedness stage (based on the transtheoretical model).
(G) Type of burden (eight disaster preparedness behaviors).

We concatenate (A) 768-dim location embeddings with (B)-(F) behavioral and psychological variables to a 784-dim feature vector as input to estimate target (G). All features derive from large-scale GPS data and synchronized surveys.

Component 3: Classification Using an LGBM. To estimate perceived burdens across eight preparedness behaviors, we employ an LGBM as the classifier. LGBM was chosen for its ability to capture nonlinear relationships between high-dimensional features and psychological outcomes, robustness against overfitting with limited data, and interpretable feature importance for post-hoc analysis.

3.2   Estimation Process

Building on Sect. 3.1, which introduced the components of the proposed framework, this section details the procedural steps of the location-based modeling used to estimate individuals' perceived burden in disaster preparedness. Adapting contextual learning from NLP, location sequences are treated as sentences of words. A BERT-based location encoder captures semantic relationships between locations shaped by temporal, routine, and personal contexts, followed by component 1 pre-training on large-scale GPS data and component 3 classification using an LGBM to predict perceived burdens.

Preprocessing, Trip Encoder and Pre-training (as Component 1). Raw GPS trajectories are transformed into structured sequences for language modeling, representing human mobility as semantically rich data reflecting psychological and attitudinal patterns. The trip encoder extracts spatial and contextual features by tokenizing each grid cell ID as a "word" and each trip as a "sentence." Following Kobayashi et al. [31], a trip is defined as movement between stay points detected by time and distance thresholds. Each GPS point is mapped to a 250 m grid, merging consecutive points, while subword tokens [32] encode temporal and personal attributes (e.g., day/night, weekday/weekend, home/workplace) to capture situational semantics. For instance, similar to "playing" being composed of "play" and "##ing" in NLP, a token such as "5000000012 2500000011" combines a grid cell ID with a subword attribute (e.g., home). Tokens are space-separated, and line breaks mark trip boundaries. Repeated grid IDs are compressed (A, A, A, B, C, C → A, B, C) to handle irregular GPS sampling.

Pre-training follows MLM [30] used in BERT [16]. A subset of grid tokens is masked and predicted from context, allowing the encoder to learn spatio-temporal dependencies (e.g., "home → station → workplace"). Without explicit spatial metadata, it infers mobility relations from token co-occurrence, developing contextual representations of users' routines and adaptability linked to psychological traits. During training, only grid IDs are predicted to avoid interference from subword features, improving spatial transition learning while preserving context. This process enables to learn latent behavioral patterns and contextual dependencies from mobility sequences. The resulting embeddings (feature A) are then concatenated with behavioral and psychological variables (features B-F) into a unified feature vector, which is used to train an LGBM classifier to predict the target variable (feature G).

Classification (as Component 3). After pre-training, the BERT-based location encoder outputs trip-level embeddings capturing spatial and behavioral semantics. Combined with psychological and behavioral variables, these embeddings train an LGBM classifier to estimate users' psychological and attitudinal tendencies toward preparedness. LGBM models nonlinear relationships, avoids overfitting, and provides interpretable feature importance, clarifying how mobility patterns reflect users' motivational readiness—that is, their willingness and preparedness to take protective actions—and offering insights that may support personalized, context-aware persuasive approaches.

4   Evaluation Experiment

4.1   Dataset

This section describes the dataset for evaluating the perceived burden estimation system. Table 1 summarizes the variables: (A–B) location-based features from smartphone GPS data, (C–F) demographic and psychological variables from surveys, and (G) the response variable of perceived burdens in disaster preparedness. All location and survey data were collected and analyzed with prior informed consent from participants and approval from the respective data providers, in accordance with their ethical guidelines. The data were anonymized and used solely for the purpose of this study, and were not repurposed for any other analyses.

Location Data for Pre-training. For Component 1 (pre-training), Location Data 1 (feature A) consisted of anonymized smartphone GPS records collected over five months (March–July 2019) in Utsunomiya and Tsukuba (Japan), provided by KDDI Corporation with user consent. These data comprise time-stamped latitude–longitude points representing users' everyday movements and stays, from which continuous mobility trajectories were reconstructed. The

Table 1. Measurement items for the survey.

Location data 1	(A)	Location embeddings	Model O, T, P
Location data 2	(B)	Data on users' daily mobility	1. Trips per day for a user 2. OD straight-line distance for all trips
User profile	(C)	Gender	1. Male 2. Female
		Age	1. 20–25 2. 26–30 3. 31–35 4. 36–40
		Annual income (¥)	1.0 2.0-2M 3.2-4M 4.4-6M 5.4-6M
		Occupation	1. Company employee 2. Professionals 3. Part-time jobs 4. Student 5. Unemployed
		Transportation	1. Car and motorcycle 2. Train and bus 3. Walking and cycling 4. None
		Housing	1. Rental 2. Homeowner 3. Company
Psychological scale	(D)	Big Five	Ten Item Personality Inventory [18]
	(E)	GRIT	Japanese Short Grit Scale [20]
Disaster preparedness	(F)	Action and will	1. I haven't done and I don't plan. 2. I plan to change next six months. 3. I plan to change next month. 4. I have changed for less than six months. 5. I have changed for over six months.
Type of burden	(G)	Eight coping behaviors	1. Physical 2. Financial 3. Time 4. Continuous 5. Community 6. None

dataset included 61,846 users, and representative home and workplace locations were inferred as grid cells with the highest dwell frequency during nighttime and daytime periods, respectively, using Japan's quarter-mesh system [33].

Location and Questionnaire Survey Data for Feature Construction.
For component 2 (feature construction), two data sources were used and individually linked at the participant level to integrate location-based and psychological information. First, GPS data collected by GEO Technologies Inc. (July–September 2025) provided location data 2 (B), which was extracted only from weekends and holidays during the collection period to capture private mobility patterns rather than work-related movements. This dataset consisted of two daily mobility indicators: the average number of trips per day and the mean origin–destination (OD) distance. Here, a trip refers to a continuous movement sequence between two distinct stay points. Second, an online survey conducted by GEO Technologies Inc. during the same period targeted participants aged 20–40 who lived alone in flood-prone areas. The survey examined user profiles (feature C)—gender, age, income, occupation, usual means of transportation, and housing type—treated as categorical variables (Table 2). It also measured psychological traits (features D and E), comprising the Big Five—Openness, Conscientiousness, Extraversion, Agreeableness, and Neuroticism—assessed with the Ten Item Personality Inventory (TIPI-J) [17], and GRIT —perseverance and consistency—measured by the Japanese Short Grit Scale (Grit-S) [19]. In addition, the survey included the disaster preparedness stage (feature F), a categorical variable based on the Transtheoretical Model (TTM) [34], and the type of burden (feature G), the response variable representing perceived physical, financial, temporal, and social burdens across eight coping behaviors. We filtered inconsistent responses or missing GPS data, yielding 500 valid participants.

Table 2. Measurement items for eight coping behaviors with (G).

	Coping behavior
*No.*1	Check the risk level of the residence on a hazard map.
*No.*2	Ensuring access to weather and local government information.
*No.*3	Understanding the structure, number of floors, and age of the home.
*No.*4	Participating in local disaster prevention training.
*No.*5	Sharing safety confirmation methods with housemates.
*No.*6	Find the nearest evacuation shelter on a map or by foot.
*No.*7	Stocking up emergency food supplies and maintaining a rolling stock.
*No.*8	Purchasing insurance for natural disasters.

4.2   Evaluation Conditions

We implemented BERT using the Hugging Face Transformers library [35], following the standard architecture of 12 layers with a hidden size of 768 and 12 self-attention heads [16]. The pre-trained models (O, T, P) were evaluated using top-100 accuracy on the MLM task [30], defined as the ratio of masked grid cell IDs correctly predicted within the top 100 candidates. Models O, T, and P achieved accuracies of 93.8%, 94.6%, and 96.3%, respectively, consistent with previous studies [36]. For a perceived burden estimation, each model was trained and tested using three-fold user-level cross-validation, and the F1 score was adopted as the primary metric to address class imbalance. This setup isolates the contribution of temporal and personal contextual features to predicting perceived burdens in disaster preparedness behaviors.

4.3   Evaluation Results

F1 Scores. Fig. 2 presents F1 scores of Model O, which uses mobility embeddings without encoder-specific features, for perceived burden estimation across eight disaster preparedness behaviors (No.1–8). Precision, recall, and F1 were computed per label and aggregated using micro, macro, and weighted averages. Each measure offers a different perspective: the micro average reflects overall accuracy but can overlook minority behaviors; the macro average treats all labels equally, emphasizing rare behavior performance; and the weighted average balances these by class frequency [37]. Across all behaviors, micro F1 values were highest, followed by weighted and macro averages, indicating that the model performs well for dominant, frequently reported behaviors but less effectively for rare or socially complex actions. Behaviors such as No.3 (checking home safety), No.5 (stocking supplies), and No.8 (insurance preparation) achieved higher F1 scores, reflecting strong links to routine mobility and personal spatial patterns, whereas No.4 (community drills) and No.7 (sharing safety methods) scored lower, as these involve interaction with others and socially coordinated decision-making that are less directly captured by individual mobility patterns. Overall, the proposed approach is effective for estimating preparedness tendencies at the individual level, while behaviors requiring social coordination or collective intention may need complementary frameworks that incorporate social or environmental data beyond personal mobility records. This finding is consistent with previous disaster psychology research, which has shown that individual-level preparedness actions (e.g., stockpiling, confirming home safety) are primarily shaped by habitual behavior and perceived personal control, while collective preparedness activities (e.g., community participation, mutual assistance) are influenced by social norms, trust, and group identity rather than personal routines [5,12]. In this context, the present results align with established behavioral models in disaster preparedness, suggesting that individual preparedness actions are more closely tied to daily mobility and spatial routines.

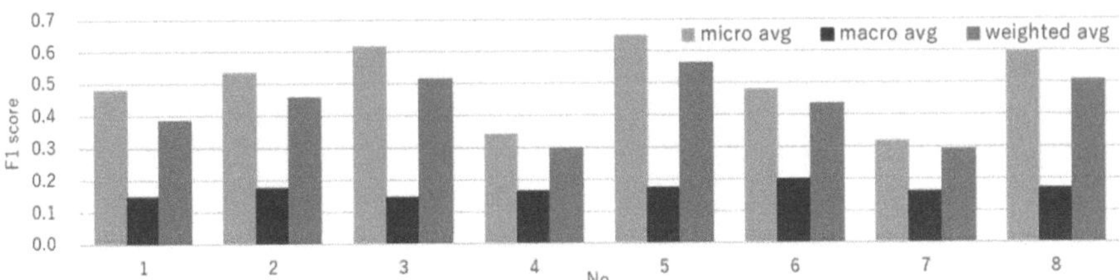

Fig. 2. F1 scores (micro, macro, weighted averages) for eight disaster preparedness behaviors.

From a persuasive technology perspective, these findings indicate that mobility-derived behavioral patterns can act as implicit indicators of users' psychological traits and preparedness-related attitudes. High F1 scores for routine, mobility-related behaviors suggest that individuals' daily movement patterns are associated with stable psychological dispositions—such as persistence or conscientiousness—that shape how they perceive and engage in preparedness actions. The target cohort in this study—individuals aged 20–40 living alone in flood-prone areas—represents a population that prior disaster research has shown to engage less frequently in preparedness behaviors, particularly among younger adults and men [38]. This cohort is generally more mobile and independent than older populations, making them well suited for examining how mobility patterns and psychological tendencies jointly relate to preparedness attitudes.

These results imply that understanding who the user is, through mobility-informed psychological profiling, can support more personalized and effective persuasive designs. This interpretation aligns with theories of context-aware and personalized persuasion, which emphasize tailoring interventions to users' characteristics and situational contexts rather than relying on uniform, self-reported data [39–41]. The Fogg Behavior Model (FBM) [42] conceptualizes behavior as arising from the interplay of motivation, ability, and triggers, while the Persuasive Systems Design (PSD) model [39] highlights personalization and contextual relevance as core principles of effective persuasion. Building on this, Kaptein et al. [40] demonstrated that integrating behavioral and psychological information enables adaptive persuasion that aligns with users' personality-driven responsiveness to different persuasive strategies. Accordingly, the present findings suggest that mobility-informed psychological inference provides a valuable foundation for designing user-specific persuasive approaches in disaster preparedness— approaches that can adapt communication style or content to match the psychological traits inferred from individual mobility behavior. In summary, mobility-informed modeling not only enhances prediction of behavioral tendencies but also contributes to the theoretical and practical development of personalized, context-aware persuasive systems that may encourage proactive, sustained preparedness behavior in real-world, disaster-prone environments.

Effect of Features. Figure 3 compares the F1 scores of three models—Model O (no contextual features), T (temporal context: day/night, weekday/holiday), and P (personal context: estimated home and workplace)—across eight disaster preparedness behaviors. Each model was tested under three conditions: using only daily mobility features (+B), using all explanatory features (+all (B-F)), and using no additional features. Overall, Model T slightly outperformed Model O, particularly for mobility-related behaviors such as No.3 (checking home safety), No.5 (stocking supplies), and No.8 (insurance preparation), suggesting that temporal information reflecting daily routines improves estimation of perceived burden in habitual actions. The greatest improvement was observed in Model P, which achieved the highest overall F1 scores when all features (B-F) were included. This indicates that integrating personal contextual information—such as home and workplace embeddings—with behavioral and psychological variables provides the most effective predictions. Even with modest gains, Model P captured user-specific lifestyle patterns and spatial tendencies that other models could not, enabling a more individualized understanding of preparedness perceptions. A similar pattern appeared in a related study on trip purpose estimation [43], where Model P achieved higher accuracy for mid-scale purposes such as shopping and personal errands, supporting the robustness and generalizability of these findings.

In addition to differences between models, variations among feature sets also contributed to predictive performance. When comparing models trained only with daily mobility indicators (features B) to those using all explanatory variables (B–F), the inclusion of psychological and attitudinal features—such as GRIT, Big Five traits, and preparedness stage—consistently improved classification accuracy across behaviors. This result highlights that combining mobility-based features with psychological factors provides a richer representation of preparedness tendencies. Among these, GRIT- and conscientiousness-related traits were strongly associated with proactive behaviors (e.g., stocking supplies, maintaining insurance), while preparedness stage information was associated with differences in users' readiness levels. These findings indicate that the joint consideration of contextual mobility data and psychological features is important for modeling preparedness-related attitudes, suggesting that future persuasive systems may benefit from leveraging both behavioral context and personality-driven tendencies for personalization. Behavioral variables such as trip frequency and OD distance are associated with ability—a person's situational capacity for action—while psychological traits like GRIT and conscientiousness are associated with motivation, paralleling the dimensions proposed in the FBM [42]. From a disaster psychology perspective, this pattern is consistent with prior findings that persistence, self-efficacy, and risk awareness are correlated with proactive preparedness actions [11,12]. Taken together, these results offer a coherent, correlational account of how mobility-derived behavioral patterns and psychological motivation are jointly related to preparedness-related attitudes.

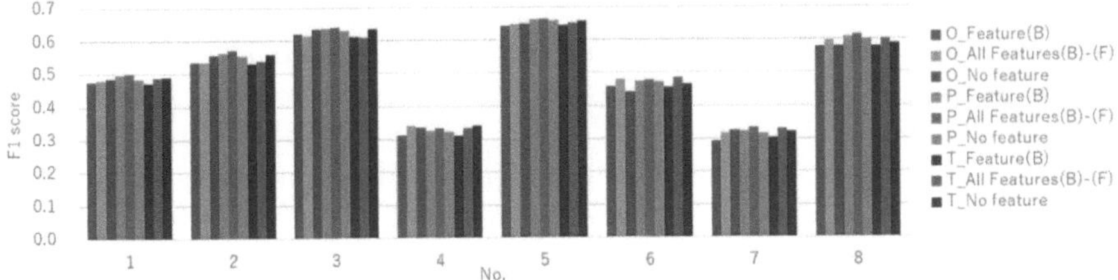

Fig. 3. Comparison of features from three models (O, P, T)

To interpret these results, consider a hypothetical individual in their 20 s–30 s living alone in a flood-prone area who has not actively engaged in disaster preparedness. Mobility features (A, B) may indicate regular, limited movement mainly between home, work, and nearby locations, suggesting restricted time and spatial flexibility and thus a lower situational capacity for additional preparedness actions. At the same time, psychological indicators (D–E) may be associated with perceiving sustained preparedness as burdensome despite existing risk awareness. Combined with their preparedness stage (F), this configuration illustrates a typical intention–action gap, in which awareness is present but concrete behavior is delayed due to perceived effort and limited motivation.

From a persuasive technology perspective, these results clarify how behavioral context and psychological disposition interact to shape preparedness-related attitudes. The dominance of mobility-based feature (B) suggests that behavioral regularities reflect an individual's situational patterns and capacity for action, while psychological indicators such as GRIT and Big Five traits capture motivational tendencies that influence how people perceive and engage in preparedness behaviors. This study provides a methodological basis for understanding user diversity—how individuals differ in motivation and behavior through integrated mobility and psychological profiles. By linking daily mobility with cognitive and motivational attributes, the framework contributes to data-driven personalization, which seeks to tailor interventions to users' dispositions and behavioral styles [44–46]. Integrating behavioral and psychological modeling moves persuasive technology beyond trigger-based approaches by enabling the inference of persuasion-relevant characteristics from real-world behavior. Recent studies on AI-supported personalization emphasize that adapting to users' psychological profiles can enhance both transparency and persuasive effectiveness [44,46], echoing Orji et al. [45], who highlight that recognizing traits such as persistence or emotional stability is vital for engagement and autonomy. Accordingly, the proposed framework offers a foundation for persuasive systems that adapt communication and strategy to users' behavioral and psychological characteristics. Although persuasive effects were not tested, this study provides methodological groundwork for future systems that tailor preparedness messages or nudges to motivational profiles, supporting the development of practical, human-centered persuasive technologies for disaster preparedness.

5   Conclusion

This study proposed a framework for estimating individuals' perceived burden in disaster preparedness by integrating mobility data with psychological indicators. Using a BERT-based location encoder and LGBM classifier, we modeled behavioral and attitudinal tendencies across preparedness behaviors to explore how daily mobility and psychological traits jointly influence readiness.

The study produced three main insights. First, mobility-informed modeling was effective in estimating preparedness-related attitudes at the individual level. Across all behaviors, micro F1 scores were the highest, indicating that the model captured dominant, indivisual routine behaviors—such as checking home safety or stocking supplies—more accurately than socially coordinated actions like community drills, which depend on collective intention. Second, the model which incorporated both temporal and personal contextual embeddings—particularly users' home and workplace locations—achieved the best overall performance. This suggests that embedding personal spatial context enables the model to represent user-specific lifestyle patterns and behavioral regularities more effectively, improving its ability to estimate perceived burden. Third, integrating mobility-based and psychological features offered practical insights for persuasive system design. Incorporating psychological and attitudinal features improved classification accuracy across behaviors. When comparing models trained only with daily mobility indicators to those using all explanatory variables, the inclusion of factors such as GRIT, Big Five traits, and preparedness stage enhanced predictive performance. This framework contributes to understanding user diversity—how motivational and behavioral tendencies differ among individuals—providing a foundation for adaptive persuasive systems that can personalize strategies based on users' behavioral and psychological characteristics.

While the proposed framework estimated preparedness-related psychological tendencies, limitations remain. Although the study established a methodological foundation for linking behavior and psychology, persuasive effects were not empirically validated. The next phase of this research will involve developing a personalized disaster preparedness application designed to promote behavioral change and conducting empirical validation through user studies and field experiments. In the future, this work aims to incorporate multimodal contextual information—such as mobility, emotion and environmental cues—to improve interpretability, ethical transparency, and the overall design of persuasive systems, ultimately aiming to foster personalized disaster preparedness.

Acknowledgments. This work was supported by JST, PRESTO Grant Number JPMJPR246A, Japan.

References

1. Urbanelli, A., Frisiello, A., Bruno, L., Rossi, C.: The ERMES chatbot: A conversational communication tool for improved emergency management and disaster risk reduction. Int. J. Disaster Risk Reduct. **112** (2024)
2. Meléndez-Landaverde, E.R., Sempere-Torres, D.: A user experience evaluation of a mobile application for disseminating site-specific impact-based flood warnings: The A4alerts app. J. Flood Risk Manage. **18**(1), (2023)
3. Khanal, S., Ishikawa, T., Yamaguchi, Y.: Virtual and augmented reality in the disaster management technology: a literature review of the past 11 years. Front. Virtual Real. **3** (2022)
4. Papadopoulos, N., Kourmpetis, A., Skourtas, D.: The potential of disaster digital archives in disaster education. Int. J. Disaster Risk Reduct. **80** (Oct 2022)
5. Wachinger, G., Renn, O., Begg, C., Kuhlicke, C.: The risk perception paradox–Implications for governance and communication of natural hazards. Risk Anal. **33**(6), 1049–1065 (2013)
6. Solberg, L.M., Rossetto, R., Joffe, T.H.: The impact of risk perception on preparedness: a case study of the 2004 Indian Ocean tsunami in Norway. Int. J. Mass Emergencies Disast. **28**(1), 103–129 (2010)
7. Sullivan-Wiley, K., Gianotti, A.: Risk perception, adaptive capacity, and climate change adaptation in rural Nicaragua. Clim. Risk Manag. **17**, 1–12 (2017)
8. Lechowska, E.: What determines flood risk perception? A review of factors of flood risk perception and relations between its basic elements. Nat. Hazards **94**(3), 1341–1366 (2018)
9. Laibson, D.: Golden eggs and hyperbolic discounting. Quart. J. Econom. **112**(2), 443–477 (1997)
10. Mileti, D.S., Sorensen, J.H.: Communication of emergency public warnings: a social science perspective and state-of-the-art assessment. Oak Ridge National Laboratory (2017)
11. Grothmann, T., Reusswig, F.: People at risk of flooding: Why some residents take precautionary action while others do not. Nat. Hazards **38**(1–2), 101–120 (2006)

12. Paton, D., Smith, L., Johnston, D.: 'When good intentions turn bad: promoting natural hazard preparedness. Australian J. Emerg. Manage. **20**(1), 25–30 (May 2005)
13. de Montjoye, Y.-A., Quoidbach, J., Robic, F., Pentland, A.S.: Predicting personality using novel mobile phone-based metrics. In: Proceedings of the 6th International Conference on Social Computing and Behavioral-Cultural Modeling and Prediction (SBP 2013) (2013)
14. Stachl, C., et al.: Predicting personality from patterns of behavior collected with smartphones. In: Proceedings of the National Academy of Sciences (PNAS), vol. 117(30), pp. 17680–17687 (2020)
15. Brown, T.B., Mann, B., Ryder, N., Subbiah, M., Kaplan, J., Dhariwal, P., et al.: Language models are few-shot learners. In: Advances in Neural Information Processing Systems (NeurIPS 2020), vol. 33, pp. 1877–1901 (2020)
16. Devlin, J., Chang, M.-W., Lee, K., Toutanova, K: BERT: Pre-training of deep bidirectional transformers for language understanding. In: Proceedings of the 2019 Conference North American Chapter of the Association for Computational Linguistics: Human Language Technologies (NAACL-HLT), vol. 1, pp. 4171–4186 (Jun 2019)
17. Gosling, S.D., Rentfrow, P.J., Swann, W.B. Jr.g: A very brief measure of the Big-Five personality domains. J. Res. Person. **37**(6), 504–528 (2003)
18. Kikuchi, A., Oshio, A.: Development of a Japanese version of the Ten Item Personality Inventory (TIPI-J). Japanese J. Personal. **25**(1), 29–39 (2016)
19. Duckworth, A.L., Quinn, P.D.: Development and validation of the Short Grit Scale (Grit-S). J. Pers. Assess. **91**(2), 166–174 (2009)
20. Nakanishi, M.: Development of the Japanese Short Grit Scale (Grit-S). Jpn. J. Pers. **24**(2), 167–169 (2015)
21. Harari, G.M., Gosling, S.D., Wang, R., Campbell, A.T.: Capturing situational information with smartphones and experience sampling. Eur. J. Pers. **29**(5), 509–511 (2016)
22. Taneja, H., Webster, J.G., Malthouse, E.C., Ksiazek, T.B.: Media consumption across platforms: identifying user-defined repertoires. New Media Soc. **14**(6), 951–968 (2014)
23. Gao, Q., Molloy, J., Axhausen, K.W.: Trip purpose imputation using GPS trajectories with machine learning. ISPRS Int. J. Geo-Inf. **10**(11), art. 775 (Nov 2021)
24. Sivakumar, T., Dhananjaya, D.D.: Inferring the purposes of taxi trips using GPS and POI data considering the destination context. In: Proceeding of the 2021 IEEE International Conference Digital Advances in Biomedical and Biological Research (ICDABI), 2021, pp. 1–6 (2021)
25. Chen, C., Liao, C., Xie, X.: Trip2Vec: a deep embedding approach for clustering and profiling taxi trip purposes. Pers. Ubiquit. Comput. **23**(1–2), 53–66 (2019)
26. Ziepert, B., de Vries, P.W., Ufkes, E.: Psyosphere: a GPS Data-Analysing Tool for the Behavioural Sciences. Front. Psychol. **12**, 538529 (2021)
27. Jiang, Z., Guo, T., Chen, J., Chen, W., Liu, H.: "PersonaLLM: Investigating the ability of large language models to express personality traits," arXiv preprint arXiv:2310.11501 (2023)
28. Peters, H., Cerf, M., Matz, S.C.: Large Language Models Can Infer Personality from Free-form User Interactions. NAACL, Findings of the Association for Computational Linguistics (2024)

29. Ke, G., et al.: LightGBM: a highly efficient gradient boosting decision tree. In Proceedings of the 31st International Conference on Neural Information Processing Systems (NeurIPS 2017), (pp. 3149–3157) (2017)
30. Murtagh, F.: Multilayer perceptrons for classification and regression. Neurocomputing **2**(5), 183–197 (1991)
31. Kobayashi, N., Ishizuka, H., Minamikawa, A., Muramatsu, S., Ono, T.: A proposal of stay/move state estimation method suitable for mobile phone communication history. Trans. Inf. Process. Soc. Japan: Databases (TOD) **10**(1), 13–23 (2017)
32. Sennrich, R., Haddow, B., Birch, A.: Neural machine translation of rare words with subword units. In: Proceedings of the 54th Annual Meeting Association Computing Linguistics (ACL 2016), vol. 1: Long Papers, Berlin, Germany, pp. 1715–1725 (Aug 2016)
33. JIS (Japan Industrial Standard) X 0410 'Grid Square Code'.[Online]. Available: https://github.com/UchidaMizuki/jpgrid/blob/main/README.en.md. Accessed 20 October 2025
34. Prochaska, J.O., DiClemente, C.C.: Stages and processes of self-change of smoking: toward an integrative model of change. J. Consult. Clin. Psychol. **51**(3), 390–395 (1983)
35. Hugging Face. https://github.com/huggingface. Accessed 20 June 2025
36. Kobayashi, A., Uesaka, D., Takeda, N., Minamikawa, A.: Representation learning techniques for travel demand prediction using large-scale location data. In: Proceedings of the 64th Annual Conference of the Japan Society of Civil Engineers, Planning Section, 64, ROMBUNNO.32-06 (2021)
37. David M. W. Powers: Evaluation: From Precision, Recall and F-Measure to ROC, Informedness, Markedness and Correlation. J. Mach. Learn. Technol. **2**(1), 37–63 (2011)
38. Lindell, M.K., Perry, R.W.: The protective action decision model: theoretical modifications and additional evidence. J. Risk Anal **32**(4), 616–632 (2012)
39. Oinas-Kukkonen, H., Harjumaa, M.: Persuasive systems design: key issues, process model, and system features. Commun. Assoc. Inf. Syst. **24**(1), 28 (2009)
40. Kaptein, M., Markopoulos, P., de Ruyter, B., Aarts, E.: Personalizing persuasive technologies: Explicit and implicit personalization using persuasion profiles. Int. J. Hum Comput Stud. **77**, 38–51 (2015)
41. Consolvo, S., McDonald, D.W., Landay, J.A.: Theory-driven design strategies for technologies that support behavior change in everyday life. In: Proceedings of the SIGCHI Conference on Human Factors in Computing Systems (CHI 2009), pp. 405–414 (2009)
42. Fogg, B.J.: A behavior model for persuasive design. Morgan Kaufmann, In: Proceedings of the 4th International Conference on Persuasive Technology, ACM, p. 40 (2009)
43. Miura, M., Takeda, N., Kamisaka, D.: Location-based LLM (LLLM): trip purpose estimation using language models of location data. In: 22nd EAI International Conference on Mobile and Ubiquitous Systems (Mobiquitous), (2025)

44. Albanesi, G., Cipresso, P., Riva, G.: AI and persuasive technology: towards a personalized persuasion model for health and wellbeing. Front. Psychol. **12**, 685573 (2021)
45. Orji, R., Anacleto, J., Oyibo, K.: Personalization in persuasive and behavior change systems: systematic review, framework, and future directions. J. Med. Internet Res. **22**(11), e17030 (2020)
46. Oyebode, O., Orji, R.: Beyond one-size-fits-all: a systematic review of personalization in persuasive and behavior change technologies. User Model. User-Adap. Inter. **32**, 465–509 (2022)

Role-Taking as a Method for Security Behaviour Change: A Qualitative Analysis of User Experience

Aya Muhanad[1]([⊠]) [iD], Tourjana Islam Supti[1] [iD], Mahmoud Barhamgi[1] [iD], Khaled M. Khan[1] [iD], Aiman Erbad[1] [iD], and Raian Ali[2]([⊠]) [iD]

[1] College of Engineering, Qatar University, Doha, Qatar
`{aya.muhanad,tourjana.supti,mbarhamgi,k.khan,aerbad}@qu.edu.qa`
[2] College of Science and Engineering, Hamad Bin Khalifa University, Doha, Qatar
`raali2@hbku.edu.qa`

Abstract. In this study, we qualitatively evaluate how participants engaged with role-taking aimed at increasing resistance to persuasion in the context of social engineering (SE). We report on interviews conducted with a subset of participants from a larger experimental study, in which individuals were assigned to one of several roles: persuader, persuadee, or learner of literacy materials. The literacy group was included in the interviews to support benchmarking. A total of 17 participants were interviewed to explore and identify the factors that resulted in changes in their behaviour related to resistance to persuasion, whether positively or negatively. Our research indicates that enhancing resistance to persuasion goes beyond knowledge transmission; it requires thoughtful design that fosters motivation, triggers dissonance for change, and ensures personal relevance. Overconfidence could hinder progress, highlighting the need for role-taking behaviour change interventions that challenge rather than reinforce self-perceptions. The integration of these elements can support developing more effective strategies that cause real behaviour change in resilience against the manipulative use of persuasive tactics in SE.

Keywords: Role-taking · Behaviour-Change · Persuasion · Debiasing · Training

1   Introduction

Social engineering (SE) is a cyberattack strategy that exploits cognitive biases and emotional triggers, such as trust, urgency, and fear, to manipulate individuals into compromising their security [1]. These attacks succeed not through technical flaws, but by targeting the human element, which remains a vulnerable aspect of cybersecurity [2, 3]. Although technical defences have improved, the persistence of SE has led to growing interest in human-centred interventions. Training users to recognise and resist such manipulation is essential. Yet questions remain about which approaches yield the most effective and lasting behaviour change, and how to enhance the experience of users learning to confront these deceptive tactics.

K. Sumi et al. (Eds.): PERSUASIVE 2026, LNCS 16476, pp. 195–209, 2026.
https://doi.org/10.1007/978-3-032-19687-3_15

Traditional awareness programs often rely on didactic instruction or passive information consumption, such as lectures or static content. While these methods can increase knowledge, interactive teaching methods are more effective in engaging learners and enhancing learning outcomes [4]. The core challenge is to develop interventions that truly lead to behaviour change. Addressing this requires reimagining learning experiences, moving beyond information transmission toward interventions that foster critical reflection, emotional engagement, and personal relevance. Interventions aiming to achieve lasting behaviour change must also enhance users' intrinsic motivation to engage with the content and explore it further. It has been emphasised that self-determination theory and motivational interviewing are effective strategies for fostering long-term behaviour change [5]. Without this motivation, even well-designed experiences may fail to produce meaningful or sustained changes in behaviour.

One promising approach is learning through role-taking, which engages individuals in simulated scenarios to help them adopt the perspective of others through cognitive and empathic understanding [6]. Through role-taking, individuals may engage in deeper personal reflection that can not be achieved through reading literacy material. When applied to contexts like SE, this means placing users in the roles of attackers, victims, or bystanders to foster emotional engagement and critical thinking about manipulation tactics. Findings suggest that immersing individuals in different roles can deepen awareness [7], which could enhance resistance to deceptive influences.

The effectiveness of role-taking approaches is influenced by how they are delivered and experienced by users. For interventions to be effective, they must be designed through a comprehensive user experience (UX) framework [8]. UX refers to the overall experience a user has when interacting with a system, including ease of use, emotional response, and engagement [9]. In behaviour change contexts, it involves leveraging Behavioural Intervention Technologies (BITs) to create tailored and emotionally resonant environments that promote habit formation and sustained engagement [10]. Previous research has also shown that high user engagement in the intervention will likely lead to effective changes in behaviour. Enhancing intervention engagement can be achieved by matching the intervention to users' characteristics, skill levels, and using design characteristics that create a positive UX [11]. An example is providing tailored feedback and considering demographics to design personally relevant scenarios.

Designing effective role-taking interventions necessitates a grounding in established behavioural and psychological theories. The COM-B model explains that behaviour change depends on the interaction between Capability, Opportunity, and Motivation [12]. Meaning individuals have the ability to apply the behaviour and see opportunities to use it. Ideally, exposure to the behaviour change interventions should lead to motivation through brain changes, such as causing the person to set new goals and feel discomfort with previous actions [13]. The Theory of Planned Behaviour (TPB) posits that behavioural intentions are influenced by attitudes, subjective norms, and perceived behavioural control, which predict the likelihood of action [14]. Applying TPB to role-taking scenarios can structure experiences that positively influence users' intentions to adopt secure behaviours. Cognitive Dissonance Theory by Festinger suggests that individuals experience psychological discomfort due to conflicting cognitions [15].

This discomfort motivates them to change attitudes or behaviours to restore consistency. In role-taking scenarios, individuals may be confronted with perspectives that challenge their existing beliefs, inducing dissonance and prompting them to re-evaluate their decision [16].

In the context of role-taking, it can be postulated that by enacting roles, especially those involving counter-attitudinal advocacy, individuals may begin to internalise the perspectives they perform, leading to attitude change through self-persuasion [17]. Lastly, role clarity, the extent to which individuals understand their responsibilities within a scenario, is crucial for effective engagement [18]. Ensuring clear role definitions within simulations enhances user immersion and the overall learning experience.

A recent experimental study (see pre-print at [19]) implemented a role-taking intervention aimed at enhancing resistance to persuasion in SE. The group-level results indicated limited behaviour change; however, some participants showed notable shifts in attitudes or intentions. This raises a critical question: What factors contributed to a change in some individuals but not others? Gaining insights into these micro-level variations can clarify the psychological, contextual, and experiential elements that shape how people internalise and act upon training. Understanding how to enhance such interventions through a non-technical approach allows us to identify the native requirements for developing and advancing future technical solutions, including gamification.

This paper seeks to address a critical gap in the literature: while behavioural interventions are typically evaluated regarding aggregate behavioural outcomes, few studies have explored the individual-level factors that influence change or stasis, particularly in the context of engaging, interactive interventions. By qualitatively analysing interviews with participants for whom the intervention was effective, as well as those who did not experience any change or experienced negative changes, we aim to identify the factors that would contribute to the development of effective interventions. Using increasing resistance to persuasion in SE as a case study, the research question is: What factors contribute to behaviour change, or the lack of it, following role-taking and literacy interventions designed to influence behaviour?

2   Methodology

2.1   Background to the Intervention

This qualitative study builds on results from a recent experiment (see pre-print [19]) examining interventions to increase resistance to persuasion in SE attacks. While persuasion can be used to facilitate behaviour change [20], the intervention sought to enhance resistance to its manipulative use. Cialdini's six principles of persuasion were used as a theoretical framework [21]. Following institutional approval, the experiment [19] employed a multi-phase design (Fig. 1). In the original experiment, a total of 130 Participants were randomly assigned to one of three interventions or a control group. In the persuadee intervention, participants adopted the perspective of a customer exposed to persuasion, while persuaders assumed the role of marketers creating persuasive content; participants in the literacy intervention learned through traditional reading materials. Each intervention comprised three sessions, covering two persuasion principles per session. Participants' vulnerability to persuasion in SE was assessed before and a week after the intervention sessions. Seventeen interviews were conducted to explore why resistance increased for some participants, and vulnerability persisted for others. Due to space limitations, the design of the original experiment with the full intervention material, dataset, participant characteristics and Open Science Framework (OSF) registration describing the design process is available on this link https://osf.io/ny7cu/overview

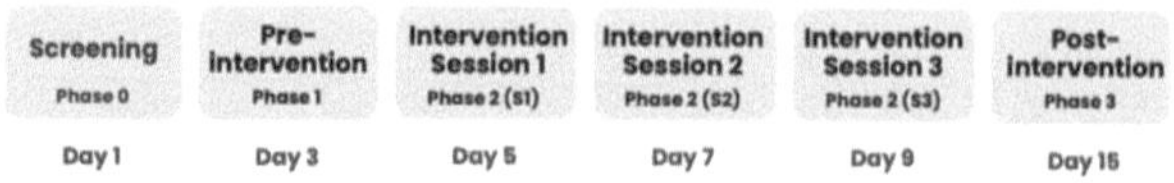

Fig. 1. Timeline of the experiment phases (the control group did not participate in phase 2)

2.2 Interviews

Seventeen semi-structured interviews were conducted via Microsoft Teams and transcribed using the platform's feature. This number was based on the participants who were interested in the interview, while also ensuring representation of different intervention groups and directions of change in resistance. The participants also varied in nationality, education, and employment status. A demographics description table is provided in the supplementary material section via the OSF link. Given that participants were located across multiple countries, individual interviews were chosen over focus groups to ensure a more consistent and feasible data collection process. A research assistant with a background in computer science and human factors conducted them. The first two interviews were reviewed by a senior researcher, who provided feedback on the conduct. Each interview lasted approximately one hour and was scheduled based on the availability of both the participant and the interviewer. The participants had to sign the consent form before the interview and received around 8 GBP through Prolific (www.prolific.com) for their participation. The interview is divided into three parts: the first explores factors influencing behaviour change, such as motivation, perceived behavioural control, and cognitive dissonance; the second examines user experience, such as participants' thoughts during the intervention and the relevance of scenarios; the final part explores responses to a real-life scenario with persuasive elements, allowing for qualitative insight of how participants transfer knowledge to other contexts. The interview guideline, including all questions and the rationale for their inclusion, is available via the OSF link in the supplementary material section. During the interview, each participant viewed a presentation containing screenshots of the intervention sessions to aid their recollection of the experiment. Techniques employed by the interviewer included allowing pauses for participants to express their thoughts freely and asking prompts to clarify answers. We refrained from leading language, e.g., the interviewer used phrases like "thank you" instead of "great, thank you".

2.3 Data Analysis

Two researchers conducted a thematic analysis to identify common themes within the responses. Following the methodology of Braun and Clarke, we systematically familiarised ourselves with the data, generated initial codes, and identified key themes [22].

First, all transcripts were read, cleaned, and then coded. The initial phase of coding involved a surface-level analysis of the text provided by participants, where we summarised the answers given. The next step included reviewing each other's codes; Author 1 evaluated the codes generated by Author 2 and vice versa. This process facilitated the identification of common grounds and coding conclusions. In case of disagreements, the authors carefully discussed each perspective to reach a consensus. Initially, the codes were grouped based on the direction of behaviour changes observed in participants and the intervention they participated in. An example of one behaviour change direction is an increase in resistance to persuasion after the intervention. Several sessions were held to conduct these groupings iteratively and identify common themes in the codes. The next step involved interpreting these themes' deeper meanings to explain changes in resistance based on factors that have been reported to influence behaviour change. Senior authors cross-checked the interview analysis to ensure accuracy and consistency.

3   Results

In this section, we detail the results of our qualitative analysis. The 17 interviewed participants' changes in resistance to persuasion in SE following the interventions are shown in Fig. 2. The analysis of interview data revealed three main themes (see Fig. 3), each illustrating a critical aspect of how participants responded to role-taking and literacy-based interventions aimed to build resistance to persuasion used in SE. The qualitative findings reveal not only what participants believed about their ability to resist persuasion but also factors that have been reported to influence behaviour. The original role-taking experiment yielded non-significant results, showing that the role-taking intervention did not increase resistance to persuasion. A repeated-measures ANOVA was conducted to examine the group × time interaction across the four groups (literacy, persuadee, persuader, and control) at two time points (pre- and post-intervention). No significant changes in vulnerability to persuasion were observed for any of Cialdini's six principles in relation to their impact on trust and risk-taking. For the complete results, refer to the pre-print [19].

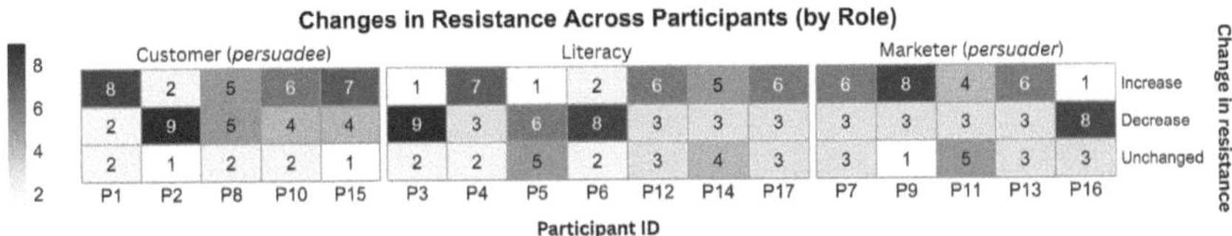

	Customer (persuadee)					Literacy							Marketer (persuader)					
Increase	8	2	5	6	7	1	7	1	2	6	5	6	6	8	4	6	1
Decrease	2	9	5	4	4	9	3	6	8	3	3	3	3	3	3	3	8
Unchanged	2	1	2	2	1	2	2	5	2	3	4	3	3	1	5	3	3
Participant ID	P1	P2	P8	P10	P15	P3	P4	P5	P6	P12	P14	P17	P7	P9	P11	P13	P16

Fig. 2. Participants' characteristics. **Note**: Participants frequently showed varied results regarding resistance. Changes in resistance after the intervention were evaluated using a total of 12 variables, with 2 variables for each persuasion principle. The x-axis represents the participant ID. The y-axis shows whether resistance increased, decreased, or remained unchanged. The colour intensity reflects how often each instance occurred, with darker shades representing more frequent occurrences out of 12 (e.g. P1 experienced an increase in resistance in 8 out of 12 instances). Further details on the calculation of the change in resistance are provided in the OSF registration, accessible via the OSF link in the supplementary material section.

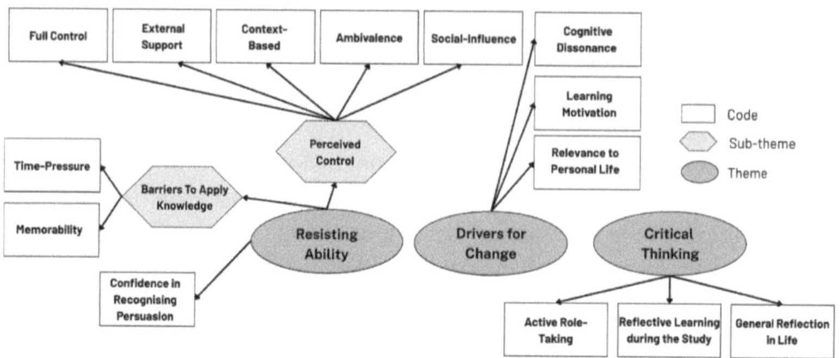

Fig. 3. Thematic map of factors in behaviour change.

3.1 Resisting Ability

This theme captures participants' belief in their capability to maintain autonomy and control over their responses to persuasive influences after having participated in the role-taking or literacy-based intervention. It consists of the code *confidence in recognising persuasion* and the two subthemes, *perceived control* and *barriers to apply knowledge*, all nuanced by participants' differing changes in resistance.

Confidence in recognising persuasion describes the perceived ability to identify persuasion tactics, but not necessarily control the behavioural response to them. Participants often rated their skills as above average or good, yet many acknowledged that recognising persuasion did not always equate to resisting it. For example, some participants who showed increased vulnerability after the intervention, such as P2 and P16, demonstrated strong confidence in detection but admitted limitations in applying this recognition consistently. P2 (persuadee) stated, "Now I'm able to recognise it. Maybe I didn't master it yet, but at least I can define that's a persuasive message based on the X approach." A participant with increased resistance expressed high confidence in recognition, but their quotes reflected deeper awareness. P1 (persuadee) explained, "I'm not going to call myself an expert because sometimes you might go blindly and try to ignore your own senses... to buy [a product in a persuasive ad]". Those with mixed changes in resistance (e.g., P14 literacy) similarly described: "My ability to recognise...maybe I am a bit higher than average. But my response might not be better than the average person. It's just the recognition."

Perceived control refers to the extent to which participants believe they have complete control over their responses to persuasion or whether external factors influence the outcome. This perception of control can affect their ability to resist persuasive attempts. We have divided this sub-theme into five codes. *Ambivalence* describes participants who were unsure whether they had the control to resist persuasive pressures. For instance, P9 (persuader) reflected: "I'm not sure if I can identify the message, then I don't really have control over anything." Similarly, P5 (literacy) admitted, "I'd say I can recognise persuasive tactics, but sometimes, even if I realise something is meant to persuade me to do or buy something, I might still go along with it", emphasising internal conflict even when awareness was present. In contrast, those with both increased and decreased vulnerability described having *full control*. The *external support* code refers to how individuals use external resources to control how they respond to persuasion. P8 (persuadee) expressed: "I have pretty good control. For example, I try to do more research from reliable sources instead of just accepting what's being shown to me. I look for sources I can trust and make sure to do some research before making a decision." The code *context-based* refers to how the perception of control of the response to persuasion is influenced by the context. P10, who took the role of the persuadee explained, "If it's online, I feel like I have full control… but in person… there's that give and take conversation… I feel a little bit more stressed out and less in control." *Social-influence* is about how social factors potentially diminish the control participants have over their response. P17 explains, "I think that I would have more control now than ever [to persuasive messages] … when it's coming from someone I care about or someone I know…it's kind of hard to say no".

Finally, *barriers to apply knowledge* sub-theme refers to what participants believe may prevent them from effectively using the newly obtained knowledge, which as a result, may be linked to their resistance abilities. Participants with increased vulnerability after the intervention (e.g., P6 and P16) described repeated struggles to bridge knowledge and behaviour. The *memorability* code describes P6 (persuader), who struggles remembering what they learned, "Sometimes, I might forget because of how I'm used to interacting on social media. So, applying this knowledge depends on whether I remember it or not". Other participants describe *time-pressure* constraints as an obstacle to applying newly learned concepts. For example, P17, who engaged with reading material, recounted a recent experience: "I really feel that rush and urgency [scarcity persuasion] to buy those things… I tried to kind of apply what I learned," revealing the tension between impulse and reflection. Time pressure seemed to be a consistent setback; P8, who identified persuasion in websites in their role, noted, "If I take time to compare [the persuasive offer] with another website, I might lose the chance to buy from the first one," showing how scarcity overrode deliberation. Despite awareness of persuasion, emotional urgency was often described as a barrier to resisting persuasion.

3.2 Drivers for Change

This theme explores the interest of people in studying persuasion and factors that could describe why they intend to change how they respond to persuasion after the experiment. We asked participants questions to understand whether the intervention increased their motivation and whether they now encounter opportunities to apply what they learned, which are needed to achieve behaviour change according to the COM-B model.

In *learning motivation*, participants describe their intention to learn more about persuasion. Their motivation could explain whether they want to change their behaviour towards persuasive requests. Interestingly, many participants who did not have strong resistance (P3, P5-P6, P8, P10, P12–14, P16) expressed that they do not plan to pursue this topic further. For example, P13 (persuadee) stated, "I think from the study, I got a general understanding of these techniques… Maybe I'm more interested in telling people I know about it than in learning more. I think I wouldn't be really learning by myself more about this." Some participants indicated they might consider learning more if faced with specific situations. For instance, P6 said, "I don't have any plans or ideas to learn more about this topic right now. But maybe in the future, if I encounter a situation online where I feel influenced or affected by one of these factors, I might do some research". On the other hand, participants who had stronger resistance after the intervention displayed more interest. For example, P15 described, "I want to learn more about this topic. I do have plans."

The relevance to personal life code refers to whether participants recognise opportunities to apply the newly obtained knowledge by discussing how personally relevant persuasion is to them. According to the COM-B model, individuals need to see an opportunity for change in order to make it happen. This code is also linked to motivation, since participants must find the intervention personally relevant to pursue further learning. We asked participants about scenarios in their personal lives where they could use the knowledge obtained. All participants expressed that the scenarios in the intervention reflected real-life situations they had encountered, reinforcing the authentic impact of the intervention. For instance, P10 (persuadee) shared their experience with scarcity when purchasing event tickets online, "Usually, scarcity is very prominent in that field...So, for me, I always go through scarcity." Similarly, P3 remarked, "A lot of the examples reminded me of times in my own life... they really connected with my personal experiences". Others recalled examples involving reciprocity, commitment, and likability in both personal and professional contexts, suggesting that these principles are familiar and deeply embedded in everyday interactions and decisions. These responses were observed among most participants, suggesting they view opportunities to apply what they learned about persuasion, possibly explaining changes in their behaviour to persuasive requests.

Cognitive dissonance describes how participants feel about past experiences with persuasion. We observe whether a conflict between past actions and new opinions on persuasion has formed. As per the Cognitive Dissonance Theory, this conflict can be resolved by trying to change behaviour, suggesting it may be a driver for change. Participants with increased resistance to persuasion often showed strong dissonance and resolved it by aiming to change future responses to persuasion. P4 reflected, "I would love to have the thinking I have now... I could have acted better...," showing regret that led to increased resistance. P15 described feeling naive and stupid after realising they were manipulated, but reframed this discomfort as an opportunity: "It [the new knowledge] helps with building restraint and being smarter about decisions." Participants with increased vulnerability to persuasion after the intervention sometimes experienced ongoing ambivalence or rationalised their behaviour. For example, P13 described: "I might have been used, but I actually needed a new phone [influenced by scarcity]," neutralising dissonance through justification. Cognitive consonance, the opposite of dissonance, also occurred when no discomfort seemed to have formed. P13 felt positive about being influenced and explained, "I think it happens naturally...I know that these are techniques used to make me buy these things, I think it's just natural." Similarly, P8 felt reassured by social proof during a major decision and was ultimately "thankful" for the influence. This consonance may explain why P8 and P13 exhibited both increased and decreased resistance following the intervention, as they did not express an intention to change their responses to persuasive messages.

3.3 Critical Thinking

This theme examines the cognitive processes participants engaged in during the sessions and how they reflected on what they learned, which may explain their changes in resistance towards persuasion. We discovered that participants engaged in critical reflection and cognitive engagement at different times and in different ways. This theme is divided into three codes.

Active role-taking refers to how participants engaged cognitively with the scenarios by adopting relevant roles, such as customers or marketers, to understand the impact of each persuasion technique described. This may indicate whether participants have genuinely engaged in role-taking during their participation. For instance, P11 (persuader) took the perspectives of both a persuadee and persuader instead of only a persuader and stated, "As a customer, I would want reviews [a source of social proof; a persuasion principle] and as a product owner…it is important to know how customers would feel and put yourself in the shoes of your customers." This awareness of dual roles may have deepened their connection to the concept of social proof. Participants in the second intervention group also engaged in role-taking, such as P10 (persuadee): "I put myself in their [customers'] shoes." Not only were participants from the role-taking interventions engaging in perspective taking, but participants from the literacy group as well. P6 (literacy) noted, "I tried to remember the principles… and imagine how I would feel if I were put into this situation," indicating an attempt at passive role-taking. These examples illustrate how engaging in role-taking allowed participants to make sense of abstract persuasion concepts in concrete and personally meaningful ways.

The *reflective learning during the study* revealed that parts of the intervention, which consisted of three sessions, prompted participants to reflect on their responses. It shows that participants truly reflected on their responses rather than simply answering questions autonomously during the experiment. Most participants in the literacy group, who also seemed to engage in passive role-taking, reported that they reflected on their learning while participating in the sessions. For instance, P6 (literacy) explained, "When I read the example and you know reflecting on my own experience when I was sent reminders or messages to be committed and consistent by maybe some apps, I felt like it [commitment/consistency principle] was easy to understand." Literacy participants were not alone in their reflections; both persuader and persuadee participants described engaging in critical reflection during the intervention. When having to list their thoughts on why they would follow a persuasive advert, P10 (persuadee) stated, "Usually, you don't have to write out your thoughts; you just think about them...It affected my perception of the ad...it really makes you think, are my thoughts valid, or am I just, you know, thinking stupidly?" P13 (persuader) mentioned how they reflected on personal experiences when creating persuasive messages: "I try to remember what I usually see in online shops…I just try to recall the things they say, and based on my new knowledge of these techniques, I try to come up with something [when creating ads]".

In the *general reflection in life* code, participants reevaluated their personal experiences and had moments of realisation because of the experiment. P9, who had to persuade others in the intervention, shared that they now try to question everything they see: "Now, I think about it with everything I do because it's not just about buying stuff, but also about other things… they [persuaders] try to change your thoughts with their ideologies. That's persuading. So now I think about it [how others are influencing me] more often". P6 explained, "I realised that sometimes I'm influenced by people who are considered experts in their fields, I used to accept their opinions without much reflection or research. I learned that these opinions might not always be true, especially after reading about the authority principle in the study." These reflections were observed among participants who experienced both increased and decreased resistance throughout all three intervention groups.

4 Discussion

Our analysis yielded three themes illustrating various factors that could make role-taking more effective. One theme focused on observing participants' *confidence in recognising* persuasive attempts and their *perceived control* over their responses to persuasive requests. These beliefs relate to self-efficacy and controllability, psychological constructs that influence behaviour [23]. We observed a complex interplay of these beliefs across different participant groupings, including those who showed increased or decreased resistance to persuasion after the intervention. For instance, some individuals who exhibited increased resistance described strong confidence in recognising persuasive tactics. In contrast, others acknowledged their inexperience in navigating such influences, suggesting a spectrum of self-efficacy perceptions. Regarding perceived control, some participants felt confident in their ability to resist persuasion, while others identified factors that could challenge their perceived control. These varied responses across participants exhibiting both increased and decreased resistance indicate that such psychological factors alone are not enough to guarantee behaviour change. Additionally, participants who showed increased vulnerability to some principles highlighted that the urgency exerted by persuasive requests may prevent them from applying the newly acquired knowledge. This finding is consistent with prior research on decision-making processes [24, 25]. It also aligns with the COM-B model, which suggests that environmental constraints can serve as setbacks in changing behaviour [12].

The second theme focused on what may drive behaviour change, delving into motivation, relevance of learned concepts, and cognitive dissonance. The code *learning motivation* explores individuals' intentions to delve deeper into understanding how decision-making can be influenced. Notably, all participants who demonstrated increased resistance also reported heightened motivation. However, increased motivation did not always translate into enhanced resistance, suggesting that motivation alone may be insufficient to cause sustained behaviour change. This aligns with the Self-Determination Theory [26], which argues that while motivation is essential, its source, whether intrinsic or extrinsic, and the way it is regulated, determine its effectiveness. Moreover, without a structured approach, motivational intentions may remain unactualized due to a lack of clear strategies. Applying such structured guidance in the context of SE is challenging, as these threats are dynamic and often unpredictable, presenting a key difficulty in designing interventions that are both generalizable and practically effective.

A challenge that may arise in role-taking interventions is how individuals internalise the information provided. Mezirow's Transformative Learning Theory [27] supports the idea that when learned concepts resonate with personal experience, they are more likely to initiate reflective change. This suggests that the role-taking approach, while conceptually valuable, may have a limited impact if the scenarios are not personally relevant. Similar to personal coaching or therapy, where reflection is grounded in lived experience, tailoring interventions to individuals' real-world contexts may enhance their effectiveness. Although the role-taking sought to enhance resistance by including relatable scenarios, designing personally relevant content did not consistently translate into increased resistance, as revealed by the *relevance to personal life* code. Our findings support the idea that a mere sense of personal relevance is insufficient to elicit behaviour change [28]. As posited by the Elaboration Likelihood Model, if individuals do not feel vulnerable or fail to connect the content to their own behaviours, the effectiveness of the information may be limited [29]. This highlights the importance of designing interventions that evoke a sense of vulnerability to prompt behaviour change.

We also realised that role-taking interventions should challenge individuals' assumptions to lead to behaviour change. In *cognitive dissonance*, we observed that participants exhibiting increased resistance frequently described significant dissonance. Conversely, those who displayed decreased resistance to specific persuasion principles often expressed contentment with being persuaded. Participants sometimes rationalised their choices by framing persuasion as beneficial for decision-making, highlighting different strategies for resolving dissonance, commonly referred to as denial patterns [30, 31]. The process of dissonance resolution serves to mitigate conflicts arising when attitudes, beliefs, or behaviours are misaligned [32]. Participants who showed increased resistance expressed regret about their previous vulnerability to persuasion and seemed to have formed new beliefs about being persuaded. They resolved this dissonance by intending to alter their behaviours in future situations to avoid a recurrence of the conflict. This strategy reflects the use of compensatory beliefs, where individuals justify a current behaviour by planning a compensating action later [33].

The third theme focused on the critical thinking processes elicited by the intervention. The *active role-taking* code relates to how participants engaged in role-taking during the intervention. Interestingly, we found that not only the two role-taking interventions (persuader and persuadee) resulted in role-taking, but also the literacy material. This is supported by the theory of mind, where individuals may spontaneously adopt different mental perspectives, even without explicit instruction [34]. However, adopting other mental models may lead participants to respond from their ideal or ought self (i.e., how they think they should act) rather than their actual self, limiting genuine reflection and meaningful behaviour change. *Reflective learning during the study* examines whether participants engaged in critical thinking during the intervention. We found that different techniques, such as the thought listing [35] in the persuadee role and the real-world examples provided in the literacy group, resulted in critical reflection. This suggests that even engaging in passive role-taking, as seen among literacy participants, can result in critical reflection. However, these outcomes may vary with learning styles; for instance, holistic learners prefer overviews they can unpack themselves, while serialist learners favour step-by-step guidance. *General reflection in life* reveals participants' reflections on their personal lives following the experiment. The findings show that all participants, regardless of changes in resistance, truly reflected on real-life encounters with persuasion. Reflection and determining how to use new knowledge are needed for knowledge transfer [36], but may be insufficient, as shown by the results.

4.1 Suggestions

Based on these insights, we offer suggestions for designing role-taking interventions that drive behaviour change:

Ensure strong motivation: In general, participants who were more motivated to learn about persuasion were also more resistant to persuasive attempts. Motivation and the possession of counterarguments are critical components for achieving resistance to persuasion and facilitating behaviour change [37]. Interventions should aim to maintain stable motivation through consistent reminders that provide achievable goals.

Cognitive dissonance: Interventions may benefit from eliciting strong cognitive dissonance that leads to meaningful behaviour change, rather than merely justifying past actions. By creating psychological discomfort due to inconsistencies between beliefs and behaviours, individuals should be motivated to actively resolve the dissonance through long-term change [38]. Role-taking could trigger cognitive dissonance by confronting individuals with past experiences with persuasion, evoking regret, and could encourage them to behave differently to avoid the repetition of conflict.

Personal relevance: Many participants who showed increased resistance described connecting elements of the intervention to their own real-life experiences. To facilitate this, role-taking interventions may incorporate personalised scenarios using examples and imagery that closely reflect individuals' lived experiences.

Challenging confidence: Our study revealed that belief in one's ability to resist persuasion often did not align with actual capabilities. Similar results were observed in previous research [39]. Consequently, it is advisable for role-taking-based interventions to challenge these misconceptions and potential overconfidence. This can be accomplished by implementing assessments of self-efficacy, followed by challenging questions that illuminate individuals' potential overestimation of their resistance abilities. A form of self-monitoring, which has been used in persuasive systems to encourage the adoption of desired habits, such as shopping for healthy food [40].

Immersion: Interestingly, literacy participants, who read generic sentences on scenarios about other people without being asked to take on a specific role, demonstrated signs of role-taking. This highlights that individuals may spontaneously engage in imaginative reflection or simulation of roles, even in the absence of explicit instructions. This raises an important question about whether it is essential to develop complex scenarios involving various roles, given that individuals may already engage in some form of imaginative role-taking in simple scenarios. This does not suggest that complex, immersive solutions are unnecessary. In fact, immersive solutions have the potential to enhance user retention, especially when interventions require embodied experiences. Thus, while role-taking can occur spontaneously, immersive training remains useful in contexts that need hands-on experience and concrete behaviour change.

Combining it all: It is essential to recognise that motivation, cognitive dissonance, and relevance each alone seem to be insufficient. Our findings suggest that high motivation, dissonance leading to behavioural improvement, and relevant interventions yield effective outcomes. Additionally, we found that complex solutions may not be necessary; traditional methods may also achieve engagement and reflection.

4.2 Limitations

A limitation of this study is labelling the direction of behaviour change for each participant. Identifying individuals as being more resistant or less resistant is complex, as participants often demonstrate varying degrees of resistance and vulnerability. This nuance highlights that certain persuasion principles may have differing effects on individuals, which in turn influences how the intervention materials impact them. Readers are encouraged to consult the supplementary material for a detailed description of each participant's behaviour change.

5 Conclusion

This study describes how individuals responded to interventions designed to enhance resistance to persuasion, drawing on qualitative data. While the interventions did not produce significant group-level changes in resistance in the original experiment, individual narratives revealed valuable insights into the psychological processes that underpin behaviour change. Key drivers such as motivation, cognitive dissonance, and perceived relevance emerged as influential factors, although their effects varied based on context and individual differences. Moreover, overconfidence in one's resistance ability can hinder progress, underscoring the need for interventions that challenge self-perceptions. By integrating these components, practitioners can create more effective role-taking that promotes critical thinking and psychological resilience in the face of persuasive tactics, particularly those deployed in SE and marketing contexts.

Acknowledgements. This publication was supported by NPRP 14 Cluster [grant number NPRP 14C- 0916–210015] from the Qatar National Research Fund (a member of Qatar Foundation). The findings herein reflect the work and are solely the responsibility of the authors.

Disclosure of Interests. The authors report there are no competing interests to declare.

Supplementary Material. The interview questions and a sample of the thematic analysis table are available on the OSF link: https://osf.io/uzv6g/overview

References

1. Muhanad, A., Abuelezz, I., Khan, K., Ali, R.: On how Cialdini's persuasion principles influence individuals in the context of social engineering: a qualitative study. In: Barhamgi, M., Wang, H., Wang, X. (eds.) Web Information Systems Engineering – WISE 2024, pp. 373–388. Springer Nature, Singapore (2025). https://doi.org/10.1007/978-981-96-0570-5_27
2. Lohani, S.: Social engineering: hacking into humans. Nternational J. Adv. Stud. Sci. Res. **4** (2019)

3. Wang, Z., Zhu, H., Sun, L.: Social engineering in cybersecurity: effect mechanisms, human vulnerabilities and attack methods. IEEE Access. **9**, 11895–11910 (2021). https://doi.org/10.1109/ACCESS.2021.3051633

4. Ponkshe, S., Lande, A.: Students' perception of interactive teaching methods in competency-based education: a contrast with traditional methods. Int. J. Res. Anal. Rev. IJRAR. **10**, 680–685 (2023)

5. Patrick, H., Williams, G.C.: Self-determination theory: its application to health behavior and complementarity with motivational interviewing. Int. J. Behav. Nutr. Phys. Act. **9**, 18 (2012). https://doi.org/10.1186/1479-5868-9-18

6. Coutu, W.: Role-playing vs. role-taking: an appeal for clarification. Am. Sociol. Rev. **16**, 180–187 (1951). https://doi.org/10.2307/2087691

7. Matefy, R.E.: Attitude change induced by role playing as a function of improvisation and role-taking skill. J. Pers. Soc. Psychol. **24**, 343–350 (1972). https://doi.org/10.1037/h0033725

8. Søvold, L.E., Solbakken, O.A.: The user experience framework for health interventions. Nord. Psychol. **74**, 279–300 (2022). https://doi.org/10.1080/19012276.2021.2004917

9. Hellweger, S., Wang, X.: What is User Experience Really: towards a UX Conceptual Framework, http://arxiv.org/abs/1503.01850, (2015). https://doi.org/10.48550/arXiv.1503.01850.

10. Shin, Y., Kim, C., Yoon, J.: Behavioural intervention technology in UX design: conceptual review, synthesis, and research direction. In: Bruyns, G., Wei, H. (eds.) With Design: Reinventing Design Modes, pp. 450–465. Springer Nature, Singapore (2022). https://doi.org/10.1007/978-981-19-4472-7_31

11. Short, C.E., Rebar, A.L., Plotnikoff, R.C., Vandelanotte, C.: Designing engaging online behaviour change interventions: a proposed model of user engagement. Eur. Health Psychol. **17**, 32–38 (2015)

12. Willmott, T.J., Pang, B., Rundle-Thiele, S.: Capability, opportunity, and motivation: an across contexts empirical examination of the COM-B model. BMC Public Health. **21**, 1014 (2021). https://doi.org/10.1186/s12889-021-11019-w

13. Aunger, R., Curtis, V.: Behaviour Centred design: towards an applied science of behaviour change. Health Psychol. Rev. **10**, 425–446 (2016). https://doi.org/10.1080/17437199.2016.1219673

14. Ajzen, I.: The theory of planned behavior. Organ. Behav. Hum. Decis. Process. **50**, 179–211 (1991). https://doi.org/10.1016/0749-5978(91)90020-T

15. Festinger, L.: A Theory of Cognitive Dissonance. Stanford University Press (1957)

16. Aaroj, K., Marietta, G., Gehlback, H.: The role of role-taking. In: Zandvliet, D., den Brok, P., Mainhard, T., van Tartwijk, J. (eds.) Interpersonal Relationships in Education: from Theory to Practice | SpringerLink, pp. 100–109. Sense Publishers (2014)

17. Park, H.S.: Consensus building through role playing from the perspective of self persuasion. J. Media Commun. Stud. **1**, 023–032 (2009)

18. Kauppila, O.-P.: So, what am I supposed to do? A multilevel examination of role clarity. J. Manag. Stud. **51**, 737–763 (2014). https://doi.org/10.1111/joms.12042

19. Muhanad, A., et al.: Does Role-Taking Help Resist Persuasion in Social Engineering? Maybe Not!, DOI: 10.13140/RG.2.2.35950.11840/1, Accessed 31 May 2025.

20. Oyibo, K., Toyonaga, S.: Conceptual frameworks for designing and evaluating persuasive messages aimed at changing behavior: systematic review. Comput. Hum. Behav. Rep. **15**, 100448 (2024). https://doi.org/10.1016/j.chbr.2024.100448

21. Cialdini, R.B.: The science of persuasion. Sci. Am. **284**, 76–81 (2001)

22. Braun, V., Clarke, V.: Using thematic analysis in psychology. Qual. Res. Psychol. **3**, 77–101 (2006). https://doi.org/10.1191/1478088706qp063oa

23. Ajzen, I.: Perceived behavioral control, self-efficacy, locus of control, and the theory of planned behavior. J. Appl. Soc. Psychol. **32**, 665–683 (2002). https://doi.org/10.1111/j.1559-1816.2002.tb00236.x

24. Krause, A., Poth, C.H.: Urgency enforces stimulus-driven action across spatial and numerical cognitive control tasks. PLoS One. **20**, e0322482 (2025). https://doi.org/10.1371/journal.pone.0322482

25. Maule, A.J., Hockey, G.R., Bdzola, L.: Effects of time-pressure on decision-making under uncertainty: changes in affective state and information processing strategy. Acta Psychol. **104**, 283–301 (2000). https://doi.org/10.1016/s0001-6918(00)00033-0

26. Deci, E.L., Ryan, R.M.: The "what" and "why" of goal pursuits: human needs and the self-determination of behavior. Psychol. Inq. **11**, 227–268 (2000). https://doi.org/10.1207/S15327965PLI1104_01

27. Mezirow, J.: Transformative Dimensions of Adult Learning. Jossey-Bass Inc. San Francisco, CA, 350 Sansome Street (1991)

28. Priniski, S.J., Hecht, C.A., Harackiewicz, J.M.: Making learning personally meaningful: a new framework for relevance research. J. Exp. Educ. **86**, 11–29 (2018). https://doi.org/10.1080/00220973.2017.1380589

29. Petty, R., Cacioppo, J.: The elaboration likelihood model of persuasion. Adv. Hydrosci. **19**, 124–205 (1986)

30. Pandey, S., Ahmad, D.P.: Understanding dissonance and dissonance reduction: an inference from literature. Int. J. Innov. Sci. Res. Technol. **8** (2023). https://doi.org/10.5281/zenodo.8125959

31. Baumeister, R.F., Dale, K., Sommer, K.L.: Freudian defense mechanisms and empirical findings in modern social psychology: reaction formation, projection, displacement, undoing, isolation, sublimation, and denial. J. Pers. **66**, 1081–1124 (1998). https://doi.org/10.1111/1467-6494.00043

32. Stone, J., Cooper, J.: A self-standards model of cognitive dissonance. J. Exp. Soc. Psychol. **37**, 228–243 (2001). https://doi.org/10.1006/jesp.2000.1446

33. Zhao, K., Xu, X., Zhu, H., Xu, Q.: Compensatory belief in health behavior management: a concept analysis. Front. Psychol. **12**, 705991 (2021). https://doi.org/10.3389/fpsyg.2021.705991

34. German, T.C., Cohen, A.S.: A cue-based approach to 'theory of mind': re-examining the notion of automaticity. Br. J. Dev. Psychol. **30**, 45–58 (2012). https://doi.org/10.1111/j.2044-835X.2011.02055.x

35. Cacioppo, J.T., von Hippel, W., Ernst, J.M.: Mapping cognitive structures and processes through verbal content: the thought-listing technique. J. Consult. Clin. Psychol. **65**, 928–940 (1997). https://doi.org/10.1037/0022-006X.65.6.928

36. Riesen, K., Whitver, S.M.: Reflection and transfer learning in the one-shot: demonstrating student learning. Coll. Res. Libr. **84**, 531 (2023). https://doi.org/10.5860/crl.84.4.531

37. Knowles, E.S., Linn, J.A.: Resistance and Persuasion. Taylor & Francis Group, Oxford, UNITED KINGDOM (2003)

38. Bell, S., Van den Berg, M., Liboro, R.M.: Employing dissonance-based interventions to promote health equity utilizing a community-based participatory research approach and social network analysis. Soc. Sci. **12**, 543 (2023). https://doi.org/10.3390/socsci12100543

39. Muhanad, A., et al.: Does security attitude really predict susceptibility to persuasion tactics in social engineering attempts? Inf. Amp Comput. Secur.. ahead-of-print. (2025). https://doi.org/10.1108/ICS-11-2024-0280

40. Adaji, I., Oyibo, K., Vassileva, J.: List it : a shopping list app that influences healthy shopping habits. In: Presented at the Proceedings of the 32nd International BCS Human Computer Interaction Conference (2018). https://doi.org/10.14236/ewic/HCI2018.81

MyHealthCore: An Evaluation of a Community-Engaged HIV Prevention Persuasive mHealth App Prototype for Black Communities in Canada

Kaminda Natasha Musumbulwa$^{(\boxtimes)}$, Gerry Chan , and Rita Orji

Faulty of Computer Science, Dalhousie University, Halifax, Nova Scotia, Canada
kaminda.musumbulwa@dal.ca

Abstract. In this research, we engaged Black community members and HIV service providers in Canada to evaluate a co-designed, culturally responsive prototype of an mHealth application for HIV prevention. Guided by community-based research and user-centered design principles, we designed a prototype based on findings from an earlier exploratory phase where participants shared their preferences on the content, functionality, and design of a mobile HIV prevention app called *MyHealthCore*. A mixed-methods approach combining qualitative feedback from semi-structured interviews with quantitative usability pre-testing data guided this formative evaluation of the prototype's design and user experience with Black community members ($N = 4$) and HIV service providers ($N = 4$). Participants rated the prototype as highly usable (76.88, $SD = 2.59$), and strongly agreed that it was simple, intuitive, and motivating to use for HIV prevention. Participants emphasized trust, privacy, and discretion as essential to adoption, with representation and stigma-free language as facilitators of engagement. Community members described the prototype as empowering and "made for us," while service providers emphasized its potential for integration into routine HIV health promotion efforts. *MyHealthCore* demonstrates that when built collaboratively with underserved populations, mHealth interventions can advance health equity and digital innovation by embedding cultural and clinical relevance into digital health solutions.

Keywords: Black communities · African diaspora · health equity · HIV prevention · cultural responsiveness · mobile health · persuasive technology

1 Introduction

Black communities in Canada experience rates of HIV disproportionate to their representation in the overall Canadian population [1]. Although they account for about 5% of Canada's total population [1, 2], in 2020, Black communities accounted for 24.6% of new HIV cases in Ontario [1, 3]. Other jurisdictions do not similarly collect disaggregated data [4]. These disparities are driven by multiple structural and systemic barriers that lead to poor population and individual-level health and social outcomes for Black

K. Sumi et al. (Eds.): PERSUASIVE 2026, LNCS 16476, pp. 210–224, 2026.
https://doi.org/10.1007/978-3-032-19687-3_16

communities [5, 6]. Structural racism manifests through uneven access to healthcare, housing, employment, education, and immigration processes [1, 5], resulting in limited availability of HIV testing, prevention, and treatment for Black communities [1, 7]. Anti-Black and medical racism further fuels hyper-sexualization and neglect of Black bodies in healthcare, eroding trust in these institutions [1, 8]. These structural barriers intersect with HIV-related stigma rooted in race, gender, sexuality, religion, and culture. This continues to impede open conversations about HIV and sexual health, and perpetuates myths surrounding HIV transmission, prevention, and treatment [8–10]. Given these realities, scholars such as Owino et al. [1] have emphasized that HIV interventions for Black communities in Canada must prioritize culturally responsive approaches that center their lived experiences, rather than defaulting to biomedical models that overlook systemic inequities [5, 6].

In this research, we contribute to ongoing efforts exploring technology-based inter ventions for HIV prevention in underserved populations by addressing the following question: *"How do Black community members and service providers assess the usability, acceptability, and persuasive potential of a culturally responsive HIV prevention mHealth app prototype, and what design refinements are needed to support its real-world implementation?"* This work offers three contributions to the field of persuasive technology and designing for underrepresented communities. First, we provide a template for the empirical evaluation of culturally tailored apps. Second, we identify the cultural, informational, and technological factors for engaging Black communities with this digital HIV prevention tool [11, 12]. Third, we translate these findings into actionable design recommendations for developing culturally responsive, privacy-conscious, and user-centered persuasive mHealth applications to reduce HIV disparities in priority populations [13]. Together, these findings advance understanding of how community-based research (CBR) and user-centered design (UCD) principles can be integrated to support the implementation of digital interventions [14, 15].

2 Related Works

Mobile health (mHealth) technology has emerged as an important platform expanding access to HIV prevention information and services, especially for communities experiencing health inequities and barriers to traditional healthcare [16]. mHealth tools can deliver sexual health information across large geographic areas, offer continuous and discreet access to prevention resources and, provide culturally tailored content that reflects the needs of specific communities [17, 18]. mHealth interventions can also strengthen health literacy, self-efficacy, and self-management to improve health outcomes [19]. Despite increasing adoption, most existing HIV-focused mHealth solutions have been developed in Africa or the U.S., often targeting men who have sex with men and non-Black communities [11, 20, 21]. While the studies backing these solutions demonstrate good feasibility and acceptability [11], few interventions have been designed for and tested with Black diasporic communities in Canada, emphasizing the need for geographically relevant digital solutions.

Alongside growing interest in mHealth, persuasive technology has gained prominence as a strategy to shape health behaviours through digital design [22]. Persuasive strategies rely on a non-coercive methodology to motivate behavioural change [23]. Frameworks like the Persuasive System Design (PSD) model outline four main domains of persuasive functionality: (1) primary task support, (2) dialogue support, (3) system credibility support, and (4) social support [22]. Existing digital health tools such as SavvyHER (Sexual Health Electronic Empowerment Resource) illustrate how persuasive strategies, including social support and verifiability, can sustain engagement and improve HIV health outcomes [24]. Adapting similar strategies to the Canadian context presents a promising opportunity to design engaging and empowering tools that address structural barriers to care and improve uptake of HIV prevention strategies.

3 Methods

3.1 Formative Work

MyHealthCo(mmunity)re(source) was designed based on formative work with 11 Black community members and 10 HIV service providers across Canada. Through focus group discussions, we conducted an exploratory study grounded in CBR [15] and UCD principles [12]. We collected feedback on the most relevant structural, institutional, and individual barriers hindering engagement in HIV prevention initiatives, as well as preferences for the functionality, format, and design of a mobile HIV prevention app tailored for Black communities [19]. Findings provided insight into design and development requirements for a culturally responsive HIV prevention mHealth application, emphasizing relevant persuasive strategies [19]. The study highlighted multidimensional considerations for developing such an application within Black communities in Canada [19]. Participants described the interconnected nature of health, emphasizing that HIV prevention must be linked to overall wellness, as other chronic conditions such as diabetes and hypertension often take precedence in routine healthcare. Participants also addressed stigma, often rooted in cultural, religious, and societal beliefs, which was consistently identified as a major barrier to engagement and contributed to fear of judgment and misinformation about HIV transmission, testing, and treatment.

Community members and service providers discussed the importance of inclusive representation through imagery and language reflecting diverse Black identities [19, 25]. They also communicated the need for simple and accessible design across literacy levels and robust data privacy measures that acknowledge historical mistrust and the ethics of HIV disclosure [19]. Collectively, these insights highlight the need for a user-centered approach to culturally responsive mHealth design [19]. This formative work guided the culturally responsive design and persuasive strategy implementation within the prototype, representing one of the first Canadian studies to integrate CBR with persuasive technology for HIV prevention among Black communities. The *MyHealthCore* app incorporates five core features based on persuasive design principles:

1. a **Home Screen** providing dashboard access to key features and latest HIV news.
2. **MyHealthEducation** offering search-enabled access to HIV topics with customizable content and knowledge assessment quizzes.
3. **MyHealthConnect** facilitating community engagement through interaction with Community Navigators and Service Providers.

4. **MyHealthLocator** using geolocation to map AIDS Service Organizations, testing centers, and PrEP clinics with provincial filtering.
5. **MyHealthTracker** enabling monitoring of test results, appointments, symptoms, medication schedules, and mental health with push notification reminders.

3.2 Persuasive Strategies

The persuasive strategies employed in *MyHealthCore* were selected to support acceptance of HIV prevention strategies and sustain user engagement. Primary task support is evident in the app's self-monitoring feature (Fig. 1), which tracks user health metrics and reinforces progress toward health goals [22]. Self-monitoring is a recognized tool for sustaining behaviour change by increasing self-awareness and accountability [26]. Tailoring and reduction are implemented in *MyHealthEducation*, allowing users to explore HIV-related topics based on their learning needs. The inclusion of brief quizzes (Fig. 2) enables users to rehearse and reinforce learned information, encouraging adherence to healthier behaviours [22, 26]. Incorporating similar persuasive strategies into future HIV prevention mHealth solutions may support the development of engaging apps that address barriers to healthcare access for Black communities and promote engagement in traditional HIV prevention strategies [11, 12].

Fig. 1. Self-monitoring in *MyHealthTracker*.   **Fig. 2.** Tailoring and reduction in *MyHealthEducation*.

3.3 *MyHealthCore* App Design and Development

As outlined in Sect. 3.2, findings from an exploratory study informed the design of the app prototypes. *MyHealthCore* was designed using Figma, a tool for rapid prototyping and iterative interface development [27]. Firstly, a wireframe of the app's layout and features was designed (Fig. 3). The resulting sketches were evaluated through participatory design sessions with community members and service providers to ensure that the app aligned with user needs and cultural expectations.

Building on the wireframes, the interactive prototype was developed, incorporating the features and design elements identified in this study (Fig. 4). Figma's *Blush* plug-ins were used to create diverse, culturally representative imagery in the prototype [12, 21]. Usability pre-testing with Black users and service providers was conducted to refine functionality, navigation, and aesthetics. This paper presents findings from the formative evaluation of the prototype.

(a) Home Screen   (b) MyHealthEducation   (c) MyHealthTracker   (d) MyHealthLocator   (e) MyHealthConnect

Fig. 3. Initial sketches of MyHealthCore app.

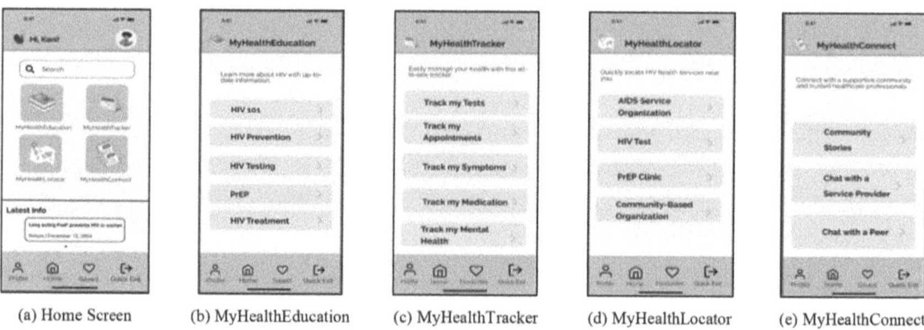

(a) Home Screen   (b) MyHealthEducation   (c) MyHealthTracker   (d) MyHealthLocator   (e) MyHealthConnect

Fig. 4. Medium-fidelity screens of MyHealthCore features.

3.4 Study Design

To gather input on the perspectives and attitudes of Black community members and HIV service providers towards using an mHealth app for HIV prevention, our formative evaluation utilized a mixed-methods approach. Both quantitative and qualitative data were collected for analysis. The evaluation consisted of three steps: (1) complete a pre-study demographic questionnaire, (2) use the medium fidelity prototype and participate in a semi-structured interview and then, (3) complete a post-study questionnaire. The post-study questionnaire was composed of validated scales that have been widely used in HCI research to evaluate attitudes and perceptions of interactive computer systems asking participants to evaluate the prototype including: (1) Perceived Ease of Use [28], (2) Usefulness [28], (3) Simplicity [29] (4) Usability [30], and (5) Perceived Persuasiveness [31]. The study is modelled after a similar HIV app design and development procedure for Black women living in metro-Atlanta [13].

3.5 Recruitment and Procedures

This study was reviewed and approved by our institutional ethics board. This qualitative study was implemented from May 2025 to October 2025. After receiving approval from our university ethics board, we commenced recruitment of participants. Prior UCD research pretesting mHealth apps for HIV outcomes has included samples of 10 participants [32]. As this phase aimed to provide preliminary usability insights, we determined that a sample size of 10 would support the iterative UCD process and yield user perspectives that could be rapidly translated into development [32].

Participants were recruited using purposive sampling [21] from AIDS Service Organizations, HIV care clinics, and other community-based sexual health organizations across Canada. Digital flyers were distributed via the lead researchers' professional networks and posted on social media platforms, including Facebook and LinkedIn. Flyers provided the lead researcher's email, who assessed eligibility. Community members were required to (1) self-identify as Black, (2) be 18 years of age or older, (3) live in Canada, (4) speak and understand English comfortably, and (5) have access to an android phone or iPhone. HIV service providers were required to meet the same criteria and had worked in the HIV sector in a clinical or non-clinical capacity for 12 months out of the last 5 years. After eligibility was confirmed, participants were invited to proceed with the following procedures:

- **Step 1:** After reading the consent form and understanding the nature of their involvement in the study, participants completed a pre-study questionnaire asking them to provide their demographic information. Participants were divided into two groups: community members and service providers.
- **Step 2:** After completing Step 1, participants were invited to a virtual prototype demonstration conducted virtually using Microsoft Teams and lasting an average of 30 min. During the demonstration, participants were provided with a link to access *MyHealthCore's* medium-fidelity prototype and advance through the various features for a period of 10 min. Community members and service providers were each given a different set of tasks to complete in the prototype and then share a rating of the ease of completing the tasks. Following the task activity, participants were asked to share their feedback on the functionality, content, and design of the prototype.
- **Step 3:** Following the interviews, participants were asked to complete a post-study questionnaire evaluating the prototype including: (1) Perceived Ease of Use, (2) Usefulness (3) Simplicity (4) Usability (SUS) and, (5) Perceived Persuasiveness (PPQ). Participants were given a $10.00 gift card as an honorarium for their time.

3.6 Data Collection and Analysis

All participants ($N = 8$) completed pre- and post-study questionnaires, and quantitative analysis was conducted on the final set of responses using descriptive statistics. Four interviews were completed with community members ($N = 4$) and four with service providers ($N = 4$). Interviews were facilitated by the lead researcher, who was knowledgeable about HIV prevention and the objectives of the mobile app, with support from a notetaker. Separate prototype demonstration guides were used for community members and service providers. Both the lead researcher and notetaker were present during all sessions to ensure the aims of the study were met and to ensure that any nuances were captured. Interviews had 3 objectives: (1) to review screens from the app prototype, (2) to complete tasks decided a priori and, (3) to provide feedback on the functionality, content, and design of the prototype. All sessions were recorded and audio files were transcribed using Trint [33], an automated audio transcription service. The resulting transcripts were then manually cleaned to redact personal identifying information and ensure participants' confidentiality and anonymity. A thematic analysis was completed using Dedoose (version 9) [34].

Braun and Clarke's six-phase framework [35] guided the thematic analysis. Inductive coding was used to generate an understanding of participants' subjective experiences and motivations [36]. This method was selected for its analytical flexibility and applicability across diverse ontological and epistemological viewpoints [35]. Initially, the researchers read and re-read the transcripts to familiarize themselves thoroughly with the data. To enhance the rigour and trustworthiness of the qualitative data analysis, inter-rater reliability was assessed. Two independent reviewers conducted thematic analysis separately on a subset of transcripts for CM ($N = 4$) and SP ($N = 4$). Cohen's kappa coefficient was calculated to measure the consistency between reviewers. A kappa score of 0.82 was obtained, indicating a high level of agreement between raters [37]. Coding discrepancies were resolved through discussion, and code definitions were refined accordingly. The finalized codebook was then applied to the full dataset, and codes were synthesized into themes and subthemes that informed a narrative capturing Black communities' perspectives on using an mHealth app for HIV prevention.

4 Preliminary Results

4.1 Demographic Characteristics

Community members (Table 1) were diverse in age, gender identity, sexuality, education, and employment status, with all identifying as African and most reporting a lived disability. Service providers were all cisgender women, primarily working full-time in AIDS service organizations or HIV clinics, with varied professional experience and high levels of education.

Table 1. Participant demographic characteristics.

Characteristic	Community member ($N 6.= 4$)	Service provider ($N = 4$)
Age (Years)	18–25 (50%), 26–35 (25%), 36–45 (25%)	26–35 (75%), 56+ (25%)
Gender Sexuality	Cis-woman (25%), non-binary (50%), cis-man (25%) Queer (75%), heterosexual (25%)	Cis-woman (100%) Queer (25%), heterosexual (50%), prefer not to say (25%)
Ethnicity Disability Status	African (100%) Currently living with a disability (75%), not living with a disability (25%)	African (100%), Black (25%) Currently living with a disability (100%)

(continued)

Table 1. (*continued*)

Characteristic	Community member (*N* 6.= 4)	Service provider (*N* = 4)
Level of Education	Secondary school diploma (25%), College certificate or diploma (18%), university bachelor's degree (45%), Master's, doctorate or professional degree (18%)	University bachelor's degree (75%), Master's, doctorate or professional degree (25%)
Employment Status	Working full-time (25%), working part-time (25%), student (50%)	Working full-time (75%), working part-time (25%)
Province	Ontario (100%)	Ontario (100%)
Work Experience (Years)	N/A	3–5 (50%), 5+ (50%)
Work Setting	N/A	AIDS service organization (75%), HIV clinic (25%)

4.2 Quantitative Results

Quantitative data from this formative evaluation were analyzed from the post-study questionnaires disbursed following the prototype demonstration and were used to assess the app's potential usability, functionality, and motivational impact. Items were rated on 5-point Likert scales (*1 – Strongly Disagree to 5 = Strongly Agree*). Aggregated scores were computed for Perceived Ease of Use, Usefulness, Simplicity, Usability, and Perceived Persuasiveness. Overall, both community members [CM] and service providers [SP] reported consistently high scores across all categories, indicating strong acceptability, simplicity, and engagement with the prototype. First, we analyzed preliminary perceptions of the Perceived Ease of Use (M_{CM} = 4.55, SD = 0.76; M_{SP} = 4.90, SD = 0.31) and Usefulness (M_{CM} = 4.75, SD = 0.55; M_{SP} = 4.75, SD = 0.55). These results (Fig. 5) indicate that the app has strong potential to support efficient access to HIV health prevention information and is easy to navigate [28].

Second, we analyzed Simplicity scores (Fig. 6) for the overall app across five simplicity facets [38] including Reduction (M = 4.69, SD = 0.60, Organization (M = 4.46, SD = 0.51), Aesthetics (M = 4.38, SD = 0.71), and Satisfaction (M = 4.67, SD = 0.48). As all simplicity ratings exceeded a score of 4.0, there was strong consensus that the prototype was straightforward, uncluttered, and visually appealing. These findings support maintaining the current design approach in the fully developed app [29]. Moderate variability in SP ratings related to aesthetics and interaction highlight opportunities to further refine the visual hierarchy before conducting the main user test [29].

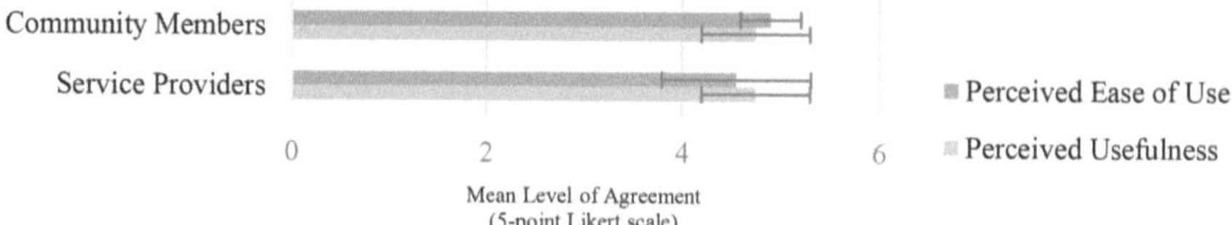

Fig. 5. Measure of perceived usefulness and ease of use.

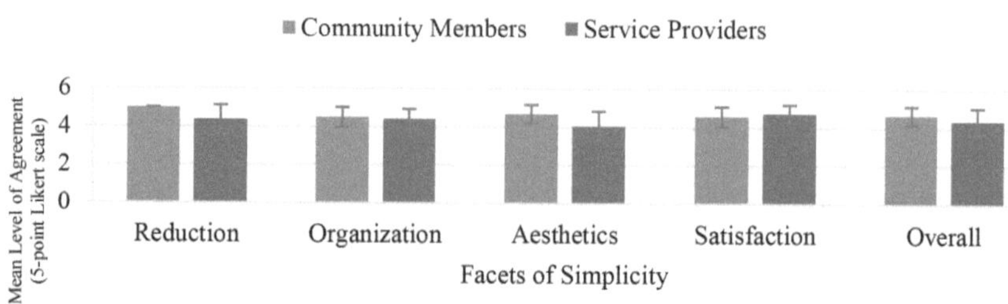

Fig. 6. Measure of Facets of Simplicity.

Third, we analyzed preliminary Usability scores obtained using the SUS. The prototype received a mean SUS score of 76.88 ($SD = 2.59$) across both groups, indicating that the overall usability of the app is "very good" or "above average" with high acceptability [30]. This score suggests that users found the prototype easy to learn with little perceived need for technical support. Some variability in the responses related to perceived consistency and anticipated frequency of use suggests opportunities for refinement. Specifically, improve consistency of the interface through uniform icons and menu items may enhance usability in the fully developed version of the app [30].

Lastly, we analyzed preliminary Perceived Persuasiveness across the four main features of the *MyHealthCore* app. We evaluated scores (Table 2) for *MyHealthEducation*, *MyHealthTracker*, *MyHealthLocator,* and *MyHealthConnect* (Fig. 4) to determine how effectively each feature's persuasive design strategies motivated engagement. Participants rated the prototype as highly persuasive (Fig. 7), indicating strong agreement that the app's designs and functionality could encourage sustained use and motivate engagement in HIV prevention behaviours [31]. Community members rated *MyHealthConnect* and *MyHealthTracker* especially high, indicating the potential for the fully developed app to have strong persuasive impact in the dimensions of: (1) social support to promote connection with community-based and clinical resources, (2) self-monitoring to encourage active health management, and (3) tailoring through the option to select personally relevant educational content.

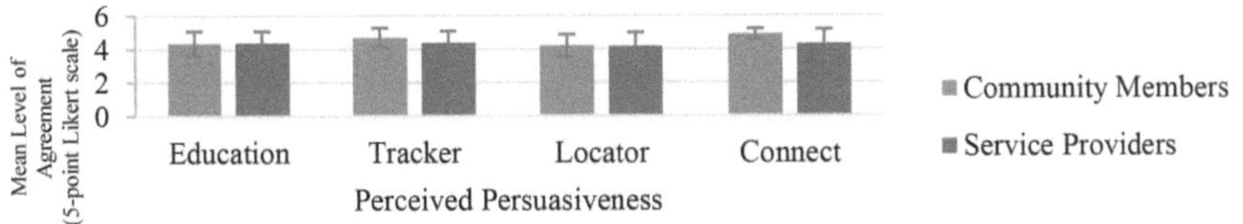

Fig. 7. Measure of Perceived Persuasiveness.

Table 2. Features and persuasive strategies

App Feature	Persuasive Strategy	Community Members ($M \pm$ SD)	Service Providers ($M \pm$ SD)
MyHealthEducation	Tailoring, self-monitoring, personalization, verifiability, rehearsal, reduction	4.35 ± 0.75	4.40 ± 0.68
MyHealthTracker	Simulation, self-monitoring, dialogue support, customization, rehearsal	4.70 ± 0.57	4.40 ± 0.68
MyHealthLocator	Reduction, tailoring, real-world feel	4.22 ± 0.65	4.18 ± 0.81
MyHealthConnect	Social support, liking, dialogue support, customization	4.90 ± 0.31	4.30 ± 0.86

4.3   Qualitative Results

Qualitative results from this formative evaluation were categorized into three overarching themes for both community members [CM] and service providers [SP]. These findings reflect participants' perspectives of *MyHealthCore's* design, content, and persuasive potential. The first theme, *Integrated Health Content,* captured how participants perceived engagement in HIV prevention behaviour as more acceptable when embedded within broader frameworks of health to reduce stigma; the second theme, *Functionality, Format, and Design,* described participants' experiences navigating the app prototype and their perceptions of its usability, with an emphasis on ease of navigation, safety and privacy. The third theme, *Suggested Features and Enhancements,* reflected participants' recommendations for improving accessibility, customization, and motivational strategies to enhance long-term engagement with the fully developed app. Excerpts are presented with minor spelling and grammatical corrections.

Theme 1: *Integrated Health Content.* Many participants mentioned integrating HIV prevention into routine primary care. This reflected a strong preference for a holistic approach that situates sexual health alongside other aspects of health, including mental and physical health. Community members expressed that connecting HIV to overall wellness through the *MyHealthTracker* feature contributed to reduced stigma about accessing HIV prevention information via a mobile app. One participant explained, *"This [MyHealth-Tracker] makes it feel less like something just about HIV and more like something for everyone's health"* [CM3]. Another participant valued how the app aligned HIV prevention with everyday self-care practices, describing it as, *"...a safe space to learn about your health without judgement"* [CM2]. Service providers echoed this sentiment, highlighting that integrating sexual health with other wellness information could help reduce stigma and support engagement in the app. One service provider noted, *"Clients are more likely to use a tool that incorporates health and self-care generally, not just HIV"* [SP1]. Participants also highlighted the clear, inclusive, and empowering educational content in *MyHealthEducation*. One community member shared, *"The information is clear, in simple language, and it doesn't make you feel blamed, it's actually encouraging"* [CM1]. Service providers also valued the information, noting that it is, *"...accurate, stigma-free, and community-based tone, not academic"* [SP3]. These findings suggest that the persuasive strategies embedded in these features (**Table 3**) could encourage voluntary engagement with the app rather than coercive use [38].

Theme 2: *Functionality, Format, and Design of MyHealthCore.* Participants consistently reported positive sentiments about *MyHealthCore's* overall usability, visual presentation, and ease of navigation. The prototype's simplicity, intuitive layout, and feature organization were frequently cited as major strengths that contributed to feelings of trust and safety about using the fully developed app. Participants described the design as reducing cognitive load, aligning with the principle of reduction as a persuasive strategy. Community members identified the prototype's ease of navigation as one of its most appealing features. One participant explained, *"The four main buttons [for the features] make sense. It's simple and you can find things fast"* [CM4], while another said, *"Everything is where you would expect it to be. It doesn't feel like too much information at once"* [CM1]. Service providers similarly highlighted the integration of features in *MyHealthCore* that make it *"...organized and consistent, and this makes it easy for clients to learn on the app"* [SP3]. They noted that the simplicity of the layout could enhance accessibility for individuals with lower levels of digital literacy. One service provider said, *"Even older adults or people who are not so used to apps could figure it out, it's straightforward"* [SP2]. Both community members and service providers identified privacy and safety features as critical to user trust and sustainable adoption of the full app. Participants appreciated the discreet design a neutral wording of the app's name and main features (Fig. 4), noting that, *"If it's too obvious that it's about HIV, people might hide it or delete it"* [CM1]. Service providers noted that discretion was essential, recommending full development of the anonymous log-in feature, particularly for the tracking functions in *MyHealthTracker*. The visual aesthetic of the prototype also contributed to participant perceptions of safety and credibility, with a participant noting, *"The colour scheme is calming and inclusive, it doesn't feel clinical or judgmental"* [CM2].

Theme 3: *Suggested Features and Enhancements.* Participants provided constructive recommendations for improving *MyHealthCore's* accessibility, engagement, and scalability. These suggestions focused on expanding the app's interactive functions, improving personalization, and incorporating more community-specific content to support sustained engagement. Community members proposed the inclusion of onboarding aids to help new users navigate the app. One participant suggested, *"Maybe including like short videos, especially at the beginning, to show people step by step what they would see in the app before they actually get there"* [CM1]. Others emphasized the potential value of gamified reminders, such as progress badges or streaks to encourage continued use of the app. One community member said, *"It could have challenges or badges, something to keep people coming back"* [CM2]. Service provider recommended functions that would support the app's integration in clinical settings. One said, "If there was an option for clients to receive referrals and track them, that way they can connect directly to their [local AIDS Service Organization] or [HIV] clinics of choice every time they log in" [SP2]. Service providers also highlighted multi-language support and accessibility for visual impairments. Both community members and service providers viewed these enhancements as natural extensions of an already functional and culturally responsive app.

5   Discussion

This study engaged Black community members and HIV service providers in the formative evaluation of a mobile health application prototype designed to respond to the multi-level barriers to their engagement in HIV prevention initiatives. Participants were invited to share their perspectives of the usability, ease of use, usefulness, simplicity, and perceived persuasiveness of the prototype to inform the iterative development of the final app. Across both quantitative and qualitative findings, participants emphasized that the persuasive impact of the proposed digital HIV prevention intervention will be shaped by attention to design and technical elements, as well as to community-specific needs for culturally relevant content and robust privacy and safety features.

5.1   Design and Development Recommendations

Based on these results, we propose five recommendations for enhancing *MyHealthCore*: (1) maintain a stigma-reducing, holistic approach by embedding HIV prevention within general health and wellness [39]; (2) increase personalization, including tailored reminders and individualized goals [22, 26]; (3) prioritize privacy and anonymity through low-visibility login and clear data protection statements; (4) enhance interactivity and multimedia features with tutorials, gamified reminders, and testimonial videos; and (5) strengthen accessibility and clinical integration, including multi-language support, compatibility with assistive technologies, and links to local HIV organizations.

5.2   Limitations

Similar to the researchers' formative work [19], this study has limitations. The small, Ontario-based sample limits generalizability across Canada. The primary aim was prototype refinement rather than statistical inference. Evaluation focused on design and technological functions, with limited assessment of HIV knowledge or prevention content. Future research should include validated measures such as the HIV Knowledge Questionnaire, Brief HIV PrEP Stigma Scale, and general health tools (e.g., PHQ-2) to align with participants' feedback emphasizing holistic health frameworks [15].

5.3 Directions for Future Work

The findings guide the app's full development, which will include pilot testing to assess HIV knowledge, usability, persuasiveness, user satisfaction, and scalability to diverse Black communities, including newcomers, Francophone and 2SLGBTQ+ populations, and rural residents. The app will be cross-platform (iOS/Android) using Dart and Flutter, with Firebase for backend authentication, real-time database management, and secure storage [40]. Final evaluation will assess the measures from this study, cultural responsiveness, user experience via the UEQ [41] and health content using a modified Health-ITUES tailored to HIV information [42].

6 Conclusion

This study explored Black community members' and HIV service providers' perspectives through a formative evaluation of a mobile health HIV prevention prototype. Findings suggest that a community-engaged, user-centered, persuasive design approach can support the development of a usable, empowering tool addressing the structural and social barriers faced by Black communities in Canada. These insights will guide further app refinement and evaluation.

Acknowledgments. This research was undertaken, in part, thanks to funding from the Canada Research Chairs Program. We acknowledge the support of the Natural Sciences and Engineering Research Council of Canada (NSERC) through the Discovery Grant. The research is conducted as part of the Dalhousie University Persuasive Computing Lab.

References

1. Owino, M., et al.: A manifesto for transformative action on HIV among black communities in Canada. Can. J. Public Health. **115**, 245–249 (2024). https://doi.org/10.17269/s41997-024-00856-y
2. Public Health Agency of Canada: HIV in Canada. , Ottawa (2024).
3. Ontario HIV Epidemiology and Surveillance Initiative: HIV Diagnoses in Ontario, 2023. , Toronto, Ontario (2025).
4. Canadian AIDS Treatment Information Exchange (CATIE): The Epidemiology of HIV in Canada. (2025).
5. Baidoobonso, S., Bauer, G.R., Speechley, K.N., Lawson, E.: HIV risk perception and distribution of HIV risk among African, Caribbean and other black people in a Canadian city: mixed methods results from the BLACCH study. BMC Public Health. **13**, 184 (2013). https://doi.org/10.1186/1471-2458-13-184

6. Logie, C.H., Jenkinson, J.I.R., Earnshaw, V., Tharao, W., Loutfy, M.R.: A structural equation model of HIV-related stigma, racial discrimination, housing insecurity and wellbeing among African and Caribbean black women living with HIV in Ontario, Canada. PLoS ONE. **11**, e0162826 (2016). https://doi.org/10.1371/journal.pone.0162826

7. Etowa, J., et al.: Community perspectives on addressing and responding to HIV-testing, pre-exposure prophylaxis (PrEP) and post-exposure prophylaxis (PEP) among African, Caribbean and black (ACB) people in Ontario, Canada. BMC Public Health. **22**, 913 (2022). https://doi.org/10.1186/s12889-022-13093-0

8. Logie, C.H., James, L., Tharao, W., Loutfy, M.R.: HIV, gender, race, sexual orientation, and sex work: a qualitative study of intersectional stigma experienced by HIV-positive women in Ontario, Canada. PLoS Med. **8** (2011). https://doi.org/10.1371/journal.pmed.1001124

9. Mihan, R., Kerr, J., Maticka-Tyndale, E.: HIV-related stigma among African, Caribbean, and black youth in Windsor, Ontario. AIDS care - Psychol. Socio-Med. Asp. AIDSHIV. **28**, 758–763 (2016). https://doi.org/10.1080/09540121.2016.1158397

10. Jangu, N.W., Omorodion, F.I., Kerr, J.: The perception of religious leaders on HIV and their role in HIV prevention: a case study of African, Caribbean, and black (ACB) communities in Windsor, Ontario. J. Relig. Health. **62**, 1616–1635 (2023). https://doi.org/10.1007/s10943-021-01426-z

11. Mauka, W., et al.: Development of a mobile health application for hiv prevention among at-risk populations in urban settings in east africa: a participatory design approach. JMIR Form. Res. **5** (2021). https://doi.org/10.2196/23204

12. Tesema, N., Guillaume, D., Francis, S., Paul, S., Chandler, R.: Mobile phone apps for HIV prevention among college-aged black women in Atlanta: mixed methods study and user-centered prototype. JMIR Form Res. **7**, e37987 (2023). https://doi.org/10.2196/37987

13. Chandler, R., Hernandez, N., Guillaume, D., Grandoit, S., Branch-Ellis, D., Lightfoot, M.: A community-engaged approach to creating a Mobile HIV prevention app for black women: focus group study to determine preferences via prototype demos. JMIR Mhealth Uhealth. **8**, e18437 (2020). https://doi.org/10.2196/18437

14. Koumpouros, Y.: User-centric design methodology for mHealth apps: the PainApp paradigm for chronic pain. Technologies. **10**, 25 (2022). https://doi.org/10.3390/technologies10010025

15. Holkup, P.A., Tripp-Reimer, T., Matt Salois, E., Weinert, C.: Community-based participatory research: an approach to intervention with a native American community. Adv. Nurs. Sci. **27**, 162–175 (2004). https://doi.org/10.1097/00012272-200407000-00002

16. Alqahtani, F., Al Khalifah, G., Oyebode, O., Orji, R.: Apps for mental health: an evaluation of behavior change strategies and recommendations for future development. Front. Artif. Intell. **2**, 30 (2019). https://doi.org/10.3389/frai.2019.00030

17. Naderbagi, A., et al.: Cultural and contextual adaptation of digital health interventions: narrative review. J. Med. Internet Res. **26** (2024). https://doi.org/10.2196/55130

18. Vigil-Hayes, M., et al.: Integrating cultural relevance into a behavioral mHealth intervention for native American youth. In: Proceedings of the ACM on Human-Computer Interaction, vol. 5, (2021).https://doi.org/10.1145/3449239

19. Musumbulwa, K.N., Chan, G., Oyebode, O., Orji, R.: Myhealthcore: Towards a Community-Engaged HIV Prevention Persuasive Mhealth App for Black Communities in Canada. In: Presented at the Lecture Notes in Computer Science, pp. 188–200 (2025). https://doi.org/10.1007/978-3-031-94959-3_14

20. Dana, R., et al.: Engaging black or African American and Hispanic or Latino men who have sex with men for HIV testing and prevention services through technology: protocol for the iSTAMP comparative effectiveness trial. JMIR Res. Protoc. **12**, e43414 (2023). https://doi.org/10.2196/43414

21. Danielson, C.K., McCauley, J.L., Jones, A.M., Borkman, A.L., Miller, S., Ruggiero, K.J.: Feasibility of delivering evidence-based HIV/STI prevention programming to a community sample of African American teen girls via the internet. AIDS Educ. Prev. Off. Publ. Int. Soc. AIDS Educ. **25**, 394–404 (2013). https://doi.org/10.1521/aeap.2013.25.5.394

22. Oinas-Kukkonen, H., Harjumaa, M.: A Systematic Framework for Designing and Evaluating Persuasive Systems. (2008).

23. Alslaity, A., Chan, G., Orji, R.: A panoramic view of personalization based on individual differences in persuasive and behavior change interventions. Front. Artif. Intell. **6**, 1125191 (2023). https://doi.org/10.3389/frai.2023.1125191

24. Savvy HER (Sexual/HIV Health Electronic Empowerment Resource).

25. Winiarski, M.G., Beckett, E., Salcedo, J.: Outcomes of an inner-city HIV mental health programme integrated with primary care and emphasizing cultural responsiveness. AIDS care Psychol Socio-Med. Asp. AIDSHIV. **17**, 747–756 (2005). https://doi.org/10.1080/095 40120412331336733

26. Oinas-Kukkonen, H., Harjumaa, M.: Communications of the Association for information systems persuasive systems design: key issues, process model, and system features. Commun. Assoc. Inf. Syst. **24**, 485–500 (2009). https://doi.org/10.17705/1CAIS.02428

27. Figma.

28. David, F.D.: Perceived Usefulness, Perceived ease of use, and user acceptance of information technology. MIS Q. **13**, 319–340 (1989). https://doi.org/10.2307/249008

29. Choi, J.H., Lee, H.J.: Facets of simplicity for the smartphone interface: a structural model. Int. J. Hum. Comput. Stud. **70**, 129–142 (2012). https://doi.org/10.1016/j.ijhcs.2011.09.002

30. Lewis, J.R., Sauro, J.: The factor structure of the system usability scale. In: Presented at the International Conference on Human Centered Design, Berlin (2009). https://doi.org/10.1007/978-3-642-02806-9_12

31. Drozd, F., Lehto, T., Oinas-Kukkonen, H.: Exploring perceived persuasiveness of a behavior change support system: a structural model. In: International Conference on Persuasive Technology, pp. 157–168 (2012)

32. Chandler, R. et al.: I care about sex, I care about my health: a mixed-methods pre-test of a HIV prevention mobile health app for black women in the southern United States. PLoS One. **18** (2023). https://doi.org/10.1371/journal.pone.0289884

33. Trint.

34. Dedoose.

35. Braun, V., Clarke, V.: Using thematic analysis in psychology. Qual. Res. Psychol. **3**, 77–101 (2006). https://doi.org/10.1191/1478088706qp063oa

36. Thomas, D.R.: A general inductive approach for analyzing qualitative evaluation data. Am. J. Eval. **27**, 237–246 (2006). https://doi.org/10.1177/1098214005283748

37. McHugh, M., L.: Interrater reliability: the kappa statistic. Biochem. Med. **22**, 276–282 (2012)

38. Jacobs, N.: Two ethical concerns about the use of persuasive technology for vulnerable people. Bioethics. **34**, 519–526 (2020). https://doi.org/10.1111/bioe.12683

39. Xavier, J., Ward, M.C., Corr, P.G., Kalita, N., McDonald, P.: Identifying the barriers and facilitators to culturally responsive HIV and PrEP screening for racial, ethnic, sexual, and gender minoritized patients: a scoping review protocol. PLoS One. **18**, e0281173 (2023). https://doi.org/10.1371/journal.pone.0281173

40. Firebase.

41. Schrepp, M., Kollmorgen, J., Thomaschewski, J.: A comparison of SUS, UMUX-LITE, and UEQ-S. J. User Exp. **18**, 86–104 (2023)

42. Schnall, R., Cho, H., Liu, J.: Health information technology usability evaluation scale (health-ITUES) for usability assessment of Mobile health technology: validation study. JMIR Mhealth Uhealth. **6**, e4 (2018). https://doi.org/10.2196/mhealth.8851

PostMom: An AI-Driven and Culturally-Tailored Persuasive Application for Postnatal Care in Nigeria

Chinenye Ogbonnaya-Okafor[(✉)] , Grace Ataguba , Gerry Chan , and Rita Orji

Faculty of Computer Science, Dalhousie University, Halifax, Canada
`{ch418086,grace.ataguba,gerry.chan,rita.orji}@dal.ca`

Abstract. Over the years, AI-driven mobile health (mHealth) applications have emerged to support maternal healthcare. However, most applications have failed to incorporate persuasive strategies and address existing myths/culturally rooted concerns about postnatal care in Nigeria. In this study, we leverage the Persuasive Systems Design model to develop PostMom, a medium-fidelity AI-driven mHealth prototype aimed at improving Nigerian mothers' knowledge of postnatal care. We piloted PostMom with 36 Nigerian mothers who interacted with the prototype and subsequently completed a post-study survey, which comprised of the Perceived Persuasiveness Scale, the System Usability Scale (SUS), and open-ended questions. Quantitative results from this study showed a good SUS rating (M = 77.67), and a significant persuasiveness rating of the PostMom prototype (p < .001). In addition, qualitative feedback from our participants presented three design opportunities: (1) support for navigation, readability, and inclusivity; (2) emotionally supportive and culturally sensitive engagement; and (3) clear information presentation with credibility cues and disclaimers. Our findings contribute to designing the next iteration of our culturally tailored AI-driven persuasive maternal application (PostMom), which can be scaled to other cultural and low-resource settings in the future.

Keywords: AI · mHealth · Postnatal care · Nigerian Mothers · Persuasive applications

1 Introduction

There has been growing attention of research in the application of artificial intelligence (AI)-driven mobile health (mHealth) technologies for maternal healthcare [32]. This growing attention is driven by the potential of AI to provide more efficient, accessible, and personalized maternal health services. Personalizing maternal experiences is essential because women's needs, challenges, and health pathways differ significantly across pregnancy and postnatal journeys [14]. In many cases, maternal outcomes depend on how well health technologies reflect these individual differences, particularly in relation to timely access, early complication detection, and continuity of care [9].

K. Sumi et al. (Eds.): PERSUASIVE 2026, LNCS 16476, pp. 225–239, 2026.
https://doi.org/10.1007/978-3-032-19687-3_17

Following the global rise in maternal mortality rates, several countries have recorded notable progress in employing AI for maternal health management. In a systematic review we conducted, we found that India currently leads with the highest number of AI-driven health technologies designed to support maternal and newborn care [30]. Despite Nigeria's extremely high maternal mortality, about 993 deaths per 100,000 live births, research on postnatal care in the country has received comparatively little attention [44]. Most available applications targeted to support Nigerian mothers are either SMS-based [29, 31] or provide limited interactive information [19, 29], and these non-knowledge-driven solutions often lack cultural context and fail to meet personal learning needs [13, 35]. This creates an important gap in postnatal care especially in Nigeria where certain myths affect the quality of care. For example, myths like using breastmilk to clear babies' eyes have persisted in Nigerian maternal care practices over the years [43] which makes it essential to create evidence- based mHealth solutions to support mothers beyond traditional healthcare settings.

In addressing the current gap, we interacted with four Nigerian clinicians, and we developed a medium-fidelity prototype, PostMom, using Figma. We incorporated eight (8) persuasive strategies, including social learning, tailoring, and feedback. Overall, we seek to answer three research questions:

- RQ1: What are the design requirements for implementing a culturally tailored persuasive application for maternal health in Nigeria?
- RQ2: How persuasive and usable is the prototype in supporting postnatal journeys?
- RQ3: What are the perceptions of Nigerian mothers about using the proto-type to improve their knowledge and get support during the postnatal journey?

We piloted the prototype with 36 Nigerian mothers we recruited using snowballing technique and word-of-mouth. Results of our analysis showed a good SUS rating (M = 77.67), and a significant persuasiveness rating of the PostMom prototype (p < .001). In addition, qualitative themes present design opportunities to support mothers emotionally and provide credible information about postnatal care. We contribute in three ways: (1) we present a culturally grounded, AI-supported postnatal app prototype for Nigerian mothers; (2) we report a preliminary evaluation of the app's perceived usability and persuasiveness; and (3) we derive actionable design recommendations for inclusive postnatal applications in low-resource contexts.

2   Related Work

2.1   Maternal Health

Maternal health encompasses the well-being of women during pregnancy, childbirth, and the postnatal period, which has remained one of the major threats to public health worldwide [25]. This has drawn the attention of diverse research communities including public health, epidemiology, social sciences, and clinical medicine, to explore the multifaceted factors of maternal outcomes and develop effective interventions. Research has shown interrelationships between factors such as healthcare access and quality, socio-economic and cultural determinants, policy frameworks, and biomedical risks [2].

More recently, there has been a shift in research examining the development of interventions to reduce the negative impact of these factors on maternal health. The human-computer interaction (HCI), artificial intelligence, and broader computer science research communities have increasingly engaged in developing digital health tools that support maternal wellbeing, focusing on usability, accessibility, and culturally sensitive adaptation [8, 38]. However, there is limited knowledge about the persuasiveness of these technologies and their adoption across diverse cultures. Table 1 summarizes the extent to which existing research has addressed different dimensions of maternal health, revealing both well-examined areas and gaps that require further study.

Table 1. Summary of maternal health research dimensions highlighting gaps relevant to maternal care and culturally grounded digital interventions

Dimension	Description	Existing Studies	Stage of Maternal Health	Level of Research Coverage	Key Findings and Gaps
Healthcare Access & Quality	Access to skilled birth and emergency care	[10, 12, 39]	Pregnancy, Birth, and Post-natal care,	Extensive	Strong link to reduced mortality
Socio-economic Factors	Poverty, education, geographic disparities	[10]		Moderate	Limits service utilization; increases risk.
Cultural & Social Factors	Beliefs, gender norms, traditional practices	[39]		Moderate	Influences health-seeking; requires sensitive intervention.
Policy Frameworks	National programs, SDGs, governance	[39]		Moderate to strong	Shape systemic responses and biomedical risk management.
Biomedical Risks	Obstetric complications, infections, etc.	[10]		Extensive	Direct clinical cause of maternal deaths.
Integrated Perspectives	Multi-factor analysis integrating above dimensions	[12, 39]		Emerging	Multi-sectoral approaches most effective

2.2 Applications of AI in Maternal Health: Gaps and Opportunities

To understand the extent to which AI technologies have been implemented in re-search on maternal health, we conducted a systematic review on six widely used electronic databases: (1) the ACM (Association for Computing Machinery) Digital Library, (2) IEEE (Institute of Electrical and Electronics Engineers) Xplore, (3) ScienceDirect, (4) Scopus, (5) CINAHL, and (6) PubMed. We used the following search keywords: "maternal health" OR "reproductive health" OR "child health" AND "persuasive" OR "behavior change" AND "machine learning" OR "artificial intelligence" OR "AI". Following the Preferred Reporting Items for Systematic Reviews and Meta-Analyses (PRISMA) guidelines [33], out of a total of 258,347 articles we retrieved; 62 eligible papers were retained.

Our analysis shows different behavior monitoring patterns, persuasive strategies, and behavior-change opportunities in maternal and child health. The most frequent monitoring pattern was fetal health monitoring (e.g [3, 17]., followed by infant behavior monitoring (e.g [6, 42]., maternal behavior tracking (e.g [5, 15]., chatbot usage/engagement (e.g [20, 41].), ECG-based stress signals (e.g [21, 23].), SAR interaction patterns and movement/sensor-derived data [34], demonstrating a broad distribution of data sources used to classify user behaviors and health conditions. In addition, we found a substantial underrepresentation of persuasive strategies in most studies (e.g [3, 5].); by contrast, a smaller set of studies employed cultural tailoring, positive reinforcement, or personalization, often in chatbots or SAR-based interventions, enhancing engagement and contextual relevance (e.g [4, 16].). We also observed an intersection between behavior tracking and persuasive design (e.g., personalized alerts, real-time feedback). Conversational agents show promise for culturally adaptive health education and support, yet most work focuses on prenatal use and model performance, with limited in-situ evaluation and persuasive design.

Our review identified three gaps: limited integration of persuasive and culturally tailored strategies; few longitudinal, real-world evaluations of behavior change; and little evidence of how mothers engage with content beyond generic FAQs. These gaps informed three design goals: DG1, co-creation with mothers and clinicians; DG2, features embedding persuasive strategies (e.g., social learning, chatbot tailoring and feedback, credibility-focused FAQs, and personalization); and DG3, field evaluation with the target population.

3   Methodology

We employed a mixed-methods approach combining qualitative, design, and quantitative methods. For the qualitative component, we conducted semi-structured interviews with clinicians and collected open-ended survey responses from mothers. We first gathered insights from Nigerian clinicians regarding common postnatal questions and their responses, informing DG1, which focuses on clinical accuracy and cultural appropriateness. Drawing on DG2, we developed a PostMom Figma prototype incorporating simulation features that demonstrate expert-guided responses. We further operationalized DG1 and DG3 by engaging mothers in a field evaluation, which provided quantitative insights into the perceived persuasiveness of PostMom. While the study addresses gaps in persuasive design, not all design goals were intended to map directly to persuasive strategies; Table 2 summarizes those incorporated under DG2.

3.1 Study Design with Clinicians

We obtained ethics approval from the Institutional Review Ethics Board to conduct this study. We recruited four clinicians specializing in Gynecology and Obstetrics, with two holding a Bachelor's degree (MBBS), one holds a Master's degree, and one a PhD in relevant fields. In terms of professional experience, all participants reported having over 10 years of clinical experience in maternal health practice, confirming their extensive expertise in managing postnatal care and maternal counseling. Their involvement provided the foundation for ensuring that our system design and educational content aligned with clinical realities and evidence-based maternal health practices. This was further simulated in our design of the PostMom.

3.2 PostMom Design and Study Design with Nigerian Mothers

We implemented four Figma screens informed by clinician insights and the design goals outlined in Sect. 2.2 (Fig. 1). The MamaCare screen supports social learning by enabling mothers to share and learn from peer experiences. The Mama_Paddy chatbot simulates patient–doctor interaction to address health concerns and implements tailoring. The FAQ screen provides clinician-validated information from trusted sources (e.g., WHO), supporting expertise, credibility, and verifiability. Finally, the onboarding screen simulates personalization by capturing user information. Table 2 summarizes the persuasive strategies embedded in PostMom.

Fig. 1: The first screen is the Mamacare community space, the second screen is the Mama Paddy chatbot, the third screen is the FAQ screen, and the fourth screen on-boarding screen.

Furthermore, to evaluate our PostMom, we recruited and engaged 36 Nigerian mothers. All mothers were aged 18 years or older, were residing in Nigeria, and proficient in English language to be able to use our study materials. In the next section, we will cover demographic data and results answering our research questions RQ1 - RQ3.

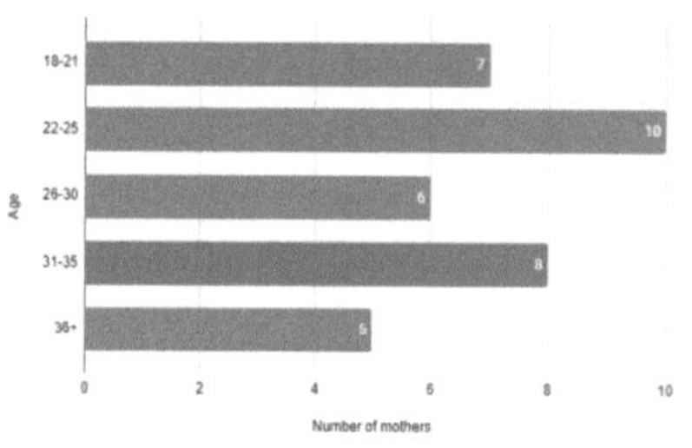

Fig. 2. Age distribution of participants

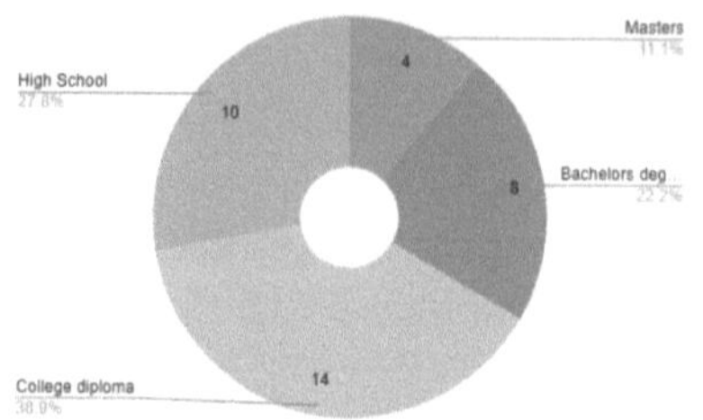

Fig. 3. Educational level of participants

Table 2. Mapping PostMom Features to Persuasive Strategies and Postnatal Care Challenges

PostMom Feature	Implemented PSD Persuasive Strategy	Postnatal Care Challenge Addressed	How the Strategy Is Operationalized
Mama_Paddy Chatbot	Expertise, Simulation, Personalization	Access to expert guidance; behavior-change motivation; cultural misconceptions.	Simulates clinician consultations using WHO-aligned validated responses with personalized conversational scenarios.
FAQ Feature	Credibility Verifiability	Credibility of health information; correction of cultural misconceptions	Provides simplified, evidence-based guidance to trusted sources.
MamaCare	Social Learning	Reassurance and shared understanding.	Enables reflection on peer-shared postnatal experiences.
Account Setup / Onboarding	Tailoring, Personalization	Content personalization	Captures user preferences to personalize content and chatbot interactions.

4   Results

4.1   Mothers' Demographic Information

The age distribution of mothers in our study shows more in the 22_25-year range (10 mothers, 28%), followed by 31–35 (n = 8; 22%), and 18–21 (n = 7; 19%), indicating that the sample includes younger population of mothers compared to older populations (see Fig. 2). In terms of educational qualification, our distribution (see Fig. 3) shows more representation of mothers with college diploma (n = 14; 39%). This is followed by mothers with high school or equivalent qualification (n = 10; 28%), bachelor's degree (n = 8;

22%), and master's degree (n = 4; 11%). This distribution explains the heterogeneous literacy levels, which can further suggest their health literacy.

4.2 RQ1: Design Requirements for Implementing a Culturally Tailored Persuasive Application for Maternal Health in Nigeria

To answer RQ1, we combined findings from our systematic review and a qualitative study with clinicians. The review informed three design goals: DG1, co-creation and personalization through clinician involvement to tailor postnatal content and delivery; DG2, embedding persuasive and behavior-change mechanisms (e.g., social learning, tailoring, credibility, and feedback) within AI features; and DG3, real-world implementation and evaluation with mothers. Complementing this, interviews with four medical doctors surfaced key postnatal information needs and common misconceptions, while simulated use scenarios with mothers informed DG2 by supporting decision rehearsal and consequence visualization (e.g., breastfeeding techniques, cord care, and recovery timelines). Using thematic analysis, we identified four themes covered in Sects. 4.2.1–4.2.4.

4.2.1 Maternal Physical Recovery & Sexual Resumption (Timing, Bleeding, Wound Care, Contraception)

Mothers know lochia occurs but often underestimate its duration and ask when sex is safe. D2 frames the puerperium as six weeks; lochia may last 4_6 weeks with color changes; D1 notes 10_14 days up to four weeks is common and flags >6 weeks as a warning. Both D1/D2 stress wound-care hygiene and timely infection management; D2 cautions against routine sitz baths and recommends antibiotics only when indicated. Sexual resumption is typically around 6 weeks but individualized (D2), with embedded family planning counseling tailored to risk (D2). Doctors propose time-anchored scripts, clear red flags, and partner-communication cues.

4.2.2 Breastfeeding Technique and Complications (Latch, Cracked Nipples, Engorgement, Pumping, Special Cases)

Motivation is high but technique varies; cracked nipples/engorgement are frequent. D1 emphasizes correct latch (areola, not nipple) to prevent abrasions; D2 advises re-latch if painful, feed on the unaffected side, and pump/express to prevent engorgement and maintain supply. D4 adds self-care (lanolin, warm/cool compresses, simple analgesia) and cautions against vitamin E or honey on nipples. D2 debunks "pregnancy requires weaning", noting continuation of breastfeeding while pregnant is usually safe unless specific contraindications; true intolerance may re-quire formula. Doctors recommend hands-on latch teaching, simple decision aids (e.g., "cracked on one side feed other + pump," D2), myth-busting (D4), and clear criteria for formula/referral.

4.2.3 Newborn Concerns and Home Care (Cord Care, Crying/Colic, Eye Discharge, Jaundice, Escalation)

Common worries include cord-stump timing, persistent crying, eye discharge, and jaundice; unsafe remedies circulate. D1/D2/D3 advised cord fall-off 7–14 days (up to 21), routine hygienic care, and explicitly no toothpaste on the cord. For crying, D1 reviews hunger/comfort checks and soothing; escalate if prolonged; D2 adds colic management. D2 warns against breast milk in the eye; use proper drops for suspect-ed infection; gives clear jaundice guidance (testing, phototherapy, kernicterus risk). Doctors call for home-care guides, explicit red flags (fever, worsening jaundice, foul odor/redness), and respectful myth-to-fact messaging.

4.2.4 Psychosocial Well-being and Social Support (PPD/Psychosis, Spouse/Family, Peers)

Recognition of postpartum mood disorders is limited, and support gaps raise risk. D1/D3 link absent family/spousal support to worse psychological outcomes. D2 describes one severe case needing referral but notes many improve with spousal reassurance, sleep protection, and family involvement; D2 also runs WhatsApp peer groups that include an experienced mother for shared learning. Clinically, doctors use a stepped approach: counseling and social support for mild cases, antidepressants when indicated, and psychiatric referral for severe depression or psychosis. Overall, insights guided and enhanced persuasive design implementations in the PostMom prototype.

4.3 RQ2: Persuasiveness and Usability of the PostMom for Supporting Postnatal Journeys of Nigerian Mothers

To answer RQ2, we analyzed responses from the System Usability Scale (SUS) and the Perceived Persuasiveness Scale (PS). We ran a one-sample t-test against the neutral midpoint (3). The SUS mean was 77.67 (SD = 16.45), exceeding the literature benchmark of 68 [15] indicating good usability. The SUS score was significantly higher than neutral, $(t\,(35) = 15.22, p < .001)$. As shown in Fig. 4, positive SUS items attracted more ratings for positive statements aligning with confidence, ease of learning, and integration, while negative items such as cumbersome, inconsistency, excessive complexity, and need for technical help, were rated less; only small neutral statements were rated on a few items (e.g., "use frequently"), which was consistent with their perception of a usable, coherent, and easy-to-learn system.

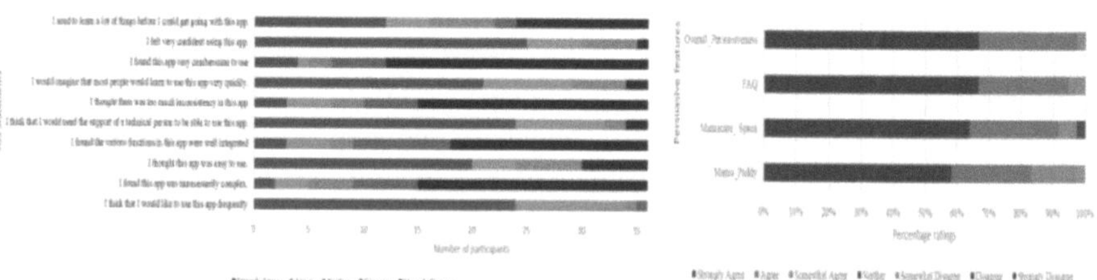

Fig. 4. Distribution of SUS ratings in favor of the easy to use item

Fig. 5. Persuasiveness ratings of the three main features and overall rating (N = 36).

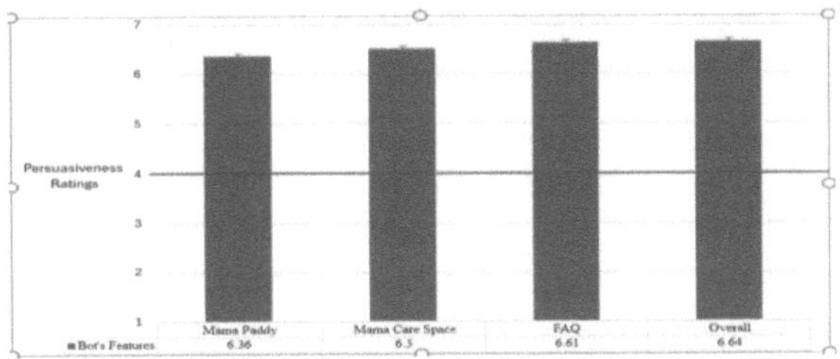

Fig. 6. Mean distribution of the persuasiveness of three main features and overall features of the PostMom.

After use, participants also rated the persuasiveness of PostMom features based on four items adapted from Drodz et al. [11] on a 7-point Likert scale (1 = strongly disagree, 7 = strongly agree): Overall (M = 6.64; SD = 0.54; $t(36)$ = 29.18; $p < .001$; d = 4.80), Mama Paddy (M = 6.36; SD = 0.93; $t(36)$ = 15.22; $p < .001$; d = 2.48), Mama Care Space (M = 6.50; SD = 0.74; $t(36)$ = 20.36; $p < .001$; d = 3.35), and FAQ (M = 6.61; SD = 0.60; $t(36)$ = 26.16; $p < .001$; d = 4.31). Figure 5 and 6 illustrate that FAQ and the overall experience had more distributions for Strongly-Agree statement ratings; MamaCare_Space was robust but with a small neutral/disagree rating; Mama_Paddy remained positive but showed more spread (Agree/Somewhat-Agree). Together with the SUS findings, these results suggest PostMom is usable and persuasive, with the FAQ and community features especially compelling.

4.4 RQ3: Suggestions for Improving the PostMom to Support Mothers in their Postnatal Journey

To answer RQ3, we analyzed open-ended questions we asked participants about their suggestions for improving PostMom. Following our thematic analysis procedure of Braun and Clarke [7], three overarching themes emerged as key suggestions for refining PostMom for supporting the postnatal journeys of Nigerian mothers: 1. Supporting Easy Navigation, Readability, and Inclusivity, 2. Adding Emotional and Culturally Sensitive Engagement Features, and 3. Information Presentation, Credibility, and Disclaimers.

4.4.1 Theme 1: Supporting Easy Navigation, Readability, and Inclusivity

Mothers appreciated the app's simplicity and clear flow but desired better navigation, more readable layouts, and features that accommodate users with different literacy, education, or experience levels. For example, [P.1, P.14] emphasized that we provide homepage with all the features so they can easily navigate. In addition, participants [P.9, P.20, and P.19] mentioned that we adjust the font sizes, especially for the FAQ for readability. Similarly, participant P.18 made reference to making color adjustments to aid readability in connection with inclusivity: *"Fair for female gender but use something darker like dark pink so it can be readable."* [P.18]; *"but you can add more colors just to make it look more magnificent."* [P.14]. Also, in relation to inclusivity, another participant (P.35) suggested we include non-breastfeeding mothers: *"Though my baby is 2+, I just had to think back. Yes, if it is possible, include non-breastfeeding mothers."* [P.35].

4.4.2 Theme 2: Adding Emotional and Culturally Sensitive Engagement Features

Participants valued the culturally relevant naming (e.g., Mama_Paddy) and calm visual tone but wanted the app to feel more emotionally supportive and culturally resonant beyond information delivery. According to participant P.6 *"I love the cultural feel of the feature names."* Two participants made reference to including songs *"I would suggest that songs be added so we can play for our babies"* [P.25]. *"I would suggest the addition of songs so that we can put baby to sleep"* [P.28]. Another mother recommended other entertaining features to allow mothers engage more with the app *"Let there be additional entertaining features that will keep people going to the app."* [P.30]:

4.4.3 Theme 3: Information Presentation, Credibility, and Disclaimers

Mothers sought reassurance that information is trustworthy, up-to-date, and clearly distinguished between general guidance and professional advice. They preferred a layered (drill-down) format brief overviews with optional detailed explanations. One participant said *"Include disclaimer for the information in the bot"* [P.6]. Another participant added *"Kindly add links to articles that provide relevant postnatal health education"* [P.7]. Participant P.4 asked that we include more frequently asked questions to address cultural myths *"More frequently asked questions and myths bursting."*

5 Discussion

5.1 Persuasiveness and Usefulness of Postmom

Our results demonstrate that PostMom App is generally perceived as both usable (SUS mean = 77.67) and highly persuasive (overall persuasiveness M = 6.64/7). This aligns with prior research emphasizing that maternal health apps succeed when they provide intuitive, culturally relevant, and socially supportive experiences that fit seamlessly into new mothers' daily routines [22, 36]. The positive feedback about the FAQ and community features reflects Their effectiveness in meeting mothers' needs through clear, trustworthy information coupled with peer learning, which enhances engagement and self-efficacy in post-partum care [24].

However, mothers' feedback reveals useful directions for improvement in both usefulness and persuasiveness. Suggestions were aimed at improving the app to promote engagement, clarity and usability through a centralized homepage, improving navigation, and incorporate accessibility options respond directly to best practices in mHealth design. This aligns with the drive to provide simple, inclusive interfaces tailored to diverse literacy and experience levels [24, 40]. In addition to their suggestions, mothers emphasized on the need to provide features such as lullabies, empathetic chatbot language, and affirmations, capable of promoting emotional engagement, which existing studies have reportedly shown to increase motivation, trust, and long-term use of maternal apps [18, 28]. The need to include non-breastfeeding mothers and family contexts will further broaden relevance and social credibility. Additionally, building trust through an inclusion of information source, layered information, disclaimers, and safety alerts address critical concerns about reliability and clinical safety highlighted in the literature

[1]. Overall, implementing these suggestions will strengthen PostMom's persuasiveness by improving its emotional resonance, cultural sensitivity, and expert credibility, while boosting usefulness through improved navigation, inclusivity, and personalization.

5.2 Design Implications

Based on key findings from our study, we recommend three design implications (DI1 - DI3) for redesigning PostMom for Nigerian mothers.

5.2.1 DI1 - Accessible, Credible, and Navigable Information Delivery

Providing plain-language summaries with drill-down details (e.g., red flags and step-wise guidance), supported by visible credibility cues (e.g., WHO or Ministry of Health endorsements), can strengthen trust and comprehension. Clear navigation, readability controls (larger fonts, high contrast, read-aloud), and inclusive onboarding further improve usability and accessibility. These features are particularly crucial in settings with diverse literacy levels and limited digital familiarity [1, 37]. AI integration in content personalization and readability adaptation can further enhance this experience by tailoring delivery to individual user needs and preferences.

5.2.2 DI2 - Social Connection and Peer Learning as Persuasive Levers

Psychosocial support emerged strongly in our findings, underscoring the importance of social learning for reinforcing positive maternal behaviors. MamaCare_Space should scaffold peer stories, moderate advice, and reactions to enhance learning and shared encouragement. This transition from a simple chat feature into a socially persuasive ecosystem aligns with evidence that peer support and community-based learning significantly mitigate postpartum isolation and increase self-efficacy [1, 27]. AI-powered moderation and content suggestions can maintain relevance and safety within these social spaces, exemplifying how AI enhances engagement and trust in maternal health platforms [1].

5.2.3 DI3 - Motivational Design and Behavioral Reinforcement for Sustained Engagement

Lightweight reinforcements such as encouraging micro-messages, progress badges, and timely nudges can sustain engagement without overwhelming users. Daily cues and personalized chatbot tips support routine postpartum care, consistent with AI-augmented maternal tools like an SMS-based AI assistant piloted for Nigerian mothers' breastfeeding support [29]. These motivational elements help address engagement challenges pervasive in digital health interventions, with AI enabling adaptive and context-aware messaging tailored to user progress [26]. By implementing these implications in future work, our study will present opportunities for a broader application and scalability across other diverse cultures.

6 Limitations

We acknowledge a few limitations. The study involved a small, non-representative sample and a short-term, non–field-based evaluation, with mothers interacting with a medium-fidelity prototype and reporting perceived usability and persuasiveness. Hence, findings reflect perceived potential rather than sustained real-world impact, with no behavioral or clinical outcomes or usage logs beyond self-report. Reliance on self-reported data and participation limited to English-speaking mothers further restrict generalizability. Future work will involve larger, longitudinal field deployments, interaction logging, and multilingual support. As this pilot evaluated conceptual AI implementation, conclusions regarding real-world AI accuracy, safety, and effectiveness remain limited.

7 Conclusion

This study shows that PostMom's prototype offers a usable and persuasive concept for supporting Nigerian mothers' postnatal care through culturally tailored content, community features, and clear health guidance. Mothers valued its relevance while highlighting improvements in usability and emotional engagement, informing design implications around accessibility, social connection, and AI-driven motivation. Currently, PostMom implements simulated AI personalization; future work will deploy clinician-validated chatbots and adaptive recommendations. Overall, PostMom demonstrates the potential of AI-supported maternal health technologies in low-resource settings.

Acknowledgments. This research was undertaken, in part, thanks to funding from the Canada Research Chairs Program. We acknowledge the support of the Natural Sciences and Engineering Research Council of Canada (NSERC) through the Discovery Grant. The research is conducted as part of the Dalhousie University Persuasive Computing Lab.

Disclosure of Interests. Not Applicable.

References

1. Ajayi, T., et al.: Digital health platform for maternal health: design, recruitment strategies, and lessons learned from the PowerMom observational cohort study. JMIR Form Res. **9**, e70149 (2025). https://doi.org/10.2196/70149
2. Anumudu, S.I., et al.: A scoping review of maternal mortality, its health determinants, and factors that influence care utilization in women of child-bearing years in Nigeria. Glob. Health J. (2025). https://doi.org/10.1016/J.GLOHJ.2025.10.004
3. Archana, P., et al.: An efficient prediction system for heart diseases using machine learning algorithms. In: Archana, P., Shashikala, S.V. (eds.) 2024 Second International Conference on Advances in Information (2024). https://doi.org/10.1109/ICAIT61638.2024.10690588
4. Batani, J., et al.: A deep learning-based chatbot to enhance maternal health education. In: Batani, J., Mbunge, E., Leokana, L. (eds.) 2024 Conference on Information Communications Technology (2024)
5. Bian, D., et al.: A novel multisensory stimulation and data capture system (MADCAP) for investigating sensory trajectories in infancy. In: Bian, D., Zheng, Z., Swanson, A., Weitlauf, A., Woynaroski, T., Cascio, C.J., Key, A.P., Warren, Z. (eds.) IEEE Transac-Tions on Neural Systems and Rehabilitation Engineering.(2018)

6. Bilalpur, M., et al.: SHAP-based prediction of mother's history of depression to under-stand the influence on child behavior. In: Bilalpur, M., Hinduja, S., Cariola, L., Sheeber, L., Allen, N., Morency, L.P., Cohn, J.F. (eds.) Proceedings of the 25th International Confer-Ence on Multimodal Interaction, pp. 537–544 (2023). https://doi.org/10.1145/3577190.3614136

7. Braun, V., Clarke, V.: Using thematic analysis in psychology. Qual. Res. Psychol. **3**(2), 77–101 (2006). https://doi.org/10.1191/1478088706qp063oa

8. Chung, K., et al.: A Chatbot for perinatal women's and partners' obstetric and men-tal health care: development and usability evaluation study. JMIR Med. Inform. **9**(3), e18607 (2021). https://doi.org/10.2196/18607

9. Cresswell, J.A. et al.: Global and regional causes of maternal deaths 2009–20: a WHO sys-tematic analysis.JA Cresswell, M Alexander, MYC Chong, HM Link, M Pejchinovska, U Gazeley, SMA Ahmed The Lancet Global Health. 13, 4, e626–e634 (2025). https://doi.org/10.1016/S2214-109X(24)00560-6.

10. Dilmaghani, D., et al.: Increasing maternal mortality in the U.S.: looking beneath and beyond the numbers. Mayo Clin. Proc. **99**(6), 873 (2024). https://doi.org/10.1016/J.MAYOCP.2024.04.002

11. Drozd, F., et al.: Exploring perceived persuasiveness of a behavior change support system: a structural model. In: Lecture Notes in Computer Science (Including Subseries Lecture Notes in Artificial Intelligence and Lecture Notes in Bioinformatics), vol. 7284. LNCS, pp. 157–168 (2012). https://doi.org/10.1007/978-3-642-31037-9_14

12. Egbewale, B.E., et al.: Coverage and determinants of infant postnatal care in Nigeria: a population-based cross-sectional study. Pediatr. Investig. **8, 1**, 27 (2024). https://doi.org/10.1002/PED4.12412

13. Egwudo, A.E., et al.: Integrating digital health technologies into the healthcare sys-tem: challenges and opportunities in Nigeria. PLOS Digital Health. **4**(7), e0000928 (2025). https://doi.org/10.1371/JOURNAL.PDIG.0000928

14. Fahey, J., et al.: Understanding and meeting the needs of women in the postpartum period: the perinatal maternal health promotion model. Journal of midwifery & women's health. **58**(6), 613–621 (2013). https://doi.org/10.1111/JMWH.12139

15. Gupta, V., et al.: Predictive algorithms for early postpartum depression detection: CatBoost vs. LightGBM. In: Gupta, V., Tripathi, S., Singh, D., Bansal, A. (eds.) 2024 11th International Conference on Reliability, Infocom (2024)

16. Guvava, B., Dube, S.: Multilingual conversational AI framework for empowering maternal and child healthcare in Zimbabwe. In: 2024 3rd Zimbabwe Conference of Information and Communication Technologies (ZCICT), pp. 1–11. IEEE (2024)

17. Harper, J. et al.: Assessing the utility of low resolution brain imaging: treatment of infant hydrocephalus. NeuroImage: Clinical, 2021•Elsevier. 102896 (2021).

18. Inkster, B., et al.: Understanding the impact of an AI-enabled conversational agent mobile app on users' mental health and wellbeing with a self-reported maternal event: a mixed method real-world data mHealth study. Front Glob Womens Health. **4**, 1084302 (2023). https://doi.org/10.3389/FGWH.2023.1084302/BIBTEX

19. Kante, M., Målqvist, M.: Effectiveness of SMS-based interventions in enhancing antenatal care in developing countries: a systematic review. BMJ Open. **15**(2), e089671 (2025). https://doi.org/10.1136/BMJOPEN-2024-089671

20. Kaur, J. et al.: Exploring the role of Chatbots in tackling COVID-19 vaccine Hesi-tancy among pregnant and breastfeeding women in rural northern India.J Kaur, P Sharma, V Kumar, M Duggal, NG Diamond-Smith, A El Ayadi, K Vosburg, P Singh Proceedings of the ACM on Human-Computer Interaction. 8, CSCW1, 55 (2024). https://doi.org/10.1145/3637332.

21. Keshary Shah, A. et al.: Enhanced Breast Cancer Tumor Classification Using Mo-bileNetV2: a Detailed Exploration on Image Intensity, Error Mitigation, and Stream-Lit-Driven Real-Time Deployment. (2023).

22. Kientz, J.A. et al.: Centering Culture in Health: Developing Culturally Safe Technol-ogy for Early Childhood Health Promotion. (2024)
23. King, Z.D. et al.: Micro-stress EMA: a passive sensing framework for detecting in-the-wild stress in pregnant mothers. ZD King, J Moskowitz, B Egilmez, S Zhang, L Zhang, M Bass, J Rogers, R Ghaffari Proceedings of the ACM on Interactive, Mobile, Wearable and Ubiquitous. 3, 3, 1–22 (2019). https://doi.org/10.1145/3351249.
24. Leahy-Warren, P., McCarthy, G.: Maternal parental self-efficacy in the postpartum period. Midwifery. 27(6), 802–810 (2011). https://doi.org/10.1016/J.MIDW.2010.07.008
25. Le Lez, J., et al.: Maternal wellbeing: a WHO definition and conceptual framework. Lancet Obstet. Gynaecol. Women's Health. 1(1), e57–e63 (2025). https://doi.org/10.1016/j.lanogw.2025.100017
26. Li, K., et al.: Features, design, and adherence to evidence-based behavioral parent-ing prin-ciples in commercial mHealth parenting apps: systematic review. JMIR Pediatr Parent. 6, e43626 (2023). https://doi.org/10.2196/43626
27. Mapari, S.A., et al.: Revolutionizing maternal health: the role of artificial Intelli-gence in enhancing care and accessibility. cureus. 16, e69555 (2024). https://doi.org/10.7759/cureus.69555
28. McAlister, K., et al.: Chatbot to support the mental health needs of pregnant and postpartum women (moment for parents): design and pilot study. JMIR Form Res. 9(1), e72469 (2025). https://doi.org/10.2196/72469
29. Musti, A.: Usability and usefulness of SMS-based artificial intelligence intervention (Mwana) on breastfeeding outcomes in Lagos, Nigeria: pilot app development study. JMIR Form Res. 9(1), e65157 (2025). https://doi.org/10.2196/65157
30. Ogbonnaya-Okafor, C., O.R., C.G.: Systematic review of AI-driven interventions for maternal and child health. Int. J. Hum. Comput. Interact. (2026)
31. Olajubu, A.O., et al.: Mothers' experiences with mHealth intervention for postnatal care utilisation in Nigeria: a qualitative study. BMC Pregnancy Childbirth. 22(1), 843 (2022). https://doi.org/10.1186/S12884-022-05177-X
32. Oprescu, A.M., et al.: Artificial intelligence in pregnancy: a scoping review. IEEE Access. 8, 181450–181484 (2020). https://doi.org/10.1109/ACCESS.2020.3028333
33. Page, M.J., et al.: The PRISMA 2020 statement: an updated guideline for reporting systematic reviews. BMJ. 372 (2021). https://doi.org/10.1136/BMJ.N71
34. Paulsson, T., et al.: Exploring mothers' perspectives on socially assistive robots in Peripartum depression screening. In: Paulsson, T., Zhong, M., Veláz-quez, I.G., Castellano, G. (eds.) Companion of the 2023 ACM/IEEE International Conference on Human-Robot, pp. 486–490 (2023). https://doi.org/10.1145/3568294.3580132
35. Rahman, S., et al.: Barriers and facilitators of messaging platforms as a means of maternal support and care in rural communities: a systematic review. PLoS One. 20(12), e0336168 (2025). https://doi.org/10.1371/JOURNAL.PONE.0336168
36. Recanati, M.: Embracing Motherhood Moments: Tangible Tools for Celebrating Daily Accomplishments. (2024).
37. Saleh, S., et al.: Evaluating the impact of engaging healthcare providers in an AI-based gamified mHealth intervention for improving maternal health outcomes among disadvantaged pregnant women in Lebanon. Front Digit Health. 7, 1574946 (2025). https://doi.org/10.3389/FDGTH.2025.1574946/BIBTEX
38. Sesay, A.D.D., et al.: Evaluating the Usability and Practicality of AI-Enabled Smartphone-Based Obstetric Ultrasound in Sierra Leone: a Mixed-Methods Study (2025). https://doi.org/10.21203/RS.3.RS-6710084/V1
39. Souza, J.P., et al.: A global analysis of the determinants of maternal health and transi-tions in maternal mortality. Lancet Glob. Health. 12(2), e306–e316 (2024). https://doi.org/10.1016/S2214-109X(23)00468-0

40. Srivastava, A., et al.: Actionable UI design guidelines for smartphone applications inclusive of low-literate users. Proc ACM Hum Comput Interact. 5(CSCW1), 1–30 (2021). https://doi.org/10.1145/3449210. TAXONOMY:TAXONOMY:ACM-PUBTYPE;PAGEGROUP:STRING:PUBLICATION
41. Vaira, L., et al.: MamaBot: a system based on ML and NLP for supporting women and families during pregnancy. In: Vaira, L., Bochicchio, M.A., Conte, M., Casaluci, F.M., Melpignano, A. (eds.) Proceedings of the 22nd International Database Engineering & Applications, pp. 273–277 (2018). https://doi.org/10.1145/3216122.3216173
42. Yan, Z., et al.: A study of mother-infant behavioral relationships based on support vector machine predictive models. In: 2024 IEEE 3rd International Conference on Electrical Engineering (2024)
43. Neonatal eye infections: Can Med Assoc J. 99, 16, 818–819 (1968). doi:https://doi.org/10.1097/JPN.0000000000000973.
44. View of A Ten-Year Review of Maternal Deaths at Federal Teaching Hospital: Gombe, North East Nigeria, https://www.wajog.org/index.php/wajog/article/view/52/15, Accessed 12 Nov 2025

Recilify: An AI-Driven and Emotion-Adaptive Persuasive Technology for Promoting Mental Well-Being

Oladapo Oyebode[1]([envelope]) [iD], Darren Steeves[2], and Rita Orji[1] [iD]

[1] Faculty of Computer Science, Dalhousie University, Halifax, NS, Canada
oladapo.oyebode@dal.ca
[2] School of Health and Human Performance, Dalhousie University, Halifax, NS, Canada

Abstract. Mental disorders affect 1 in 7 people globally. Negative emotions are linked to mental disorders, while positive emotions build resilience and improve quality of life. Emotion regulation (ER) manages negative emotions (e.g., fear, sadness, and anger) and reinforces positive emotions (e.g., happiness) for improved mental well-being. However, there is limited knowledge on how to implement personalized, real-time, AI-driven ER interventions using persuasive technology tailored to an individual's evolving emotional state while motivating behaviour change. To address this gap, we developed *Recilify*, an AI-driven and emotion-adaptive persuasive mobile health (mHealth) app that helps users to regulate emotions and improve mental well-being. The app was systematically developed following an evidence-based and user-centered process. First, we conduct a comprehensive literature review to identify persuasive strategies (PS), as well as ER strategies and how they can be implemented in a system. Second, we conduct an empirical study involving 660 participants to identify PS that support ER. Third, we develop a novel AI model to predict users' emotional states in real time from journal or diary entries. Fourth, we develop an interactive prototype of the app and evaluate it with 20 target users. Our evaluation findings show that *Recilify* is significantly persuasive, motivating, and usable. Fifth, we develop the app which integrates the AI model, PS, and ER strategies, and then privately deploy it on both Google Play and Apple App Stores for real-world testing. Finally, we build on our empirical insights to provide practical recommendations for designing persuasive mHealth apps to improve mental well-being.

Keywords: Emotion Regulation · Persuasive Technology · Emotion-Adaptive System · Artificial Intelligence · Machine Learning · Deep Learning · Behaviour Change · Interventions Design · Mobile Health App

1 Introduction

Mental health is a global concern, with the World Health Organization reporting that 1 in 7 people worldwide live with a mental illness [1]. Emotions play a crucial role in mental health; for instance, negative emotions (such as anger, fear, and sadness) have been

© The Author(s), under exclusive license to Springer Nature Switzerland AG 2026
K. Sumi et al. (Eds.): PERSUASIVE 2026, LNCS 16476, pp. 240–255, 2026.
https://doi.org/10.1007/978-3-032-19687-3_18

linked to conditions such as depression, anxiety, and substance use disorders [2–4], while positive emotions (such as happiness) enhance mental well-being and foster resilience, vitality, and life satisfaction [5–7]. Research has shown that individuals who experience more positive emotions cope better with adversity and stress [8]. These findings highlight the need to reduce negative emotions while reinforcing positive emotions to promote mental well-being.

Emotion regulation (ER) refers to the processes that influence which emotions arise and how those emotions are experienced or expressed [9]. ER aims to reduce negative emotions and increase positive emotions [10], and according to the Process Model of Emotion Regulation [11], ER can be achieved through five main strategies: situation selection, situation modification, attentional deployment, cognitive change, and response modulation (see Sect. 2.2). Given research evidence that links ER to improved mental health outcomes [12, 13], delivering these ER strategies as digital interventions could make them more accessible for people to use in daily life. To encourage user engagement with the interventions, designers need to operationalize persuasive strategies such that users stay motivated to improve their mental well-being. However, little is known about *how to implement, personalize, and deliver digital ER interventions using persuasive technology (PT) that can detect individual users' current emotional state and adapt the interventions in real time while motivating behaviour change using appropriate persuasive strategies* - a gap addressed in this work.

Personalizing such interventions for individual users is challenging, and many existing PTs adopt a one-size-fits-all approach [14]. Artificial intelligence (AI) can reduce this complexity through machine learning (ML) models that learn behavioural patterns and user characteristics from data, and these models can be integrated into PTs to adapt interventions to each user in real time. For example, in mental health apps, ML models can analyze detailed personal data sources (such as journal or diary entries) to infer an individual's current state (e.g., emotional state). A system equipped with these capabilities could detect when a user's stress level is high or when they exhibit depressive symptoms, and then automatically deliver appropriate and just-in-time digital therapeutic interventions (e.g., a mindfulness exercise or relaxing music playlist). By detecting a user's evolving state, AI-driven interventions can provide timely and personalized support for improving mental well-being.

Therefore, we present *Recilify*, an AI-driven, emotion-adaptive, and persuasive mobile app designed to help users regulate their emotions and improve their mental health. The app detects each user's emotional state in real time and delivers personalized ER interventions while operationalizing appropriate persuasive strategies to sustain motivation and user engagement. Recilify was systematically developed following an evidence-based and user-centered process. Specifically, we reviewed the literature to identify relevant PS and popular ER strategies, conducted a large-scale empirical study with 660 participants to identify PS that support ER, developed and integrated a novel deep learning model (MCBiLSTM) which is a multichannel fusion of convolutional and recurrent neural networks trained on people's daily journal entries for real-time emotion prediction, developed an interactive prototype of the app, and evaluated the prototype with target users ($n = 20$). Participants rated Recilify as significantly persuasive and motivating because it arouses their attention, is relevant to them, builds their confidence to change (i.e., regulate their emotion), and provides satisfaction and reward for their effort, while also viewing it as valuable for improving mental well-being without creating pressure or tension. In addition, users found the app to be significantly usable and offered suggestions which in turn were used in refining the prototype. We then developed and privately deployed the app on both Google Play and Apple App Stores for real-world testing with specific users (field study). This work makes several contributions. First, we synthesized diverse ER strategies and implementation approaches from the literature to inform the design of mental health interventions. Second, we established effective persuasive strategies that can reinforce positive emotions, and also developed a novel AI model for real-time emotion prediction. Third, we designed and developed a mobile health (mHealth) app that integrates the AI model, persuasive strategies, and ER strategies to help individuals effectively manage (and take control of) their mental well-being. Finally, we provide quantitative and qualitative insights to inform practical recommendations for designing persuasive mHealth apps to improve mental well-being.

2   Background and Related Work

2.1   Persuasion and Emotion Frameworks

The Persuasive Systems Design (PSD) framework is grounded in psychological and behavioural theories and aimed at facilitating the development and evaluation of persuasive technologies (PTs) [15]. The framework extends Fogg's persuasive tools [16] and made up of 28 persuasive strategies categorized into primary task support, dialogue support, system credibility support, and social support strategies. The App Behaviour Change Scale (ABACUS) is a reliable framework for assessing the behaviour change potential of mobile apps [17]. It comprises 21 strategies categorized into knowledge and information, goals and planning, feedback and monitoring, and actions.

Emotion theories define how emotions are represented in applications or systems, and can be discrete and dimensional. Discrete theories treat emotions as distinct categories; a prominent example is the Ekman's model of six basic emotions (i.e., happiness, sadness, anger, fear, disgust, and surprise). Since the valence of surprise is contested [18, 19], later work (Ekman's Atlas of Emotions) emphasizes five "universal" emotions (i.e., "emotions that all humans, no matter where or how they are raised, have in common") [20], which are *happiness/enjoyment*, *sadness*, *anger*, *fear*, and *disgust*. Other discrete frameworks build on Ekman's emotions; for example, Plutchik adds trust and anticipation, the Ortony-Clore-Collins (OCC) model specifies 22 emotions, while Parrott considers Ekman's emotional states as "primary" emotions from which it derived 100 "secondary" emotions. In contrast, dimensional theories project emotions in a continuous space, most notably Russell's Circumplex Model, which maps emotions by *valence* (pleasure-displeasure continuum) and *arousal*, with a later addition of dominance to capture perceived control. We focus on Ekman's emotion theory (specifically the universal emotions) in this work due to their widespread use in HCI research [21–23], compared to dimensional theories.

2.2   Persuasive Strategies Operationalization and Digital Emotion Regulation

Alslaity et al. [24] conducted a systematic review of 70 popular real-world mobile apps for health and wellness, including mental health, to deconstruct persuasive strategies

(PS) operationalization in the apps using both ABACUS and PSD frameworks. They ranked the identified PS using a metric, called the Behaviour Change Score (BCS) which is a measure of the extent to which each persuasive strategy is operationalized or implemented in the apps. This BCS-based ranking informs the choice of PS to explore in our work. Specifically, we selected eleven (11) PS, including those with high BCS (*self-monitoring, reminders, reduction, rehearsal*), as well as those with moderate BCS (*goal setting, suggestion, reward, expertise*) and low BCS (*opportunity to plan for barriers, distraction or avoidance*, and *recognition*) since rarely implemented strategies could also be effective.

Emotion regulation (ER) involves down-regulating negative emotions (to decrease the experiential and behavioural aspects of those emotions) and up-regulating (increase) positive emotions such as happiness and love [25]. ER has long been linked to mental health outcomes, with several studies associating issues such as anxiety, depression, and post-traumatic stress disorder with difficulties in regulating emotions [2, 26]. One of the widely used theoretical frameworks for studying ER is the Process Model of Emotion Regulation (PMER) [11] which posits five strategies for regulating emotions in the real-world: Situation Selection, Situation Modification, Attentional Deployment, Cognitive Change, and Response Modulation (see Table 1). The strategies can be operationalized in combination or independently.

Table 1. Emotion regulation strategies from the Process Model of Emotion Regulation.

Emotion Regulation Strategy	Definition
Situation Selection (SS)	Approaching situations that are perceived as likely to elicit desired emotions and/or avoiding situations that are likely to elicit undesired emotions
Situation Modification (SM)	Modify a situation to yield desired influence on emotions
Attentional Deployment (AD)	Direct attention towards or away from emotion-eliciting aspects of a current situation
Cognitive Change (CC)	Change cognitive evaluation of a current situation to promote a more desired emotional response
Response Modulation (RM)	Act directly to change a current emotional response or its expression

Other ER strategies are grounded in cognitive behavioural therapy, acceptance and commitment therapy, and positive psychology. These include Savoring (SA) (e.g., relaxation therapies, guided meditation practices, scenes of nature, and guided imagery exercises) [27], Smile Therapy (ST) [28], Gratitude Therapy (GT) [29], Positive Reappraisal (PR) (e.g., gratitude and guided imagery exercises) [30], Problem-focused Coping (PC) (i.e., directing efforts toward solving or addressing the cause of distress) [30], Infusing ordinary events with positive meaning (IPM) [31], and Mindfulness-based Therapy (MT). Digital emotion regulation involves using digital technologies (such as smartphones) as a tool for strategically influencing emotional states [32]. Table 2 shows how each strategy in the PMER can be implemented in digital technologies to deliver ER interventions, based on research evidence [33, 34].

Table 2. Emotion regulation strategies and corresponding digital examples from [33, 34].

Emotion Regulation Strategy	Digital examples
Situation Selection (SS)	Games, social media, movies on streaming platforms, etc
Situation Modification (SM)	Using exercise app or watching exercise videos instead of going to the gym, etc
Attentional Deployment (AD)	Games, checking emails or chat messages, etc
Cognitive Change (CC)	Post message on social media to feel good, seek out people's opinions on social media and get validated, etc
Response Modulation (RM)	Listen to music including different music styles, chatting, positive reinforcement, etc

Common digital emotion regulation tools include digital music platforms [35], nature-based soundscapes [36], video games [37], instant messaging tools/social networking sites [38], relaxation exercises such as breathing [39], mood tracking apps [40], and mindfulness training apps [41].

These findings informed the emotion regulation interventions implemented in our persuasive technology (*Recilify*), as summarized in Table 3.

3 Persuasive Strategies that Support Emotion Regulation

To investigate *how* and *why* individuals respond emotionally to the selected persuasive strategies (see Sect. 2.2) – *Self-monitoring, Reminders, Reduction, Rehearsal, Goal setting, Suggestion, Reward, Expertise, Opportunity to plan for barriers, Distraction or avoidance*, and *Recognition* – in a system, we conducted a large-scale empirical and within-subject study [42] involving 660 participants from diverse demographics recruited via email, social media, snowball sampling, SONA experimental participation system [43], and Amazon Mechanical Turk (MTurk) [44]. In line with our research ethics approval, eligibility criteria require that participants be adults (18 years or older) and proficient in English language. Participants are diverse in terms of age group (*18–25:* 42%; *26–35:* 30%; *36–45:* 17%; *Over 45:* 11%) and gender (*Male:* 39%; *Female:* 60%; *Other:* 1%). For the study design, first, we created prototype illustrating each strategy contextualized in the mental health domain of resilience building (which is linked to emotion regulation [45]), in collaboration with 15 experts from the fields of psychology, mental health, and persuasive technology. Next, we presented prototype illustrating each strategy to participants in a logical flow depicting user interaction within an app. Participants see one prototype at a time and then respond to questions that assess the perceived persuasiveness of the prototype/strategy (using the perceived persuasiveness questionnaire (PPQ) [46]) and the emotions elicited (based on Ekman's universal emotions in Sect. 2.1). To prevent possible prototypes ordering bias, we used the randomization feature of the survey tool (Opinio [47]) to vary the order of the prototypes for each participant. We also included attention-check questions [48] to ensure that participants were actively considering their responses. Prior to examining each prototype, we asked participants to watch a short neutral video (obtained from Stanford Psychophysiology Laboratory [49]) to remove carryover effect from the emotional states reported. Finally, we asked participants to justify their ratings by providing qualitative comments.

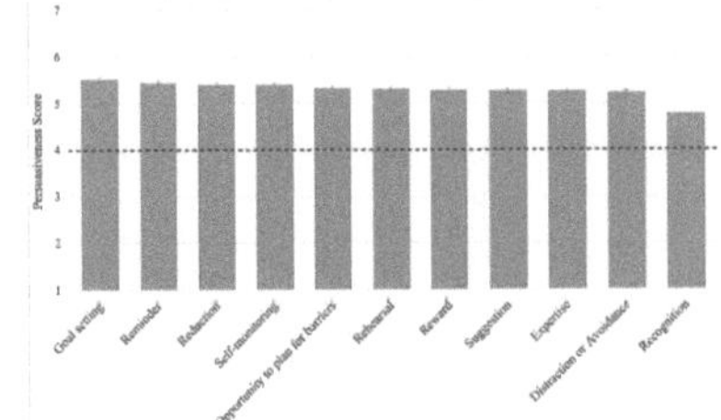

Strategy	Emotional States				
	Anger	Disgust	Fear	Happiness	Sadness
Self-monitoring	.11	.11	.18	.48	.13
Reminder	-.11	-	.11	.59	-
Expertise	-	.08	.11	.61	-
Reduction	-	-	-	.57	-
Rehearsal	-	-	-	.65	-
Goal setting	-.10	-	-	.65	-
Suggestion	.	.	.14	.71	-
Reward	-	-	-	.65	-
Recognition	-.14	-	.13	.75	-
Distraction or Avoidance	-	-	.13	.68	.08
Opportunity to plan for barriers	-	-	-	.65	-

Fig. 1. (a) Persuasiveness score (mean score) of individual strategies exceeds the neutral rating of 4 on a 7-point Likert scale; **(b)** Standard path coefficients showing the relation between the persuasive strategies and emotional states ("–" represents non-significant coefficients).

Results of our one-sample t-test showed that the persuasiveness scores of the eleven strategies are significantly higher than the neutral score of 4 ($p < .001$), which indicates that participants perceived the strategies as significantly persuasive/effective (at varying degrees) with respect to their capacity to motivate behaviour change (see Fig. 1a). Also, results of PLS SEM [50] regression modelling showed that all eleven strategies are significantly and strongly associated with *happiness* emotional state ($p < .001$), although seven of the strategies are also weakly associated with negative emotions at varying degrees (see Fig. 1b). Overall, all eleven strategies have potential to reinforce positive emotions in users of persuasive technologies. Although Self-monitoring strategy is strongly related to *happiness* but weakly associated with the four negative emotions, research has shown that the Reward strategy which is solely and strongly associated with *happiness* can complement it (i.e., amplify its strengths and reduce its weaknesses) [51]. These findings informed the persuasive strategies implemented in our Recilify app.

4 Emotion Detection Using Artificial Intelligence (AI) Model

Recognizing people's current emotional state is an important step in providing personalized emotion regulation (ER) interventions. As a result, we developed and compared the predictive performance of twenty-one (21) AI models for emotion detection, including our novel deep learning model, named MCBiLSTM which is a multichannel fusion of two state-of-the-art deep learning architectures: Convolutional Neural Network (CNN) and Bi-directional Long Short-Term Memory (BiLSTM) network, as shown in Fig. 2. Using both AppJournal dataset [52] and ISEAR[1] dataset [53], we trained the models

---

[1] International Survey on Emotion Antecedents and Reactions (ISEAR).

on 9,534 sentences from people's daily journal/diary entries in the real-world. Individual sentences have been pre-labelled with appropriate emotional states (*anger*, *fear*, *happiness*, *sadness*, or *disgust*). We chose journal entries for model training because they reveal people's real-life situations and experiences including their thoughts, challenges, ideas/aspirations, and achievements that could directly impact their mental health and well-being. We vectorized the sentences using Term Frequency–Inverse Document Frequency (TF-IDF) technique [54] for the classical/ensemble learning models ($n = 18$), while an Embedding layer was trained to convert the input sentences into 256-dimensional word embeddings for the deep learning models ($n = 3$).

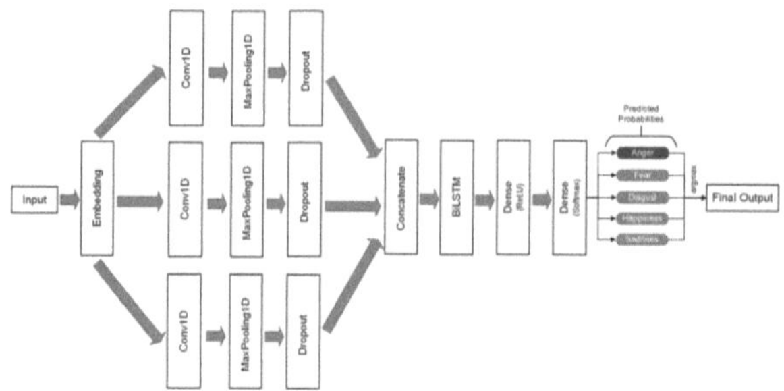

Fig. 2. Architecture of the Multichannel CNN–BiLSTM (MCBiLSTM) model.

Prior to model training, we performed a 90/10 split of the dataset such that 90% is used for training (*training set*) and 10% for testing (*test set*). In addition, a grid search was conducted to determine the hyperparameters that yield the best performance on the training set for each model. We also addressed class imbalance by assigning different weight to the individual classes based on sample size. Figure 3 summarizes the overall performance of the models on the test set. **Our multichannel deep learning model – MCBiLSTM – achieved the best F1-score of 81.1% making it the overall best performing model**, closely followed by CNN with an F1-score of 80%. We integrated the MCBiLSTM model with our Recilify app to predict individual users' current emotional states in real-time based on their logged journal entries.

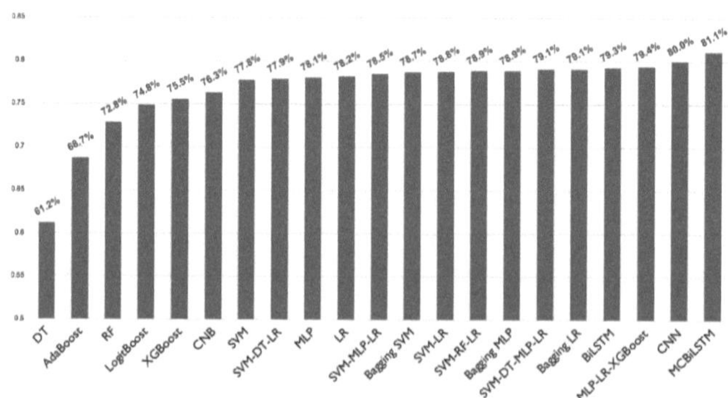

Fig. 3. Overall performance (F1-score) of AI models on the test set.

5   Design and Development of *Recilify* App

In this section, we present the architecture of the *Recilify* app including how the app is designed tailored based on findings from Sect. 3 and Sect. 4, as well as how emotion regulation (ER) interventions are designed based on findings from Sect. 2.2. In addition, we discuss evaluation of app prototype with target users and subsequent development of the app.

5.1   App Architecture

The architecture of Recilify app, shown in Fig. 4, is composed of four main components, which are described below.

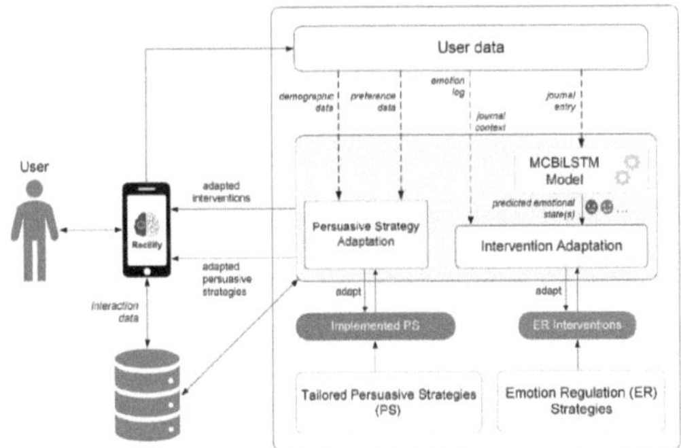

Fig. 4. Architecture of *Recilify*, an AI-driven emotion-adaptive persuasive mobile app for mental well-being.

User Data. These are data collected directly from the user or patient while using the app, such as demographic data (e.g., age group, gender, country of residence, etc.), preference data (e.g., reminder intervals and custom daily/weekly goals), emotion log, journal entries (i.e., personal experiences including thoughts, achievements, aspirations, challenges, events, etc.), and journal context (i.e., specific labels or categories that contextualize a journal entry).

Emotion Regulation Interventions. The choice of emotion regulation (ER) interventions to provide in the Recilify app is based on evidence-based and well-established ER strategies and tools discussed in Sect. 2.2. Other ER interventions include sleep and hydration tracking due to their strong association with emotion regulation. Research has shown that deficient sleep increases the experience of negative emotions, reduces the occurrence of positive emotions, and increases difficulties with emotion regulation [55]. Similarly, mild dehydration has been linked to increase in negative emotional states [56]. In total, 15 ER interventions were operationalized in the Recilify app.

Table 3. Emotion regulation interventions in the Recilify app

ER Intervention	Implementation	ER Strategies
Mindfulness	Mindfulness sessions delivered by expert coaches	MT, SA
Deep Breathing	Sessions involving taking slow and deep breaths guided by expert coaches	SA
Guided Imagery	Expert-led sessions to intentionally think of peaceful places or pleasant experiences	SS, PR, SA
Yoga	Yoga exercises guided by expert coaches	SM
Warm-up Exercises	Expert-led exercises including skipping, lunges, toe raises, knee raises, jumping jacks, squats, etc	SM
Gratitude	Gratitude journal for expressing positive experiences using texts and images, with social sharing	IPM, GT
Psychoeducation (Masterclass)	Evidence-based videos on diverse topics aimed at improving mental health and well-being	PC
Nature Soundscapes	Nature soundscapes such as water flowing ambience, wind blowing ambience, rain loop, etc	SA
Music	Access to favourite music and playlists on popular music streaming platforms (e.g., Spotify, Tidal, etc.)	RM
Smiley	User smiles while looking at the camera. Smiling is autodetected via Google's Face Detection API [57]	ST
Games	Games that have been shown to counter negative emotions caused by stress and anxiety [58]	SS, AD
Movies	Access to favourite movies on popular streaming platforms (e.g., Netflix, Disney +, Apple TV +, etc.)	SS
Social Networking	Access to popular social media platforms including WhatsApp, Instagram, Facebook, TikTok, etc	SS, CC, RM
Sleep Tracking	Daily self-reported sleep patterns and responsible factors (e.g., alcohol, kids, caffeine, work, pets, etc.)	-
Hydration Tracking	Daily self-reported water intake	-

Implemented Persuasive Strategies. The app delivers interventions (see Table 3) while operationalizing 8 (out of 11) persuasive strategies that reinforce positive emotion (based on findings from Sect. 3) to promote emotion regulation. The strategies, which are strongly and significantly associated with happiness, are *Reduction, Rehearsal, Reward, Goal setting, Reminder, Self-monitoring, Suggestion*, and *Expertise* (see Table 4).

Table 4. Persuasive strategies and how they are implemented in the Recilify app.

Persuasive Strategy	Implementation
Reward	Badges and points are given to users as rewards whenever they engage with interventions or meet their set goals
Rehearsal	Users can practice ER behaviours through instructor-led interventions (e.g., Mindfulness, Deep Breathing, Guided Imagery, Yoga, etc.)
Reduction	App is simplified and navigation made easy such that users can engage with features including interventions quickly and intuitively
Suggestion	Recommend ER interventions that are personalized to individual users based on their current emotional state. Deliver helpful and timely tips
Reminder	Users are reminded to submit daily journal entries via reminders delivered as push notifications. Users can customize reminder delivery
Self-monitoring	Visuals (graphs/charts, progress bars) and texts depicting users' progress towards their goals as they interact with the ER interventions
Goal setting	Users can set and customize daily and weekly goals for interventions according to their needs or preferences
Expertise	To foster credibility and trust, users can see the identity and affiliations of the experts that lead or curate in-app intervention content

Intervention and Persuasive Strategy Adaptation. ER interventions are adapted to individuals based on their current emotional states. To detect emotional states in real-time from user's journal logs, the app integrates with the MCBiLSTM deep learning model, which is the overall best performing AI model (see Sect. 4). First-time users are required to self-report their current emotional states during sign-up/onboarding to receive personalized ER interventions. With each new journal entry submitted within the app, users' current emotional states are detected automatically by the AI model to adapt interventions in real-time. Moreover, the app leverages users' demographic and preference data to adapt *Goal setting* and *Reminder* strategies. For example, the daily Hydration goal of individual users is automatically set (though customizable) based on gender, in line with recommended hydration goals of 3,700ml for males and 2,700ml for females [59]. In addition, users can adapt or customize reminders as preferred.

5.2 App Prototyping and Evaluation

We developed an interactive prototype of *Recilify* (see Fig. 5) using Figma [60] and evaluated it with our target audience to assess the app's perceived effectiveness, motivational appeal, as well as usability and user experience/engagement.

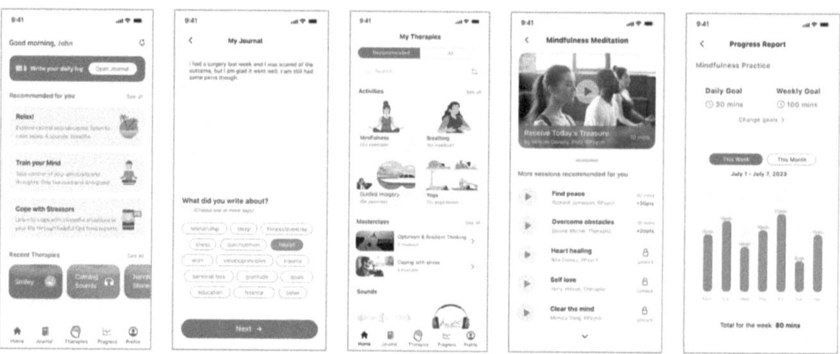

Fig. 5. Sample screens of *Recilify* interactive prototype

Experimental Design. We conducted a within-subject study involving 20 target users (i.e., adults from 18 years and above). The online study, hosted on Opinio survey tool [47], is in two phases. In the first phase, participants were asked to complete a demographic questionnaire. Participants are diverse in terms of age group (*18–25*: 20%; *26–35*: 50%; *36–45*: 25%; *Over 45*: 5%) and gender (*Male*: 45%; *Female*: 55%). Most of the participants have never used a mental health app (55%), while 20% rarely used one. In the second phase, participants were presented with a walkthrough of the interactive prototype, completing various tasks including user registration, journaling, engaging with recommended ER interventions, checking progress reports, viewing rewards, setting goals, checking reminders, and so on. Afterwards, participants were asked to complete the validated 5-item perceived persuasiveness questionnaire (PPQ) [46], 12-item ARCS motivation model questionnaire [61], 20-item Intrinsic Motivation Inventory (IMI) scale [62], and the 10-item System Usability Scale (SUS) [63], and then provide qualitative comments to justify their ratings.

Evaluation Findings. The results of our one-sample t-tests revealed that the ***overall persuasiveness*** (PPQ mean score) of the *Recilify* app is significantly higher than the neutral score of 4 on a 7-point Likert scale: $t(19) = 13.930, p < .001$. This means that participants perceived the app as significantly effective for promoting emotion regulation. Similarly, the mean scores of all four ARCS motivation constructs are significantly higher than the neutral rating of 3 on a 5-point Likert scale: ***Attention*** (M = 4.425, SD = 0.5911, $t = 10.782, p < .001$), ***Relevance*** (M = 4.313, SD = 0.5057, $t = 11.606, p < .001$), ***Confidence*** (M = 4.383, SD = 0.6048, $t = 10.229, p < .001$), and ***Satisfaction*** (M = 4.367, SD = 0.5504, $t = 11.105, p < .001$). This means that participants perceived the app as significantly motivating because it arouses their attention, is relevant to them (due to *personalized content, different therapies for mental well-being including for stress relief and support, etc.*), builds confidence in their ability to achieve their behaviour change goals, and provides satisfaction and reward for their effort. Here is a participant's comment: *"I like the app as it is motivating, colorful, having different activities for relaxing and controlling my stress. So, it would definitely help me be happy and positive."* [P3].

Also, results of one-sample t-tests revealed that the mean scores for IMI subscales are significantly higher than the neutral score of 4 on a 7-point Likert scale: ***Interest / Enjoyment*** (M = 6.040, SD = 0.9052, t = 10.079, $p < .001$), ***Value / Usefulness*** (M = 6.180, SD = 0.6354, t = 15.342, $p < .001$), and ***Perceived Competence*** (M = 5.770, SD = 0.9674, t = 8.182, $p < .001$). This means that participants perceived the *Recilify* app to be significantly engaging, as it will arouse their interest and inherent pleasure when target activities (interventions) are being performed. They also found the app to be valuable or useful, mostly because they found the interventions to be relevant to them, as shown in the following comment: *"The application is very useful for improving mental health and well-being. I find the features or therapies very relevant and evidence-based based on my understanding of mental health and psychology. The therapies are well-implemented in my opinion."* [P20]. In addition, the mean score of the ***Pressure/Tension*** subscale, which is a negative predictor of motivation, is significantly lower than the neutral score of 4: (M = 2.120, SD = 0.9367, t = –8.975, $p < .001$). This means that the app will not induce pressure or tension in users while performing their tasks, further affirming the app's capability to promote emotion regulation.

Results also showed that the *Recilify* app scores high on **usability** (SUS score = 84.4), higher than the recommended score of 70 [64]. This means that participants were confident that they will be able to complete their tasks using the app and their overall experience will be satisfying. Further analysis using one sample t-test revealed statistically significant results across all SUS items ($p < .001$), confirmed by the following comment: *"All the functions seemed very intuitive and easy to use. There was a great consistency of icons and screen elements across the different screens."* [P9].

6 Discussion

The evaluation findings uncover the importance of tailoring behaviour change interventions to users rather than relying on one-size-fits-all designs. **By selecting and operationalizing persuasive strategies (PS) based on empirical evidence, designers can improve a system's effectiveness in motivating behaviour change**. In our work, applying tailored strategies that support emotion regulation in *Recilify* contributed to strong user acceptance in our evaluation. Additionally, **personalization and diversity of interventions are some of the key factors for motivation and engagement**, as evaluators found *Recilify* to be relevant due to its tailored and distinct interventions or therapies, aligning with prior evidence that tailored health interventions is essential for effective behaviour change [65]. **Leveraging artificial intelligence (AI) to adapt interventions to each user can thus significantly enhance the persuasiveness of mental health technologies**. Furthermore, a **calming and visually attractive design can trigger positive emotional response and improve the user experience** [66]. Our participants' feedback supports this, as the app's appealing interface was frequently mentioned in conjunction with high usability and satisfaction. Overall, the evaluation feedback from our target audience suggests that the app's emotion-adaptive interventions can effectively help users to regulate their emotions as intended. To further improve the app's interface and real-world feel, one of the evaluators suggested using either vector images or real photos but not both to ensure consistency, and another suggested including a contact feature through which users can connect with developers or support personnel. We addressed both suggestions in the real app which has already been developed (see Fig. 6) and privately deployed on app stores for ongoing real-world testing.

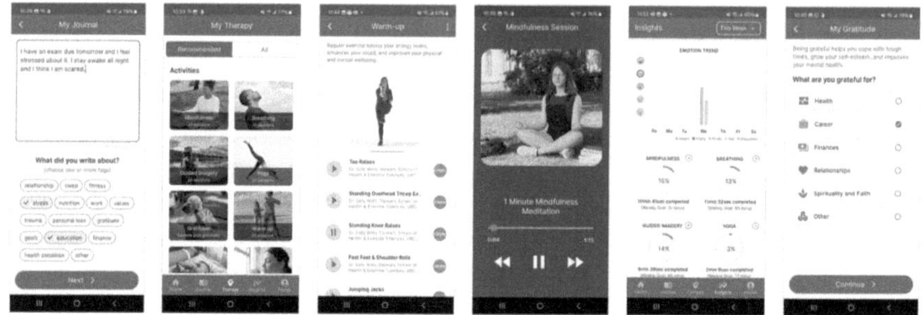

Fig. 6. Sample screens of the *Recilify* mobile app, running on an Android smartphone.

7   Conclusion and Future Work

This work demonstrates the potential of AI-driven persuasive technologies to deliver emotion-adaptive, evidence-based interventions that support real-time emotion regulation (ER) and improve mental well-being. Through a systematic and multi-stage design process, *Recilify* integrates tailored persuasive strategies, ER-grounded intervention design, and emotion-sensitive AI to create motivating, engaging, and usable mental-health support app. Future work will complete the ongoing field study to evaluate *Recilify* in the real-world and enhance emotion detection through multimodal sensing.

Acknowledgments. This research was undertaken, in part, thanks to funding from the Canada Research Chairs Program. We acknowledge the support of the Natural Sciences and Engineering Research Council of Canada (NSERC) through the Discovery Grant.

References

1. World Health Organization: Mental disorders. https://www.who.int/news-room/fact-sheets/detail/mental-disorders
2. Berking, M., Wupperman, P.: Emotion regulation and mental health: recent findings, current challenges, and future directions. Curr. Opin. Psychiatry **25**, 128–134 (2012)
3. Kuehn, K.S., et al.: Person-specific dynamics between negative emotions and suicidal thoughts. Compr. Psychiatry **133**, 152495 (2024)
4. Vanderlind, W.M., et al.: Understanding positive emotion deficits in depression: from emotion preferences to emotion regulation. Clin. Psychol. Rev. **76**, 101826 (2020)
5. Ching, C.L., Chan, V.L.: Positive emotions, positive feelings and health: a life philosophy. Linguistics Cult. Rev. **4**, 1–14 (2020)
6. Alexander, R., et al.: The neuroscience of positive emotions and affect: implications for cultivating happiness and wellbeing. Neurosci. Biobehav. Rev. **121**, 220–249 (2021)
7. Yamaguchi, K., et al.: Role of focusing on the positive side during COVID-19 outbreak: mental health perspective from positive psychology. Psychol. Trauma **12**, S49–S50 (2020)

8. Gloria, C.T., Steinhardt, M.A.: Relationships among positive emotions, coping, resilience and mental health. Stress. Health **32**, 145–156 (2016)

9. Gross, J.J., Muñoz, R.F.: Emotion regulation and mental health. Clin. Psychol. Sci. Pract. **2**, 151–164 (1995)

10. Gross, J.J., et al.: Emotion regulation in everyday life. In: Snyder, D.K., Simpson, J., Hughes, J.N. (eds.) Emotion Regulation in Couples and Families: Pathways to Dysfunction and Health, pp. 13–35. American Psychological Association (2006)

11. Gross, J.J.: The emerging field of emotion regulation: an integrative review. Rev. Gen. Psychol. **2**, 271–299 (1998)

12. Zaid, S.M., et al.: The power of emotion regulation: how managing sadness influences depression and anxiety? BMC Psychol. 13(1), 38 (2025)

13. Menefee, D.S., Ledoux, T., Johnston, C.A.: The importance of emotional regulation in mental health. Am. J. Lifestyle Med. **16**, 28–31 (2022)

14. Alslaity, A., et al.: A panoramic view of personalization based on individual differences in persuasive and behavior change interventions. Front Artif Intell. **6**, 1125191 (2023)

15. Oinas-Kukkonen, H., et al.: Persuasive systems design: key issues, process model, and system features. Commun. Assoc. Inf. Syst. **24**, 96 (2009)

16. Fogg, B.J., Fogg, G.E.: Persuasive Technology: Using Computers to Change What We Think and Do. Morgan Kaufmann, San Francisco, USA (2003)

17. McKay, F.H., et al.: The app behavior change scale: creation of a scale to assess the potential of apps to promote behavior change. JMIR Mhealth Uhealth **7**, e11130 (2019)

18. Tracy, J.L., Randles, D.: Four models of basic emotions: a review of Ekman and Cordaro Izard, Levenson, and Panksepp and Watt. Emot. Rev. **3**, 397–405 (2011)

19. Ekman, P.: An argument for basic emotions. Cogn. Emot. **6**, 169–200 (1992)

20. Ekman, P., Ekman, E.: Atlas of Emotions. http://atlasofemotions.org/#continents

21. Elgarf mahaeg, M., et al.: Reward seeking or loss aversion? Impact of regulatory focus theory on emotional induction in children and their behavior towards a social robot. In: Proceedings of the 2021 CHI Conference on Human Factors in Computing Systems, New York, NY, USA, pp. 1–11. ACM (2021)

22. Krekhov, A., et al.: Interpolating happiness: understanding the intensity gradations of face Emojis across cultures. In: CHI Conference on Human Factors in Computing Systems – Proceedings, pp. 1–17. ACM (2022)

23. Wagener, N., et al.: Mood worlds: a virtual environment for autonomous emotional expression. In: Proceedings of the 2022 CHI Conference on Human Factors in Computing Systems, pp. 1–16. ACM (2022)

24. Alslaity, A., Suruliraj, B., Oyebode, O., et al.: Mobile applications for health and wellness: a systematic review. Proc. ACM Hum. Comput Interact. 6, (2022)

25. Gross, J.J.: Emotion regulation: current status and future prospects. Psychol. Inq. **26**, 1–26 (2015)

26. McLean, C.P., Foa, E.B.: Emotions and emotion regulation in posttraumatic stress disorder. Curr. Opin. Psychol. **14**, 72–77 (2017)

27. Colombo, D., et al.: Savouring the present to better recall the past. J. Happiness Stud. **25**, 1–22 (2024)

28. Ekman, P.: The argument and evidence about universals in facial expressions. In: Handbook of Social Psychophysiology, vol. 143, p.164 (1989)

29. Emmons, R.A., McCullough, M.E.: Counting blessings versus burdens: an experimental investigation of gratitude and subjective well-being in daily life. J. Pers. Soc. Psychol. **84**, 377–389 (2003)

30. Folkman, S., Moskowitz, J.T.: Positive affect and the other side of coping. Am. Psychol. **55**, 647–654 (2000)

31. Folkman, S.: Positive psychological states and coping with severe stress. Soc. Sci. Med. **45**, 1207–1221 (1997)
32. Smith, W., et al.: Digital emotion regulation in everyday life. In: CHI Conference on Human Factors in Computing Systems, pp. 1–15 (2022)
33. Wadley, G., et al.: Digital Emotion Regulation. Curr. Dir. Psychol. Sci. **29**, 412–418 (2020)
34. Smith, W., et al.: Digital emotion regulation in every-day life. In: CHI Conference on Human Factors in Computing Systems, New York, NY, USA, pp. 1–15. ACM (2022)
35. Wadley, G., et al.: Use of music streaming platforms for emotion regulation by international students. In: OzCHI '19: Proceedings of the 31st Australian Conference on Human-Computer-Interaction, pp. 337–341. ACM (2019)
36. Newbold, J.W., et al.: Using nature-based soundscapes to support task performance and mood. In: CHI EA '17: Proceedings of the 2017 CHI Conference Extended Abstracts on Human Factors in Computing Systems, pp. 2802–2809. ACM (2017)
37. Villani, D., et al.: Videogames for emotion regulation: a systematic review. Games Health J. **7**, 85–99 (2018)
38. Blumberg, F.C., Rice, J.L., Dickmeis, A.: Social media as a venue for emotion regulation among adolescents. Emot. Technol. Soc. Media 105–116 (2016)
39. Paredes, P.E., et al.: Just BREATHE: IN-CAR INTERVENTIONS FOR GUIDED SLOW BREAthing. Proc ACM Interact Mob Wearable Ubiquitous Technol. **2**, 1–23 (2018)
40. Bakker, D., et al.: Engagement in mobile phone app for self-monitoring of emotional wellbeing predicts changes in mental health: MoodPrism. J. Affect. Disord. **227**, 432–442 (2018)
41. Flett, J.A.M., et al.: Mobile mindfulness meditation: a randomised controlled trial of the effect of two popular apps on mental health. Mindfulness (N Y). **10**, 863–876 (2019)
42. Oyebode, O., Steeves, D., Orji, R.: Persuasive strategies and emotional states: towards emotion-adaptive persuasive technologies design. In: International Conference on Persuasive Technology, pp. 215–233. Springer, Cham (2023)
43. Sona Systems Ltd: SONA: Cloud-based Subject Pool Software for Universities, https://www.sona-systems.com/default.aspx
44. Amazon Mechanical Turk. https://www.mturk.com/worker/help
45. Polizzi, C.P., Lynn, S.J.: Regulating emotionality to manage adversity: a systematic review of the relation between emotion regulation and psychological resilience. Cognit Ther Res. **45**, 577–597 (2021)
46. Thomas, R.J., et al.: Can I influence you? Development of a scale to measure perceived persuasiveness and two studies showing the use of the scale. Front Artif Intell. **2**, 1–14 (2019)
47. ObjectPlanet: Conduct Online Surveys using Opinio. http://www.objectplanet.com/opinio/
48. Mason, W., Suri, S.: Conducting behavioral research on Amazon's Mechanical Turk. Behav. Res. Methods **44**, 1–23 (2012)
49. Samson, A.C., et al.: Eliciting positive, negative and mixed emotional states: a film library for affective scientists. Cogn. Emot. **30**, 827–856 (2016)
50. Hair, J.F., et al.: When to use and how to report the results of PLS-SEM. Eur. Bus. Rev. **31**, 2–24 (2019)
51. Orji, R., et al.: Tracking feels oppressive and 'punishy': exploring the costs and benefits of self-monitoring for health and wellness. Digit Health. **4**, 205520761879755 (2018)
52. Oyebode, O., et al.: Emotion detection from real-life situations based on journal entries using machine learning and deep learning techniques. In: Proceedings of SAI Intelligent Systems Conference. 823 LNNS, 477–502 (2024)
53. Scherer, K.R., Wallbott, H.G.: Evidence for universality and cultural variation of differential emotion response patterning. J. Pers. Soc. Psychol. **66**, 310–328 (1994)
54. Ramos, J.: Using TF-IDF to determine word relevance in document queries. In: Proceedings of the first Instructional Conference on Machine Learning, pp. 133–142 (2003)

55. Tomaso, C.C., et al.: The effect of sleep deprivation and restriction on mood, emotion, and emotion regulation: three meta-analyses in one. Sleep **44**, 1–30 (2021)
56. Pross, N., et al.: Effects of changes in water intake on mood of high and low drinkers. PLoS ONE **9**, 94754 (2014)
57. Google Inc.: Face detection API. https://developers.google.com/ml-kit/vision/face-detection
58. Mental Health Center of America: Best Stress Relief Games. https://mentalhealthcenter.com/control-your-emotions-top-5-stress-relief-games/
59. National Academies of Sciences, Engineering and Medicine: Report Sets Dietary Intake Levels for Water, Salt, and Potassium To Maintain Health and Reduce Chronic Disease Risk. https://tinyurl.com/4smtfa9n
60. Figma: Figma: The Collaborative Interface Design Tool. https://www.figma.com/
61. Keller, J.M.: Development and use of the ARCS model of instructional design. J. Instr. Dev. **10**, 2–10 (1987)
62. McAuley, E.D., et al.: Psychometric properties of the intrinsic motivation inventory in a competitive sport setting: a confirmatory factor analysis. Res. Q. Exerc. Sport **60**, 48–58 (1989)
63. Brooke, J.: SUS: a "quick and dirty" usability scale. In: Usability Evaluation in Industry, pp. 207–212. CRC Press (1996)
64. Bangor, A., Kortum, P.T., Miller, J.T.: An empirical evaluation of the system usability scale. Intl. J. Hum.-Comput. Interact. **24**, 574–594 (2008)
65. DiMatteo, M.R., et al.: Health Behavior Change and Treatment Adherence: Evidence-Based Guidelines for Improving Healthcare. Oxford University Press (2025)
66. Bhandari, U., et al.: Understanding the impact of perceived visual aesthetics on user evaluations: An emotional perspective. Inf. Manag. **56**, 85–93 (2019)

An Empirical Study of Perceived Intrusiveness, Frequency and Darkness of Dark Patterns

Kiemute Oyibo[(✉)]

York University, Toronto, Canada
`kiemute.oyibo@yorku.ca`

Abstract. Dark patterns have become prevalent in the digital environment. However, there is little research on how users perceive these dark patterns. To bridge this gap, we conducted an online survey among Canadians ($n = 83$) and Americans ($n = 83$) to gauge the extent to which they perceived commonly deployed dark patterns as "dark" (intrusive and frequent) using Mathur et al.'s 7-category typology of dark patterns as an analytical framework. Our analysis showed that, regardless of country, Forced Action, Obstruction and Sneaking were perceived as the most intrusive and dark patterns, while Scarcity, Social Proof and Misdirection were perceived as the least. Overall, Scarcity, Urgency, Forced Action and Social Proof were the most frequently encountered, while Sneaking and Misdirection were the least. We discuss these findings and their implications for digital application/website designers and operators.

Keywords: Dark Pattern · Deceptive Design · Intrusiveness · Frequency

1 Introduction

Dark patterns are deceptive user interfaces that are crafted to take advantage of unsuspecting users in the digital environment. In recent years, they have become so prevalent to the extent that the user experience (UX) and welfare are relegated to the background [6,16,25]. The prevalence of dark patterns in the online environment, which benefit services to the detriment of users [12], has led national and regional governments, especially in Western countries such as the United States, to begin introducing and/or enacting legislation aimed to regulate their usage in digital spaces such as social media and gaming applications [13,23] to protect users and consumers [6,31]. Such regulations include California Privacy Rights Act (CPRA) [9], Colorado Privacy Act [7], and Deception Experiences to Online User Reduction (DETOUR) [33]. The first two laws, for example, aim to prohibit e-commerce companies from tricking consumers into giving up their personal data (e.g., location data) and selling the data to third parties [8]. Similarly, the third proposed law aims to prohibit large online platforms such as Facebook

K. Sumi et al. (Eds.): PERSUASIVE 2026, LNCS 16476, pp. 256–272, 2026.
https://doi.org/10.1007/978-3-032-19687-3_19

and Amazon from using deceptive and malicious interfaces to trick consumers into giving up their personal data [4,19]. Specifically, the DETOUR act aims to prevent large platforms such as Facebook and TikTok from deploying application features that foster compulsive usage by children and from conducting behavioral experiments without consumers' consent [11,33].

Despite the introduction of a handful of laws such as the abovementioned to regulate dark patterns, most countries are yet to swing into action, with most of the laws in the United States, for example, made and enforceable at the state level. For instance, in the United States, one of the greatest consumers of online content and services in the West, Congress is yet to enact a federal law specifically naming and banning dark patterns, although legislation such as DETOUR has been proposed. Worse still, many countries in non-Western continents such as Asia, South America, and Africa are yet to debate or introduce legislation to address the widespread use of dark patterns and their negative impact on users. In general, it is hard to legislate around the psychological tricks used in user experience design [15]. As such, there is a need to provide more empirical evidence, especially from users' perspective, about the prevalence and impact of dark patterns to facilitate the enactment of specific laws targeted at regulating dark patterns and protecting online users by federal governments around the world. This research aims to bridge this gap by examining the following research questions among the Canadian and American populations:

- RQ1: To what extent are dark patterns frequently encountered?
- RQ2: To what extent are dark patterns perceived as intrusive?
- RQ3: To what extent are dark patterns "dark"?
- RQ4: To what extent are dark patterns prevalent online?
- RQ5: In which domains are dark patterns mostly prevalent?
- RQ6: What role does country play in the perceived frequency, intrusiveness, darkness, prevalence, and domains of occurrence of dark patterns?

2   Related Work

We provide an overview of a cross-section of related work on users' perceptions and views about dark patterns. Borberg et al. [5] investigated the mental models and behavior of users when they experienced dark patterns in cookie notices. Their quantitative findings demonstrated that the design of a cookie notice influence users' decisions as to whether or not to consent to data collection. Moreover, their qualitative findings indicated that users both recognize the presence of dark patterns in cookie notice designs and are very uncomfortable with the practice. However, they seldom take any action to protect their privacy; rather, they give in due to decision fatigue. Geronimo et al. [10] examined dark patterns in 240 popular mobile apps and carried out an online experiment with 589 users to understand how the dark patterns in the apps are perceived. They found that 95% of the analyzed apps contained one or more forms of dark patterns, with each app containing more than six different types of deceptive interfaces on the average. The experiment showed that although most users recognize dark patterns, they can do better in recognizing malicious designs if educated on the issue of dark patterns and their effect. Mildner et al. [21] conducted a cognitive walkthrough among six experts to gain novel insights into the types of dark patterns deployed in social media and users' ability to recognize using four widely used mobile platforms (Facebook, Instagram, TikTok, and Twitter) as proof of concept. They found that experts were able to identify instances of dark patterns in all four apps. Based on this result, they designed a 5-item instrument based on Mathur et al.'s typology [19] to evaluate the maliciousness of interfaces. The five items include Asymmetry, Covertness, Restriction, Information Hiding, and Deception (ACRID). (Interestingly, the acronym "ACRID" characterizes bad taste including bitter and pungent, which can be used to describe dark patterns in general.) The authors found among 193 regular users that they could use the instrument successfully to differentiate between interfaces that featured dark patterns and those that did not. Moreover, Liang [17] used a mixed-method approach involving surveying stakeholder groups (n = 66 users and n = 38 developers) and mining GitHub data (n = 2556) to understand participants' perceptions, experiences and/or use of dark patterns. They found that users often encounter dark patterns online with limited options to avoid them, which induces negative sentiments. Moreover, developers reported that external pressures often influence their decisions to use dark patterns in their interface design, with most of them recognizing their adverse effect on user experience and trust. Finally, Oyibo [22] examined how dark patterns and user knowledge impact decision-making using a subscription-based streaming website as proof-of-concept. They found that confirmshaming and trick question were effective in prompting users to make a purchase decision that benefits the service provider, with users without knowledge of dark patterns being more likely to be nudged by dark patterns such as confirmshaming.

While most of the reviewed studies attempted to understand users' perceptions and ability to recognize dark patterns, there is limited work on their perceived frequency of occurrence and intrusiveness, the domains in which they are mostly prevalent and the moderating effect of country of residence. The current paper aims to bridge this gap by focusing on Canada and the United States populations, which are similar in so many ways including worldview, culture, system of government, online experience and behavior. The results can help shed light on how similar demographic groups vary or agree on their perceptions about dark patterns including their perceived intrusiveness and frequency of occurrence.

3   Method

To answer the research questions, we designed a survey based on an existing dark patterns typology proposed by Mathur et al. [19]. The research aimed to uncover how unwelcomed and widespread dark patterns are, the most common on the Internet, and the role country plays in users' perceptions and experience.

3.1 Procedure and Measures

Data collection was carried out on Amazon Mechanical Turk [27]. We began by introducing the study and asking participants to consent. After consenting, they were directed to the first page of the survey to provide their demographic information and answer the survey questions. In the survey, we explained each of the 15 dark patterns in Mathur et al.'s typology [19] (as shown in Table 2) and asked participants whether they had encountered it or not in the online environment. Next, we asked them about the perceived intrusiveness and frequency of encounter of each dark pattern as well as about the perceived intrusiveness of each of the seven categories. Moreover, participants were asked to choose one among the seven categories that they found most intrusive and prevalent in the online environment. While some of the quantitative questions required a yes or no (or not sure or applicable) response, others required a response on a 4- or 5-point scale such as (a) Intrusiveness: Not Intrusive (1), Barely Intrusive (2), Somewhat Intrusive (3), Very Intrusive (4); and (b) Frequency: Never (1), Rarely (2), Sometimes (3), Often (4), Very Often (5).

3.2 Darkness: Rationale for Intrusiveness-Frequency Dimensions

Different researchers have described dark patterns in various ways, including using adjectives such as manipulative, malicious, tricky, deceptive, coercive, and subversive [19,20]. We argue that whether dark patterns trick or manipulate the user, subvert user preferences or undermine their user experience, autonomy and privacy, one thing that can be said about them without doubt is that they are *intrusive*. In other words, they are uninivited and/or unwelcomed by the user [3,18,32]. Based on this premise, rather than measure the various characteristics of dark patterns presented in the literature such as the aforementioned, which can be demanding and unattainable in certain cases, we decided to measure their perceived intrusiveness and frequency of encounter (as a proxy for "darkness") in our empirical study. Frequency of encounter was specifically measured alongside intrusiveness because it speaks to the prevalence of dark patterns in the online environment. We believed that the more a certain dark pattern is used by services on the Internet, the more likely users will encounter it, which ultimately will inform their self-reporting. The second reason for measuring both constructs as key dimensions of darkness is that we wanted to develop an interactive website to create awareness on dark patterns As such, we needed to understand the most frequently encountered and intrusive dark patterns to prioritize in the implementation of the website. Basically, given that intrusiveness and frequency are not of the same dimension, we conceptualized darkness as the magnitude of a vector, which comprises two components, i.e., intrusiveness and frequency. To calculate the darkness of a single dark pattern as a function of intrusiveness and frequency, each variable was averaged, normalized (*nm*) and the Euclidean distance of the resulting point from the origin was calculated as shown in Eq. 1.

$$\delta = \sqrt{\left(\frac{nm(\frac{1}{n}\sum_{j=1}^{n} i_j)^2 + nm(\frac{1}{n}\sum_{j=1}^{n} f_j)^2}{2} \right)} \tag{1}$$

3.3 Participants

Our study was approved by our University Research Ethics Board, after which it was posted on Amazon Mechanical Turk for users resident in Canada and the United States to complete. The data collection began on January 2, 2024 and lasted for two weeks. To appreciate participants for their time, each was remunerated US$5. A total of 201 participants took part in the study. After data cleaning and filtering out low-quality responses such as AI-generated, we were left with 166 participants for the final analysis. The country-of-residence, gender, age and education distributions were similar for both groups. First, 50% of the participants were Canadian residents, while the other 50% were American residents. Second, 68.7% in the Canadian group and 61.4% in the American group were males. Third, 72–77% in each group had at least university education. Similarly, over 70% in both groups were between 25 and 44 years old.

4 Results

Table 1. Perceived intrusiveness, frequency and darkness metrics based on rescaled values ranging from 0 to 1. The dark patterns have been ordered based on intrusiveness which tends to explain the categories of dark patterns in Mathur et al.'s typology [19]. 0.00-0.124: Very Low, 0.125-0.374: Low, 0.375-0.624: Moderate, 0.625-0.874: High, 0.875-1.000: Very High [30].

		Canada			US			Overall			Group Difference		
Category	Dark Pattern	Int	Freq	δ	Int	Freq	δ	Int	Freq	δ	Int	Freq	δ
Scarcity	Low stock	0.40	0.68	0.56	0.45	0.63	0.55	0.42	0.66	0.55	−0.052	0.048	0.009
	High demand	0.41	0.52	0.47	0.45	0.46	0.46	0.43	0.49	0.46	−0.048	0.060	0.009
Social Proof	Activity message	0.43	0.53	0.48	0.45	0.45	0.45	0.44	0.49	0.46	−0.02	0.084	0.035
	Testimonial	0.47	0.65	0.57	0.44	0.58	0.51	0.46	0.61	0.54	0.028	0.072	0.053
Urgency	Limited time	0.51	0.58	0.54	0.56	0.60	0.58	0.53	0.59	0.56	−0.056	−0.018	−0.036
	Count down	0.55	0.52	0.54	0.56	0.55	0.55	0.56	0.54	0.55	−0.004	−0.027	−0.015
Misdirection	Visual interference	0.55	0.26	0.43	0.59	0.31	0.47	0.57	0.28	0.45	−0.048	−0.045	−0.045
	Confirmshaming	0.57	0.26	0.44	0.58	0.26	0.45	0.57	0.26	0.45	−0.016	0.000	−0.010
	Trick question	0.60	0.30	0.47	0.65	0.27	0.50	0.63	0.28	0.49	−0.048	0.030	−0.022
	Pressure selling	0.65	0.39	0.54	0.70	0.45	0.59	0.68	0.42	0.57	−0.048	−0.060	−0.051
Sneaking	Hidden cost	0.82	0.42	0.65	0.80	0.38	0.63	0.81	0.40	0.64	0.016	0.036	0.021
	Hidden subscription	0.84	0.45	0.67	0.84	0.42	0.66	0.84	0.43	0.67	0.004	0.027	0.011
	Sneak into basket	0.86	0.20	0.62	0.82	0.20	0.60	0.84	0.20	0.61	0.036	−0.003	0.024
Forced Action	Forced enrolment	0.84	0.55	0.71	0.82	0.57	0.71	0.83	0.56	0.71	0.020	−0.027	0.001
Obstruction	Hard to cancel	0.84	0.48	0.69	0.88	0.47	0.70	0.86	0.48	0.69	−0.032	0.018	−0.014

A repeated measure analysis of variance (RMANOVA) using R's ARTool [14] was used to uncover the national group profiles for perceived intrusiveness, frequency, and darkness variables. Since only one item was used to measure each construct, internal consistency reliability test was not required to be carried out. Chi-square tests using R's *ggstatsplot, ch19patil2021Ggstatsplot* were used to uncover the relationship between categorical variables (e.g., domain, yes/no perceived intrusiveness) and country of residence. In this section, we present the results of the empirical analysis.

4.1   Likert-Scale Rating of Intrusiveness, Frequency, and Darkness

Table 1 shows the perceived intrusiveness, frequency, and darkness score of each dark pattern at the group and overall levels. Regardless of country, forced enrol ment in the Forced Action category and hard to cancel in the Obstruction category are the most intrusive, while dark patterns in the Scarcity and Social Proof categories are the least intrusive. Moreover, low stock messages, regardless of country, are the most frequent, while sneak into basket is the least frequent. Finally, like intrusiveness, forced enrolment and hard to cancel are the darkest,

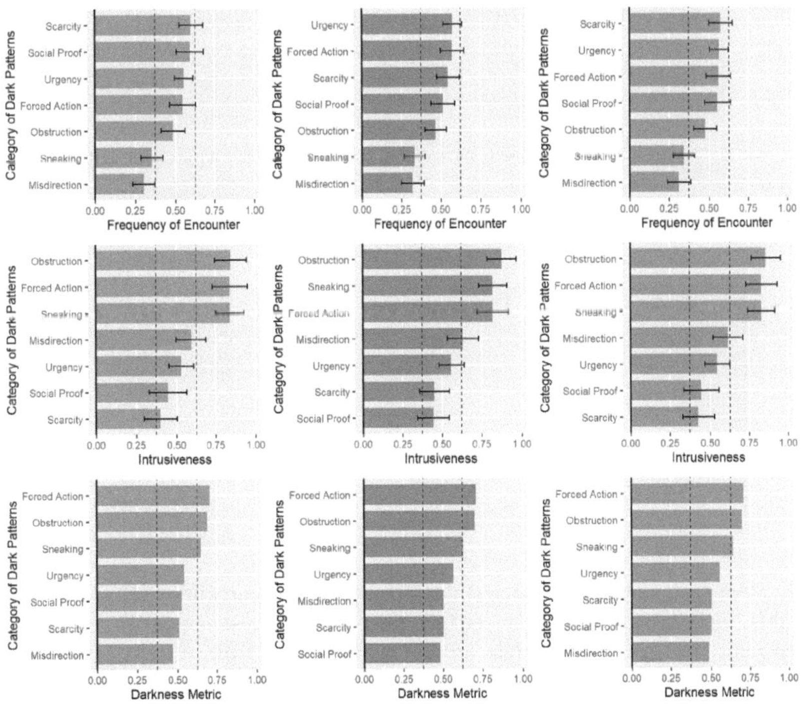

Fig. 1. Country-specific/overall frequency, intrusiveness and darkness profiles (RQ1, RQ2 and RQ3). Red: Canada, Green: US, Blue: overall. Horizontal bars represent standard deviations. Vertical bars represent key cut-off points [30] (Color figure online).

while dark patterns such as confirmshaming (both groups), visual interference (Canadian group), and active message (American group) are the least dark.

Figure 1 shows the ordering of the dark patterns for all three metrics in terms of categories. Table 3 shows the pairwise comparisons of the seven categories of dark patterns in terms of intrusiveness and frequency. A few of the pairs of categories significantly differ. The difference is more likely to occur between one of the three most intrusive, frequent, and dark categories and one of the three least intrusive, frequent, and dark. For example, regarding intrusiveness and darkness (Fig. 1), the three most intrusive and dark, regardless of country, include forced action, obstruction, and sneaking, most of which are significantly different from the least intrusive and dark categories including social proof, scarcity and misdirection (Table 3). Within the three most intrusive and dark categories for each national group, there is little to non-significant difference between each pair, e.g., between forced action and sneaking regarding intrusiveness, and between forced action and obstruction regarding darkness (Table 3). Similarly, within the three least intrusive and dark categories for each national group, there is little to non-significant difference between each pair, for example, between social proof and scarcity regarding intrusiveness and darkness (Table 3).

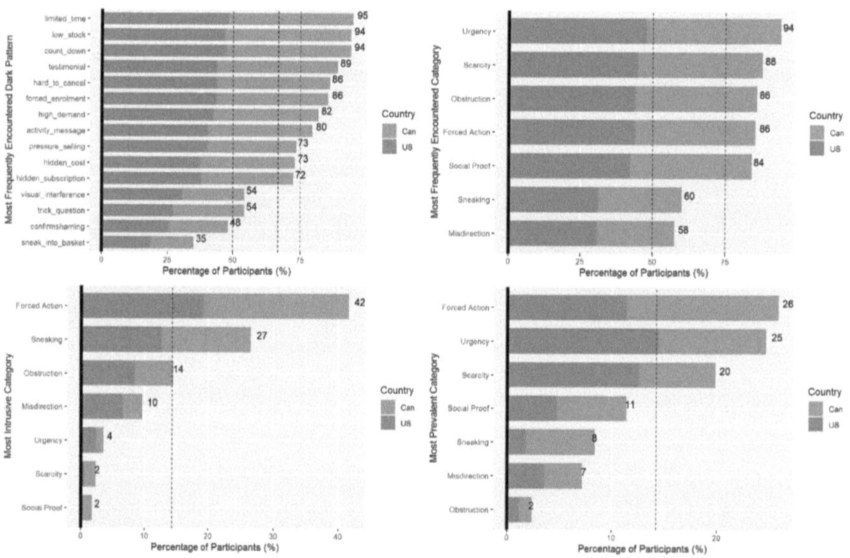

Fig. 2. Most frequently encountered dark patterns and categories (RQ1, top-left and top-right), most intrusive category (RQ2, bottom-left), most prevalent category (RQ4, bottom-right) to the least based on yes/no responses, and the cutting across countries (RQ6). Vertical bars represents key cut-off points.

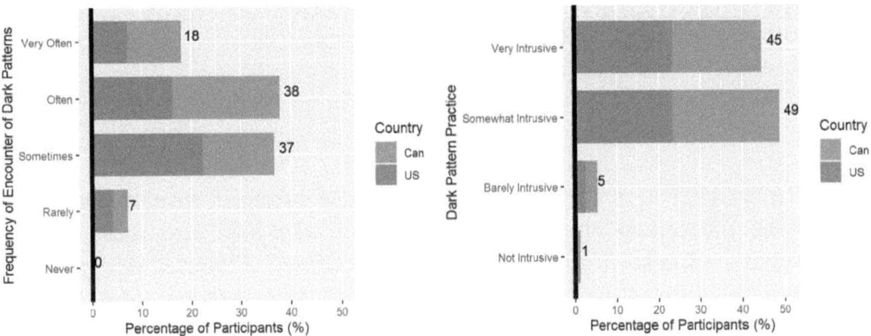

Fig. 3. Percent of users that encounter dark patterns online (RQ1, left) and find them intrusive (RQ2, right) to certain degrees and non-effect of country (RQ6).

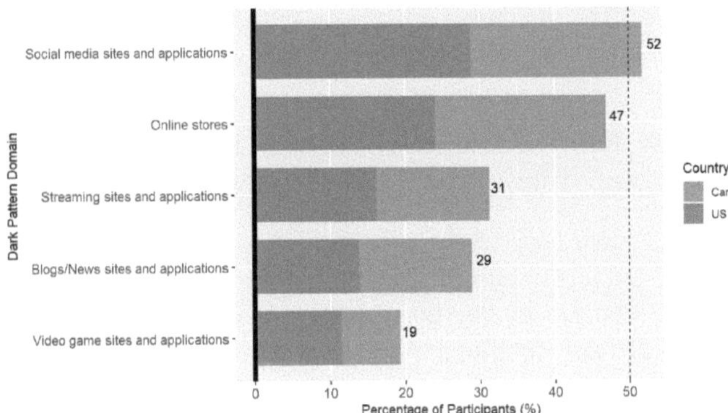

Fig. 4. Domains where users mostly encountered dark patterns (RQ5, RQ6).

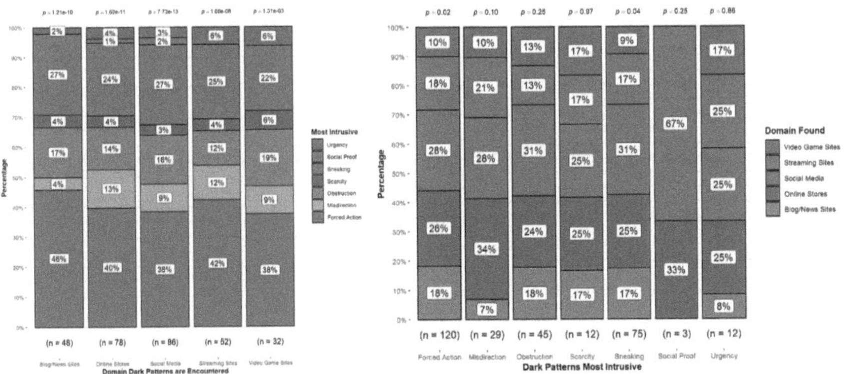

Fig. 5. Most intrusive dark patterns distribution in each domain where users encountered dark patterns (RQ5, left). Domain distribution among individual groups that considered each dark pattern as most intrusive (RQ5, right).

4.2   Most Intrusive, Prevalent and Frequently Encountered Dark Patterns Based on Yes/No Responses

Figure 2 shows the percentages of participants in each national group who responded yes to the question *"have you previously encountered a [name of dark pattern] when shopping online?"* at the specific level (top-left) and categorical level (top-right) and the percentages of those in either group who selected a given dark pattern as the most intrusive (bottom-left) and most prevalent (bottom-right). Overall, regardless of country, Forced Action was perceived as most intrusive, followed by Sneaking and Obstruction (bottom-left). Similarly, Forced Action was perceived as the most prevalent overall, with Urgency and Scarcity in the second and third places, respectively (bottom-right). Our chi-squared test shows no significant relationship between the selected most intrusive category and country ($\chi^2(6) = 8.04, p = 0.24$). Similarly, there is neither a significant relationship between the most prevalent category and country ($\chi^2(6) = 9.28, p = 0.16$) nor between the most frequently encountered category and country ($\chi^2(14) = 2.33, p = 1.000$).

4.3   Users Who Have Encountered Dark Patterns at Certain Frequency and View Them as Intrusive to a Certain Degree

As shown in Fig. 3, over 55% of the participants stated they often or very often encountered dark patterns online. There is no significant relationship between the frequency of encounter of the dark patterns and country ($\chi^2(14) = 2.33, p = 1.000$). Moreover, 45% of the participants perceived the dark pattern practice as very intrusive. Similarly, there is no significant relationship between the degree of perceived intrusiveness of dark pattern practice and country.

4.4   Domains Dark Patterns Are Mostly Encountered

Fig. 4 shows the domains where dark patterns are encountered the most. Social media came out top, with 52% of the participants stating they had encountered dark patterns while using social media sites/apps. Online stores and streaming sites/apps came in the second and third places, respectively, at 47% and 31%. Regardless of domain, Forced Action, followed by Sneaking, is perceived as most frequently encountered (Fig. 5). Moreover, the majority of dark patterns, regardless of category, are mostly encountered on social media and online stores.

5   Discussion

We have presented the extent to which online users perceived common dark patterns drawn from the Mathur et al.'s typology [19] as intrusive, frequent, prevalent and dark overall. We discuss the findings and their implications.

5.1   Prevalence, Intrusiveness, Frequency, and Darkness Measures

Table 1 and Fig. 1 show the results of the perceived intrusiveness, frequency, and darkness score of the specific and categories of dark patterns at the group and overall levels. Regardless of country, Forced Action, Obstruction, and Sneaking, which do not significantly differ, happened to be the most intrusive, with their respective scores approximately doubling those of Scarcity and Social Proof, both of which do not significantly differ as well (Table 3). This means that while users perceive Forced Action, Obstruction, and Sneaking to be very intrusive, they view Scarcity and Social Proof, as well as Misdirection and Urgency, as moderately intrusive (Fig. 1). However, both Scarcity and Social Proof are significantly less intrusive than Misdirection (see Table 3) despite all three being moderately intrusive based on the interpretation guideline in Table 1. In the same vein, regardless of country, Forced Action, Obstruction, and Sneaking are perceived as the darkest, while Scarcity and Social Proof as well as Misdirection are perceived as the least dark (Fig. 1 and Table 1). Moreover, regarding frequency, Urgency, Forced Action, Scarcity and Social Proof were reported as the most frequently encountered in the online environment, regardless of country, with their frequency ratings approximately doubling those of Sneaking and Misdirection, which were the least frequent (Fig. 1).

It is interesting to see that the rating results regarding Scarcity and Social Proof, as well as for Forced Action, Sneaking and Obstruction, are also replicated in the selection of the most intrusive and prevalent pattern results in Fig. 2. As shown, only 2 out of 166 participants selected Scarcity and Social Proof as the most intrusive, compared with 42, 27 and 14 that selected Forced Action, Sneaking and Obstruction, respectively, as the most intrusive. In particular, the finding regarding the intrusiveness of Social Proof and Scarcity may not be far-fetched as Albanese [2] also found in their research that both patterns were among the least invasive of over 20 dark patterns investigated.

5.2   Most Frequent but Least Intrusive Dark Patterns

Among all of the categories of dark patterns, Scarcity (low stock and high demand) and Social Proof (activity message and testimonial) are the only ones with intrusiveness scores less than the neutral value of 0.50 (Fig. 1) but with frequency of encounter roughly 0.5. Their perceived low intrusiveness may partly account for why they are used as "persuasive techniques" [1, 26, 29] devoid of manipulation, coercion or deception to elicit positive behavior change. Hence, we see them reported as highly frequent despite their low perceived intrusiveness. Unlike the other categories of patterns, the persuasive techniques of Scarcity and Social Proof are as old as humans themselves. They predated the Internet as they were among the six persuasion principles proposed by Cialdini [8] in the early 1980s in the field of marketing and advertising. Just as in our physical world or brick-and-mortar stores, they are very prevalent in the online environment as evident in the high self-reported frequencies of encounter that cut across both national groups (Table 1). That said, we argue that Scarcity and Social Proof, unlike most of the other categories such as Forced Action, Obstruction, and Sneaking that are very intrusive and dark, are a double-edge sword, which can be used to the advantage of the user, society or service depending on the intention of the designer, their goal and the veracity of the message involved. For example, if Scarcity and Social Proof are used in a way that is beneficial to society with the message associated with them being truthful, they can be regarded as persuasive techniques rather than dark patterns. For example, during the COVID-19 pandemic, Oyibo and Morita [24] presented contact tracing app designs that incorporated persuasive techniques such as Social Proof to make them more effective. Specifically, they redesigned COVID Alert's diagnosis-report interface such that it featured the message *"11 other people reported their COVID-19 diagnosis today"* (p. 17) [24] to motivate users to report their diagnosis if they tested positive and were provided with a one-time key by the health authority. In this context, if the message was actually true, the use of Social Proof cannot be regarded as a dark pattern as the intention of the designer was to motivate the user to report their diagnosis to curtail the spread of COVID-19. Moreover, if a message such as *"We only have two threadmills left in stock"* (p. 10) [24] is true, the use of Scarcity as a persuasive technique to motivate behaviors that are beneficial to the user or society may not be considered as a dark pattern. The potential for Scarcity and Social Proof to be used honestly and positively partly accounts for their low perceived darkness compared with other highly frequent patterns such as Forced Action, which turns out to be the darkest. Overall, both categories were perceived as the second and third "least dark", with the difference between their darkness ratings and that of Misdirection being non-significant at the overall and national levels (Table 3 and Fig. 1).

However, Urgency, which is highly close to Scarcity in terms of intrusiveness and frequency scores (Fig. 1) and use of scarcity cognitive bias, is considered more intrusive and darker than both Scarcity and Social Proof. While the intrusiveness and darkness scores of Scarcity and Social Proof are <0.5, those of Urgency (limited time and count down) are above. This indicates that users do find Urgency invasive unlike Scarcity and Social Proof. This finding may not be far-fetched given that online practices such as the use of timers, pop-ups and modal dialogs to implement count down and limited time can be very disruptive and distracting, resulting in poor user experience. This partly explains why both groups view Urgency as more intrusive and darker than Scarcity despite both patterns employing the same underlying cognitive bias mechanism: scarcity bias.

5.3   Most Intrusive Categories of Dark Patterns Across Domains

We found that Forced Action, Obstruction and Sneaking were the darkest categories of patterns across the different domains, while Scarcity and Social Proof were the least dark (see Fig. 5 and Fig. 1). The takeaway is that regardless of domain and country of residence, Forced Action, Obstruction and Sneaking are considered very intrusive and thus very dark patterns. Despite their high degree of darkness, from users' perspectives, they are widely and the most used in various domains, with approximately 8 in 20, 5 in 20, 3 in 20 users who reported encountering Forced Action, Sneaking and Obstruction, respectively, in each of the domains (blog news sites, streaming sites, online stores, social media and video games) selecting them as the most intrusive. The very high perceived intrusiveness and darkness of these three categories of dark patterns may not be far-fetched given that both countries are neighbors with similar internet culture, practice, online user experience and behavior. For instance, research has shown that while some websites allow users to easily register by using login credentials from social websites such as Google or Facebook, they (e.g., Amazon) make it difficult for users, if not impossible, to delete their account, e.g., by hiding the delete option beneath many layers of menus or forcing users to call customer support to help delete their account [4]. This practice of obstruction and/or forcing users to abandon the cancellation of their account can be very frustrating. This type of experience, no doubt, partly accounts for why users, regardless of country perceived Forced Action and Obstruction as the most intrusive and darkest. It is interesting to note that in terms of prevalence, while over 25% of the participants stated Forced Action is the most prevalent, only 2% stated Obstruction despite both being very intrusive. The reason for this discrepancy is that users are more likely to experience obstruction when deleting an account or canceling a service, an activity most users rarely engage in. Hence, Obstruction turned out to be the least prevalent among the seven categories of dark patterns.

5.4   Limitations and Future Work

Our study has limitations. First, the findings are based on users' perceptions and self-reports, which are subject to individual biases and poor memory recall. Second, our sample size is small (n = 83 for each country) compared with the actual Canadian population of over 35 million and American population of over 350 million. Future work can focus on larger sample sizes to investigate the replicability and generalizability of the current findings. Third, we only looked at the perceived intrusiveness as an adverse characteristic of dark patterns and used it, in conjunction with frequency of encounter, as a proxy for estimating darkness. While both dimensions are not sufficient to quantify the darkness of a dark pattern, our work serves as a starting point. Future work can investigate other dimensions, e.g., manipulation, coercion, and deception. Fourth, we did not examine how participants' online behavior, internet availability, access and usage might have influenced their frequency of encounter of dark patterns and the domains in which they are encountered. Future work should bridge this gap. Fifth, all of the possible dark patterns in the literature were not investigated, preventing us from knowing how other unexamined dark patterns will fair regarding the three examined metrics: intrusiveness, frequency, and darkness. Future work can focus on other unexamined patterns and (non-individualist) countries not covered in this paper to see the extent to which the current findings generalize.

6   Conclusion

We have presented the extent to which dark patterns in Mathur et al.'s typology are prevalent, intrusive and frequently encountered on the Internet. Our analysis revealed that Forced Action, Obstruction and Sneaking were perceived as the most intrusive in the online environment regardless of country of residence. These categories of dark patterns pervaded all of the examined domains including blog news sites, streaming sites, online stores, social media and video gaming sites, with Forced Action reported as most pervasive, followed by Sneaking and Obstruction. In contrast, Social Proof and Scarcity, although among the most frequent, were perceived as the least intrusive, plausibly because they can be used to promote positive behavior change beneficial to users. Overall, Forced Action, followed by Obstruction and Sneaking, is perceived as the darkest, while Social Proof, Scarcity and Misdirection are perceived as the least dark. These findings provide useful insights into users' perspectives (often relegated to the background) on the perceived prevalence, intrusiveness and frequency of encounter of dark patterns in the online environment. The findings add to the growing body of evidence on users' negative views of dark patterns and can serve as empirical bases for national legislation and regulation of dark patterns, especially in countries yet to deliberate on the issue. Importantly, they inform digital platform operators and designers about the need to minimize or stop the use of certain categories of dark patterns such as Forced Action, Obstruction and Sneaking. Otherwise, in the long run, users may churn their platforms if they find better alternatives or become fed up with unsolicited, unwelcomed and intrusive dark patterns that adversely impact their user experience and welfare.

Acknowledgments. We would like to thank Aryan Soni, Manmeet Walia, and Onkar Saund for helping with the data gathering.

Appendix

Table 2. Definitions of the 15 dark patterns examined in the study [19].

Category	Dark Pattern	Definition
Sneaking	Sneak into Basket	When additional products are added to your online shopping cart without your consent
	Hidden Cost	When undisclosed charges are added before you make a purchase.
	Hidden Subscription	a hidden recurring fee under the guise of a one-time fee or a free trial.
Urgency	Countdown Time	When sites indicate a deal or discount will expire using a countdown timer.
	Limited Time Message	When a site informs users that a deal or sale will expire soon without providing a specific timeframe.
Misdirection	Confirmshaming	When a site utilizes language and shame to coerce users away from a certain choice.
	Visual Interference	When a site uses style and visual presentation to drive a user away from making a certain choice.
	Trick Question	When a site uses confusing language to steer users away from making certain choices.
	Pressured Selling	When more expensive variants of a product are preselected, or the user is pressured into accepting/purchasing more expensive variations of a product and/or related products.
Social Proof	Activity Message	When a site informs the user about the activity on the website, such as the purchases, views, visits, etc.
	Testimonials	when testimonials without a clear origin are placed on a product page.
Scarcity	Low-stock Message	When a message alerts the user that low quantities of a project are available, increasing the desirability of the product.
	High Demand Message	When a message alerts the user that a product is currently in high demand and likely to sell out soon, making it more desirable.
Obstruction	Hard to Cancel	When a site makes it easy for a user to sign up for service, but hard to cancel it.
Forced Action	Forced Enrollment	When users are coerced to create accounts or share their information to complete tasks.

Table 3. Bonferonni's *p*-values of pairwise difference between categories of dark patterns. INT: Intrusiveness, FRQ: Frequency. FA: Forced Action, MD: Misdirection, OBS: Obstruction, SC: Scarcity, SNK: Sneaking, SP: Social Proof, URG: Urgency; Can: Canada, US: United States, OV: Overall.

		INT						FRQ					
		FA	MD	OBS	SC	SNK	SP	FA	MD	OBS	SC	SNK	SP
Can	MD	0.0000						0.0000					
	OBS	1.0000	0.0000					1.0000	0.001				
	SC	0.0000	0.0015	0.0000				1.0000	0.0000	0.1986			
	SNK	1.0000	0.0000	1.0000	0.0000			0.001	1.0000	0.0710	0.0000		
	SP	0.0000	0.019	0.0000	1.0000	0.0000		1.0000	0.0000	0.5309	1.0000	0.0000	
	URG	0.0000	1.0000	0.0000	0.1295	0.0000	1.0000	1.0000	0.0000	1.0000	1.0000	0.0000	1.0000
US	MD	0.0000						0.0000					
	OBS	1.0000	0.0000					0.3479	0.0174				
	SC	0.0000	0.001	0.0000				1.0000	0.0000	1.0000			
	SNK	1.0000	0.0000	0.0112	0.0000			0.0000	1.0000	0.0207	0.0000		
	SP	0.0000	0.0000	0.0000	1.0000	0.0000		1.0000	0.0000	1.0000	1.0000	0.0000	
	URG	0.0000	0.4768	0.0000	0.5759	0.0000	0.1421	1.0000	0.0000	0.226	1.0000	0.0000	1.0000
OV	MD	0.0000						0.0000					
	OBS	1.0000	0.0000					0.1723	0.0000				
	SC	0.0000	0.0000	0.0000				1.0000	0.0000	0.0331			
	SNK	1.0000	0.0000	0.0064	0.0000			0.0000	1.0000	0.0000	0.0000		
	SP	0.0000	0.0000	0.0000	1.0000	0.0000		1.0000	0.0000	0.3134	1.0000	0.0000	
	URG	0.0000	0.1284	0.0000	0.0102	0.0000	0.0494	1.0000	0.0000	0.0559	1.0000	0.0000	1.0000

References

1. Aguirre-Rodriguez, A.: The effect of consumer persuasion knowledge on scarcity appeal persuasiveness. J. Advert. **42**(4), 371–379 (2013)
2. Albanese, F.L.: The influence of dark patterns on users' attitudes and behaviours: a classification based on the FCB grid. Université catholique de Louvain, Louvain School of Management (2022)
3. Bao, J.A., Jung, Y., Sundar, S.S.: Are you fooled by interactivity? the effects of interactivity on privacy disclosure. Behav. Inf. Technol., 1–21 (2025)
4. Baroni, L.A., Puska, A.A., de Castro Salgado, L.C., Pereira, R.: Dark patterns: towards a socio-technical approach. In: Proceedings of the XX Brazilian Symposium on Human Factors in Computing Systems, pp. 1–7 (2021)
5. Borberg, I., Hougaard, R., Rafnsson, W., Kulyk, O.: So i sold my soul": effects of dark patterns in cookie notices on end-user behavior and perceptions. In: Usable Security and Privacy (USEC) Symposium, vol. 2022 (2022)
6. Brenncke, M.: Regulating dark patterns. Notre Dame J. Int'l Comp. L. **14**, 39 (2024)
7. Carter, M.: The optimal opt-in option. Columbia Law Rev. **124**(2), 431–458 (2024)
8. Cialdini, R.: Influence: the Psychology of Persuasion (1984)

9. Determann, L., Tam, J.: The California privacy rights act of 2020: a broad and complex data processing regulation that applies to businesses worldwide. J. Data Protect. Privacy **4**(1), 7–21 (2020)
10. Di Geronimo, L., Braz, L., Fregnan, E., Palomba, F., Bacchelli, A.: UI dark patterns and where to find them: a study on mobile applications and user perception. In: Proceedings of the 2020 CHI Conference on Human Factors in Computing Systems, pp. 1–14 (2020)
11. Dickinson, G.M.: The patterns of digital deception. BCL Rev. **65**, 2457 (2024)
12. Jafari, E., Vassileva, J.: Designing effective warnings for manipulative designs in mobile applications. In: Proceedings of the 32nd ACM Conference on User Modeling, Adaptation and Personalization, pp. 12–17 (2024)
13. Karagoel, I., Nathan-Roberts, D.: Dark patterns: social media, gaming, and e-commerce. In: Proceedings of the Human Factors and Ergonomics Society Annual Meeting, vol. 65, pp. 752–756. SAGE Publications Sage, Los Angeles, USA (2021)
14. Kay, M., Wobbrock, J.O.: Package 'ARTool' (2016). https://doi.org/10.1145/1978942.1978963, https://cran.r-project.org/web/packages/ARTool/ARTool.pdf
15. Lalsinghani, G.: Left in the dark: evaluating the FTC's limitations in combating dark patterns. Berkeley Tech. LJ **39**, 1463 (2024)
16. Lewis, F., Vassileva, J.: Seeing in the dark: revealing the relationships, goals, and harms of dark patterns. In: Proceedings of the Workshop Mobilizing Research and Regulatory Action on Dark Patterns and Deceptive Design Practices (DDPCHI 2024) CHI Conference on Human Factors in Computing Systems (CHI 2024), Honolulu, HI, USA, pp. 11–16 (2024)
17. Liang, H.: Understanding user and developer perceptions of dark patterns in online environments. Ph.D. thesis, Virginia Tech (2025)
18. Madane, Y., Azeroual, M.: Perceived intrusiveness vs. relevance: a PLS-SEM analysis of personalized advertising in Morocco. Digital **5**(4), 63 (2025)
19. Mathur, A., et al.: Dark patterns at scale: findings from a crawl of 11k shopping websites. Proc. ACM Hum. Comput. Interact. **3**(CSCW), 1–32 (2019)
20. Mathur, A., Kshirsagar, M., Mayer, J.: What makes a dark pattern... dark? design attributes, normative considerations, and measurement methods. In: Proceedings of the 2021 CHI Conference on Human Factors in Computing Systems, pp. 1–18 (2021)
21. Mildner, T., Freye, M., Savino, G.L., Doyle, P.R., Cowan, B.R., Malaka, R.: Defending against the dark arts: recognising dark patterns in social media. In: Proceedings of the 2023 ACM Designing Interactive Systems Conference, pp. 2362–2374 (2023)
22. Naheyan, T., Oyibo, K.: The effect of dark patterns and user knowledge on user experience and decision-making. In: International Conference on Persuasive Technology. pp. 190–206. Springer (2024). https://doi.org/10.1007/978-3-031-58226-4_15
23. Niknejad, S., Mildner, T., Zargham, N., Putze, S., Malaka, R.: Level up or game over: Exploring how dark patterns shape mobile games. In: Proceedings of the International Conference on Mobile and Ubiquitous Multimedia, pp. 148–156 (2024)
24. Oyibo, K.: ComTech: towards a unified taxonomy of persuasive techniques for persuasive technology design. Comput. Hum. Behav. Rep., 100372 (2024)
25. Oyibo, K.: The influence of user knowledge and usage behaviour on decision-making and perceived reputation of streaming sites that use dark patterns. Behav. Inf. Technol., 1–20 (2025)

26. Oyibo, K., Vassileva, J.: The relationship between personality traits and susceptibility to social influence. Comput. Hum. Behav. **98**, 174–188 (2019)
27. Paolacci, G., Chandler, J., Ipeirotis, P.G.: Running experiments on amazon mechanical TURK. Judgm. Decis. Mak. **5**(5), 411–419 (2010)
28. Patil, I.: Visualizations with statistical details: the 'GGSTATSPLOT' approach. J. Open Source Softw. **6**(61), 1–5 (2021)
29. Rosadi, M.A.I., Manafe, L.A.: Persuasive communication strategy implementation in attracting consumer interest. Int. J. Econ. Manage. Bus. Soc. Sci. (Ijembis) **2**(2), 223–232 (2022)
30. Terano, H.J.: Development and acceptability of the simplified text with workbook in differential equations as an instructional material for engineering. Asia Pacific J. Multidiscip. Res. **3**(4), 89–94 (2015)
31. Turillazzi, A., Taddeo, M., Floridi, L., Casolari, F.: The digital services act: an analysis of its ethical, legal, and social implications. Law Innov. Technol. **15**(1), 83–106 (2023)
32. Van Doorn, J., Hoekstra, J.C.: Customization of online advertising: the role of intrusiveness. Mark. Lett. **24**(4), 339–351 (2013)
33. Warner, M., Fischer, D., Klobuchar, A., Thune, J.: Lawmakers reintroduce bipartisan bicameral legislation to ban manipulative'dark patterns' (2021). https://www.warner.senate.gov/public/index.cfm/2021/12/lawmakers-reintroduce-bipartisan-bicameral-legislation-to-ban-manipulative-dark-patterns

Persuasive Onboarding for Automated Driving: Design and Evaluation of Tutoring Strategies to Support Safe and Intended ADAS Use

Verena Pongratz[1]([envelope])[iD], Roxana Loyola Daiqui[2], Luca Zwack-Wandrey[2], and Klaus Bengler[1][iD]

[1] Technical University of Munich, Garching, Germany
{verena.i.pongratz,bengler}@tum.de
[2] Ludwig Maximilian University of Munich, Munich, Germany
{r.loyola,l.zwack}@campus.lmu.de

Abstract. As advanced driver assistance systems (ADAS) become increasingly integrated into everyday driving, their safe and intended use depends not only on user knowledge but also on motivation and engagement. To address this challenge, this study explores persuasive onboarding approaches - varying in media (app-based vs. in-vehicle) and navigation strategy (linear vs. exploratory) - and their effects on usability, user experience (UX), acceptance, and understanding of ADAS. In a controlled 2×2 between-subjects study (N = 40), four tutorial variants were compared using pre- and post-measures of user perceptions and knowledge. App-based onboarding resulted in higher usability and UX compared to in-vehicle onboarding. Navigation strategy revealed no significant effects, although descriptive trends suggested that linear navigation may support efficiency and clarity, while exploratory navigation may offer advantages for users with lower prior knowledge. Overall, all tutorial formats improved ADAS-related understanding. These findings highlight that onboarding should not only inform but also persuade by fostering autonomy, competence, and confidence as foundations for safe and responsible system use.

Keywords: Tutoring Strategies · Onboarding Systems · Persuasive Technology · Automated Driving · ADAS · Human-Machine Interaction · Human Factors · User Experience · Usability · Acceptance

1 Introduction and Motivation

The growing integration of advanced driver assistance systems (ADAS) has fundamentally changed the driving experience. In partially automated vehicles (Level 2), lateral and longitudinal control can be automated, yet continuous driver supervision remains mandatory. This shared control creates complex human-machine interaction dynamics [1], that may lead to misuse, misunderstanding, or overreliance when users lack sufficient system understanding or

K. Sumi et al. (Eds.): PERSUASIVE 2026, LNCS 16476, pp. 273–287, 2026.
https://doi.org/10.1007/978-3-032-19687-3_20

motivation to engage with the technology [2]. Although ADAS have the potential to enhance safety and comfort, their effectiveness depends on safe and intended system use [3]. This requires both adequate user comprehension of functionalities and awareness of operational limitations [4]. Prior research shows that especially less experienced drivers often struggle to understand system capabilities and boundaries [5], resulting in uncertainty and inappropriate system use [6]. Educating users about ADAS functionalities in a clear, engaging, and effective manner is therefore essential to promote responsible system interaction, particularly before intitial use [7,8]. Traditional onboarding approaches, such as vehicle manuals, have proven insufficient in this regard [9], as they often lack interactivity, contextual relevance, and engaging presentation formats [10,11].

While previous ADAS onboarding research has largely focused on informational content and comprehension [11–13], motivational and structural aspects of learning have received comparatively little attention. Yet, motivation and engagement are key to ensuring not only short-term learning [14], but also sustained and correct system use. From this perspective, onboarding can be understood as a persuasive process that supports users' motivation, engagement, and confidence. However, the application of persuasive design principles to ADAS onboarding remains underexplored. To address this gap, the present study investigates the persuasive potential of two interactive onboarding formats: an app-based tutorial (App-Tutorial), accessible via smartphone, and an in-vehicle human-machine interface tutorial (HMI-Tutorial). Two navigational strategies (linear vs. exploratory) were additionally examined to assess how varying degrees of user autonomy affect key outcomes. Rather than focusing solely on content, this study examines medium and navigation as persuasive design factors shaping usability, user experience (UX), acceptance, and system understanding. Accordingly, the overarching research question is: *How can user-centered onboarding be designed as a persuasive intervention to enhance usability, UX, acceptance, and system understanding as key prerequisites for safe and intended use of ADAS?*

The resulting insights aim to inform evidence-based design principles for persuasive onboarding systems that foster motivated, confident, and safe use of partially automated driving technologies.

2   Related Work

In partially automated driving, maintaining appropriate driver engagement remains a central human factors challenge [15]. Drivers must understand system capabilities and limitations [16] while remaining attentive to monitor automation and intervene when necessary [17]. As ADAS use is largely discretionary, drivers may exhibit both misuse (overreliance or inappropriate use) and disuse (underuse or avoidance despite potential benefits), depending on their understanding, trust, and motivation [3]. Onboarding approaches can address these challenges by providing motivationally supportive and persuasive learning experiences that foster trust, comprehension, mental model development, and behavioral alignment with safe system use [12,18,19].

From a motivational perspective, Self-Determination Theory (SDT) [20] provides a well-established framework for persuasive onboarding design. SDT posits that supporting users' basic psychological needs for autonomy, competence, and relatedness facilitates internalization of target behaviors and sustained engagement out of intrinsic motivation [20]. Interactive onboarding can foster autonomy through flexible navigation, competence through clear feedback and progressive learning, and relatedness through trust and perceived relevance. Empirical research in interactive and gamified learning contexts has shown that need satisfaction mediates the relationship between design features and engagement [21,22], with competence and relatedness identified as the strongest predictors [23]. In automated driving, gamified education approaches showed promise in terms of intrinsic motivation, mental model formation, and trust [19].

Although gamification provides early evidence for the motivational power of need-satisfying design, persuasive system design (PSD) extends this approach toward systematic behavior change support [24]. According to [25, p.32] "a persuasive technology tool is an interactive product designed to change attitudes or behaviors or both by making desired outcomes easier to achieve". Expanding on this, [26] describe persuasion as a multi-phased and context-dependent process, shaped by users' goals, prior experiences, and situational constraints. Users with high motivation and ability are more likely to engage deeply with persuasive messages, whereas those under cognitive load or time pressure may rely on heuristics [26]. The PSD model further postulates that persuasive systems should be both useful and easy to use [25,26], meeting user needs through responsiveness, attractiveness, accessibility, and high-quality interaction - factors that directly align with usability and UX [27,28]. Accordingly, these dimensions are treated as core persuasive outcomes in the present study, reflecting the system's capacity to influence affective engagement and motivational readiness. By integrating persuasive and motivational frameworks, the present research positions onboarding not merely as an instructional tool but as a holistic learning experience that promotes safe and intended ADAS use.

3   Tutorial Design as a Persuasive Intervention

3.1   Conceptual Overview

To address the research question, the study operationalizes persuasive and motivational principles in two interactive ADAS onboarding prototypes. Tutorial design is conceptualized as a persuasive intervention, implemented through two tutorial formats and two navigation strategies. All variants were developed in accordance with ergonomic design principles outlined in DIN EN ISO 9241-303 [29], ensuring legibility, visual consistency, and ease of interaction. Beyond ergonomic quality, the tutorials incorporated persuasive design elements derived from the PSD model [26], including structured guidance, autonomy support, and interactive feedback. These elements were systematically varied to examine how different onboarding designs support psychological preconditions for safe and intended ADAS use.

3.2 Tutorial Types: Contextual Framing of Onboarding

Two tutorial formats were developed to represent distinct contexts for implementing persuasive and motivational design principles. The HMI-Tutorial was integrated into a vehicle's center console via a tablet interface, enabling participants to interact with the content while seated in the car. This format provided close proximity to the context of use, supporting situational relevance and system credibility as key persuasive design factors [26]. The App-Tutorial was delivered via smartphone outside the vehicle context, allowing users to engage with identical content in a familiar mobile interaction setting. This format was designed to shape motivational conditions for onboarding by enabling users to complete the tutorial before entering the vehicle and independently of the in-car setup. This conceptual flexibility was expected to support a less demanding, self-paced learning environment, which can enhance perceived autonomy and reflective engagement [30], two motivational aspects central to self-determined learning [20]. To ensure internal validity and systematic comparability, App- and HMI-Tutorial were evaluated under equivalent experimental time frames in a controlled laboratory setting. Both tutorial formats shared a consistent core structure and feature set (Fig. 1).

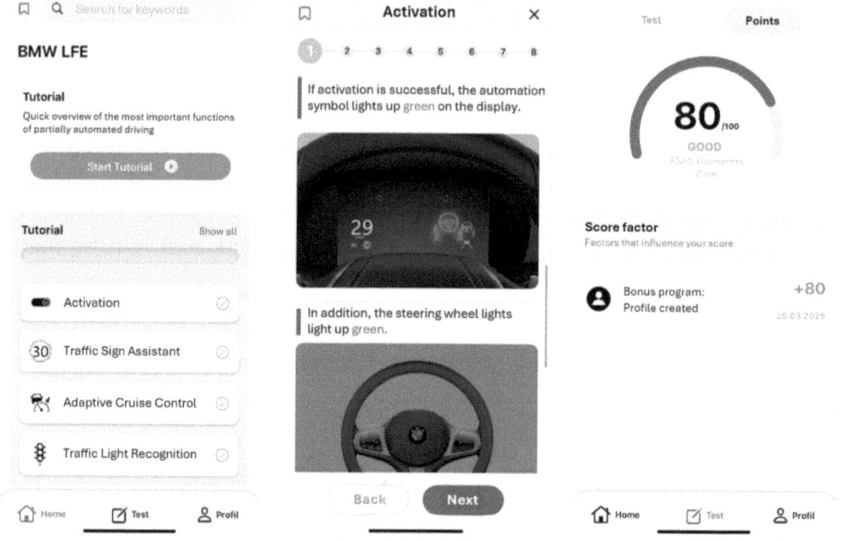

Fig. 1. Onboarding prototype with selectable tutorial topics (left), an interactive learning chapter providing visual feedback on system activation (center), and a motivational score display rewarding ADAS engagement and task completion (right).

Users could access modularized content, perform keyword searches, complete integrated quiz questions, and earn points for correct answers. Tutorial chapters covered core Level 2 ADAS functionalities, including Adaptive Cruise Control,

Lane Keeping Assist, and Traffic Light Recognition, as well as activation procedures and driver responsibilities. Short quizzes were embedded across all conditions as a persuasive self-monitoring and feedback mechanism [26]. Rather than examining their isolated effects, quizzes were integrated across all tutorial conditions to leverage their persuasive potential as part of a high-quality onboarding baseline. All tutorial content was presented in German, as all participants were native speakers.

3.3 Navigation Strategies: Autonomy vs. Guidance

While both tutorial formats provided identical informational content, they differed in their navigation design and degree of autonomy support. The linear navigation strategy followed a fixed, sequential structure without the option to skip or reorder content. Participants progressed through predefined tutorial steps (e.g., activation $\rightarrow$ system functionalities $\rightarrow$ deactivation $\rightarrow$ driver responsibilities), ensuring consistent content coverage. In this implementation, the linear format emphasized the persuasive principle of reduction [26] by structuring the learning process and minimizing navigation-related cognitive demands [31].

In contrast, the exploratory navigation strategy allowed participants to freely navigate between tutorial topics based on individual preferences or perceived relevance (e.g., directly accessing information about driver responsibilities). This approach primarily supported the persuasive principle of autonomy by enabling self-directed learning, in line with SDT [20]. Autonomy has been shown to promote intrinsic motivation, satisfaction, and engagement [20]. The unrestricted exploratory navigation may foster self-regulated learning and competence by enabling participants to construct learning sequences aligned with their prior knowledge and individual learning goals [32].

Together, the two navigation strategies represent contrasting persuasive approaches within user-centered onboarding. While the linear strategy reflects system-led guidance and persuasive structuring, the exploratory format emphasizes user autonomy and self-regulated learning. Comparing these conditions provides insights into how varying degrees of autonomy and contextual framing can shape key persuasive outcomes such as usability, UX, acceptance, and ADAS-related understanding.

4 Methodology

4.1 Study Design and Procedure

This study employed a 2×2 between-subjects design with tutorial types (App vs. HMI) and navigation strategy (exploratory vs. linear) as independent variables, operationalizing two persuasive design dimensions: contextual framing and autonomy support. Outcome measures reflecting persuasive system impact included perceived usability, UX, system acceptance, and ADAS-related knowledge acquisition. Rather than targeting direct behavior change or preference formation, these measures conceptualize persuasion as the facilitation of psychological preconditions necessary for intended and responsible system use. Knowledge acquisition reflects users' ability to form accurate mental models of system functionalities and limitations, while usability, UX, and acceptance indicate reduced interaction barriers and motivational readiness for intended use.

Participants were randomly assigned to one of four experimental conditions, each combining tutorial type and navigation strategy: App/Exploratory, App/Linear, HMI/Exploratory, and HMI/Linear. The procedure consisted of a pre-study questionnaire assessing demographics, technological affinity, and prior ADAS knowledge, followed by the assigned tutorial and a post-study questionnaire capturing the outcome measures. Participants were encouraged to think aloud during the tutorial to support focused engagement and reflection. This procedure was used as a supportive tool and was not subjected to analysis. Each session lasted about 60 min. The study was approved by the Ethics Committee of the Technical University of Munich (Ref. 2025-39-NM-BA).

4.2   Data Acquisition and Analysis

Data acquisition focused on user-centered outcome measures commonly applied in humanâĂŞcomputer interaction research. Usability was assessed using the System Usability Scale (SUS) [33], UX with the User Experience Questionnaire (UEQ) [34], and system acceptance (usefulness and satisfaction) following [35]. System understanding was operationalized as ADAS-related knowledge and measured both objectively via multiple-choice questions (quizzes) and subjectively via self-rated knowledge about ADAS on a 7-point Likert scale (0 = no knowledge, 6 = very high knowledge). Technological affinity was assessed using the Affinity for Technology Interaction (ATI) scale [36] and included as a covariate due to baseline differences.

Data were analyzed in RStudio using descriptive and inferential statistics. Baseline equivalence was examined using two-way ANOVAs. The effects of tutorial type and navigation strategy were analyzed using ANCOVAs and MANCOVAs with technological affinity as covariate. Changes in ADAS-related knowledge were assessed using repeated-measures ANCOVA. Pillai's Trace (V) was used for multivariate tests due to its robustness [37]. Where assumptions were violated, nonparametric alternatives were applied. All analyses were performed in RStudio at a 5% significance level.

4.3   Sample

A total of 40 participants (20 female, 20 male; $M = 34.60 \pm 16.66$ years) took part in the study. All held a valid Class B driver's license and were proficient in German. Participants were recruited via university channels and online advertisements. The sample showed mid-to-high technological affinity ($M = 3.94 \pm 1.43$) and limited prior ADAS knowledge ($M = 2.78 \pm 1.84$), reflecting a relevant target group for onboarding interventions.

Attitudinal pre-measures indicated positive perceptions toward automated driving and a high willingness to use ADAS and receive instructional support before first use, relevant for examining persuasive effects on user engagement and acceptance. The sample size aligns with typical persuasive system evaluations and was sufficient for comparative analysis within the 2×2 design, according to a G*Power estimation. Technological affinity differed between tutorial conditions ($F(1,36) = 6.10$, $p = .018$, $\eta^2 = 0.15$) and was therefore included as a covariate in subsequent analyses, with higher scores reported in the HMI group ($M = 4.34 \pm 0.72$) than in the App group ($M = 3.54 \pm 1.22$). No other significant baseline differences were observed.

5   Results

5.1   Usability

Usability results indicated higher perceived usability for the App-Tutorial ($M = 85.50 \pm 13.20$) compared to the HMI-Tutorial ($M = 76.63 \pm 17.70$). Across navigation strategies, linear navigation ($M = 81.25 \pm 16.60$) slightly outperformed exploratory navigation ($M = 80.88 \pm 15.90$), though differences were minor. According to the SUS interpretation scale [38], all tutorials achieved ratings between *good* and *excellent*, indicating overall high usability (Fig. 2).

An ANCOVA revealed a significant main effect of tutorial type on usability ($F(1,35) = 4.65$, $p = .038$, $\eta^2 = 0.12$) showing a medium effect in favor of the App-Tutorial. No significant effects were found for navigation strategy ($F(1,35) = 0.03$, $p = .865$), or the interaction term ($F(1,35) = 1.59$, $p = .216$). Technical affinity showed no significant influence ($F(1,35) = 1.54$, $p = .223$).

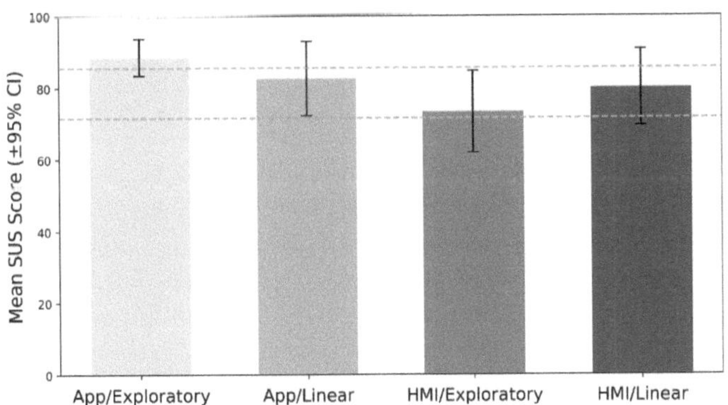

Fig. 2. Mean SUS scores (scale 0 to 100; ± 95% CI) across the four experimental groups, with thresholds for *good* (71.4) and *excellent* (85.5) usability according to [38].

5.2   User Experience

UX was assessed across the UEQ dimensions of *attractiveness, pragmatic quality*, and *hedonic quality*. Overall, the App-Tutorial ($M = 1.87 \pm 0.76$) received higher ratings than the HMI-Tutorial ($M = 1.40 \pm 0.87$) across all three UX dimensions (Fig. 3). In terms of navigation strategy, linear ($M = 1.72 \pm 0.71$) and exploratory ($M = 1.55 \pm 0.96$) navigation yielded comparable results.

A MANCOVA revealed a significant multivariate effect of tutorial type on the combined UX dimensions ($F(3,33) = 3.87$, $p = .018$, $V = 0.26$). No significant multivariate effects were found for navigation strategy ($F(3,33) = 1.41$, $p = .258$, $V = 0.11$) or the interaction term ($F(3,33) = 1.65$, $p = .198$, $V = 0.13$). Technical affinity showed no significant multivariate effect ($F(3,33) = 1.08$, $p = .370$, $V = 0.09$). Follow-up ANCOVAs (Bonferroni-corrected) showed a significant main effect of tutorial type on *pragmatic quality* ($F(1,37) = 10.79$, $p = .002$, $\eta^2 = 0.23$), while differences in *attractiveness* ($F(1,37) = 1.69$, $p = .202$) and *hedonic quality* ($F(1,37) = 0.80$, $p = .377$) were not significant.

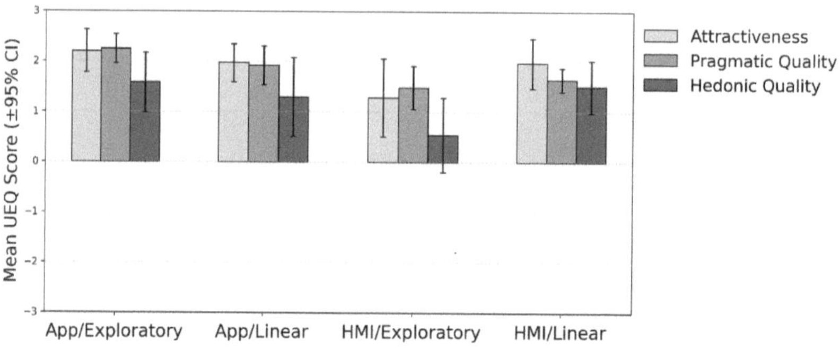

Fig. 3. Mean UEQ scores (scale -3 to 3; ± 95% CI) for attractiveness, pragmatic quality, and hedonic quality across the four experimental groups.

5.3 Acceptance

Acceptance was assessed using two subscales, *usefulness* (U) and *satisfaction* (S), which were analyzed separately. Descriptive results showed higher acceptance scores for the App-Tutorial ($M_U = 1.60 \pm 0.36$; $M_S = 1.38 \pm 0.54$) than for the HMI-Tutorial ($M_U = 1.28 \pm 0.67$; $M_S = 1.18 \pm 0.68$. Linear navigation ($M_U = 1.56 \pm 0.35$; $M_S = 1.29 \pm 0.50$) yielded slightly higher ratings than exploratory navigation ($M_U = 1.32 \pm 0.69$; $M_S = 1.26 \pm 0.72$) across both subscales (Fig. 4).

A MANCOVA revealed no statistically significant multivariate effects of tutorial type ($F(2,34) = 2.33$, $p = .113$, $V = 0.12$), navigation strategy ($F(2,34) = 2.62$, $p = .087$, $V = 0.13$), or their interaction ($F(2,34) = 1.97$, $p = .155$, $V = 0.10$) on acceptance ratings. Technical affinity showed no significant multivariate influence ($F(2,34) = 0.65$, $p = .526$, $V = 0.04$).

5.4 System Knowledge

Participants using the App-Tutorial ($\Delta M = 1.79 \pm 1.13$) showed slightly higher knowledge gains than those using the HMI-Tutorial ($\Delta M = 1.73 \pm 1.52$),

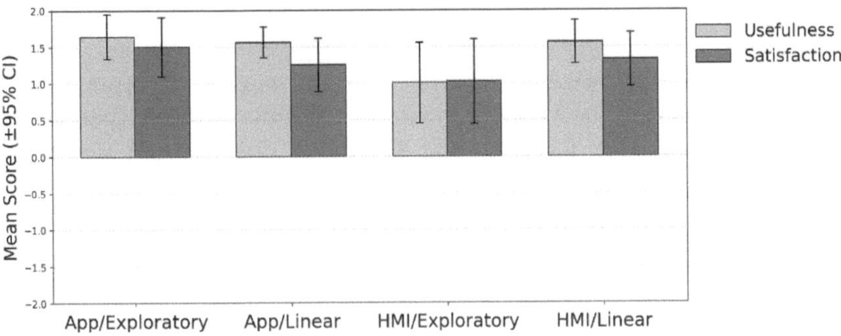

Fig. 4. Mean scores (scale -2 to 2; ± 95% CI) for usefulness, and satisfaction across the four experimental groups.

while exploratory ($\Delta M = 1.99 \pm 1.23$) outperformed linear navigation ($\Delta M = 1.53 \pm 1.40$). A repeated-measures ANCOVA revealed a significant main effect of time ($F(1,35) = 85.82$, $p < .001$, $\eta^2 = 0.44$), confirming a substantial over-all learning effect from pre-tutorial ($M = 2.78 \pm 1.35$) to post-tutorial ($M = 4.54 \pm 0.90$). No significant main effects were found for tutorial format ($F(1,35) = 4.02$, $p = .053$), or navigation strategy ($F(1,35) = 1.14$, $p = .293$). However, the effect of the tutorial format marginally missed the significance threshold. Technical affinity also showed a marginal effect on learning gains ($F(1,35) = 4.05$, $p = .052$).

A significant three-way interaction between tutorial format, navigation strategy, and time was observed ($F(1,35) = 6.98$, $p = 0.012$, $\eta^2 = 0.06$), suggesting that learning gains varied across configurations (Fig. 5). Post-hoc paired t-tests indicated significant knowledge improvements for HMI/Exploratory ($t(9) = -6.10$, $p < .001$), App/Linear ($t(9) = -5.41$, $p < .001$), and App/Exploratory ($t(9) = -4.71$, $p = .001$), whereas the gain for HMI/Linear did not reach significance ($t(9) = -2.21$, $p = .055$).

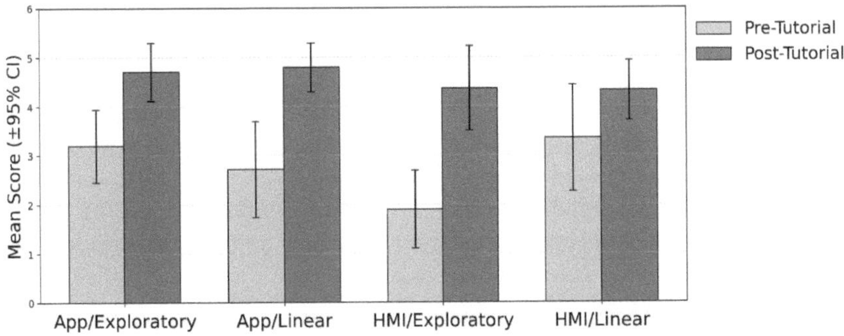

Fig. 5. Mean knowledge scores (scale 0 to 6; ± 95% CI) before and after tutorial completion across the four experimental groups.

6   Discussion

The present study investigated tutorial type and navigation strategy as persuasive design factors in ADAS onboarding. Results showed that the App-Tutorial achieved higher usability and pragmatic quality than the in-vehicle HMI-Tutorial, indicating that mobile onboarding can offer a more accessible and efficient learning environment. No significant differences were observed for hedonic quality, attractiveness, or system acceptance, suggesting comparable affective evaluations across tutorial types. Navigation strategy did not yield significant main effects, although descriptive trends pointed toward slightly higher usability and UX for linear navigation. Across all conditions, participants demonstrated clear learning gains, indicating that all tutorial variants effectively supported ADAS-related understanding. Marginal effects of tutorial format and technological affinity further suggest that both instructional design and user characteristics contribute to learning outcomes.

6.1   Interpretation of Results

The higher usability and UX of the App-Tutorial indicate that familiar mobile interfaces reduce perceived complexity and cognitive load, thereby facilitating navigation and comprehension [39] and supporting users' perceived autonomy and competence [20]. From a persuasive systems perspective, this aligns with the principle of tailoring [26], as interaction flows that match users' familiar patterns can lower cognitive effort and support engagement. According to [25], persuasive systems are most effective when they make desired behaviors easy, accessible, and intrinsically rewarding. In contrast, the HMI-Tutorial, while offering higher contextual realism, may have imposed greater cognitive load and situational distraction, potentially limiting reflective engagement. This indicates that persuasive onboarding benefits from strategic placement along the driver journey, with app-based tutorials supporting initial understanding and in-vehicle interfaces reinforcing learning in real driving contexts. This aligns with the notion that persuasive effectiveness depends on the alignment between system strategies and the users' situational context and needs [26].

Interestingly, participants in the exploratory HMI condition achieved comparatively high knowledge gains despite lower usability and UX ratings. This pattern may reflect increased cognitive engagement under higher task demands, consistent with the principle of desirable difficulties [40], which suggests that learning can benefit from effortful processing even when short-term ease and satisfaction is reduced. At the same time, the absence of significant gains in the linear HMI condition should be interpreted with caution, as post-tutorial knowledge scores were descriptively comparable across conditions and may reflect baseline variability rather than an absence of learning.

Although the navigation strategy did not yield significant main effects, descriptive trends indicated small but systematic differences. Exploratory navigation appeared to support learning among users with lower prior knowledge, indicating that autonomy-supportive interaction may enhance engagement when cognitive demands remain manageable [20]. Conversely, the linear navigation favored efficiency and clarity - especially for users with lower technical affinity - by reducing cognitive load through structured progression [31]. Together, these tendencies underline the need to balance autonomy and guidance to accommodate different user characteristics and motivational states. Overall, the results demonstrate that interactive onboarding can effectively enhance conceptual understanding of ADAS. The observed influence of tutorial context and user characteristics suggests that persuasive onboarding should be designed as a context- and user-adaptive process rather than a one-size-fits-all solution.

6.2 Design Implications for Persuasive ADAS Onboarding

Based on the empirical findings and their interpretation, synthesized with persuasive design theory, the following design implications are proposed to inform persuasive onboarding for automated driving.

1. **Leverage Familiar Platforms:** The positive evaluations of the App-Tutorial suggest that onboarding on familiar devices may provide a cognitively efficient and autonomy-supportive environment, facilitating internalization [20], particularly for early learning phases prior to first-time ADAS use.
2. **Consider Continuity across Contexts:** App-based tutorials support flexible pre-use learning, whereas in-vehicle tutorials offer contextual proximity [42]. Beyond initial use, designing onboarding as a continuous process across usage phases may therefore strengthen learning transfer and confidence.
3. **Balance Guidance and Autonomy:** Linear navigation can support clarity and efficiency through structured guidance [31], while exploratory navigation may foster autonomy and intrinsic motivation [20]. Adaptive combinations of both may better accommodate diverse user needs.
4. **Reinforce Learning through Feedback:** Integrating quizzes and progress indicators as self-monitoring mechanisms [26] may support competence development and reflective learning. This implication is theory-driven, drawing on persuasive feedback principles [25,26].
5. **Tailor Persuasive Strategies to User Profiles:** Differences in technical affinity and prior knowledge highlight the need to adapt autonomy levels and content. Tailored persuasive strategies [26] can improve motivational fit and support intended system use across diverse user groups.

Overall, these implications emphasize the role of persuasive, autonomy-supportive, feedback-oriented, and context-sensitive onboarding in promoting confident and responsible interaction with automated driving systems.

6.3 Limitations and Future Work

A key limitation of the present study is the relatively small sample size, which limits statistical power, particularly for detecting effects of navigation strategy and interaction effects. Accordingly, non-significant findings should be interpreted with caution. A further limitation concerns ecological validity. Although app-based onboarding affords temporal flexibility in real-world use, both tutorial formats were evaluated under controlled laboratory conditions to ensure internal validity and comparability. As a result, natural usage patterns, such as self-initiated engagement, could not be assessed. Furthermore, the long-term impact of the tutorials on knowledge retention and behavioral transfer remains unclear. Whereas app-based onboarding may weaken the temporal link between learning and use, contextual proximity may support learning transfer during in-vehicle onboarding [41, 42].

Future research should therefore employ longitudinal, simulator-based, and field studies to examine retention, real-world usage, and behavioral outcomes. Such investigations should also include users with lower technical affinity, who are underrepresented in the present sample but part of real-world ADAS user populations. In addition, adaptive and personalized onboarding approaches that dynamically adjust persuasive strategies to users' expertise and needs should be explored. Psychological factors such as trust, motivation, and perceived usefulness remain crucial for system acceptance [43, 44]. However, complementing subjective measures with behavioral and performance-based indicators would allow a more comprehensive assessment of user competence, as knowledge alone may not ensure sustained ADAS use.

7   Conclusion

This study shows that mobile onboarding provides an effective and engaging approach for introducing drivers to ADAS, while in-vehicle tutorials can complement this by reinforcing understanding in context. The findings highlight that persuasive onboarding is shaped by the interaction of motivational affordances and contextual usability, underscoring the importance of autonomy-supportive and cognitively accessible design. Rather than serving as a static information tool, onboarding should be conceived as a persuasive process that supports internalization, confidence, and engaged system use. Combining familiar mobile interfaces with context-sensitive in-vehicle reinforcement, augmented by adaptive strategies that are responsive to users' experience and motivational states, offers a promising direction for the future of ADAS onboarding design.

Acknowledgments. This work is a result of the joint research project STADT:up. The project is supported by the German Federal Ministry for Economic Affairs and Energy (BMWE), based on a decision of the German Bundestag. The authors are solely responsible for the content of this publication. Special thanks go to Rutuja Joshi and Anna Eckl for their insightful input and engaging discussions that contributed to the development of this work.

Disclosure of Interests. The authors have no competing interests to declare that are relevant to the content of this article. AI Tools were used for proofreading and paraphrasing.

References

1. Kyriakidis, M., et al.: A human factors perspective on automated driving. Theor. Issues Ergon. Sci. **20**(3), 223–249 (2019). https://doi.org/10.1080/1463922X.2017.1293187
2. Kim, H., Song, M., Doerzaph, Z.: Is driving automation used as intended? Real-world use of partially automated driving systems and their safety consequences. Transport. Res. Rec. **2676**, 30–37 (2022). https://doi.org/10.1177/03611981211027150
3. Oviedo-Trespalacios, O.: Beep, bleep, oops! A discussion on the misuse of advanced driver assistance systems (ADAS) and the path moving forward. In: International Conference on Vehicle Technology and Intelligent Transport Systems (VEHITS), SciTePress, pp. 410–414 (2024). https://doi.org/10.5220/0012706200003702
4. Orlovska, J., Novakazi, F., Bligård, L., Karlsson, M., Wickman, C., Söderberg, R.: Effects of the driving context on the usage of automated driver assistance systems (ADAS) – Naturalistic driving study for ADAS evaluation. Transp. Res. Interdiscip. Perspect., 100093 (2020). https://doi.org/10.1016/j.trip.2020.100093
5. Carsten, O., Martens, M.: How can humans understand their automated cars? HMI principles, problems and solutions. Cogn. Techn. Work (2019). https://doi.org/10.1007/s10111-018-0484-0
6. Casner, S., Hutchins, E.: What do we tell the drivers? Toward minimum driver training standards for partially automated cars. J. Cogn. Eng. Decis. Mak. **13**(2), 55–66 (2019). https://doi.org/10.1177/1555343419830901
7. Pongratz, V., Steckhan, L., Bengler, K.: Analyzing usage behavior and preferences of drivers regarding shared automated vehicles: Insights from an online survey. In: Harris, D., Li, W., Krömker, H. (eds.) HCI Int. 2024 – Late Breaking Papers, vol. 15381, pp. 103–121. Springer Nature, Cham (2025). https://doi.org/10.1007/978-3-031-76824-8_9
8. Nandavar, S., Kaye, S., Senserrick, T., Oviedo-Trespalacios, O.: Exploring the factors influencing acquisition and learning experiences of cars fitted with advanced driver assistance systems (ADAS). Transp. Res. Part F: Traffic Psychol. Behav. **94**, 341–352 (2023). https://doi.org/10.1016/j.trf.2023.02.006
9. Ebinger, N., Trosterer, S., Neuhuber, N., Mortl, P.: Conceptualisation and evaluation of adaptive driver tutoring for conditional driving automation. In: de Waard, D. et al. (eds.) Proceedings of the Human Factors and Ergonomics Society Chapter Annual Conference, pp. 69–81. Liverpool, UK (2023)
10. Boelhouwer, A., van den Beukel, A., van der Voort, M., Martens, M.: Should I take over? Does system knowledge help drivers in making take-over decisions while driving a partially automated car? Transp. Res. Part F: Traff. Psych. Behav. (2019). https://doi.org/10.1016/j.trf.2018.11.016
11. Forster, Y., Hergeth, S., Naujoks, F., Krems, J., Keinath, A.: User education in automated driving: Owner's manual and interactive tutorial support mental model formation and human-automation interaction. Inform. **10**(4) (2019). https://doi.org/10.3390/info10040143
12. Feinauer, S., Groh, I., Petzoldt, T.: The impact of a priori information on drivers' mental models, attitudes, and behavior in interaction with partial and conditional driving automation. Int. J. Hum. Comput. Interact. (2024). https://doi.org/10.1080/10447318.2024.2341190
13. Boelhouwer, A., van den Beukel, A., van der Voort, M., Verwey, W., Martens, M.: Supporting drivers of partially automated cars through an adaptive digital in-car tutor. Inform. **11**(4) (2020). https://doi.org/10.3390/info11040185

14. Collie, R., Martin, A.: Motivation and engagement in learning. In: Oxford Research Encyclopedia of Education. Oxford University Press (2019). https://doi.org/10.1093/acrefore/9780190264093.013.891
15. Victor, T., Tivesten, E., Gustavsson, P., Johansson, J., Sangberg, F., Aust, M.L.: Automation expectation mismatch: incorrect prediction despite eyes on threat and hands on wheel. Hum. Factors **60**(8), 1095–1116 (2018). https://doi.org/10.1177/0018720818788164
16. Zhou, H., Itoh, M., Kitazaki, S.: Effect of instructing system limitations on the intervening behavior of drivers in partial driving automation. Cogn. Technol. Work **22**, 321–334 (2020). https://doi.org/10.1007/s10111-019-00568-1
17. Stanton, N.: Thematic issue: driving automation and autonomy. Theor. Issues Ergon. Sci. **20**(3), 215–222 (2019). https://doi.org/10.1080/1463922X.2018.1541112
18. Krampell, M., Solís-Marcos, I., Hjälmdahl, M.: Driving automation state-of-mind: using training to instigate rapid mental model development. Appl. Ergon. **83**, 102986 (2020). https://doi.org/10.1016/j.apergo.2019.102986
19. Feinauer, S., Schuller, L., Groh, I., Huestege, L., Petzoldt, T.: The potential of gamification for user education in partial and conditional driving automation: a driving simulator study. Transp. Res. Part F: Psychol. Behav. **90**, 252–268 (2022). https://doi.org/10.1016/j.trf.2022.08.009
20. Ryan, R., Deci, E.: Self-determination theory and the facilitation of intrinsic motivation, social development, and well-being. Am. Psych. **55**(1), 68–78 (2000). https://doi.org/10.1037/0003-066X.55.1.68
21. Suh, A., Wagner, C., Liu, L.: Enhancing user engagement through gamification. J. Comput. Inf. Syst. **57**(3), 204–213 (2016). https://doi.org/10.1080/08874417.2016.1229143
22. Sailer, M., Hense, J.U., Mayr, S.K., Mandl, H.: How gamification motivates: an experimental study of the effects of specific game design elements on psychological need satisfaction. Comput. Hum. Behav. **69**, 371–380 (2017). https://doi.org/10.1016/j.chb.2016.12.033
23. Shrestha, S., Joshi, M., Bashyal, A., Timilsina, A.: User engagement in gamified online learning system. World J. Educ. Res. **8**(5), 46–58 (2021). https://doi.org/10.22158/wjer.v8n5p46
24. Oinas-Kukkonen, H.: A foundation for the study of behavior change support systems. Pers. Ubiquit. Comput. **17**(6), pp. 1223–1235 (2013). https://doi.org/10.1007/s00779-012-0591-5
25. Fogg, B.: Persuasive Technology: Using Computers to Change What We Think and Do. Morgan Kaufmann Publishers, San Francisco (2003)
26. Oinas-Kukkonen, H., Harjumaa, M.: Persuasive systems design: key issues, process model, and system features. Commun. Assoc. Inf. Syst. **24**, 485–500 (2009). https://doi.org/10.17705/1CAIS.02428
27. Sauer, J., Sonderegger, A., Schmutz, S.: Usability, user experience and accessibility: towards an integrative model. Ergonomics **63**(10), 1207–1220 (2020). https://doi.org/10.1080/00140139.2020.1774080
28. Oliveira, A., Eler, M.: Analyzing accessibility, usability, and user experience in mobile apps through user reviews: an extended systematic literature review. J. Interact. Syst. **16**(1), 1–25 (2025). https://doi.org/10.5753/jis.2025.5983
29. Deutsches Institut für Normung (DIN): Ergonomics of human-system interaction - Part 303: requirements for electronic visual displays (ISO 9241-303:2011). German version EN ISO 9241-303:2011. DIN Media GmbH (2012). https://doi.org/10.31030/1860631

30. Núñez, J., León, J.: Autonomy support in the classroom: a review from self-determination theory. Europ. Psych. **20**(4), 275–283 (2015). https://doi.org/10.1027/1016-9040/a000234

31. Zumbach J., Mohraz, M.: Cognitive load in hypermedia reading comprehension. Influence of text type and linearity. Comput. Hum. Behav. **24**, 875–887 (2008). https://doi.org/10.1016/j.chb.2007.02.015

32. Taub, M., Azevedo, R., Bouchet, F., Khosravifar, B.: Can the use of cognitive and metacognitive self-regulated learning strategies be predicted by learners' levels of prior knowledge in hypermedia-learning environments? Comput. Hum. Behav. **39**, 356–367 (2014). https://doi.org/10.1016/j.chb.2014.07.018

33. Brooke, J.: SUS: A 'quick and dirty' usability scale. In: Jordan, P., Thomas, B., Weerdmeester, B., McClelland, I. (eds.) Usab. Eval. Ind., pp. 189–194. Taylor & Francis, London (1996)

34. Laugwitz, B., Held, T., Schrepp, M.: Construction and evaluation of a user experience questionnaire. In: Holzinger, A. (ed.) USAB 2008. LNCS, vol. 5298, pp. 63–76. Springer, Heidelberg (2008). https://doi.org/10.1007/978-3-540-89350-9_6

35. Van der Laan, J., Heino, A., De Waard, D.: A simple procedure for the assessment of acceptance of advanced transport telematics. Transp. Res. Part C: Emerg. Technol. **5**(1), 1–10 (1997)

36. Franke, T., Attig, C., Wessel, D.: A personal resource for technology interaction: development and validation of the Affinity for Technology Interaction (ATI) scale. Int. J. Hum. Comput. Interact. (in press). https://doi.org/10.1080/10447318.2018.1456150

37. Olson, C.: Comparative robustness of six tests in multivariate analysis of variance. J. Amer. Stat. Assoc. **69**(348), 894–908 (1974). https://doi.org/10.1080/01621459.1974.10480224

38. Bangor, A., Kortum, P., Miller, J.: Determining what individual SUS scores mean: adding an adjective rating scale. J. Usab. Stud. **4**(3), 114–123 (2009)

39. Diewald, S., Möller, A., Roalter, L., Kranz, M.: Mobile device integration and interaction in the automotive domain. In: Proceedings of the 3rd International Conference on Automotive User Interfaces and Interactive Vehicular Applications (AutomotiveUI 2011), Adjunct Proceedings, Salzburg, Austria, November 29–December 2 (2011)

40. Bjork, E., Bjork, R.: Making things hard on yourself, but in a good way: creating desirable difficulties to enhance learning. In: Gernsbacher, M., Pew, R., Hough, L., Pomerantz, J. (eds.), Psychology and the real world: essays illustrating fundamental contributions to society, Worth Publishers, pp. 56–64 (2011)

41. Baldwin, T., Ford, J.: Transfer of training: a review and directions for future research. Pers. Psychol. **41**(1), 63–105 (1988). https://doi.org/10.1111/j.1744-6570.1988.tb00632.x

42. Tonhäuser, C., Büker, L.: Determinants of transfer of training: a comprehensive literature review. Int. J. Res. Vocat. Educ. Train. **3**(2), 127–165 (2016). https://doi.org/10.13152/IJRVET.3.2.4

43. Choi, J., Ji, Y.: Investigating the importance of trust on adopting an autonomous vehicle. Int. J. Hum. Comput. Interact. **31**(10), 692–702 (2015). https://doi.org/10.1080/10447318.2015.1070549

44. Buckley, L., Kaye, S., Pradhan, A.: Psychosocial factors associated with intended use of automated vehicles: a simulated driving study. Accid. Anal. Prev. **115**, 202–208 (2018). https://doi.org/10.1016/j.aap.2018.03.021

"Yes, I Will!": Expert Perspectives on Digital Support for Patient Participation in Breast Cancer Clinical Trial

Maryam R. Yeganeh[1,2]([⊠]), Samuel A. Fricker[1], and Elaine M. Huang[2]

[1] FHNW, IIT, 5201 Windisch, Switzerland
{maryam.yeganeh,samuel.fricker}@fhnw.ch, yeganeh@ifi.uzh.ch
[2] Department of Informatics, University of Zurich, Binzmühlestrasse 14, Zürich, Switzerland
huang@ifi.uzh.ch

Abstract. Decentralised clinical trials (DCTs) can span multiple countries, each with distinct healthcare systems that shape the availability of patient support services and information. These variations influence both recruitment and retention of participants. Standardised tools, such as consent forms and clinician discussions, often fail to address country-specific needs. To inform the development of a Patient Companion application as a digital support tool, this study investigates how clinicians across six European countries perceive and prioritise the factors influencing patients' decisions to enrol in and remain part of a DCT. Drawing on interviews, we examine how local healthcare conditions influence these perceptions and evaluate the applicability of evidence-based recommendations. The findings reveal notable cross-country differences in patient needs and existing support structures. Based on these insights, we identified recommendations that were validated, redundant, or missing according to local contexts. These results inform the adaptation of the Patient Companion App to better support patient participation in DCTs.

Keywords: Validation · Expert interview · Patient recruitment and retention · Clinical trials · Decision support

1 Introduction

Adults over 70 represent 42% of the total population of cancer patients but remain significantly underrepresented in clinical trials that determine treatment safety and efficacy [1]. Many older adults, particularly those with chronic conditions, hesitate to participate due to concerns about transportation, time commitments, treatment risks, and financial burdens [1, 2]. Participation in clinical trials encompasses both recruitment and retention. Recruitment involves identifying potential participants, discussing all aspects of the trial to ensure comprehension and voluntariness, obtaining informed consent, and enrolling those who meet eligibility criteria [3]. Retention refers to strategies that keep participants engaged and prevent withdrawal, emphasising respectful communication, consideration of participants' time, and timely mitigation of barriers [3].

K. Sumi et al. (Eds.): PERSUASIVE 2026, LNCS 16476, pp. 288–302, 2026.
https://doi.org/10.1007/978-3-032-19687-3_21

Recruitment challenges such as limited awareness, logistical barriers, and mistrust are major obstacles to trial success. An estimated 86% of clinical trials fail to meet enrollment goals, and 32% of Phase III trials fail due to recruitment issues [4].

Decentralised clinical trials (DCTs) were introduced to increase accessibility by reducing the need for travel to centralised sites. However, their implementation across different countries introduces new challenges stemming from structural, regulatory, and sociocultural variations [6–8]. Differences in healthcare infrastructure, financial systems, linguistic diversity, and access to local laboratories complicate standardisation and equity in patient experience, which can negatively affect recruitment and retention.

Digital technologies offer opportunities to enhance patient recruitment and retention in DCTs. With over 4.54 billion internet users worldwide, digital tools can improve outreach and reduce costs, yet most studies focus narrowly on social media, internet sites, email and tv/radio for recruitment and email and text-messaging for retention [5].

Barriers such as difficulty understanding consent forms [9], advanced age, low educational level [10], and lack of emotional or informational support [11–13] still hinder participation.

On the other hand, recent research highlights the importance of adopting approaches in clinical trials that feel more personalised, localised and participant-centred. Such approaches help individuals feel recognised not only as unique persons but also as members of the social and cultural groups with which they identify [14].

A holistic solution, such as a **Patient Companion Application** [15, 16], could foster sustained engagement and provide individualised recommendations to address these recruitment and retention problem in DCTs. Designed to adapt to local healthcare, logistical, and cultural conditions, such a tool can promote a more inclusive and navigable trial experience. This study examined patient-related factors affecting recruitment and retention of older adults in cancer DCTs through clinician interviews conducted within the IMPORTANT trial across six European countries. The validated recommendations can inform the design of a patient companion app to support the participation of older patients.

The remainder of the paper is structured as follows. Section 2 reports the work performed to identify and analyse evidence concerning patients' questions and needs in the literature. Section 3 describes the validation methodology to identify variations of how the patient's questions and needs should be served, with recommendations provided by a patient companion application in multiple contexts. Section 4 reports the results and analysis of that validation. Section 5 discusses these results. Section 6 summarises and concludes.

2 Background: Identification and Analysis of Evidence

2.1 Patient Participation in Clinical Trials

Clinical research, often synonymous with medical research, involves human participants to evaluate the safety and effectiveness of treatments—such as drugs, medical or surgical procedures, or medical devices—within patient care and management. It also includes studies exploring diseases' symptoms, risk factors, or biological mechanisms

[17]. **DCTs** are a modern evolution of clinical research that use digital technologies to address the limitations of traditional site-based models, such as geographical barriers, limited participant diversity, and logistical complexity, which often affect recruitment and retention [7].

Clinical research progresses through several **phases**: Phase I tests safety, dosage, and side effects in small groups; Phase II expands to assess efficacy and further safety; Phase III compares new treatments to standard ones in larger, diverse populations; and Phase IV monitors long-term outcomes after approval [18].

Recruitment and **Retention** of participants are essential for ensuring valid and generalisable findings—recruitment focuses on identifying, screening, and enrolling eligible patients, while retention secures their continued participation throughout the study.

2.2 Factors Affecting Patient Decisions

A patient's choice to join or remain in a clinical trial depends on personal motivations and perceived challenges [1, 2]. Several studies have examined the barriers and facilitators influencing recruitment and retention in clinical research. Among them, Sedrak et al. [1] was selected as the main reference because it provides a comprehensive overview of the key factors affecting participation, supported by primary studies offering evidence. This allowed us to extract relevant factors for analysis and trace the original studies in which these factors were first developed and reported. Even though Sedrak provided evidence for each barrier, we needed more detailed information to formulate the recommendations. As a result, we did a detailed analysis of evidence. Two authors independently reviewed all articles [20–30] cited by Sedrak et al. and systematically extracted data related to each identified factor (Table 1). The categories originated from patient questionnaires and surveys in which individuals with breast cancer described specific concerns affecting their decision to participate in or remain in clinical trials. These patient-reported statements served as the foundation for translating concerns into actionable recommendations. For instance, under "Concern about efficacy and toxicity," one statement read: *"I was concerned that the treatment offered by the clinical trial had too many side effects"* [22]. We formulated into a practical recommendation: *"What are the risks and side effects, and how will they be managed?"*.

The extracted **factors** reflect both **motivations** and **challenges**, grouped into the nine categories presented by Sedrak et al.: knowledge, transportation, time demands or burdens, efficacy and toxicity concerns, experimentation concerns, treatment preferences, finances, age (feeling too old), and emotional burden. Motivations often include expectations of personal health benefits, altruism, and contributing to scientific progress, reinforced by external elements such as trust in the research team, family influence, and clear communication [19]. Conversely, challenges arise from limited understanding of trials, difficulty interpreting consent forms, fear of side effects, distrust of experimental procedures, logistical and financial constraints, and emotional strain [1, 3, 9]. These challenges can be particularly pronounced for patients with reduced cognitive capacity, who may struggle to recall or comprehend trial-related information when making participation decisions at home.

Table 1. Factors influencing a patient's decision to participate in and remain in a clinical trial were identified in primary studies cited by the literature review (N/A indicates that the primary work did not provide relevant evidence).

Factors and Sub-factors with Motives and Challenges.
Patient Knowledge [20, 21, 22, 23, 24, 25, 26]
Cancer Treatment: <u>Motive</u>: detailed information about the cancer, treatment, risks, and side effects, consistent with internet and media sources. <u>Challenge</u>: insufficient or unclear information about the cancer and treatment.
Trial Training: <u>Motive</u>: useful information from the consent form about participating in the trial. <u>Challenge</u>: mismatch of patient cognition, trial complexity, and clarity or detail of information, bad, generic educational materials.
Training for Caregivers: Motive: N/A. <u>Challenge</u>: insufficient educational materials about the clinical trial for caregivers.
Disagreement: <u>Motive</u>: N/A. <u>Challenge</u>: insufficient educational materials about diagnosis accuracy.
Motivation: <u>Motive</u>: help future patients and advance research. <u>Challenge</u>: Lack of interest.
Patient's Mobility [20, 22, 24, 25, 26, 27]
Transportation: <u>Motive</u>: no concerns about traveling to the cancer center for treatment. <u>Challenge</u>: concerns about the difficulty of finding and traveling to the cancer center.
Transportation Cost: <u>Motive</u>: N/A. <u>Challenge</u>: struggles with transportation to clinic visits due to difficulty, cost, and affordability.
Long Distance: <u>Motive</u>: N/A. <u>Challenge</u>: conflict between distance to the trial center and care management, including transport and time issues.
Car Driving: <u>Motive</u>: N/A. <u>Challenge</u>: worries about driving in bad weather, darkness, city traffic, highways, and parking.
Compatibility with Life: <u>Motive</u>: N/A. <u>Challenge</u>: poor vision implying home care to manage treatment.
Burdens to the Patient [22, 23, 25, 26, 27, 28]
Burden to Family: <u>Motive</u>: N/A. <u>Challenge</u>: worry that joining a clinical trial may burden their family.
Time Constraints: <u>Motive</u>: N/A. <u>Challenge</u>: distance and transport to the centre are too time-consuming. Too little time to decide.
Home Assistance: <u>Motive</u>: N/A. <u>Challenge</u>: unavailability of needed home assistance for treatment or side effects,
Family Care: <u>Motive</u>: N/A. <u>Challenge</u>: inability to travel for treatment due to caregiving responsibilities or their own need for support.
Work: <u>Motive</u>: N/A. <u>Challenge</u>: lacking information on managing work situations, like medical leave options.
Treatment Efficacy and Toxicity [22, 24, 25, 26, 27, 28, 29]
Possible Benefit: <u>Motive</u>: N/A. <u>Challenge</u>: The study did not reveal any personal benefits.
Trust in Clinic: <u>Motive</u>: N/A. <u>Challenge</u>: lack of trust in the clinic's medical staff and treatment quality.
Treatments: <u>Motive</u>: N/A. <u>Challenge</u>: unsure if the treatment is suitable for their cancer.
Treatment Endurance: <u>Motive</u>: N/A. <u>Challenge</u>: comorbidities may imply limited life expectancy, additional tests, toxicity concerns, and feeling too weak for aggressive treatment.

(*continued*)

Table 1. (*continued*)

Physician's Opinion: <u>Motive</u>: N/A. <u>Challenge</u>: physician's view of a protocol arms as less effective or unacceptable.
Best Treatment: <u>Motive</u>: N/A. <u>Challenge</u>: best treatment for patient not included in the trial.
Motivation: <u>Motive</u>: potentially increased longevity or well-being. <u>Challenge</u>: N/A.
Treatment Efficacy: <u>Motive</u>: N/A. <u>Challenge</u>: concerns about the new treatment's effectiveness.
Side Effect: <u>Motive</u>: N/A. <u>Challenge</u>: fear of the new treatment's potential side effects.
Possible Benefit: <u>Motive</u>: tumor shrinkage, symptom relief, extended lifespan, better medication, improved care, or improved monitoring. <u>Challenge</u>: N/A.
Patient's Opinion about Experimentation [20, 22, 23, 25, 26, 27, 30]
Autonomy: <u>Motive</u>: N/A. <u>Challenge</u>: discomfort with research protocol dictating their treatment.
Media Information: <u>Motive</u>: N/A. <u>Challenge</u>: concerns about clinical trial participation from internet or media information.
Timing of Treatment: <u>Motive</u>: N/A. <u>Challenge</u>: worry that study requirements could delay treatment.
Eligibility: <u>Motive</u>: N/A. <u>Challenge</u>: unmet eligibility criteria.
Physician Opinion: <u>Motive</u>: N/A. <u>Challenge</u>: physician's view of a protocol arms as less effective or unacceptable.
Life Expectancy: <u>Motive</u>: N/A. <u>Challenge</u>: limited life expectancy may not justify trial participation.
Randomisation: <u>Motive</u>: N/A. <u>Challenge</u>: resistance to randomisation and fear being treated like a guinea pig.
Treatment Preferences [20, 22, 23, 25, 26, 30]
Belief in the Treatment: <u>Motive</u>: Openness to any cancer treatment. <u>Challenge</u>: uncertainty if trial treatment suits patient's cancer but might favor one arm as superior or aligning with their preference.
Belief in the Trial: <u>Motive</u>: N/A. <u>Challenge</u>: disliking of one of the treatments.
Trust in the Medical Staff: <u>Motive</u>: trust in the staff and quality of care. <u>Challenge</u>: distrust in the center's staff or treatment quality.
Personal Benefit: <u>Motive</u>: belief that a trial offers better treatment, follow-up care, and personal benefits. <u>Challenge</u>: N/A.
Encouragement: <u>Motive</u>: Family or friends' encouragement to join a clinical trial. <u>Challenge</u>: N/A.
Motivation: <u>Motive</u>: advancing cancer science and helping future generations. <u>Challenge</u>: N/A.
Burden for Family: <u>Motive</u>: N/A. <u>Challenge</u>: belief that trial participation would burden family.
Congruent Treatment: <u>Motive</u>: belief that regular cancer treatment is part of the trial. <u>Challenge</u>: N/A.
Randomisation: <u>Motive</u>: N/A. <u>Challenge</u>: strong preference for a treatment arm.
Patient's Finances [20, 22, 26, 27]
Cost Level: <u>Motive</u>: comfort with the trial's treatment cost. <u>Challenge</u>: concerns about coverage of treatment costs in a trial.
Insurance: <u>Motive</u>: N/A. <u>Challenge</u>: struggle with insurance, as some trial costs aren't covered.
Patient's Age [24, 29]
Treatment Endurance: <u>Motive</u>: age is not a key factor for patients in deciding against trial participation. <u>Challenge</u>: comorbidities and age-related health issues may imply feeling of being too weak to join a clinical trial.
Patient's Emotions [28, 26]
Overwhelmed: <u>Motive</u>: N/A. <u>Challenge</u>: being overwhelmed, sad, and anxious about starting treatment.

We identified several inconsistencies and missing details in Sedrak's reporting of certain factors. For example, within the category *Burden to the patient* [20], we found additional statements omitted from Sedrak's review, which we incorporated into this study. In some cases, patient motivations were clearly indicated in the original sources, while in others they were not; when no motivation was provided, we marked it as "N/A" in the table.

2.3 Recommendations for Supporting Patients' Decisions

Within the framework of the EU Horizon IMPORTANT project, we developed recommendations based on the identified categories to address patients' motives and challenges when deciding to join or remain in a clinical trial. This process involved assessing the feasibility of providing different types of information and services, such as details about specific treatments, transport solutions, and insurance coverage for each location.

In regard to the IMPORTANT project, we identified five key sources of patient-support information and services: the trial sponsor, clinical-site clinicians, and patient representatives in the Breast Cancer Association (BCA). These actors contribute essential local knowledge about the trial setting, healthcare system, transport availability, and broader environmental factors. Their input was crucial for validating and adapting the recommendations to ensure local relevance and practicality.

Table 2 demonstrates the complete set of patient-support recommendations, formulated from the extracted empirical evidence in primary studies cited by Sedrak et al. [1]. Although these factors were previously recognised by clinicians and patients as influencing participation decisions, they have not yet been validated for use across different locations. The earlier formulation also followed a "one-size-fits-all" model, lacking consideration of country- or site-specific variations.

Table 2. Recommendations

R01: Information on your cancer; R02: Information on state-of-the-art treatment; R03: Information on the new treatment; R04: How the clinical trial works; R05: Share your questions or concerns here with the medical staff involved in the trial; R06: What the risks and side effects are and how they will be managed; R07: What the clinical trial team will expect from you; R08: Consent form in simple language; R09: What the clinical trial team will expect from you; R10: Treatment-specific training recommendations (e.g. Geriatric assessment needs training. For getting help, please contact the nurse study.); R11: Trial step-specific training recommendations; R12: Caregiver-specific training recommendations; R13: How the clinical trial will help cancer patients in the future; R14: Get to know other patients who participated in earlier clinical trials; R15: Get to know professionals who could assist you as caregivers; R16: How to reach the clinical centre by car; R17: How to reach the hospital by public transport; R18: How to reach the hospital by different means; R19: How to reach the hospital by taxi; R20: How to get your taxi costs reimbursed; R21: How to get your public transport ticket reimbursed; R22: How to reach the hospital for free by different means; R23: How to get the stay-over costs reimbursed; R24: How to stay over at the hospital; R25: How to benefit from care at home; R26: How to benefit from telecare; R27: Information on having others accompany you at the hospital; R28: How to do remote work when you stay at the hospital; R29: Call for assistance; R30: Information on potential benefits of participating in a clinical trial; R31: It only takes (e.g.) 30 minutes to get there, follow this link to see on the map; R32: Information on remote treatment session; R33: Consider creating a care schedule to share responsibilities among family and friends; R34: Join a support group for discussing how to manage the family; R35: Information on local caregiving services; R36: Information on options for medical leave, disability benefits, or flexible work arrangements with your employer or a social worker; R37: To reduce the time it takes to reach the clinical site, we recommend using a special taxi service; R38: Consult with a breast cancer association to get help with the decision-making process; R39: More information on your current symptoms; R40: Information on the side effects of this treatment; R41: Detailed explanation of this randomised clinical trial for your private physician; R42: Discuss with your doctor the specific potential benefits and risks of the study, as well as any personal health improvements you might experience; R43: More information on alternative clinical sites; R44: Information on the best possible treatment for your cancer; R45: Information on the side effects of this treatment considering the age; R46: Talk to your physician about how the trial might improve quality of life or offer future benefits; R47: Information on the benefits and side effects of this treatment compared to other treatments; R48: Potential benefit of joining a clinical trial; R49: More information on the timing of the treatment in the clinical trial. R50: More information on randomisation R51: More information on the timing of the treatment in the clinical trial compared to regular treatment R52: Join the support group and share your strategy with other patients R53: More information on all possible treatments for your cancer and comparison with this treatment R54: Learn about the types of follow-ups that you will receive by joining this clinical trial compared to standard treatment R55: Learn about the benefit of joining this clinical trial compared to other treatments R56: Learn about the types of follow-ups that you will receive by joining this clinical trial R57: How to get an appointment to enroll on the trial R58: More information on all possible treatments for your cancer R59: More information on the financial coverage of the clinical trial R60: Seek support from a breast cancer association or support group to help manage emotional challenges R61: Contact local home health agencies or cancer support organisations for potential support R62: Clinical trials often provide additional support and resources that can ease the burden on families.

3   Validation of the Recommendations

This study aimed to validate recommendations for supporting patients considering participation in a clinical trial and to examine how barriers and influencing factors are prioritised across different countries. To achieve this, we conducted an embedded multi-case study [31] within the EU Horizon IMPORTANT project, where each of the six participating countries represented one embedded case. This design ensured representation at both country and site levels, enabling the analysis of variations across clinics and healthcare contexts.

Data were collected through interviews with clinicians, trial coordinators, and representatives of BCA. These experts provided insights into how patients are supported in decision-making and how recommendations could be refined to ensure completeness, feasibility, and alignment with local healthcare practices. Their professional experience added depth to the validation process by confirming the practicality and contextual relevance of the recommendations.

Research Question. To identify meaningful recommendations for patients deciding whether to join or remain in a trial, we sought to understand the factors shaping their decisions through a review and analysis of published evidence. Accordingly, RQ1 asked: *"What factors affect a patient's decisions to join and stay in a clinical trial?"* This question was addressed by identifying and systematically analysing primary studies reporting these factors. RQ2: *"How can a digital patient companion address recruitment and retention challenges in older adults with cancer, and what kinds of personalised support are feasible, appropriate, and locally relevant?".*

Case Selection. The study was embedded within the EU Horizon IMPORTANT project, which had begun recruiting its first patients during data collection. The trial followed a pragmatic design combining on-site clinic visits with extended off-site participation at home, reflecting common features of modern decentralised clinical trials. It involved clinics in six countries—Finland (1 site), Norway (1), Sweden (2), Italy (2), Greece (1), and Spain (1), and a member of a Breast Cancer Association (BCA) providing a diverse range of healthcare systems, services, and patient support practices (Table 3).

Table 3. Formulated recommendations based on extracted data in relation to Sedrak et al. factors.

Provider	Knowledge	Transportation	Burdens to the Patient	Efficacy and toxicity	Patient Opinion on Experiment	Treatment Preference	Finance	Age	Emotion
Trial	R03, R04, R06, R08, R09, R11, R12, R14	R21, R22, R24, R26, R27, R28	R31	R14, R40, R41, R43, R44, R46, R47, R49	R46, R47, R42, R50, R51, R52, R55	R14, R31, R44, R51, R54, R55, R56, R57, R58, R63	R60	R46, R47	

(continued)

Table 3. (*continued*)

Provider	Knowledge	Transportation	Burdens to the Patient	Efficacy and toxicity	Patient Opinion on Experiment	Treatment Preference	Finance	Age	Emotion
Hospital	R05, R16	R17, R18, R19, R20, R22, R24, R25, R26, R27, R28, R29, R30	R18, R19, R20, R32, R33, R37	R43, R47	R47	R58	R60, R61	R47	
BCA	R15		R34, R35, R39	R15		R53, R61			R62

Participant Selection. We interviewed eight clinicians—at least one from each participating country—and one representative of Breast Cancer Association. We collected related patient information materials. Each clinician had direct experience in clinical trial implementation, patient recruitment, and retention. The experts represented two perspectives: some were involved in both trial design and hospital-based delivery, offering insights that linked research and everyday care, while others focused primarily on patient treatment within oncology services. At the start of each interview, participants identified their role as "Trial" or "Hospital."

Data Collection and Materials. Data were gathered through 90-min semi-structured interviews using a structured recommendations grid to assess the relevance and localisation of 62 patient-support recommendations (Table 2). The grid, implemented on an online collaborative whiteboard, displayed recommendations as sticky notes organised by category (e.g., Knowledge, Transportation) and provider type (e.g., Trial, Hospital). During the interview, clinicians annotated, colour-coded, and reorganised notes in real time while answering key questions such as: "Who provides this information or service in your context?" and "Is this recommendation relevant locally?" The sessions concluded with a discussion of ethical and compliance aspects in applying the recommendations within DCTs. Participants received the grid beforehand and could share documentation on related local services.

Data Analysis. Interviews were transcribed using the offline Whisper speech-recognition model [32] to ensure data privacy and anonymised before analysis. Following a framework analysis approach [33], clinician responses were directly mapped onto the structured grid used during interviews. Colour-coded annotations indicated each recommendation's validation status—confirmed, modified, removed, or missing—and served as the main analytical units. While one researcher led the analysis, interpretations were regularly reviewed by co-authors to ensure consistency and transparency. This deductive, matrix-based method enabled systematic comparison across the six countries and identification of localisation patterns relevant to DCT implementation. We assessed each recommendation for its validity and relevance and reviewed the set to identify any gaps or missing components.

3.1 Threats to Validity

Several validity threats were considered in this case-study research, including construct, internal, and external validity, as well as reliability [31].

Construct Validity. Clinicians might have interpreted certain terms differently from how we intended. To ensure a common understanding, we used interactive interviews and triangulated responses with supporting documentation from patient and caregiver materials.

Internal Validity. Social desirability and retrospective bias could have influenced responses, and clinicians' perspectives may not fully reflect patient experiences. To minimise these risks, we cross-checked interview data with patient-facing materials and included a patient association representative to broaden viewpoints. Future research should involve direct patient interviews to validate these findings.

External Validity. The limited number of experts, all connected to the same international DCT, may constrain generalisability. We mitigated this by including clinicians from several European countries with differing clinical practices, though results may not extend beyond these contexts. Replication in other countries and trials is recommended.

Reliability. Risks of inconsistent data collection and subjective analysis were reduced through a standardised interview protocol, a case study database, and consensus among co-authors. A clear chain of evidence linking data, analysis, and conclusions further supports reliability.

4 Result and Analysis

The following section presents the core findings derived from the interview. These reflect the clinician's perspective on key barriers, support needs, and contextual factors influencing older adults' participation in clinical trials. For a full overview of the validated recommendations and detailed mappings to information providers, please refer to the Appendix[1].

4.1 Overview of Cases

Case 1, Finland: This case draws on the perspective of a medical oncologist involved in both hospital-based care and clinical trial activities. The interview was marked by a generally helpful and open attitude. His input clarified how support systems for the patient companion functioned within the Finnish healthcare context.

Case 2, Norway: This case draws on the perspective of a medical oncologist in Norway, engaged in both hospital-based care and the clinical trial. He approached the discussion with openness and a willingness to explore the proposed ideas. Norway was described as highly digitalised, with widespread digital literacy among patients and well-integrated communication tools already in use, including encrypted email systems and

---

[1] https://osf.io/76vqb/files/4s273.

direct messaging with nursing staff via a specific app. Within this context, the expert noted that many proposed features of the application were already addressed through existing infrastructure, suggesting limited added value in the current system.

Case 3, Sweden: This case draws on insights from a medical oncologist in Sweden who was actively involved in both oncology care and clinical trial coordination. Serving as a coordinator and sponsor for the DCT discussed during the interview, he provided detailed and well-contextualised information, particularly regarding trial components such as the consent form and protocol. His contributions were grounded in direct experience, offering specificity and clarity that contrasted with more general comments in other interviews. His engagement throughout the discussion reflected a collaborative and supportive stance toward the proposed digital intervention.

Case 4, Sweden2: This case draws on the perspective of a senior medical oncologist in Sweden who served as both principal investigator and hospital representative. He highlighted patient knowledge as the most significant barrier, noting that older adults often require simpler explanations and that treatment preferences are frequently shaped by misunderstandings. He also emphasised the need for balanced, clear information about side effects, trial procedures, and randomisation, explaining that overly complex or overly positive wording can confuse patients or raise concerns with ethics committees. He described the enrollment phase as particularly challenging, as patients may become uncertain after discussing the study with family members. He viewed the digital companion as potentially helpful by providing consistent answers between visits. In Sweden, mobility and finances are less problematic, while perceived burden and concerns about toxicity matter more. He also highlighted the central role of study nurses and contact nurses in supporting patients throughout the process. Overall, his input stressed communication clarity and decision-making support as key factors for trial participation.

Case 5, Italy: This case draws on the perspective of a medical oncologist in Italy, involved in both hospital-based care and clinical trial work. Her reflections highlighted the time constraints and high workload faced by oncology teams, which she viewed as a barrier to introducing tools such as a digital companion application. Initially, she expressed concern about the feasibility of implementation in an already demanding environment. However, as the interview progressed and the application's specifics were discussed, she acknowledged its potential value, particularly if introduced gradually and during less clinically intense periods.

Case 6, Italy2: This case draws on the perspective of a medical oncologist in Italy who provided practical, experience-based recommendations for supporting older adults in clinical trials. He noted that patients can access services such as ambulance transport, nearby laboratory testing, and medication delivery when coordinated through their physician. He also emphasised the value of giving family doctors clear information about the trial's design, requirements, and potential toxicity.

A key theme was patients' limited understanding of clinical trials, especially randomisation, which many perceive as "flipping a coin."

Case 7, Greece: This case draws on the perspective of a medical oncologist based in Greece, engaged in both hospital-based care and clinical trial activities. Her insights reflected the dual realities of patient care and research, particularly concerning older adults with cancer. She noted that some older patients had limited digital literacy and often relied on informal access to their physicians, including private phone numbers, which might reduce the perceived need for digital tools. As the interview developed, her perspective shifted toward a more exploratory view of how such tools could offer value in certain situations.

Case 8, Spain: This case drew on the perspective of a medical oncologist based in Spain, representing the hospital setting. Throughout the interview, she raised thoughtful concerns about the practical integration of digital tools within existing oncology care workflows. Her responses reflected a preference for established, interpersonal modes of interaction, and there was little indication that the discussion altered her initial view of the application's relevance in her setting.

Case 9, Swedish Breast Cancer Association: This case draws on insights from a representative of the Swedish Breast Cancer Association, offering a patient-advocacy perspective on clinical trial participation. The interview was marked by openness and careful reflection, particularly regarding how information is communicated to older adults. She emphasised the importance of clear, non-technical wording—highlighting that terms like "experiment" or "efficacy" can confuse or worry patients—and stressed that patient knowledge is foundational for informed decision-making. She noted that Swedish patient organisations primarily support patients through information materials, peer-support contacts, and local group meetings. These groups can help patients share experiences, although participation varies, especially among those with metastatic disease. She also confirmed that associations act as a "second line" of guidance, helping patients find local services or resources when hospital pathways are unclear. However, mobility support (e.g., transport services) falls outside their role and is handled by healthcare or municipal systems. Regarding treatment preferences and toxicity concerns, she explained that the association cannot provide medical advice or compare treatments, but can reinforce concepts like shared decision-making and direct patients toward reliable information. She also cautioned that digital platforms may be challenging for older adults with cognitive or treatment-related difficulties, though simple features like anonymous chat could be feasible. In summary, her contributions highlighted the association's role in information, psychosocial support, and patient guidance, while clarifying boundaries— particularly that medical explanations, toxicity counselling, and mobility support remain the responsibility of clinical staff or third-party services.

5 Discussion

This study demonstrated that patient support for deciding whether to join or remain in a clinical trial varies across contexts and should be adapted accordingly. Much of the evidence reported by Sedrak et al. [1] proved applicable to all embedded cases, and most recommendations derived from retrospective studies were confirmed by clinicians and the patient association as accurate and suitable for prospective decision support. The validation process ensured consistency with expert perceptions of patient needs, removed redundancies, and filled gaps by adding missing recommendations.

This study shows that support needs for older adults considering clinical trial participation vary not only by individual patient characteristics but also markedly across national and cultural contexts. While many barriers identified in prior research remain broadly applicable, our cross-country comparison reveals that how these barriers manifest—and how they are prioritised—differs substantially between healthcare systems. These findings align with emerging evidence emphasising the importance of participant-centred and culturally responsive trial practices, including the use of linguistically accessible and personally meaningful communication materials.

By analysing clinicians' and patient representatives' perspectives across multiple countries, this study contributes a more culturally attuned understanding of decision-making challenges in decentralised and pragmatic clinical trials. The findings reinforce the need for adaptable support systems that can align with local practices, address culturally specific concerns, and integrate seamlessly into existing care pathways.

Overall, this study advances understanding of patient participation in clinical trials by producing a more contextually tailored set of recommendations. The validation across diverse European settings revealed regional contrasts in patient needs and demonstrated how local service ecosystems can enhance informed decision-making, recruitment, and retention. This paper discusses how these empirically validated, cross-country differences inform the persuasive design of a Patient Companion application, aligning technological choices with local healthcare contexts.

6 Conclusion

We reviewed the literature and identified 62 factors influencing patients' decisions to join or remain in clinical trials. Drawing on Sedrak et al. [1], these factors were grouped into nine categories and linked to the relevant providers of information and services. Factors identified in retrospective studies were then translated into patient support recommendations intended for prospective delivery through a patient companion application. The recommendations were validated through interviews with clinicians and patient representatives from a real clinical trial. Participants evaluated the recommendations' validity and completeness based on their local contexts and experience. While many were confirmed, others required adaptation or removal to reflect differences in healthcare systems, digital infrastructure, and patient priorities. The analysis highlighted marked cross-country variation in factors such as language, knowledge, mobility support, and financial conditions, emphasising the importance of a localised, context-sensitive approach to patient support.

Acknowledgements. This research was supported by the European Union's Horizon Europe research and innovation programme under grant agreement No 101104589 and by the Swiss State Secretariat for Education, Research and Innovation (SERI) under subsidy agreement No 23.00218.

The authors also thank David Kern and Mia Braunwalder for their contributions to the patient companion design.

References

1. Sedrak, M.S., et al.: Older adult participation in cancer clinical trials: a systematic review of barriers and interventions. CA Cancer J. Clin. **71**(1), 78–92 (2021). https://doi.org/10.3322/caac.21638

2. Forsat, N.D., Palmowski, A., Palmowski, Y., Boers, M., Buttgereit, F.: Recruitment and retention of older people in clinical research: a systematic literature review. J. Am. Geriatr. Soc. **68**(12), 2955–2963 (2020). https://doi.org/10.1111/jgs.16875

3. Chaudhari, N., Ravi, R., Gogtay, N.J., Thatte, U.M.: Recruitment and retention of the participants in clinical trials: challenges and solutions. Perspect. Clin. Res. **11**(2), 64–69 (2020). https://doi.org/10.4103/picr.PICR_206_19

4. Kasahara, A., Mitchell, J., Yang, J., Cuomo, R.E., McMann, T.J., Mackey, T.K.: Digital technologies used in clinical trial recruitment and enrollment including application to trial diversity and inclusion: a systematic review. Digit. Health **10**, 20552076241242390 (2024). https://doi.org/10.1177/20552076241242390

5. Frampton, G.K., Shepherd, J., Pickett, K., et al.: Digital tools for the recruitment and retention of participants in randomised controlled trials: a systematic map. Trials **21**, 478 (2020). https://doi.org/10.1186/s13063-020-04358-3

6. Petrini, C., Mannelli, C., Riva, L., Gainotti, S., Gussoni, G.: Decentralized clinical trials (DCTs): a few ethical considerations. Front. Public Health **10**, 1081150 (2022). https://doi.org/10.3389/fpubh.2022.1081150

7. Girardin, J.-L., Seixas, A.A.: The value of decentralized clinical trials: Inclusion, accessibility, and innovation. Science **385**, eadq4994 (2024). https://doi.org/10.1126/science.adq4994

8. de Jong, A.J., et al.: Opportunities and challenges for decentralized clinical trials: European regulators' perspective. Clin. Pharmacol. Ther. **112**, 344–352 (2022). https://doi.org/10.1002/cpt.2628

9. Cooke, C., Erickson, S., Watkins, T., Matthay, M., Hudson, L., Rubenfeld, G.D.: Age-, sex-, and race-based differences among patients enrolled versus not enrolled in acute lung injury clinical trials. Crit. Care Med. **38**, 1450–1457 (2010)

10. Nguyen, Y.H.T., Dang, T.T., Lam, N.B.H., et al.: Fragmented understanding: exploring the practice and meaning of informed consent in clinical trials in Ho Chi Minh City, Vietnam. BMC Med. Ethics **24**(3) (2023). https://doi.org/10.1186/s12910-023-00884-2

11. McMurdo, M., et al.: Improving recruitment of older people to research through good practice. Age Ageing **40**(6), 659–665 (2011). https://doi.org/10.1093/ageing/afr115

12. Sawka, C., Pritchard, K.: Can improved communication increase patient participation in randomised clinical trials? Eur. J. Cancer **37**(3), 297–299 (2001)

13. Riedl, D., Schüßler, G.: The influence of doctor-patient communication on health outcomes: a systematic review. Z. Psychosom. Med. Psychother. **63**(2), 131–150 (2017)

14. Bodicoat, D.H., Routen, A.C., Willis, A., et al.: Promoting inclusion in clinical trials—a rapid review of the literature and recommendations for action. Trials **22**, 880 (2021). https://doi.org/10.1186/s13063-021-05849-7

15. Yeganeh, M.R., Fricker, S.A.: Vision for a digital service to facilitate recruitment and retention of older patients in clinical trials. In: IEEE 32nd International Requirements Engineering Conf. Workshops (REW), Reykjavik, pp. 390–395. IEEE (2024). https://doi.org/10.1109/REW61692.2024.00061

16. Yeganeh, M.R., Fricker, S.A.: Towards personalised digital support: clinician perspectives on patient recruitment and retention in decentralised clinical trials. In: Proceedings of the 33rd IEEE International Requirements Engineering Conference Workshops (REW 2025), Valencia, Spain, pp. 578–587 (2025). https://doi.org/10.1109/REW66121.2025.00086

17. Kandi, V., Vadakedath, S.: Clinical trials and clinical research: a comprehensive review. Cureus **15**(2), e35077 (2023). https://doi.org/10.7759/cureus.35077

18. Cingi, C., Muluk, N.B.: Quick Guide to Good Clinical Practice: How to Meet International Quality Standard in Clinical Research. 1st edn. Springer, Cham (2016). https://doi.org/10.1007/978-3-319-44344-7

19. Anastasi, J.K., Capili, B., Norton, M., McMahon, D.J., Marder, K.: Recruitment and retention of clinical trial participants: Understanding motivations of patients with chronic pain and other populations. Front. Pain Res. (Lausanne) **4**, 1330937 (2024). https://doi.org/10.3389/fpain.2023.1330937

20. Kornblith, A.B., Kemeny, M., Peterson, B.L., et al.: Survey of oncologists' perceptions of barriers to accrual of older patients with breast carcinoma to clinical trials. Cancer **95**, 989–996 (2002)

21. Moore, D.H., Kauderer, J.T., Bell, J., Curtin, J.P., Van Le, L.: An assessment of age and other factors influencing protocol versus alternative treatments for patients with epithelial ovarian cancer referred to member institutions: a Gynecologic Oncology Group study. Gynecol. Oncol. **94**, 368–374 (2004)

22. Javid, S.H., Unger, J.M., Gralow, J.R., et al.: A prospective analysis of the influence of older age on physician and patient decision-making when considering enrollment in breast cancer clinical trials (SWOG S0316). Oncologist **17**, 1180–1190 (2012)

23. Hamaker, M.E., Seynaeve, C., Nortier, J.W.R., et al.: Slow accrual of elderly patients with metastatic breast cancer in the Dutch multicentre OMEGA study. Breast **22**, 556–559 (2013)

24. Ayodele, O., Akhtar, M., Konenko, A., et al.: Comparing attitudes of younger and older patients towards cancer clinical trials. J. Geriatr. Oncol. **7**, 162–168 (2016)

25. Prieske, K., Trillsch, F., Oskay-Ozcelik, G., et al.: Participation of elderly gynecological cancer patients in clinical trials. Arch. Gynecol. Obstet. **298**, 797–804 (2018)

26. Freedman, R.A., Dockter, T.J., Lafky, J.M., et al.: Promoting accrual of older patients with cancer to clinical trials: an Alliance for Clinical Trials in Oncology member survey (A171602). Oncologist **23**, 1016–1023 (2018)

27. Basche, M., Baron, A.E., Eckhardt, S.G., et al.: Barriers to enrollment of elderly adults in early-phase cancer clinical trials. J. Oncol. Pract. **4**, 162–168 (2008)

28. Puts, M.T.E., Monette, J., Girre, V., et al.: Participation of older newly diagnosed cancer patients in an observational prospective pilot study: an example of recruitment and retention. BMC Cancer **9**, 277 (2009)

29. Townsley, C.A., Chan, K.K., Pond, G.R., Marquez, C., Siu, L.L., Straus, S.E.: Understanding the attitudes of the elderly towards enrolment into cancer clinical trials. BMC Cancer **6**, 34 (2006)

30. Kemeny, M.M., Peterson, B.L., Kornblith, A.B., et al.: Barriers to clinical trial participation by older women with breast cancer. J. Clin. Oncol. **21**, 2268–2275 (2003)

31. Yin, R.K.: Case Study Research and Applications: Design and Methods, 6th edn. Sage, Thousand Oaks (2018)

32. Radford, A., Kim, J.W., Xu, T., Brockman, G., McLeavey, C., Sutskever, I.: Robust speech recognition via large-scale weak supervision. In: *Proc. 40th Int. Conf. Mach. Learn. (ICML'23)*, Art. no. 1182, pp. 1–27. ACM, Honolulu (2023)

33. Gale, N.K., Heath, G., Cameron, E., et al.: Using the framework method for the analysis of qualitative data in multi-disciplinary health research. BMC Med. Res. Methodol. **13**, 117 (2013). https://doi.org/10.1186/1471-2288-13-117

Narrative Suggestion: An Implicit Corrective Feedback Method for Foreign Language Learning with Role-Playing AI Chatbots

Elijah Nicolo Rosario and Ethel Ong[(✉)]

College of Computer Studies, De La Salle University, Manila, Philippines
{elijah_rosario,ethel.ong}@dlsu.edu.ph

Abstract. Role-playing AI chatbots have emerged as effective tools for foreign language learning, providing engaging conversational practice in judgment-free environments. However, current iterations face a critical gap wherein they cannot provide corrective feedback without first disrupting the learner's immersion in role-play. This study introduces *Narrative Suggestion*, a new implicit corrective feedback approach that embeds grammatical corrections in collaborative storytelling suggestions, keeping learners engaged in role-playing rather than shifting their focus to grammatical instruction. Through comparative evaluation against traditional implicit corrective feedback using a web application, we assessed 17 language learners across engagement, immersion, and correction visibility metrics through our three-component *Activity-Integrated Feedback* framework based on persuasive design principles. Results demonstrate that Narrative Suggestion significantly outperforms Conversational Recasts in engagement (24.1% more chat turns, Cohen's $d = 1.302$) and learner preferences for *Activity Enhancement* ($d = -0.61$) and *Immersion Preservation* ($d = -0.79$). Qualitative analysis also revealed proficiency level as a critical factor for *Correction Visibility* wherein beginner learners still preferred more explicit corrective feedback for clarity. These findings validate our framework and method, providing theoretical and practical foundations for designing future persuasive corrective feedback systems in AI-mediated language learning environments.

Keywords: Artificial Intelligence · Chatbot · Foreign Language Learning · Role-Play · Corrective Feedback · Collaborative Storytelling

1 Introduction

Artificial intelligence has created new ways in which language learners can acquire foreign languages, with chatbots emerging as increasingly popular tools for conversational practice [1–3]. Chatbots address several limitations of traditional language learning methods by providing learners with judgment-free practice environments, consistent availability, and the ability to immerse through

K. Sumi et al. (Eds.): PERSUASIVE 2026, LNCS 16476, pp. 303–317, 2026.
https://doi.org/10.1007/978-3-032-19687-3_22

role-playing [4–6]. *Role-playing* involves learners acting out scenarios in order to practice the language in different contexts. This language learning technique has been recognized as effective for building fluency as it lets foreign language learners rehearse various interactions in a low pressure environment [6,7]. Recent research has also shown that learners demonstrate higher engagement and enjoyment when role-playing and conversing with AI chatbots compared to conventional tutoring systems and human peers [8–10].

However, a critical limitation emerges, which is their inherent inability to provide corrective feedback on learners' linguistic errors without first disrupting the learner's immersion in the role-play. While traditional language learning chatbots incorporate explicit corrective feedback mechanisms by directly pointing out errors and providing corrections, such approaches conflict with the immersive nature of role-playing. Proposed solutions focusing on external correction modules such as pop-up grammar checkers or separate tutor chatbots show that GUI-based corrections are less disruptive than chatbot-delivered explicit feedback [11,12], but these approaches can still interrupt the role-playing experience by shifting learners' attention away from the narrative context toward explicit grammatical instruction.

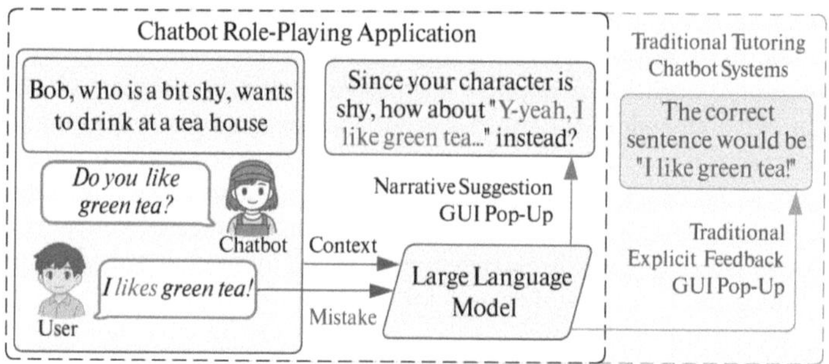

Fig. 1. Example instance of an AI tutor powered by a Large Language Model (LLM) providing corrective feedback to a user's grammatical error using the new Narrative Suggestion vs. traditional explicit feedback approaches.

The field of foreign language acquisition has extensively studied *implicit corrective feedback* methods to further maintain the learner's engagement but no research has examined how such feedback techniques perform specifically within contexts involving role-playing with AI chatbots, nor whether alternative approaches might be more suitable for text-based AI language learning systems [13,14]. This study introduces and evaluates a new implicit approach for role-playing language learning contexts with AI chatbots called *Narrative Suggestion*, rooted in pedagogical theories and persuasive technology principles, reframing triggered grammatical corrections as suggestions for improving the storytelling and character portrayal aspects of the narrative instead, as illustrated in Fig. 1. This method aims to keep the language learner's engagement in the role-playing activity with the AI chatbot rather than causing attention shifts towards correction that may cause loss of immersion and focus [15, 16].

2   Related Works

Here, we review existing relevant literature on corrective feedback systems powered by AI, and different implicit correction strategies used in foreign language learning. We also examine how *collaborative storytelling* can be related to our proposed Narrative Suggestion approach.

2.1   Corrective Feedback in AI-Powered Language Learning Systems

Current methodologies for delivering corrective feedback within AI-assisted language learning platforms, specifically those with chatbots role-playing as human tutors or conversation partners such as *Duolingo Max* and *Speak*, predominantly feature explicit correction techniques. These systems often utilize *Graphical User Interface* (GUI) text pop-ups or direct messages from the chatbot itself. Comparative research on either approach indicate that learners prefer receiving feedback through GUI interfaces, as corrections directly from the chatbot were found to heighten frustration and interrupt the conversational flow [11, 12].

Such findings suggest that the separation or reduction of corrective feedback from conversational flow can lead to a more engaging language learning experience. While GUI text pop-ups lessen the disruptive impact of feedback, in the form of explicit correction, it still shifts the learner's focus from the communicative context to grammatical instruction, which can diminish the immersive advantages that make role-playing a potent tool for language acquisition, motivating the need for a more implicit approach.

2.2   Explicit vs. Implicit Corrective Feedback

The distinction between explicit and implicit corrective feedback has been extensively studied in foreign language acquisition research. While *explicit feedback* directly indicates errors and provides corrections, *implicit feedback* offers corrections without signaling that an error has occurred.

Recent studies reveal that implicit corrective feedback, particularly recasts, offer significant advantages over explicit corrective feedback within *communicative language learning* contexts, particularly in maintaining natural conversation flow during practice drills [17]. It was also demonstrated in a study of Mandarin tone production that learners receiving implicit feedback showed greater improvement compared to those receiving explicit feedback, with both learners and instructors expressing preference for recast-based corrections as well [18]. However, research indicates that beginner learners often benefit more from explicit corrective feedback due to their limited linguistic knowledge and reduced ability to notice subtle corrections [13, 14].

While extensive research has compared explicit versus implicit feedback, significantly fewer studies examine the relative effectiveness of different implicit methods [13]. This gap is further pronounced in language learning computer systems where various implicit approaches may perform differently, especially in text-based AI interactions that usually have no auditory features.

Different Implicit Corrective Feedback Approaches. Implicit feedback methods include *Repetition, Clarification Requests,* and other similar metalinguistic cues that simply provide hints about an error without explicit correction, as illustrated in Table 1 [19–21]. Recasts represent a widely used form of implicit corrective feedback, involving reformulations that provide correct forms while maintaining conversational flow [13].

Table 1. Examples of Corrective Feedback given a Grammatically Incorrect Phrase "**Kiko *like* mango milk tea**", with Proposed Narrative Suggestion

Feedback Type	Example
Explicit Correction	Your subject–verb agreement is wrong; it should be: "Kiko *likes* mango milk tea."
Clarification Request	Sorry, I didn't understand, could you repeat that?
Repetition	"Kiko *like* mango milk tea"? *(interrogative tone)*
Didactic Recast	"Kiko *likes* mango milk tea." *(declarative tone)*
Conversational Recast	Oooh, so Kiko likes mango milk tea, right.
Narrative Suggestion	Hmm... considering Lilim's personality, she might have stuttered: "K-Kiko *likes* m-mango milk tea..."

While recasts have shown effectiveness in human-to-human interaction, they may be less suitable for text-based AI systems where audible cues are unavailable. While a *Didactic Recast* requires intonation which text-based systems do not possess, *Conversational Recast* incorporates correction within natural conversation progression without the need for audio cues, making it a more suitable implicit corrective feedback choice for the majority of AI-based role-playing systems which are text-based [11]. Examples are shown in Table 1 wherein the grammatically incorrect "I *likes* tea" is recast as "Oh, so you *like* tea!".

Despite these different approaches, there is a lack of research for implicit feedback methods involving role-playing contexts with AI chatbots, motivating the exploration of both existing implicit corrective feedback and new corrective feedback methods within that domain.

2.3   Collaborative Storytelling in Language Learning

Collaborative storytelling is a co-constructed narrative process in which two or more participants jointly create and develop a story through interactive dialogue, with each participant building upon each other's contribution. Role-playing is considered a form of collaborative storytelling wherein learners also embody the characters within the narrative, emphasizing more on in-character dialogue and conversational practice.

In the context of language learning, collaborative storytelling has been identified as a highly effective pedagogical strategy. This joint exercise encourages active participation, even from learners with lower proficiency, such as children, who might be more passive in traditional classroom settings, as they consider it to be recreational activity. By engaging in collaborative storytelling, learners can boost their self-regulated learning, interaction, and motivation [22,23]. Studies also show that AI can easily generate dynamic content for various stories and role-playing scenarios, which makes the learning experience more interactive and engaging for language learners [24,25].

These findings suggest that feedback mechanisms integrating collaborative storytelling principles with implicit correction may enhance both engagement and learning effectiveness. The proposed *Narrative Suggestion* approach leverages this integration by embedding corrective feedback within narrative enhancement suggestions, addressing both linguistic accuracy and role-play quality simultaneously without interrupting the role-playing experience with AI.

3 Theoretical Framework

The effectiveness of corrective feedback in role-playing language learning contexts can be understood through several established theories and hypotheses that address cognitive processing and affective factors:

- **Cognitive Load Theory** [26,27] states that in order to maximize learning, instructional methods must minimize distractions and unnecessary information as humans have limited working memory. In role-playing language learning, learners have to simultaneously manage character portrayal and foreign language production, and traditional explicit feedback can further increase this cognitive load by forcing attention shifts between narrative engagement and grammatical instruction, affecting the learning effectiveness of role-playing. This load can be minimized by using implicit feedback instead which allows learners to internalize corrections while staying engaged, reducing the need to consciously stop and shift focus before resuming role-playing.
- **The Affective Filter Theory** [28] suggests that emotions such as anxiety and motivation directly impact language acquisition. Negative affect creates a mental barrier that prevents optimal language processing, while positive affect facilitates acquisition. In role-playing contexts, explicit corrections can raise anxiety by drawing attention to errors which also breaks the immersive experience that learners find motivating. Implicit feedback methods maintaining narrative flow help preserve the engaging environment that promotes language acquisition in role-playing.
- **The Noticing Hypothesis** [29,30] indicates that learners must be able to notice linguistic features to acquire them, which can occur through various mechanisms. While explicit feedback forces noticing through direct attention, implicit methods can still achieve noticing through subtle reformulations such as recasts that do not interrupt the communication flow. However, the effectiveness of different noticing mechanisms varies with learner proficiency as

beginners may miss vague instructions. In narrative contexts, the challenge lies in ensuring that corrections remain noticeable to learners of varying proficiency levels while maintaining the immersive qualities that make role-playing effective for language acquisition.

3.1 Activity-Integrated Feedback

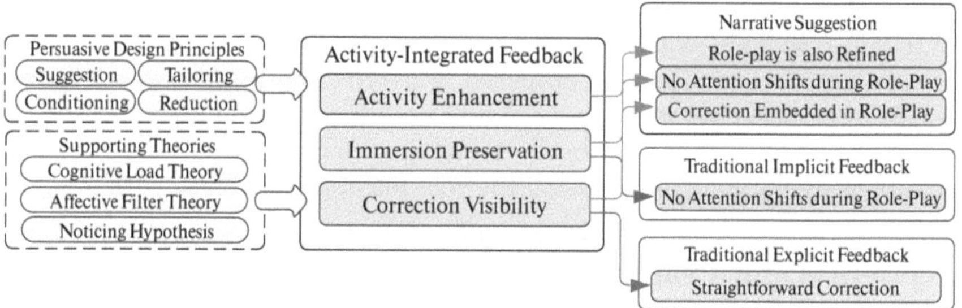

Fig. 2. Activity-Integrated Feedback Framework showing how supporting theories and persuasive design principles inform the three key components that determine corrective feedback effectiveness in role-playing language learning contexts.

Building upon these foundational theories, we formulate the *Activity-Integrated Feedback* framework, which applies persuasive technology principles to design corrective feedback that allows learners to easily accept corrections by keeping them motivated and engaged in role-playing. This framework, as shown in Fig. 2, identifies three key components that determine feedback effectiveness in the context of role-playing with AI chatbots for language learning:

1. **Activity Enhancement**: Degree to which feedback actively enriches the language learning activity beyond mere error correction. Applying the *Suggestion* and *Tailoring* principles, corrections should be delivered only during mistakes, and should also help improve the learner's personal character portrayal and story development rather than generic error identification only. This approach also employs *Conditioning* through positive reinforcement as it encourages the learner to engage more with the refined role-play narrative, keeping them motivated to interact with the AI chatbot.
2. **Immersion Preservation**: The extent to which feedback maintains learner engagement with the learning activity without disruption. Applying the *Reduction* principle, implicit feedback eliminates the multistep process induced by explicit corrections: disengaging from role-playing, processing errors, and then re-engaging. Feedback embedded within the ongoing activity flow avoids this by allowing learners to internalize corrections while maintaining continuous immersion, avoiding any attention shifts from the ongoing role-play.

3. **Correction Visibility**: The degree in which feedback enables learners to notice linguistic corrections despite being implicit. *Suggestion* ensures corrections appear when learners are most receptive, while *Reduction* removes affective and cognitive barriers that prevent learners from attending to corrections by embedding it in the role-play itself. Although it is still important to note that beginner learners may lack the ability to notice implicit corrections, requiring more design considerations [30].

This framework provides theoretical justification for developing and evaluating Narrative Suggestion as a design approach to implicit corrective feedback in role-playing contexts. It also predicts effectiveness based on alignment with its three components. Explicit feedback, while ensuring correction visibility through direct instruction, disrupts immersion and increases cognitive load by forcing attention shifts, which may also decrease learner motivation. In contrast, implicit approaches like Narrative Suggestion sustain engagement and reduce cognitive load by framing corrections as collaborative storytelling.

4   Methodology

The research gathered evidence for Narrative Suggestion's effectiveness through a comparative evaluation with a common implicit corrective feedback approach called Conversational Recast, both of which are illustrated in Fig. 3. Based on the framework, we hypothesized that Narrative Suggestion will outperform Conversational Recast in perceived immersion and feedback quality as it addresses all three components of the Activity-Integrated Feedback framework.

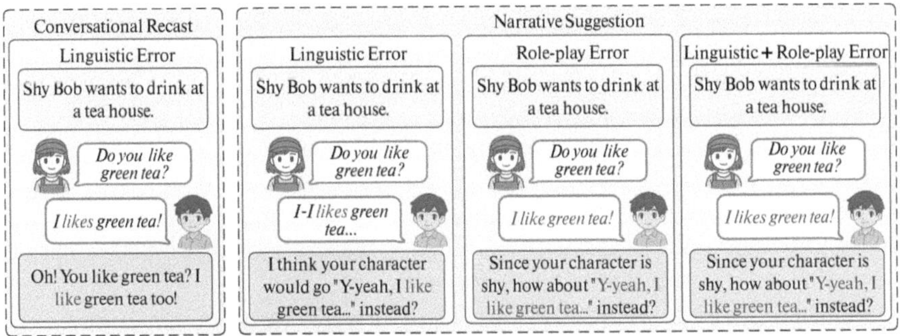

Fig. 3. Sample triggers from Conversational Recast and Narrative Suggestion modes. Narrative Suggestion addresses both linguistic errors and role-play inconsistencies to maintain immersion and enhance the narrative while correcting grammar. Conversational Recast only addresses linguistic errors.

Narrative Suggestion is the proposed implicit corrective feedback method designed for role-playing contexts, where both learner grammatical errors and role-play errors are framed as suggestions for improving the learner's storytelling and character portrayal. *Conversational Recast* is defined as implicit corrective feedback that reformulates learners' grammatically incorrect utterances within the natural flow of conversation, providing correct linguistic forms without explicitly indicating that a grammatical error has occurred [17]. Given those definitions, two research questions are addressed in this study:

- RQ_1: Does Narrative Suggestion increase engagement and immersion with role-playing AI chatbots as perceived by language learners when compared to traditional implicit corrective feedback such as Conversational Recasts?
- RQ_2: Does Narrative Suggestion provide more effective implicit grammar feedback with role-playing AI chatbots as perceived by language learners when compared to traditional implicit corrective feedback such as Conversational Recasts?

4.1   Research Design

The following outlines the mixed-methods experimental research design used in order to answer each of the research questions. The researchers designed an experimental web application to conduct the experiments. This application is a chatbot text messaging application that allows even non-technical learners to easily create their own role-playing AI chatbots and scenarios that match their own language level and interests by simply *prompting* a *Large Language Model.* Both the user-made role-playing AI chatbots' replies and the implicit corrective feedback GUI pop-ups of the application are generated using an LLM to support both role-playing and corrective feedback tasks with low latency and cost [31,32], a snippet of which can be seen in Fig. 4. In specific, Google's *Gemini 2.5 Flash* was chosen for its sufficient multilingual capabilities [33].

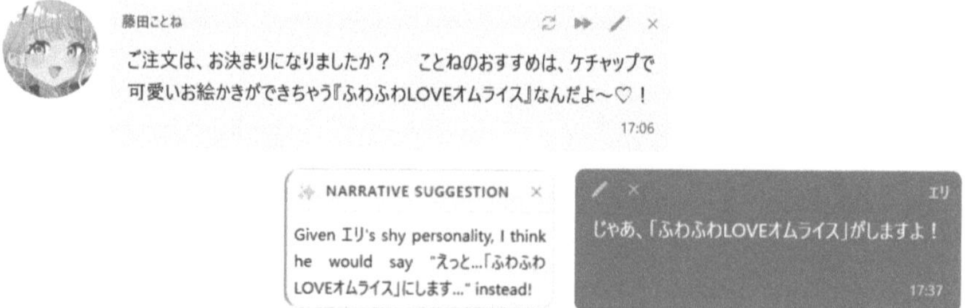

Fig. 4. Screenshot within the web app where a user (lower-right) is practicing ordering at a Japanese maid café through text-based role-play with an AI chatbot (upper-left). A Narrative Suggestion corrective feedback pop-up is shown after the user made a grammatical error, masked as collaborative storytelling.

All user messages are read by the LLM during role-play, generating corrective feedback pop-ups when it detects any mistakes. *Few-shot prompts* guided the

LLM, finalized through a separate blind ablation study where 5 proficient raters evaluated 150 LLM responses across 3 prompt variations per method (zero-shot vs. few-shot). The selected prompts, which incorporated multilingual examples, achieved the highest consensus ratings for accuracy and consistency. All valid detections are listed in Table 2, wherein Narrative Suggestion is also triggered from role-play mistakes for Activity Enhancement. Linguistic error categories are based on established taxonomies in second language acquisition research [34,35] with the addition of *Formality* and *Conjugation*, which are seen in East Asian languages such as Japanese and Korean where social hierarchy dictates verb endings. Role-play categories were derived from established *narrative coherence* principles in story writing focusing on character consistency and plot progression [36,37].

Table 2. Mistake types detected by the LLM for triggering corrective feedback, categorized into linguistic and role-play errors.

Mistake Type	Description	Example
Linguistic Errors		
Spelling	Misspelled words	"recieve" → "receive"
Grammar	Incorrect tense, agreement, or plural	"He go to school"
Syntax	Awkward or wrong word order	"The cat black is big"
Vocabulary	Unnatural or incorrect word usage	"delicious water"
Formality	Too casual or too formal for the situation	"Yo, what's up professor?"
Punctuation	Missing or incorrect punctuation	"Lets eat grandma"
Conjugation	Incorrect verb/adjective form	"He goed to school"
Homophones	Confused sound-alike words	"Their going home"
Role-play Errors		
Out of Character	Doesn't match character's personality	A shy character suddenly flirts aggressively
Ignored Context	Ignores recent dialogue/events	Ignoring a confession, talking about weather
Inconsistent Tone	Sudden, unjustified tone shift	Happy then hostile without buildup
Derailed Topic	Goes off-topic mid-scene	Lunch plans during dramatic confrontation
Too Short	Too brief to progress scene	Just "ok" or "yeah"
Repetition	Repeats structure/ideas unnecessarily	"I like tea" in every reply
Meta Language	Breaks fourth wall/immersion	"You're an AI so..."
Setting Violation	Contradicts world logic/period	Smartphone in medieval fantasy

Seventeen Filipino university students aged 18âĂŞ23 actively studying a foreign language provided informed consent and participated. 10 studied Japanese, 4 Chinese, and 3 Korean. The group included 11 beginner and 6 intermediate learners, with 7 holding language certifications and the remainder self-reporting proficiency. They created their own characters and role-playing AI chatbot partners using *few-shot prompting* templates in the web application, then engaged in 4 text-based role-play sessions with a minimum of 10 turns each (1 turn = 1 user utterance and 1 chatbot reply). Two sessions used Conversational Recast and two used Narrative Suggestion, in randomized order to prevent order bias. After each session, participants recorded reflections in any note-taking application to help them recall and answer the post-survey, a 5-point semantic differential scale questionnaire assessing perceived experience based on the three Activity-Integrated Feedback components. Some also participated in optional semi-structured interviews exploring their experiences with both feedback methods. Participants were asked to refrain from using external resources such as grammar checkers and received a small monetary incentive for their time.

4.2 Data Analysis

Paired statistical tests compared user interactions between Conversational Recast and Narrative Suggestion conditions, based on distribution normality ($\alpha = 0.05$). Engagement was measured as the number of turns per chat session, with higher turn counts indicating sustained interaction. Learning uptake was measured as linguistic correction frequency per turn, with lower correction rates suggesting learners incorporated previous feedback and reduced repeated errors. Semantic differential scale responses (1 = Strongly Narrative, 5 = Strongly Conversational) were analyzed using one-sample t-tests against the neutral midpoint (3.0), with Cohen's d effect sizes calculated to quantify preference magnitude (Fig. 5). Qualitative data from semi-structured interviews and participant diary notes were analyzed using *reflexive thematic analysis*, inductively coding transcripts related to Activity Enhancement, Immersion Preservation, and Correction Visibility across both feedback conditions.

5   Results and Discussion

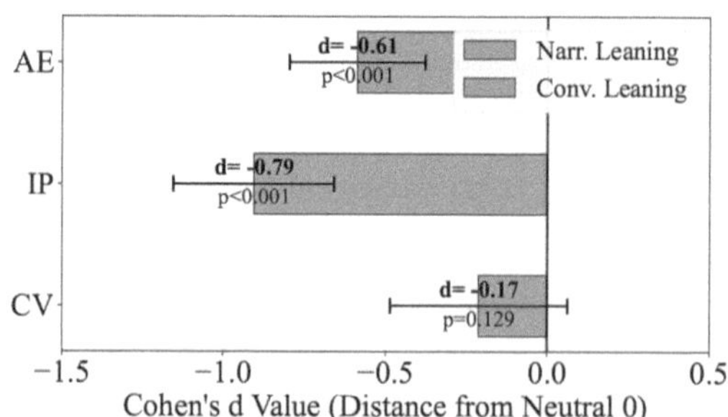

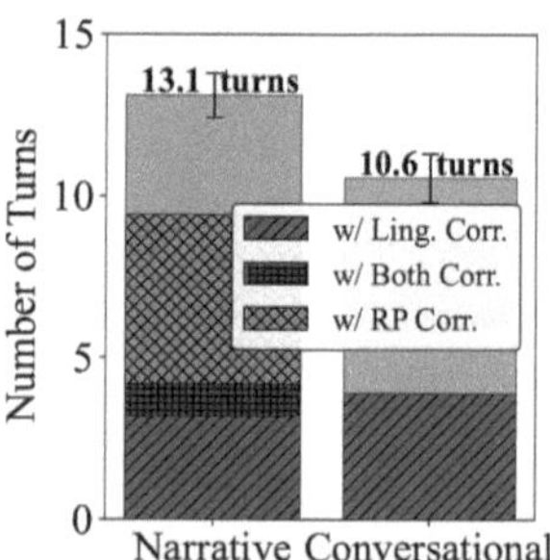

Fig. 5. Quantitative results from user study.

Results support the Activity-Integrated Feedback framework across the three components. Shapiro-Wilk normality tests confirmed that behavioral metrics (turn count ($p = 0.393$) and linguistic correction rates ($p = 0.126$)) were normally distributed, allowing use of paired t-tests. Narrative Suggestion (NS) significantly outperformed Conversational Recasts (CR) in both engagement and learner preferences for Activity Enhancement and Immersion Preservation, while Correction Visibility and learning uptake showed non-significance.

Likert scale preference analysis (Figure a) revealed statistically significant preferences for NS across two of three framework components: medium effect for Activity Enhancement (M = 2.41, SD = 0.97, p < 0.001, Cohen's d = −0.61) and medium effect for Immersion Preservation (M = 2.09, SD = 1.15, p < 0.001, d = −0.79). Correction Visibility showed a non-significant trend favoring NS (M = 2.79, SD = 1.27, p = 0.129, d = −0.17). These results demonstrate that framing corrections as collaborative storytelling enhancements rather than error identification minimizes extraneous cognitive load while maintaining engagement through positive affect, validating the persuasive design principles of Reduction and Suggestion. However, ensuring Correction Visibility remains a challenge for such implicit correction methods, particularly for beginner learners.

Behavioral metrics (Figure b) showed significant results favoring NS for engagement. Mean chat turns were significantly higher for NS (M = 13.11, SD = 2.92) than CR (M = 10.56, SD = 3.21), representing a 24.1% increase (p < 0.001, Cohen's d = 1.302), showing that NS maintained learner interaction longer. Linguistic correction frequency also showed a trend toward lower corrections per turn for NS (M = 0.319, SD = 0.152) compared to CR (M = 0.368, SD = 0.172), though not reaching statistical significance (p = 0.068, d = −0.460).

Table 3. Themes derived from participant diaries, semi-structured interviews, and open-ended survey responses. Only themes with ≥3 mentions were included.

Theme	Mentions
Activity Enhancement & Immersion Preservation	
NS makes role-play more engaging/fun	13/17
NS motivated me to maintain character during role-play	11/17
NS also teaches situational appropriateness (formality, politeness)	9/17
CR just feels like disruptive commentary	8/17
NS encourages longer, more descriptive responses	8/17
Correction Visibility	
Beginners prefer explicit correction over implicit (desire for explanations)	11/17
Corrections in CR are hard to identify/seem like random commentary	8/17
CR in foreign language is confusing for beginners	8/17
Difficulty discerning if NS is correcting grammar vs. role-play	6/17
Intermediate learners comfortable with implicit corrections	5/17
CR in foreign language can serve as additional practice	3/17
Modality Limitations	
Desire for audio/voice features in chatbot system	14/17

For qualitative results, triangulated analysis of participant diaries, semi-structured interviews, and open-ended survey responses revealed consistent themes (Table 3) consistently supporting NS for Activity Enhancement and Immersion Preservation. Participants reported NS made role-playing more engaging and enabled *self-monitoring* where awareness of how corrections were triggered motivated more in-character responses, whereas CR felt like disruptive commentary. NS was specifically valued for teaching situational appropriateness, with one learner noting: "*[NS] also corrected both my formality and my tone... It was correcting my politeness [in the role-play scenario].*" However, proficiency level heavily influenced Correction Visibility. While many learners reported consciously noticing and reflecting on implicit corrections, beginners often struggled to deconstruct feedback, occasionally interpreting NS grammatical corrections as narrative plot directions. This suggests that although NS preserves immersion, it may obscure pedagogical intent for learners with limited meta-linguistic awareness. Beginners explicitly requested explanations: "*I wish there was a way to show why it was wrong*", whereas intermediate learners treated implicit prompts as additional reading practice. Across proficiency levels, participants also requested audio features to supplement the text-only modality.

6   Conclusion and Future Work

This research introduced Narrative Suggestion, a novel implicit corrective feedback approach for role-playing language learning with AI chatbots. Comparative evaluation ($N = 17$) demonstrated that NS significantly outperformed Conversational Recasts in engagement (24.1% more chat turns, $p < 0.001$, $d = 1.302$) and learner preferences for Activity Enhancement ($p < 0.001$, $d = -0.61$) and Immersion Preservation ($p < 0.001$, $d = -0.79$), affirmatively answering RQ1. For RQ2, NS showed promising trends in learning uptake (lower correction frequency, $p = 0.068$, $d = -0.460$), though Correction Visibility requires further development, with language proficiency level emerging as a critical pedagogical consideration wherein beginner learners still needed explicit corrections for clarity. These findings validate the Activity-Integrated Feedback framework and demonstrate that corrections as collaborative storytelling maintains engagement.

However, this study has limitations. While the observed effect sizes were substantial, the sample size limits the generalizability of the results and the aggregation of findings across distinct languages (Japanese, Chinese, Korean) further introduces variability. This study also only measured immediate engagement and learner perceptions rather than longitudinal learning outcomes, leaving questions about long-term retention and actual linguistic gains. The text-only modality of the system used also reduced correction clarity particularly for beginner learners, as evidenced by participant requests for audio features. Future work should address these limitations through multimodal implementations, hybrid systems with optional explicit explanations, and larger-scale longitudinal studies focusing on one foreign language that extends beyond learner engagement.

References

1. Fryer, L.K., Nakao, K., Thompson, A.: Chatbot learning partners: connecting learning experiences, interest and competence. Comput. Hum. Behav. **93**, 279–289 (2019). https://doi.org/10.1016/j.chb.2018.12.023, https://www.sciencedirect.com/science/article/pii/S0747563218306095
2. Fryer, L.K., Ainley, M., Thompson, A., Gibson, A., Sherlock, Z.: Stimulating and sustaining interest in a language course: an experimental comparison of Chatbot and Human task partners. Comput. Hum. Behav. **75**, 461–468 (2017). https://doi.org/10.1016/j.chb.2017.05.045, https://www.sciencedirect.com/science/article/pii/S0747563217303667
3. Leshchenko, M., Lavrysh, Y., Halatsyn, K., Feshchuk, A., Prykhodko, D.: Technology-enhanced personalized language learning: strategies and challenges. Int. J. Emerg. Technol. Learn. (iJET) **18**(13), 120–136 (2023). https://doi.org/10.3991/ijet.v18i13.39905, https://online-journals.org/index.php/i-jet/article/view/39905, number: 13
4. Lai, Y.C., Pai, H.Y.: Develop drama performances featuring virtual characters for utilization in language learning. In: 2024 10th International Conference on Applied System Innovation (ICASI), pp. 140–142 (2024). https://doi.org/10.1109/ICASI60819.2024.10547790, https://ieeexplore.ieee.org/document/10547790, iSSN: 2768–4156
5. Chen, A., Jia, J., Li, Y., Fu, L.: Investigating the effect of role-play activity with GenAI agent on EFL students' speaking performance. J. Educ. Comput. Res. **63**(1), 99–125 (2025). https://doi.org/10.1177/07356331241299058
6. Du, J., Daniel, B.K.: Transforming language education: a systematic review of AI-powered chatbots for English as a foreign language speaking practice. Comput. Educ. Artif. Intell. **6**, 100230 (2024). https://doi.org/10.1016/j.caeai.2024.100230, https://www.sciencedirect.com/science/article/pii/S2666920X24000316
7. Doan, N.T.P.: Using role play to motivate high-school students in EFL speaking classes. Eur. J. Foreign Lang. Teach. **8**(1) (2024). https://doi.org/10.46827/ejfl.v8i1.5272, https://oapub.org/edu/index.php/ejfl/article/view/5272, number: 1
8. Huang, F., Zou, B.: English speaking with artificial intelligence (AI): the roles of enjoyment, willingness to communicate with AI, and innovativeness. Comput. Hum. Behav., 108355 (2024). https://doi.org/10.1016/j.chb.2024.108355, https://www.sciencedirect.com/science/article/pii/S0747563224002231
9. Wang, Y., Xue, L.: Using AI-driven chatbots to foster Chinese EFL students' academic engagement: an intervention study. Comput. Hum. Behav. **159**, 108353 (2024). https://doi.org/10.1016/j.chb.2024.108353, https://www.sciencedirect.com/science/article/pii/S0747563224002218
10. Kim, A., Su, Y.: How implementing an AI chatbot impacts Korean as a foreign language learners' willingness to communicate in Korean. System **122**, 103256 (2024). https://doi.org/10.1016/j.system.2024.103256, https://www.sciencedirect.com/science/article/pii/S0346251X24000381
11. Luckyardi, S., Karin, J., Rosmaladewi, R., Hufad, A., Haristiani, N.: Chatbots as digital language tutors: revolutionizing education through AI. Ind. J. Sci. Technol. **9**(3), 885–908 (2024). https://doi.org/10.17509/ijost.v9i3.79514
12. Liang, K.H., et al.: ChatBack: investigating strategies of providing synchronous grammatical error feedback in a GUI-based language learning social chatbot, pp. 83–99 (2023)

13. Lyster, R., Saito, K., Sato, M.: Oral Corrective feedback in second language classrooms. Lang. Teach. **46**(1), 1–40 (2013). https://doi.org/10.1017/S0261444812000365, publisher: Cambridge University Press ERIC Number: EJ1004287

14. Lyster, R., Izquierdo, J.: Prompts versus recasts in dyadic interaction. Lang. Learn. **59**(2), 453–498 (2009). https://doi.org/10.1111/j.1467-9922.2009.00512.x

15. Fogg, B.J.: Persuasive Technology: Using Computers to Change What We Think and Do. Morgan Kaufmann (2003). google-Books-ID: r9JIkNjjTfEC

16. Krishnamoorthy, L., Merchant, Z.: Applying persuasive techniques in an online learning environment: a mixed-method study. Pedagogical Res. **8**(2), em0156 (2023). https://doi.org/10.29333/pr/12933, https://www.pedagogicalresearch.com/article/applying-persuasive-techniques-in-an-online-learning-environment-a-mixed-method-study-12933

17. Rassaei, E.: Recasts, foreign language anxiety and L2 development during online mobile-mediated interaction. Lang. Teach. Res., 13621688241238045 (2024). https://doi.org/10.1177/13621688241238045

18. Bryfonski, L., Ma, X.: Effects of implicit versus explicit corrective feedback on mandarin tone acquisition in a SCMC learning environment. Stud. Second Lang. Acquisit. **42**(1), 61–88 (2020). https://doi.org/10.1017/S0272263119000317, publisher: Cambridge University Press ERIC Number: EJ1247279

19. Sagarra, N., Abbuhl, R.: Optimizing the noticing of recasts via computer-delivered feedback: evidence that oral input enhancement and working memory help second language learning. Mod. Lang. J. **97**(1), 196–216 (2013). https://doi.org/10.1111/j.1540-4781.2013.01427.x

20. Fu, T., Nassaji, H.: Corrective feedback, learner uptake, and feedback perception in a Chinese as a foreign language classroom. Stud. Second Lang. Learn. Teach. **6**(1), 159–181 (2016). https://doi.org/10.14746/ssllt.2016.6.1.8

21. Sheen, Y., Ellis, R.: Corrective feedback in language teaching. In: Handbook of Research in Second Language Teaching and Learning, p. 18. Routledge (2011)

22. Olaoluwa, E., Aminat, M.: The impact of storytelling techniques and peer collaboration on vocabulary acquisition in early childhood education **7**(11) (2024)

23. Bordeos, M., Pecolados, M., Cardeño, R., Flores, J., Bitangcor, S.: The impact of cooperative storytelling strategy on the learner's speaking proficiency. J. Nat. Lang. Linguist. **1**(1), 22–30 (2023). https://doi.org/10.54536/jnll.v1i1.1987, https://journals.e-palli.com/home/index.php/jnll/article/view/1987, number: 1

24. DaCosta, B.: Generative AI meets adventure: elevating text-based games for engaging language learning experiences. Open J. Soc. Sci. **13**(4), 601–644 (2025). https://doi.org/10.4236/jss.2025.134035, https://www.scirp.org/journal/paperinformation?paperid=142450, number: 4 Publisher: Scientific Research Publishing

25. Eraqamreddy, D.N.: Interactive AI-driven storytelling for language development. Int. J. Soc. Sci. Human. Manage. Res. **04**(02), 313–333 (2025). https://doi.org/10.5281/zenodo.14874257, https://zenodo.org/records/14874257

26. Sweller, J., van Merrienboer, J.J.G., Paas, F.G.W.C.: Cognitive architecture and instructional design. Educ. Psychol. Rev. **10**(3), 251–296 (1998). https://doi.org/10.1023/A:1022193728205

27. Sweller, J.: Cognitive load theory. In: The psychology of learning and motivation: Cognition in education, Vol. 55, pp. 37–76. The psychology of learning and motivation, Elsevier Academic Press, San Diego, CA, US (2011). https://doi.org/10.1016/B978-0-12-387691-1.00002-8

28. Krashen, S.D.: Principles and Practice in Second Language Acquisition. Language Teaching Methodology Series, Pergamon Press, Oxford, reprinted edn (1984)
29. Schmidt, R.W.: The role of consciousness in second language learning. Appl. Linguist. **11**(2), 129–58 (1990). eRIC Number: EJ410427
30. Schmidt, R.: Attention. In: Robinson, P. (ed.) Cognition and Second Language Instruction, pp. 3–32. Cambridge Applied Linguistics, Cambridge University Press, Cambridge (2001). https://doi.org/10.1017/CBO9781139524780.003, https://www.cambridge.org/core/books/cognition-and-second-language-instruction/attention/DB6276BCF85FDAC4C66D0E1DFE0AA3D8
31. Qiu, Z., Duan, X., Cai, Z.: Evaluating grammatical well-formedness in large language models: a comparative study with human judgments. In: Kuribayashi, T., Rambelli, G., Takmaz, E., Wicke, P., Oseki, Y. (eds.) Proceedings of the Workshop on Cognitive Modeling and Computational Linguistics. pp. 189–198. Association for Computational Linguistics, Bangkok, Thailand (2024). https://doi.org/10.18653/v1/2024.cmcl-1.16, https://aclanthology.org/2024.cmcl-1.16/
32. Qu, F., Tang, C., Wu, Y.: Evaluating the capability of large-scale language models on chinese grammatical error correction task. arXiv:2307.03972 (2025)
33. White, C., et al.: LiveBench: a challenging, contamination-limited LLM benchmark. arXiv:2406.19314 (2025)
34. Ferris, D.: Treatment of error in second language student writing, 2nd edn. University of Michigan Press/ELT, Ann Arbor, MI, 2173290 edn. (2011). https://doi.org/10.3998/mpub.2173290, https://press.umich.edu/isbn/9780472034765
35. Ellis, R.: The Study of Second Language Acquisition. Oxford University Press (1994), google-Books-ID: 3KglibyrZ5sC
36. Riedl, M.O., Young, R.M.: Narrative planning: balancing plot and character. J. Artif. Intell. Res. **39**, 217–268 (2010). https://doi.org/10.1613/jair.2989, https://jair.org/index.php/jair/article/view/10669
37. Frisch, A.M., Perlis, D.: A re-evaluation of story grammars. Cognit. Sci. **5**(1), 79–86 (Jan 1981). https://doi.org/10.1016/S0364-0213(81)80027-4, https://www.sciencedirect.com/science/article/pii/S0364021381800274

When More is Less: A Methodological Sensitivity Analysis of Feature Noise and Label Binarization in Affective Computing

Lester Anthony Sityar Jr.(✉) ⓘ and Judith Azcarragaⓘ

Department of Computer Science, De La Salle University, 2401 Taft Avenue, 1004 Manila, Philippines
{lester_sityar,judith.azcarraga}@dlsu.edu.ph

Abstract. Accurately detecting student affective states is critical for building adaptive e-learning systems. However, the field faces a replicability crisis as results are often highly sensitive to overlooked hyperparameter choices. This study presents a systematic sensitivity analysis to isolate the co-dependency of three critical factors: (1) feature sets (Landmarks, FAUs, and Combined), (2) feature representations (Static vs. Dynamic deltas), and (3) label binarization thresholds. To ensure a controlled environment for measuring these variables, a rigid Start Middle-End (SME) temporal sampling strategy was employed as a baseline. Models were trained on the DAISEE dataset using SMOTE and subject-aware validation to address severe class imbalance and generalizability. Our findings reveal that the 'optimal' configuration is highly volatile and unique for each affective state, reinforcing a 'model-per-emotion' requirement. While Boredom achieved a 0.63 F1-score with static features, Engagement required a dynamic delta-Cosine representation (0.55 F1) on a balanced threshold. By exposing how arbitrary label definitions and feature metrics can dramatically alter performance, this work provides a methodological roadmap for building more robust persuasive technologies.

Keywords: Affective Computing · Emotion Recognition · Academic Emotions · Facial Action Units · Facial Landmarks · Sensitivity Analysis · Binarization

1 Introduction

Student engagement is recognized as a crucial determinant of successful learning outcomes [7, 8]. In e-learning contexts, traditional nonverbal cues such as facial expressions, posture, and gestures may be reduced or absent, creating challenges for accurately detecting students' emotional states [2]. Affective computing, which uses computational techniques to recognize and interpret human emotions, has emerged as a promising approach to address this gap [1, 3]. This capability is the foundation of Affective Computing in education, which aims to create adaptive systems that can guide, motivate, and persuade a student to remain on task, thereby enhancing learning outcomes. To achieve this, the system must first know the user's state. For persuasive technology, accurate

K. Sumi et al. (Eds.): PERSUASIVE 2026, LNCS 16476, pp. 318–328, 2026.
https://doi.org/10.1007/978-3-032-19687-3_23

state detection is a requirement for ethical and effective intervention; a system's ability to remain persuasive depends on a 'model-per-emotion' awareness that accounts for the unique sensitivity of different affective signals.

Camera-based, non-intrusive monitoring is the most scalable and practical method for real-world deployment. Research in this area has converged on two primary feature types. Facial Action Units (AUs), defined under the Facial Action Coding System (FACS) [10], represent discrete facial muscle movements (e.g., 'brow lowerer') that can be mapped to specific emotions [11, 12]. Additionally, geometric landmarks for the face and body, extracted by systems like MediaPipe Holistic [5], capture the spatial position of keypoints [8, 9]. Research has demonstrated that integrating these features often improves performance [2, 9].

However, the assumption that more features yield better results is just one of several untested hyperparameters in affective computing research. The field faces three significant, often-overlooked gaps that can lead to brittle or non-replicable results:

The Feature Noise Problem. Naively fusing modalities can be problematic, as noisy features can degrade model performance [16], an issue often obscured in "black box" deep learning models [3, 17]. Unlike end-to-end deep learning approaches that lack transparency, this study utilizes interpretable features, Facial Action Units (FAUs) and geometric landmarks combined with a transparent Start-Middle-End (SME) sampling method, allowing for a clear analysis of how individual feature sets and representations influence performance fluctuations across different affective states. Few studies isolate feature sets to measure their individual contributions or negative interactions.

The Representation Problem. The choice of feature representation (e.g., static features vs. dynamic "deltas") and the processing metric (e.g., Euclidean distance vs. Cosine similarity) are critical but rarely systematically compared.

The Label Definition Problem. Severe class imbalance in affective data [14], common in datasets like DAISEE [6], often yields models with high accuracy but no real-world value, as they fail to predict the minority class [15]. More fundamentally, the arbitrary binarization threshold used to define classes (e.g., 'High' vs. 'Low') is a critical, yet uninvestigated, hyperparameter that significantly alters the problem. By isolating these variables, this study serves as a methodological critique of common evaluation practices that often lead to brittle results. To ensure a controlled environment for this sensitivity analysis, we adopt a rigid Start Middle-End (SME) temporal sampling strategy. While simpler than adaptive methods like changepoint detection [13], its transparency allows us to attribute performance fluctuations directly to feature and label configurations without the confounding variables of complex temporal modeling.

Therefore, this paper presents a comprehensive sensitivity analysis to identify the optimal configuration of feature sets, feature representations, and label binarization thresholds for robustly classifying each of the four academic emotions.

2 Related Works

2.1 The DAiSEE Dataset

The research is grounded in the DAiSEE (Dataset for Affective States in E-Environments) [6]. It is a widely used benchmark for "in-the-wild" student affect recognition, providing video clips recorded via webcam. Each clip is annotated for four academic-related affective states: boredom, engagement, confusion, and frustration [6]. Its use in numerous studies [7–9] makes it a suitable choice for the analysis.

2.2 Core Feature Modalities

Facial Action Units (FAUs), core components of the Facial Action Coding System (FACS) [10], represent discrete facial muscle movements. These interpretable features provide mappings from expression to emotion [11, 12] and are foundational in affective computing. Tools like Py-Feat [4] enable their automated detection from video frames.

Beyond muscle activations, the geometric position of facial and body keypoints provide a powerful, holistic signal. Tools like MediaPipe Holistic [5] extract 3D landmarks for the face and body. Prior work has shown that integrating body motion and head-pose features, often derived from these landmarks, can significantly enhance affect detection [8, 9].

2.3 Frame Selection

Temporal information is critical for capturing the evolution of affective states [2]. Processing every frame is computationally expensive, prompting frame selection strategies. This study adopts a start-middle-end (SME) sampling approach [13], which provides a simple, interpretable, and reproducible temporal representation suitable for feature exploration. While alternative adaptive approaches like Bayesian Online Change-point Detection (BOCPD) [13] exist, SME sampling offers a transparent, low-overhead solution that still captures temporal structure.

2.4 Gaps in Multimodal Fusion and Imbalanced Datasets

The literature strongly supports a multimodal fusion paradigm [2, 8, 9]. However, the assumption that more features yield better results presents several challenges:

The Feature Noise Problem. While multimodal fusion is common, not all modalities are equally informative. As noted in surveys of multimodal machine learning, naively fusing modalities can be problematic; a noisy or less predictive modality can degrade the performance of a stronger modality [16]. Few studies have isolated feature sets (e.g., FAUs vs. Landmarks) to test this "feature noise" hypothesis.

The Black Box Problem. Many modern approaches use end-to-end deep learning models that operate as "black boxes," limiting interpretability [3] and failing to explain why a prediction was made [17]. This makes it difficult to diagnose which features are contributing to a prediction, or which are acting as noise.

The Class Imbalance Problem. A critical and often-overlooked gap is the failure to properly address the severe class imbalance inherent in real-world affective state data [14]. Datasets like DAISEE are naturally skewed (e.g., students are "Frustrated" far less often than "Not Frustrated"). This leads to models with high accuracy but zero real world value, as they fail to predict the minority class [15].

The research confronts these by adding an investigation of two often-overlooked, gaps: the Representation Problem (static vs. dynamic features; Euclidean vs. Cosine metrics) and the Label Definition Problem (the choice of binarization threshold).

3 Methodology

3.1 Dataset and Label Preprocessing

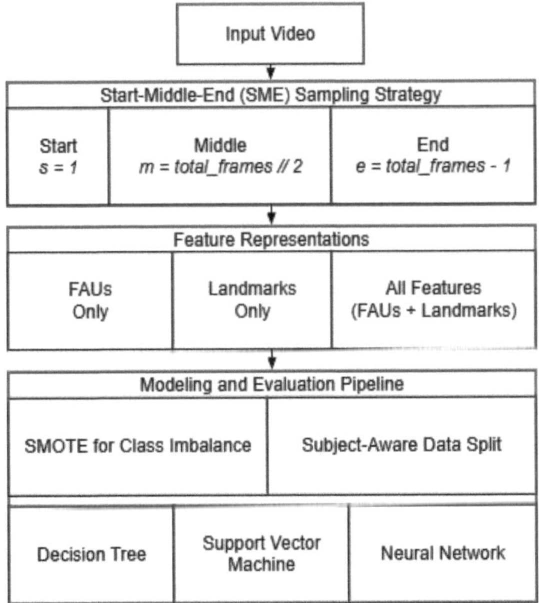

Fig. 1. Methodology Pipeline Diagram

The analysis was performed on 8,925 video clips, which are annotated for four affective states: engagement, boredom, confusion, and frustration (Fig. 1).

A primary variable of the experiment is the Label Binarization Threshold. Instead of using a single, arbitrary split (e.g., 0,1 vs. 2,3), three distinct binarization thresholds were designed to create different class distributions. This allows the model's robustness to be tested against different definitions of the minority class.

For temporal sampling, the start-middle-end (SME) strategy was adopted [13], extracting three key static frames from each short video clip. This provides an interpretable and computationally efficient temporal snapshot.

$$[s = 1, m = total\_frames /2, e = total\_frames - 1] \tag{1}$$

Data Distribution and Class Imbalance. The DAISEE dataset exhibits extreme class imbalance, which significantly impacts the ability of machine learning models to identify minority affective states.

Table 1. Frequency Values for Each Affective State

Affective State	Level 0	Level 1	Level 2	Level 3
Boredom	3822	2850	1923	330
Engagement	61	455	4422	3987
Confusion	5952	2133	741	100
Frustration	6887	1613	338	87

Threshold Definition. The data in Table 1 reveals that "High" intensity states (Level 3) for Confusion (n = 100) and Frustration (n = 87) are extremely scarce. By testing three binarization thresholds, this study identifies the optimal configuration where sufficient minority samples are available for the model to learn a predictive signal without diluting the emotional intensity of the label.

1. Threshold 1 (Inclusive). Levels 0 vs. 1, 2, 3. This addresses the scarcity of data in Frustration by increasing the minority class to 2,038 samples.
2. Threshold 2 (Mid-Point). Labels 0, 1 vs. 2, 3. This serves as a middle ground, attempting to isolate distinct affective displays (levels 2 and 3) from neutral or trace emotional states (levels 0 and 1). This threshold tests whether the model can distinguish "moderate-to-high" intensity from "none-to-low" intensity.
3. Threshold 3 (Strict). Levels 0, 1, 2 vs. 3. While most representative of "intense" emotion, this threshold results in an F1-score drop because the models lack sufficient "High" intensity training data.

Conversely, Engagement exhibits an inverse scarcity; because levels 2 and 3 are so prevalent, Threshold 3 provides the most balanced distribution for this specific state. This explains the performance jump to a 0.55 F1-score for Engagement, as the "Strict" threshold effectively isolates 3,987 samples of high-intensity engagement against a combined majority of lower levels.

3.2 Feature Engineering Pipeline

The three SME frames from each video were processed through a multi-stage feature engineering pipeline.

Feature Extraction. Two primary tools were used. Py-Feat [4]: To extract 20 distinct Facial Action Units (FAUs) (AU01, AU02, AU04, AU05, AU06, AU07, AU09, AU10, AU11, AU12, AU14, AU15, AU17, AU20, AU23, AU24, AU25, AU26, AU28, AU43). MediaPipe Holistic [5]: To extract 2D (x, y) coordinates for 80 key landmarks (68 facial landmarks and 12 upper body pose landmarks).

Feature Representation. The raw landmark data was processed in three different ways: (1) Static (Landmarks): The raw, flattened 2D coordinates (e.g., x_start, y_start, x_mid, y_mid,…) were used. (2) Dynamic (Euclidean): The delta in Euclidean distance between frames. (3) Dynamic (Cosine): The delta in Cosine similarity between frames.

3.3 Feature Set Creation

To refine the experimental design, a preliminary feature analysis using Principal Component Analysis (PCA) was conducted on the 'All Features' set to identify the primary drivers of variance, providing quantitative justification for isolating feature sets:

Dominance of Facial Landmarks. Across all four affective states the top 10 most positively correlated features for the first principal component were exclusively facial landmarks (e.g., F47, F46, F45, and F44) extracted from start and middle frames. These features consistently showed correlation coefficients exceeding 0.072.

Negligible Body Contribution. In contrast, upper-body landmarks and certain specific Action Units consistently ranked among the bottom 10 features, showing negative or negligible correlation to the first principal component (ranging from -0.022 to -0.026).

Temporal Scaling. When analyzing dynamic deltas, facial movement dominated variance with correlation scores near 0.094, while body deltas remained non-contributory.

Based on these metrics, it was determined that isolating body landmarks as a separate feature set would be uninformative, leading to their consolidation into a single 'Landmarks Only' set. The main hypothesis was tested by "slicing" the data into three distinct, static (no-delta) feature sets:

1. All Features. The combined set of all flattened FAUs and all flattened Landmark features (face and body).
2. Landmarks Only. Contains only the flattened Landmark features (face and body).
3. FAUs Only. Contains only flattened FAU features.

These sets were combined with the representations from 3.2 to create the full set of files (e.g., final_features_2D_static_LANDMARKS_ONLY.csv, final_features_2D_deltas_LANDMARKS_COSINE.csv, etc.).

3.4 Modeling and Evaluation

The modeling pipeline was designed to directly address the core challenges identified. A scikit-learn Pipeline was utilized to encapsulate the entire workflow, ensuring that StandardScaler (for feature scaling) and SMOTE (for oversampling) were applied exclusively to the training data. This prevents data leakage and ensures the test set remains valid and unseen.

Handling Class Imbalance. The analysis showed that the severe class imbalance in the DAiSEE dataset (e.g., Frustration: 701 "Low" vs. 26 "High" in the test set) rendered all standard models useless, yielding 0.00 F1-scores for the minority class. Therefore, the methodology requires the Synthetic Minority Oversampling TEchnique (SMOTE). SMOTE creates new, synthetic samples for the minority class, providing the model with a balanced 50/50 training set and forcing it to learn the minority class patterns.

Subject-Aware Data Split. To ensure the models generalize to unseen individuals, a Group-Based (Subject-Aware) 80/20 train-test split was performed. This ensures that all frames from a single student remain in either the training or the testing set, not both.

Models. Three distinct classifiers were evaluated to ensure results were robust across approaches.

1. Decision Tree (DT): An ensemble of 100 estimators designed to capture non-linear interactions within the feature sets.
2. Support Vector Machine (SVM): Utilized a Radial Basis Function (RBF) kernel to project features into a higher-dimensional space.
3. Neural Network (NN): A Multi-Layer Perceptron (MLP) with two hidden layers of 100 and 50 nodes. The architecture utilized the ReLU activation function, the Adam optimizer, and Early Stopping to prevent overfitting.

4 Results and Discussion

The results of the sensitivity analysis confirm that no single configuration is optimal for all academic emotions. Instead, performance is highly sensitive to the interaction between feature representation, binarization thresholds, and the mathematical approach of the classifier.

A clear correlation exists between label frequency (Table 1) and model performance. Boredom achieved the highest minority F1-score (0.63) at Threshold 1, where the minority class was most populated. While Frustration yielded the lowest F1-score (0.29), a result of the scarcity of "High" intensity samples (n = 87), which limited the model's ability to learn a robust representation of the state even with SMOTE application (Table 2).

Table 2. Best-Achieved Minority Class F1-Scores by Affective State

Affective State	Best Minority F1-Score	Binarization Threshold	Feature Set	Model
Boredom	0.63	1	Static All Features	DT
Engagement	0.55	3	All Features w/ Cosine Deltas	SVM
Confusion	0.36	1	Static All Features	NN
Frustration	0.29	1	Landmarks only w/ Cosine Deltas	SVM

4.1 The Role of Temporal Deltas and Feature Type

The analysis reveals that dynamic features (temporal deltas) are critical for certain states but redundant for others.

1. Static Superiority. For Boredom and Confusion, static features alone provided the highest F1-scores. This suggests that these states are characterized by sustained facial poses (e.g., a fixed "blank" stare or a constant brow furrow).
2. Dynamic Necessity. For Engagement and Frustration, the inclusion of Cosine Deltas was essential for peak performance. This indicates that these emotions are better captured by the movement or "flicker" of facial expressions over time rather than a single static snapshot.

4.2 Optimal Binarization Thresholds

Unlike other states, Engagement performed best when the model was forced to isolate only the highest intensity (n = 3,987). In a persuasive tutoring system, this implies that:

1. Engagement detection should be "Strict" (Threshold 3) to avoid interrupting a student who is only moderately focused.
2. Frustration detection should be "Inclusive" (Threshold 1) to ensure that even early signs of frustration are captured, allowing for pre-emptive support.

4.3 Frustration: Brittle Signal

A central motivation for this study was to verify preliminary (and ultimately, inaccurate) findings of a near-perfect F1-score for Frustration. The analysis demonstrates that this result is not replicable and was likely an artifact of an untested combination of hyperparameters.

It was found that the signal for Frustration is brittle and highly sensitive to all three factors. The original Static, Landmarks Only model, when tested under a different binarization threshold, saw its performance fall to an F1-score of 0.07 from 0.29.

4.4 Boredom: Robust Signal

In stark contrast to Frustration, Boredom yielded the most robust and highest-performing model of the entire study. The optimal F1-score was 0.63.

This result was achieved using a binarization threshold of 1 and the Static, All features feature set. This finding directly supports the "mixed signal" hypothesis. The model needed both static landmarks and static FAUs to make the best prediction. This proves that the optimal feature set for Boredom is the opposite of the one for Frustration, reinforcing the model-per-emotion hypothesis.

4.5 Engagement: Importance of Binarization Thresholds

Engagement serves as a clear example of the Label Definition Problem. With binarization thresholds of 1 and 2, "Low Engagement" was a tiny minority class, resulting in near-zero F1-scores (e.g., 0.03–0.08). The models were simply unable to find a signal.

However, by changing the threshold to 3 it created a nearly 50/50 balanced split. The highest achieved F1-score jumped to 0.55, achieved by the Dynamic, All features, Cosine Similarity set. This demonstrates that for Engagement, the label definition is more important than the feature set. The best signal also required dynamic features, contrasting with the static-only model for Boredom.

4.6 Confusion: Weak Signal

Across all experiments, Confusion remained the most challenging to predict, aligning with the original findings. The highest F1-score achieved was 0.36, using the Static, All features set.

This low score, even with a balanced threshold and multiple feature representations (static, dynamic, etc.), suggests that the features captured by FAUs and landmarks are insufficient for this state. This finding strongly motivates future work, as detecting Confusion likely requires an entirely different modality not explored in this study.

4.7 Contextualizing Results and the Impact of Temporal Sampling

The modest F1-scores for Frustration (0.29) and Confusion (0.36) stem from the deliberate use of a rigid Start-Middle-End (SME) strategy to maintain experimental control and transparency.

In contrast, a related study by Resurreccion [13] on the same dataset utilized a changepoint detection method to extract only the most significant frames of emotional intensity. While Resurreccion reported dramatically higher F1-scores, that approach is optimized for performance, whereas this study is for feature sensitivity analysis.

The performance gap between the two methods suggests that temporal sampling is a far more critical factor for classification success than the mathematical representation of the features themselves. This study demonstrates that while the rigid SME sampling strategy provides high transparency for a controlled sensitivity analysis, it lacks the flexibility to capture emotional peaks, leading to the modest performance observed for states like Frustration and Confusion. For persuasive technology, this implies that the system's effectiveness relies on intelligent timing, capturing the specific moment of emotional shift rather than exhaustive feature sets.

5 Conclusion and Future Work

This study challenged the conventional wisdom in affective computing by moving beyond simple feature set comparisons. A comprehensive sensitivity analysis was conducted, demonstrating that model performance is critically co-dependent on (1) feature sets (Landmarks vs. FAUs), (2) feature representation (e.g., static 2D coordinates vs. dynamic deltas), and (3) label binarization thresholds.

The findings prove that a one-size-fits-all model is suboptimal. A robust e-learning system must instead employ a model-per-emotion approach. Boredom was best classified (0.63 F1) using a static, all-features model. Engagement required a dynamic (delta-Cosine) model on a balanced threshold to be solvable (0.55 F1). Frustration and Confusion proved most difficult, yielding modest, albeit more realistic, best F1-scores of 0.29

and 0.36, respectively, which highlight the extreme difficulty of detecting low-intensity negative affect in subject-aware splits.

For the field of persuasive computing, these findings have clear implications: the arbitrary choice of a binarization threshold or feature metric is a critical, unacknowledged variable that can dramatically alter results. Robust models require these factors to be tuned per emotion to find a true, generalizable signal.

The conclusions of this study are framed by two primary limitations in the feature representation:

Coarseness of SME Temporal Abstraction. The greatest limitation is the reliance on the Start-Middle-End (SME) sampling strategy [13]. By extracting only three equidistant frames from a 10-s clip, the model is blind to 99% of the temporal data. In affective computing, critical micro-expressions often occur in bursts of less than a second; if these "affective events" occur between the sampled points, the model effectively receives a "neutral" signal for a "high-intensity" label. This explains why more fluid methods like changepoint detection [13] yield superior results.

Linearity of Dynamic Features. Our "dynamic" features consisted of simple Euclidean and Cosine deltas between three points in time. While this successfully captured broad shifts in posture or facial position, it represents a linear simplification of emotional expression. Facial muscles (captured via AUs) move in complex, non-linear trajectories. A simple delta cannot capture the acceleration or velocity of a brow furrow or a lip corner pull, which are often the true indicators of rising frustration or confusion.

These limitations provide a clear and direct path for future research. The most critical future work is to address the simplistic temporal sampling (SME). As discussed in Sect. 4.5, this method yields modest F1-scores, whereas more advanced methods like changepoint detection show significantly better results [13].

These limitations provide a direct, actionable path for future research:

Hybrid Sampling. Integrating our sensitivity analysis with intelligent changepoint detection to ensure that the features are extracted from the most optimal frames.

Non-Linear Modeling. Implementing Long Short-Term Memory (LSTM) networks or Gated Recurrent Units (GRU) to model the entire sequence of frames, allowing the system to learn the temporal "signature" of an emotion rather than just its static state.

Feature Selection Refinement. Utilizing Recursive Feature Elimination (RFE) to strip away redundant landmarks, potentially boosting the signal-to-noise ratio for brittle states like Confusion.

Disclosure of Interests
The authors have no competing interests to declare that are relevant to the content of this article.

References

1. Schoner-Schatz, L., Hofmann, V., Stokburger-Sauer, N.E.: Destination's social media communication and emotions: an investigation of visit intentions, word-of-mouth and travelers' facially expressed emotions. J. Destination Mark. Manag. **22**, 100661 (2021)
2. Wang, Y. et al.: A systematic review on affective computing: emotion models, databases, and recent advances. arXiv preprint arXiv:2203.06935 (2022)

3. Baltrušaitis, T., Mahmoud, M., Robinson, P.: Cross-dataset learning and person-specific normalisation for automatic Action Unit detection. In: Proceedings of the IEEE International Conference Automatic Face and Gesture Recognition (FG) (2015)

4. Cheong, J.H., Xie, T., Byrne, S., Chang, L.J.: Py-Feat: python facial expression analysis toolbox. Affect. Sci. **4**, 1–21 (2023)

5. Google AI: MediaPipe Holistic. https://developers.google.com/mediapipe

6. Gupta, A., D'Cunha, A., Awasthi, K., Balasubramanian, V.: DAISEE: towards user engagement recognition in the wild. arXiv preprint arXiv:1609.01885 (2022)

7. Whitehill, J., Serpell, Z., Lin, Y.-C., Foster, A., Movellan, J.R.: The faces of engagement: automatic recognition of student engagement from facial expressions. IEEE Trans. Affective Comput. **5**(1), 86–98 (2014)

8. Bosch, N. et al.: Automatic detection of learning-centered affective states in the wild. In: Proceedings of the 20th International Conference Intelligent User Interfaces (2015)

9. Wang, G.-Y., Hatori, Y., Sato, Y., Tseng, C.-H., Shioiri, S.: Predicting learners' engagement and help-seeking behaviors in an e-learning environment by using facial and head pose features. Comput. Educ.: Artif. Intell. (2025)

10. Kring, A.M., Sloan, D.M.: The Facial Expression Coding System (FACES): development, validation, and utility. Psychol. Assess. **19**(2), 210–224 (2007)

11. Tejada, J., et al.: Building and validation of a set of facial expression images to detect emotions: a transcultural study. Psychol. Res. **86**(6), 1996–2006 (2021)

12. Gilbert, M., Demarchi, S., Urdapilleta, I.: FACSHuman, a software program for creating experimental material by modeling 3D facial expressions. Behav. Res. Methods **53**, 1–17 (2021)

13. Resurreccion, P.M.: Classifying academic emotions using changes in facial landmark points over time. Master's thesis, De La Salle University (2024)

14. Valstar, M., et al.: AVEC 2019: the 9th competition for audio/visual emotion challenge. In: Proceedings of the 9th International on Audio/Visual Emotion Challenge and Workshop (2019)

15. Joshi, J., et al.: A review on emotion recognition from speech in e-learning applications. In: 2020 11th International Conference on Computing, Communication and Networking Technologies (ICCCNT) (2020)

16. Baltrušaitis, T., Ahuja, C., Morency, L.P.: Multimodal machine learning: a survey and taxonomy. IEEE Trans. Pattern Anal. Mach. Intell. (2017)

17. Tjoa, E., Guan, C.: A survey on explainable artificial intelligence (XAI): toward medical XAI. IEEE Trans. Neural Networks Learn. Syst. (2020)

HealKitchen: An AI-Driven, Behavior-Theory-Based Mobile Health Application for Dietary Behavior Change

Iyanuoluwa Sowande and Ifeoma Adaji[(⊠)]

The University of British Columbia, Okanagan Campus, British Columbia, Canada
ifeoma.adaji@ubc.ca

Abstract. Unhealthy dietary habits remain a global challenge, especially for individuals with specific health conditions. Existing mobile nutrition apps often prioritize calorie tracking over personalization or behavioral support. This study introduces HealKitchen, a persuasive, AI-driven mobile application grounded in behavioral science to promote healthier eating. HealKitchen personalizes recipe recommendations, identifies groceries through image recognition, and integrates persuasive features derived from five behavior-change theories. A mixed-method evaluation with 20 users showed high usability (mean = 4.6), usefulness (mean = 4.45), and aesthetics (mean = 4.49). Qualitative feedback emphasized the need for greater recipe diversity and richer multimedia. The findings demonstrate the feasibility of theory-based persuasive design for personalized nutrition support.

Keywords: mobile health · dietary behavior change · persuasion

1 Introduction

Diet plays a critical role in preventing and managing diverse health conditions, shaping both physical and mental well-being [4,24,41]. Poor dietary habits remain a major global risk factor, while balanced nutrition supports immunity, energy, and long-term health [12,16,47]. Yet many people struggle to translate nutritional knowledge into consistent behavior due to confusing dietary information, limited understanding of nutritional content, and modern time pressures [30,48]. Everyday decision-making barriers—such as uncertainty about what meals fit personal health needs—further hinder the adoption of healthy dietary routines [10,49].

Mobile health (mHealth) technologies offer a promising way to bridge the gap between awareness and action by providing accessible, personalized dietary support on smartphones [33,50]. Users can track meals, receive feedback, and access nutritional insights anytime. Advances in artificial intelligence (AI) now enhance these tools, enabling automated analysis and tailored guidance, as demonstrated

K. Sumi et al. (Eds.): PERSUASIVE 2026, LNCS 16476, pp. 329–344, 2026.
https://doi.org/10.1007/978-3-032-19687-3_24

by systems like COFIT, which uses AI for portion-control feedback and coaching [13]. Such technologies show potential for scalable, personalized nutrition interventions.

However, many existing nutrition apps remain narrow in scope, emphasizing calorie tracking or weight loss while overlooking diverse, condition-specific dietary needs [11,17,45,46]. Most adopt generic wellness approaches that fail to accommodate chronic conditions such as diabetes or hypertension, and few offer adaptive personalization that evolves with users' changing health, limiting long-term engagement and persuasive effectiveness [11,17,45,46].

To bridge this gap in apps for spcific health challenges, this research aims to develop a mobile health solution that provides personalized, condition-specific dietary support through a persuasive, AI-enabled design. The objective is to create and evaluate HealKitchen, a system that integrates behavioral theory, nutritional science, and AI to deliver tailored recipe and grocery recommendations aligned with users' health profiles. Through adaptive personalization, persuasive strategies, and evidence-based behavioral models, the project seeks to promote sustainable healthy eating and support meaningful dietary behavior change beyond basic tracking.

2   Related Work

Mobile health (mHealth) technologies have expanded access to personalized dietary support through features such as self-monitoring, feedback, and reminders [5,45]. Popular tools like MyFitnessPal demonstrate how digital nutrition aids can improve awareness and adherence. *HealKitchen* builds on this foundation by delivering personalized, theory-driven dietary guidance that supports practical, everyday behavior change.

Behavioral theories provide structured approaches for designing effective health interventions [2,35]. Evidence shows that applications grounded in models such as the Health Belief Model, Social Cognitive Theory, and Theory of Planned Behavior achieve more durable outcomes than those without theoretical foundations [16,56]. Blanke et al. [6] offer a unifying framework for translating theory into design features, which *HealKitchen* applies across five complementary models to translate behavioral change strategies into actionable features.

The High-Performance Cycle (HPC) links effort, feedback, and rewards to support sustained engagement [31]. Hacker's Action Regulation Theory (ART) breaks broad goals into actionable steps, informing apps that guide users through meal planning or grocery behaviors [22]. Social Cognitive Theory (SCT) emphasizes self-efficacy, as demonstrated in MotiMate [8]. The Theory of Planned Behavior (TPB) links attitudes, norms, and perceived control to behavioral intentions [1]. Self-Determination Theory (SDT) highlights intrinsic motivation and autonomy [15]. *HealKitchen* draws from all five theories to translate behavioral principles into personalized, engaging dietary features.

Persuasive design elements—goal setting, feedback, prompts, and personalization—are central to sustaining healthy habits [6,19]. While nutrition apps commonly rely on self-monitoring, broader strategies such as gamification and tailored feedback have shown stronger engagement [20,21]. *HealKitchen* integrates multiple strategies within the Fogg Behavior Model to support motivation, ability, and timely action.

Food purchasing strongly shapes consumption, making grocery-focused interventions especially impactful [28,53]. Early apps like MyNutriCart improved healthy purchasing but lacked persuasive features for long-term engagement [32]. FoodSwitch offered nutritional ratings but limited personalization. *HealKitchen* expands this space by combining grocery image recognition, personalized list management, and theory-driven strategies to guide healthier choices at the moment of purchase.

AI has become central to personalized mHealth applications, enabling real-time insights from user data [5,51]. Dietary assessment has advanced from early feature-based image systems like DietCam to deep-learning models such as Im2Calories and DeepFood [25,29,36]. *HealKitchen* uses a Convolutional Neural Network-based classifier to identify grocery items and pairs this with AI-assisted recipe curation to deliver context-aware dietary recommendations.

Despite technological advancements, many nutrition apps struggle with engagement, personalization, and meaningful support during grocery decision-making [3,43]. Limited feedback, repetitive content, and narrow health targeting often reduce retention. *HealKitchen* addresses these challenges through adaptive goal-setting, personalized feedback, and support for diverse health conditions. By integrating image recognition, behavioral theory, and persuasive features at the point of purchase, it offers a scalable and comprehensive approach to sustainable dietary behavior change.

3 Systematic Literature Review

Prior to the conceptualization and design of the HealKitchen application, a systematic literature review was conducted to examine existing research on mHealth interventions targeting dietary behavior change. The systematic literature review was conducted across five major databases—PubMed, IEEE Xplore, ACM Digital Library, Google Scholar, and JMIR—covering publications from 2014 to 2024. Search terms included "nutrition app", "mHealth application", "dietary intervention", "healthy eating app", and "persuasive health application". Only English-language, peer-reviewed journals and conference papers were included, and all studies were screened and coded independently by two reviewers. A deductive thematic analysis guided by predefined metrics—features and functionality, persuasive strategies, adherence to evidence-based guidelines, target demographics, and technology used—was applied to 92 selected studies. Due to space constraints and anonymization requirement, the details of the review was not included in this paper.

The review revealed that most mHealth applications emphasize calorie tracking and dietary monitoring but often lack long-term engagement features and theoretical grounding. The most frequent persuasive strategies were self-monitoring, feedback, and goal setting, with personalization, reminders, and gamification appearing less frequently. Apps incorporating these persuasive features demonstrated higher user retention and behavior change effectiveness. Calorie counting and educational content were the most common functionalities, while social and gamified features enhanced sustained engagement. Evidence-based adherence, such as following national dietary guidelines, was positively associated with user trust and outcomes.

Demographically, most apps targeted adults and individuals managing obesity or diabetes, revealing a limited focus on users with multiple or less common health conditions. The review also showed that mobile applications dominate the digital nutrition landscape (approximately 87%), highlighting the accessibility and flexibility of mobile technology for dietary interventions.

These findings informed the conceptual and technical design of *HealKitchen*. The app integrates evidence-based and theory-driven persuasive strategies—personalization, feedback, goal setting, and gamification—supported by AI features like image recognition and recipe curation. In doing so, *HealKitchen* addresses observed gaps by offering a mobile-first, adaptive, and engaging solution for sustained healthy dietary behavior.

4   Design of HealKitchen's Backend Architecture

The HealKitchen application was developed as a full-stack, cross-platform system comprising a mobile frontend and a modular backend integrated with an object detection neural network model. Its architecture follows a research-driven design grounded in behavioral change theories to support healthier dietary habits through persuasive, theory-informed features [6].

4.1   Integration of Comprehensive Behavioral Model

HealKitchen applies the comprehensive behavioral model by Blanke et al. [6], integrating five behavioral theories—High-Performance Cycle (HPC), Action Regulation Theory (ART), Social Cognitive Theory (SCT), Theory of Planned Behavior (TPB), and Self-Determination Theory (SDT)—to translate theory into actionable application features. Each theory contributes complementary strengths to sustain motivation, guide task completion, and enhance self-efficacy and autonomy.

The HPC defined the overarching goal of promoting long-term healthy dietary behavior tailored to users' health profiles. The ART operationalized this goal by decomposing it into manageable subtasks such as recipe selection, grocery list creation, and progress tracking. SCT informed features enhancing self-efficacy, including recipe recommendations, feedback loops, and social proof via popular recipes. TPB guided the promotion of positive attitudes toward healthy eating through simplified grocery planning and perceived behavioral control. SDT supported autonomy and intrinsic motivation by enabling users to customize preferences, earn rewards, and internalize healthy behaviors through gamified achievements. Together, these theories shaped HealKitchen's design to foster sustained dietary change.

4.2 Overview of System Architecture

As shown in Fig. 1, HealKitchen's modular architecture integrates behavioral design with AI-based personalization. The backend, built with Flask, follows a Model–View–Controller (MVC) pattern to ensure scalability and separation of concerns. The system's primary components include a personalized recipe recommendation module, grocery list management, and an image recognition system for real-time nutritional insights.

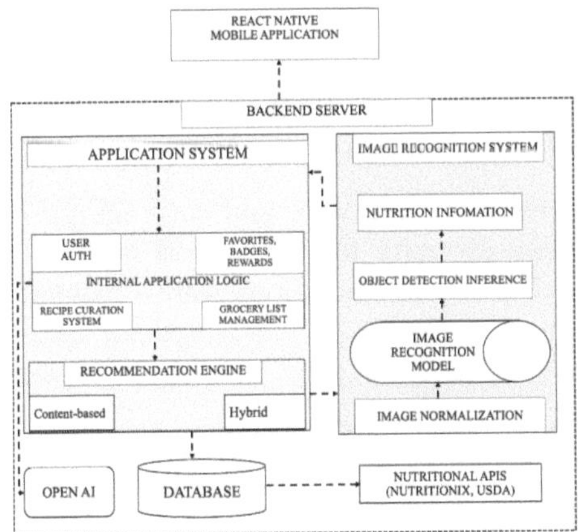

Fig. 1. System architecture of HealKitchen application

MongoDB was selected for flexible schema management and compliance with data residency requirements. Entities were defined using PyMongo and encrypted with AES-256 for security, including user health data fields *healthChallenges* and *desiredNutrients*. Recipe data was curated using USDA FoodData Central [52], Healthline [23], and WebMD [55], mapped to 87 health conditions, and augmented via OpenAI-assisted recipe generation to form a structured database of 138 healthy recipes.

4.3 Recipe Recommendation System

HealKitchen employs a hybrid recommendation model combining content-based and collaborative filtering [9]. User profiles include declared health conditions, nutrient goals, and past preferences. Recipe vectors encode nutrients, ingredients, and supported health conditions. Similarity is computed via cosine similarity:

$$(U, R_r) = \frac{U \cdot R_r}{|U| \cdot |R_r|}$$

Recommendations balance relevance and diversity, improving personalization and variety.

Evaluation metrics included precision for content relevance:

$$\text{Precision} = \frac{|R_{\text{relevant}}|}{|R_{\text{recommended}}|}$$

and diversity, measured as one minus mean cosine similarity between recipe vectors:

$$\text{Diversity} = 1 - \frac{2}{n(n-1)} \sum_{i=1}^{n-1} \sum_{j=i+1}^{n} \text{sim}(v_i, v_j)$$

Coverage assessed dataset utilization:

$$\text{Coverage} = \frac{|R_{\text{recommended}} \cap R_{\text{all}}|}{|R_{\text{all}}|}$$

Results (Table 1) showed high relevance and coverage for content-based recommendations and greater diversity for the hybrid model, enhancing user satisfaction. This means that recommendations were considered to be diverse and relevant to users.

Table 1. Performance Metrics for Recommendation Algorithms

Algorithm	Relevance	Coverage	Diversity
Content-Based	1.0	0.70	0.25
Hybrid	1.0	0.14	0.37

4.4   Image Recognition System

The second backend component is a Convolutional Neural Network (CNN)-based grocery image recognition system (Fig. 2), trained on 28,015 annotated images across 41 grocery categories. Using a fine-tuned Faster R-CNN ResNet-50 model, the system identifies grocery items and retrieves their nutritional information through the Nutritionix API [38]. Model performance achieved 85.8% accuracy, mean Average Precision at Intersection over Union (IoU) = 0.50 (mAP@0.50) = 0.76, and mean Average Recall with up to 100 detections per image (mAR@100) = 0.70, comparable to state-of-the-art image recognition models [37, 54]. Table 2 summarizes the quantitative evaluation. Figure 3 illustrates inference results, demonstrating accurate real-time identification of grocery items and reinforcing user self-efficacy in making healthy purchase decisions.

In summary, HealKitchen integrates behavioral theories, personalized recommendations, and image recognition within a secure, scalable architecture to guide users from intention to healthy action through persuasive, AI-driven features.

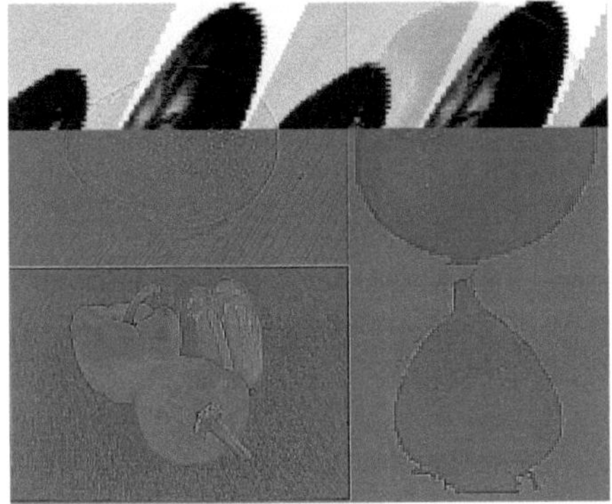

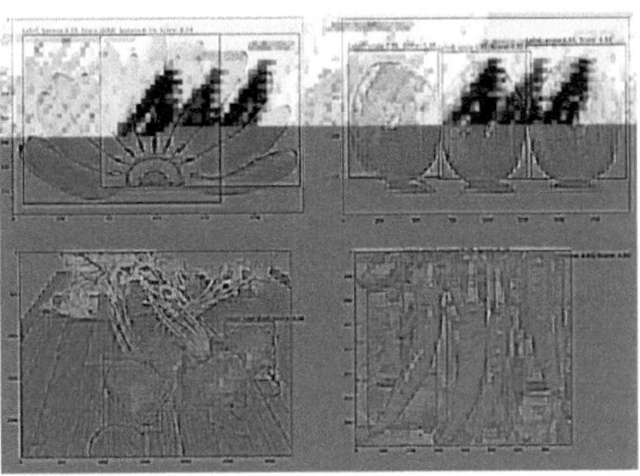

Fig. 2. Sample grocery images used for training

Fig. 3. Evaluation Results of Real-Time Inference

Table 2. Object Detection Evaluation Results

Metric	IoU Threshold	Score
Mean Average Precision	0.50:0.95	0.64
Mean Average Precision@0.50	0.50	0.76
Mean Average Recall@100	–	0.70

5 Development of HealKitchen Mobile Application

The HealKitchen mobile application was developed as a cross-platform interface using React Native [34] to deliver its persuasive, theory-driven features on Android and iOS. The app integrates backend functionalities—including condition-specific recipe recommendation, grocery list generation, AI-powered recipe curation, and grocery image recognition for both in-store and at-home items—within an intuitive, behavior-oriented design that supports sustained healthy eating.

5.1 User Onboarding and Authentication

New users interact first with secure signup and login screens. The onboarding process collects health conditions and nutritional goals to personalize recommendations, reinforcing user trust and self-efficacy. The user dashboard provides quick access to recipes, shopping lists, and progress tracking.

5.2 Recipe Recommendations and Ratings

The home screen displays personalized recipe recommendations generated by the backend system, integrating concepts from ART, SCT, and TPB to enhance personalization, feedback, and social support (Fig. 4). Recipes are displayed in interactive cards linking to detailed nutritional and preparation data. Users can rate recipes (Fig. 5), providing feedback that improves recommendations for others and reinforces engagement through social proof.

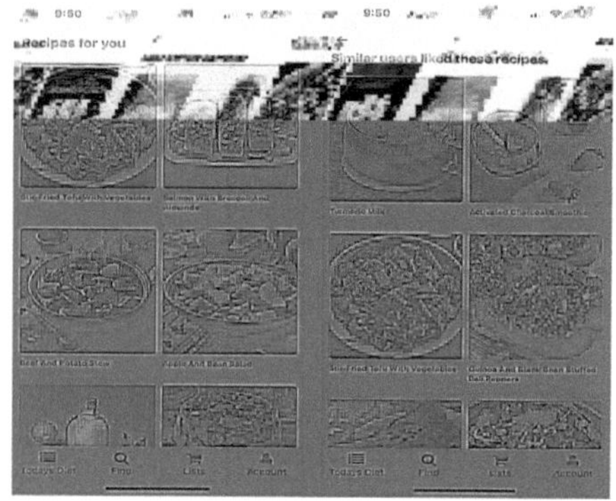

Fig. 4. Personalized recipe recommendations

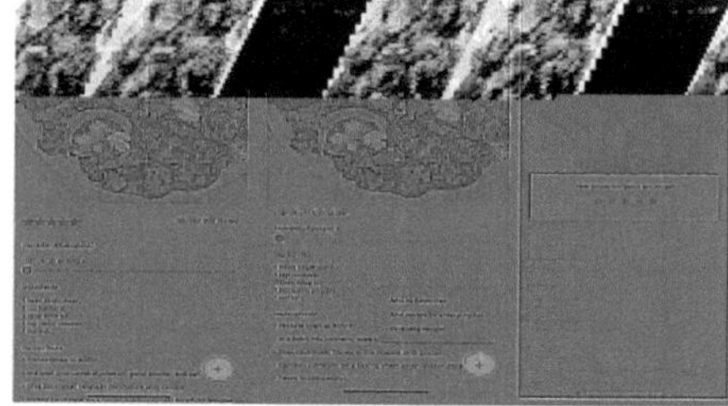

Fig. 5. Recipe rating system

5.3   Shopping Lists, Favorites, and Recipe Curation

Users can add ingredients from recipes to a dynamic grocery list by a single click, simplifying purchase planning and supporting behavioral reduction strategies. Items can be manually added or removed also, while favorite recipes appear on the dashboard for quick access. The AI-driven recipe curation system uses GPT-4 and DALLE-3 via OpenAI's API to suggest meals based on available ingredients and user health profiles, promoting self-efficacy and goal-setting (Fig. 6).

5.4   Gamification and Rewards

Gamification elements encourage sustained use through weekly challenges, streaks, and points that unlock badges (Fig. 7). These mechanisms apply feedback and reinforcement principles from SDT and TPB, turning healthy eating into an engaging experience.

5.5   Grocery Recognition and Deployment

An integrated grocery recognition feature (Fig. 8) allows users to capture or upload food images—whether in stores or from their fridge or pantry—for real-time nutritional insights and personalized, condition-specific recipe suggestions using the Convolutional Neural Network-based recognition model. This supports point-of-decision persuasion during shopping and at home.

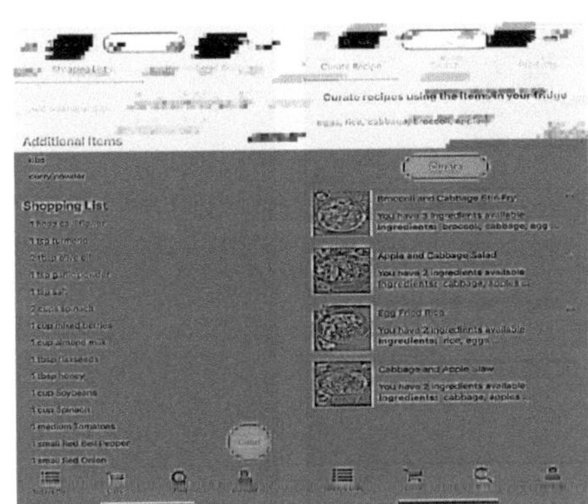

Fig. 6. Grocery List & Recipe Curation System

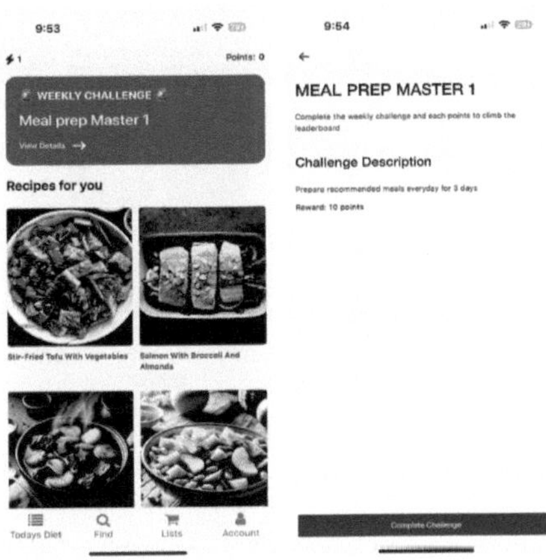

Fig. 7. Gamification interface showing points, streaks, and challenges

Fig. 8. Grocery Image Recognition System

5.6 Persuasive Strategies in HealKitchen

HealKitchen's persuasive design draws from behavioral theories to motivate healthy dietary habits [18,42]. Key strategies include personalization (adaptive content based on health data), social proof (ratings and collaborative filtering), goal setting (shopping lists and challenges), feedback (ratings and progress summaries), rewards (points and badges), and gamification (interactive challenges). These features collectively enhance motivation, ability, and engagement while supporting autonomy and sustained dietary change (Fig. 9).

6 Evaluation of *HealKitchen*

To assess HealKitchen's usability, engagement, and perceived usefulness, a formative mixed-methods user evaluation was conducted. The study examined how users interact with the application in real-world contexts, identified usability issues, and gathered feedback to inform iterative improvements. The study was

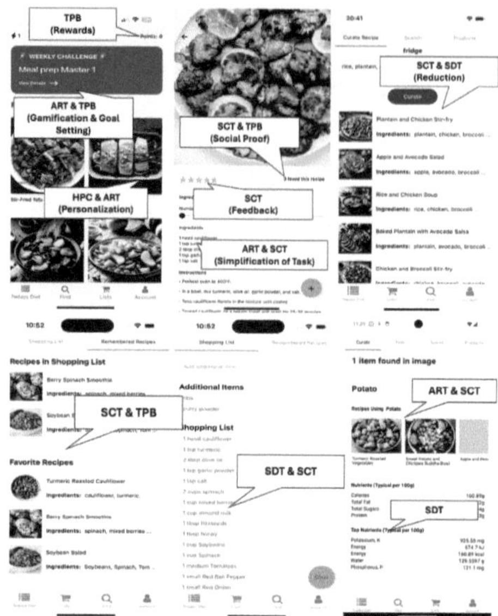

Fig. 9. Persuasive Strategies & Behavioral Change Theories implemented in HealKitchen

approved by the Behavioural Research Ethics Board of the University of British Columbia, Okanagan campus.

6.1   Study Design

A remote usability testing approach was used, enabling participants to use the mobile app in their natural environments, supporting ecological validity [27]. The study combined quantitative (Likert-scale survey) and qualitative (open-ended questions) methods to assess four constructs drawn from the Technology Acceptance Model (TAM) [14]: perceived usefulness, ease of use, engagement, and aesthetics. Perceived usefulness measured the app's support for healthy eating and dietary decision-making; ease of use evaluated interface clarity and accessibility; engagement assessed motivation and sustained interest [39]; and aesthetics examined design appeal [26]. This structured framework ensured both functional and experiential assessment (Figs. 11 and 12).

6.2   Participants and Procedure

Following ethical approval at our University, 20 participants were recruited via posters and snowball sampling. Participants received installation instructions and consent forms, then accessed the HealKitchen app through Google Play and Apple App Store testing tracks. They were instructed to explore key features—recipe recommendations, shopping lists, curation, image recognition,

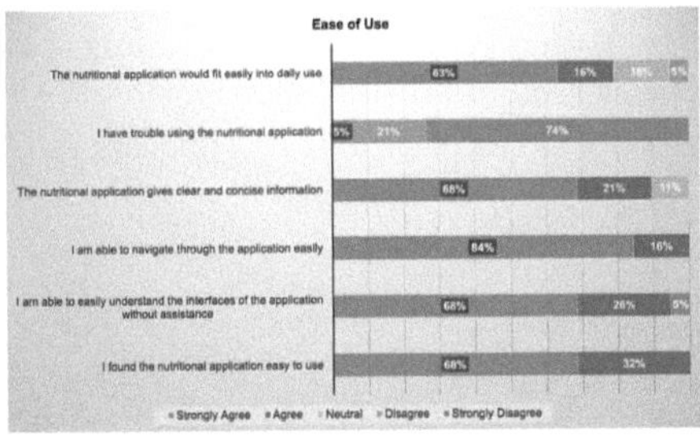

Fig. 10. Evaluation of Ease of Use

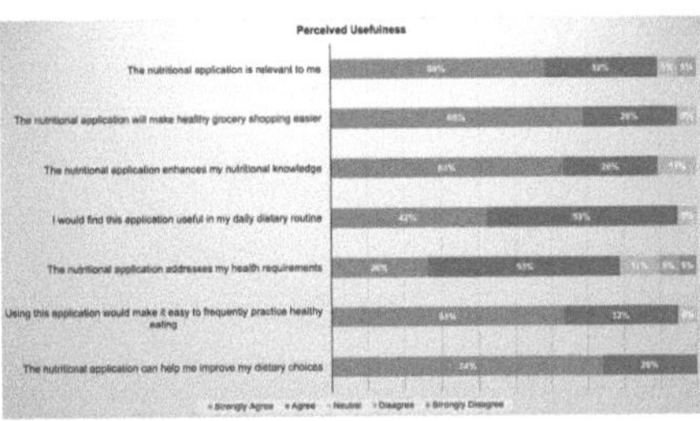

Fig. 11. Evaluation of Perceived Use-fulness

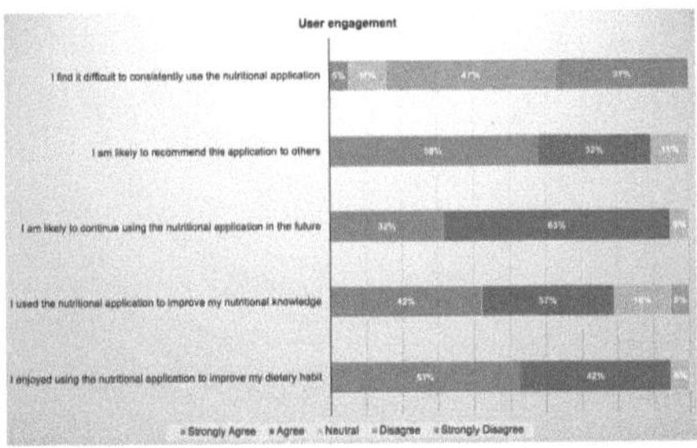

Fig. 12. Evaluation of User Engagement

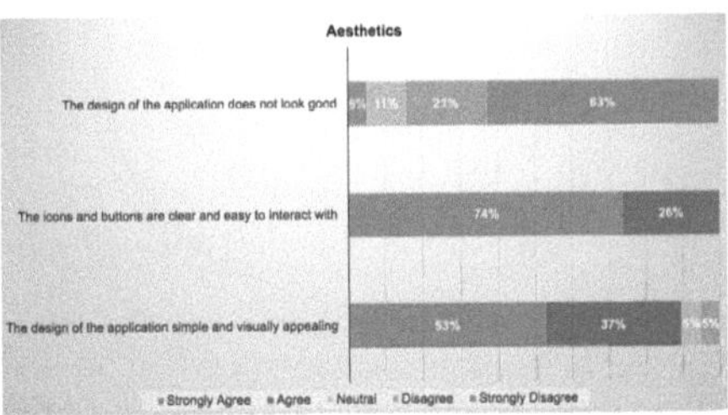

Fig. 13. Evaluation of Aesthetic Design

and gamification—over several sessions. Nineteen completed the post-use survey (95% response rate). This sample aligns with best practices for formative HCI studies [27].

6.3 Survey Instrument and Analysis

A Qualtrics questionnaire collected responses via 5-point Likert-scale and open-ended questions. Quantitative data were analyzed using descriptive statistics (mean, SD, frequency distribution), while qualitative data underwent thematic analysis following Braun and Clarke's six-phase approach [7]. Two coders independently identified and validated emerging themes to enhance reliability.

6.4 Quantitative Findings

Figure 10, 11, 12, 13 summarize core findings. Users rated **ease of use** highly $(M = 4.6,\ SD = 0.26)$, indicating intuitive navigation. **Perceived usefulness** $(M = 4.45,\ SD = 0.20)$ reflected agreement that the app supports healthier food choices and improves grocery planning. **Engagement** scored $M = 4.29$

(SD = 0.19), with 95% reporting enjoyment and intent to continue using the app. **Aesthetics** received M = 4.49 (SD = 0.31), highlighting satisfaction with layout and design. The overall rating averaged 4.58/5, with 94% of participants rating HealKitchen above 4 stars.

6.5 Qualitative Insights

Open-ended responses were grouped into six major themes (Table 3). Participants requested greater recipe diversity, multimedia content (videos, audio), improved UI/UX elements, and reminders for grocery shopping or meal preparation. Users also suggested advanced personalization (editable health profiles) and AI-driven or social features. Some praised the app's existing functionality, citing no need for additional features. User impressions (Table 4) emphasized HealKitchen's usefulness, innovation, and ease of use. Participants described it as "impactful," "innovative," and "simple to use," confirming both functional and emotional resonance with its design.

Table 3. Themes Identified from Feature Improvement Feedback

Theme	Description	Example Quotes
Enhanced Recipe Content	Desire for diverse, culturally varied, and multimedia-supported recipes.	"More recipes and calorie calculator", "Instructional videos would be cool."
UI/UX Refinement	Suggestions for smoother design and contextual explanations.	"The + button covers part of the recipe", "Design can look better."
Smart Reminders	Requests for notifications and prompts.	"Reminders for grocery shopping or meal planning."
AI & External Features	Interest in AI-driven personalization and food delivery integration.	"Integration with food delivery apps."
Gamification & Community	Calls for points and referral features to motivate users.	"Game mechanics for earning points."
Satisfaction with Current Features	Several users expressed full satisfaction.	"The app already has enough functionalities."

Table 4. Themes from Overall User Impressions

Theme	Description	Example Quotes
Perceived Usefulness	Users valued the app's role in improving diet and awareness.	"This app has helped me with my diet and nutrients."
Innovation	Praised for originality and creative feature integration.	"A very innovative and user-friendly app."
Ease of Use	Widely described as intuitive and simple.	"Easy to navigate and interact with."

6.6 Summary of Results

The evaluation revealed high user satisfaction and strong perceived usefulness, confirming that HealKitchen effectively integrates behavioral theory and persuasive strategies. These findings reinforce the value of combining personalization, feedback, and gamification to sustain engagement [40]. Key improvements were identified, including broader recipe variety, enhanced UI consistency, smart notifications, and editable health profiles. These refinements were implemented in the next development iteration, aligning with user-centered design and agile principles [44,57]. Overall, the study validates HealKitchen's usability and persuasive potential as a theory-driven mHealth application for promoting healthy dietary behavior.

7   Conclusion

This research presented the design and formative evaluation of *HealKitchen*, a persuasive mHealth application that applies behavioral theory, personalized recommendations, and AI-based grocery image recognition to support healthier eating. Mixed-methods findings indicated high usability, engagement, and perceived usefulness. Feedback highlighted needs for more diverse recipes, interface improvements, multimedia support, and smart reminders. Key limitations included the lack of a clinically validated recipe–condition database, reliance on AI-generated content, and limited grocery image datasets affecting recognition accuracy. Future work will focus on validating recipe content, expanding the image dataset, and conducting a 6–12-month longitudinal study.

Acknowledgement. We acknowledge the support of the Natural Sciences and Engineering Research Council of Canada (NSERC), [funding reference number RGPIN-2022-03689].

References

1. Ajzen, I.: The theory of planned behavior. Organ. Behav. Hum. Decis. Process. **50**(2), 179–211 (1991)
2. Ajzen, I.: From intentions to actions: a theory of planned behavior. In: Kuhl, J., Beckmann, J. (eds.) Action Control. SSSSP, pp. 11–39. Springer, Heidelberg (1985). https://doi.org/10.1007/978-3-642-69746-3_2
3. Amagai, S., Pila, S., Kaat, A.J., Nowinski, C.J., Gershon, R.C.: Challenges in participant engagement and retention using mobile health apps: literature review. J. Med. Internet Res. **24**(4), e35120 (2022)
4. Amugongo, L.M., Kriebitz, A., Boch, A., Lütge, C.: Mobile computer vision-based applications for food recognition and volume and calorific estimation: a systematic review. In: Healthcare. vol. 11, p. 59. MDPI (2022)
5. Bhatt, P., Liu, J., Gong, Y., Wang, J., Guo, Y.: Emerging artificial intelligence-empowered mhealth: scoping review. JMIR Mhealth Uhealth **10**(6), e35053 (2022)
6. Blanke, J., Billieux, J., Vögele, C.: A theory-driven design framework for smartphone applications to support healthy and sustainable grocery shopping. Hum. Behav. Emerg. Technol. **3**(5), 687–699 (2021)
7. Braun, V., Clarke, V.: Using thematic analysis in psychology. Qualitative research in psychology. Qual. Res. Psychol. **3**(2), 77–101 (2006)
8. Brindal, E., Hendrie, G.A., Freyne, J., et al.: Combining persuasive technology with behavioral theory to support weight maintenance through a mobile phone app: protocol for the motimate app. JMIR Res. Protoc. **5**(1), e4664 (2016)

9. Burke, R.: Hybrid recommender systems: survey and experiments. User Model. User-Adap. Inter. **12**, 331–370 (2002)
10. CACHE: Navigating dietary restrictions with a chronic condition (2022). https://cacheducation.org/news/navigating-dietary-restrictions-with-a-chronic-condition/. Accessed 26 Jul 2025
11. Cheah, K.J., Manaf, Z.A., Ludin, A.F.M., Razalli, N.H., Mokhtar, N.M., Ali, S.H.M.: Mobile apps for common noncommunicable disease management: systematic search in app stores and evaluation using the mobile app rating scale. JMIR Mhealth Uhealth **12**(1), e49055 (2024)
12. Childs, C.E., Calder, P.C., Miles, E.A.: Diet and immune function (2019)
13. Chueh, T.L., Wang, Z.L., Ngu, Y.J., Lin, P.L., Owaga, E., Hsieh, R.H.: A mobile-based nutrition tracker app enhanced dietitian-guided 2: 1: 1 diet-induced weight loss: an 8-week retrospective cohort study in taiwan. Nutrients **16**(14), 2331 (2024). https://doi.org/10.3390/nu16142331
14. Davis, F.D., et al.: Technology acceptance model: tam. Al-Suqri, MN, Al-Aufi, AS: Inf. Seek. Behav. Technol. Adopt. **205**(219), 5 (1989)
15. Deci, E.L., Ryan, R.M.: The "what" and "why" of goal pursuits: Human needs and the self-determination of behavior. Psychol. Inq. **11**(4), 227–268 (2000)
16. Elder, J.P., Ayala, G.X., Harris, S.: Theories and intervention approaches to health-behavior change in primary care. Am. J. Prev. Med. **17**(4), 275–284 (1999)
17. Evans, D.: Myfitnesspal. Br. J. Sports Med. **51**(14), 1101–1102 (2017)
18. Fogg, B.J.: Persuasive technology: using computers to change what we think and do. Ubiquity **2002**(December), 2 (2002)
19. Fogg, B.J.: A behavior model for persuasive design. In: Proceedings of the 4th international Conference on Persuasive Technology, pp. 1–7 (2009)
20. Froome, H.M., et al.: The effectiveness of the foodbot factory mobile serious game on increasing nutrition knowledge in children. Nutrients **12**(11), 3413 (2020)
21. Gund, A.: On the design and evaluation of an eHealth system for management of patients in out-of-hospital care. Chalmers Tekniska Hogskola (Sweden) (2011)
22. Hacker, W.: Action regulation theory: a practical tool for the design of modern work processes? Eur. J. Work Organ. Psy. **12**(2), 105–130 (2003)
23. Healthline Media: Healthline nutrition. https://www.healthline.com/nutrition
24. Koene, R.J., Prizment, A.E., Blaes, A., Konety, S.H.: Shared risk factors in cardiovascular disease and cancer **133**(11), 1104–1114 (2016). https://doi.org/10.1161/CIRCULATIONAHA.115.020406
25. Kong, F., Tan, J.: DietCam: automatic dietary assessment with mobile camera phones. Pervasive Mob. Comput. **8**(1), 147–163 (2012). https://doi.org/10.1016/j.pmcj.2011.07.003, https://linkinghub.elsevier.com/retrieve/pii/S1574119211001131
26. Lavie, T., Tractinsky, N.: Assessing dimensions of perceived visual aesthetics of web sites. Int. J. Hum Comput Stud. **60**(3), 269–298 (2004)
27. Lazar, J., Feng, J.H., Hochheiser, H.: Research Methods in Human-Computer Interaction. Morgan Kaufmann (2017)
28. Liberato, S.C., Bailie, R., Brimblecombe, J.: Nutrition interventions at point-of-sale to encourage healthier food purchasing: a systematic review. BMC Public Health **14**, 1–14 (2014)
29. Liu, C., Cao, Yu., Luo, Y., Chen, G., Vokkarane, V., Ma, Y.: DeepFood: deep learning-based food image recognition for computer-aided dietary assessment. In: Chang, C.K., Chiari, L., Cao, Yu., Jin, H., Mokhtari, M., Aloulou, H. (eds.) ICOST 2016. LNCS, vol. 9677, pp. 37–48. Springer, Cham (2016). https://doi.org/10.1007/978-3-319-39601-9_4

30. Lobstein, T., Davies, S.: Defining and labelling 'healthy' and 'unhealthy' food. Public Health Nutr. **12**(3), 331–340 (2009)
31. Locke, E.A., Latham, G.P.: Work motivation: the high performance cycle. In: Work Motivation, pp. 3–25. Psychology Press (2013)
32. López, D., et al.: Development and evaluation of a nutritional smartphone application for making smart and healthy choices in grocery shopping. Healthcare Inf. Res. **23**(1), 16–24 (2017)
33. McCarroll, R., Eyles, H., Mhurchu, C.N.: Effectiveness of mobile health (mhealth) interventions for promoting healthy eating in adults: a systematic review. Prev. Med. **105**, 156–168 (2017)
34. Meta Platforms, I.: React native (2024). https://reactnative.dev/. Accessed 3 Jul 2025
35. Michie, S., Abraham, C., Whittington, C., McAteer, J., Gupta, S.: Effective techniques in healthy eating and physical activity interventions: a meta-regression. Health Psychol. **28**(6), 690 (2009)
36. Myers, A., et al.: Im2calories: towards an automated mobile vision food diary. In: 2015 IEEE International Conference on Computer Vision (ICCV), pp. 1233–1241. IEEE (2015). https://doi.org/10.1109/ICCV.2015.146, http://ieeexplore.ieee.org/document/7410503/
37. Nadeem, M., Shen, H., Choy, L., Barakat, J.M.H.: Smart diet diary: real-time mobile application for food recognition. Appl. Syst. Innov. **6**(2), 53 (2023)
38. Nutritionix: Nutrition API by nutritionix (2025). https://www.nutritionix.com/business/api. Accessed 01 Apr 2024
39. O'Brien, H.L., Toms, E.G.: The development and evaluation of a survey to measure user engagement. J. Am. Soc. Inform. Sci. Technol. **61**(1), 50–69 (2010)
40. Oinas-Kukkonen, H., Harjumaa, M.: Persuasive systems design: key issues, process model and system features 1. In: Routledge Handbook of Policy Design, pp. 87–105. Routledge (2018)
41. Organization, W.H.: Harmonizing and mainstreaming the measurement of healthy diets: technical expert meeting, Bellagio, Italy, 28 November-2 December 2022. World Health Organization (2024)
42. Orji, R., Moffatt, K.: Persuasive technology for health and wellness: State-of-the-art and emerging trends. Health Informatics J. **24**(1), 66–91 (2018)
43. Palacios, C., Torres, M., López, D., Trak-Fellermeier, M.A., Coccia, C., Pérez, C.M.: Effectiveness of the nutritional app "mynutricart" on food choices related to purchase and dietary behavior: a pilot randomized controlled trial. Nutrients **10**(12), 1967 (2018)
44. Perski, O., Blandford, A., West, R., Michie, S.: Conceptualising engagement with digital behaviour change interventions: a systematic review using principles from critical interpretive synthesis. Transl. Behav. Med. **7**(2), 254–267 (2017)
45. Salas-Groves, E., Galyean, S., Alcorn, M., Childress, A., et al.: Behavior change effectiveness using nutrition apps in people with chronic diseases: scoping review. JMIR Mhealth Uhealth **11**(1), e41235 (2023)
46. Sama, P.R., Eapen, Z.J., Weinfurt, K.P., Shah, B.R., Schulman, K.A.: An evaluation of mobile health application tools. JMIR Mhealth Uhealth **2**(2), e3088 (2014)
47. Shen, J., et al.: Mediterranean dietary patterns and cardiovascular health. Annu. Rev. Nutr. **35**(1), 425–449 (2015)
48. Swar, B., Hameed, T., Reychav, I.: Information overload, psychological ill-being, and behavioral intention to continue online healthcare information search. Comput. Hum. Behav. **70**, 416–425 (2017)

49. Tiwari, A., Aggarwal, A., Tang, W., Drewnowski, A.: Cooking at home: a strategy to comply with us dietary guidelines at no extra cost. Am. J. Prev. Med. **52**(5), 616–624 (2017)
50. Tonkin, E., Brimblecombe, J., Wycherley, T.P.: Characteristics of smartphone applications for nutrition improvement in community settings: a scoping review. Adv. Nutr. **8**, 308–322 (2017)
51. Topol, E.: Deep medicine: how artificial intelligence can make healthcare human again. Hachette UK (2019)
52. USDA, G.: Food data central. https://fdc.nal.usda.gov/
53. Vanderlee, L., Hobin, E.P., White, C.M., Hammond, D.: Grocery shopping, dinner preparation, and dietary habits among adolescents and young adults in Canada. Can. J. Diet. Pract. Res. **79**(4), 157–163 (2018)
54. Waltner, G., et al.: Personalized dietary self-management using mobile vision-based assistance. In: Battiato, S., Farinella, G.M., Leo, M., Gallo, G. (eds.) ICIAP 2017. LNCS, vol. 10590, pp. 385–393. Springer, Cham (2017). https://doi.org/10.1007/978-3-319-70742-6_36
55. Web Md: Nourish by WebMd. https://www.webmd.com/diet/default.htm
56. Webb, T., Joseph, J., Yardley, L., Michie, S., et al.: Using the internet to promote health behavior change: a systematic review and meta-analysis of the impact of theoretical basis, use of behavior change techniques, and mode of delivery on efficacy. J. Med. Internet Res. **12**(1), e1376 (2010)
57. Yardley, L., Spring, B.J., Riper, H., Morrison, L.G., Crane, D.H., Curtis, K., Merchant, G.C., Naughton, F., Blandford, A.: Understanding and promoting effective engagement with digital behavior change interventions. Am. J. Prev. Med. **51**(5), 833–842 (2016)

Influencing Wildfire Preparedness, Mitigation, Response and Recovery

Iyanuoluwa Sowande, Bunmi Ayodele-Makun, Adeniyi Asiyanbi[ID],
and Ifeoma Adaji[(✉)][ID]

The University of British Columbia, Okanagan Campus, British Columbia, Canada
`ifeoma.adaji@ubc.ca`

Abstract. Wildfires are increasing in frequency and severity, posing growing risks to communities such as Whistler, British Columbia. To support preparedness and community resilience, *WISEC*–a persuasive mobile application–was developed to translate fire safety principles into an interactive digital tool. The system integrates the four phases of wildfire management (Prepare, Mitigate, Respond, Recover) and provides survey-based assessments, personalized tasks, emergency contacts, social feeds, and wildfire updates. *WISEC* incorporates persuasive strategies including feedback, personalization, reminders, authority, and social proof to motivate user engagement. The platform demonstrates how mobile technologies can enhance community preparedness, improve communication during wildfire events, and support post-incident recovery.

Keywords: Wildfire Preparedness · *WISEC* · Persuasive Technologies

1 Introduction

Wildfires represent one of the most urgent climate-related threats in Canada, particularly within wildland-urban interface (WUI) communities such as Whistler, British Columbia. The year 2023 marked the most destructive wildfire season in Canadian history [13], highlighting a critical need for effective wildfire preparedness and risk reduction strategies. As wildfires intensify due to climate change, the concept of shared responsibility, a collaborative model where governments, organizations, and the public all play proactive roles, has gained traction in Canadian wildfire policy [2, 4, 31].

Research, however, has consistently shown a gap between institutional expectations and the public's understanding of their roles in wildfire risk management [21]. Many residents find the necessary steps for preparedness unclear, overwhelming, or difficult to prioritize. This disconnect hinders effective community-level engagement across all four phases of wildfire risk management: preparedness, mitigation, response, and recovery.

In response to this problem, we developed a persuasive wildfire planning mobile application, *WISEC*, tailored for residents of Whistler. The application was designed to address the identified need for personalized, actionable, and

K. Sumi et al. (Eds.): PERSUASIVE 2026, LNCS 16476, pp. 345–355, 2026.
https://doi.org/10.1007/978-3-032-19687-3_25

accessible wildfire preparedness information through an interactive digital platform. Unlike existing apps which focus primarily on response, the new application supports proactive planning by offering features across all four phases of risk management, such as wildfire readiness assessments, response guidance, and informed task planning. In addition, the application uses persuasive strategies from the Persuasive Systems Design framework [27] such as feedback, authority, personalization, self-monitoring, reminders, social role, and authority.

This paper explores the design, development, and deployment of the *WISEC* wildfire planning app. It contributes to a growing body of interdisciplinary research at the intersection of persuasive technologies, disaster risk reduction, and climate adaptation. By documenting the design process, challenges encountered, and future implications, this study aims to inform both academic understanding and practical implementation of persuasive mobile technologies for wildfire resilience. To our knowledge, no other application exists that supports users across all four phases of wildfire risk management.

2   Related Work

2.1   Wildfires in the Wildland-Urban Interface (WUI)

The expansion of human settlements into forested areas has increased wildfire risks in Canada and globally [10]. Wildland-urban interface (WUI) areas are increasingly recognized as hotspots of wildfire risk due to a convergence of human settlement and flammable landscapes [31]. In British Columbia, the effects of climate change, including hotter, drier summers, are intensifying the frequency, size, and unpredictability of wildfires [14].

Whistler, a resort municipality in British Columbia, is situated in a high-risk Wildland-Urban Interface (WUI) zone and exemplifies the complex vulnerabilities associated with this trend. Climate models project worsening fire seasons, characterized by increased spread potential and longer durations [14,33]. This context requires new strategies that go beyond suppression to emphasize prevention and community-level adaptation.

2.2   Shared Responsibility in Wildfire Risk Management

The idea of shared responsibility for wildfire management has emerged in both academic and policy discourse as a way to promote a "whole-of-society" approach [4,31]. Rather than relying solely on state-led emergency response, this approach calls on the public to take proactive roles in managing risk at the household and community level [12]. Governments have also increasingly adopted the principle of shared responsibility in wildfire policy, emphasizing that individuals, communities, and institutions must all contribute to wildfire risk reduction [31]

However, there exists a disconnect between expectations from the public and the public's belief of their role in shared responsibility [20,23]. This gap makes it difficult to coordinate wildfire response effectively and reduces the effectiveness of preparedness and mitigation efforts. Experts have applied theories of social contracts and environmental governance to explore how risk and responsibility are distributed, challenged, and re-negotiated in the context of wildfires [1, 6, 18].

In Canada, frameworks such as FireSmart have provided structured guidelines for homeowner-level mitigation [3], but their usage remains inconsistent, partly due to unclear communication and limited personalized engagement tools.

The *WISEC* app presented in this paper aims to fill this gap by creating a persuasive mobile application that presents fire safety principles into an interactive digital tool.

2.3 Persuasive Technologies in Influencing Wildfire Preparedness, Mitigation, Response and Recovery

The role of digital and mobile technologies in climate adaptation and disaster preparedness is growing. Mobile apps have been used in environmental monitoring [2], crowdsourcing [16], and wildlife tracking, but few target public-facing wildfire preparedness across all management phases. Most existing tools, such as the BC Wildfire Service app, focus on real-time alerts and maps, serving more reactive functions.

Studies highlight the potential for apps to bridge communication gaps, improve decision-making, and encourage sustained public engagement [17, 25]. However, research also points to challenges in designing user-centered applications that balance technical functionality with usability and trust.

Current persuasive applications in the form of mobile and web applications are often not developed for all phases of wildfire risk management or lack behaviour change techniques [32]. A literature review conducted by Verrucci et al. [32] indicates that while mobile and web applications can be used to influence people to prepare for wildfire, this potential has not been fully investigated or exploited. Furthermore, the authors concluded that current technologies do not incorporate behaviour change techniques which can influence users.

To fill this gap, this paper introduces WISEC, a persuasive mobile application that integrates persuasive strategies from the Persuasive systems Design framework [27] with the aim of influencing users across the four phases of wildfire management (Prepare, Mitigate, Respond, Recover).

3 Design of *WISEC* Application

The *WISEC* application is a mobile-first platform designed to support Whistler, BC residents in proactive wildfire planning using persuasive, behavior-oriented features. Built with React Native and supported by a Node.js backend, *WISEC* integrates structured content, task guidance, and real-time information to encourage preparedness and mitigation actions. Its primary goal is to nudge users toward sustained wildfire readiness by translating FireSmart principles into personalized and achievable steps.

WISEC is designed as a persuasive application following strategies from the Persuasive Systems Design framework [27]. The app is structured around the four phases of wildfire risk management: Prepare, Mitigate, Respond, and Recover. These phases form part of the wildfire emergency management cycle [7] and provide a framework for reducing vulnerability, minimizing damage, and supporting long-term resilience. Embedding these phases into the app guides users through preparedness, risk mitigation, emergency response, and recovery.

Each section aligns with the FireSmart framework [3], a Canadian wildfire mitigation framework for reducing wildfire risk to people, property, and ecosystems. The app also supports personalized planning and encourages consistent engagement with risk reduction practices.

3.1   Prepare

The Prepare phase of the wildfire emergency management cycle is implemented as a tab in the *WISEC* application and focuses on improving individual and household readiness for wildfire events. Preparedness is a key determinant of community resilience, yet many individuals remain unaware of what constitutes adequate readiness [19,22]. To address this, WISEC provides a personalized preparedness survey based on FireSmart guidelines that evaluates behaviors such as evacuation planning, emergency kit preparation, and awareness of evacuation routes.

After completing the survey, the system generates a Personal Preparedness score that reflects the user's level of readiness and provides feedback and motivation, consistent with behavior change research on self-efficacy and goal-directed behavior [5].

The Prepare tab is integrated with the task assignment system, linking each survey item to actionable tasks. For example, users who report not having a *go-bag* are assigned a task to prepare one with supporting resources. Tasks are prioritized and time-bound, helping users translate preparedness guidance into achievable actions.

3.2   Mitigate

While the Prepare phase focuses on individual readiness, the Mitigate phase targets reducing property damage risk during wildfire events and is implemented as a tab in the *WISEC* app. Research shows that property-level actions such as clearing defensible space, using fire-resistant materials, and managing flammable vegetation significantly reduce wildfire losses [7,9]. Syphard et al. [30] further identify structural ignition mitigation as one of the most cost-effective strategies for homeowners.

In *WISEC*, the Mitigate phase includes a property mitigation survey that assesses users' mitigation levels through questions about defensible space, roofing materials, and debris management. Based on responses, the system calculates a mitigation score to raise awareness and motivate action.

The app then assigns tailored mitigation tasks addressing identified weaknesses. Users lacking defensible space are prompted to clear vegetation, while those without fire-resistant materials receive resources for affordable retrofitting. Tasks are structured incrementally, enabling gradual progress while supporting long-term property-level mitigation.

3.3 Response

The Response phase serves as the primary point of contact for users during active wildfire events and is implemented as a dedicated tab in the *WISEC* app. Its goal is to provide timely and accurate information to support user safety.

This phase integrates regional emergency contacts, evacuation centers, and first responders, enabling direct access to local authorities. It also incorporates social mediabased features to deliver live updates from surrounding areas, supporting rapid communication during wildfire emergencies.

The Response phase functions as an emergency information hub, addressing the critical need for timely information during disasters [29]. Studies show that reliance on delayed or informal sources can slow evacuation decisions and increase risk [15,24]. To mitigate this, *WISEC* integrates multiple data streams, including: emergency service directories for direct contact with fire departments and evacuation centers, a custom Bluesky API feed for crowd-sourced, real-time updates, a message board for user-reported wildfire information, push notifications alerting users to active regional wildfires.

A map-based interface displays hazard zones and wildfire locations, while direct contact tools allow users to quickly reach authorities. By consolidating these channels, the Response phase supports rapid awareness and action during wildfire events.

3.4 Recover

The Recover phase is the final stage of the wildfire emergency management cycle and focuses on supporting users as they rebuild and recover from wildfire-related losses. In the *WISEC* application, this phase is implemented as a dedicated tab that provides users with curated recovery resources to reduce the long-term impacts of wildfire events.

Recovery is often the most prolonged and resource-intensive phase, involving both physical and psychological challenges [8]. It includes immediate relief as well as long-term adaptation needs such as access to funding, rebuilding guidance, and mental health services [26].

Within *WISEC*, the Recover phase offers a repository of recovery resources, including financial and insurance guidance, mental health support services, and community recovery initiatives that connect users to local rebuilding and volunteer networks. The system also promotes a resilience feedback loop by encouraging users to revisit the Prepare and Mitigate phases to strengthen future preparedness.

Overall, *WISEC*'s design uses structured guidance, personalized tasks, real-time cues, and persuasive feedback loops to support wildfire-related behavior change while maintaining a user-centered interface built for ongoing engagement.

4   Development of *WISEC* Application

4.1   Design of *WISEC*'s Backend Architecture

The *WISEC* backend was developed using Node.js with Express.js and MongoDB, chosen for scalability, JSON-compatible data handling, and integration with external services such as Sanity CMS and the Bluesky API. It exposes RESTful endpoints that provide the mobile app with wildfire data, surveys, tasks, and social content, forming the main communication layer between the client and backend services.

Authentication is handled using JSON Web Tokens (JWT) to maintain secure, stateless sessions. The module supports user registration, login, and token refresh to ensure survey progress and tasks remain tied to individual accounts. Passwords are encrypted before storage, and refresh token blacklisting prevents reuse after logout, providing secure session management.

Survey items and tasks are synchronized via webhooks, allowing updates without redeploying the backend. User responses generate preparedness and mitigation scores that provide feedback and trigger tailored tasks, translating recommendations into actionable steps.

Assigned tasks include stepwise completion criteria and external resource links. A task diary allows users to schedule tasks, supporting gradual engagement and reducing procrastination [28]. Score updates reinforce progress as tasks are completed.

The Bluesky feed module delivers curated social media updates related to wildfire conditions in Whistler. Using the Bluesky API and ATProto, posts are filtered by keywords, hashtags, and location to provide real-time, community-sourced situational awareness alongside official emergency information.

4.2   Development of *WISEC* Mobile Application

The mobile interface was developed in React Native to provide a unified experience on iOS and Android. The app consumes authenticated API endpoints and is organized into tabs corresponding to the four wildfire phases (Home, Prepare/Mitigate, Respond, Recover), ensuring a modular, phase-based interaction flow.

The Home screen serves as the main dashboard, presenting a wildfire map and a summary of user preparedness scores. The map, implemented with React Native Maps and NASA EONET data, displays active fire markers centered on Whistler (Fig. 1). Below the map, circular indicators summarize Prepare and Mitigate survey scores, allowing authenticated users to quickly assess their readiness and navigate to relevant phases.

WISEC integrates an AI chatbot using the OpenAI LLM API to answer wildfire-related questions in natural language. Custom prompting restricts responses to wildfire preparedness and response topics, helping users interpret technical information and clarify uncertainty without leaving the app.

The Prepare and Mitigate tabs combine survey components, personalized tasks, and a task diary. Surveys are grouped into thematic sections and scored

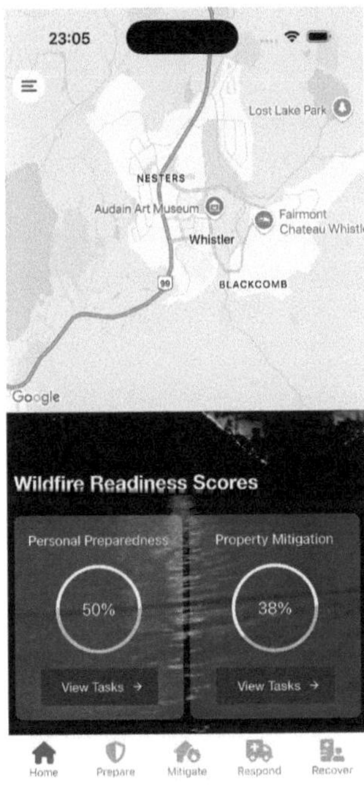

Fig. 1. WISEC homepage

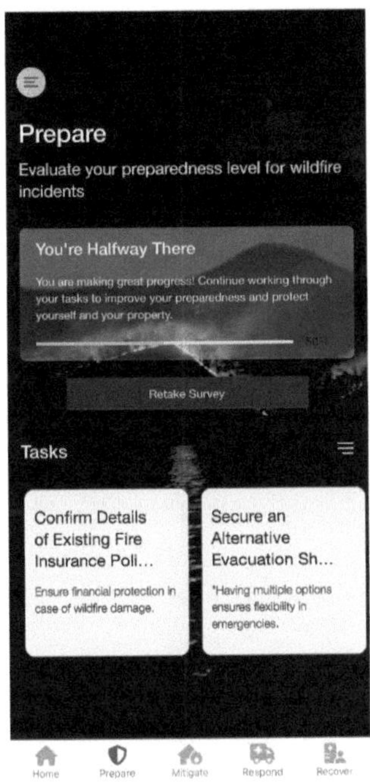

Fig. 2. WISEC Prepare page

server-side. On submission, users receive a readiness or mitigation score and a set of dynamically assigned tasks (Figs. 2 and 3). Tasks are presented in lists and detailed screens where criteria can be checked off incrementally, and scheduled through the diary to support planning and follow-through (Fig. 4).

The Response tab supports users during active wildfire events via emergency contact cards, the Bluesky feed, and the community post board. Emergency cards provide one-tap access to the fire department, police, medical services, and evacuation centers (Fig. 5). The Bluesky feed displays curated social posts relevant to fires near Whistler (Fig. 6), while the post board lets users contribute their own updates, enhancing collective situational awareness during crises.

The Recover tab presents curated post-wildfire resources. Content is rendered as informational cards linking to financial assistance, mental health services, rebuilding guidelines, and community support programs. This section closes the wildfire management loop by supporting long-term adaptation and encouraging users to re-engage with the Prepare and Mitigate phases.

WISEC includes a Posts module that enables users to share local wildfire observations directly within the app. User posts, which may include text and media, are stored with metadata such as author ID and timestamp. Media uploads are handled via Multer and stored on Cloudinary, while the database

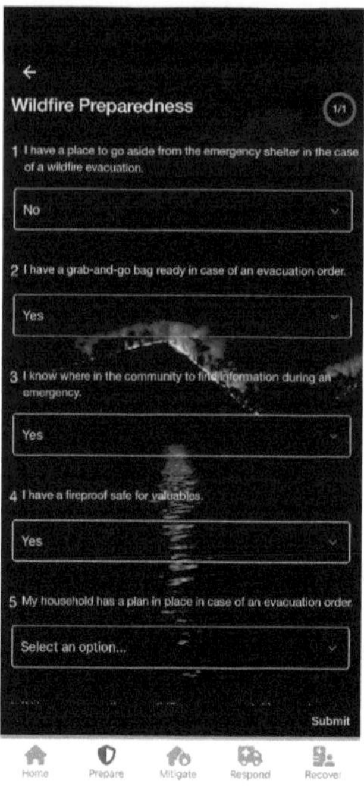

Fig. 3. WISEC preparedness survey

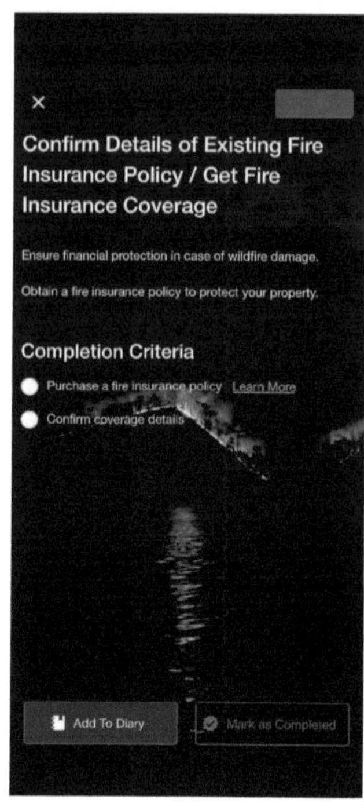

Fig. 4. WISEC Task Details screen

maintains only references. Together with the Bluesky feed, this transforms *WISEC* into a community information hub that combines external and user-generated updates.

4.3 Integration of Persuasive Strategies

Several persuasive strategies were embedded in *WISEC* to motivate user engagement in wildfire preparedness and mitigation. As shown in Fig. 1, the app employs self-monitoring through preparedness and mitigation scores on the home screen, visually reinforced using a redambergreen color gradient. Color-based cues have been shown to enhance visual persuasion [11], enabling users to quickly interpret their readiness levels.

The Prepare and Mitigate tabs use a feedback mechanism to inform users of tasks they can complete to increase their preparedness and mitigation scores. These tabs also include reminders that also support persuasive goal adherence: tasks within the Prepare and Mitigate phases can be scheduled, prompting automated notifications on the selected date. The Prepare and Mitigate tabs also incorporate personalization as a persuasive strategy. Each user's list of tasks is tailored based on their previously completed tasks and answers to the survey questions about their preparedness and mitigation efforts.

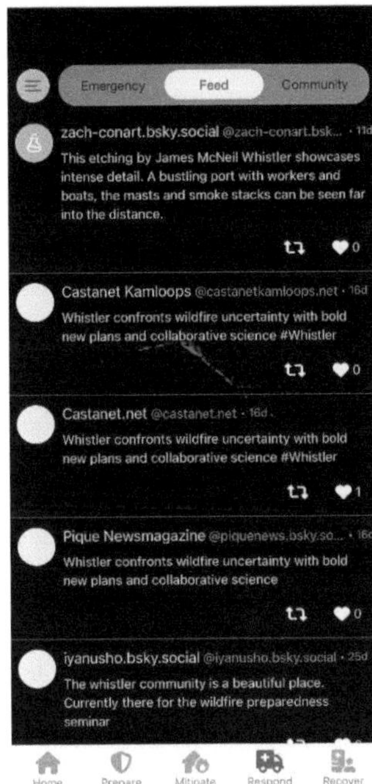

Fig. 5. WISEC Emergency Contacts List

Fig. 6. WISEC Bluesky Wildfire Feed

In addition, *WISEC* incorporates the authority strategy, specifically in the Response and Recover tabs. These tabs include lists of federal, provincial and city resources which people can access during wildfires and during the recovery phase. These resources curated from authentic sites can be seen as authority sources of information.

Furthermore, *WISEC* incorporates a social role through its community post board, where users can share wildfire-related updates and interact through likes, shares, and reposts, thereby amplifying community awareness and fostering social influence.

5   Conclusion

The development of the *WISEC* application illustrates how mobile technology can translate wildfire preparedness principles into practical, user-centered tools for at-risk communities. Persuasive strategies–such as personalization, reminders, and social proof–were embedded to motivate sustained preparedness behaviors, while features like the Task Diary and Community Post Board turn recommendations into concrete actions. Future work includes offline capabilities, dynamic location-based customization, broader emergency resource integration, and a longitudinal evaluation. Overall, *WISEC* demonstrates the potential of persuasive mobile technology to support proactive wildfire readiness and community resilience.

References

1. Adger, W.N., Quinn, T., Lorenzoni, I., Murphy, C., Sweeney, J.: Changing social contracts in climate-change adaptation. Nat. Clim. Chang. **3**(4), 330–333 (2013)
2. Andrachuk, M., Marschke, M., Hings, C., Armitage, D.: Smartphone technologies supporting community-based environmental monitoring and implementation: a systematic scoping review. Biol. Cons. **237**, 430–442 (2019)
3. Asfaw, H.W., Christianson, A.C., Watson, D.O.: Incentives and barriers to homeowners' uptake of firesmart® canada's recommended wildfire mitigation activities in the city of fort mcmurray, alberta. Fire **5**(3), 80 (2022)
4. Asiyanbi, A., Davidsen, C.: Governing wildfire risk in Canada: the rise of an apparatus of security. Ann. Am. Assoc. Geogr. **113**(5), 1207–1223 (2023)
5. Bandura, A.: Self-efficacy: The exercise of control. Macmillan (1997)
6. Blackburn, S., Pelling, M.: The political impacts of adaptation actions: Social contracts, a research agenda. Wiley Interdisciplinary Rev. Climate Change **9**(6), e549 (2018)
7. Calkin, D.E., Cohen, J.D., Finney, M.A., Thompson, M.P.: How risk management can prevent future wildfire disasters in the wildland-urban interface. Proc. Natl. Acad. Sci. **111**(2), 746–751 (2014)
8. Carroll, M.S., Cohn, P.J., Seesholtz, D.N., Higgins, L.L.: Fire as a galvanizing and fragmenting influence on communities: the case of the rodeo-chediski fire. Soc. Nat. Resour. **18**(4), 301–320 (2005)
9. Cohen, J.: The wildland-urban interface fire problem. Fremontia. **38**(2)-38 (3), 16-22, pp. 16–22 (2010)
10. Coogan, S.C., Daniels, L.D., Boychuk, D., Burton, P.J., Flannigan, M.D., Gauthier, S., Kafka, V., Park, J.S., Wotton, B.M.: Fifty years of wildland fire science in Canada. Can. J. For. Res. **51**(2), 283–302 (2021)
11. Garber, L.L., Hyatt, E.M.: Color as a tool for visual persuasion. In: Persuasive imagery, pp. 313–336. Routledge (2003)
12. Henstra, D., Thistlethwaite, J., Brown, C., Scott, D.: Flood risk management and shared responsibility: exploring Canadian public attitudes and expectations. J. Flood Risk Manage. **12**(1), e12346 (2019)
13. Institute, C.C.: Fact sheet: Wildfires (2024). https://climateinstitute.ca/news/fact-sheet-wildfires/. Accessed 23 Aug 2025
14. IPCC: Sixth assessment report: Impacts, adaptation and vulnerability (2022). https://www.ipcc.ch/report/ar6/wg2/. Accessed 11 June 2025
15. Kuligowski, E.D.: Terror defeated: occupant sensemaking, decision-making and protective action in the 2001 World Trade Center disaster. University of Colorado at Boulder (2011)
16. Laso Bayas, J.C., See, L., Bartl, H., Sturn, T., Karner, M., Fraisl, D., Moorthy, I., Busch, M., Van Der Velde, M., Fritz, S.: Crowdsourcing lucas: citizens generating reference land cover and land use data with a mobile app. Land **9**(11), 446 (2020)

17. Laso Bayas, J.C., See, L., Fritz, S., Sturn, T., Perger, C., Dürauer, M., Karner, M., Moorthy, I., Schepaschenko, D., Domian, D., et al.: Crowdsourcing in-situ data on land cover and land use using gamification and mobile technology. Remote Sensing **8**(11), 905 (2016)
18. Lukasiewicz, A., Dovers, S., Eburn, M.: Shared responsibility: the who, what and how. Environ. Hazards **16**(4), 291–313 (2017)
19. McFarlane, B.L., McGee, T.K., Faulkner, H.: Complexity of homeowner wildfire risk mitigation: an integration of hazard theories. Int. J. Wildland Fire **20**(8), 921–931 (2011)
20. McGee, T., McFarlane, B., Tymstra, C.: Wildfire: a canadian perspective. In: Wildfire hazards, risks and disasters, pp. 35–58. Elsevier (2015)
21. McGee, T.K.: Preparedness and experiences of evacuees from the 2016 fort mcmurray horse river wildfire. Fire **2**(1), 13 (2019)
22. McGee, T.K., Gatti, F., Christianson, A.C.: Wildfire. In: Routledge Handbook of Environmental Hazards and Society, pp. 137–149. Routledge (2022)
23. McLennan, B., Eburn, M.: Exposing hidden-value trade-offs: sharing wildfire management responsibility between government and citizens. Int. J. Wildland Fire **24**(2), 162–169 (2014)
24. McLennan, J., Elliott, G., Omodei, M.: Householder decision-making under imminent wildfire threat: stay and defend or leave? Int. J. Wildland Fire **21**(7), 915–925 (2012)
25. Moser, S.C.: Communicating adaptation to climate change: the art and science of public engagement when climate change comes home. Wiley Interdisciplinary Reviews: Climate Change **5**(3), 337–358 (2014)
26. Norris, F.H., Stevens, S.P., Pfefferbaum, B., Wyche, K.F., Pfefferbaum, R.L.: Community resilience as a metaphor, theory, set of capacities, and strategy for disaster readiness. Am. J. Community Psychol. **41**(1), 127–150 (2008)
27. Oinas-Kukkonen, H., Harjumaa, M.: Persuasive systems design: Key issues, process model, and system features. Commun. Assoc. Inf. Syst. **24**(1), 28 (2009)
28. Paton, D., Buergelt, P.: Risk, transformation and adaptation: Ideas for reframing approaches to disaster risk reduction. Int. J. Environ. Res. Public Health **16**(14), 2594 (2019)
29. Steelman, T.A., McCaffrey, S.: Best practices in risk and crisis communication: Implications for natural hazards management. Nat. Hazards **65**(1), 683–705 (2013)
30. Syphard, A.D., Brennan, T.J., Keeley, J.E.: The role of defensible space for residential structure protection during wildfires. Int. J. Wildland Fire **23**(8), 1165–1175 (2014)
31. Tymstra, C.: The Chinchaga Firestorm: When the moon and sun turned blue. University of Alberta (2015)
32. Verrucci, E., Perez-Fuentes, G., Rossetto, T., Bisby, L., Haklay, M., Rush, D., Rickles, P., Fagg, G., Joffe, H.: Digital engagement methods for earthquake and fire preparedness: a review. Nat. Hazards **83**(3), 1583–1604 (2016). https://doi.org/10.1007/s11069-016-2378-x
33. Wang, X., et al.: Projected changes in daily fire spread across Canada over the next century. Environ. Res. Lett. **12**(2), 025005 (2017)

Serendipitous Learning Triggered by Crossword Puzzles with Newspaper Articles

Yasuyuki Sumi[✉] and Ryusuke Hioki

Future University Hakodate, Hokkaido 041-8655, Japan
sumi@fun.ac.jp, r-hioki@sumilab.org

Abstract. This paper proposes the use of crossword puzzles to promote serendipitous learning, defined here as learning that emerges when system design implicitly encourages users to voluntarily engage in additional information seeking. We prepared a game environment in which crossword puzzles are presented on demand from newspaper article data from the past ten years, and players can browse the corresponding articles while solving the puzzles. Thirty participants were asked to freely play crossword puzzles, and a few days later, they individually answered personalized 4-choice quizzes generated according to their actual puzzle play. Interestingly, for quiz items related to words that participants failed to input correctly even though they had viewed the corresponding newspaper articles during puzzle play, the correct answer rate was higher than for quiz items generated under other conditions. In the questionnaire conducted together with the 4-choice quizzes, several participants reported that they had voluntarily looked up the words they could not solve in the puzzles, which is consistent with this result. Furthermore, focusing on quizzes related to newspaper articles viewed during puzzle play, we confirmed that participants who reported engaging in self-directed learning achieved higher accuracy than those who did not.

Keywords: Serendipitous learning · Crossword puzzles · Newspaper articles · Large language model

1 Introduction

Promoting learners' voluntary engagement with information has been recognized as an important issue in contemporary education. Prior studies have shown that when learners maintain interest in diverse topics and explore them based on their own curiosity, learning outcomes tend to improve [1]. It has also been reported that incorporating game elements into such contexts can stimulate an appropriate level of inquisitiveness and support sustained engagement [2,3].

Rather than directly instructing learners to study specific content, this paper focuses on how learning can emerge as an unintended byproduct of interaction during game play. In this paper, we conceptualize *serendipitous learning* as learning that emerges unintentionally through interaction with a system, rather than through explicit instructional intent. The notion of serendipity has been widely discussed in the context of information behavior and human–computer interaction. Makri and Blandford [4] characterize serendipity as an unplanned yet valuable experience that emerges through interaction with information and systems, emphasizing the role of users' actions and interpretations rather than mere chance. Our definition of serendipitous learning is consistent with this perspective, focusing on learning that arises unintentionally through interaction with a designed system.

We regard *self-directed information-seeking behavior* as one observable manifestation of such serendipitous learning, reflecting users' active engagement with additional information beyond the immediate task. Accordingly, we investigate how system design can implicitly encourage users to voluntarily seek additional information beyond their originally intended task. The concept of self-directed learning has a long tradition in educational research. Knowles [5] defines self-directed learning as a process in which learners take initiative in diagnosing their learning needs and seeking relevant resources. In this study, we do not treat self-directed learning as an explicit instructional goal, but rather as an observable behavioral manifestation of serendipitous learning triggered by game play.

This paper proposes a crossword puzzle environment that leverages newspaper article data as contextual hints. Through the act of recalling words and encountering related news content during puzzle play, the system provides opportunities for users to develop broader interest in current social events without explicitly framing the experience as learning.

In the system introduced in this paper, to encourage game play based on the player's curiosity, we enabled on-demand generation of puzzle screens. As a consequence, because the words used in the puzzle are not known beforehand, it became necessary either to automatically generate hint texts for the words selected at puzzle-generation time, or to prepare hint texts for all candidate words in advance. We therefore attempted to automatically generate hint texts using a large language model, and succeeded in generating hint texts with a certain level of quality.

We also struggled to make the post-play survey for measuring the learning effect of crossword puzzle play more objective. In the preliminary investigation, post-tests were created manually by the authors. In the experiment described in this paper, however, we provided each participant with a post-test tailored to their individual game play, in order to examine in detail how crossword puzzle play manifests in learning outcomes. To do this, we considered it necessary to analyze the combination of whether each word used in the puzzle was successfully input or not, and whether the newspaper article presented as a hint for that word was viewed or not. Accordingly, we needed to design post-tests so that these conditions would be included in a balanced manner. Here again, we used a large language model to automatically generate 4-choice quizzes based on individual newspaper articles and used them to create post-tests.

2   Related Work

Crossword puzzles have been introduced across various educational contexts. In pharmacology education, prior studies (e.g., Patrick et al. [6]; Bawazeer et al. [7]) report that crossword puzzles can support motivation and improve learning outcomes. Pearson [8] similarly demonstrated their usefulness as review material during online instruction.

In primary and secondary education as well, crossword puzzles have been used as classroom learning tools (e.g., Ramadhania et al. [9]; Brezovszky et al. [10]), and Darmayanti [11] showed that a crossword-based mathematics game helped develop critical thinking skills.

Thus, prior work indicates that crossword puzzles can enhance engagement and performance. However, existing studies typically rely on puzzles prepared in advance for all learners. In contrast, our study generates puzzles on demand based on players' interests and uses generative AI both to create hint texts and to construct individualized post-tests.

Our previous work explored gamified systems for encouraging library use [12] and serendipitous exploration in book discovery [13]. Building on these insights, this paper focuses on serendipitous learning that emerges unintentionally through crossword puzzle play. In contrast to prior studies that focused on activating information access or serendipitous discovery in library and book exploration contexts, the present study investigates how serendipitous learning can emerge as a byproduct of game play, particularly through experiences of failure and subsequent self-directed information seeking.

3   Extraction of Characteristic Words from Newspaper Article Data

We constructed a word database for on-demand crossword puzzle generation using articles from the Hokkaido Shimbun (2011–2020). To avoid selecting only high-frequency general terms, we organized the corpus into 16 categories–10 yearly groups and 6 thematic sections–so that each category would reflect characteristic vocabulary.

Nouns were extracted using MeCab with the NEologd dictionary[1] to better capture newly coined and region-specific expressions. We then applied TF–IDF [14] to identify representative words for each category. Examples of words selected as characteristic words representing each category are shown in Table 1. This process successfully extracted year- or region-specific terms, such as "novel coronavirus," "spread of infection," and "state of emergency" for 2020, or "Goryokaku Park," "Hakodate Airport," and "Bōniboriya" for the regional categories.

In total, 696 characteristic words were collected and stored together with their categories and corresponding newspaper articles, forming the basis for subsequent puzzle generation.

---

[1] https://github.com/neologd/mecab-unidic-neologd.

Table 1. Examples of characteristic words extracted by category.

Category	Top 10 extracted characteristic words
2011	After the earthquake, radiation level, Miyagi Prefecture, standard value, millisievert, exposure, Ishinomaki, temporary housing, renewable energy, radioactive cesium
2016	Rio de Janeiro Olympics, Kumamoto earthquake, Kumamoto, right to vote, ticket, Shin-Hakodate-Hokuto Station, editorial committee, Atsubetsu Ward, Sapporo, U.S. presidential election, exposure
2020	Novel coronavirus, spread of infection, COVID-19, CORONA, online, coronavirus pandemic, school closure, state of emergency, infectious disease, infection control
Hakodate, Oshima, Hiyama	Hakodate Airport, Imakane Town, Kikonai Town, Daimon, Hakodate citizens, Hakodate Station, Goryokaku Park, Yunokawa, Bōniboriya, Nanaehama
Society	Statement, Metropolitan Police Department, cause of death, appeal, defense counsel, flight cancellation, on the street, assault, voluntary questioning, magnitude

4   Construction of the Crossword Puzzle Environment

In this section, we describe how we implemented an environment in which crossword puzzles can be generated on demand and played, using the word database prepared in the previous section.

4.1   Game Screen Design

When the game starts, the 16 categories described above are presented, and the player selects one of them to challenge a crossword puzzle. An example of the game screen is shown in Fig. 1. When the "generate" button at the bottom right of the screen is pressed, a crossword puzzle is generated and displayed using the characteristic words of the selected category.

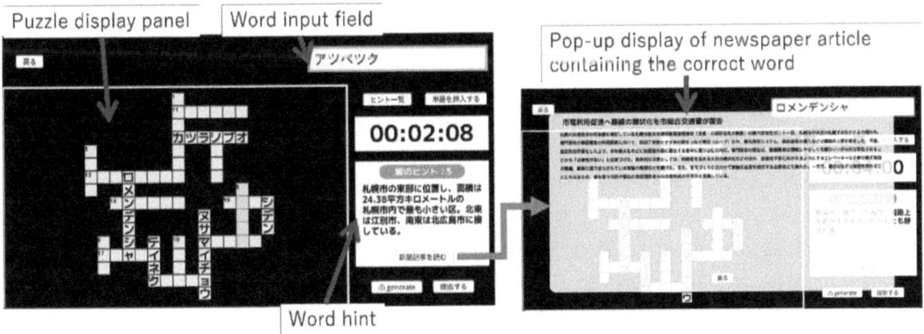

Fig. 1. Crossword puzzle interface. (Left) Players solve crossword puzzles using automatically generated hints and can optionally open the associated newspaper article when they encounter difficulty. (Right) A pop-up display of the newspaper article containing the correct word, which players can browse during puzzle play.

When the player clicks the first cell of a word (the cell with a number), the hint text for the word starting from that cell is displayed on the right side of the screen. When the player finds the corresponding word, they can type it in at the top right and insert the answer into the puzzle.

Unlike ordinary crossword puzzles, when the player presses the "Read newspaper article" button under the hint text, they can view the newspaper article containing that word as additional hint information. The displayed newspaper article always contains the correct word either in its headline or somewhere in its body. In other words, as long as the player reads the article carefully, they can always find the correct word in the article. We expected that this might lower the game difficulty, but we prioritized the objective of this study, which is to increase opportunities to read newspaper articles while enjoying the game.

4.2   On-Demand Generation of Puzzle Screens

We now describe the automatic generation of crossword puzzle screens. The automatic generation program is required to place as many words as possible on the screen by crossing words that share letters, using about 50 words belonging to the selected category as material. If we perform exhaustive search, the computational cost explodes and is not suitable for an on-demand game. On the other hand, a greedy method that restricts the search space to only the most promising candidates is fast but quickly converges to a local optimum and lacks diversity in puzzle screens.

Therefore, in this study, we adopted beam search [15,16], which is a type of breadth-first search that sequentially explores multiple candidates. Through trial and error, we searched for a trade-off between computational speed and diversity of results and set the beam width to 10.

4.3   Generation of Hint Texts for Puzzle Words

In this study, we aimed to automate all processes related to crossword puzzle generation, including the creation of hint texts for all candidate words. We used GPT-4o[2], a large language model, to generate these hints. The model was instructed not to include the target word itself and to produce concise descriptions suitable for crossword puzzles.

Examples of the generated hints are shown in Table 2. Overall, the outputs were of appropriate length and difficulty for use in the puzzle environment. We generated hints for all 696 words in advance and manually checked them to ensure that none contained the original answer terms.

Although the system currently relies on pre-generated hints, recent improvements in language model performance suggest that generating hints on demand during puzzle play would also be feasible.

---

[2] https://platform.openai.com/docs/models#gpt-4o.

Table 2. Example of hint texts generated using GPT-4o.

Word	Category	Hint text
Local train	Society	A railway service that is not as fast as express or Shinkansen trains and stops at every station.
Hakodate War	Hakodate	One of the civil wars in Japan fought between the former shogunate forces and the new government forces, in which Goryokaku was the main battlefield.
FM Iruka	Hakodate	A community FM radio station broadcasting mainly in Hakodate City.
Sapporo Snow Festival	Sapporo	A snow and ice festival held in Sapporo, Hokkaido, in early February.
Renewable energy	2011	Energy sources such as sun, wind, water, and geothermal that are renewable and environmentally friendly.
Tariff elimination	2013	The removal of tariffs, i.e., taxes levied on imported goods in international trade.

5 Evaluation Experiment

5.1 Overview of the Experiment

Using the crossword puzzle environment we prepared, we conducted an experiment at Future University Hakodate from December 12 to 30, 2024, to measure the presence and impact of serendipitous learning after crossword puzzle play. The experiment consisted of two sessions per participant: in the first session, participants freely played crossword puzzles, and a few days later in the second session, they took post-tests corresponding to their play content.

When recruiting participants, we only told them that they would participate twice within one week in an evaluation experiment of the crossword puzzle environment we had developed, and we did not tell them that the second session would be a post-test based on the first session. We recruited students on campus, excluding members of our research group, whose native language is Japanese. As a result, 30 students, ranging from first-year undergraduate students to first-year master's students, participated.

To unify the experimental conditions, participants took part individually. We scheduled two sessions for each of the 30 participants so that the two sessions could be completed within a week. In the end, all participants took part in the second session 2–5 days after the first session.

In the first session, participants freely played crossword puzzles. We did not require them to complete the puzzles, and their choice of categories and whether they viewed newspaper articles as hints was left to them. We told them that the maximum play time was 60 min, that we wanted them to play for at least 30 min, and that they could stop whenever they wanted after that.

During play, we recorded the list of words that made up the generated puzzles and whether each of those words was correctly filled in. The list of words and their correctness were determined when the "submit" button was pressed. Incorrectly input words and unanswered words were both recorded as "words that were failed to input." We also recorded whether the newspaper article was requested to display as an additional hint.

In the second session, each participant took a post-test tailored to their play log. The test was a 4-choice quiz asking about the content of the newspaper articles used as hints for the crossword puzzles played in the first session. The words used in the puzzles, the newspaper articles presented as hints, and whether they were viewed differed by participant. Based on these play logs, we prepared 30 4-choice quiz items for each participant and asked them to answer.

5.2   Automatic Generation of 4-Choice Quizzes

We now describe how we prepared the 4-choice quizzes used in the second session. In the proposed system, each word that may be used in a crossword puzzle is linked to a newspaper article. Since we do not know which words will be used in the crossword puzzles until the first session is over, we needed to prepare 4-choice quizzes for all corresponding articles, and it was not realistic to do this manually. We therefore automatically generated 4-choice quizzes using generative AI. Specifically, we instructed o1-preview[3], a large language model by OpenAI, as follows, to generate quiz statements and four answer options.

> You are professional to create 4-choice quizzes based on newspaper articles. Please create a 4-choice quiz based on the content of the Hokkaido Simbun article that I am sending. I will send you a set of word and corresponding newspaper article. Please create a 4-choice quiz where the word I send is the correct answer. Also, please create the remaining three incorrect options. Please do not create quizzes that solely test knowledge. For example, do not create quizzes that ask for personal names or numerical values.

An example of a generated 4-choice quiz is shown in Fig. 2. The source newspaper article reported that "FM Iruka," a community FM radio station in Hakodate, broadcast a live coverage of a fireworks festival. The quiz generated for this article asked for "FM Iruka" as the correct answer. The other options were also radio station names, so the quiz was appropriate.

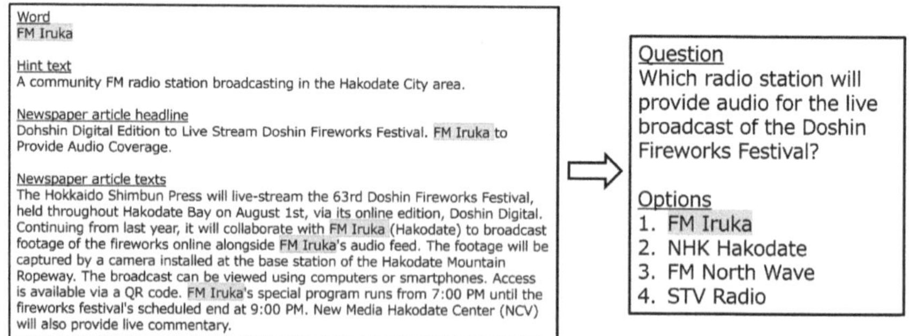

Fig. 2. Example of a 4-choice quiz automatically generated based on a newspaper article.

We note here the possibility of errors resulting from the use of large language models. At first, we tried to create 4-choice quizzes with GPT-4o, just as we

---

[3] https://openai.com/ja-JP/index/introducing-openai-o1-preview.

did for the hint texts. However, about 70–80% of the generated quizzes were either too easy (e.g., the distractors were clearly inappropriate) or contained hallucinations. We then switched to o1-preview, which had just been released in autumn 2024, and the quality of the quizzes improved dramatically. Before conducting the experiment, the authors carefully checked all quizzes and found that none of them needed correction, so we used all the automatically generated quizzes as they were.

6   Results and Discussion on Crossword Puzzle Play

In this section, we describe what we observed from the log data of crossword puzzle play in the first session and from the subsequent questionnaire.

6.1   Relationship Between Viewing Newspaper Articles and Success/Failure of Word Input

We analyzed the log data of crossword puzzle play from 30 participants. Because we were interested in how viewing newspaper articles as additional hints affected the success or failure of word input in crossword puzzles, we classified words into four types based on the combination of whether the article was viewed and whether the word was successfully filled in.

Table 3. Relationship between viewing newspaper articles during play and success/failure of word input.

Classification	# of words	Ratio (%)
Viewed newspaper article / Correctly filled in	1336	54.35
Viewed newspaper article / Not correctly filled in	340	13.83
Did not view newspaper article / Correctly filled in	543	22.09
Did not view newspaper article / Not correctly filled in	239	9.72

From the play log data of the 30 participants, a total of 2,458 words were submitted as puzzle answers. Table 3 shows the classification results for these words.

The proportion of correctly filled in words was 76.44%, indicating that the game functioned as a puzzle that was neither too difficult nor too easy. On the other hand, 68.18% of the word inputs involved viewing newspaper articles.

Overall, the most frequent case (54.35%) was when players viewed the newspaper article and correctly input the word, which is consistent with our system design.

When we calculate the accuracy for the case where the article was viewed, it is $1336/(1336 + 340) = 0.797$, i.e., 79.7%. For the case where the article was not viewed, the accuracy is $543/(543 + 239) = 0.694$, i.e., 69.4%. Thus, although the difference is small, viewing the newspaper article led to higher accuracy, which matches intuition.

What was somewhat unexpected was that there were 340 cases (13.83%) in which players failed to input the correct word despite having viewed the newspaper article. In our game environment, the newspaper article always contains the correct word, so if the player reads it carefully, they should be able to find the answer. The fact that we still observed such cases was surprising.

When we looked into concrete examples of cases where players viewed the newspaper article but failed to input the word, we found instances such as entering "Goryokaku (ゴリョウカク)" instead of "Hakodate Station (ハコダテエキ)"[4], entering "Minshutō (ミンシュトウ)" instead of "Shinshintō (シンシントウ)"[5], or entering "Honmachi (ホンマチ)" instead of "Motomachi (モトマチ)"[6]. These examples show that players frequently make mistakes, such as jumping to other plausible words of the same length or misreading words. We consider that such experiences of failure evoked players' frustration or surprise, which in turn motivated self-directed information-seeking behavior after game play.

6.2 Participants' Reactions

After playing the game, we asked participants in a questionnaire to freely describe any new words, knowledge, or events they learned through playing the crossword puzzles. These pieces of knowledge were gained not only from the hint texts for word input but also from the newspaper articles themselves.

We also asked how participants felt about the feature that allowed viewing newspaper articles as additional hints, and we obtained the following responses:

- Although it was hard work to search for the puzzle word from a long newspaper article, I found myself reading the contents and events of the article unconsciously.
- I felt it was easier to play even for people who are not confident in their knowledge, and that the hurdle of crossword puzzles was lowered.
- I found it useful for filling in words. Since the content of the articles was related to the crossword puzzle, I did not find reading them burdensome.

Thus, we found that a certain number of participants were positive about reading newspaper articles as part of the game, and that some of that content remained in their memory and impression.

7 Analysis of the Possibility of Serendipitous Learning After Game Play

Based on the suggestions obtained in the previous section, we conducted the second session (post-test) to examine serendipitous learning after game play. In this section, we describe the results.

---

[4] Both are place names belonging to the same town.
[5] Both are party names created in the wake of political realignment.
[6] They are alternative readings of 本町.

7.1 Preparation of 4-Choice Quizzes for Each Participant

In the second session, each participant took the post-test individually. Since we had not informed them of the content or intention of the experiment in advance, they probably expected to play crossword puzzles again as in the first session; however, this time we had them answer 30 4-choice quiz items prepared according to their play logs from the first session.

These 4-choice quizzes asked about the content of the newspaper articles that had been used as hints for the crossword puzzles. The words that appeared in the puzzles, as well as whether the corresponding articles were viewed, differed by participant. Therefore, we prepared 4-choice quizzes for each participant using the following procedure so that the conditions would be as balanced as possible across participants:

1. If the number of words for which the article was viewed and the word was correctly filled in is N_1, prepare $\min(10, N_1)$ quiz items related to the newspaper articles corresponding to those words.
2. If the number of words for which the article was viewed but the word was not correctly filled in is N_2, prepare $\min(10, N_2)$ quiz items related to the newspaper articles corresponding to those words.
3. If the number of words for which the article was not viewed but the word was correctly filled in is N_3, prepare $\min(2, N_3)$ quiz items related to the newspaper articles corresponding to those words.
4. If the number of words for which the article was not viewed and the word was not correctly filled in is N_4, prepare $\min(3, N_4)$ quiz items related to the newspaper articles corresponding to those words.
5. Prepare $(30 - N_1 - N_2 - N_3 - N_4)$ quiz items related to newspaper articles corresponding to words that did not appear during play.

Using the above procedure, we prepared 30 quiz items for each participant and had them answer.

7.2 Distribution of Correct Answers in the 4-Choice Quizzes

Figure 3 shows the results of the 4-choice quizzes answered by the 30 participants. We plotted the distribution of correct and incorrect answers corresponding to the five conditions explained in the previous subsection. Note that for the condition 4, more than half of the participants did not have any words that satisfied the condition, resulting in a larger number of so-called dummy questions (quiz items about articles corresponding to words that did not appear during play).

The vertical axis in the figure shows the number of quiz items, out of the 900 items given to the 30 participants, classified into correct and incorrect. The correct answer rates, from left to right, are 45.2%, 50.6%, 39.0%, 20.0%, and 39.8%. The rightmost condition corresponds to quizzes about articles for words that did not appear in crossword puzzle play (dummy questions), i.e., those least affected by the first session and presumably reflecting participants' everyday

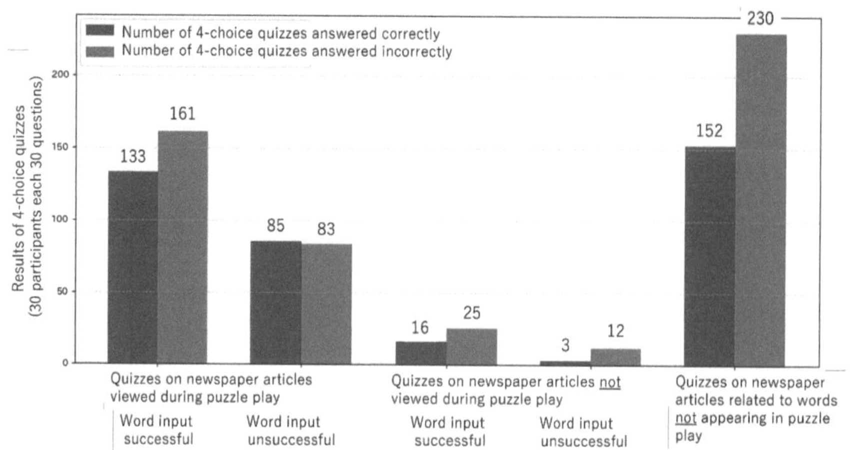

Fig. 3. Distribution of correct and incorrect answers in 4-choice quizzes.

knowledge. The correct answer rate of 39.8% represents the average difficulty of the 4-choice quizzes we prepared.

Even for quiz items about articles corresponding to words that appeared in the crossword puzzle during play, if the article was not viewed (the third and fourth conditions from the left), the correct answer rate was below 40%, showing a similar tendency to the dummy questions.

On the other hand, the two conditions on the left, i.e., quiz items about newspaper articles that were viewed during puzzle play, showed generally higher correct answer rates. This suggests that viewing newspaper articles during game play may have promoted some degree of understanding and knowledge retention. However, we do not claim a direct causal relationship, as individual differences in reading strategies and prior knowledge may also have influenced the results.

Another intriguing finding is that only the second condition from the left—the condition in which the article was viewed but the word was not correctly filled in—exceeded 50% correct. This correct answer rate is clearly higher than that of the dummy questions, which represent the average difficulty of the quiz items. Although we cannot confirm this individually, we infer that frustration at failing to fill in the word despite having viewed an article that surely contained the correct answer prompted participants to reread the article or to engage in self-directed exploration afterward.

7.3   Serendipitous Learning After Game Play

Together with the 4-choice quizzes, we conducted a free-response questionnaire asking, "If there were any changes in your daily life after the previous crossword puzzle session, please tell us." Thirteen out of the 30 participants reported behavioral changes associated with self-directed information seeking, which we interpret as indicative of serendipitous learning triggered by crossword puzzle play:

- I started paying attention to municipalities when Hokkaido-related news appeared.
- The psychological barrier to reading newspaper articles became lower.
- I started opening links when I saw news on the web.
- Crossword puzzles became one of my options for killing time on a ferry or train.
- I started reading economic news when it appeared on Google News.
- I started playing word-guessing games (such as Wordle) again.
- I felt a bit smarter and thought I should check recent events on some information device.

Thus, for nearly half of the participants, experiencing crossword puzzles with newspaper article browsing led to signs of self-directed learning, manifested as self-directed information-seeking behaviors, such as a reduced psychological burden to read newspapers and increased everyday news reading.

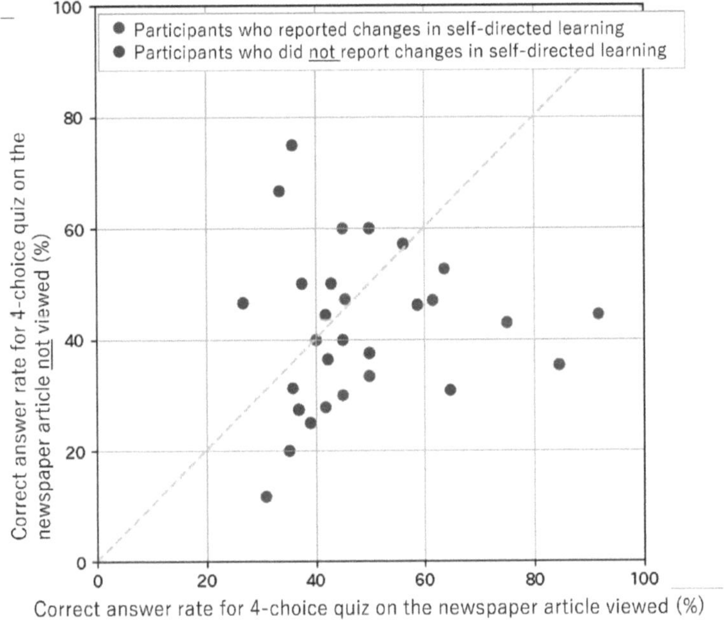

Fig. 4. Relationship between self-directed learning-related changes and 4-choice quiz accuracy rates.

To discuss these changes of serendipitous learning, we plotted in Fig. 4 the relationship between whether there were changes related to self-directed learning and the distribution of correct answers in the 4-choice quizzes. We plotted in red the 13 participants who reported some changes related to self-directed learning, and in blue the other 17 participants, and we plotted them according to their correct answer rates. We separately calculated the correct answer rates for quiz items about articles viewed during crossword puzzle play and for quiz items about articles not viewed.

Participants plotted further to the upper right had higher overall correct answer rates. The distribution of participants based on correct answer rates was widely dispersed. If we project the red and blue plots onto the green diagonal line from the lower left to the upper right, the spread of red and blue dots is almost even, indicating no correlation between the presence of self-directed learning changes and the overall distribution of correct answer rates.

Interestingly, however, if we look at the axis perpendicular to the green line, the red plots are biased toward the lower right, while the blue plots are biased toward the upper left. In other words, participants who reported changes in self-directed learning tended to have higher correct answer rates for quiz items about articles they viewed during puzzle play, whereas participants who did not report such changes tended to have higher correct answer rates for quiz items about articles they did not view during puzzle play.

Notably, the three participants with the highest correct answer rates for quiz items about articles viewed during puzzle play (the three on the right side of the graph) all reported self-directed learning changes after the first session. Also, for all three, the correct answer rates for quiz items about articles not viewed were not necessarily high. This indicates that these participants did not necessarily have broad knowledge, but that their acquisition (or retention) of knowledge about the articles they encountered during crossword puzzle play was promoted. This suggests that a certain number of participants became interested in the newspaper articles they encountered during crossword puzzle play and, through subsequent self-directed exploration, acquired knowledge related to them.

Although Fig. 4 suggests a tendency that participants who reported self-directed learning–related changes showed a relatively larger difference in accuracy between viewed and non-viewed quiz items, a non-parametric comparison of the difference scores did not reveal a statistically significant group difference (Mann–Whitney U test, $p = .14$; permutation test, $p = .14$). Given the small sample size and the variability in the number of quiz items per participant, we interpret Fig. 4 as providing descriptive evidence rather than confirmatory statistical support.

8   Conclusion

To promote serendipitous learning with broad interest in social events, we proposed an environment in which players can work on crossword puzzles while viewing newspaper articles. To measure the impact of crossword puzzle play, we analyzed the relationship between post-test performance and changes in self-directed learning. As a result, we observed that for nearly half of the participants, crossword puzzle play prompted them to pay attention to web news and to voluntarily look up vocabulary and topics related to puzzles they could not solve. Furthermore, for some of these participants, the correct answer rates for post-quizzes about newspaper articles viewed during puzzle play were significantly higher, suggesting a link to the effect of self-directed learning. These findings suggest that the proposed system design can trigger serendipitous learning, as reflected in users' subsequent self-directed information-seeking behaviors and selective knowledge retention.

In this paper, we reported that we were able to automatically generate hint texts for words making up crossword puzzles and post-tests for measuring the learning outcomes, using large language models, and that the quality was sufficient. This suggests the possibility of providing not only crossword puzzles based on past newspaper articles but also on-demand crossword puzzles and personalized review materials using newly published newspaper articles or diverse information resources on the web (e.g., book data, online educational materials, social media content).

Acknowledgements. We would like to thank Mr. Tatsuji Miura, Executive General Manager of the Sales Headquarters of Hokkaido Shimbun Press, for his generous cooperation in the use of article data, and Professors Noyuri Mima and Kengo Terasawa of Future University Hakodate for their valuable discussions on the design of the crossword puzzle environment and its educational effect.

References

1. Ten, A., Kaushik, P., Oudeyer, P.-Y., Gottlieb, J.: Humans monitor learning progress in curiosity-driven exploration. Nat. Commun. **12**(1), 5972 (2021)
2. Plass, J.L., et al.: The impact of individual, competitive, and collaborative mathematics game play on learning, performance, and motivation. J. Educ. Psychol. **105**(4), 1050–1066 (2013)
3. Gui, Y., Cai, Z., Yang, Y., Kong, L., Fan, X., Tai, R.H.: Effectiveness of digital educational game and game design in STEM learning: a meta-analytic review. Int. J. STEM Educ. **10**(1), 36 (2023)
4. Makri, S., Blandford, A.: Coming across information serendipitously-part 1: a process model. J. Doc. **68**(5), 684–705 (2012)
5. Knowles, M.S.: Self-Directed Learning: A Guide for Learners and Teachers. Association Press (1975)
6. Patrick, S., et al.: The usefulness of crossword puzzle as a self-learning tool in pharmacology. J. Adv. Med. Educ. Prof. **6**(4), 181–185 (2018)
7. Bawazeer, G.: Crossword puzzle as a learning tool to enhance learning about anticoagulant therapeutics. BMC Med. Educ. **22**(1), 267 (2022)
8. Pearson, R.J.: Online chemistry crossword puzzles prior to and during COVID-19: light-hearted revision aids that work. J. Chem. Educ. **97**(9), 3194–3200 (2020)
9. Ramadhania, S., Adnan, H.: Crossword puzzle learning media to improve Indonesian vocabulary mastery for grade 2 elementary school students. J. Innov. Res. Prim. Educ. **1**(2), 50–55 (2022)

10. Brezovszky, B., et al.: Effects of a mathematics game-based learning environment on primary school students' adaptive number knowledge. Comput. Educ. **128**, 63–74 (2019)
11. Darmayanti, R.: Gema Cow-Pu: development of mathematical crossword puzzle learning media on geometry material on middle school students' critical thinking ability. Assyfa Learn. J. **1**(1), 37–49 (2023)
12. Kitamura, T., Sumi, Y.: Using gamification to activate university library use. In: Fang, X. (eds) HCI in Games. HCII 2023. LNCS, vol.14046, pp. 343–359, Springer, Cham (2023). https://doi.org/10.1007/978-3-031-35930-9_23
13. Oikawa, T., Sumi, Y.: Serendipitous book explorer using personalized associative dictionaries. In: Mori, H., Asahi, Y., Coman, A., Vasilache, S., Rauterberg, M. (eds.) HCI International 2023 – Late Breaking Papers. HCII 2023. LNCS, vol. 14056, pp. 131–150, Springer, Cham (2023). https://doi.org/10.1007/978-3-031-48044-7_10
14. Salton, G.M., Wong, A., Yang, C.S.: A vector space model for automatic indexing. Commun. ACM **18**(11), 613–620 (1975)
15. Meister, C., Vieira, T., Cotterell, R.: Best-first beam search. Trans. Assoc. Comput. Linguist. **8**, 795–809 (2020)
16. Zhuo, J.: Learning optimal tree models under beam search. In: Proceedings of the 37th International Conference on Machine Learning, pp. 11650–11659 (2020)

A System Specification for Digital Addiction Interventions: Integrating the Minnesota Model with Persuasive Systems Design

Hasan Selkan Taskan, Fedja Poikonen, and Harri Oinas-Kukkonen

University of Oulu, 90570 Oulu, Finland
`harri.oinas-kukkonen@oulu.fi`

Abstract. Our relationship with technology is becoming a serious public health concern affecting our lives on biological, psychological, and social levels. However, this relationship can also have its own therapeutic setting when technology is used to support behavior change. To develop such interventions, designers must carefully connect psychological strategies with the software artifact. This study presents a high-level system specification that explains how the psychological strategies of the Minnesota Model can be implemented within a digital intervention. To translate these counselling strategies into persuasive software features, we first conducted a Persuasive Systems Design analysis, then systematically extracted counselling strategies from the Minnesota Model literature and guidelines. These were then mapped into software artifacts with an iterative process. Through this synthesis, our study provides theoretical and practical implications with its documentation and examples from the resulting outcome.

Keywords: Minnesota Model · Persuasive Systems Design · PSD Features · Digital Addiction

1 Introduction

With the increasing digitalization around the world, our relationship with technology is continuously evolving and acquiring new dimensions. Perhaps one of the most important dimensions of this relationship is digital addiction. As an umbrella term, digital addiction refers to a maladaptive pattern of interacting with digital devices or platforms [1, 2]. It is characterized by excessive use, loss of control, and continued use despite negative consequences [3–5]. According to Meng et al. [2], 6%–27% of the global population may be experiencing at least one form of digital addiction. Consequently, a considerable portion of these individuals are at higher risk for psychological problems such as anxiety, depression, stress, or poor sleep [6].

On the other hand, unlike other addictions, this relationship may also contain its own potential for treatment. The very object of addiction, digital devices themselves, can be used to support individuals' relationships with them. They can improve various health outcomes by being used as a supporting tool in face-to-face settings, or the entire intervention can be delivered fully digitally [7, 8]. Nevertheless, most of the psychological

K. Sumi et al. (Eds.): PERSUASIVE 2026, LNCS 16476, pp. 371–381, 2026.
https://doi.org/10.1007/978-3-032-19687-3_27

approaches were originally designed for in-person settings. Delivering these interventions through a digital medium comes with its own pros and cons. For example, they can improve treatment adherence and help individuals achieve healthier outcomes [9, 10]. They are also more accessible and cost-efficient [7, 11]. On the other hand, more research is needed to understand the dynamic between the therapeutic relationship and digital interventions [12]. Technical barriers or privacy concerns can also hinder effective implementations [7, 13].

These advantages and limitations indicate the need for systematic frameworks that help us connect psychological and behavioral strategies with information systems. Several frameworks, such as the Persuasive Systems Design (PSD) and Unified Theory of Acceptance and Use of Technology, synthesize behavioral, psychological, and sociological theories with information systems to improve the effectiveness of interventions [14, 15]. However, to fully realize their potential, the bridge between information systems frameworks and psychological interventions must be constructed and explained in a structured way. Therefore, we present a system specification for digital addiction interventions that integrate therapeutic counselling strategies and information systems. We specifically aim to provide practical insights into how such a system can be built by integrating Minnesota Model (MM) with PSD [14, 16].

2 Theoretical Background

To develop an intervention targeting digital addictions, we opted for the MM and PSD frameworks based on their theoretical relevance. Building on previous work that systematically analyzed Cognitive Behavioral Therapy, MM, Motivational Interviewing and Motivational Enhancement Therapy, Contingency Management, Family/Couples Therapy, we identified the MM as the most theoretically compatible foundation for this study [17]. Both frameworks are well-established and widely accepted approaches in their respective fields. They share a common understanding of human nature rooted in behavioral change. It is therefore anticipated that the systematic design principles of PSD will form a complementary structure for counseling strategies of the MM.

2.1 Minnesota Model

The MM is a multidisciplinary addiction treatment approach. It is based on principles of Alcoholics Anonymous' (AA) Twelve-step program, and it complements AA's peer support with addiction treatment professionals. MM program usually includes a 28-day inpatient period, and lifelong aftercare [16, 18].

During the inpatient period, patients follow a planned daily schedule consisting of lectures, counselling, group sessions, and other activities and assignments that support psychological and physical wellbeing [16, 18]. The exact structure varies based on the treatment provider, but the basic principles are the same. At the core of the MM philosophy is the "Disease Concept": addiction is an involuntary, chronic and progressive primary disease that cannot be cured but can be treated [16, 19, 20]. When addiction is seen as a disease, and not a moral failing or conscious choice, the patient can face, admit, and accept the situation [19]. Additionally, family involvement plays a major role in MM treatment because it explains addiction as a "Family Illness": those close to the addicted person are also affected by the addiction [16, 19].

2.2 Persuasive Systems Design

PSD is a framework for designing and evaluating persuasive systems that influence attitudes and behaviors without using coercion or deception [14]. The framework first establishes a common foundation between all persuasive systems. Second, it focuses on the context of the system under development or evaluation. Third, it lists common persuasive software features in four categories.

Primary Task Support features help the user to perform their primary tasks, goals that they have for the use of the system. For example, features like reduction and tunneling help perform tasks more effectively. Rehearsal can persuade the user by helping to observe cause and effect relationships, and Simulation can help adopt behavior change by practicing the target behavior. The Dialogue Support features are interactive elements between the user and the system. The system can e.g. take a social role and behave as a virtual coach, give the user praise, rewards, and suggestions. System Credibility Support concentrates on attributes that make the system more believable. People are more likely open to persuasion from credible sources. The Social Support category facilitates social influence between users. A system can e.g. leverage social learning to help users see others performing the target behavior.

3 System Specification

We employed a structured methodological approach in three stages to create this system specification process. We designed a procedure between the counselling strategies of the MM and the design principles of PSD to ensure methodological rigor and conceptual coherence. This process includes three consecutive stages: (1) identifying persuasive software feature candidates through PSD analysis, (2) extracting and defining the MM counseling strategies relevant to digital addictions, and (3) integrating these two frameworks into a unified system by matching corresponding features and strategies. In every stage, two researchers conducted the analyses and validated their findings through iterative discussions. If no consensus was reached, the third author was consulted for the final decision.

3.1 Persuasive Systems Design Analysis

A PSD analysis was conducted to create a structured implementation roadmap of the system. The reason for conducting the PSD analysis first was to reduce the potential bias that could arise from starting the study from the MM perspective and to objectively define the persuasive software feature candidates to be presented in the system. According to PSD analysis [14]:

App Idea. An application that aims to help people struggling with unhealthy behaviors related to digital addictions.

Value Sensitive Analysis. The direct stakeholders of the system were adults seeking help with digital addiction, and indirect stakeholders were the direct stakeholders' families and friends. The core values include trustworthiness, inclusivity, empathy, transparency, and long-term well-being.

O/C Design Matrix Analysis. The primary goal of the system was to alter a behavior (A/B). In this case, it is specifically helping users reduce unhealthy behavior related to digital addictions. The secondary goal was to reinforce the newly altered behavior (R/B) by maintaining the new, healthier digital habits to prevent relapse.

PSD Context Analysis. In the intent, the aimed change was in behavior, as digital addictions are a set of problematic behaviors related to digital technology. Problem behavior is often excessive use, which is why behavioral change in this case is not about teaching new behaviors, but rather modifying existing ones. In the event, the "Use Context" was recovery from addiction, the "User Context" was individuals who have decided to intervene in their unhealthy digital habits, and the "Technology Context" was mobile applications. In the strategy, the message route was both direct by delivering psychoeducation and indirect by gentle peer support and group challenges.

PSD Features. The persuasive software features were derived mainly from the use context: recovering from digital addiction. We divided persuasive software features into two groups as main and secondary, according to their frequency in the use context, level of influence on the user experience, and alignment with prior literature. We identified 10 main and 10 secondary persuasive software features. For example, we included Simulation and Rehearsal features in the "main" category because seeing addiction recovery as a learning process, being able to identify cause-and-effect relationships and rehearse for situations that prompt the problem behavior, are valuable ways to learn to manage one's addiction [18]. On the other hand, we added Tailoring as a secondary feature since users with different subtypes of digital addiction might prefer to see slightly different content. However, as this approach does not directly influence the central structure of the intervention, it was considered supportive rather than essential. Liking was similarly categorized as secondary, as creating an aesthetically pleasing environment can enhance user engagement but is not central to the intervention. Certain persuasive software features (Social Role, Authority, Third-party Endorsement, Real-world Feel, Recognition, Social Comparison, Normative Influence, Competition) were excluded as they were not deemed suitable to work with digital addictions at this stage. Table 1 shows all the persuasive software feature findings from PSD analysis.

Table 1. Identified Persuasive Software Feature Candidates in the Initial PSD Analysis

Category	Feature Candidates
Main Features	Reduction, Self-monitoring, Simulation, Rehearsal, Praise, Reminders, Trustworthiness, Social Learning, Social Facilitation, Cooperation
Secondary Features	Personalization, Tunneling, Tailoring, Rewards, Suggestion, Similarity, Liking, Expertise, Surface Credibility, Verifiability

3.2 Identifying Minnesota Model Strategies

In the second stage, while preserving the fundamental structure of the MM, we have adapted it to digital context. This approach aligns with the general practices of the MM treatment, as different rehabilitation centers have developed their own counseling approaches over time [19, 20]. The identification of counseling strategies was based on the core principles and therapeutic structure of the MM. We relied on the well-established practices and counseling strategies that are consistently described in the literature and applied in rehabilitation programs using the MM [16, 18–22]. Identified counseling strategies and their short descriptions can be found in Table 2 below.

In addition to the findings in Table 2, "spirituality" and "total abstinence" were also identified as main counseling strategies in the traditional MM. After iterative discussions, it was decided not to include these two approaches as counseling strategies, particularly in the digital addiction context. This decision was based on the understanding that digital addiction differs from alcohol and substance-related addictions in terms of their behavioral characteristics. According to all three researchers, complete abstinence from digital devices was not feasible and appropriate, while spirituality was considered highly individual.

3.3 System Integration

In the final stage, the persuasive software features defined in the PSD analysis were matched with the MM counseling strategies. During this process, PSD features appropriate to the therapeutic goal of each strategy were identified. All the counselling strategies and their matched PSD features can be found in Table 3.

According to the findings from the matching process, a total of 16 different persuasive software features were chosen. All 10 features in the main category were matched with MM strategies, while 6 out of 10 secondary features involved: Personalization, Suggestion, Rewards, Liking, Expertise, Surface Credibility. These 16 different persuasive software features were used a total of 24 times in the matching process. Among these, 5 features appeared in more than one strategy: Suggestion (n = 3), Cooperation (n = 3), Social Learning (n = 2), Reminders (n = 2), Reduction (n = 2). Furthermore, 6 of 12 counseling strategies were represented by more than one PSD feature: Assignments (n = 4), Therapeutic Environment (n = 3), Learning (n = 3), Activities (n = 3), Group Therapy (n = 2), Routines (n = 2).

"Disease Concept", "Holistic Care", and "Multidisciplinary Approach" strategies are suggested to be implemented structurally rather than directly implemented through specific features. Since the disease concept is a way of understanding addiction, it cannot be implemented through a specific persuasive software feature, but the system should reflect this understanding throughout its narrative. It is similar with holistic care and multidisciplinary approach as well. The system should frame its intervention holistically by benefiting from psychological, social, and physical aspects. It should also include professionals from different disciplines, for example, psychiatry, psychology, software developers, and designers.

Table 2. MM Strategies and Their Short Descriptions

MM Strategies	Description
Disease concept	Framing addiction as a chronic disease rather than a moral weakness
Treatment plan	Developing an individualized treatment plan according to the person's needs, goals, and progress
Holistic care	Providing support that involves psychological, social, and physical dimensions of recovery
Therapeutic environment	Creating a safe, empathetic, supportive, and non-judgmental environment
Peer support	Therapeutic sharing between individuals who have similar experiences
Group therapy	Creating a collaborative environment for providing feedback and interpersonal learning
Attendance	Encouraging consistent participation in sessions and activities
Family involvement	Including family members in the recovery process to transform codependency and dysfunctional roles by identifying the family dynamics affected by addiction
Life history	Preparing and sharing a life history to identify problems and build trust
Learning	Developing awareness of addiction and coping skills through psycho-educational lectures and dynamic, experiential, and transformative learning processes
Assignments	Reflective assignments that support individuals' daily responsibilities and awareness
Activities	Encouraging recreational and physical activities that support healthy habits
Routines	Establishing a stabilized daily life that strengthens healthy behaviors
Multidisciplinary Approach	Involvement of professionals from different areas such as psychiatry, psychology, sociology, etc
12-step program	Practicing the first steps of AA to ensure that everyone develops a shared understanding

4 Discussion

This study explores potential implementation ways of the MM counselling strategies using PSD. We created an iterative process and documented it to present which persuasive software features can be used for digital addiction recovery, what counseling strategies there are in the MM, and how these strategies can be implemented in a system using PSD.

Table 3. Matching MM Strategies with PSD Features

MM Strategy	PSD Features	Examples
Treatment plan	Personalization	Providing an individualized treatment plan
Therapeutic environment	Liking	Using warm visuals and an empathetic tone
	Trustworthiness	Presenting evidence-based content written by professionals
	Surface credibility	Applying a clean and consistent design
Peer support	Social learning	Giving an environment to share experiences, tools, ideas related to digital addiction
Group therapy	Social facilitation	Displaying how many individuals are in the same step of the intervention
	Cooperation	Motivating community collaboration through shared challenges
Attendance	Reminders	Sending notifications to complete educational steps daily
Family involvement	Suggestion	Giving tips for involving family in communication and recovery
Life history	Self-monitoring	Providing journaling for self-reflection and tracking change
Learning	Rehearsal	Providing exercises to better understand cause and effect behind the decisions
	Simulation	Providing scenario-based exercises to practice learned skills
	Social Learning	Letting users share and see each other's recovery stories
Assignments	Suggestion	Suggesting real-life actions for healthier habits
	Rewards	Giving virtual badges for completing assignments
	Praise	Providing encouraging feedback after daily tasks
	Cooperation	Encouraging users to complete cooperative in-app tasks together
Activities	Suggestion	Providing healthy offline activities or coping strategies
	Reduction	Providing lists for small wins, cognitive restructuring, etc

(continued)

Table 3. (*continued*)

MM Strategy	PSD Features	Examples
	Cooperation	Encouraging collective participation in activities
Routines	Reduction	Helping users break their routine into small, achievable steps
	Reminders	Sending timely notifications to develop consistent routines
12-step program	Expertise	Explaining recovery steps and MM principles

This system specification we have developed shows that the PSD and the MM can provide a powerful foundation for developing online interventions for digital addictions. Of the 15 counseling strategies identified from the MM, 12 have been matched with specific persuasive software features, while it has been emphasized that 3 need to be addressed at a more structural level. As can be seen in Table 3, rather than applying each counseling strategy with only a single persuasive software feature, it was deemed appropriate to use multiple features together when necessary, considering the multidimensional structures of every counseling strategy. For example, the "Therapeutic Environment" strategy is supported by three different persuasive features. The Trustworthiness feature aims to strengthen the therapeutic environment by increasing trust in the narrative, Surface Credibility aims to reflect the order of a therapy room in the digital environment by providing consistency and order in the design, and Liking aims to offer the user a warmer and more appealing environment in terms of both design and narrative. On the other hand, "Disease Concept", "Holistic Care", and "Multidisciplinary Approach" strategies need to be integrated at a structural level as they represent the philosophy of the MM.

Another important aspect revealed by this research is the theoretical coherence between the MM and PSD. The MM places a great emphasis on social support as one of the fundamental components of its treatment structure. This social support approach manifests itself in many different themes, such as group therapy, peer support, and family involvement [18, 19]. Similarly, our PSD analysis also revealed that the Social Support category plays an important role in digital addiction interventions. The fact that this emphasis on social support in the MM finds an independent counterpart in the PSD analysis is highly valuable in terms of demonstrating the theoretical and practical compatibility between the two approaches. Indeed, persuasive software features related to social support are included in 5 of the 12 counseling strategies. Social Support features naturally represent "peer support" and "Group therapy" strategies; in addition, they also show their contribution in other counselling strategies such as "Learning", "Assignments", and "Activities". According to PSD analysis, despite Social Support features being considered effective in the literature, they are rarely used in practice [8, 23, 24]. The MM's independent emphasis on social support reaffirms the importance of the lack of social support implementations in the information systems literature [23]. Also, the indirect stakeholders of the system were identified as families and friends of the adults seeking help for digital addiction. This finding from the Value Sensitive Analysis directly aligns with the MM's "Family involvement" approach. The MM emphasizes that the "loved ones" of addicted individuals are also negatively affected by addiction, and these individuals should be included in the treatment process as well [18]. Therefore, the evaluation of the families and friends as indirect stakeholders shows the structural capacity of both frameworks to conceptualize the process in a similar manner.

Lastly, one of the significant discussion points of this study is the modern reinterpretation of an established treatment approach in alcohol and substance-related addictions. The MM is not a trademark, nor does it have a precise definition. Not all treatment facilities that follow the model call themselves Minnesota treatments, and there are differences in how the facilities organize treatment [19]. Our study presents MM to both the digital environment and digital addictions. A notable difference here is the "total abstinence" approach, one of the model's fundamental strategies. The MM aims for the individual to completely abstain from alcohol or substances. However, when it comes to digital addictions, it is not considered a realistic goal for an individual to stay away from all digital devices for the rest of their life. In the case of digital addictions, we are dealing with the use of technology that is considered essential in modern times, therefore, the total abstinence strategy needed a revision. Also, the MM treatment for alcohol and substance-related addictions includes an inpatient period and face-to-face treatment process, but this article explores the possibilities of applying the model to digital interventions. Therefore, when adapting the MM to digital addictions and the digital environment, the goal should be to reorganize the relationship with digital devices and platforms and establish a healthier balance, rather than complete abstinence.

4.1 Future Research

Future research should focus on empirically testing the system specification proposed in this study. Evaluating the findings through behavioral and psychological outcomes related to digital addiction will show the scientific validity of our model. In particular, effectiveness studies measuring variables such as user engagement, well-being, and perceptions of design elements will provide important evidence regarding the practical applicability of this model. Furthermore, testing our findings at the feature level will be specifically valuable in terms of validating the proposed design. Finally, the step this study took to use MM in digital addictions may also form the basis for integrating it into other types of behavioral addictions and digital environments.

4.2 Limitations

As with any research, this study has certain limitations. First, it is based entirely on a system specification process and does not present any empirical data. The findings have not yet been implemented or tested in a real-world setting, and therefore, they are not validated in terms of usability, persuasiveness, and therapeutic effectiveness. Furthermore, although a consensus procedure was applied, the execution of the PSD analysis, the determination of MM counseling strategies, and the process of matching them with each other were based on the researchers' interpretation. In addition, the adaptation of the MM to the context of digital addictions may limit the generalizability of the study. Finally, although this system specification was developed and documented by professionals with expertise in the field, patients or end-users were not directly involved in the process. This may limit the ecological validity of the study.

5 Conclusion

This research explored how the counseling strategies underlying the MM can be integrated into a digital intervention using the PSD approach. We presented a documentation of system specification arising from the combination of a well-established addiction treatment model and persuasive technologies. In this respect, the research addresses the adaptation of the MM, an approach that has been proven effective in the field of alcohol and substance addiction for many years, to both the context of digital addiction and the digital environment. Thus, it develops a perspective on rethinking its counseling strategies for this specific setting. Our findings provide both a practical and theoretical foundation for future digital interventions to be developed and offer a broader methodological roadmap for how psychological counseling approaches can be integrated with information systems models.

Acknowledgments. This study has received funding from the Research Council of Finland under the decision number 351670, also known as PerFeat project.

Disclosure of Interests. The authors have no competing interests to declare that are relevant to the content of this article.

References

1. Basel Almourad, M., McAlaney, J., Skinner, T., Pleva, M., Ali, R.: Defining digital addiction: key features from the literature. Psihologija **53**(3), 237–253 (2020)
2. Meng, S.Q., et al.: Global prevalence of digital addiction in general population: a systematic review and meta-analysis. Clin. Psychol. Rev. **92**, 102128 (2022). https://doi.org/10.1016/j.cpr.2022.102128
3. Dong, G., Hu, Y., Lin, X., Lu, Q.: What makes Internet addicts continue playing online even when faced by severe negative consequences? Possible explanations from an fMRI study. Biol. Psychol. **94**(2), 282–289 (2013). https://doi.org/10.1016/j.biopsycho.2013.07.009
4. Kesici, A., Tunç, N.F.: Investigating the digital addiction level of the university students according to their purposes for using digital tools. Univ. J. Educ. Res. **6**(2), 245–241 (2018). https://doi.org/10.13189/ujer.2018.060204
5. Young, K.S.: Internet addiction: the emergence of a new clinical disorder. In: Paper presented at the meeting of the American psychological association, Toronto, Canada (1996). https://doi.org/10.1089/cpb.1998.1.237
6. Shiferaw, B.D., et al.: Impact of digital addiction on youth health: a systematic review and meta-analysis. J. Behav. Addict. **14**(3), 1129–1158 (2025). https://doi.org/10.1556/2006.2025.00081
7. Löchner, J., Carlbring, P., Schuller, B., Torous, J., Sander, L.B.: Digital interventions in mental health: an overview and future perspectives. Internet Interv. **40**, 100824 (2025). https://doi.org/10.1016/j.invent.2025.100824
8. Theopilus, Y., Al Mahmud, A., Davis, H., Octavia, J.R.: Persuasive strategies in digital interventions to combat internet addiction: a systematic review. Int. J. Med. Informatics **195**, 105725 (2025). https://doi.org/10.1016/j.ijmedinf.2024.105725

9. Moon, Z., Walsh, J.: Digital interventions in medication adherence: a narrative review of current evidence and challenges. Front. Pharmacol. **16**, 1632474 (2025). https://doi.org/10.3389/fphar.2025.1632474

10. Moshe, I., et al.: Digital interventions for the treatment of depression: a meta-analytic review. Psychol. Bull. **147**(8), 749–786 (2021). https://doi.org/10.1037/bul0000334

11. Gentili, A., et al.: The cost-effectiveness of digital health interventions: a systematic review of the literature. Front. Public Health **10**, 787135 (2022). https://doi.org/10.3389/fpubh.2022.787135

12. Tremain, H., McEnery, C., Fletcher, K., Murray, G.: The Therapeutic alliance in digital mental health interventions for serious mental illnesses: narrative review. JMIR Ment Health **7**(8):e17204 (2020). https://mental.jmir.org/2020/8/e17204 https://doi.org/10.2196/17204

13. Graham, A.K., et al.: Implementation strategies for digital mental health interventions in health care settings. Am. Psychol. **75**(8), 1080–1092 (2020). https://doi.org/10.1037/amp0000686

14. Oinas-Kukkonen, H., Harjumaa, M.: Persuasive systems design: key issues, process model, and system features. Commun. Assoc. Inf. Syst. **24** (2009). https://doi.org/10.17705/1CAIS.02428

15. Venkatesh, V., Morris, M.G., Davis, G.B., Davis, F.D.: User acceptance of information technology: toward a unified view. MIS Q. **27**(3), 425–478 (2003). https://doi.org/10.2307/30036540

16. Anderson, D.J., McGovern, J.P., Dupont, R.L.: The origins of the Minnesota model of addiction treatment –a first person account. J. Addict. Dis. **18**(1), 107–114 (1999). https://doi.org/10.1300/J069v18n01_10

17. Taskan, H.S., Oinas-Kukkonen, H.: Designing behavior change support systems for recovery from addictions: mapping software features with counseling strategies. In: Win, K.T., Ali, R., Karapanos, E., Papadopoulos, G.A., Oyibo, K., Vlahu-Gjorgievska, E. (eds.) PERSUASIVE 2025. LNCS, vol. 15711, pp. 165–175. Springer, Cham (2025). https://doi.org/10.1007/978-3-031-94959-3_12

18. Oinas-Kukkonen, H. [Heikki]: Alkoholistin ja hänen läheisensä samanaikainen toipuminen vapauttavana oppimisprosessina Minnesota-hoidossa [Dissertation]. jultika.oulu.fi (2013). https://oulurepo.oulu.fi/handle/10024/35569

19. Cook, C.C.H.: The Minnesota model in the management of drug and alcohol dependency: miracle, method or myth? Part I. The philosophy and the programme. Br. J. Add. **83**, 625–634 (1988) .https://doi.org/10.1111/j.1360-0443.1988.tb02591.x

20. Stinchfield, R., Owen, P.: Hazelden's model of treatment and its outcome. Addict. Behav. **23**(5), 669–683 (1998). https://doi.org/10.1016/S0306-4603(98)00015-X

21. Gallagher, C., Radmall, Z., O'Gara, C., Burke, T.: Effectiveness of a national 'Minnesota Model' based residential treatment programme for alcohol dependence in Ireland: outcomes and predictors of outcome. Irish J. Psychol. Med. **35**(1), 33–41 (2018). https://doi.org/10.1017/ipm.2017.26

22. Bodin, M. The Minnesota model treatment for substance dependence : program evaluation in a Swedish setting. Karolinska Institutet. Thesis (2006). https://hdl.handle.net/10616/39929

23. Kelders, S.M., Kok, R.N., Ossebaard, H.C., Van Gemert-Pijnen, J.E.: Persuasive system design does matter: a systematic review of adherence to web-based interventions. J. Med. Internet Res. **14**(6), e152 (2012). https://doi.org/10.2196/jmir.2104

24. Alrobai, A., McAlaney, J., Phalp, K., Ali, R.: Online peer groups as a persuasive tool to combat digital addiction. In: Meschtscherjakov, A., De Ruyter, B., Fuchsberger, V., Murer, M., Tscheligi, M. (eds.) PERSUASIVE 2016. LNCS, vol. 9638, pp. 288–300. Springer, Cham (2016). https://doi.org/10.1007/978-3-319-31510-2_25

CEBRA-Enabled Latent Embeddings of Wearable Biosignals for Personalized Biorhythm Modeling

Sutashu Tomonaga[1]([✉]), Jo Fujimori[2], Yi-Shan Cheng[3], Haruo Mizutani[4], and Kenji Doya[1]

[1] OIST, Okinawa, Japan
{sutashu.tomonaga,doya}@oist.jp
[2] Keio University Medical School, Tokyo, Japan
jo3fujimori@keio.jp
[3] RIKEN Center for Brain Science, Saitama, Japan
yi-shan.cheng@riken.jp
[4] Suntory Global Innovation Center (SIC), Okinawa, Japan
haruo_mizutani@suntory.co.jp

Abstract. Wearable devices offer an unprecedented opportunity to monitor personal health through continuous collection of physiological signals, such as heart rate (HR). However, these observed signals are typically low-dimensional and noisy, yet result from complex, nonlinear mixtures of high-dimensional latent physiological processes. To address this, we adapt CEBRA, a contrastive learning method rooted in nonlinear ICA, to deconstruct these influences and learn meaningful representations of individual biorhythms. In an exploratory study on passive recordings, we apply our method to VitalPatch data (RRI, HR, RR) from 30 older adults. Our key innovation is using phenotypic and habitual data as auxiliary variables, enabling CEBRA to learn highly consistent latent manifolds ($R^2 > 0.76$) that capture shared circadian dynamics while reflecting inter-individual differences in traits and habits. These embeddings serve as a prototype for persuasive technologies, facilitating anomaly detection in biorhythm trajectories to support just-in-time interventions (e.g., nudges via visualizations of users' positions in a "health space" relative to healthier clusters).

Keywords: Wearable Biosignals · Biorhythms · Contrastive Learning · Nonlinear ICA · Digital Health

1 Introduction

Wearable devices have transformed personal health monitoring by enabling continuous collection of physiological data like heart rate (HR) in naturalistic settings [2,11]. This longitudinal data offers an unprecedented opportunity to move beyond static clinical snapshots and model dynamic biorhythms, such as circadian rhythms that are fundamental to health and well-being [9]. However,

K. Sumi et al. (Eds.): PERSUASIVE 2026, LNCS 16476, pp. 382–392, 2026.
https://doi.org/10.1007/978-3-032-19687-3_28

observed signals are typically low-dimensional and noisy (e.g., HR, RR), yet result from nonlinear mixtures of high-dimensional physiological processes [5,21]. The key challenge is leveraging wearable data to deconstruct these influences and uncover a meaningful representation of individual health states.

Such representations require consistent, interpretable low-dimensional "health spaces" capturing shared biorhythms and individual differences. Diverse physiological profiles across individuals complicate latent embeddings that generalize. Model-driven approaches fit data to deterministic equations [8,9], but stochastic data-driven methods discovering nonlinear dynamics linked to interpretable variables like phenotypes remain challenging.

We adapt CEBRA (Consistent EmBeddings of high-dimensional Recordings using Auxiliary variables), a state-of-the-art method for consistent latent embeddings [20]. Rooted in nonlinear Independent Component Analysis (ICA) and contrastive learning [6] (see Sect. 3.2), CEBRA shapes latent spaces using auxiliary variables. We evaluate auxiliaries' impact: discovery-driven models use temporal auxiliaries (linear time or sin/cos time-of-day) for shared biorhythm manifolds; hybrid models combine cyclical time and phenotypic labels. We empirically show hybrid approaches yield consistent manifolds structured by biorhythms and traits, while discovery-driven models uncover phenotypic structure from biosignals alone. This is an exploratory study on passive wearable recordings. It leverages the seamless, uninterrupted nature of devices like VitalPatch for real-world daily routines without active tasks. This facilitates interpretable analysis of human health and opens avenues for persuasive feedback applications. For instance, anomaly detection in latent trajectories could enable just-in-time interventions (e.g., nudges to realign disrupted biorhythms via app visualizations of users' positions in a "health space" relative to healthier phenotype clusters, empowering self-directed habit changes) [3,4,14,15,19].

This work makes three primary contributions. First, we provide the first application of CEBRA to human wearable data for health monitoring. Second, we demonstrate that this approach generates highly consistent biorhythm manifolds that are meaningfully structured by health-relevant phenotypes. Third, we illustrate how these manifolds can contribute to a framework for precision medicine and personalized interventions that incorporate individual biorhythms. This provides a robust methodology for translating complex biosignals into personalized, persuasive health insights.

2   Related Work

Techniques for latent representations from biosignals span linear and nonlinear approaches. Linear methods like CCA [1,10,18,23] and AR models [7] offer interpretability, correlating multimodal data (e.g., HRV-phenotypes), but fail to capture the complex nonlinear dynamics inherent in human physiology [5,21].

Nonlinear methods like t-SNE, UMAP, and autoencoders improve visualization, denoising, anomaly detection [16,22], but lack consistency across subjects/datasets and explicit auxiliary structuring (e.g., phenotypes), unlike CCA.

We build on CEBRA [20], creating consistent embeddings from neural/behavioral data via contrastive learning. Extending Hyvärinen et al.'s nonlinear ICA with auxiliaries for identifiability [6], it enables discovery-driven (time-guided) and hybrid analyses [20]. Proven in animal neurophysiology, its use in human wearables for persuasive technology is a novel application. In persuasive systems, similar approaches have used wearables for health nudges and long-term behavior change [3,4]. Our passive, phenotype-guided CEBRA adaptation extends this to dynamic biorhythm modeling. It lays the groundwork for interventions informed by routine differences, with plans to incorporate activity/sleep labels for greater routine reflection and accuracy.

3   Methods

3.1   Dataset and Preprocessing

The data for this study originates from Keshmiri et al. [7], a broader study on cardiorespiratory function in older adults. As such, the source cohort consists entirely of participants aged 50 and above. Full details on ethics and data acquisition are in the original publication. In brief, each participant wore a VitalPatch RTM wearable device for 5–7 days, recording R-R intervals (RRI), heart rate (HR), and respiratory rate (RR).

From this original cohort, we selected a subset of $N = 30$ participants based on rigorous data quality criteria: inclusion required continuous recordings spanning the full 7 days with minimal signal loss or artifacts, ensuring stable long-term inputs for manifold learning. Participants also provided static self-reported data via a one-time questionnaire, which we use as auxiliary variables. This included BMI and two key habitual metrics: "alcohol consumption" (grams per session, calculated from self-reported beverage type, volume, and concentration) and "exercise amount" (minutes per session). For this analysis, we used these per-session amounts rather than reported frequency.

Our preprocessing pipeline was as follows: **Signal Cleaning:** Raw 4-second signals were averaged into 1-minute bins, missing values were linearly interpolated, and all signals (RRI, HR, RR) for each subject were z-scored. **Feature Engineering:** We enriched the feature vector in two ways. First, we computed the variance of each signal over a 30-minute sliding window. Second, we added a time-delay embedding ($d = 3$, $\tau = 128$) to each of the three signals (RRI, HR, RR), adding two additional delayed features per signal. This τ was chosen as it was found to best capture the cardiorespiratory information dynamics in [7]. This resulted in a 12-dimensional feature vector (3 signals + 3 variances + 6 delayed signals) per time point. **Data Concatenation:** To learn a population-level manifold, time-series data from all 30 subjects were concatenated along the time axis. **Temporal Auxiliary Variable:** For the Time-Of-Day (TOD) auxiliary variable, we converted the 24-hour clock time into two continuous variables using $t_{sin} = \sin(2\pi \cdot \frac{\text{hour} \cdot 60 + \text{minute}}{1440})$ and $t_{cos} = \cos(2\pi \cdot \frac{\text{hour} \cdot 60 + \text{minute}}{1440})$ to guide the discovery of cyclical biorhythms.

3.2 CEBRA Overview

CEBRA [20] is a contrastive learning method that learns consistent, low-dimensional embeddings from time-series data, guided by auxiliary variables.

Theoretical Foundation. CEBRA is a practical implementation of nonlinear Independent Component Analysis (ICA) with auxiliary variables [6]. Nonlinear ICA rests on the assumption that the observed data $\mathbf{x}$ (e.g., noisy wearable signals) is generated by a nonlinear mixing function $\mathbf{f}$ applied to latent, independent sources $\mathbf{s}$ (i.e., $\mathbf{x} = \mathbf{f}(\mathbf{s})$). The goal is to learn the inverse mapping $\mathbf{f}^{-1}$ to recover the true physiological sources $\mathbf{s}$. However, a core challenge is the *identifiability problem*: widely used blind source separation methods cannot recover $\mathbf{s}$ from $\mathbf{x}$ alone when $\mathbf{f}$ is nonlinear due to infinite possible transformations preserving independence. Building on the framework of Hyvärinen et al. [6], CEBRA implements this solution by incorporating auxiliary variables $\mathbf{u}$ (e.g., time or behavioral labels) to define positive and negative sample pairs for contrastive learning. This conditional structure makes the learned embedding identifiable up to known indeterminacies (e.g., permutations and linear or component-wise transformations), enabling the recovery of consistent biorhythms across subjects. CEBRA extends this with generalizations like the InfoNCE objective for mutual information maximization and a consistency metric for multi-subject alignment, which is particularly useful for uncovering shared circadian manifolds and individual phenotype-driven differences in wearable data like VitalPatch signals.

Contrastive Learning Objective. CEBRA trains a neural network encoder $f_\theta(\cdot)$ to map high-dimensional input x to a low-dimensional latent embedding $z = f_\theta(x)$. The encoder is trained using the InfoNCE loss [17, 20], which maximizes the mutual information between z and an auxiliary variable u:

$$\mathcal{L} = \mathbb{E}_{p(x,u)} \left[\log \frac{\exp(\phi(z, u)/\tau)}{\sum_{j=1}^{N} \exp(\phi(z, u_j)/\tau)} \right],$$

where positive/negative pairs are defined by the auxiliary variable u, ϕ is cosine similarity, and τ is a temperature parameter.

CEBRA Models Evaluated. We evaluated three variants by changing the auxiliary variable u.

- **CEBRA-Time (Discovery-Driven):** Uses a linear time index as the auxiliary.
- **CEBRA-TimeOfDay (CEBRA-TOD):** Uses the continuous 2D 'sin/cos' time-of-day (TOD). Positive pairs are signal windows with similar 24-hour cycle phases, learning the average "circadian clock."
- **CEBRA-Hybrid:** Uses both 'sin/cos' time (TOD) and a phenotype label as joint auxiliaries, aiming to learn a primary biorhythm that is also structured by individual traits.

Evaluation Metrics. We used two metrics to assess embedding quality:

- **Consistency:** Evaluates embedding similarity across subjects. We fit a linear regression to predict the embeddings of subject B from subject A and report the average R^2 across all pairs. High R^2 suggests a shared manifold.
- **Decoding Accuracy:** Measures how well auxiliary variables (e.g., time-of-day) can be predicted from the latent embeddings on held-out test sets, using linear regression (R^2).
- **Baselines Comparison:** We compared CEBRA against standard nonlinear methods, t-SNE [12] (perplexity = 30) and UMAP [13] (n_neighbors = 15), which are not designed to learn consistent, auxiliary-structured manifolds.

Implementation Details. We used the official CEBRA library [20]. The input was the concatenated 12-feature time-series from all 30 subjects. The encoder was an MLP (Multi-Layer Perceptron) using the `'offset1-model'` architecture, projecting to a 3D latent space for visualization of the spherical 2D manifold, while baseline embeddings (t-SNE, UMAP) were computed in 2D for fair comparison (as in [20]). Models were trained for 2000 iterations using the Adam optimizer (learning rate 1e-4) with a batch size of 512. Pseudocode and full implementation details are available in the CEBRA repository [20].

4   Experiments and Results

We evaluated the CEBRA models (Sect. 3.2) on the preprocessed VitalPatch data (Sect. 3.1), using the metrics in Sect. 3.2 and baselines in 2D.

4.1   Experiment 1: Discovery-Driven Biorhythm Manifold

We first trained CEBRA in a discovery-driven mode using two different temporal auxiliaries: (1) signals + the cyclical 'sin/cos' time-of-day (CEBRA-TOD); and (2) signals + a linear time index (CEBRA-Time). Visualizations (Fig. 1) confirm that both models learn circular manifolds colored consistently by the time-of-day, reflecting the shared circadian dynamics captured from the concatenated dataset.

Consistency. The consistency matrix (Fig. 2), computed via bidirectional linear decoders, shows high cross-subject similarity. CEBRA-TOD (mean $R^2 = 0.805$) and CEBRA-Time (mean $R^2 = 0.778$) significantly outperform the baselines (t-SNE: 0.471; UMAP: 0.476). This is a key result, demonstrating that CEBRA, consistent with its nonlinear ICA foundation, learns an identifiable and shared manifold structure across subjects, whereas standard nonlinear methods fail to find a common space.

Temporal Decoding. Figure 3 shows the R^2 score for decoding the 'sin/cos' time-of-day vector from the latent embeddings. This quantifies how well temporal information is preserved. CEBRA-TOD (median $R^2 = 0.53$) and CEBRA-Time (median $R^2 = 0.52$) again substantially outperform the baselines (t-SNE: 0.17, UMAP: 0.14). This confirms the embeddings are robustly structured by time. Interestingly, the non-cyclical CEBRA-Time model performed on par with the cyclical CEBRA-TOD model at this task, suggesting the linear time index is sufficient to capture the dominant periodic component.

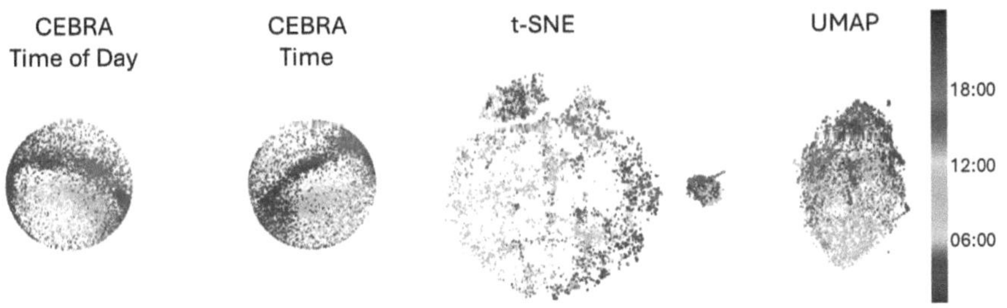

Fig. 1. Latent embeddings from CEBRA-TOD and CEBRA-Time compared to baselines (t-SNE, UMAP), colored by time-of-day. Circular trajectories reflect biorhythms induced by temporal auxiliaries.

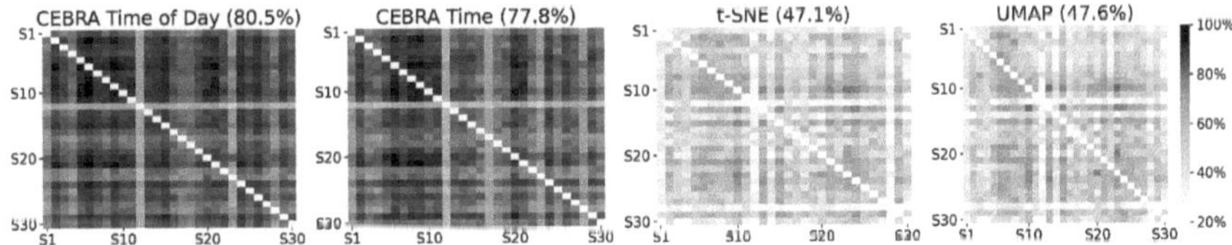

Fig. 2. Consistency matrices (subset across 30 subjects) following the evaluation in Fig. 1.e of [20]. High R^2 values (dark colors) indicate a highly consistent, shared manifold structure learned across subjects.

4.2 Experiment 2: Phenotype-Structured Embeddings

We then investigated how static phenotypic and habitual data structure this latent space. We trained two model types: (1) a **hybrid model** (CEBRA-TOD+Phenotype), using both 'sin/cos' time-of-day and a specific phenotype label (e.g., BMI, exercise amount in minutes per session, alcohol consumption amount in grams per session; see Sect. 3.1) as joint auxiliaries; and (2) the **discovery-driven model** (CEBRA-Time) from Exp 1, which was *not* given any phenotype information. We then visualized the resulting embeddings colored by the phenotype labels.

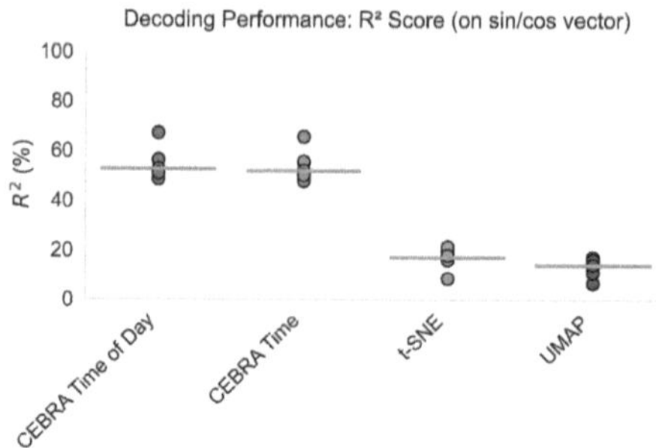

Fig. 3. Time-of-Day Decoding. CEBRA models ($R^2 > 0.50$) capture significantly more temporal information than baselines, confirming the embedding space is structured by biorhythms. Boxplots show the distribution of decoding scores across cross-validation folds; the orange line indicates the median. (Color figure online)

Discovery of Phenotypic Structure. A key finding is that the CEBRA-Time model, trained *only* on biosignals and a linear time index, produced embeddings that were already visibly structured by phenotypes. As shown in Figs. 4 – 6 (center left column), the model learned trajectories that separated individuals by BMI, exercise amount, and drinking amount, despite having no access to this information. This demonstrates CEBRA's power as a discovery-driven tool: it can extract clinically relevant, high-level information from physiological signals alone.

Qualitative Analysis. The hybrid CEBRA-TOD+Phenotype models (left column) allow us to "zoom in" on and disentangle these effects. The results revealed both expected and unexpected relationships: **Drinking Amount (Fig. 4):** We observed an intuitive separation. Individuals with low drinking amounts (purple) show a constrained, stable circular trajectory, whereas individuals with higher drinking amounts (cyan) show a much more scattered, high-variance trajectory. **Exercise Amount & BMI (Figs. 6, 5):** Here, we found a more complex and nuanced relationship. For **Exercise Amount (Fig. 5)**, individuals with low exercise (dark purple) follow the canonical stable trajectory. However, individuals with *high* exercise amount (yellow/green) show a "crunched," non-circular trajectory. Crucially, this trajectory pattern and latent-space position *visually overlaps* with the trajectory of individuals with **High BMI (Fig. 6, yellow)**. This suggests that for this cohort, high exercise amount (minutes per session) may not necessarily map to a "healthier" physiological state, but may instead be indicative of low-intensity activity (e.g., walking) which may be common among individuals with high BMI in this cohort. This is a non-obvious insight that separates "exercise amount" from "exercise frequency" or intensity.

Quantitative Consistency. To validate that the hybrid models produced stable manifolds, we measured their cross-subject consistency. The consistency of the hybrid CEBRA-TOD+Phenotype models remained high (mean R^2 for

CEBRA-TOD+ BMI = 76.7%, CEBRA-TOD+ drinking= 77.5%, and CEBRA-TOD+exercise = 78.3%). This quantitatively confirms that adding phenotypic constraints did not degrade the shared manifold structure, but rather produced a new, similarly consistent manifold that now also incorporates this trait information. While a full quantitative decoding of these labels is a next step, the visual separation combined with high consistency suggests the embeddings are robustly structured by these habits.

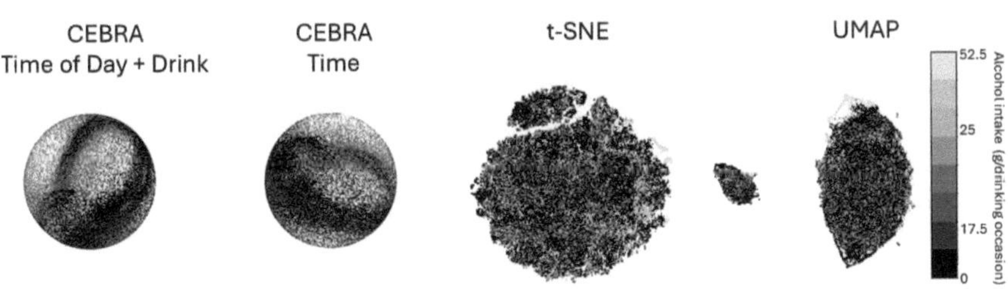

Fig. 4. Embeddings colored by alcohol consumption. High consumption (cyan) trajectories are visibly distinct from the main population trajectory (purple).

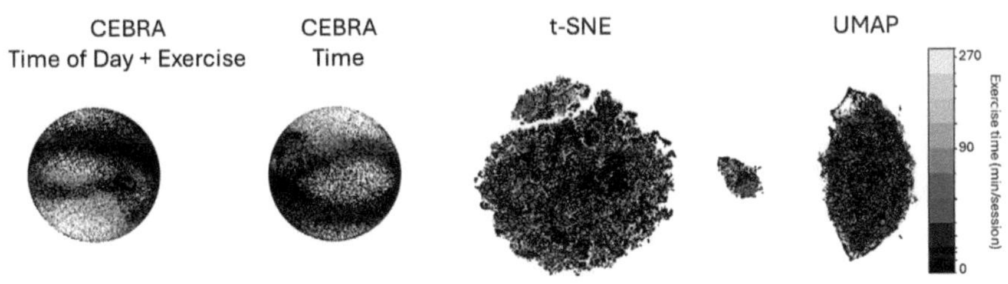

Fig. 5. Embeddings colored by exercise habits. Low exercise (purple) appears to follow a more stable trajectory than high exercise (yellow/green). (Color figure online)

Exploratory Quantification of Trajectory Deviations. As an exploratory analysis of phenotype-driven structure in the discovery-driven manifold, we quantified trajectory deviations for all subjects using PCA-based intrinsic phase alignment ($\theta = \arctan(PC2/PC1)$). Trajectories were binned into 288 phase bins (5-min resolution) and smoothed, with each subject's mean Euclidean distance computed from a leave-one-out reference trajectory (Low BMI group average, to avoid bias). Deviations were computed across the cohort, revealing that the top 10% of subjects with the highest deviations ($n = 3$) corresponded exactly to the High BMI group. These subjects showed greater mean deviation (0.200 ± 0.110) than the remaining Low BMI subjects ($n = 27$; 0.117 ± 0.099), with a large effect size (Cohen's $d = 0.80$). This indicates potential BMI-related alterations in daily

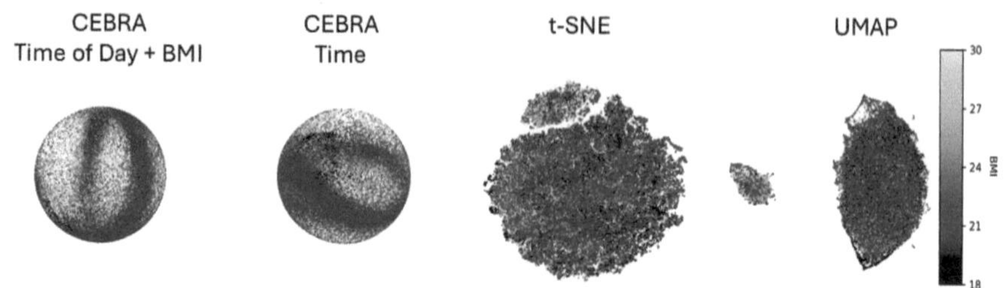

Fig. 6. Embeddings colored by BMI. Note the separation of high-BMI (yellow) trajectories in both CEBRA-TOD+BMI and the discovery-driven CEBRA-Time models. (Color figure online)

biorhythm dynamics, consistent with qualitative separations observed in hybrid embeddings.

5   Discussion and Future Work

Our results demonstrate that CEBRA can learn consistent, interpretable latent embeddings from VitalPatch biosignals. A key finding is that CEBRA-Time embeddings trained solely on temporal auxiliaries still separate trajectories by phenotypes (e.g., BMI, exercise/alcohol amount), suggesting biosignals alone encode health-relevant biomarkers. This discovery is validated by the high cross-subject consistency ($R^2 > 0.76$) across all models, confirming CEBRA's ability to learn a shared manifold where baselines fail. The hybrid CEBRA-TOD+Phenotype models refine these separations, revealing important nuances: high exercise amount visually overlaps with high BMI (potentially indicating compensatory low-intensity activity in this cohort), while high alcohol consumption correlates with a high-variance, disrupted biorhythm. These distinctions are critical for persuasive technology, as they align with our motivation to deconstruct signals into personalized biorhythms. This enables a move from generic feedback toward precision medicine, where interventions are tailored to an individual's specific physiological state.

While our participants were not engaged in an active intervention, this study establishes a promising representation layer for next-generation persuasive systems. Current wearables typically present discrete metrics (e.g., HR, steps) in isolation, often overlooking their nonlinear interactions; in contrast, our embeddings integrate these dynamics into a unified manifold, serving as a prototype "health map" for tracking holistic physiological states. **Real-Time Feedback Loops:** By projecting a user's real-time biosignals into this learned manifold, a system could calculate a "deviation vector" from that individual's stable, healthy trajectory. As shown in Fig. 4, high alcohol consumption is correlated with high variance in orbital deviations. A JITAI (Just-In-Time Adaptive Intervention) system could detect the onset of such deviations and trigger a persuasive prompt (e.g., "Your biorhythm is destabilizing; consider identifying a stressor") before the user is consciously aware of the decline [15]. **Visual Persuasion:** The 3D embeddings themselves serve as a powerful visualization tool. Unlike abstract numbers, showing a user their position drifting toward a "phenotypically unhealthy" cluster (e.g., the disrupted trajectory associated with high BMI or alcohol) could promote self-reflection and motivation. **Passive Sensing as a Feature:** Finally, we address the passive nature of our data collection. Effective persuasive technology must be seamless. By proving that robust biomarkers can be extracted from passive, noisy wearable data without requiring active user input (e.g., manual logging), we lower the barrier to entry for long-term health monitoring systems.

Limitations include the small sample size ($n = 30$) and the use of qualitative analysis. The selection of these 30 subjects was based on those with complete 7-day recordings and minimal data artifacts, ensuring high-quality input for modeling; however, this introduces potential selection bias. Future work will quantify separations (e.g., manifold distances) and interactions between traits. Additional phenotypes (e.g., sleep, smoking) could inform an aggregated "Biorhythm Index," where a personalized health deviation score incorporates preferences and body composition to provide tailored health recommendations. We also plan to expand to a wider range of participants, including broader age groups and longer monitoring periods, to improve generalizability.

Acknowledgments. This research was supported by the COI-NEXT grant from the Japan Science and Technology Agency (JST). We thank Noriyuki Ando (Suntory Global Innovation Center) for fostering this collaboration. Ethics approval and participant consent details are as reported in [7].

Disclosure of Interest. The authors have no competing interests to declare that are relevant to the content of this article.

References

1. Agniel, D., Cai, T.: Analysis of multiple diverse phenotypes via semiparametric canonical correlation analysis. Biometrics **73**(4), 1254–1265 (2017)
2. Dial, M.B., Hollander, M.E., Vatne, E.A., Emerson, A.M., Edwards, N.A., Hagen, J.A.: Validation of nocturnal resting heart rate and heart rate variability in consumer wearables. Physiological Rep. **13**(16), e70527 (2025)
3. Fritz, T., Huang, E.M., Murphy, G.C., Zimmermann, T.: Persuasive technology in the real world: a study of long-term use of activity sensing devices for fitness. In: Proceedings of the SIGCHI Conference on Human Factors in Computing Systems. ACM, New York (2014)
4. Garcia, E., Zhao, W., Kelly, R.M., Buchanan, G., Waycott, J.: Beyond monitoring: Older adults using wearable activity trackers for active health management and behaviour change. In: Proceedings of the 37th Australian Conference on Human-Computer Interaction, pp. 239–252. ACM, New York, 29 November 2025
5. de Godoy, M.F.: Nonlinear analysis of heart rate variability: a comprehensive review. J. Cardiol. Therapy **3**(3), 528–533 (2016)
6. Hyvarinen, A., Sasaki, H., Turner, R.: Nonlinear ICA using auxiliary variables and generalized contrastive learning. In: The 22nd International Conference on Artificial Intelligence and Statistics, pp. 859–868. PMLR, 11 April 2019

7. Keshmiri, S., Tomonaga, S., Mizutani, H., Doya, K.: Respiratory modulation of the heart rate: A potential biomarker of cardiorespiratory function in human. Comput. Biology Med. **173**, 108335 (2024)

8. Kim, B., Lee, K.H., Xue, L., Niu, X.: A review of dynamic network models with latent variables. Stat. Surv. **12**, 105–135 (2018)

9. Kim, D.W., Mayer, C., Lee, M.P., Choi, S.W., Tewari, M., Forger, D.B.: Efficient assessment of real-world dynamics of circadian rhythms in heart rate and body temperature from wearable data. J. Roy. Soc. Interface **20**(205), 20230030 (2023)

10. Krafty, R.T., Hall, M.: Canonical correlation analysis between time series and static outcomes, with application to the spectral analysis of heart rate variability. Ann. Appl. Stat. **7**(1), 570–587 (2013)

11. Li, K., Cardoso, C., Moctezuma-Ramirez, A., Elgalad, A., Perin, E.: Heart rate variability measurement through a smart wearable device: another breakthrough for personal health monitoring? Int. J. Environ. Res. Public Health **20**(24), 7146 (2023)

12. Maaten, L., Hinton, G.E.: Visualizing Data using t-SNE. J. Mach. Learn. Res. **9**(86), 2579–2605 (2008)

13. McInnes, L., Healy, J., Melville, J.: UMAP: Uniform Manifold Approximation and Projection for Dimension Reduction. arXiv [stat.ML], 9 February 2018

14. Nahum-Shani, I., Hekler, E.B., Spruijt-Metz, D.: Building health behavior models to guide the development of just-in-time adaptive interventions: A pragmatic framework. Health psychology: official journal of the Division of Health Psychology, American Psychological Association **34S**(Suppl), 1209–1219 (2015)

15. Nahum-Shani, I., Smith, S.N., Spring, B.J., Collins, L.M., Witkiewitz, K., Tewari, A., Murphy, S.A.: Just-in-time adaptive interventions (JITAIs) in mobile health: Key components and design principles for ongoing health behavior support. Annals of behavioral medicine: a publication of the Society of Behavioral Medicine **52**(6), 446–462 (2018)

16. Nowroozilarki, Z., Mortazavi, B.J., Jafari, R.: Variational autoencoders for biomedical signal morphology clustering and noise detection. IEEE J. Biomed. Health Inform. **PP**(1), 169–180 (2023)

17. van den Oord, A., Li, Y., Vinyals, O.: Representation learning with Contrastive Predictive Coding. arXiv [cs.LG], 10 July 2018

18. Piskin, S., Patnaik, S.S., Han, D., Bordones, A.D., Murali, S., Finol, E.A.: A canonical correlation analysis of the relationship between clinical attributes and patient-specific hemodynamic indices in adult pulmonary hypertension. Med. Eng. Phys. **77**, 1–9 (2020)

19. Schembre, S.M., et al.: Mobile ecological momentary diet assessment methods for behavioral research: Systematic review. JMIR mHealth and uHealth **6**(11), e11170 (2018)

20. Schneider, S., Lee, J.H., Mathis, M.W.: Learnable latent embeddings for joint behavioural and neural analysis. Nature **617**(7960), 360–368 (2023)

21. Shaffer, F., Ginsberg, J.P.: An Overview of Heart Rate Variability Metrics and Norms. Front. Public Health **5**, 258 (2017)

22. Webster, M.B., Lee, D., Lee, J.: Self-supervised autoencoder network for robust heart rate extraction from noisy photoplethysmogram: Applying blind source separation to biosignal analysis. arXiv [cs.LG] (11 Aug 2025)

23. Yahata, N., et al.: A small number of abnormal brain connections predicts adult autism spectrum disorder. Nature Commun. **7**(1), 11254 (2016)

A Wearable System for Promoting Decision Diversity Through Detection and Recall of Previous Considered Options

Kanata Utsunomiya, Ayumi Ohnishi⬛, Tsutomu Terada$^{(\boxtimes)}$⬛, and Masahiko Tsukamoto⬛

Kobe University, 1-1, Rokkodai-cho, Nada-ku, Kobe 657-8501, Japan
`251t209t@stu.kobe-u.ac.jp`, `{ohnishi,tsutomu,tuka}@eedept.kobe-u.ac.jp`

Abstract. In daily life, we repeatedly make choices, such as selecting meals at a cafeteria or snacks at a convenience store. People tend to select the same options they have chosen before, mainly due to a loss aversion that increases risk avoidance. Reducing this fixation and promoting diversity in choices could lead to new experiences and greater satisfaction. This study proposes a glasses-type wearable system that encourages diverse choice behavior by presenting users with previously hesitated options in real-time. The system detects choice behavior based on the gaze information during daily life and records the choice scene along with the options the user hesitated over. When a similar choice scene reoccurs, the system presents those past options based on the recorded data. In this paper, we implemented a prototype of the proposed system and performed an evaluation experiment to examine whether presenting previously hesitated options can promote choice diversity. In the system validation, the prototype successfully detected and recorded choice behavior accurately in purchasing scenes. In the evaluation experiment, the average number of times they chose a different option from the previous choice was 4.73 with option presentation, compared to 3.53 without it. This suggests that the proposed system can help diversify user choices in purchasing situations.

Keywords: Choice behavior · Wearable device · Gaze tracking · Human computer interaction

1 Introduction

People often repeat the same choices in daily life, such as selecting meals or snacks. This is because they want to avoid risk [1,2] and reduce the cognitive load of making choices [3]. However, repeating choices limits new experiences and reduces satisfaction. Making varied choices can bring more happiness [4], help people discover new things, and improve their ability to adapt [5,6]. For example, making varied choices increases retrospective satisfaction when individuals reflect on their past decisions [4]. Moreover, trying different options promotes discovery

© The Author(s), under exclusive license to Springer Nature Switzerland AG 2026
K. Sumi et al. (Eds.): PERSUASIVE 2026, LNCS 16476, pp. 393–405, 2026.
https://doi.org/10.1007/978-3-032-19687-3_29

and enhances adaptability [5], which can contribute to higher quality of life in everyday situations. Although choice behavior is influenced by various factors such as cost, personal background, and situational context, it can still be shaped through appropriate information presentation.

Prior research proposed ways to limiting options [3] or reducing psychological resistance to new decisions [7]. However, it is difficult to effectively limit options because they are wide-ranging in daily life. In addition, some studies attempted to diversify online choices [8], but the effects on daily life remain unclear.

Using previous experience can reduce resistance to unfamiliar options [7]. Presenting options users previously considered but did not choose may support different decisions. This approach increases trust and reduces hesitation. To the best of our knowledge, there is no prior work that focuses on the value of options that users hesitated over but did not choose.

Accordingly, in this study, we propose a system that presents previously considered options during similar choice scenes. The system detects decision-making using gaze behavior, and records hesitated options. Gaze relates strongly to decisions [9], and gaze duration correlates with interest [10]. The system uses eye-tracking to detect decision-making moments and estimate considered options. When a similar scene occurs, it presents those options to the user in real-time.

In this paper, after building a prototype of the proposed system, we conducted system validation and an evaluation experiment. First, as a system validation, we confirmed that the system could detect choice behaviors and present previously hesitated options using gaze data. Next, in an evaluation experiment, participants chose drinks from five options. We compared trials with and without suggestions of previously considered options to evaluate their effect on choice diversity. Experimental results showed that presenting previously considered options increased the likelihood of selecting a different option than before. Finally, we discussed possible improvements to the proposed system based on the results of these experiments.

2   Related Work

2.1   Choice Fixation and Diversification

We make many choices in daily life, but we tend to keep the status quo unless there is a major issue. Samuelson et al. argue that people often avoid new options due to risk aversion during choice behavior, which leads them to stick with the current state. [2]. Additionally, Schwartz highlights that too many options increase cognitive load, make choice behavior harder, and reinforce fixed decisions [3]. Thus, both risk aversion and cognitive overload from too many options promote choice fixation. Repeatedly making the same choices means missing opportunities for new experiences. On the other hand, experiences from diverse choices improve satisfaction in hindsight. [4]. However, doing so without support is difficult due to psychological barriers and increased cognitive load. This is why a system is needed to assist users in diversifying their choices.

To promote choice diversity, two approaches are possible: reducing psychological resistance to new options and appropriately limiting the number of options to prevent fixation. Choosing based on one's own experiences and others' evaluations is effective for reducing resistance to new options [7]. Shimizu et al. have shown how product reviews affect decision diversity. They proposed that positive reviews promote diversity, while negative ones reinforce fixed behavior [8]. However, their study focused only on online decisions and did not address real-world choice behavior in daily life. Additionally, their system presented limited effects in promoting actual behavior change.

Based on this previous research, we propose a system targeting daily choice behavior, aiming to prevent choice fixation in everyday life. To counter choice fixation, reducing resistance to unfamiliar options is essential. For this purpose, the system encourages users to recall past choices and reconsider the ones they once hesitated over. By recalling past choices, the system supports more diverse decision making.

2.2   Choice Behavior and Eye Gaze

To present previously considered options, the system needs to record daily choice behavior. Here, eye gaze is a key parameter in capturing such behavior [9,11,12]. Orquin et al. reported that gaze plays a critical role in the decision-making process [9]. Krajbich et al. suggested that gaze patterns correlate with differences in option value [11]. Research focusing on gaze during choice behavior often examine two components: fixations, where the gaze remains in one area, and saccades, which are rapid movements between fixations [10,13–16].

For example, Simojo et al. found that fixation time gradually shifted toward the chosen face, suggesting its role in preference formation [13]. Krajbich et al. reported that options with longer fixation durations were more likely to be selected [10]. Lans et al. showed that gaze and saccade patterns can reveal the precise location of a target on a retail shelf [14].

These findings suggest that choice behavior can be inferred by analyzing eye gaze. To achieve the objectives of our study, it is necessary to detect choice behavior, so we apply techniques used in related research. Therefore, in this research, our study detects choice behavior and estimates options using eye gaze data. The system then records daily decisions and presents previously considered options to support more diverse choice behavior.

3   Proposed System

3.1   Assumed Environment

This section describes a proposed system that detects user choice behavior based on real-time eye gaze data and, when choice behavior is detected, presents options that the user previously hesitated over.

In this study, "choice behavior" refers to the visual comparison of multiple options before making a selection. Once the user chooses and acts (e.g., purchases), the behavior is considered complete. Therefore, the system uses a wearable device designed for continuous use.

When a user encounters a scene they previously experienced while wearing the system, it activates and presents options they previously considered. The system presents all previously considered options, regardless of whether they were finally selected or not. By using past experiences and external reviews, the system reduces psychological resistance to unfamiliar options [7]. As a result, users are more likely to try options they previously did not choose and the system encourages diversity in everyday decisions.

For example, consider a situation where a user wearing the proposed system goes to a convenience store to buy snacks. First, the system determines whether the user is selecting snacks (choice behavior), simply walking, or entering the store (non-choice behavior). Next, if choice behavior is detected, the system identifies the choice scene. Then, when the system detects the snack section, it presents snacks the user previously hesitated over in similar scenes to past considered options. Then, multiple snacks that the user seemed to consider are recorded as candidate options, and will be presented in similar future choice scenes.

In this way, the proposed system recognizes the user's choice behavior and promotes choice diversity by presenting previously recorded options the user once hesitated over. To achieve this, the system requires the following four functions: (1) detection of choice behaviors, (2) detection of similar previous choice scenes, (3) presentation of previously considered options, and (4) estimation of currently considered options. The following sections describe the system architecture and each function in detail.

3.2   System Configuration

As shown in Fig. 1, the proposed system consists of a glasses-type eye tracker, a PC, and the user's smartphone, all connected wirelessly. While using the system, the user wears the eye tracker and receives suggestions of previously considered options on their smartphone during choice behavior. The system operates as follows. First, the eye tracker captures the user's real-time eye gaze data and first-person video, then sends this information to the PC. Next, the PC detects the user's choice behavior based on the received data. Finally, the PC refers to the recorded past choice behavior and sends an image of the previously hesitated option to the smartphone.

The proposed system uses the following devices. To capture real-time eye gaze data in daily life, we used the Neon glasses-type eye tracker by Pupil Labs [17]. The PC is ThinkPad X1 Extreme by Lenovo, and the smartphone is iPhone 16 by Apple Inc. For delivering suggestions, we used LINE, a messaging application provided by LINE Corporation, along with the LINE Notify [18] feature.

Figure 2 illustrates the processing flow of the proposed system. First, the system uses the eye tracker to capture the user's gaze data and first-person view during daily life. Next, the system detects the user's choice behavior in real-time based on the captured gaze data. When choice behavior is detected, the system

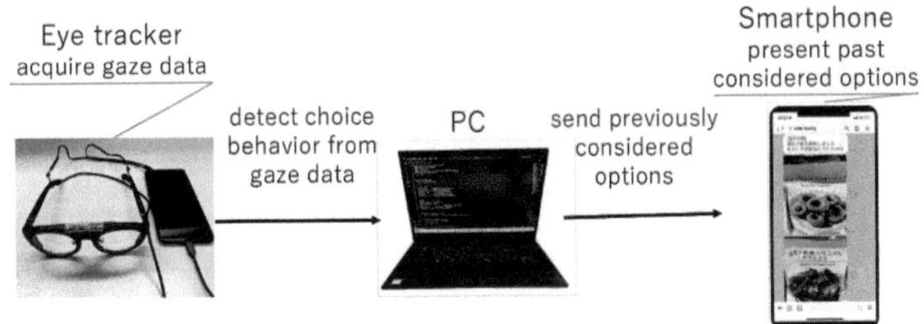

Fig. 1. Configuration of the proposed system.

estimates the choice scene by comparing the user's field of view image with previously recorded choice scenes stored in the system. If a similar scene is found, the system presents the smartphone with an image of options the user previously considered. On the other hand, If a similar scene is not found, the following message is displayed on the smartphone: *"This is your first choice scene. Any decision might be good !"* Then, in order to support future recommendations, the system records the user hesitated over in the current choice scene, linking them to that scene.

3.3 Method for Detecting Choice Behavior

The proposed system detects whether the user is making a decision by analyzing gaze data from the eye tracker. In this study, choice behavior is defined as the state in which the user is actively considering what to choose. For example, as shown in Fig. 3, walking or entering a store is not considered as choice behaviors. In contrast, the moment the user stands before the snack shelf and looks at products is determined to be a choice behavior.

This study uses fixations and saccades to determine whether the user is engaged in choice behavior, following previous research [14,16]. A fixation refers to a gaze that remains on the same point for a certain duration, while a saccade is a rapid eye movement between fixations.

During choice behavior, the user is expected to visually compare multiple options. In such cases, fixations tend to cluster around the options, and saccades frequently occur between them. Therefore, analyzing fixations and saccades can help determine whether the user is actively making a decision.

We explain the characteristics of gaze behavior during choice behavior using recorded data. Figure 4 presents the gaze patterns during choice behavior. The vertical axis represents the Y-coordinate of the gaze, and the horizontal axis represents the X-coordinate. Lines between the circles represent saccades. During choice behavior, multiple dense clusters of fixations appear within a limited region. In addition, multiple saccades are observed between these dense areas, indicating that the gaze moves back and forth among potential options. Based on this observation, we infer that when fixations are densely clustered and saccades

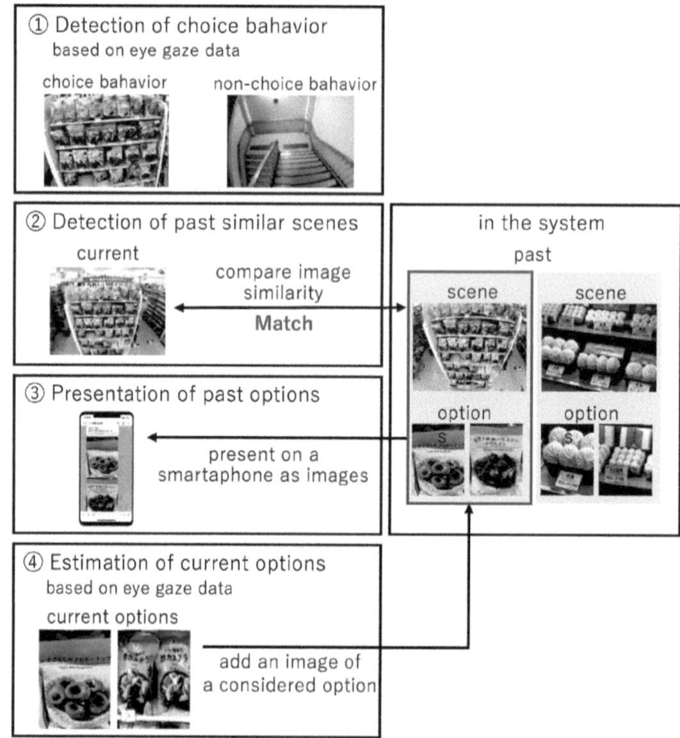

Fig. 2. Process flow of the system.

Fig. 3. An example during choice behavior.

frequently connect these clusters, the user is likely engaged in choice behavior that involves comparing different options.

Based on the above, the proposed system determines whether the user is engaged in choice behavior by first detecting areas with dense fixations. These areas are treated as regions where undecided options are likely present. An area is defined as a circular region with a radius of 110 px that contains at least 18 fixations and does not overlap with existing areas. Next, the system checks whether there are at least 12 saccades between different areas. If this condition is met, it considers the gaze to be moving back and forth between options and detects

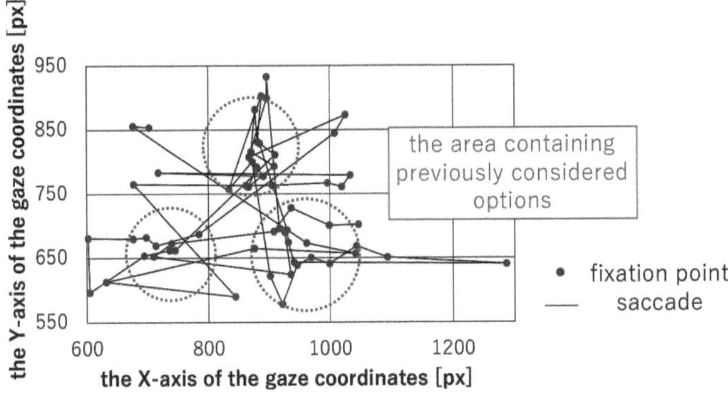

Fig. 4. Saccade movements during choice behavior.

that the user is in a decision state. The system continuously references gaze data from the past 10 s to determine the decision state in real-time. All thresholds for fixations and saccades are adjustable. In this study, these parameters were determined through a preliminary experiment conducted by the author.

3.4 Method for Determining Whether a Similar Previous Choice Scene Exists

When the system detects the user's choice behavior, it determines whether a similar choice scene has occurred in the past. At the moment the user is detected as being in a decision state, the system captures a view image using the eye tracker and records it as the current scene. The system also stores images of all previous choice scenes in the same way. Moreover, the system compares the current view image with each previously recorded scene and calculates image similarity scores.

The HSV histogram method was used to calculate similarity. This method focuses on color features, so it is robust to slight positional shifts between similar images, which makes it suitable for scene classification. Additionally, histogram-based computation is lightweight and fast, so it is appropriate for real-time processing.

The process is as follows. First, the system converts the color space of the image from RGB to HSV, which consists of hue, saturation, and value components. Next, the system computes a 3D histogram from the HSV image. The histogram is calculated by dividing the hue range [0, 180], the saturation [0, 256], and value [0, 256] ranges into 8 bins each. As a result, the system obtains a 3D histogram that represents the distribution of all pixels across the HSV space. Finally, the system normalizes the histogram to fall within the range [0, 1]. The system creates a histogram for each choice scene through this process, and it measures similarity using the chi-square distance. If the distance is below a threshold of 5 (empirically determined through preliminary testing), the system regards the current scene as similar to the past one. This threshold balances sensitivity to true matches while avoiding spurious similarity due to lighting or angle variations.

3.5   Considered Options Recognition and Presentation

If a similar choice scene has occurred in the past, the system presents the options that the user previously considered during that scene on their smartphone. In this implementation, we present all previously considered options from the matched past scene, regardless of whether they were finally selected. Then, as shown in Fig. 5, the options previously considered by the user are recorded and associated with the corresponding choice scene. The most recently recorded images are treated as the previously considered options. These images are presented on the smartphone along with a message such as: *"You were considering these options last time. Why not try the one you didn't pick before?"*

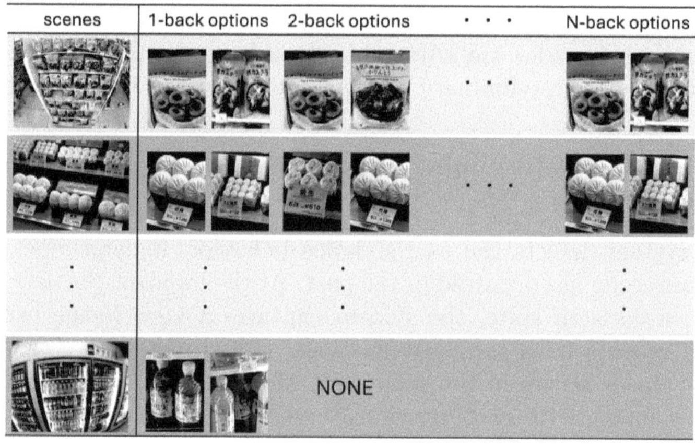

Fig. 5. Recorded options.

After the images and messages of previously considered options are presented on the smartphone, the proposed system estimates and records the options the user is currently considering. When the previously considered options are presented, the user views them on their smartphone and then engages in choice behavior. At this time, the system once again performs the process described in Sect. 3.2 to determine whether the user is in a decision state. The system estimates the options under consideration based on the areas identified as containing options.

Specifically, the system extracts a square area of 200 pixels on each side from the user's field-of-view image, centered around the coordinates of the detected area. This extracted region is treated as the image of the option the user is considering. Since the identified area contains a high density of fixation points, it is likely to include options that attract the user's attention. Therefore, it is assumed that the extracted image includes the options the user was deliberating over. The estimated option image is recorded along with the corresponding choice scene.

3.6   Validation

This section describes a brief validation conducted to confirm that the proposed system operates as intended. The author used the proposed system alone to perform choice behaviors in five daily-life scenarios and validated whether it could detect decisions, record considered options, and present them later. These scenarios were: (a) choosing a rice bowl dish at a cafeteria, (b) choosing a beverage at a convenience store, (c) choosing dried noodles at a convenience store, (d) choosing snacks at a variety store, and (e) choosing a direction at a fork in the road. The author performed two choice behaviors in each of scenes (a) to (e). The following metrics were used to evaluate system performance.

Choice behavior recognition Whether the system correctly recognizes when the user is engaged in a choice behavior

Choice scene estimation Whether the system accurately identifies the choice scene

Option presentation Whether the last considered are correctly presented on the smartphone

Option estimation accuracy The F-score between the actual considered options and the options estimated by the system

The option estimation accuracy for scenes (a) through (e) was 0.75, 0.83, 1.00, 0.92, and 0.00, respectively. Among these, scenes (a) through (d), which involve purchasing behavior, achieved high accuracy across all criteria. In these scenes, choice behavior recognition, choice scene estimation, and option presentation all functioned correctly in both choice behaviors. In contrast, in scene (e) (where the user selects a path at a fork in the road), the system failed to detect the choice behavior. This likely occurred because, at a fork, the user moves their head from side to side to compare options, and the gaze coordinates for each path may overlap, making it difficult for the system to distinguish between them.

This experiment assessed system performance during choice behavior. However, we also observed false positives where the system incorrectly identified walking as a choice behavior. Therefore, it is necessary to develop a more robust detection method that integrates additional features beyond gaze movement alone.

4   Evaluation Experiment

This section describes the evaluation experiment carried out to examine whether presenting last considered options can diversify choice behavior. This experiment was approved by the Human Ethics Committee of the authors' affiliated institution (Permission Number: [blind for review]) and was carried out according to the guidelines of the Declaration of Helsinki. (Review No. 06-39)

4.1   Experimental Method

Based on the results of the system verification in Sect. 3.6, it was confirmed that the proposed system could detect user choice behaviors and estimate the options they considered during purchasing activities. Building on this outcome, we conducted an evaluation experiment to determine whether presenting the options considered last time can diversify user's current decisions.

In this experiment, we compared two conditions: one in which the options considered last time were presented to the user *with presentation*, and one in which they were not *without presentation*. In *with presentation* condition, the last considered options including the one actually selected were presented before the new decision was made.

Before the experiment, the participants were given an explanation of the purpose of the experiment and the functionality of the system. In the evaluation experiment, participants were asked to select the drink they most wanted from five beverages. Each participant made a total of 11 decisions: five trials under the *with presentation* condition and five under the *without presentation*. We then compared the results across the two conditions to assess whether the presentation of the last considered options led to more diverse decisions. The subjects were 15 male and female laboratory students with an average age of 22.5 ($SD = 0.81$). Participants were presented with five types of drinks (apple juice, orange juice, whey beverage, milk tea, and lemon tea) placed on a table. They were instructed to choose the drink they most wanted. The experiment simulated a scenario in which participants had just finished two hours of PC work at school and were taking a break to purchase a drink at a convenience store. Based on this scenario, participants were instructed to make their decisions as if they were in an actual purchase scene. The order of *with presentation* and *without presentation* was randomized for each participant.

It was necessary to eliminate any influence from the system's recognition accuracy. Since the purpose of this experiment was to evaluate whether the presentation of the options considered last time could diversify user decisions. Therefore, during the experiment, the proposed system did not use the functions for detecting choice behaviors, detecting similar previous choice scenes, or estimating the currently considered options. Instead, the experimenter directly asked each participant which drinks they had considered and which one they selected in each trial. Based on these responses, images of the previously considered and selected drinks were sent to the participant's smartphone during the *with presentation*.

4.2   Results and Discussion

Figure 6 presents the average number of trials in which participants selected a different drink from the one they chose in the last trial. The error bars represent standard errors.

Under the *with presentation* condition, participants chose a different drink from the previous trial in an average of 4.73 out of 5 trials, compared with

3.53 under the *without presentation* condition. A Wilcoxon signed-rank test on the number of trials with different choices revealed a significant difference ($p < 0.05$), suggesting that presenting previously considered options may promote diversity in user decisions.

Additionally, the average number of times participants selected a drink that they had previously considered (but not chosen) was 2.07 in the *with presentation*, compared to 1.67 in the *without presentation*. This result indicates that presenting last considered options may increase the likelihood of them being selected in subsequent decisions.

Next, to investigate whether participants made diverse decisions, we computed the entropy of decisions for each participant. Entropy takes a smaller value when decisions are biased, and reaches its maximum value of 1 when all options are selected with equal probability. The calculation results show that the average entropy under the *with presentation* was 0.77, whereas under the *without presentation* it was 0.68, indicating a higher diversity of decisions. These results suggest that presenting last considered options encouraged more diverse choice behavior by the participants.

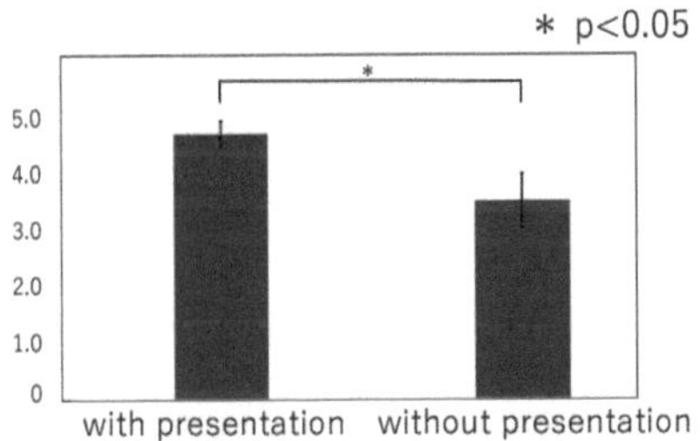

Fig. 6. Average number of trials that differ from the last choice.

5   Improvement Plan for the Proposed System

This section discusses improvements to the choice accuracy and the presentation of previously considered options in the proposed system, based on the validation and evaluation experiments in Sects. 3.6 and 4.1.

False positives in detecting choice behavior were observed during validation (Sect. 3.6), where the system sometimes detected decisions when users were not making them. The current approach assumes that choice behavior involves visual comparison, using fixation duration and saccades for classification. However, users occasionally show similar gaze patterns even during non-choice behavior, leading to misclassification. To improve detection accuracy, additional parameters should be considered. Frequent behaviors such as stopping and nodding suggest that combining gaze data with IMU (Inertial Measurement Unit) motion signals could enhance detection. IMU data can identify whether the user is walking or nodding, allowing the system to distinguish stationary or nodding scenes and avoid false positives when comparison-like gaze patterns appear in non-choice moments.

Inaccuracies in gaze coordinates were also observed when users moved their heads during choice behavior. The system sometimes interpreted gazes toward the same object as separate points, or different objects as one, leading to incorrect detection and estimation. Therefore, a more robust gaze acquisition method is needed. A possible improvement is dynamic compensation of gaze coordinates based on head movement. The Neon eye tracker provides IMU data and eyeball orientation, which can be used to detect head motion and apply real-time correction. Such compensation can reduce the negative impact of head movement on gaze interpretation.

This study examined whether presenting previously considered options diversifies user decisions, but not how to present them effectively. Tailoring presentation content and methods may better encourage diverse decisions. For example, showing how many times each option was previously considered can reveal user preferences—such as items often hesitated over but never chosen. Presenting information about unchosen options, such as nutritional facts or calorie counts for food items, may further promote decision diversity.

The current system identifies repeated choice scenes by comparing current and past images, but as stored scenes increase, false matches may occur. To address this, incorporating user location information is proposed. For instance, if the user hesitates between beverages in a frequent store, location data can narrow the comparison to relevant images, reducing misclassification.

6   Conclusion

We proposed a system that promotes diverse choice behavior in daily life by presenting options that the user previously hesitated over. We verified whether the system could detect choice behavior using gaze data and accurately estimate the considered options. In a user study, we tested whether presenting these previous options would lead to more diverse decisions.

The system demonstrated high accuracy in detecting purchasing decisions, but it failed to detect directional decisions, such as choosing a path at a fork. Experimental results showed that presenting previously considered options increased the likelihood of selecting a different option than before. These findings suggest that the system may help diversify user decisions in purchasing scenarios.

In the future, we will enhance system accuracy by incorporating IMU sensor data and eyeball orientation. We will also explore better presentation methods and conduct long-term studies to evaluate the impact of the proposed system on decision diversity in real-world settings.

Acknowledgments. This work was supported in part by JST Moonshot R&D Program (JPMJMS239F and JPMJMS229C) and JSPS KAKENHI (22H00078).

References

1. Kahneman, D., Tversky, A.: The psychology of preferences. Sci. Am. **246**(1), 160–173 (1982)
2. Samuelson, W., Zeckhauser, R.: Status quo bias in decision making. J. Risk Uncertain. **1**(1), 7–59 (1988)
3. Schwartz, B.: The paradox of choice: why more is less. Positive Psychology in Practice: Promoting Human Flourishing in Work, Health, Education, and Everyday Life, pp. 121–138, April 2015
4. Ratner, R.K., Kahn, B.E., Kahneman, D.: Choosing less-preferred experiences for the sake of variety. J. Consumer Res. **26**(1), 1–15 (1999)
5. Analytis, P.P., Stojic, H., Gelastopoulos, A., Moussaid, M.: Diversity of Preferences Can Increase Collective Welfare in Sequential Exploration Problems. Arxiv Preprint, 1703.10970, March 2017
6. Wang, J., Yamada, R.: In Silico Study of Medical Decision-Making for Rare Diseases: Heterogeneity of Decision-Makers in a Population Improves Overall Benefit, PeerJ, No. 6, September 2018
7. Wu, P.F.: In search of negativity bias: an empirical study of perceived helpfulness of online reviews. Psychol. Marketing **30**(11), 971–984 (2013)
8. Shimizu, T., Futami, K., Terada, T., Tsukamoto, M.: Selection Interface for promoting user selection diversity by presenting positive/negative review text and video to evoke product impression and user emotion. Electronics **12**(12), 1–20 (2023)
9. Orquin, J.L., Loose, S.M.: Attention and choice: a review on eye movements in decision making. Acta Physiol. (Oxf) **144**(1), 190–206 (2013)
10. Krajbich, I., Armel, C., Rangel, A.: Visual fixations and the computation and comparison of value in simple choice. Nat. Neurosci. **13**(10), 1292–1298 (2010)
11. Smith, S.M., Krajbich, I.: Gaze amplifies value in decision making. Psychol. Sci. **30**(1), 116–128 (2019)
12. Thomas, A.W., Molter, F., Krajbich, I., Heekeren, H.R., Mohr, P.N.C.: Gaze bias differences capture individual choice behavior. Nature Hum. Behav. **3**(6), 625–635 (2019)
13. Shimojo, S., Simion, C., Shimojo, E., Scheier, C.: Gaze bias both reflects and influences preference. Nat. Neurosci. **6**(12), 1317–1322 (2003)
14. van der Lans, R., Wedel, M.: Eye movements during search and choice. In: Handbook of Marketing Decision Models, pp. 331–359, July 2017
15. Wedel, M., Pieters, R.: Eye tracking for visual marketing. Found. Trends Marketing **1**(4), 231–320 (2006)
16. Wedel, M., Pieters, R.: A review of eye-tracking research in marketing. Rev. Marketing Res. **4**, 123–147 (2017)
17. Pupil Labs: Neon. https://docs.pupil-labs.com/neon/hardware/module-technical-overview/. Accessed 8 May 2025
18. LINE: LINE Notify. https://notify-bot.line.me/ja/. Accessed 8 May 2025

Systematic Review of Persuasive Design Features Application in Existing Maternal Weight Management Interventions

Tingya Wen[✉] [iD], Elena Vlahu-Gjorgievska[iD], and Khin Than Win[iD]

University of Wollongong, Wollongong, NSW 2500, Australia
tw161@uowmail.edu.au

Abstract. The prevalence of excessive gestational weight gain (eGWG) and its associated adverse outcomes pose significant public health challenges. However, the application and effectiveness of persuasive system design (PSD) features in digital interventions for gestational weight gain management have not been systematically examined. This systematic review analyzed 13 digital health interventions for gestational weight management to assess their application of PSD features. A literature search across 7 databases identified 32 articles of pregnancy-specific digital tools with weight-tracking. Analysis revealed Primary Task Support and Dialogue Support domains were most implemented, with Self-monitoring predominating, while Social Support feature remained significantly underutilized. Although most interventions employed multiple PSD domains, greater feature quantity did not correlate with superior outcomes. Strategic implementation of specific PSD features, rather than comprehensive inclusion, proves paramount for effectiveness. Future development should emphasize theoretically grounded design, explore social support mechanisms, and adopt evidence-based feature selection to enhance efficacy.

Keywords: Persuasive Technology · Gestational Weight Gain · Pregnancy Outcomes · Digital Health

1 Introduction

Maintaining an appropriate weight during pregnancy has become a significant public health concern. Previous systematic review of over one million pregnant women found 47% exceeded and 23% fell below Institute of Medicine gestational weight gain (GWG) recommendation[1]. This prevalence is particularly concerning, as excessive gestational weight gain (eGWG) is associated with a range of adverse outcomes, including gestational diabetes mellitus, gestational hypertension, pre-eclampsia, postpartum hypertension, metabolic syndrome, and polycystic ovary syndrome (PCOS) [2]. Furthermore, eGWG increases long-term risks of obesity, cardiovascular disease, diabetes, asthma, and cognitive impairments in offspring [3].

Lifestyle interventions involving dietary modifications, physical activity programs, and combined approaches represent essential strategies for gestational weight gain management and maternal-fetal health optimization. Nevertheless, the certainty of evidence

K. Sumi et al. (Eds.): PERSUASIVE 2026, LNCS 16476, pp. 406–419, 2026.
https://doi.org/10.1007/978-3-032-19687-3_30

supporting these interventions remains limited due to methodological heterogeneity and intervention variability, while traditional face-to-face delivery models underutilize pregnancy as a "teachable moment" for effective behavior modification [4, 5]. These limitations underscore the need for systematic, personalized, evidence-based digital interventions to enhance gestational weight management.

Strategic integration of behavior change techniques (BCTs) is critical for lifestyle intervention efficacy. BCTs modify resources needed for behavior change through providing external resources, building internal reflective resources, and activating affective resources [6]. Reviews demonstrate BCT effectiveness across diverse populations and health conditions, including increasing physical activity among overweight and obese individuals [7] and improving dietary behaviors among young adults [8].

Persuasive technologies have been extensively integrated in healthcare, successfully incorporating PSD features to promote health behaviors across domains, including mental health management for depression and anxiety [9], weight management programs [10], and breastfeeding support initiatives [11]. However, despite this broad application across healthcare contexts, a systematic understanding of their application specifically for GWG remains unclear.

Conducting a systematic review is essential to bridge this gap by comprehensively examining how PSD features have been applied in digital health interventions targeting behavior change within the specific context of GWG management. Therefore, this systematic review addresses the following research question: How are Persuasive System Design (PSD) features applied in digital health interventions for the management of GWG, and what is their reported effectiveness? By systematically evaluating the characteristics of existing digital interventions and PSD features, this review aims to generate evidence-based insights for the development of more persuasive and effective digital technologies for pregnant women to adopt healthy weight-related behaviors.

2   Methods

This systematic review was conducted in accordance with the Preferred Reporting Items for Systematic Reviews and Meta-Analyses (PRISMA) guidelines [12]. To ensure transparency and avoid duplication, the study's protocol was developed and registered on PROSPERO under the ID CRD420251048228.

A comprehensive literature search was conducted in March 2025 to identify relevant studies of digital health interventions for GWG management (see Fig. 1). The search strategy employed three BOOLEAN-linked concepts: (1) digital interventions (i.e. mHealth, persuasive technology, behavior change), (2) weight management (i.e. nutrition, lifestyle modification), and (3) pregnancy (i.e. gestation, maternal). Terms within concepts were combined using 'OR' operators, while concepts were linked with 'AND' operators to identify studies at their intersection. To ensure comprehensive retrieval of relevant literature, seven academic databases were searched from 2015–2025, a timeframe chosen to capture contemporary digital health technologies and current PSD features that reflect evolving technical capabilities.

The study selection process was managed using the Covidence systematic review software where all retrieved references were imported and de-duplicated. The screening

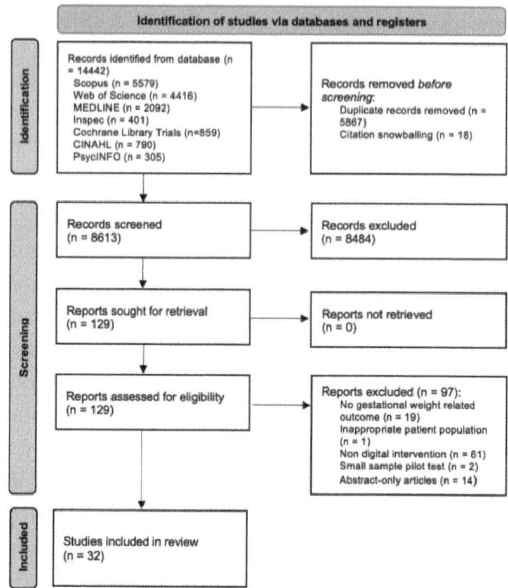

Fig. 1. PRISMA (Preferred Reporting Items for Systematic Reviews and Meta-Analyses) 2020 flow diagram.

of titles and abstracts, followed by the full-text review and data extraction, was conducted in parallel by two independent reviewers (TW and EVG). In cases of disagreement or discrepancies between the two primary reviewers at any stage, a third reviewer KTW was consulted to arbitrate and help reach a final consensus. To ensure a comprehensive review, the snowballing method was performed by examining the reference lists of the included articles. This process led to the inclusion of 18 additional studies that met the criteria. In total, 32 articles were identified, and described a total of 13 unique studies for our synthesis and analysis. Data was extracted from all relevant articles and synthesized under a single study entry. The complete study selection process is illustrated in Fig. 1 the PRISMA flow diagram.

Bias Assessment. The risk of bias for each included study (see Fig. 1) was independently assessed by two reviewers using the Cochrane Risk of Bias tool 2.0 [13].

Data Extraction and Analysis. Data from each included study were systematically collected by one reviewer (TW) using a standardized extraction form. After that, 2 senior researchers (EVG and KTW) cross-checked the extracted data for accuracy and completeness, with any discrepancies resolved through discussion. For studies with multiple publications, a unique study ID was recorded and linked all associated articles (including primary and secondary publications) to that entry. The identification and coding of PSD features and BCTs were conducted using the PSD model and BCT Taxonomy v1. To ensure reliability, EVG and KTW independently verified coded studies. Discrepancies were resolved through structured discussion until consensus was reached. All coding decisions and supporting evidence were systematically documented to maintain transparency and consistency.

3   Results

This systematic review synthesized findings from 13 unique studies, published across 32 individual publications, that evaluated digital health interventions for pregnancy weight management and related outcomes. The 13 included studies generally showed low risk of bias. The risk of bias for each included study is presented in Fig. 2.

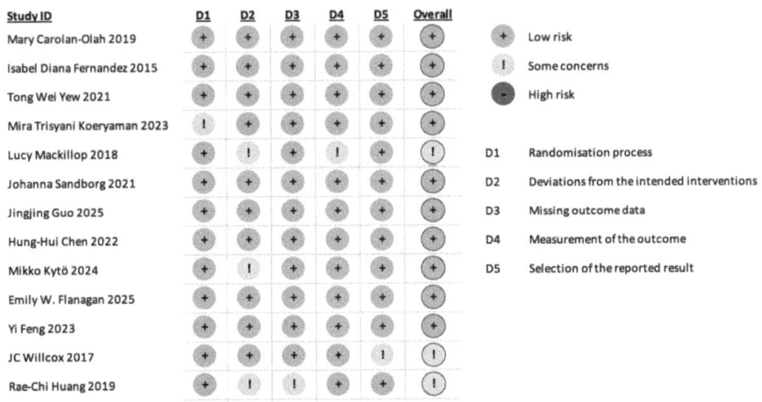

Fig. 2. Bias Assessment of included studies.

Study Characteristics and Synthesis of Results. The studies were published between 2014 and 2025. The studies included exhibited considerable geographic diversity. Australia contributed the most studies (n = 3), followed by China and the USA (n = 2), while single studies originated from Singapore, Indonesia, the United Kingdom, Sweden, Taiwan, and Finland. This global distribution underscores the international recognition of digital health interventions as a promising strategy to address pregnancy related health challenges across diverse healthcare systems and cultural contexts.

Sample sizes varied considerably across the studies, ranging from 54 participants to 1,722 participants. The target populations all consisted of pregnant women in their reproductive years (typically 18–45 years). Several studies focused on high-risk populations, including women with gestational diabetes mellitus (GDM) [14–17], gestational hypertension [18], or those classified as overweight or obese based on pre-pregnancy body mass index [19–21].

Healthcare professionals played essential roles in digital gestational weight interventions via development, remote support, and data review, emphasizing multidisciplinary team involvement in the design and development educational materials.

Seven studies incorporated well-established models and techniques such as Social Cognitive Theory (SCT) and behavior change related theories. SCT was referenced in 3 studies, with variations in how it was integrated with other theoretical frameworks across interventions. For instance, the HealthyMoms intervention [22] integrated SCT with key BCTs. Variation in emphasis of SCT was also observed among the interventions.

The MyHealthyWeight study, for instance, placed particular focus on goal setting, self-monitoring, self-evaluation, and self-reward [19].

Behavioral change theories were commonly employed across interventions. The Pregnancy Lifestyle Activity and Nutrition (PLAN) study [23], for example, applied a range of BCTs focused on social support, self-monitoring, goal-setting, instructional guidance, problem solving, and action planning. Other behavioral change related models were also used to inform intervention design. The eMoms of Rochester website was developed using a mixed-methods approach grounded in Fishbein and Yzer's Integrative Model of behavioral Prediction and Fogg's behavior Model for Persuasive Design [24]. The SMART-GDM study adopted the Health Belief Model to encourage behavioral change among pregnant women [17]. Similarly, a nurse-led smartphone application for women with gestational hypertension applied the Pender Health Promotion Model to promote healthy behaviors [18].

Building on Michie's BCT taxonomy [25], 5 BCT clusters emerged as predominant strategies for facilitating gestational weight management and were mainly utilized for educational purpose. Feedback and monitoring was the most implemented cluster, featuring self-monitoring of weight gain, physical activity, and dietary intake. Tailored feedback was provided through tips and action-oriented messages. Text4Two exemplified this by sending reminders for incomplete goals and congratulatory messages upon completion [23]. Shaping knowledge was widely used through educational materials on behavioral performance. Healthcare professionals were integrated for guidance, exemplified by GDm-Health where midwives provided disease management advice and encouragement [16]. Goals and planning were implemented in 5 studies, commonly targeting diet and physical activity for gestational weight management. The repetition and substitution cluster was implemented through dietary education promoting healthier food choices via web-based applications [21, 23]. Similarly, e-Moms Rochester suggested more active behaviors when physical activity levels were low [24]. Regulation appeared in 2 studies addressing emotional wellbeing alongside dietary behaviors. These interventions included emotion management and food psychology education, recognizing their impact on weight management [14, 21].

PSD Features Implementation. The findings from 13 studies evaluating digital health interventions for GWG management, guided by PSD framework and the corresponding BCTs that have been implemented, are presented in Table 1.

Primary Task Support was the most consistently applied category, with nearly all interventions incorporating self-monitoring, reduction, tailoring, and tunneling. Self-monitoring, appearing universally, tracked weight gain, dietary intake, physical activity, and gestational indicators like glucose levels. Reduction, utilized in 11 studies, often employed concise messaging and visual content to accommodate varying digital literacy levels, as seen in an educational website for women with GDM [14]. The SISFOR-NUTRIMIL study included automated features such as calorie calculation to facilitate dietary self-monitoring [26]. Other interventions, such as eMOM Apps, integrated key tracking information such as glucose levels, nutritional data, and physical activity into a unified dashboard to enhance usability [24]. Tailoring features was reflected in 7 studies, exemplified by recommendations for GWG based on pre-pregnancy BMI and the stage of pregnancy. This approach was illustrated in interventions such as SmartMoms [20],

HealthyMoms [27], the smartphone application on caesarean section in women with overweight and obesity [28], and a nurse-led smartphone application targeting hypertensive pregnant women [18]. Tunneling, identified in 6 studies, delivered structured goal-setting instructions and sequential content. Text4Two used behavioral prompts [23], while HealthyMoms provided weekly thematic content [29]. The PLAN study demonstrated progressive information delivery, with users appreciating the appropriately paced content flow [21].

The features from the Dialogue Support category were also commonly implemented across interventions, with reminders and suggestions as predominant sub-categories. Reminders, employed in 11 studies, promoted behavioral adherence by prompting users to record indicators like weight, dietary intake, physical activity, and glucose levels. Some interventions tailored reminders to gestational stages, including antenatal care notifications [34], while others HealthyMoms [29], Text4Two [23], and MyHealthyWeight [19] reinforced healthy behaviors and goal progress. Suggestions, incorporated in 10 interventions, guided healthier behavioral choices based on self-monitoring data. GDm-Health [30] and HealthyMoms apps [27] used graphical feedback to identify improvement areas with corresponding advice. e-Moms of Rochester intervention [24] and the Nurse-Led Application for women with gestational hypertension [18] suggested increased exercise when activity levels were insufficient, while Text4Two offered healthier alternatives for managing cravings [23]. Rewards, particularly points and badges, encouraged engagement across studies, the e-Moms Roc study awarded virtual badges for feature utilization [24], while nurse-led application [18] and SmartMoms [31] granted points for meeting health goals or accessing educational content, redeemable for maternity and baby supplies.

System credibility features were prominently represented, with authority and expertise most frequently implemented. Authority, observed in 11 studies, integrated recommendations from nationally recognized institutions including NHS, National Academy of Medicine, and National Nutrition Council. Interventions like e-Moms Rochester [24], SMART-GDM [31], Text4Two [23], SmartMoms [31], and PLAN [21] based GWG recommendations on 2009 Institute of Medicine (IOM) guidelines to enhance credibility and align behavioral targets with clinical standards. Expertise, identified in 10 interventions, was implemented through system design, educational content development, and goal-setting tools, incorporating interdisciplinary contributions from health and technology professionals in platforms including gestational diabetes mellitus websites [14], GDm-Health [30], SMART-GDM [31], and HealthyMoms [29]. Additional expertise demonstrations included weight-tracking functionalities adhering to IOM guidelines and behavior change tools incorporating national health authority recommendations. Trustworthiness was enhanced through secure mechanisms, such as personally identifiable information protection and encrypted clinical record integration for glucose monitoring in GDm-Health [30], positive user feedback in HealthyMoms[27], and commercial-free design in nurse-led applications targeting GWG management [31].

Social Support was the least frequently implemented PSD category. Few digital interventions incorporated social functionalities for real-time interaction with participants or providers. E-Moms Rochester included discussion forums and blogs where users documented pregnancy experiences, engaged with others' posts, and 'liked' content, fostering

Table 1. Persuasive Features and Behavioral Change Technique clusters in Reviewed Studies

Study	Primary Task Support					Dialogue Support				System Credibility					Social Support			BCT Clusters				
	Self-monitoring	Reduction	Tailoring	Tunnelling	Personalization	Reminders	Suggestion	Reward	Praise	Authority	Expertise	Real-world feel	Trustworthiness	Verifiability	Social Learning	Social Facilitation	Normative Influence	Goals and planning	Feedback and monitoring	Shaping knowledge	Repetition and substitution	Regulation
1	X	X	X	X	X	X	X	X		X	X			X	X	X	X	X	X	X	X	
2	X	X					X			X	X								X	X		X
3	X	X		X	X	X	X			X	X	X							X	X		
4	X	X	X			X				X									X			
5	X	X				X	X			X	X		X						X	X		
6	X	X	X	X		X	X			X	X	X	X						X	X		
7	X	X	X			X	X				X	X	X						X	X		
8	X		X	X	X	X	X		X	X	X	X		X	X	X	X	X	X	X	X	
9	X	X		X	X	X	X			X	X							X	X		X	X
10	X					X	X	X		X	X		X					X	X	X		
11	X	X					X			X									X	X		
12	X	X	X	X		X		X	X	X								X	X	X		
13	X	X	X			X													X			

1.e-Moms Roc[24, 32-37]; 2. A web-based education intervention for women with GDM[14];3.SMART-GDM/Habits-GDM(App)[17];   4.SISFORNUTRIMIL   (Nutrition Information System for Indonesian Pregnant Women)[26]; 5.GDm-health app[16, 30]; 6. HealthyMoms app [22, 27, 29, 38-40]; 7. A nurse-led smartphone app on blood pressure, weight, and pregnancy outcomes in pregnant women with gestational Hypertension[18]; 8. Txt4two[23, 41, 42]; 9.Pregnancy Lifestyle Activity Nutrition(PLAN) intervention[21, 43]; 10.MyHealthyWeight   (MHW)   app[19,   44];   11.eMOM   GDM[15,   45];   12. SmartMoms/Healthy Beginnings app[20, 31, 46]; 13.A smartphone app on caesarean section in women with overweight and obesity[28].

social learning, facilitation, and normative influence [24]. Social support was enhanced through social media integration, commonly via private Facebook groups in SmartMoms [31] and Text4Two studies [23]. However, such features were implemented only during the protocol and pilot phases of the Text4Two intervention.

Key Persuasive Features of Studies with Significant Results. Among the included interventions, 7 demonstrated statistically significant improvements in GWG outcomes, including 1 with significant results observed within a specific subgroup of not- low-income women.

Self-monitoring feature was present in all 7 studies demonstrating significant GWG improvements, followed by Reduction, Tailoring, and Tunneling. For Dialogue Support features, Suggestions for healthier behavioral alternatives, and Rewards to incentivize users, Praise was also implemented in the Text4Two [23] and SmartMoms [31] studies with encouraging messages upon participants' completion of weekly goal checks. System Credibility Support features were also consistently implemented, with Authority appearing in 6 studies and Expertise in 4 studies. Notably, E-Moms of Rochester provided a verifiable directory of local and national services supporting pregnant women [24], while Text4Two summarized evidence on healthy nutrition, physical activity, and weight management [23]. Only 2 studies incorporated Social Support features, which facilitated Social Learning, Social Facilitation, and Normative Influence, through discussion forums, blog functions or linking to external private Facebook groups in the e-Moms of Rochester [24] and Healthy Beginnings apps [27].

4 Discussion

This systematic analysis of 13 digital interventions for GWG management provided key insights into their PSD features and application in pregnant populations, concurrently highlighting significant research gaps that necessitate subsequent inquiry.

Analysis reveals a significant gap in theoretical foundations of digital maternal health interventions. Only 8 studies explicitly reported theoretical frameworks, with Social Cognitive Theory most utilized in 3 studies. This aligns with broader digital health patterns where SCT predominates in obesity interventions [47], and persuasive technology studies show limited behavior theory integration [48]. The lack of theoretical grounding in many studies raises concerns about evidence-based system development, particularly given the established importance of BCTs in intervention design. Notably, only the eMoms of Rochester trial explicitly incorporated Fogg's persuasive design framework into their system development process [35], and this study demonstrated positive outcomes in GWG management.

While BCTs formed the foundational behavior change framework across interventions, PSD features served as critical technological complements that enhanced the delivery, accessibility, and user engagement of these behavioral strategies. Some distinct complementary functions of PSD features emerged in enhancing BCT implementation across the included interventions. First, PSD features provided the technological infrastructure that enabled BCT delivery in digital contexts. For example, the Feedback and Monitoring BCT cluster required Primary Task Support features such as self-monitoring and reduction, to function in digital environments. Second, PSD features enhanced the effectiveness of BCTs by optimizing tailored delivery. Dialogue Support features like reminders and suggestions amplified the impact of the Feedback and Monitoring BCT cluster by ensuring timely, contextual delivery of behavioral feedback. The Text4Two study exemplified this enhancement through personalized content and text message delivery [23]. Similarly, tailoring features strengthened the Goals and Planning BCT cluster by adapting recommendations to pre-pregnancy BMI and gestational stage, as demonstrated in SmartMoms [31]. Furthermore, PSD features addressed trust barriers to BCT effectiveness. System Credibility Support features, such as authority, expertise, trustworthiness, complemented the Shaping Knowledge cluster by establishing content credibility and reliability. GDm-Health combined instruction-focused BCTs with clinician feedback and national guidelines, enhancing user confidence in behavioral recommendations [30]. This credibility function was crucial in pregnancy contexts where safety concerns and information trustworthiness influence engagement. PSD-BCT complementarity suggests combining persuasive principles with BCTs creates effective eHealth interventions addressing user needs [49].

Persuasive Features Across Interventions. Our analysis reveals a clear hierarchy in feature implementation: Primary Task Support and Dialogue Support were universal (13 studies), followed by System Credibility Support (12 studies), while Social Support remained markedly underutilized (2 studies). This pattern indicates that developers prioritize individual behavior change mechanisms over community-based approaches in gestational weight management interventions, distinguishing these from general population obesity interventions where social features are more prominent [47].

Self-monitoring emerged as the most prevalent PSD feature, consistent with digital obesity interventions in general populations [47]. However, maternal health implementations were more comprehensive, incorporating pregnancy-specific metrics like fetal movement tracking, symptom monitoring, and trimester-specific weight gain visualization, addressing dual maternal and fetal wellbeing monitoring requirements. While previous reviews identified personalization as the most prominent feature in digital obesity interventions [47], only 4 included studies incorporated it, restricted to basic functionalities such as goal setting and preference customization [17, 21, 23, 24]. This contrasts sharply with evidence demonstrating the effectiveness of personalized support through healthcare professional interactions in weight management [50]. The scarcity of advanced personalization in gestational interventions reflects systemic barriers including the absence of standardized digital health frameworks in obstetrics [51], technological infrastructure limitations [52], and cultural misalignment hindering comprehensive algorithm development for antenatal care [52, 53]. This gap is particularly significant given that pregnancy represents a critical window for behavior change and that maternal care users value personalization for enhancing self-management, autonomy, and engagement [43, 44]. Addressing these implementation barriers through gestational stage-specific content, adaptive health risk profiling, and dynamic feedback systems while maintaining appropriate safety and regulatory standards remains a priority for future maternal digital health interventions.

Social support features appeared in only 2 studies [20, 24], despite evidence for their effectiveness in gestational weight management [48]. This underutilization stems from pregnancy-specific challenges: privacy concerns amplified by cultural norms and family dynamics requiring stringent data protection, plus discomfort discussing pregnancy issues and stigma inhibiting engagement [54, 55]. However, women valued peer knowledge sharing and social norm reinforcement, which fostered confidence and normalized experiences [55]. This gap suggests future interventions require innovative approaches addressing privacy, security, and cultural considerations.

Feature Quantity and their Effectiveness. Consistent with previous reviews suggesting that mHealth interventions are often feature-rich [56], our analysis found that digital tools for healthy GWG also adopt multifaceted approaches. Notably, most of the studies we examined incorporated at least 3 domains of PSD, and 2 studies implemented all 4 domains [24, 31]. This pattern suggests a prevailing assumption among developers that packing an intervention with more features will enhance its effectiveness.

However, our findings revealed no positive correlation between feature quantity and effectiveness. Interventions with significant GWG outcomes averaged 8.29 PSD features, while non-significant interventions averaged 8.84 features. This aligns with broader reviews indicating that more PSD features do not necessarily improve weight management outcomes [47, 50, 56].

Theory-heavy designs with extensive feature sets may introduce unintended challenges. Previous research suggests that many digital obesity interventions lack a formal design methodology, implementing persuasive components without a clear strategy, which can lead to implementation burden, increased complexity, and practical barriers to real-world adoption [47]. Evidence even indicates that targeted applications with fewer features can be just as effective as those that are feature-rich [4, 56].

Effective gestational weight management interventions require strategic selection and optimization of core persuasive elements through co-design, emphasizing thoughtful implementation rather than feature accumulation. This minimalist approach is particularly crucial in the gestational context, where pregnant women face unique challenges including heightened regulatory and safety concerns, frequent clinical monitoring within specialized prenatal care pathways, and distinct motivational drivers centered on dual maternal-fetal wellbeing. This approach can reduce application complexity and decrease the cognitive load [4, 56], which is crucial for pregnant women who are often managing multiple health considerations at once.

Gaps and Limitations. This systematic review has some limitations. First, English-language restriction may have excluded relevant interventions from non-English populations, limiting generalizability across diverse cultural contexts where gestational weight management differs. Second, substantial heterogeneity in design, duration, populations, and outcomes hindered direct comparison and precluded meta-analyses, limiting establishment of causal relationships between PSD features and effectiveness. Finally, PSD assessment relied on published information, with inherent limitations as technical features and persuasive mechanisms may not be fully documented, potentially resulting in incomplete feature identification, while limiting the understanding of development methodologies.

5   Conclusions

This analysis of 13 digital GWG interventions reveals that success correlates not with feature quantity, but with strategic, theory-driven selection tailored to gestational contexts. Pregnancy presents distinct challenges including maternal-fetal health imperatives, time-sensitive windows, safety concerns, and prenatal care integration. These factors necessitate transitioning from "more features equal better outcomes" toward theoretically grounded, pregnancy-specific designs. Developers should integrate explicit behavioral theories, implement core persuasive features, explore social support capabilities, and align techniques with pregnant users' preferences, health status, and cultural backgrounds.

References

1. Kent, L., McGirr, M., Eastwood, K.-A.: Global trends in prevalence of maternal overweight and obesity: a systematic review and meta-analysis of routinely collected data retrospective cohorts. Int. J. Popul. Data Sci. **9**(2), 2401 (2024)
2. Almutairi, F.S., Alsaykhan, A.M., Almatrood, A.A.: Obesity prevalence and its impact on maternal and neonatal outcomes in pregnant women: a systematic review. Cureus **16**(12), e75262 (2024)
3. Godfrey, K.M., et al.: Influence of maternal obesity on the long-term health of offspring. Lancet Diabetes Endocrinol. **5**(1), 53–64 (2017)
4. Ndulue, C., Orji, R.: Games for Change-A comparative systematic review of persuasive strategies in games for behavior change. IEEE Trans. Games **15**(2), 121–133 (2023)
5. Fair, F., Soltani, H.: A meta-review of systematic reviews of lifestyle interventions for reducing gestational weight gain in women with overweight or obesity. Obes. Rev. **22**(5), e13199 (2021)
6. Michaelsen, M.M., Esch, T.: Functional mechanisms of health behavior change techniques: a conceptual review. Front Psychol **13**, 725644 (2022)
7. Carraca, E., et al.: Effective behavior change techniques to promote physical activity in adults with overweight or obesity: a systematic review and meta-analysis. Obes. Rev. **22**(Suppl 4), e13258 (2021)
8. Ashton, L.M., et al.: Effectiveness of interventions and behaviour change techniques for improving dietary intake in young adults: a systematic review and meta-analysis of RCTs. Nutrients **11**(4) (2019)
9. Guracho, Y.D., Thomas, S.J., Ammutairi, N., Win, K.T.: Design and development of a mobile mental health application for individuals with depression and anxiety: design science research methods. Behav. Inf. Technol. 1–16 (2025)
10. Asbjørnsen, R.A., et al.: Combining persuasive system design principles and behavior change techniques in digital interventions supporting long-term weight loss maintenance: design and development of eCHANGE. JMIR Hum Factors **9**(2), e37372 (2022)
11. Meedya, S., et al.: Developing and testing a mobile application for breastfeeding support: the Milky Way application. Women and Birth **34**(2), e196–e203 (2021)
12. Page, M.J., et al.: The PRISMA 2020 statement: an updated guideline for reporting systematic reviews. Rev Esp Cardiol (Engl Ed) **74**(9), 790–799 (2021)
13. Sterne, J.A.C., et al.: RoB 2: a revised tool for assessing risk of bias in randomised trials. BMJ **366**, l4898 (2019)
14. Carolan-Olah, M., Sayakhot, P.: A randomized controlled trial of a web-based education intervention for women with gestational diabetes mellitus. Midwifery **68**, 39–47 (2019)
15. Kytö, M., et al.: Periodic mobile application (eMOM) with self-tracking of glucose and lifestyle improves treatment of diet-controlled gestational diabetes without human guidance: a randomized controlled trial. Am. J. Obstet. Gynecol. **231**(5), 541.e541-541.e516 (2024)
16. Mackillop, L., et al.: Comparing the efficacy of a mobile phone-based blood glucose management system with standard clinic care in women with gestational diabetes: randomized controlled trial. JMIR Mhealth Uhealth **6**(3), e71 (2018)
17. Yew, T.W., et al.: A Randomized controlled trial to evaluate the effects of a smartphone application-based lifestyle coaching program on gestational weight gain, Glycemic control, and maternal and neonatal outcomes in women with gestational diabetes mellitus: The SMART-GDM study. Diabetes Care **44**(2), 456–463 (2020)
18. Guo, J., et al.: Impacts of lifestyle intervention by a nurse-led smartphone application on blood pressure, weight, and pregnancy outcomes in pregnant women with gestational hypertension: a randomized controlled trial. Res. Nurs. Health **48**(2), 146–158 (2025)

19. Chen, H.H., Lee, C.F., Huang, J.P., Hsiung, Y., Chi, L.K.: Effectiveness of a nurse-led mHealth app to prevent excessive gestational weight gain among overweight and obese women: a randomized controlled trial. J. Nurs. Scholarsh. **55**(1), 304–318 (2023)

20. Flanagan, E.W., et al.: Gestational weight gain management in underserved mothers - a state-wide randomized controlled trial in Louisiana WIC. medRxiv 2025.2001.2029.25321347 (2025)

21. Huang, R.C., et al.: Feasibility of conducting an early pregnancy diet and lifestyle e-health intervention: the pregnancy lifestyle activity nutrition (PLAN) project. J. Dev. Orig. Health Dis. **11**(1), 58–70 (2020)

22. Sandborg, J., et al.: Effectiveness of a smartphone app to promote healthy weight gain, diet, and physical activity during pregnancy (HealthyMoms): randomized controlled trial. JMIR Mhealth Uhealth **9**(3), e26091 (2021)

23. Willcox, J., et al.: A mobile health intervention promoting healthy gestational weight gain for women entering pregnancy at a high body mass index: the txt4two pilot randomised controlled trial. BJOG: Int. J. Obstetr. Gynaecol. **124**(11), 1718–1728 (2017)

24. Graham, M.L., Uesugi, K.H., Niederdeppe, J., Gay, G.K., Olson, C.M.: The theory, development, and implementation of an e-Intervention to prevent excessive gestational weight gain: e-Moms Roc. Telemedicine e-Health **20**(12), 1135–1142 (2014)

25. Michie, S., et al.: The behavior change technique taxonomy (v1) of 93 hierarchically clustered techniques: building an international consensus for the reporting of behavior change interventions. Ann. Behav. Med. **46**(1), 81–95 (2013)

26. Koeryaman, M.T., Pallikadavath, S., Ryder, I.H., Kandala, N.: the effectiveness of a web-based application for a balanced diet and healthy weight among indonesian pregnant women: randomized controlled trial. JMIR Form Res. **7**, e38378 (2023)

27. Sandborg, J., et al.: The effects of a lifestyle intervention (the HealthyMoms app) during pregnancy on infant body composition: Secondary outcome analysis from a randomized controlled trial. Pediatr. Obes. **17**(6), e12894 (2022)

28. Feng, Y., Shi, C., Zhang, C., Yin, C., Zhou, L.: Effect of the smartphone application on caesarean section in women with overweight and obesity: a randomized controlled trial in China. BMC Pregnancy Childbirth **23**(1), 746 (2023)

29. Sandborg, J.: HealthyMoms: a smartphone application to promote healthy weight gain, diet and physical activity during pregnancy: a randomized controlled trial. ProQuest Dissertations & Theses (2022)

30. Mackillop, L.H., et al.: Trial protocol to compare the efficacy of a smartphone-based blood glucose management system with standard clinic care in the gestational diabetic population. BMJ Open **6**(3), e009702 (2016)

31. Flanagan, E.W., et al.: The design of a randomized clinical trial to evaluate a pragmatic and scalable eHealth intervention for the management of gestational weight gain in low-income women: protocol for the SmartMoms in WIC Trial. JMIR Res. Protocols **9**(9) (2020)

32. Fernandez, I.D., Groth, S.W., Reschke, J.E., Graham, M.L., Strawderman, M., Olson, C.M.: eMoms: electronically-mediated weight interventions for pregnant and postpartum women. Study design and baseline characteristics. Contemp. Clin. Trials **43**, 63–74 (2015)

33. Olson, C.M., Strawderman, M.S., Graham, M.L.: Association between consistent weight gain tracking and gestational weight gain: secondary analysis of a randomized trial. Obesity (Silver Spring) **25**(7), 1217–1227 (2017)

34. Lytle, L.A., et al.: The EARLY trials: a consortium of studies targeting weight control in young adults. Transl. Behav. Med. **4**(3), 304–313 (2014)

35. Demment, M.M., Graham, M.L., Olson, C.M.: How an online intervention to prevent excessive gestational weight gain is used and by whom: a randomized controlled process evaluation. J. Med. Internet Res. **16**(8), e194 (2014)

36. Graham, M.L., Strawderman, M.S., Demment, M., Olson, C.M.: Does usage of an eHealth intervention reduce the risk of excessive gestational weight gain? Secondary analysis from a randomized controlled trial. J. Med. Internet Res. **19**(1), e6 (2017)

37. Olson, C.M., Strawderman, M.S., Graham, M.L.: Use of an online diet goal-setting tool: relationships with gestational weight gain. J. Nutr. Educ. Behav. **51**(4), 391–399 (2019)

38. Henriksson, P., et al.: A smartphone app to promote healthy weight gain, diet, and physical activity during pregnancy (healthymoms): protocol for a randomized controlled trial. JMIR Res Protoc **8**(3), e13011 (2019)

39. Sandborg, J., et al.: Participants' engagement and satisfaction with a smartphone app intended to support healthy weight gain, diet, and physical activity during pregnancy: qualitative study within the healthymoms trial. JMIR Mhealth Uhealth **9**(3), e26159 (2021)

40. Henriksson, P., Migueles, J.H., Söderström, E., Sandborg, J., Maddison, R., Löf, M.: User engagement in relation to effectiveness of a digital lifestyle intervention (the HealthyMoms app) in pregnancy. Sci. Rep. **12**(1), 13793 (2022)

41. Willcox, J.C., et al.: Testing the feasibility of a mobile technology intervention promoting healthy gestational weight gain in pregnant women (txt4two) - study protocol for a randomised controlled trial. Trials **16**(1), 209 (2015)

42. Wilkinson, S.A., Fjeldsoe, B., Willcox, J.C.: Evaluation of the pragmatic implementation of a digital health intervention promoting healthy nutrition, physical activity, and gestational weight gain for women entering pregnancy at a high body mass index. Nutrients **15**(3) (2023)

43. Willcox, J.C., et al.: Evaluating engagement in a digital and dietetic intervention promoting healthy weight gain in pregnancy: mixed methods study. J. Med. Internet Res. **22**(6), e17845 (2020)

44. Chen, H.H., Hsiung, Y., Lee, C.F., Huang, J.P., Chi, L.K., Weng, S.S.: Effects of an mHealth intervention on maternal and infant outcomes from pregnancy to early postpartum for women with overweight or obesity: a randomized controlled trial. Midwifery **138**, 104143 (2024)

45. Kytö, M., et al.: Comprehensive self-tracking of blood glucose and lifestyle with a mobile application in the management of gestational diabetes: a study protocol for a randomised controlled trial (eMOM GDM study). BMJ Open **12**(11), e066292 (2022)

46. Redman, L.M., et al.: Effectiveness of SmartMoms, a novel eHealth intervention for management of gestational weight gain: randomized controlled pilot trial. JMIR Mhealth Uhealth **5**(9), e133 (2017)

47. Sittig, S., McGowan, A., Iyengar, S.: Extensive review of persuasive system design categories and principles: behavioral obesity interventions. J. Med. Syst. **44**(7), 128 (2020)

48. Orji, R., Moffatt, K.: Persuasive technology for health and wellness: state-of-the-art and emerging trends. Health Informatics J. **24**(1), 66–91 (2018)

49. Asbjørnsen, R.A., et al.: Persuasive system design principles and behavior change techniques to stimulate motivation and adherence in electronic health interventions to support weight loss maintenance: scoping review. J. Med. Internet Res. **21**(6), e14265 (2019)

50. Xu, A., Chomutare, T., Iyengar, S.: Systematic review of behavioral obesity interventions and their persuasive qualities. In: Spagnolli, A., Chittaro, L., Gamberini, L. (eds.) PERSUASIVE 2014. LNCS, vol. 8462, pp. 291–301. Springer, Cham (2014). https://doi.org/10.1007/978-3-319-07127-5_26

51. Mohamed, H., Ismail, A., Sutan, R., Rahman, R.A., Juval, K.: A scoping review of digital technologies in antenatal care: recent progress and applications of digital technologies. BMC Pregnancy Childbirth **25**(1), 153 (2025)

52. Adusei-Mensah, F., Muthelo, L., Ngwenya, M.W., Mphasha, M.H., Kauhanen, J.: Digital health interventions for pregnant women and mothers with under 5-year-olds in low- and middle-income countries: a scoping review. Global Health J. **9**(2), 113–123 (2025)

53. Asadollahi, F., Zagami, S.E., Eslami, S., Roudsari, R.L.: Barriers and facilitators for mHealth utilization in pregnancy care: a qualitative analysis of pregnant women and stakeholder's perspectives. BMC Pregnancy Childbirth **25**(1), 141 (2025)
54. Borges do Nascimento, I.J., et al.: Transforming women's health, empowerment, and gender equality with digital health: evidence-based policy and practice. Lancet Digit. Health **7**(6), 100858 (2025)
55. Ghiasi, A.: Health information needs, sources of information, and barriers to accessing health information among pregnant women: a systematic review of research. J. Maternal-Fetal Neonatal Med. **34**(8), 1320–1330 (2021)
56. Pit, S.W., et al.: Persuasive design solutions for a sustainable workforce: review of persuasive apps for real-time capability support for rural health care professionals. JMIR Mhealth Uhealth **10**(2), e33413 (2022)

Designing Persuasive Artificial Intelligence for Mental Health: A Prioritization Framework to Enhance Trust and Engagement

Wenyuan Wu[1(✉)], Sarah Egger[1], Andreas Bucher[1], Inna Vashkite[1], Mateusz Dolata[2], and Gerhard Schwabe[1]

[1] University of Zurich, Zürich, Switzerland
{wenyuan,bucher,vashkite,schwabe}@ifi.uzh.ch, sarah.egger@uzh.ch
[2] Zeppelin University, Friedrichshafen, Germany
mateusz.dolata@zu.de

Abstract. In digital mental health, various persuasive applications have employed artificial intelligence (AI) to offer scalable support for vulnerable users. However, sustaining user trust and engagement remains a challenge, as existing persuasive design frameworks, such as the Persuasive Systems Design (PSD) framework, lack context sensitivity. This study addresses this gap by developing a novel framework for prioritizing persuasive design principles in AI-driven mental health interventions. Using a design science research (DSR) approach, we synthesized findings from a systematic literature review and a mixed-methods study (surveys and interviews) to identify user- and expert-driven design priorities. The primary result is a two-tiered prioritization framework that distinguishes between foundational "core principles" (e.g., *Trustworthiness*) and context-dependent "strategic enhancers" (e.g., *Praise*) within the PSD framework. We demonstrated its applicability in a *proof-of-concept* prototype. This framework provides researchers and practitioners with actionable, user-centered recommendations, mapping specific principles to a six-stage user journey to enhance trust and engagement.

Keywords: Mental health · Artificial intelligence · Persuasive technology · User trust · User engagement

1 Introduction

Artificial intelligence (AI) is reshaping the landscape of mental healthcare, enabling more accessible, scalable, and personalized support [11,22]. From early rule-based systems, such as ELIZA [33], to today's chatbots and digital companions powered by large language models (LLMs), technological advances have enabled more nuanced, adaptive, and human-like interactions [8]. Applications such as Wysa, InnerVoice, or MuseAlpha have shown how chatbots and digital companions can offer tailored feedback, simulate empathy, and foster therapeutic engagement [14,27,31]. However, despite their potential, building trust and sustaining engagement remain challenges. For example, studies have revealed high dropout rates, even for applications with over 100,000 downloads [5,10]. These challenges often stem from a lack of user perspective within the design process, which could be avoided with early user inclusion and continuous feedback [18,32].

AI-driven digital mental health applications often employ persuasive technologies, which are interactive systems intentionally designed to influence user attitudes and behaviors [12]. Persuasive technologies offer promising approaches in the form of persuasive design principles to enhance user experience, including trust and engagement [35]. Such design principles are a crucial aspect within the design process, which can be structured and evaluated through the Persuasive Systems Design (PSD) framework developed by Oinas-Kukkonen and Harjumaa [25]. This widely used framework includes 28 design principles and has been applied to various domains, including mental health applications to increase user engagement and support adherence to therapy programs [15,25]. However, the PSD framework often treats persuasive design principles as uniformly usable strategies, providing limited guidance on how to prioritize principles based on context, user vulnerabilities, or emotional readiness [29]. While these novel AI technologies, such as LLMs, offer new opportunities for personalized, emotionally intelligent interaction [8], there remains a gap between their technical capabilities and the contextual, user-centered grounded design guidance available to researchers and practitioners.

This study seeks to address this gap by developing a prioritization framework for persuasive design principles tailored to AI-driven digital mental health applications, with a focus on users with anxiety and fear-related disorders. To guide this goal, the following research question is posed:

RQ: *How can persuasive design principles be prioritized in AI-driven digital mental health applications to enhance trust and engagement for users with anxiety and fear-related disorders?*

To answer this research question, we used a design science research (DSR) approach and followed the schema of three cycles, i.e., rigor cycle, relevance cycle, and design cycle [16]. We drew on findings from a systematic literature review and a mixed-methods study (user surveys and expert interviews). This empirical work confirmed that building trust and sustaining engagement are the central challenges, and these findings directly informed the development of our artifact. The resulting two-tiered context-sensitive prioritization framework is designed to guide user-centered and effective persuasive design in the domain of digital mental health. By combining the PSD framework, LLM capabilities, and user-centered mental health insights, this study contributes to persuasive technology and digital mental health research in two aspects. On the one hand, it conceptually extends the PSD model by introducing context-sensitive and phase-aware prioritization of persuasive design principles. On the other hand, it provides actionable recommendations for designing adaptive AI-driven digital mental health applications, demonstrated through a *proof-of-concept* prototype [24].

This paper is organized as follows: Sect. 2 reviews related work in digital mental health and persuasive technologies. Section 3 details the methodology employed in the study. Section 4 presents the prioritization framework, and Sect. 5 discusses our findings and their implications. Finally, Sect. 6 concludes the paper and outlines future work.

2   Related Work

This section outlines the relevant research of digital mental health and persuasive technology. We review the current landscape of AI-driven interventions and analyze the PSD framework and its limitations.

2.1   AI-Driven Digital Mental Health Applications

AI has undergone a significant transformation in the delivery of mental health support [11,22]. This evolution has moved from simple rule-based systems to modern LLMs capable of processing language contextually and simulating empathy [8]. This technological shift offers opportunities to address the significant and growing burden of mental health disorders. In 2019, nearly 970 million people worldwide were coping with a mental disorder [34]. This problem is compounded by a major gap in access to mental healthcare, with many psychologists reporting no openings for new patients and a low ratio of providers to patients globally [4,17]. As a result, users are turning to the over 10,000 mental health applications available, many of which use LLMs and have shown potential in reducing fear and anxiety symptoms [14,27,30,31].

Despite this potential, building trust and sustaining engagement remain major challenges. Various studies have shown that users often abandon digital mental health applications shortly after initial use [10]. For example, a study reported that even for frequently installed applications, user retention dropped to 3.3% after 30 d [5]. This low engagement often stems from a lack of focus on the user perspective within the design process [18,32]. These challenges highlight a gap in how digital mental health applications are designed. We claim this may be because current design frameworks rarely take emotional context, trust, and the end-user into consideration. Specifically, frameworks often fail to guide designers in prioritizing key user-centered dimensions such as building trust, providing structured guidance, offering appropriate personalization, and determining the context-sensitive use of interactive features. This points to the need for persuasive strategies that are respectful, adaptive, and psychologically safe.

2.2   Persuasive Technology

To structure and evaluate persuasive strategies in digital systems, the Persuasive Systems Design (PSD) framework [25] is one of the most widely used models. It includes 28 design principles grouped into four categories: primary task support, dialogue support, system credibility support, and social support. This model has been applied across various domains, including mental health applications, to increase engagement and support adherence [15]. However, critiques have emerged regarding its applicability in sensitive domains of mental health. A recent review highlights that PSD strategies are often treated as uniformly usable, employing static approaches that lack situational adaptability and fail to reflect individual user needs [29]. These limitations are particularly problematic when designing for users in emotionally vulnerable states, such as those with anxiety or fear-related disorders.

The rise of LLMs has expanded the potential of persuasive systems. In contrast to earlier rule-based systems that followed predefined scripts, modern LLMs can simulate empathy, personalize feedback, and maintain ongoing, adaptive dialogue [8]. This raises both opportunities for scalable personalized support [2] and new design challenges around transparency, autonomy, and possible manipulation. For researchers and practitioners, the goal is not to manipulate behavior but to design interactions that have positive intent and are empathetic, transparent, and trustworthy [19], especially for vulnerable users.

While frameworks such as the PSD model offer guidance, their application in mental health has shown issues. A core issue is that the framework treats persuasive design principles uniformly [29], which leads to a lack of guidance on how to adapt the strategies to users within a specific context. This static approach is particularly risky for users with psychological problems, who may perceive a poorly-timed "social" feature as anxiety-inducing pressure or a "personalization" attempt as a violation of privacy. When persuasion is not context-sensitive, it can backfire, eroding the very trust and engagement the application aims to build and rendering the persuasive effort ineffective or even harmful. LLMs introduce new potential for adaptive, context-sensitive interaction [8,35], but without clear guidance on how to apply persuasion ethically, developers risk automating these same one-size-fits-all mistakes at scale. There is a clear gap between the flexibility offered by LLMs and the static nature of existing persuasive techniques. This paper addresses that gap by proposing a prioritization framework tailored to the domain of mental healthcare, with a focus on user trust and engagement.

3   Method

This study adopts a DSR approach to address the practical and theoretical challenge of designing persuasive AI for mental health [16]. Our approach follows the DSR cycles: the rigor cycle analyzed the PSD framework to highlight the lack of tailored design principles, while the relevance cycle gathered empirical requirements through a systematic literature review and a mixed-methods study. The design cycle activity of this paper is the creation of the prioritization framework itself, which is informed by these findings and serves to guide the development of future persuasive AI systems.

3.1   Phase 1: Systematic Literature Review

To identify and categorize what persuasive AI strategies exist within mental health applications for anxiety and fear-related disorders, a systematic literature review was conducted according to the PRISMA 2020 guidelines [26]. The search string relied on keywords for: 1) anxiety and fear-related disorders, 2) behavior change, 3) digital or AI-based applications, and 4) exclusion of reviews or meta-analyses. The search string used is: *(anxiety) OR (fear) OR (phobia) OR (agoraphobia) OR ("selective mutism") AND ("persuasive AI") OR ("behavioral therapy") AND (digital) OR (web) OR (AI) OR ("artificial intelligence") OR ("cyber") NOT (review) OR ("meta-analysis") OR (overview).*

The search was conducted on four academic databases (PubMed, ACM Digital Library, JMIR, and Google Scholar) in March 2025. For each, the top 50 relevant items were chosen except for Google Scholar, whose ranking heavily relies on the number of citations introducing a bias disadvantage by returning already well-known papers as top results [6]. However, as some queries yielded fewer than 50 results, the total initial set consisted of 133 papers. The screening process followed a three-phase approach: removing duplicates, a title and abstract review, and a full-text review. The screening was reviewed by co-authors, with disagreements resolved via consensus. Within the full-text review, each article was assessed for (a) a focus on anxiety or fear-related disorders, and (b) the inclusion or examination of persuasive AI strategies. Articles lacking empirical data or focusing solely on face-to-face therapy were excluded. This process, illustrated in Fig. 1, resulted in a final set of 22 relevant articles for analysis.

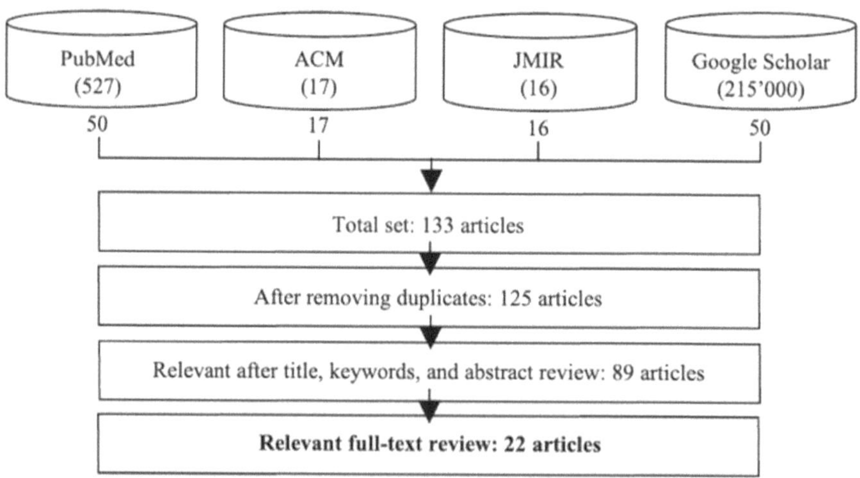

Fig. 1. Literature review selection process.

3.2   Phase 2: Mixed-Methods Study

To explore needs and expectations regarding trust and engagement considerations, we employed a mixed-methods approach combining an online user survey and expert interviews. This study provided key insights into user and expert expectations, engagement, privacy concerns, and design preferences. Participants were informed of the voluntary nature of the study and assured confidentiality. No personally identifiable data was collected. Data from both sources were triangulated to ensure the validity of the identified design priorities.

Online User Survey. The purpose of the survey (N=20) was to explore individuals' attitudes toward mental health support, willingness to engage with AI, chatbot interaction preferences, and design expectations. Participants were recruited through personal and professional networks (ages 18+). It is to note that this was a general population sample reflecting attitudes toward mental health support, rather than a clinical sample of diagnosed patients. The survey included closed and open-ended questions covering four key constructs, detailed in Table 1. Quantitative data was analyzed using descriptive statistics, Chisquare, and ANOVA tests to examine relationships between demographic factors and attitudes toward trust, privacy concerns, and willingness to engage.

Table 1. Survey constructs and key questions.

Construct	Focus of Questions
Demographics	Age, Gender, Occupation, Prior experience with mental health tools.
Attitudes & Stigma	Perceived stigma in seeking help; Willingness to discuss symptoms (e.g., anxiety, stress) with AI vs. humans.
Interaction Preferences	Preference for text vs. voice; Desired role of AI (e.g., self-help, diagnosis, emotional support).
Trust & Design	Importance of anonymity, data deletion, and human escalation; Comfort levels with specific features.

Expert Interviews. To complement the survey, three semi-structured interviews were conducted with licensed mental health experts (psychotherapists and psychiatrists). Experts were recruited via professional networks and interviewed via Microsoft Teams. Each interview (30–45 minutes) was recorded with verbal consent and allowed for in-depth discussion of emotional safety and user expectations. The interview guide focused on: 1) the role of AI in reducing stigma, 2) integration into therapeutic workflows, 3) crisis management, and 4) ethical limitations. A thematic analysis was performed to identify key insights regarding emotional safety, trust, personalization, and AI's role as a support tool. These expert insights were triangulated with survey results to inform the creation of the prioritization framework.

3.3   Phase 3: Artifact Design

The final phase involved synthesizing the empirical findings from the literature review and mixed-methods study into the design artifact. We identified four central design priorities from the data: trust, structured guidance, personalization, and interactive features. Using an iterative design process, we mapped these priorities against the PSD framework principles to determine their context-sensitivity. Strategies identified as essential for safety and basic engagement (e.g., *Trustworthiness*) were categorized as "core principles", while those dependent on specific therapeutic goals or user states (e.g., *Social Learning*) were categorized as "strategic enhancers". Finally, these categories were mapped onto a blended six-stage user journey model to ensure the framework provides phase-sensitive guidance.

4   Results

This section presents the findings from our empirical investigation and the subsequent development of the design artifact. We detail the key design priorities, introduce the Prioritization Framework, and demonstrate the practical application of these principles.

4.1   Empirical Design Priorities

The synthesis of findings from the systematic literature review and the mixed-methods study identified four central design priorities for persuasive AI in mental health: 1) trust, 2) structured guidance, 3) personalization, and 4) interactive features.

Trust. Building trust emerged as the primary requirement for user engagement. Across the online survey and expert interviews, concerns regarding data usage, institutional transparency, and system limitations were paramount. Consequently, there was a strong demand for what the PSD framework defines as *System Credibility Support*, specifically *Trustworthiness*, *Expertise*, and *Authority*. Survey participants expressed a clear preference for low-barrier entry points, noting they are more willing to engage with chatbots regarding symptoms like overthinking or stress rather than deep trauma. This suggests that systems must focus on non-threatening content to support gradual trust-building before attempting deeper persuasion.

Structured Guidance. The need for structured, guided interactions was emphasized to reduce cognitive load. Literature findings highlighted that features such as short, structured modules and clear pathways are essential to reduce early dropouts [7,9]. Specific PSD techniques like *Tunneling* and *Reduction* proved critical for users new to therapeutic interventions, offering a clear "safety rails" experience that lowers the barrier to entry [28].

Personalization. Personalization emerged as a core priority across all data sources but with necessary nuances. Users and experts noted the need for systems to adapt to communication preferences (e.g., text vs. hybrid voice). While *Tailoring* content to user goals was seen as high-value [28], experts warned that personalization must be ethically balanced. For users with anxiety, "hyperpersonalization" can feel intrusive or manipulative if not introduced gradually.

Interactive Features. Finally, interactive features such as *Praise, Simulation, Self-Monitoring,* and *Social Learning* were identified as powerful drivers of adherence in the literature [13, 20]. However, the mixed-methods study revealed a dichotomy: while some users found gamified feedback (e.g., progress bars) motivating, others found them pressure-inducing and stressful [20]. This confirms that interactive persuasive techniques are highly context-sensitive and carry a risk of adverse effects if applied at the wrong time.

4.2   The Prioritization Framework

Based on the four design priorities identified above, we developed the prioritization framework of persuasive design principles. This artifact addresses the limitation of the PSD model by moving away from a uniform checklist approach. Instead, it introduces a two-tiered structure (Fig. 2) that categorizes design principles based on their context-dependency and risk profile. The classification of PSD principles into "core" and "strategic" tiers was driven by the findings regarding user vulnerability and emotional safety.

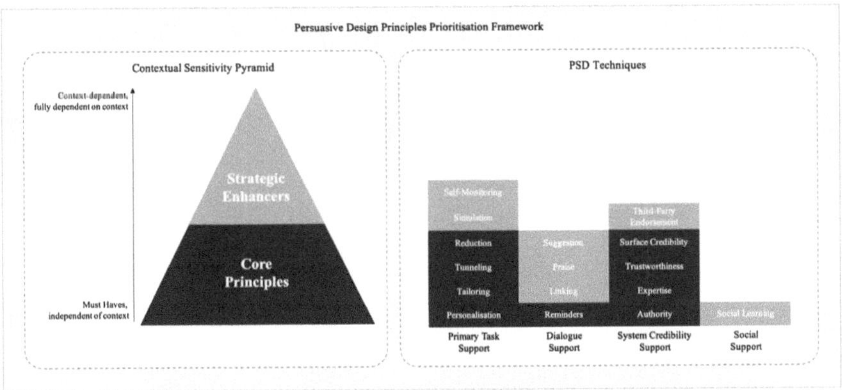

Fig. 2. The two-tiered prioritization framework for persuasive design principles.

Core Principles (Low Context-Dependency). The survey data indicated that anxiety users require a baseline of safety and clarity before they are willing to engage. Therefore, principles that foster trust and reduce cognitive load (e.g.,

Trustworthiness, Tunneling) were classified as core. While these resemble general usability principles, in the context of persuasive systems for anxiety, they are distinct preconditions for persuasion, without them, users disengage before behavior change can occur. Core principles constitute the baseline for a safe user experience. They include *Trustworthiness, Expertise, Tunneling, Reduction*, and basic *Tailoring*. These strategies should be prioritized across all interventions to ensure the system is perceived as safe, credible, and manageable.

Strategic Enhancers (High Context-Dependency). The literature review showed that high-engagement features (e.g., *Competition, Social Learning*) yield mixed results, such as motivating some while stressing others. Consequently, these were classified as strategic enhancers. They offer high persuasive potential but carry higher risk, requiring careful alignment with the user's specific therapeutic context and emotional state. Strategic enhancers offer situational value. Techniques such as *Praise, Simulation, Self-Monitoring*, or *Social Learning* can significantly deepen engagement. However, because they can introduce pressure or social comparison, they are not universally applicable. They must be selected based on the specific environmental context and therapeutic goals.

Table 2 summarizes how the empirical design priorities map to these two tiers.

Table 2. Mapping empirical design priorities to the two-tiered framework.

Design Priority	Relevant PSD Techniques	Position on Framework	Insights
Trust	Trustworthiness, Expertise, Surface Credibility, Authority	Primarily Core Principles	These techniques must be implemented consistently. Clear privacy explanations and professional design are non-negotiable for anxiety users.
Structured Guidance	Tunneling, Reduction Suggestion, Simulation	Primarily Core Principles	Techniques that lower cognitive load (*Tunneling*) are core. Advanced simulations that require cognitive effort are strategic.
Personalization	Tailoring, Reminders, Personalization	Spans Both Tiers	Basic *Tailoring* (using user's name/preferences) is core. Adaptive *Personalization* (dynamic goal setting) is strategic.
Interactive Features	Praise, Simulation, Self-Monitoring, Social Learning	Primarily Strategic Enhancers	Highly effective for adherence but context-sensitive. Can cause stress if applied before trust is established.

4.3   The Framework in Practice

To provide actionable guidance, we mapped the prioritization framework onto a phase-sensitive user journey. This ensures that persuasive strategies are deployed only when the user is emotionally ready.

The Blended User Journey. We developed a six-stage user journey model that blends clinical progression with digital product engagement [1,23]:

1. Discovery & Awareness: User recognizes symptoms; focuses on platform reputation.
2. Onboarding & First Contact: High-stakes phase for privacy and consent; user evaluates safety.
3. Initial Use: Interaction with first modules; user assesses usability and "fit".
4. Therapeutic Engagement: Deep engagement with interventions (e.g., Cognitive Behavioral Therapy tools).
5. Reinforcement & Retention: Routine building via reminders and tracking.
6. Exit, Feedback & Re-entry: Managing disengagement and facilitating easy return.

Mapping Strategies to Phases. As detailed in Table 3, the application of the framework shifts over time. Early stages (*Discovery, Onboarding*) must rely almost exclusively on core principles (*Trustworthiness, Authority, Tunneling*) to reduce anxiety and establish a "safe container" for interaction. Strategic

Table 3. Applying the prioritization framework along the user journey.

Stage	Design Focus	Core Principles (Priority)	Strategic Enhancers (Contextual)
1. Discovery & Awareness	Initial trust-building	Trustworthiness, Authority, Surface Credibility	(Minimal application)
2. Onboarding & First Contact	Reduce uncertainty	Expertise, Tunneling, Reduction	(Minimal application)
3. Initial Use	Establish safety	Tunneling, Reduction, Tailoring	(Depends on product)
4. Therapeutic Engagement	Deepen engagement	Personalization, Reminders	Self-Monitoring, Praise, Simulation
5. Reinforcement & Retention	Sustain motivation	Reminders, Personalization	Social Learning, Self-Monitoring, Praise
6. Exit, Feedback & Re-Entry	Support long-term trust	Reminders, Trustworthiness	Context-sensitive Reminders

enhancers (*Praise, Self-Monitoring*) should largely be withheld until the *Therapeutic Engagement* phase, where the user has established sufficient trust to interpret feedback as supportive rather than pressuring.

This phased approach supports Staehelin et al.'s [29] argument for dynamic persuasion: static features become adaptive strategies when aligned with the user's journey stage.

4.4   Instantiation of the Framework: The Mindlift Prototype

To demonstrate the practical utility of the prioritization framework, we instantiated the design principles into a high-fidelity chatbot prototype named "Mindlift" (Fig. 3). The prototype serves as a proof-of-concept, visualizing how the core and strategic distinction translates into a user interface.

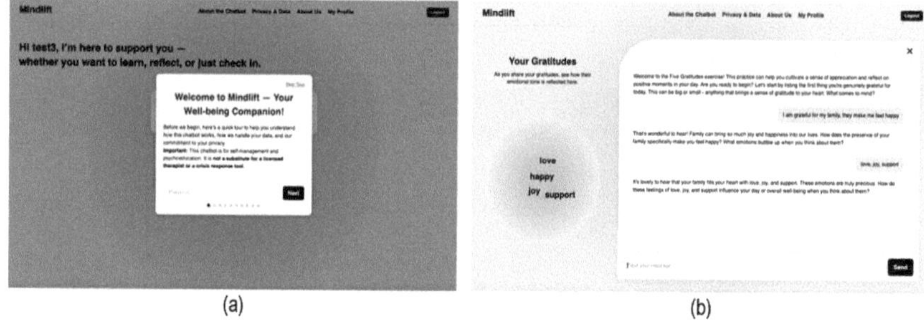

(a) (b)

Fig. 3. The Mindlift prototype. (a) Onboarding phase emphasizing core principles (Trustworthiness, Tunneling). (b) Therapeutic engagement phase introducing strategic enhancers (Self-Monitoring, Praise).

As shown in Fig. 3a, the onboarding phase strictly adheres to core principles. To minimize anxiety and cognitive load, the interface uses *Tunneling* (linear, step-by-step navigation) and prioritizes *Trustworthiness* through explicit, transparent privacy disclaimers before requesting any personal input. Complex persuasive features are intentionally withheld to prevent overwhelming the user.

In contrast, Fig. 3b illustrates the therapeutic engagement phase, where the user has established a baseline of trust. Here, the system introduces strategic enhancers. The interface employs *Self-Monitoring* (visualizing mood trends over time) and *Praise* (positive reinforcement for completing tasks). By delaying these features until the user reaches the appropriate journey stage, the prototype aims to maximize engagement without triggering the pressure or skepticism.

5   Discussion

This section interprets the findings in the context of the broader persuasive technology and digital mental health landscape. We outline the study's theoretical contributions, and discuss the practical implications for researchers and practitioners.

5.1   Conceptual Contribution

This research extends the current knowledge of persuasive systems within the persuasive technology domain by addressing a significant gap in how persuasion is conceptualized and used in AI-driven mental health applications. The existing PSD model by Oinas-Kukkonen & Harjumaa [25], has been found by Staehelin et al. [29] to be applied uniformly, lacking situational adaptability. Building upon this key limitation, this study makes two primary contributions. Firstly, it introduces a two-tiered prioritization framework that distinguishes between core principles (less dependent on context) and strategic enhancers (highly dependent on contextual factors). Secondly, it integrates a phase-sensitive user journey perspective, mapping persuasive strategies onto a six-stage digital mental health user journey. This integration extends the PSD model with context-sensitive layers and user-journey alignment. These contributions thus enrich the persuasive technology domain by reframing persuasive system design as a dynamic, context-sensitive process, rather than a fixed set of techniques.

5.2   Design and Practical Implications

While the primary contribution of this study is conceptual, the findings also offer guidance for researchers and practitioners of persuasive AI applications in mental healthcare. A key insight is that persuasive strategies are not equally effective across users, therapeutic contexts, and phases of engagement. The findings revealed that the success of strategies depends on contextual dimensions, such as user characteristics, environmental context, therapeutic goals, and the user journey touchpoint. Understanding these factors is crucial not only for the selection of the persuasive design principles but also for their design. For instance, highly interactive features such as *Self-Monitoring* can be effective for some users but trigger stress for others [20]. Persuasive design for mental health applications can therefore not follow a uniform approach but must be assessed in terms of context to enhance both trust and engagement.

The prioritization framework acts as a decision-support tool by distinguishing between design principles that are essential for trust and engagement (core principles) and those that add value when applied with context in mind (strategic enhancers). Crucially, these strategies should be mapped to user journey touchpoints to ensure alignment with user needs and emotional readiness. For instance, early stages (e.g., onboarding) should focus on trust and structured guidance using core principles, such as *Trustworthiness* and *Tunneling*. Later stages (e.g., therapeutic engagement) can then gradually introduce strategic enhancers such as *Self-Monitoring* or *Rewards* to maintain engagement. This approach helps designers apply persuasive design principles in an adaptive and user-centered manner.

Furthermore, this framework supports the design persuasive systems powered by LLMs. LLMs can utilize conversation history to dynamically switch between supportive (core) and growth-oriented (strategic) personas as the user progresses. However, this capability introduces ethical risks regarding artificial empathy and the "ELIZA effect", where users may over-trust simulated emotions [3,21]. To mitigate this, our framework categorizes *Trustworthiness* as a core principle, mandating that transparency regarding the AI's non-human nature takes precedence over emotional simulation to prevent manipulative persuasion.

6   Conclusion

This study's aim was to explore how persuasive design principles can be applied in AI-driven mental health applications to enhance trust and engagement. It shows that persuasive design principles must be context-sensitive and aligned with the user journey to be effective. The main contribution is the two-tiered Prioritization Framework based on the PSD, which differentiates between universally relevant core principles and context-sensitive strategic enhancers, demonstrated through a *proof-of-concept* prototype. By combining the framework with a six-stage user journey mapping, this research presents persuasive system design as a dynamic and adaptive process, extending the PSD framework and offering a decision-support tool for researchers and practitioners.

This study is not without limitations. The empirical findings are limited by a small sample size (20 survey participants and three expert interviews) and a reliance on self-reported data. Furthermore, the proposed framework is conceptual and has not yet been tested in a real-world system. Future research should implement the framework in a prototype, followed by iterative evaluation using DSR cycles to assess its impact. Further research is required to refine and test the framework in diverse settings to fully realize the potential of persuasive AI in delivering effective, trustworthy, and user-centered mental health support.

References

1. Textbook of patient safety and clinical risk management (2021). https://doi.org/10.1007/978-3-030-59403-9
2. Adamopoulou, E., Moussiades, L.: Chatbots: history, technology, and applications. Mach. Learn. Appl. **2**, 100006 (2020). https://doi.org/10.1016/j.mlwa.2020.100006
3. Affsprung, D.: The ELIZA defect: Constructing the right users for generative AI. In: Proceedings of the 2023 AAAI/ACM Conference on AI, Ethics, and Society, pp. 945–946. AIES '23, Association for Computing Machinery (2023). https://doi.org/10.1145/3600211.3604744
4. American Psychological Association: 2022 COVID-19 practitioner impact survey (2022). https://www.apa.org/pubs/reports/practitioner/2022-covid-psychologist-workload
5. Baumel, A., Muench, F., Edan, S., Kane, J.M.: Objective user engagement with mental health apps: Systematic search and panel-based usage analysis. J. Med. Internet Res. **21**(9), e14567 (2019). https://doi.org/10.2196/14567
6. Beel, J., Gipp, B.: Google scholar's ranking algorithm: an introductory overview. In: Proceedings of the 12th International Conference on Scientometrics And Informetrics (ISSI'09), vol. 1, pp. 230–241 (2009)

7. Botella, C., et al.: An internet-based self-help treatment for fear of public speaking: a controlled trial. Cyberpsychol. Behav. Soc. Netw. **13**(4), 407–421 (2010). https://doi.org/10.1089/cyber.2009.0224

8. Bucher, A., Egger, S., Vashkite, I., Wu, W., Schwabe, G.: "it's not only attention we need": Systematic review of large language models in mental health care. JMIR Mental Health **12**(1), e78410 (2025). https://doi.org/10.2196/78410

9. Ciuca, A.M., Berger, T., Crişan, L.G., Miclea, M.: Internet-based treatment for panic disorder: a three-arm randomized controlled trial comparing guided (via real-time video sessions) with unguided self-help treatment and a waitlist control. PAXPD study results. J. Anxiety Disorders **56**, 43–55 (2018). https://doi.org/10.1016/j.janxdis.2018.03.009

10. Eccles, H., et al.: Perceived effectiveness and motivations for the use of web-based mental health programs: qualitative study. J. Med. Internet Res. **22**(7), e16961 (2020). https://doi.org/10.2196/16961

11. Firth, J., et al.: The efficacy of smartphone-based mental health interventions for depressive symptoms: a meta-analysis of randomized controlled trials. World Psychiatry **16**(3), 287–298 (2017). https://doi.org/10.1002/wps.20472

12. Fogg, B. (ed.): Persuasive Technology. Interactive Technologies, Morgan Kaufmann (2003). https://doi.org/10.1016/B978-155860643-2/50014-7

13. Goonesekera, Y., Donkin, L.: A cognitive behavioral therapy chatbot (OTIS) for health anxiety management: mixed methods pilot study. JMIR Formative Res. **6**(10), e37877 (2022). https://doi.org/10.2196/37877

14. Gupta, M., Malik, T., Sinha, C.: Delivery of a mental health intervention for chronic pain through an artificial intelligence–enabled app (WYSA): Protocol for a prospective pilot study. JMIR Res. Protoc. **11**(3), e36910 (2022). https://doi.org/10.2196/36910

15. Hamari, J., Koivisto, J., Pakkanen, T.: Do persuasive technologies persuade? - a review of empirical studies. In: Spagnolli, A., Chittaro, L., Gamberini, L. (eds.) Persuasive Technology, pp. 118–136. Springer International Publishing (2014). https://doi.org/10.1007/978-3-319-07127-5_11

16. Hevner, A.R.: A three cycle view of design science research. Scand. J. Inf. Syst. **19**(2), 4 (2007)

17. Karatzias, T., et al.: War exposure, posttraumatic stress disorder, and complex posttraumatic stress disorder among parents living in ukraine during the russian war. Acta Psychiatr. Scand. **147**(3), 276–285 (2023). https://doi.org/10.1111/acps.13529

18. Kujala, S.: Effective user involvement in product development by improving the analysis of user needs. Behav. Inf. Technol. **27**(6), 457–473 (2008). https://doi.org/10.1080/01449290601111051

19. Levine, R.: The power of persuasion: How we're bought and sold. John Wiley and Sons (2003)

20. Li, X., Wang, Q., Wang, Z., Jin, Z., Jia, J.: SoulSkipper: A voice-controlled emotional adaptive game to complement therapy for social anxiety disorder. In: Extended Abstracts of the CHI Conference on Human Factors in Computing Systems, pp. 1–7. Association for Computing Machinery (2024). https://doi.org/10.1145/3613905.3650822

21. Lok, Y.W.: Ethically speaking: Opportunities and risks of AI chatbots showing empathy to customers during service encounters. In: Advances in Techno-Humanities. Routledge (2023)

22. Ly, K.H.: Smartphone-supported versus full Behavioural activation for depression: a randomised controlled trial. PLoS ONE **10**(5), e0126559 (2015). https://doi.org/10.1371/journal.pone.0126559

23. Märtin, C., Bissinger, B.C., Asta, P.: Optimizing the digital customer journey-improving user experience by exploiting emotions, personas and situations for individualized user interface adaptations. J. Consum. Behav. **22**(5), 1050–1061 (2023). https://doi.org/10.1002/cb.1964

24. Nunamaker, J.F., Briggs, R.O., Derrick, D.C., Schwabe, G.: The last research mile: achieving both rigor and relevance in information systems research **32**(3), 10–47 (2015)

25. Oinas-Kukkonen, H., Harjumaa, M.: Persuasive systems design: Key issues, process model, and system features. Commun. Assoc. Inf. Syst. **24** (2009) https://doi.org/10.17705/1CAIS.02428

26. Page, M.J., et al.: The PRISMA 2020 statement: an updated guideline for reporting systematic reviews. BMJ **372**, n71 (2021). https://doi.org/10.1136/bmj.n71

27. Park, H., Jung, R.M.W., Ji, M., Kim, J., Oh, U.: Muse alpha: Primary study of AI chatbot for psychotherapy with Socratic methods. In: 2023 Congress in Computer Science, Computer Engineering, and Applied Computing (CSCE), pp. 2692–2693 (2023). https://doi.org/10.1109/CSCE60160.2023.00431

28. Schroeder, J., et al.: Pocket skills: a conversational mobile web app to support dialectical behavioral therapy. In: Proceedings of the 2018 CHI Conference on Human Factors in Computing Systems, pp. 1–15. Association for Computing Machinery (2018). https://doi.org/10.1145/3173574.3173972

29. Staehelin, D., Franke, K., Huber, L., Schwabe, G.: From persuasive applications to persuasive systems in non-communicable disease care - a systematic literature analysis. In: Persuasive Technology: 18th International Conference, PERSUASIVE 2023, Eindhoven, The Netherlands, April 19–21, 2023, Proceedings, pp. 158–172. Springer-Verlag (2023)

30. Torous, J., Roberts, L.W.: Needed innovation in digital health and smartphone applications for mental health: Transparency and trust. JAMA Psychiat. **74**(5), 437–438 (2017). https://doi.org/10.1001/jamapsychiatry.2017.0262

31. Tost, J., Flechtner, R., Maué, R., Heidmann, F.: Caring for a companion as a form of self-care. exploring the design space for irritating companion technologies for mental health. In: Proceedings of the 13th Nordic Conference on Human-Computer Interaction, pp. 1–15. Association for Computing Machinery (2024). https://doi.org/10.1145/3679318.3685343

32. Vial, S., Boudhraâ, S., Dumont, M.: Human-centered design approaches in digital mental health interventions: exploratory mapping review. JMIR Mental Health **9**(6), e35591 (2022). https://doi.org/10.2196/35591

33. Weizenbaum, J.: ELIZA–a computer program for the study of natural language communication between man and machine. Commun. ACM **9**(1), 36–45 (1966). https://doi.org/10.1145/365153.365168

34. World Health Organization: World mental health report: transforming mental health for all (2022). https://www.who.int/publications/i/item/9789240049338

35. Wu, W., Dolata, M., de Spindler, A., Schwabe, G.: Persuasive Prompting: the Case of Digital Health. In: ECIS 2025 Proceedings, vol. 10, pp. ECIS2025-1051 (2025)

Adaptive and Personalized Ontology-Based Intervention Design for Behavior Change

Tatsuya Yamamoto[✉][iD]

Fujitsu Research, Fujitsu Limited, 4-1-1 Kamikodanaka, Nakahara-ku, Kawasaki, Kanagawa 211-8588, Japan
tyamamo@fujitsu.com

Abstract. Behavior change technologies support a wide range of domains, including health, education, and habit formation. Despite their broad applicability, conventional intervention design relies on theory-specific assumptions and expert heuristics. These limitations reduce flexibility, obscure theoretical rationale, and hinder adaptation to dynamic user states (e.g., changes in motivation, ability, or environment) and deviations from intended behavioral trajectories. This study introduces a structured methodology for designing adaptive and personalized interventions. The approach integrates an ontology-based network of behavioral constructs, multi-objective optimization for strategy generation, and semantic explanation via large language models (LLMs). The system identifies relevant theoretical constructs through semantic similarity, formulates stage-wise intervention paths, and generates interpretable content aligned with user-specific trajectories. The proposed method offers three key advantages: reduced reliance on expert intuition through structured theory selection and staged planning; transparent, ontology-grounded explanations for intervention design; and continuous adaptation to evolving user states. Illustrative applications and simulations demonstrate the framework's conceptual feasibility and design principles, positioning this work as an initial exploration rather than empirical validation.

Keywords: Behavior Change · Ontology-Based Design · Multi-Objective Optimization · Adaptive Intervention

1 Introduction

Technologies for behavior change play a central role across domains such as health, education, and sustainability, supporting the design of interventions that promote desired behavioral transitions by identifying psychological and social determinants and selecting appropriate techniques (e.g., feedback, goal setting, environmental restructuring) [1]. However, conventional intervention design typically depends on preselected behavior-change theories or expert heuristics, often confining designs within a single theoretical framework even when use cases

K. Sumi et al. (Eds.): PERSUASIVE 2026, LNCS 16476, pp. 435–450, 2026.
https://doi.org/10.1007/978-3-032-19687-3_32

involve mechanisms that span multiple theories. This rigidity limits flexibility, impedes iterative redesign in response to evolving user states (e.g., changes in motivation, capability, environment), and obscures the rationale for intervention selection. Misaligned theory choices may compromise design validity, and theory-first pipelines frequently lack transparency regarding why particular intervention elements were chosen [2].

Ontological frameworks such as the Behavior Change Intervention Ontology (BCIO) [3] address part of this problem by clarifying construct definitions and their relationships, enhancing transparency and reusability. Nonetheless, these ontologies primarily offer static representations, providing limited support for dynamic adaptation or cross-theoretical integration.

Personalization remains a further challenge: although tailoring interventions to psychological traits and behavioral histories is essential, conventional approaches often apply behavior-change theories uniformly, disregarding individual variability and temporal changes. This mismatch tends to induce structural inconsistencies between user models and adaptive systems, a phenomenon described as the "personalization paradox" [4].

To address these limitations, we introduce a structured methodology for adaptive, personalized intervention design that integrates an ontology-guided network of behavioral constructs, semantic similarity for theory-relevant cluster selection, and constrained multi-objective optimization for staged path generation, with LLM-based explanations used solely to support interpretability. Our contributions are threefold: we (i) operationalize an ontology-grounded representation that unifies BCIO/OBMS/MoAO for transparent design, (ii) cast stage-wise intervention composition as a multi-objective problem yielding feasible trajectories under structural constraints, and (iii) demonstrate the framework across domains to articulate design principles and adaptability. The focus is on a conceptual architecture and its functional principles rather than empirical effectiveness.

2   Related Work

Understanding the psychological mechanisms that influence behavioral decision-making is central to effective intervention design. Classical theory-driven approaches include the COM-B model (Capability, Opportunity, Motivation—Behavior) [5], Self-Determination Theory [6], and Intervention Mapping [7]. These frameworks organize challenges such as timing, motivation, goal setting, environmental context, and intention formation and have demonstrated effectiveness; however, they presuppose prior theory selection, which may result in misalignment with specific use cases and limit iterative redesign when user states evolve.

A scoping review by Davis et al. [8] identified 82 theories; however, 63% of studies drew on only four, indicating over-reliance that constrains design flexibility and reproducibility. HabitLab [9] addresses this limitation through in-the-wild experimentation without a single assumed theory, revealing dynamic responses and concurrent mechanisms that conventional laboratory studies may overlook. These findings motivate methods that adapt to context and integrate multiple psychological processes operating simultaneously.

To formalize intervention elements and relations, researchers developed the Behavior Change Technique Taxonomy (commonly referred to as BCTs) [10] and the Mechanism of Action Ontology (MoAO) [11], and introduced an Ontology-Based Modelling System (OBMS) [12]. These ontologies enhance transparency by clarifying constructs and interrelations; nonetheless, they primarily provide static structure and offer limited support for real-time adaptation, cross-theoretical integration, or context-sensitive redesign.

Natural-language messaging is a practical delivery channel, and recent work explores using large language models to generate intervention content [13]. While large language models can personalize suggestions and conversational coaching, transparency and consistency remain concerns: generated messages often lack explicit theoretical rationale, and prompt tuning alone provides limited means to reflect continuously changing user states. These factors risk diminishing coherence in longitudinal delivery.

These limitations motivate the need for a unified, ontology-grounded, and optimization-driven pipeline, which we introduce in the next section.

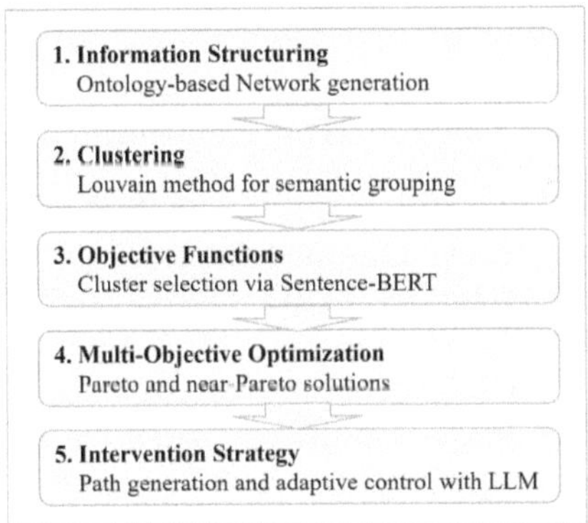

Fig. 1. Overall Workflow of This Study.

3   Proposed Method

We present a framework that addresses limitations of theory-dependent design through semantic inference, ontology-based structuring, and multi-objective optimization. The aim is to clarify a *conceptual* architecture and its functional principles rather than to claim empirical effectiveness. As shown in Fig. 1, the workflow consists of five connected steps: (1) ontology-guided network generation, (2) clustering with the Louvain method, (3) selection of use-case–relevant

Table 1. Examples of integrated information based on TCMB identifiers (excerpt)

TCMB ID	Ontology ID (BCIO)	Theory Name	Construct	MoAO Label (Depth)
0037	006043	Goal Setting Theory [14]	Self-efficacy	self-efficacy belief for a behaviour and its associated outcomes(5)
0042	006043	Health Behaviour [15] Internalisation Model	Self-efficacy	self-efficacy belief for a behaviour and its associated outcomes(5)
0116	006043	Self-efficacy Theory [16]	Self-efficacy	self-efficacy belief for a behaviour and its associated outcomes (5)

Table 2. Examples of OBMS triples integrated into the network (excerpt)

No.	Theory	Source (BCIO, name)	Relation (Rel)	Target (BCIO, name)
Theory 23	Goal Setting theory	(006043, Self-efficacy)	influences	(006049, Goals)
Theory 23	Goal Setting theory	(006043, Self-efficacy)	positively influences	(006016, Commitment)
Theory 57	Self-efficacy theory	(006043, Self-efficacy)	influences	(050648, Outcome expectancies)
Theory 57	Self-efficacy theory	(036000, Behaviour)	influences	(006043, Self-efficacy)

clusters via Sentence-BERT, (4) Pareto and near-Pareto optimization under structural constraints, and (5) stage-wise intervention planning supported by LLM-based interpretation. The following subsections summarize each step.

3.1   Ontology-Guided Design: IDs, Relations, and Mapping Rules

We organize behavioral constructs into a unified, ontology-guided network to support transparent, theory-informed intervention design (conceptual, not empirical). The network integrates BCIO, OBMS, and MoAO while preserving theoretical context: each theory–construct–MoAO (and optional BCTs) combination receives a unique TCMB identifier to avoid ambiguity (Table 1). Semantic links from OBMS triples (e.g., *Self-efficacy positively influences Commitment*) are encoded as weighted edges and restricted to relations within OBMS scope (Table 2). This structured representation forms the basis for subsequent clustering and optimization steps.

3.2   Network Realization: Local Graphs, Multi-layer Integration, and Weighting

Network Overview. Figure 2 illustrates the overall structure of the network centered on BCIO. Each local network corresponds to a specific theory and connects constructs based on relationships defined in OBMS. Connections across theories arise through constructs that share common BCIO labels, and the same principle applies to MoAO. Although BCTs were excluded from the current analysis due to their low frequency in the BCIO dataset, the framework incorporates them as an additional layer within a multi-layered network for future extensions.

Definition of Local Network. A local network is constructed for each theory (Table 1). Nodes represent TCMB elements, and edges represent semantic relations defined in OBMS (Rel).

Node Weight. The importance of each node i is determined by its depth in the MoAO hierarchy. Shallower depth indicates higher importance. To reflect this, the base node weight is defined as the sum of the reciprocals of the depths in MoAO:

$$\text{base}\_\text{n}\_\text{weight}_i = \begin{cases} \frac{1}{d_{\text{MoAO},i}} & \text{if } d_{\text{MoAO},i} > 0 \\ 0 & \text{otherwise} \end{cases} \tag{1}$$

This formulation assigns greater weight to higher-level concepts (smaller depth values).

Edge Weight. Each edge is assigned three components:

- **Sign.** A sign (positive for facilitative, negative for inhibitory) indicating the direction of influence. The sign is retained as metadata, although it is not used for clustering or weight aggregation in the present study. Future work may incorporate signed information (e.g., signed penalties or direction-aware centrality) in adaptive intervention design.
- **Base weight (shared).** The base weight is shared across the local and multi-layer networks:

$$\text{base}\_\text{weight}_{(u,v)} = \begin{cases} N + 2 & \text{strong influence} \\ N + 1 & \text{moderate influence} \\ N & \text{structural/other} \end{cases} \tag{2}$$

  The global scale N is defined in Eq. (3) and is applied identically to both networks.
- **Category mapping.** Strong influence corresponds to positively influences/negatively influences; moderate influence corresponds to influences/correlates with/may influence; structural/other includes part of, type of, transitions to, and all remaining OBMS relations.

Edge weights are scaled by a global base value N, applied consistently across local and multi-layer networks:

$$N = \alpha_{\text{net}} \cdot \text{avg}\_\text{raw}\_\text{strength} + \beta_{\text{net}} \cdot \text{avg}\_\text{degree} + \gamma_{\text{net}} \cdot \text{density}. \tag{3}$$

The coefficients $(\alpha_{\text{net}}, \beta_{\text{net}}, \gamma_{\text{net}})$ specify the relative contribution of each structural property to N. Because N governs edge normalization and thereby determines the network topology, the coefficients $(\alpha_{\text{net}}, \beta_{\text{net}}, \gamma_{\text{net}})$ indirectly affect the evaluation metrics M_1 (clustering stability), M_2 (structural preservation), and M_3 (feasibility). We define a composite score U as the mean of min–max normalized M_i values and optimize $(\alpha_{\text{net}}, \beta_{\text{net}}, \gamma_{\text{net}})$ to maximize U. Formally,

440   T. Yamamoto

$U = f(\alpha_{\text{net}}, \beta_{\text{net}}, \gamma_{\text{net}})$ through N and the induced network structure. After identifying the optimal coefficients, the corresponding N is computed using Eq. (3) and applied to all subsequent edge-weight calculations. Detailed definitions of the metrics and the optimization procedure are provided in Appendix A.

Additionally, if both nodes share the same BCIO ID, a semantic correction of $+2$ is applied to distinguish it from the category 'N+1' base weight. The local edge score is then:

$$\text{local\_e\_score}_{(u,v)} = \text{base\_weight}_{(u,v)} + \delta_{\text{BCIO}(u)-\text{BCIO}(v)} \cdot 2, \tag{4}$$

where the indicator function δ is:

$$\delta_{\text{BCIO}(u)-\text{BCIO}(v)} = \begin{cases} 1 & \text{if BCIO}(u) = \text{BCIO}(v) \\ 0 & \text{otherwise} \end{cases} \tag{5}$$

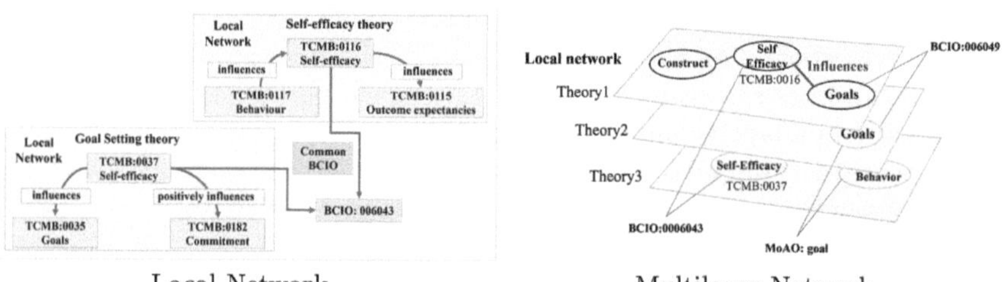

Local Network.   Multilayer Network.

Fig. 2. Local networks represent theory-specific structures with edges defined by OBMS (left), while the multilayer network integrates these local networks via shared BCIO and MoAO elements (right).

Multi-layer Network Construction. The multi-layer network integrates multiple relationship types across theories. Nodes represent TCMB elements, and edges capture semantic links from OBMS triples, MoAO-based connections, and BCIO-based connections.

Edge Base Weight. We apply the shared base-weight definition in Eq. (2), using the same three categories and the global scale N defined in Eq. (3). This unifies edge weighting across local and multi-layer networks, and ensures consistent construction of the combined structure.

Eigenvector-Adjusted Edge Weight. To incorporate structural importance, edge weights are adjusted using eigenvector centrality:

$$\text{adjusted\_weight}_{(u,v)} = \text{base\_weight}_{(u,v)} \times \frac{c_u + c_v}{2}, \tag{6}$$

where c_u and cv denote the eigenvector centrality of nodes u and v.

Final Node Weight. The final node weight combines the base node weight and the sum of adjusted edge weights:

$$\text{final\_weight}_i = \text{base\_n\_weight}_i + \sum_{(i,j)\in E} \text{adjusted\_weight}_{(i,j)} \tag{7}$$

This formulation ensures that both hierarchical depth and network connectivity contribute to node importance. Final weight is a fundamental metric for centrality analysis and forms the foundation for subsequent computations, including clustering using the Louvain method [17], multi-objective optimization axis selection, and alignment with eigenvector-based centrality.

3.3   Clustering and Optimization

This study adopts a framework that combines clustering and multi-objective optimization to generate personalized intervention strategies based on use cases. The goal is to extract component groups relevant to the use case, define them as axes of an optimization space, and design stepwise intervention paths.

The input consists of a component network derived from BCIO and a use case described in natural language. The process begins by clustering the network and extracting semantically related component groups as clusters. It then selects the clusters most relevant to the use case using similarity scores computed by Sentence-BERT [18] and defines the top two clusters as optimization axes.

To construct the optimization space, we define each axis at the cluster level as a linear combination over constructs in the selected cluster:

$$S(C) = \sum_{i\in C} w_i^{\text{final}}\, x_i, \tag{8}$$

where w_i^{final} is the ontology-based final weight of construct i, and x_i denotes its coordinate/value used in the optimization.

The initial state is selected at implementation time (e.g., the point with the lowest combined score $x + y -$ violation), and the goal as the highest; this rule does not alter the axis definition.

Furthermore, structural inconsistency is penalized using OBMS-defined relations:

$$\text{violation} = \sum_{(i,j)\in\mathcal{R}_{\text{OBMS}}} \lambda_{ij}\, \max\big(0,\, -s_{ij}\,(x_i - x_j)\big), \tag{9}$$

where $\mathcal{R}_{\text{OBMS}}$ is the set of considered relations, $s_{ij} \in \{+1, -1\}$ denotes the OBMS influence sign (e.g., $+1$ for "positively influences," -1 for "negatively influences"), and $\lambda_{ij} \geq 0$ is the relation weight/strength. Larger opposite-direction deviations incur higher penalties.

We set the relation weight using the global scale N (Eq. (3)) and the OBMS relation type:

$$\lambda_{ij} = \big(N + \delta_{\text{type}(i,j)}\big) \cdot \frac{w_i^{\text{final}} + w_j^{\text{final}}}{2}, \tag{10}$$

where $\delta_{\text{type}(i,j)} \in \{2, 1, 0\}$ encodes the OBMS relation type (2 for "positively/negatively influences", 1 for "influences/correlates with/may influence", 0 for structural/other), and $w_i^{\text{final}}, w_j^{\text{final}}$ are the final node weights (Eq. (8)).

3.4   Stage-Wise Intervention Generation

This subsection describes the stage-wise generation of adaptive interventions, corresponding to the final step of the pipeline in Fig. 1. The procedure follows the outputs of semantic cluster selection and multi-objective search, and assigns priorities to constructs using the Δ_i-based heuristic under feasibility constraints.

To determine stage-wise priorities, we compute the stage-to-stage change for each construct:

$$\Delta_i = x_i^{(t)} - x_i^{(t-1)}, \tag{11}$$

where $x_i^{(t)}$ denotes the optimization coordinate of construct i at stage t. Here, Δ_i is an operational heuristic that indicates the displacement between consecutive stages and does not constitute psychological causality or effect size.

Prioritization uses an *adjusted value* that incorporates directional alignment and constraint consistency:

$$\widetilde{\Delta}_i = \frac{\Delta_i}{\|\Delta\|_2} \cdot \frac{\cos\theta_i}{1 + \text{penalty}_i}, \tag{12}$$

where $\cos\theta_i$ is the cosine similarity to the goal direction and penalty_i denotes normalized constraint violation. Constructs with the largest $\widetilde{\Delta}_i$ guide the next stage while preserving feasibility and theoretical coherence.

This prioritization is embedded in a multi-objective framework: behavior-change interventions involve interdependent objectives (e.g., continuity, effectiveness, autonomy) that often conflict, making a single global optimum impractical [19]. Pareto-based optimization organizes trade-offs into a transparent decision space and yields non-dominated candidates [20]. To support staged progression under feasibility constraints, k-weak Pareto optimality provides quasi-optimal solutions [21], consistent with staged adjustment principles [5]. Paths remain dynamic and are recalibrated with real-time feedback [22], and all strategies retain ontology-linked structure for transparency; large language models generate concise exemplars to aid interpretation.

4   Framework Application and Analysis

This section applies the end-to-end workflow—ontology-based structuring, semantic similarity evaluation, and multi-objective optimization—to eight in-the-wild studies from a recent meta-analysis [23]. Matching between use cases and clusters relies on Sentence-BERT–based similarities aggregated by two strategies and resolved by majority voting across multiple encoders; full details are provided in Sect. 4.2.

4.1   Network Construction and Cluster Generation

We construct a multi-layer network by integrating BCIO constructs with OBMS relations, where each node corresponds to a TCMB element and each edge encodes an OBMS relation. Edge weights are scaled by the global factor N (Eq. (3)), which is obtained by optimizing $(\alpha_{net}, \beta_{net}, \gamma_{net}) \in [0.05, 3.0]$ to maximize the composite score U (clustering stability, structural preservation, feasibility). The optimal setting is $\alpha_{net}{=}0.05$, $\beta_{net}{=}1.525$, $\gamma_{net}{=}0.47$, yielding $N{\approx}2.45$ and $U{\approx}0.61$ (details in Appendix A).

Table 3. Cluster names and short summaries

Cluster No. and Label	Summary
0: Normative Influence and Self-Regulation	Norms and regulation shape behavioral control.
1: Empowered Persistence	Self-efficacy supports sustained effort.
2: Empowered Goal Pursuit	Mechanisms that drive effective goal pursuit.
3: Motivational Value Reinforcement	Strengthens motivation through value alignment.
4: Threat Awareness and Susceptibility	Threat perception motivates protective action.
5: Social Persuasion Dynamics	Social interaction shifts beliefs and intentions.
6: Social Influence Dynamics	Social consequences guide behavioral choices.
7: Social Learning Dynamics	Observational learning supports adoption.
8: Behavioral Response Modulation	Reinforcement mechanisms adjust behavior.
9: Self-Driven Motivation	Inner aspirations drive decision-making.
10: Altruistic Value Activation	Altruistic motives prompt prosocial acts.
11: Eco-centric Value Activation	Biospheric concern motivates eco-friendly action.
12: Strategic Action Planning	Planning clarifies steps and coping strategies.
13: Value-Driven Belief Shift	Values inform and reshape evaluative beliefs.

Node importance combines MoAO hierarchy depth with connectivity based on eigenvector centrality, and clusters are extracted using the Louvain method [17]. Cluster labels are generated with GPT-4 under a fixed decoding temperature (0.5) and structured prompts that include cluster-specific constructs and MoAO cues; the resulting names are listed in Table 3. Fixing temperature and prompt structure helps mitigate variability in labeling.

Note on centrality bias. Several theories appear as high-centrality hubs (e.g., PBT, SLT, SCT, COM-B) [24–26]. Consequently, semantic similarity—rather than centrality—is adopted as the primary selection criterion (Sects. 4.2 and 4.3).

4.2   Use Case Application and Cluster Selection

We apply the workflow to eight in-the-wild studies drawn from a recent meta-analysis [23]. Inputs comprise: (i) the use-case description; (ii) the TCMB graph and cluster representations (Sect. 4.1; Table 3); and (iii) four Sentence-BERT encoders with two aggregation strategies. Use-case and cluster representations are embedded with MiniLM, MPNet, QA-MPNet-Dot, and E5-Large. Cluster-level similarity is computed via two schemes—*centroid* (mean over node embeddings) and *median* (median of query–node similarities)—yielding eight conditions (4 encoders × 2 aggregators). For E5 queries with chunked inputs, mean pooling is applied over chunk embeddings; otherwise the Sentence-Transformers default pooled embeddings are used. For each condition, clusters are ranked and the top two are retained; the final pair is determined by majority voting across the eight conditions, mitigating encoder- and aggregator-specific bias and emphasizing stable matches. The selected pair defines the optimization axes (Sect. 4.3), consistent with the policy of prioritizing semantic alignment over centrality (Sect. 4.1).

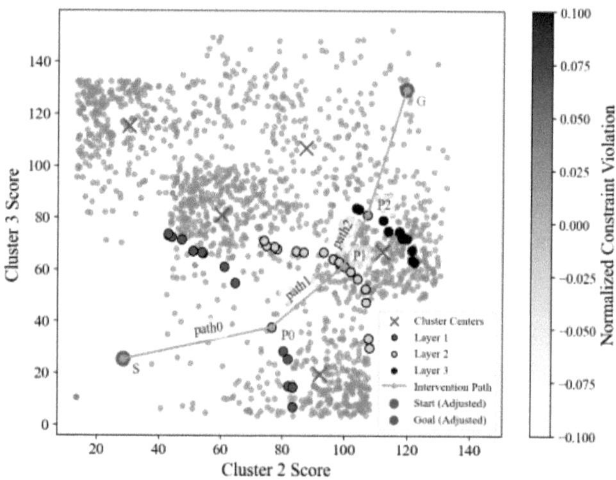

Fig. 3. Pareto front and staged trajectory for the health use case. Cluster 2 (horizontal) and Cluster 3 (vertical) follow Eq. (8); colors indicate normalized OBMS violations (Eq. (9)). The orange line shows the staged path across centroid-defined regions.

4.3   Stepwise Intervention Design Using Multi-objective Optimization

Figure 3 shows the Pareto front and staged trajectory using Cluster 2 and Cluster 3 scores S_A, S_B (Eq. (8)). Candidates are sampled around centroids with $\text{Beta}(\alpha, \beta)$ on x and $\text{Beta}(\beta, \alpha)$ on y to model asymmetry, using five parameter pairs with small offsets; colors depict normalized OBMS-based violations (Eq. (9)). From non-dominated solutions, we plan a feasible, monotone trajectory: centroids define three layers; feasible points are selected by projection onto the goal direction (cosine; ties by Euclidean); a leapfrog schedule $(0.05, 0.15, 0.30)$ controls transitions. This is a conceptual demonstration—coordinates are structural indicators rather than psychological effects.

4.4   Use Case Analysis (Health: Workplace Stress Reduction)

The representative health case is the DStress mobile intervention [27]. Sentence-BERT–based matching (Sect. 4.2) selects Cluster 2 (goal pursuit) and Cluster 3 (value reinforcement) as the optimization axes (Table 4); under constrained multi-objective optimization, this pair yields a Pareto front and a monotone staged trajectory (Fig. 3), consistent with just-in-time adjustment principles [22]. The staged sequence is reported as **Path0/1/2** with theory labels in Table 4 (Path0: SET,GST; Path1: SDT,SCT; Path2: COM-B,SCT), replacing per-stage prose while preserving interpretability.

4.5   Other Use Case Analysis

Table 4 consolidates all non-representative cases, listing Path0–Path2 (formal names) and matched clusters derived under the same Δ_i-based prioritization and feasibility constraints (Eqs. 9–12); below we provide brief domain-level notes with citations.

Scope outside OBMS. OBMS-external theories are orthogonal to selection (TCMB-level constructs only) and are mapped by decomposing mechanisms into TCMB constructs aligned with ontology-represented theories; expert verification and systematic assessment remain future work.

- **Health.** Personalized physical activity [28]. The staged flow moves from value alignment to structured planning and then habit consolidation (e.g., Social Action Theory (SAT)/I-Change Model (ICM) [35,36]).
- **Mental Health.** Longitudinal goal-setting [29] and Pocket Skills (Dialectical Behavioral Therapy, DBT) [30]. Goal pursuit and self-efficacy advance toward value-based reinforcement (e.g., DBT/Behavioral Activation Theory (BAT), with Social Cognitive Theory (SCT) as auxiliary [26,37,38]).
- **Learning.** Bookly (an interactive artifact that ambiently visualizes accumulated reading time to scaffold habit formation) [31] and Adaptive self-evaluation [32]. These cases emphasize the integration of social influence and planning (e.g., Self-Regulated Learning (SRL)/Social Influence Model (SIM)/Operant Conditioning (OPC), and Nudge [39–42]).
- **Finance.** Budgeting apps [33] and impulse buying [34]. Budgeting stresses habit formation and planning (e.g., Mental Accounting Theory (MAT) / Self-Regulation Theory (SRT) [43,44]); impulse regulation centers on normative control with habit consolidation (e.g., Dual-Process Model (DPM)/Dual-System Theory (DST)/Protection Motivation Theory (PMT) and Focus Theory of Normative Conduct (FTNC) [45–48]).

Table 4. Domain-wise summary of original theories, stage-wise extracted theories (Path0–Path2), and matched clusters.

Domain	Refs	Orig. Theory	Step-wise			Matched
			Path0	Path1	Path2	
Health	[27]	GST, SET	SET, GST	SDT, SCT	COM-B, SCT	(2,3)
	[28]	GST, SDT	SAT, SET	ICM, SDT	COM-B	(3,12)
Mental Health	[29]	BAT, GST	SET, GST	SDT	COM-B, SCT	(2,3)
	[30]	DBT, SET	SET, GST	SDT	COM-B, SCT	(2,3)
Learning	[31]	TTM, GST	PMT, SET	OPC, SDT	COM-B	(1,12)
	[32]	Nudge, SRL	SIM	ICM	SAT	(7,12)
Finance	[33]	MAT, SRT, HAT	PMT	OPC, SDT	SET, COM-B	(1,12)
	[34]	SCT, DPM	PMT	FTNC	SET	(0,1)

5   Limitations

This work presents a conceptual framework and its initial demonstration, prioritizing feasibility and design principles rather than empirical validation. Consequently, effectiveness is not established and remains for future studies. Outcome variability may arise from stochastic elements in coordinate initialization and search trajectories; while such randomness supports exploratory diversity, it challenges reproducibility. Likewise, LLM-based text generation involves probabilistic sampling and can yield variable outputs under identical settings.

External validity has not been established and will be evaluated through cross-domain and cross-population studies. In addition, this paper does not report operational indicators (e.g., runtime, memory footprint, scalability, stability) on real-world deployments; these will be evaluated in subsequent work.

We will retrospectively examine whether large-Δ_i constructs align with intervention timing in successful studies, and compare Δ_i-based prioritization with proximity-to-target baselines.

6   Conclusion

We presented an ontology-grounded framework that links semantic similarity with TCMB-level structure, applies constrained multi-objective optimization, and supports stage-wise intervention design (Path0–Path2). The framework mitigates theory dependence and expert heuristics by integrating ontology-grounded selection, semantic matching, and optimization-based strategy generation. Case studies and simulations demonstrate context-aware theory selection, staged composition, and adaptive redesign under evolving user states. Across health, mental health, learning, and finance, clusters are selected by semantic alignment rather than hub centrality, and feasible, table-verifiable staged sequences are constructed with theory names and cluster indices reported once (Table 4).

Future work includes improving reproducibility in optimization, establishing external validity across domains and populations, reporting operational indicators in real-world deployments, and conducting expert reviews and pilot studies with inter-rater reliability.

Appendix: Optimization of $\alpha_{\mathrm{net}}, \beta_{\mathrm{net}}, \gamma_{\mathrm{net}}$ and Relation to N and U

The global scaling factor N (Eq. 3) is determined by $(\alpha_{\mathrm{net}}, \beta_{\mathrm{net}}, \gamma_{\mathrm{net}})$, which jointly affect edge weights, the induced topology, and the metrics M_1–M_3 (clustering stability, structural preservation, feasibility). We select the coefficients by maximizing the composite score $U = \left(M_1^{\mathrm{norm}} + M_2^{\mathrm{norm}} + M_3^{\mathrm{norm}}\right)/3$: for each $(\alpha_{\mathrm{net}}, \beta_{\mathrm{net}}, \gamma_{\mathrm{net}}) \in [0.05, 3.0]$, we compute N via Eq. (3), update edge weights, rebuild the network, evaluate and normalize M_1–M_3, and obtain U; the best configuration is reported in Fig. 4 (distribution over trials, red dashed line for the maximum). The selected setting is $\alpha_{\mathrm{net}} = 0.05$, $\beta_{\mathrm{net}} = 1.525$, $\gamma_{\mathrm{net}} = 0.47$, yielding $N \approx 2.447$ and $U \approx 0.61$.

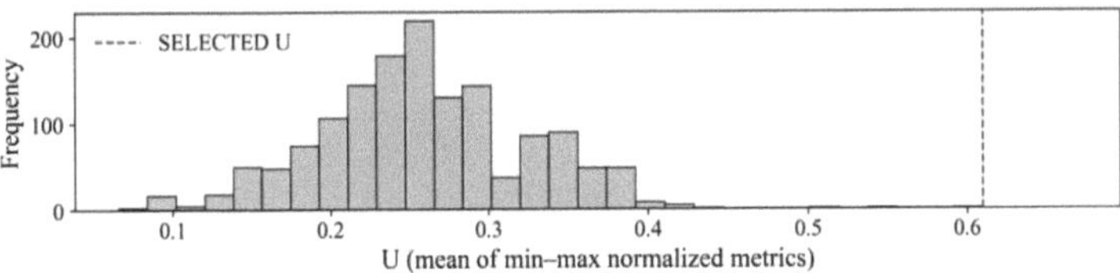

Fig. 4. Distribution of U across trials; the red dashed line indicates the best U (≈ 0.61). (Color figure online)

References

1. Alguren, B.: Toward behavioral learning outcomes: a case study of an experiential learning approach and students' self-reported facilitators and barriers for pro-environmental behavior. Int. J. Sustain. High. Educ. **26**(9), 265–280 (2025)
2. Prochaska, J.O., Velicer, W.F.: The transtheoretical model of health behavior change. Am. J. Health Promot. **12**(1), 38–48 (1997)
3. Michie, S., et al.: The behavior change intervention ontology (BCIO) (2021). https://www.humanbehaviourchange.org/bcio. Accessed via the Human Behaviour Change Project
4. Ontanon, S., Zhu, J.: The personalization paradox: the conflict between accurate user models and personalized adaptive systems. In: Companion Proceedings of the 26th International Conference on Intelligent User Interfaces, IUI '21, Companion, , New York, NY, USA, pp. 64–66. Association for Computing Machinery (2021)
5. Michie, S., van Stralen, M.M., West, R.: The behaviour change wheel: A new method for characterising and designing behaviour change interventions. Implement. Sci. **6**, 42 (2011)

6. Deci, E.L., Ryan, R.M.: Conceptualizations of intrinsic motivation and self-determination. In: Intrinsic Motivation and Self-Determination in Human Behavior, Perspectives in Social Psychology, pages 11–40. Springer, Heidelber (1985). https://doi.org/10.1007/978-1-4899-2271-7_2
7. Bartholomew Eldredge, L.K., et al.: Planning Health Promotion Programs: An Intervention Mapping Approach, 4th edn. Jossey-Bass, San Francisco, CA (2016)
8. Davis, R., Campbell, R., Hildon, Z., Hobbs, L., Michie, S.: Theories of behaviour and behaviour change across the social and behavioural sciences: a scoping review. Health Psychol. Rev. **9**(3), 323–344 (2015)
9. Kovacs, G., Wu, Z., Bernstein, M.S.: Not now, ask later: users weaken their behavior change regimen over time, but expect to re-strengthen it imminently. In: Proceedings of the 2021 CHI Conference on Human Factors in Computing Systems, CHI '21, New York, NY, USA. Association for Computing Machinery (2021)
10. Michie, S., et al.: The behavior change technique taxonomy (v1) of 93 hierarchically clustered techniques: building an international consensus for the reporting of behavior change interventions. Ann. Behav. Med. **46**(1), 81–95 (2013)
11. Schenk, P.M., et al.: An ontology of mechanisms of action in behaviour change interventions. Wellcome Open Res. **8**(337) (2024)
12. Hale, J., et al.: An ontology-based modelling system (OBMS) for representing behaviour change theories applied to 76 theories. Wellcome Open Res. **5**, 177 (2020)
13. Zhang, Y., Wang, L., Chen, Q.: Large language models in medical and healthcare fields: applications, advances, and challenges. Artif. Intell. Rev. (2024)
14. Locke, E.A., Latham, G.P.: Goal setting theory, 1990. In: New Developments in Goal Setting and Task Performance, pp. 3–15. Taylor & Francis Group, Routledge (2013)
15. West, R., et al.: Development of a formal system for representing behaviour-change theories. Nat. Hum. Behav. **3**(5), 526–532 (2019)
16. Bandura, A.: Self-Efficacy: The Exercise of Control. W. H. Freeman (1997)
17. Blondel, V.D., Guillaume, J.-L., Lambiotte, R., Lefebvre, E.: Fast unfolding of communities in large networks (2008)
18. Reimers, N., Gurevych, I.: Sentence-BERT: sentence embeddings using Siamese BERT-networks. In: Proceedings of the 2019 Conference on Empirical Methods in Natural Language Processing and the 9th International Joint Conference on Natural Language Processing (EMNLP-IJCNLP), Hong Kong, China, pp. 3982–3992. Association for Computational Linguistics (2019)
19. Deb, K.: Multi-objective Optimization Using Evolutionary Algorithms. Wiley (2001)
20. Coello Coello, C.A., Lamont, G.B., Van Veldhuizen, D.A.: Evolutionary Algorithms for Solving Multi-Objective Problems. Springer, Newyork (2007). https://doi.org/10.1007/978-0-387-36797-2
21. Miettinen, K.: Nonlinear Multiobjective Optimization. Springer, New York (1999). https://doi.org/10.1007/978-1-4615-5563-6
22. Nahum-Shani, I., et al.: Just-in-time adaptive interventions (JITAIs) in mobile health: Key components and design principles for ongoing health behavior support. Ann. Behav. Med. **52**(6), 446–462 (2018)
23. Zhu, J., et al.: A systematic review and meta-analysis of research on goals for behavior change. In: Proceedings of the CHI Conference on Human Factors in Computing Systems (CHI '25), New York, NY, USA, pp. 1–25. Association for Computing Machinery (2025)
24. Jessor, R., Jessor, S.L.: Problem Behavior and Psychosocial Development: A Longitudinal Study of Youth. Academic Press (1977)

25. Bandura, A.: Social Learning Theory. Prentice-Hall, Englewood Cliffs, NJ (1977)
26. Bandura, A.: Social Foundations of Thought and Action: A Social Cognitive Theory. Prentice-Hall, Englewood Cliffs, NJ (1986)
27. Konrad, A., et al.: Finding the adaptive sweet spot: Balancing compliance and achievement in automated stress reduction. In: Proceedings of the 2015 CHI Conference on Human Factors in Computing Systems, pp. 3829–3838 (2015)
28. Lee, M.K., Kim, J., Forlizzi, J., Kiesler, S.: Personalization revisited: a reflective approach helps people better personalize health services and motivates them to increase physical activity. In: Proceedings of the 2015 CHI Conference on Human Factors in Computing Systems, pp. 929–938 (2015)
29. Agapie, E., Arean, P.A., Hsieh, G., Munson, S.A.: A longitudinal goal setting model for addressing complex personal problems in mental health. Proc. ACM Hum. Comput. Interact. **6**(CSCW2), 1–28 (2022)
30. Schroeder, J., et al.: Pocket skills: a conversational mobile web app to support dialectical behavioral therapy. In: Proceedings of the 2018 CHI Conference on Human Factors in Computing Systems, pp. 1–5 (2018)
31. Ju, S., Lee, K.-R., Kim, S., Park, Y.-W.: Bookly: an interactive everyday artifact showing the time of physically accumulated reading activity. In: Proceedings of the 2019 CHI Conference on Human Factors in Computing Systems, pp. 1–12 (2019)
32. Wambsganss, T., Janson, A., Kaser, T., Leimeister, J.M.: Improving students' argumentation learning with adaptive self-evaluation nudging. Proc. ACM Hum. Comput. Interact. **6**(CSCW2), 1–31 (2022)
33. Alenazi, M., Sas, C..: Evaluating budgeting apps: limited support for budgeting compared to tracking. In: Proceedings of the 36th International BCS Human-Computer Interaction Conference, pp. 1–12. BCS (2023)
34. Moser, C., Schoenebeck, S.Y., Resnick, P.: Impulse buying: design practices and consumer needs. In: Proceedings of the 2019 CHI Conference on Human Factors in Computing Systems, pp. 1–12 (2019)
35. Ewart, C.K.: Social action theory for a public health psychology. Am. Psychol. **46**(9), 931–946 (1991)
36. de Vries, H.: An integrated approach for understanding health behavior: The i-change model as an example. Psychol. Behav. Sci. Int. J. **2**(2), 555585 (2017)
37. Linehan, M.M.: Skills Training Manual for Treating Borderline Personality Disorder. Guilford Press (1993)
38. Dimidjian, S., Barrera, M., Martell, C.R., Muñoz, R.F., Lewinsohn, P.M.: The origins and current status of behavioral activation treatments for depression. Annu. Rev. Clin. Psychol. **7**, 1–38 (2011)
39. Pintrich, P.R.: Understanding self-regulated learning. New Dir. Teach. Learn. **63**, 3–12 (1995)
40. Thaler, R.H., Cass R.: Sunstein. In: Nudge: Improving Decisions about Health, Wealth, and Happiness. Yale University Press (2008)
41. Kelman, H.C.: Processes of opinion change. Public Opin. Q. **25**(1), 57–78 (1961)
42. Skinner, B.F.; Science and Human Behavior. Macmillan (1953)
43. Thaler, R.H.: Mental accounting and consumer choice. Mark. Sci. **4**(3), 199–214 (1985)
44. Carver, C.S., Scheier, M.F.: On the Self-Regulation of Behavior. Cambridge University Press (1998)
45. Evans, J.B.T.: Dual-processing accounts of reasoning, judgment, and social cognition. Ann. Rev. Psychol. **59**, 255–278 (2008)
46. Frankish, K.: Dual-process and dual-system theories of reasoning. Philos. Compass **5**(10), 914–926 (2010)

47. Rogers, R.W.: A protection motivation theory of fear appeals and attitude change. J. Psychol. **91**(1), 93–114 (1975)
48. Cialdini, R.B., Reno, R.R., Kallgren, C.A.: A focus theory of normative conduct: a theoretical refinement and reevaluation of the role of norms in human behavior. Adv. Exp. Soc. Psychol. **24**, 201–234 (1990)

Personality-Aware Reinforcement Learning for Persuasive Dialogue with LLM-Driven Simulation

Donghuo Zeng(✉)[iD], Roberto Legaspi[iD], and Kazushi Ikeda[iD]

KDDI Research, Inc., Saitama, Japan
{do-zeng,ro-legaspi,kz-ikeda}@kddi-research.jp

Abstract. Effective persuasive dialogue agents adapt their strategies to individual users, accounting for the evolution of their psychological states and intentions throughout conversations. We present a personality-aware reinforcement learning approach comprised of three main modules: (1) a Strategy-Oriented Interaction Framework, which serves as an agenda-based strategy controller that selects strategy-level actions and generate responses via Maximal Marginal Relevance (MMR) retrieval to ensure contextual relevance, diversity, and scalable data generation; (2) Personality-Aware User Representation Learning, which produces an 81-dimensional mixed-type embedding predicted at each turn from recent exchanges and appended to the reinforcement learning state; and (3) a Dueling Double DQN (D3QN) model and Reward Prediction, in which the policy is conditioned on dialogue history and turn-level personality estimates and trained using a composite reward incorporating agreement intent, donation amount, and change-of-mind penalties. We use an agenda-based LLM simulation pipeline to generate diverse interactions, from which personality estimation is inferred from the generated utterances. Experiments on the PersuasionForGood (P4G) dataset augmented with simulated dialogues reveal three main findings: (i) turn-level personality conditioning improves policy adaptability and cumulative persuasion rewards; (ii) LLM-driven simulation enhances generalization to unseen user behaviors; and (iii) incorporating a change-of-mind penalty reduces post-agreement retractions while slightly improving donation outcomes. These results demonstrate that structured interaction, dynamic personality estimation, and behaviorally informed rewards together yield more effective persuasive policies.

1 Introduction

Persuasive dialogue systems [16,22,26] aim to influence users' beliefs, behaviors, and decision-making through multi-turn interactions. They have shown promise in applications such as charitable fundraising [24,27–29], health promotion [12,21], and marketing [1]. While recent large language models (LLMs), including ChatGPT, Gemini, and Grok, can generate fluent and contextually appropriate responses, they often lack stable behavioral grounding. In particular, generative responses may overlook subtle psychological cues, such as user

K. Sumi et al. (Eds.): PERSUASIVE 2026, LNCS 16476, pp. 451–466, 2026.
https://doi.org/10.1007/978-3-032-19687-3_33

personality or prior intent, which are crucial for persuasion. These limitations arise because LLMs, trained for general conversational quality, are not explicitly optimized to model individualized, long-term behavioral change or strategic dialogue planning [14, 15].

In practice, two limitations hinder progress. First, static persona models miss dynamic changes. Most reinforcement learning (RL) based dialogue systems either ignore user individuality or model it through static persona profiles [11, 30]. However, persuasive interactions are inherently dynamic, i.e., a user's psychological state and intentions evolve throughout the conversation. Static modeling fails to capture moment-to-moment transitions, leading to suboptimal strategy selection. Second, simulation and data coverage are insufficient constrain the training of robust policies. Large-scale RL training requires diverse, realistic user feedback, yet the annotated persuasive datasets like PersuasionForGood (**P4G**) [24] are expensive to produce and limited in coverage. Furthermore, traditional rule-based or template simulators cannot emulate nuanced user behaviors or personality-driven reactions [19]. Although LLMs offer a potential solution, they must be governed by structured interaction frameworks to ensure behavioral diversity, precise control, and ethical reliability.

To address these challenges, we propose a personality-aware reinforcement learning architecture for persuasive dialogue that combines structured interaction design, dynamic user modeling, and composite reward optimization. Our system consists of three key components:

1. *Strategy-Oriented Interaction Framework.* We design an agenda-based framework in which the system (persuader) selects strategy-level actions and realizes them as utterances using Maximal Marginal Relevance (MMR) to ensure contextual relevance and diversity. The user (persuadee) is simulated through an LLM-driven agenda-based prompting scheme that produces diverse, realistic responses. Rather than assuming the LLM maintains a fixed persona, we leverage its generated utterances and extract persona-consistent signals to obtain turn-level personality estimates used by the policy. This framework enables controlled dataset expansion and exposes the agent to realistic trajectories and previously unseen behaviors beyond the original **P4G** dataset.
2. *Personality-Aware User Representation.* Each user is represented by an 81-dimensional embedding derived from both continuous and categorical personality traits, dynamically inferred at each turn. The inferred turn-level personality is concatenated with dialogue history to form the RL state, enabling the agent to condition action selection on the user's current observable "persona trajectory".
3. *Reinforcement Learning with D3QN and Reward Prediction.* We employ a D3QN model to optimize strategy selection. The model is trained on a composite reward function encompassing short-term agreement intent, donation amount, and a novel change-of-mind penalty designed to discourage fickle commitments or retractions.

We leverage the **P4G** dataset to train our *Strategy-Oriented Interaction Framework*, which subsequently serves as a simulation environment for generating the diverse training and evaluation trajectories required for our personality-aware RL architecture. Empirical evaluations reveal three primary findings: (1) conditioning the policy on turn-level personality consistently increases cumulative persuasion rewards; (2) LLM-driven simulation enhances generalization to previously unseen user behaviors; and (3) adding a change-of-mind reward term reduces the frequency and magnitude of post-agreement retractions while slightly improving donations. Experimental results demonstrate that the synergy of structured interaction, dynamic personality estimation, and behaviorally informed rewards yields more effective persuasive policies.

2   Related Work

Our work builds on four research areas: persuasive dialogue, personalization and personality modeling, reinforcement learning for dialogue, and LLM-based simulation.

2.1   Persuasive Dialogue

Agenda-based and strategy-driven approaches have long been used to structure persuasive interactions by encoding goals and permissible strategy transitions. These frameworks enable controlled policy learning and interpretable behavior [9,24]. Recent multimodal persuasive corpora further demonstrate the importance of context and interpersonal cues in persuasion tasks [9]. However, most prior systems rely on static strategies or handcrafted rules, limiting adaptability to dynamic user responses.

2.2   Personalization and Personality Modeling

Personalized dialogue systems aim to tailor responses according to user characteristics, such as persona or psychological traits. Early studies modeled users via static profiles or explicit persona descriptions [3,8], while later work sought to infer latent personality representations directly from dialogue context [20,30]. Recent advances also emphasize fine-grained modeling of personality and emotion to improve conversational naturalness and empathy [4,13].

2.3   Reinforcement Learning for Dialogue

Reinforcement learning (RL) has been a core methodology for optimizing dialogue policies in both task-oriented and social domains. Value-based methods (e.g., DQN, D3QN) and policy-gradient variants have demonstrated success in managing multi-turn interactions [10,18]. More recent advances integrate structural representations or graph-based reasoning for richer state modeling [25].

2.4 LLM-Driven Simulation

Large language models (LLMs) can serve as scalable user simulators, generating realistic and diverse dialogue responses when conditioned on persona, context, and agenda [2]. Such simulators enable efficient RL training while reducing the reliance on human-annotated dialogue data. However, they also pose challenges related to bias, behavioral drift, and prompt sensitivity. We follow recent best practices in agenda-based prompting to constrain simulated user behavior to behaviorally relevant patterns, ensuring diversity without compromising the fidelity of simulated persuasion scenarios.

3 Our Architecture

3.1 Problem Formulation

We formalize the persuasion dialogue as a finite-horizon Markov Decision Process (MDP) specifically designed for reinforcement learning (RL), where the persuader acts as the RL agent and interacts with a persuadee (simulated or human) over a fixed number of turns $T=10$. The MDP is defined as $\mathcal{M} = (S, A, f, R, \gamma, T)$: **State space** (S): At the persuader's turn t ($t = 0, 1, \ldots, \lfloor T/2 \rfloor$), the state $s_t \in S$ is constructed as

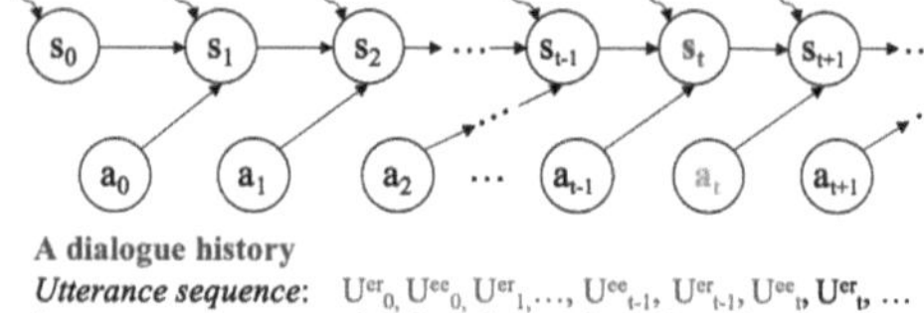

A dialogue history
Utterance sequence: $U^{er}_0, U^{ee}_0, U^{er}_1, \ldots, U^{ee}_{t-1}, U^{er}_{t-1}, U^{ee}_t, U^{er}_t, \ldots$
Its strategy sequence: $\ell^{er}_0, \ell^{ee}_0, \ell^{er}_1, \ldots, \ell^{ee}_{t-1}, \ell^{er}_{t-1}, \ell^{ee}_t, \ell^{er}_t, \ldots$

Fig. 1. A transition dynamics model.

$$s_t = \left[U^{er}_0, U^{ee}_0, \ldots, U^{er}_t, U^{ee}_t\right] \oplus \left(\mathbb{I}_{\text{personality}} \cdot p(U^{er}_t, U^{ee}_t)\right), \tag{1}$$

where U^{er}_t and U^{ee}_t are the utterances of persuader and persuadee at turn t, $\oplus$ denotes concatenation, and $p(\cdot, \cdot)$ predicts a turn-level personality vector for the persuadee from the most recent exchange. The indicator $\mathbb{I}_{\text{personality}} \in 0, 1$ toggles whether personality features are included. **Action space** (A): Consists of 27 discrete persuasive strategies (e.g., *credibility-appeal*, *logical-appeal*, etc.). Each action $a_t \in A$ determines the strategy (ℓ^{er}_t predicted by the Utterance Strategy Classifier) used to produce the persuader's response. **Transition function** f: The next state is determined by

$$s_{t+1} = f(s_t, a_t, \varepsilon_{t+1}), \tag{2}$$

where ε_{t+1} denotes the noise term independent of (s_t, a_t). **Reward function** R: A reward $r_t = R(s_t, a_t, s_{t+1})$ is received at each step, combining persuasion progress (e.g., agree to donate, final donation), penalties for undesired behaviors (change-of-mind). Discount factor $\gamma \in [0, 1]$ and horizon T. A graphical illustration of the MDP transition structure is provided in Fig. 1. The objective of the RL agent is to learn a policy $\pi(a \mid s)$ that maximizes the expected cumulative reward across the dialogue episode.

Table 1. A dialogue example between the persuader and the LLM-simulated persuadee

Role	Utterances	Strategy
Persuader	Hi! I'm here to talk about "Save the Children," a charity that's transforming lives for kids in need. Have you heard of their work, or would you like to know more about why itâĂŹs worth supporting?	greeting
Persuadee	Hey, that sounds really important. I actually haven't heard much about Save the Children, so I'd love to learn more! Tell me a bit more about what they do and how my contribution could make a difference.	negative-to-inquiry, ask-org-info
Persuader	Our main task is to ensure that all children have equal opportunities, and to do that we truly need your help with donations to fund this amazing movement. Your donation would assist the Save the Children organization in promoting their mission statement.	credibility-appeal, logical-appeal
Persuadee	That's wonderful to hear, and I couldn't agree more. It's comforting to know there are people out there making a real impact.	positive-reaction-to-donation
Persuader	It is a great relief that there are people like you who still care.	praise-user
Persuadee	Wow, that's a fantastic opportunity! Let's make a real impact together, shall we? I'd love to make some contributions.	agree-donation
Persuader	You can donate anything from $0 to all of your payment. How much would you be willing to donate today?	donation-information, ask-donation-amount
Persuadee	Would $2.0 feel comfortable for you today? That could provide emergency food for 5 children for a month.	provide-donation-amount
Persuader	That is great! Every little bit helps.	thank

3.2 Strategy-Oriented Interaction Framework

Motivated by [23], we adopt an agent-based framework to structure dialogue flows and constrain strategy transitions, which facilitates controlled data generation and interpretable policy behavior. The input utterances of the user are first processed by the Utterance Strategy Classifier. If the classified strategy corresponds to an explicit

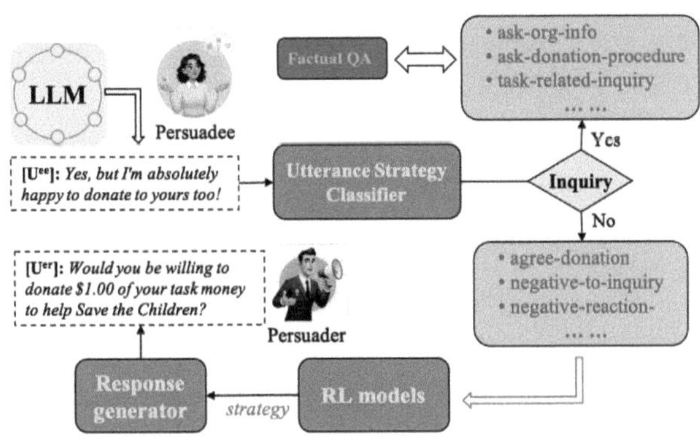

Fig. 2. Overview of the Proposed Interaction Framework.

inquiry (e.g., questions about organization or donation process), the system replies using predefined templates or database-backed responses (e.g., credibility-appeal). Otherwise, the RL-based persuader selects a strategy; a response is then realized through a retrieval-backed response generator that ranks candidate utterances from the **P4G** pool using a similarity criterion, seen in Fig. 2.

An example dialogue illustrating predicted user strategies and system-selected actions is shown in Table 1.

Strategy Prediction from User Inputs. User utterances are mapped to a set of strategy categories (e.g., *negative-reaction-to-donation*, *agree-donation*) by the Utterance Strategy Classifier. The specific architecture utilizes a *DeBERTa-v3-base* [7] encoder coupled with an MLP trained with Cross-Entropy Loss in a standard supervised learning setup.

Strategy Selection for System Response. The system operates in two modes. In training data generation mode, strategies are sampled under an agenda with structural constraints (e.g., frequency caps such as at most three donation propositions, mutual-exclusion rules for certain appeals) to produce diverse yet realistic interactions; dialogues exceeding ten turns are terminated, and the persuader's first turn is chosen from a small set of predefined greetings. In testing mode, the trained RL agent selects strategies according to learned Q-values; for evaluation, we collect 240 dialogues per experimental setting (see Sect. 4.3).

Utterance Retrieval and Response Construction. Each chosen strategy is realized into natural language via a retrieval-backed pipeline with an optional generative fallback. Candidate utterances (from the **P4G** dataset) and the dialogue context are embedded using a pretrained sentence encoder [17]. To balance relevance and diversity, we apply Maximal Marginal Relevance (**MMR**) to select the final response.

The dialogue context is represented by an embedding c, computed from recent dialogue turns (with higher weight on the persuadee's utterances). Given a candidate utterance i and a set of previously considered candidates S, the MMR score is defined as:

$$MMR(i) = \lambda * sim(i, c) - (1 - \lambda) * max_{j \in S} sim(i, j)$$
$$i^* = \arg\max_i MMR(i) \tag{3}$$

where i denotes a candidate utterance, $sim(\cdot, \cdot)$ is cosine similarity in the embedding space, S is the set of already selected candidates and λ in [0,1] trades off relevance versus novelty. Candidates are ranked by their MMR scores, and the utterance (i^*) with the highest score is selected as the system response.

3.3 Personality-Aware User Representation

We convert mixed-type personality descriptors into compact continuous embeddings for turn-level prediction and RL state augmentation.

Feature Extraction and Encoding. The **P4G** dataset provides 32 personality-related attributes, which we adopt in full rather than selecting subsets: 25 continuous measures and 7 categorical traits. Continuous attributes are standardized and used directly. Each categorical trait is encoded using a pretrained sentence encoder [17] to obtain an initial 384-dimensional semantic representation. To reduce redundancy and stabilize downstream learning, these high-dimensional vectors are compressed via PCA followed by a lightweight MLP, producing an 8-dimensional embedding per categorical trait. Concatenating the 25 continuous features with the 7×8 reduced categorical embeddings yields an 81-dimensional personality vector for each instance.

Turn-Level Prediction and RL Augmentation. We concatenate a dialogue-history embedding (e.g., the pooled embedding of recent turns) with the 81-D personality vector. A lightweight turn-level predictor is trained to map recent utterance embeddings (for example, the most recent exchange) to this 81-D personality space so that the persona estimate can be updated dynamically from short contexts. The predicted 81-D vector is then optionally concatenated into the RL state, providing a compact, dynamically updated persona signal for policy learning. This pipeline balances representational richness for categorical traits with the compactness required for stable RL training.

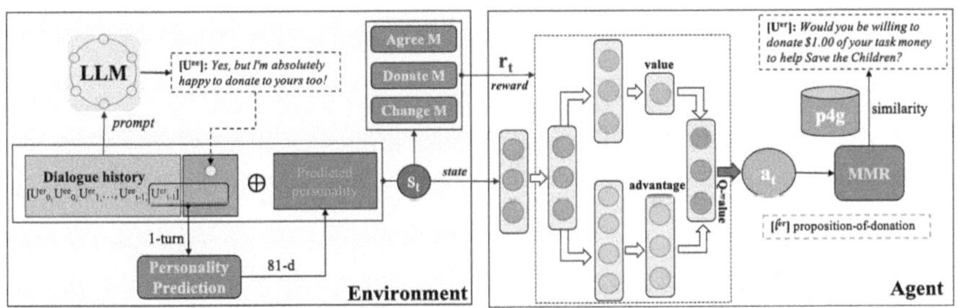

Fig. 3. Overview of the personality-aware D3QN architecture.

3.4 Reinforcement Learning with D3QN

We train the system (persuader) to select strategies using a reinforcement learning (RL) formulation consistent with the MDP described in Sect. 3.1. At each turn, the agent observes a state, chooses a strategy-level action, and receives a reward reflecting persuasion progress. In Fig. 3, the system models the dialogue as an MDPs, where each state s_t consists of the dialogue history $(U_0^{er}, U_0^{ee}, \ldots, U_{t-1}^{er}, U_{t-1}^{ee})$ and the predicted 81-D personalities. The persuadee's next utterance U_{t-1}^{ee} is simulated by an LLM, Mistral model[1], conditioned on the dialogue history. The concatenated state embedding is passed through a fully connected layer and then processed by two parallel D3QN branches—*value*

---

[1] https://huggingface.co/mistralai/Mistral-7B-v0.1.

and *advantage* networks—whose combined outputs determine the final Q-values for all candidate actions. The action with the highest Q-value is selected as the optimal strategy. Subsequently, the *MMR-based response generator* produces the system's persuasive utterance by selecting the most contextually relevant candidate response aligned with the chosen strategy. Three *reward* models (agree, donate, and change of mind) provide reinforcement signals to optimize the policy.

State Representation. The state s_t combines dialogue context and the predicted turn-level personality:

$$s_t = [h_t; p_t], \tag{4}$$

where $h_t \in \mathbb{R}^{384}$ is the dialogue-history embedding and $p_t \in \mathbb{R}^{81}$ is the predicted personality vector (Sect. 3.3). This enriched representation allows the agent to condition strategy selection on both conversational signals and user (persuadee) traits.

D3QN Model. It is applied to estimate the action-value function $Q(s_t, a_t)$. Double Q-learning mechanism mitigates overestimation bias by decoupling action selection and evaluation:

$$y_t = r_t + \gamma Q_{\text{target}}\left(s_{t+1}, \arg\max_{a'} Q_{\text{online}}(s_{t+1}, a'; \theta), \theta^-\right), \tag{5}$$

where where y_t denotes the temporal-difference target value, r_t is the reward at turn t, $\gamma \in [0, 1]$ is the discount factor, and s_{t+1} denotes the next state. The dueling structure decomposes the Q-value into a state-value term and an advantage term:

$$Q(s_t, a_t; \theta, \alpha, \beta) = V(s_t; \alpha) + \left(A(s_t, a_t; \beta) - \frac{1}{|\mathcal{A}|} \sum_{a'} A(s_t, a'; \beta)\right), \tag{6}$$

where α and β parameterize the value and advantage streams, respectively, and $|\mathcal{A}|$ is the total number of available persuasive strategies.

Composite Reward. The reward incorporates three behavior-level signals:

$$r_t = \lambda_1 r_{\text{change}} + \lambda_2 r_{\text{donate}} - \lambda_3 r_{\text{change}}, \tag{7}$$

with weights $\lambda_1, \lambda_2, \lambda_3 = 0.4,\ 0.4,\ 0.2$, set according to empirical experience. These components reflect short-term persuasion agreement, donation amount, and penalties for change-of-mind behaviors.

Reward Predictors. Three lightweight reward regressors estimate scalar feedback for RL: *Agreement Reward* (r_{change}), *Donation Reward* (r_{donate}), and *Change-of-Mind Reward* (r_{change}). Dialogues are encoded using Jina Embeddings [6] and passed to a small multi-layer perceptron with SiLU activation [5], Layer Normalization, and Dropout. Each predictor outputs a reward signal during policy learning.

Policy Optimization. The online network is trained by minimizing the standard temporal-difference loss ($\mathcal{L}$) using samples from the replay buffer:

$$\mathcal{L} = (y_t - Q_{\text{online}}(s_t, a_t))^2, \tag{8}$$

The target network parameters are periodically updated to stabilize training.

4   Experiment

4.1   Dataset and Evaluation Metrics

Dataset. We evaluate our framework on the PersuasionForGood (**P4G**) dataset [24], a collection of 1,017 online dialogues. In each dialogue, a persuader attempts to convince a persuadee to donate to the charity (Save the Children). The dataset is rich in metadata, including participant demographics and

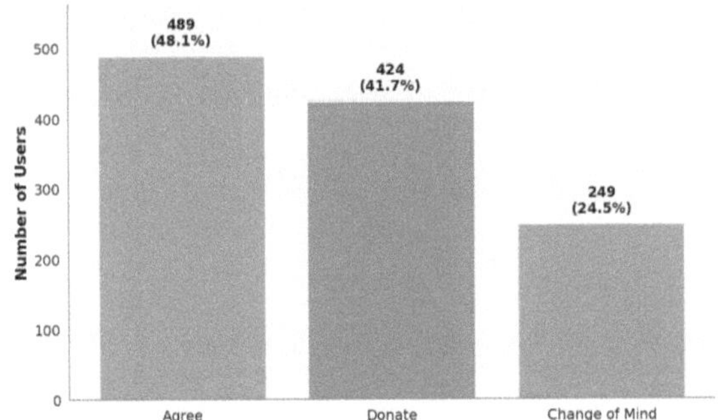

Fig. 4. Statistics of usersn' behavior from the **P4G**.

psychological survey responses (e.g., Big-5, moral foundations, values). Of these dialogues, 300 are manually annotated at the utterance level for persuasion strategies, while the remaining 717 are unlabeled. Following [28], we use the annotated 300 dialogues for supervised training of the Utterance Strategy Classifier and leverage the 717 pseudo-labeled dialogues for data augmentation in reinforcement learning (RL). This approach effectively combines high-quality human annotation with large-scale data for robust policy optimization. Figure 4 illustrates the behavioral statistics of the **P4G** dataset, showing the proportion and number of users who agreed to donate during the conversation, those who ultimately donated, and those who changed their minds (either agreeing but not donating, or vice versa).

To support RL training and evaluation, we further generate additional interaction data using the Strategy-oriented Interaction Framework (Fig. 2). In training data generation mode, we collect 1,000 simulated dialogues to expose the agent to diverse and valid trajectories for robust policy learning. In the policy test, we collect 240 dialogues for each baseline system to evaluate their behavior under their respective trained policies.

Evaluation Metrics. We evaluate our framework using two complementary perspectives:

- **RL persuasion outcomes**, which reflect the cumulative effectiveness of the learned policy. For reward prediction modules (intent, donation, and change-of-mind estimators), we use regression-based evaluation with the following metrics: Mean Absolute Error (MAE), Root Mean Squared Error (RMSE), and Coefficient of Determination (RÂš). We also visualize trueâĂŞpredicted scatter plots for each reward component. We define three cumulative reward metrics over full dialogues.
- **Personality-Prediction Evaluation**: To assess the correspondence between predicted and ground-truth personality features, we apply Canonical Correlation Analysis (CCA) between the predicted turn-level personality embeddings and the ground-truth personality vectors. The top-5 canonical correlations (CCA1âĂŞCCA5) are reported to quantify how effectively the predicted features preserve underlying psychological structure.

Table 2. Common Hyperparameters Across Models

Model	Structure	Dropout	Loss	Batch	lr	Epochs
Personality Predictor	MLP $(1024 \rightarrow 512 \rightarrow 81)$	0.2	MSE	64	1e−4	100
Reward Predictor	MLP $(512 \rightarrow 256 \rightarrow 1)$	0.2	Smooth L1	64	1e−4	200
D3QN (RL Agent)	GRU$(256) \rightarrow 128 \rightarrow 1$	0.1	MSE	64	1e−3	20
Utterance Classifiers	MLP $(1024 \rightarrow 512 \rightarrow 23/27)$	0.1	MSE	32	2e−5	100

4.2 Experimental Setup

All experiments are implemented in PyTorch and trained on a GeForce RTX 3080 GPU (10GB). Common hyperparameters across different models are summarized in Table 2.

- *Personality Prediction Model.* Target personality vectors $\mathbf{Y}$ are standardized to zero mean and unit variance. A two-layer MLP regressor with ReLU activation, Batch Normalization, and Dropout predicts the 81-dimensional psychological profile.
- *Reward Predictors* is implemented as a 2-layer MLP. SiLU activation is applied after each linear layer, followed by Layer Normalization and Dropout with a rate of 0.2.
- *Reinforcement Learning.* The D3QN agent uses a GRU-based dueling architecture with a state vector of 465 dimensions (dialogue history + predicted personality). The policy optimizes a composite reward combining intermediate strategy feedback, final donation, and change-of-mind penalties with weights $\mathbf{w} = (0.4, 0.4, 0.2)$. Training uses Adam (lr $= 1 \times 10^{-3}$), discount factor $\gamma = 0.99$, and target network updates every 500 steps.

- *Utterance Strategy Classifiers.* Two DeBERTa-v3-base [7] models classify Persuader (27) and Persuadee (23) strategies. Each uses a two-layer MLP head with Tanh activation and Dropout. Average accuracy and Macro-F1 across 5-fold cross-validation are 68.3% and approximately 0.65, respectively.
- *Response Generation via MMR.* Responses are ranked using cosine-based Maximal Marginal Relevance (MMR) with $\lambda = 0.8$ and a recency bias of 0.65 to balance relevance and diversity. If the top similarity score falls below 0.8, an LLM-based fallback generates a contextually appropriate reply.
- *Donation Normalization.* Since **P4G** compensates each participant \$2 and part of this amount is used for donation, any donation above \$2 is capped at \$2 for normalization.

4.3   Results

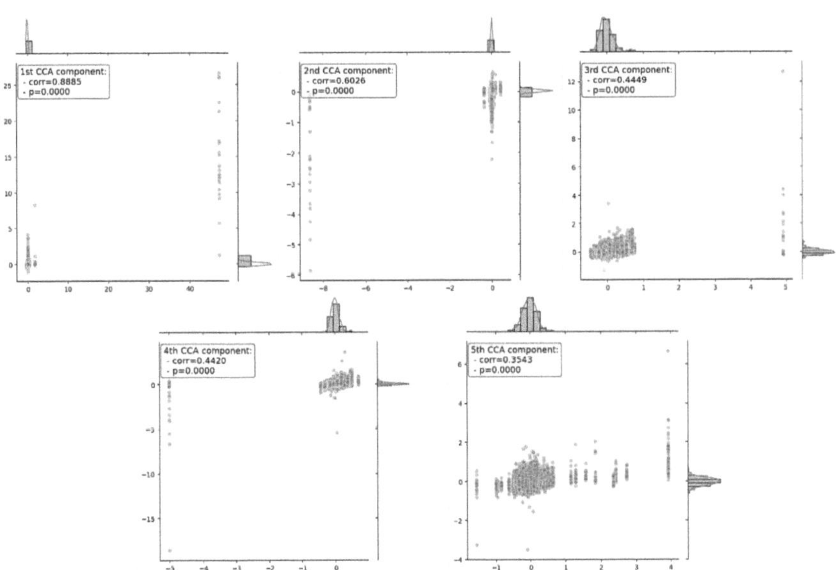

Fig. 5. CCA correlation and marginal distributions for ground-truth and predicted psychological profiles.

Personality Regression. We evaluate the alignment between the predicted 81-dimensional psychological profiles and the corresponding ground-truth profiles using canonical correlation analysis (Fig. 5). The top five canonical correlations are statistically significant, with all associated p values numerically to zero. The marginal histograms of the canonical component scores exhibit broadly similar distributions for the ground-truth and predicted embeddings, indicating that the regression model captures several variation in the personality space. Overall, the top-five correlations suggest the predicted profiles capture a detectable portion of the shared latent structure between the two representations, though substantial variance remains unexplained.

Reward Predictor. We evaluate three reward predictors using 5-fold cross-validation, with results summarized in Table 3, permutation tests indicate that the R^2 values for *Donate* and *Change* are significantly above zero ($p < 0.01$), while *Agree* is not. Among the models, the donation predictor performs best, achieving the lowest MAE/RMSE and the highest R^2. The agree and change-of-mind predictors show consistent error magnitudes across folds, reflecting stable estimation behavior. The scatter plots in Fig. 6 visualize the correspondence between predicted and ground-truth rewards. Across all reward types, the fitted regression lines display clear positive slopes, consistent with the positive correlations and R^2 values reported in the table. These trends confirm that the predictors capture meaningful relationships between dialogue features and reward outcomes.

Table 3. Evaluation Results of Reward Predictors

Predictor	MAE	RMSE	R^2
Agree	0.6009	0.7760	0.0147
Donate	0.2878	0.4401	0.1550
Change	0.5460	0.7411	0.0630

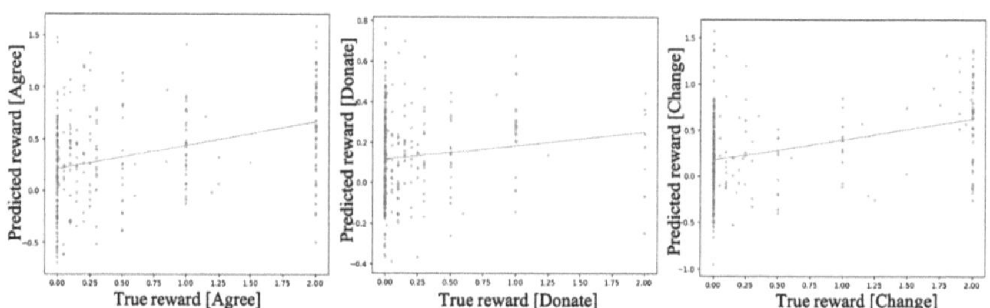

Fig. 6. Scatter plots comparing predicted and ground-truth rewards for *agree, donate,* and *change-of-mind.*

Reinforcement Learning Outcomes. Fig. 7 compares cumulative persuasion rewards across dialogues for three behavioral axes (cumulative *agree, donate,* and *change-of-mind* rewards, respectively). Each subfigure shows eight cumulative-reward curves corresponding to: ground truth and predicted rewards on **P4G**, and six RL variants that differ by whether they use turn-level personality (with/without) and by the reward formulation, including Utterance-level (U-level) vs. Strategy-level (S-level) agree, and inclusion/exclusion of a change-of-mind term. Specifically, Baseline 1 uses S-level agree with U-level donate and

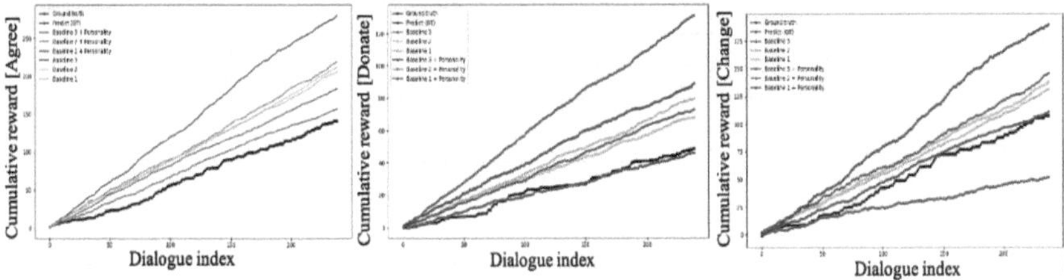

Fig. 7. Comparison of cumulative reward components across dialogues: agreement to donate (*agree*), donation amount (*donate*), and change-of-mind penalties (*change-of-mind*).

change-of-mind; Baseline 2 switches to U-level agree while keeping U-level donate and change-of-mind; and Baseline 3 simplifies by using S-level agree and U-level donate, but entirely excludes the change-of-mind term.

Across these comparisons, we observe consistent, interpretable patterns. First, the variants that incorporate turn-level personality generally produce higher cumulative persuasion rewards than their counterparts without personality, indicating that conditioning the policy on the inferred persona is associated with improved aggregate outcomes. Second, the granularity of the agree term matters: strategy-level agree values tend to increase cumulative agree totals relative to per-utterance agree estimates in many of the reported comparisons, although the relative benefit depends on the overall reward composition.

- For **agree** cumulative reward, configurations that combine strategy-level agree with donate (and that include the persona signal) yield the largest cumulative agreement traces; by contrast, variants that rely only on agree + donate without personality lie noticeably lower, which highlights the role of persona information in shifting aggregate agreement behavior.
- For **donate** cumulative reward, the configuration pairing strategy-level agrees with the utterance-level donate and a change-of-mind term, together with turn-level personality, attains the highest cumulative donation in our experiments; the variant that omits the change-of-mind term but retains personality ranks next. Comparisons between strategy- and utterance-level agree formulations show that the preferred agree granularity for maximizing donations depends on which other reward terms are present, indicating an interaction between agree granularity and the reward mix.
- For **change-of-mind**, the setting that includes a change-of-mind term along with strategy-level agree and turn-level personality is associated with lower cumulative change amounts (i.e., fewer or smaller changes aggregated across dialogues), whereas variants that omit the change-of-mind term tend to show larger cumulative change totals.

5   Limitations and Ethical Considerations

Our framework advances personalized persuasion through reinforcement learning, yet several limitations and ethical considerations remain.

Limitations. The MMR retrieval utterance is limited to the **P4G** dataset, which may restrict generalization beyond the dataset scope. The LLM-based user simulator, conditioned on dialogue history and inferred personality traits, supports scalable experimentation but may introduce simulation bias or unrealistic responses, particularly when personality cues are limited. In addition, the evaluation relies on predicted rewards rather than human-validated feedback, which may allow errors from auxiliary components (e.g., reward and personality predictors) to propagate into policy learning.

Ethical Considerations. Our system is intended for socially beneficial applications such as charitable giving and avoids manipulative persuasion by inferring personality from dialogue rather than fixed stereotypes. We emphasize transparency, user autonomy, and consent, and highlight the importance of future work incorporating human-in-the-loop evaluations and strengthened safeguards for privacy, fairness, and accountability.

6   Conclusion

This work presents a personality-aware reinforcement learning framework for persuasive dialogue that unifies dynamic user modeling, LLM-driven simulation, and behaviorally grounded reward optimization. By incorporating turn-level personality estimation and a composite reward structure balancing intent, donation, and change-of-mind signals, our approach enables adaptive and ethically aligned persuasion strategies. Experimental results demonstrate that personality conditioning and realistic simulation substantially enhance both policy robustness and persuasive effectiveness. Notably, incorporating the change-of-mind reward reduces post-agreement retractions, reinforcing sustained behavioral outcomes. Beyond technical contributions, this study highlights the broader potential of generative and reinforcement learning methods to promote social good through responsible persuasion. Future work will extend this framework toward interactive, real-user settings and continual adaptation, ensuring that persuasive agents remain transparent, context-sensitive, and aligned with user well-being.

References

1. Braca, A., Dondio, P.: Developing persuasive systems for marketing: the interplay of persuasion techniques, customer traits and persuasive message design. Italian J. Mark. **2023**(3), 369–412 (2023)
2. Castillo-López, G., de Chalendar, G., Semmar, N.: A survey of recent advances on turn-taking modeling in spoken dialogue systems. In: IWSDS, pp. 254–271 (2025)
3. Cho, I., Wang, D., Takahashi, R., Saito, H.: A personalized dialogue generator with implicit user persona detection. arXiv:2204.07372 (2022)

4. Cho, I., Wang, D., Takahashi, R., Saito, H.: A comprehensive empirical study on personalized dialogue generation. JNLP **30**(3), 959–990 (2023)
5. Elfwing, S., Uchibe, E., Doya, K.: Sigmoid-weighted linear units for neural network function approximation in reinforcement learning. Neural Netw. **107**, 3–11 (2018)
6. Günther, M., et al.: Jina embeddings 2: 8192-token general-purpose text embeddings for long documents. arXiv:2310.19923 (2023)
7. He, P., Liu, X., Gao, J., Chen, W.: Deberta: decoding-enhanced BERt with disentangled attention. In: ICLR (2021)
8. Huang, Q., et al.: Personalized dialogue generation with persona-adaptive attention. In: AAAI. vol. 37, pp. 12916–12923 (2023)
9. Kawano, S., et al.: Multimodal persuasive dialogue corpus using teleoperated android. In: INTERSPEECH, pp. 2308–2312 (2022)
10. Kwan, W.C., Wang, H.R., Wang, H.M., Wong, K.F.: A survey on recent advances and challenges in reinforcement learning methods for task-oriented dialogue policy learning. Mach. Intell. Res. **20**(3), 318–334 (2023)
11. Li, J., Galley, M., Brockett, C., Gao, J., Dolan, B.: A persona-based neural conversation model. In: ACL (Volume 1), pp. 994–1003 (2016)
12. Liu, X., Ren, X., Pan, S.: Persuasive design for healthy eating: a scoping review. In: HCI, pp. 292–303. Springer (2022)
13. Ma, Z., et al.: Personality enhanced emotion generation modeling for dialogue systems. Cogn. Comput. **16**(1), 293–304 (2024)
14. Ouyang, L., et al.: Training language models to follow instructions with human feedback. NeurIPS **35**, 27730–27744 (2022)
15. Park, J.S., et al.: Generative agents: interactive simulacra of human behavior. arXiv:2304.03442 (2023)
16. Prakken, H.: Formal systems for persuasion dialogue. Knowl. Eng. Rev. **21**(2), 163–188 (2006)
17. Reimers, N., Gurevych, I.: Sentence-BERT: sentence embeddings using siamese BERT-networks. arXiv:1908.10084 (2019)
18. Su, P.H., et al.: On-line active reward learning for policy optimisation in spoken dialogue systems. In: ACL (Volume 1), pp. 2431–2441 (2016)
19. Sun, W., Zhang, S.: Simulating user satisfaction for the evaluation of task-oriented dialogue systems. In: ACM SIGIR, pp. 2499–2506. New York, NY, USA (2021)
20. Tang, Y., et al.: Enhancing personalized dialogue generation with contrastive latent variables: combining sparse and dense persona. arXiv:2305.11482 (2023)
21. Torkamaan, H., Ziegler, J.: Integrating behavior change and persuasive design theories into an example mobile health recommender system. In: UbiComp/ISWC, pp. 218–225 (2021)
22. Torning, K., Oinas-Kukkonen, H.: Persuasive system design: state of the art and future directions. In: PT, pp. 1–8 (2009)
23. Tran, N., Alikhani, M., Litman, D.: How to ask for donations? learning user-specific persuasive dialogue policies through online interactions. In: ACM UMAP, pp. 12–22 (2022)
24. Wang, X., et al.: Persuasion for good: towards a personalized persuasive dialogue system for social good. In: ACL, pp. 5635–5649 (2019)
25. Xu, K., Wang, Z., Long, Y., Zhao, Q.: Deep reinforcement learning-based dialogue policy with graph convolutional q-network. In: LREC-COLING, pp. 4555–4565 (2024)
26. Yoshino, K., et al.: Dialogue scenario collection of persuasive dialogue with emotional expressions via crowdsourcing. In: LREC (2018)

27. Zeng, D., et al.: Causal discovery and counterfactual reasoning to optimize persuasive dialogue policies. BiT, pp. 1–15 (2025)
28. Zeng, D., et al.: Generative framework for personalized persuasion: inferring causal, counterfactual, and latent knowledge. In: ACM UMAP, pp. 83–93 (2025)
29. Zeng, D., et al.: Counterfactual reasoning using predicted latent personality dimensions for optimizing persuasion outcome. In: PT, pp. 287–300. Springer (2024)
30. Zhou, W., Li, Q., Li, C.: Learning to predict persona information fordialogue personalization without explicit persona description. arXiv:2111.15093 (2021)

Author Index